INTRODUCTION TO DESIGN AND ANALYSIS

Second Edition

INTRODUCTION TO
DESIGN AND ANALYSIS
A Student's Handbook

Second Edition

Geoffrey Keppel

William H. Saufley, Jr.
University of California, Berkeley

Howard Tokunaga
San Jose State University

W. H. Freeman and Company
New York

Library of Congress Cataloging-in-Publication Data

Keppel, Geoffrey.
  Introduction to design and analysis : A student's handbook. – 2nd
ed. / Geoffrey Keppel, William H. Saufley, Jr., Howard Tokunaga.
      p.   cm.
  Includes bibliographical references and indexes.
  ISBN 0-7167-2320-4 (hardbound). — ISBN 0-7167-2321-2 (paperback)
  1. Psychology, Experimental — Statistical methods.   2. Psychology—
Experiments.   3. Experimental design.   I. Saufley, William H.
II. Tokunaga, Howard.   III. Title.
BF198.7.K47   1992   92–1364
150′.724–dc20   CIP

Printed in the United States of America

Seventh printing, 2000

Dedicated to Professor Emeritus Benton J. Underwood,

the mentor of two of us in graduate school, who,
through his teaching, supervision, and writing,
communicated the excitement of investigating the puzzles in research,
while exhibiting the productive interplay between research design
and creative statistical analysis;

and to our parents,

Charles and Edetha Keppel
Bill and Olyn Saufley
Katsumi and Grayce Tokunaga

CONTENTS

Chapter 7
Estimating Population Means and Effect Size 169

Chapter 8
Errors of Hypothesis Testing and Statistical Power 187

PART THREE
THE ANALYSIS OF FACTORIAL DESIGNS 225

Chapter 9
Introduction to the Analysis of Factorial Experiments 227

Chapter 10
Analytical Comparisons in the Factorial Design 277

PART FOUR
THE ANALYSIS OF WITHIN-SUBJECTS DESIGNS 313

Chapter 11
The Single-Factor Within-Subjects Design 315

Chapter 12
The Mixed Within-Subjects Factorial Design 359

Chapter 13
The Two-Factor Within-Subjects Design 399

PART FIVE
ADDITIONAL STATISTICAL PROCEDURES 429

Chapter 14
The Analysis of Categorical Data 431

Chapter 15
Correlation and Regression 457

Chapter 16
Additional Topics

Appendices

TO THE INSTRUCTOR

We believe that the traditional way of teaching statistics usually results in superficial coverage of the design and analysis of experiments. Because many introductory statistics texts cover a great deal of ground, *analysis of variance* is often introduced only near the end. The resulting time constraints leave the instructor no option but to rush through one of the most frequently used analytical techniques. One consequence is that students are poorly prepared for reading the results of experiments and for devising experimental tests of hypotheses in which they are interested. Moreover, the often casual treatment of *interaction* leaves students unable to appreciate an important and practical concept that has been available to us for over 50 years. Accordingly, in this edition we continue to concentrate on the design and detailed analysis of experiments, to provide thorough discussions of statistical interaction, and to show how a judicious use of *repeated measures* on the same subject can confer advantages of economy and sensitivity to research, all in the context of meaningful research situations.

Students, both ours and others, have shown strong interest in this approach. We capitalize on their interest by introducing the design and analysis of experiments early in the text and delaying or omitting material that in many introductory books precedes these fundamental topics. We also include other important topics, such as essential *descriptive techniques, correlation and regression,* and *chi square.* We have been encouraged in this approach by reports from others using our book that their students have been able to devise factorial experiments and to address follow-up comparisons to answer specific questions of their own. After students have acquired some familiarity with these topics, they are better able to read the results sections of studies reported in the contemporary literature. We believe these insights to be an essential goal of education in each discipline that employs these techniques.

Special Features of the Second Edition

We have written our text for students who meet the standard quantitative prerequisites for entry into most colleges and universities. We cover the logic governing each analysis, explain each procedure step by step, and then work through a problem completely to illustrate the procedures. Problems of experimental design and statistical analysis are necessarily intertwined and, therefore, treated as closely related topics. This second edition is a substantial revision of the first. In preparing it, we have been guided by our own experiences in the classroom and by the fine advice given to us by students and by instructors at other universities. Some of the important changes introduced in the second edition are:

- We have reorganized the presentation of the completely randomized single-factor design and have included two new chapters: Chapter 7, in which we consider interval estimation and estimating effect size; and Chapter 8, in which we discuss errors of statistical inference, controlling cumulative type I error, and power. In Appendix A, we provide simplified power charts to encourage students to use the concept of power to estimate sample size in a variety of research situations.

- We draw attention to problems that may result from violating the assumption of equal group variances and offer a simple procedure to protect against the increase in type I error that may result from such violations.

- In Chapter 10, we have expanded our coverage of analytical procedures designed to illuminate the results of factorial experiments. We illustrate how to use these procedures to analyze factorial designs with repeated measures in Chapters 12 and 13.

- We more fully present designs with repeated measures, with revised chapters on the single-factor within-subjects design and the mixed two-factor within-subjects design (Chapters 11 and 12, respectively) and a new chapter on the complete two-factor within-subjects designs (Chapter 13). Our approach to error terms used in making focused analyses with these designs is to offer simplified, but acceptably accurate, solutions for choosing the appropriate error term, along with cautionary explanations and suggestions of where to turn when more precision is required.

- We have revised the chapter on the analysis of experiments with categorical response measures (Chapter 14) and illustrate how one can estimate the sample size necessary to achieve a desired level of power for a particular experimental outcome.

- We present linear correlation and regression in a single, new chapter (Chapter 15), in which we emphasize the interpretation of the product-moment correlation coefficient. We also show how a researcher can use sample size to control power in a correlational study.

- In another new chapter (Chapter 16), we consider a number of topics, including a description of other types of research methods used in the social and behavioral sciences and an illustration of how a popular statistical software package (SPSS) may be programmed to analyze a single-factor experiment.

- We have added appendices at the end of certain chapters in which we provide more extensive treatment of topics for those teachers who want to go into subjects in more detail.

- We have increased the number of exercises at the ends of most chapters and provide detailed answers for selected exercises in Appendix B. We include two new appendices, one instructing students how to use hand-held statistical calculators effectively in conducting statistical analyses (Appendix C), the other presenting a discussion of trend analysis (Appendix D).

- We have modified the notational system to be more compatible with other texts, while retaining capital letters — which we prefer, for their intuitive character — to represent sums in the computational formulas for the analysis of variance.

An Overview of the Second Edition

The first 14 chapters are devoted to the analysis of data from experiments. In contrast with other texts, our approach reflects the thinking of a researcher, and our explanations are verbal rather than mathematical. Our aim is to provide students with an intuitive understanding of the basic procedures involved in designing and analyzing an experiment.

In Part One, we introduce students to the logic of experimentation (Chapter 1) and to the notions of central tendency and variability (Chapter 2).

Part Two focuses on the analysis of the completely randomized single-factor experiment. We begin with a general discussion of the use of randomization to control unwanted nuisance factors and the fundamental logic of hypothesis testing (Chapter 3); students should be able to follow this discussion even with little prior statistical knowledge. In Chapters 4 and 5, we explain in detail the procedures for assessing the significance of an experimental outcome. By focusing immediately on the multilevel experiment, we encourage students very early to think in terms of designs using more than two groups — designs that are more representative of contemporary research.

In Chapter 6, we consider the detailed analysis of an experiment, stressing the analytical, meaningful analysis of the results. Our students have been intrigued by the idea of planned comparisons and feel challenged by the possibility of conducting a creative independent research project. Chapter 7 considers two topics that help researchers interpret the results of their experiments: confidence intervals and estimates of the size of the treatment effects observed in an experiment. Chapter 8 examines in detail the risks associated with hypothesis testing (type I error, type II error, and cumulative type I error). We also show how to use sample size and the concept of statistical power to achieve control — in the planning stage — over the sensitivity of a proposed experiment.

Part Three covers the design and analysis of factorial experiments. As elsewhere, our emphasis is on an intuitive understanding of the material. We introduce the concept of interaction and the overall analysis of the completely randomized two-factor design in Chapter 9. In Chapter 10, we indicate how researchers are able to extract detailed information from the results of a factorial experiment. To demonstrate these procedures, we use an example initially introduced as a single-factor manipulation in Chapter 6 and expanded into a factorial experiment in Chapter 9. This continuity enables students to see how theoretical expectations can be examined, isolated, and evaluated statistically in factorial designs.

Part Four considers within-subjects designs, in which subjects serve in more than one or even in all of the treatment conditions — designs that are widely used in the behavioral and social sciences because of their economical use of subjects and their greater statistical power. (They are also favorite designs of our students for their individual projects.) In Chapter 11, we discuss the simplest type of within-subjects design, namely, a design in which subjects receive all levels of a single independent variable. The next two chapters show how we can extend the within-subjects design to factorial experiments; both designs are commonly represented in the contemporary research literature. Chapter 12 focuses on the mixed within-subjects factorial design, in which subjects receive some but not all of the treatment combinations created by the factorial design; while Chapter 13 considers the analysis of a "pure" within-subjects factorial design, in which subjects receive all of the factorial treatment combinations.

Part Five contains three chapters covering certain additional statistical procedures. In Chapter 14, we present statistical techniques — those employing the Pearson chi square statistic — appropriate for use with data that consist of response categories rather than scores obtained from continuous measures; we focus on the analysis of experiments and the subdivision of the overall chi square statistic into a number of meaningful comparisons obtained by arranging the treatment conditions into different patterns. In Chapter 15, we shift attention from the analysis of experiments to the analysis of correlational data. We discuss two basic correlational methods, linear correlation and regression. The final chapter (Chapter 16) presents three supplemental topics: a description of several types of nonexperimental research methods, an example of using statistical software (SPSS) and the computer to analyze the results of a simple experiment, and a consideration of areas of study students might explore to widen their understanding of research and statistical analyses.

Finally, the appendices include basic statistical tables (Appendix A), detailed answers to selected chapter exercises (Appendix B), an instructional unit on using hand-held statistical calculators to facilitate calculation of means, standard deviations, and sums of squares in the analysis of variance (Appendix C), and a discussion of trend analysis (Appendix D). The Glossary provides definitions of all critical terms and concepts appearing in the text.

Acknowledgments

We wish to thank *Biometrics*, the *Biometrika* Trustees, and the *Journal of Educational and Psychological Measurement* for their permission to reproduce statistical tables in this book.

We are indebted to a number of people who provided advice and assistance in the preparation of this book. We should mention first our students and teaching assistants who have provided us useful comments over the years, individuals who have written to us with questions and ideas for improving the book, and the reviewers who offered useful suggestions for the second edition: David Brooks, Illinois School of Professional Psychology; Jane Marantz Connor, State University of New York at Binghamton; Howard F. Gallup, Lafayette College; Elyse B. Lehman, George Mason University; Glenn E. Meyer, Lewis and Clark College; and Linda Skitka, Southern Illinois University. We are particularly appreciative of the comments we received from Thomas D. Wickens, who reviewed an earlier version of Chapter 14 and prepared the table of power functions, which appears as Table A-8 of Appendix A.

We also wish to thank some of the individuals who assisted in the production of this book. Jonathan Cobb, the psychology editor for W. H. Freeman and Company, showed keen and continued interest in the development of the second edition and provided helpful advice and support during all phases of the project. Philip McCaffrey and Erica Seifert skillfully guided the manuscript through the many details of production. We give special thanks to

Richard K. Mickey, who provided expert and constructive copyediting of the manuscript. Finally, we wish to thank Sheila Keppel, who supplied ideas for the cover design; and Martha Geering and Bruce Klein, who developed these ideas into the final design.

Geoffrey Keppel
William H. Saufley, Jr.
Howard Tokunaga

TO THE STUDENT

Most students who enroll in a statistics course are familiar with the ideas of research and experimentation and are ready to learn about the statistical analysis of data generated by experiments. We have written this book to give you the opportunity to think extensively about analytical research and to gain familiarity with the way much current research in psychology and other social and behavioral sciences is designed and carried out. Throughout this book, our approach is to emphasize that a scientist's job is to try to make sense out of some aspect of nature.

We begin with a discussion of how to devise hypotheses so that they lead to tests in the form of experiments. Throughout the text, we stress how an experiment is analyzed to answer specific questions posed by a researcher. We use examples to show the relationships between research questions, the choice of specific treatment conditions, and the statistical analysis of the experiment. Our explanations of hypothesis testing and our discussions of the uses of variability are primarily verbal rather than mathematical. We introduce each new procedure with an intuitive explanation and then work through an example step by step to illustrate the procedure in detail. Any student patient enough to work through the techniques and to correct his or her errors can master the concepts and procedures covered in the text.

To gain a thorough understanding of a topic, you should completely read and reread the chapters in question. Such a task might sound unpleasant, but the reward is the satisfaction of understanding a topic that initially seemed difficult. After studying the procedure for a particular analysis, work through the examples, checking each step to make certain you understand the various operations. Errors in calculation frequently result from incorrect substitution or omitting a step in the analysis, and so we point out places where errors are likely to occur. The best safeguard against making errors is to use a systematic format for working through an analysis so that you can identify each major step and review your calculations for accuracy when necessary.

You will find that hypothesis testing and the analysis of data are remarkably valuable in the design and interpretation of research. Still, as in the study of any set of techniques, we all sometimes focus too much on the procedures themselves, especially when we do not fully understand their role. As you read this text, keep in mind that there is no substitute for knowledge of the research field you are interested in, and for common sense in conducting your research and analyzing the results.

PA T • ON

EXPERIMENTAL DESIGN AND PRELIMINARY DATA ANALYSIS

We assume that most students reading this book are undergraduate majors in psychology or related disciplines and that the course of which this book is a part is probably a requirement for the major. As a psychology major, you will be expected to understand how the empirical basis of a science is created — how data are generated, collected, and summarized statistically — and you may even work with data yourself, for a class project, in your independent study, or your honors thesis. To be able to contribute to the growth of an empirical science, no matter how modestly, you must be able to use the analytical methods and procedures of the science.

Each research field within psychology has its own collection of methodological and statistical tools, and these tools change and develop continually as the field grows through new research. As your interests become more focused and you learn more about particular methods, you will begin to acquire a critical attitude toward the inferences that you and others draw from psychological research. Fundamentally, the quality of any conclusion based on empirical evidence — new or old — depends on the logic of the research that generated it in the first place. A familiarity with specific procedures and methods will enable you to evaluate the research reports you read and study and thus to weigh the importance of the reported results.

Basic to all research is a working knowledge of statistics. Many of you will have been exposed to some of the fundamental aspects of statistics either in an introductory course in statistics or as a supplement to the material presented in content courses. This book emphasizes a particular type of research methodology, namely, the *experiment*, in which the researcher manipulates some feature of the task given to subjects (or of the conditions of testing and even of the psychological or physiological states of the subjects), called the **independent variable**, and determines the effects of these manipulations on the behavior of the subjects, called the **dependent variable**.

The authors are psychologists who are active in research and teach research methods and statistical procedures to psychology students. The book's clear bias is toward the problems facing the researcher designing and analyzing an experiment. Our primary goal is to introduce you to the *analytical* side of experimentation. A knowledge of this subject will assist you in your reading of primary resource material in psychological research journals and in designing research projects that reflect the sophistication of present-day experimentation in psychology.

We have found through our teaching of experimental design and statistical analysis that undergraduates have widely varying backgrounds, both in mathematics and in psychological experimentation. The two chapters in Part One are designed to make up for deficiencies you may have in these subjects and to set the stage for the systematic coverage of statistical analysis in later chapters.

In Chap. 1, we describe the critical features of an experiment and introduce some fundamental terms and concepts. The chapter is intended to help you think in terms of experimentation and to make clear how ideas are pursued through the critical testing ground of the experiment. In Chap. 2, we discuss the initial processing of data, which includes the calculation of two fundamental kinds of descriptive statistical measures: central tendency and variability. The material we present in Chap. 2 and later chapters does not assume any mathematical background beyond high school algebra and the calculations you will be performing consist only of the four basic arithmetical operations: addition, subtraction, multiplication, and division. All you will need to learn is when to perform each operation in a series of calculations.

Chapter • 1

INTRODUCTION TO EXPERIMENTAL DESIGN

Psychology is primarily the study of human and animal behavior. To this end, psychologists have developed a vast array of research procedures and techniques. This book concentrates on one class of such methods, namely, *designing and analyzing experiments* in psychology and related disciplines of the social and behavioral sciences. We describe the most common experimental designs in sufficient detail that you will understand how to interpret findings from studies reported in academic journals and even how to complete an original research project of your own. Conducting research is a demanding and difficult task, which requires a variety of skills: conceptual skills in developing ideas, organizational skills to collect information in a systematic way, quantitative skills to analyze this information, and communication skills to report your findings to others.

1.1 GETTING STARTED

You might have little, if any, desire to pursue a career conducting psychological research. The thought of prolonging your "studenthood" by going to graduate school might not appeal to you. Thus, it is natural to wonder why you have to learn about conducting research. First, you probably have a curiosity about human nature and what makes us tick. Understanding ourselves leads to important decisions about the ways we conduct our social and political affairs. Then there is a practical side to psychology. Throughout your life, you have been and will continue to be affected by the results of psychological research. Recently, your admission to college was based in part on scores obtained from tests developed by psychologists to gauge your chances of successfully completing your academic work. In an entirely different domain, the design of the cockpit of airplanes, along with methods used to train pilots, is substantially the result of psychological research. Activities as varied as rehabilitation therapy following head injury and marketing the many products we can buy are also influenced by research conducted by psychologists.

As the findings of research become known, how are we to know whether they are any "good"? We must be able to determine whether the research findings are repeatable and relevant to the behavior under investigation. The picture becomes more blurred whenever the topic of research is contentious and when different investigators studying the same topic present opposing conclusions. Whom are you to believe? Being able to read original research will give you the ability to critically evaluate the strengths and weaknesses of the methods employed by the researchers. In doing so, you can reasonably decide whether the conclusions a researcher has drawn are appropriate.

Understanding how research is conducted not only will help you evaluate the research of others, but will also help when you attempt to do your own. Even if you are reading this text because you have to, learning to conduct your own research gives you a means of using creativity and of satisfying your own curiosity. You will find that conducting your own research will give you a better appreciation and understanding of research in general.

Forming a Research Question

In teaching our classes, we typically have students conduct their own research projects. Students frequently find this difficult for several reasons. First, they are concerned about the techniques asking questions such as: "How should I collect my data? How should I analyze this information? How do I know whether the results are meaningful? How should I present my findings?"

Another concern of students is choosing and developing the topic of study. "What should I study? Is it an important topic? Is it interesting? Why should I study it?" There is no simple answer to the questions of what should be studied or why. The best advice is to start with a question in which you are interested and which you would have fun studying. Once you have chosen a general question, turn to library research to find out what others have done and how the topic is approached and conceptualized. We want to benefit from the hard work of others to make our job easier and relevant to the findings already reported in the literature.

Forms of Research

In addition to developing a body of empirical information, the goal of research is to develop theories that explore, describe, explain, and predict behavior. Frequently, students report that they seem to have chosen a question which, in spite of the seemingly endless number of articles published, has been ignored. Often research is conducted to explore uncharted territory. This is the purpose of **exploratory research**, research designed to provide initial insight to guide further research efforts. Once a phenomenon has been identified, we might carry out **descriptive research** to flesh out and delineate its distinguishing characteristics. A book by the statistician John W. Tukey (1977), *Exploratory Data Analysis*, provides a lively and interesting introduction to the exploratory and descriptive phase of research.

Explanatory research attempts to define cause-and-effect relationships. For example, does a particular teaching method lead to greater retention of material? Do different environments lead to differences in brain structures? How is attention affected by competing tasks? Can creativity be improved with a particular kind of practice? As you shall see, being able to make inferences to answer cause-effect questions with any degree of confidence requires certain steps.

The most efficient means we have to establish cause-effect relationships between certain events in the environment and selected forms of behavior is the **experiment**. Often the word *experiment* is used casually to refer to a test or to a trial, an attempt to try something out. However, we use a very specific set of conditions to define an experiment.[1] The basic notion is simple:

At least two groups of subjects are treated exactly alike in all ways except one — the treatment of interest. Any differences observed in the behavior of the two groups of subjects are then attributed to, or said to be caused by, the differences in the specific treatment conditions.

We consider this simple notion in some detail in the next two sections.

Finally, we often want to use available information to predict future behavior. For example, if we know that scores on the Scholastic Aptitude Test (SAT) are related to performance in college, we can use the results of this test when administered in high school to predict who will do well in the college or university environment. This is the purpose of **predictive research**. Predicting the behavior of individuals is an important part of psychological research, but beyond the scope of this book.

1.2 HOW DO PSYCHOLOGISTS CONDUCT RESEARCH?

The scientific method of inquiry is characterized by certain assumptions. The first assumption of science is that there is a sense of order and lawfulness; things do not happen randomly or without cause. Second, research involves the systematic collection of empirical data rather than reliance upon one's subjective perceptions or intuition. In this sense, the entire enterprise is public — one's ideas are shared with others, who can then test them themselves to see if they reach the same conclusions. Finally, the purpose of science is to organize and integrate individual facts in order to develop **paradigms**. Paradigms are logical systems encompassing both theoretical concepts and research techniques; a paradigm is the dominant way of thinking and working in some area of science. One example of a paradigm was the belief that the world is flat. This belief not only affected explorers, but also affected how mapmakers and astronomers conducted their business. A paradigm guides

---

[1] The definition of an experiment in psychology was developed over a period of time and expressed most clearly by Robert S. Woodworth (1938, pp. 1–4).

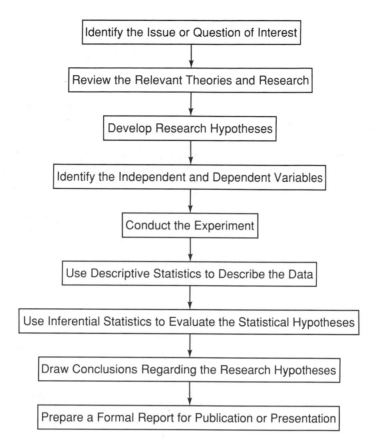

FIGURE 1-1 *A Schematic Representation of the Design and Analysis of an Experiment.*

our way of thinking about a phenomenon until we come to believe that a new paradigm provides a better explanation.

The process of doing research is presented in Fig. 1-1.[2] For the remainder of this section, we will discuss each of these steps. It is extremely important for you to keep in mind that this is an "ideal" way of doing research. The "real" way, as you will discover in your own efforts, may not resemble a smooth ride but rather one filled with starts and stops, dead ends, and right turns when you should have made left turns. Overall, you should keep in mind that conducting psychological research is basically the process of asking questions and attempting to answer them.

---

[2] This process, which is called the **hypothetico-deductive method**, is one of the defining characteristics of science and the scientific method.

Posing Questions

Most research starts with some question that the researcher has. Although this may seem simple enough, we find that students, when given the assignment of conducting their own projects, encounter the greatest difficulty at this point. For this reason it is worthwhile to discuss where ideas for research typically come from. Research often arises from one's own ideas, intuition, daily observations, and personal theories. Although this may not seem terribly scientific, there is one main advantage of using your own thoughts: you will be more interested in what you are studying. If there is one useful piece of advice we give our students attempting to develop their research projects, it is this: do something you're interested in.

Besides relying on your interests, you will often encounter research questions in examining the theories, ideas, and research of other people. As you move through your course work, you may find that you agree with some theories and theorists and disagree with others. By learning research design and statistics, you will have the tools not only to evaluate the beliefs of others, but to test them with your own research.

Reviewing Relevant Theory and Research

Once you have begun to formulate a question or issue you want to study, the next step is to find out what others have done and said in trying to answer that question. Reviewing existing theory and relevant research is the reason for doing library research. The main purpose of reviewing the psychological literature is to determine the existing paradigm. Early on in this search, you should begin to identify theories that are relevant to your topic. A **theory** is a set of propositions used to describe or explain a phenomenon. The purpose of theory is to summarize, organize, and explain a variety of specific existing facts into a logically consistent framework, as well as to generate new knowledge by focusing our thinking and identifying gaps in our current state of knowledge.

What are the characteristics of a "good" theory? The first is that it must be able to make predictions, not just explain what has already happened. Similarly, given a certain set of circumstances, a theory should make only one prediction rather than several. These are perhaps the main criticisms of classic psychoanalytic theory. For example, a child receives repeated spankings from his or her father. According to psychoanalytic theory, what might be the effect of the spankings? They may have no direct effect as the child forgets about them — this is what is referred to as *repression*. However, the child may choose to express deep anger at other people rather than at the father (*displacement*), may express great love for the father (*reaction formation*), or may hate him or herself (*internalization*). All of these predictions stem from the same situation — it is only after the child has grown up that we may determine which one was most accurate.

To be useful, a theory must also make specific predictions and be testable in terms of publicly observable evidence. This helps it meet the requirement of *replicability*: its specificity allows other researchers to attempt to discover whether they find the same results. A good theory also possesses *breadth* — it can be applied to a number of different settings — and *parsimony* in that it explains phenomena as simply and with as few principles as possible.

By learning the main characteristics and assumptions of relevant theories, you can see how they attempt to explain the phenomena in which you are interested. By placing your study within a theoretical framework, you will be able to either provide support for or refute these theories.

A second reason for reviewing the research literature is to see what research methods are typically employed within a particular paradigm. An examination of relevant experiments will give you an idea of how other investigators have approached the phenomenon you are planning to study. You may find that you can easily adapt their methods to your research project, which will help you make headway on your own project and provide an important link with the research already reported in your field. The third main reason is to learn not only what the dominant theory is but also who the dominant researchers are. Psychology is not only the study of individuals; it is based on the ideas of individuals. Becoming acquainted with these individuals will make psychology a much more interesting field of study for you.

Reviewing the literature will ultimately help you decide whether it is worth the time and energy needed to conduct your study. By seeing what others have done you may decide that the idea you wish to study has already been investigated and there is no reason to duplicate earlier efforts. However, you may decide that the ideas of others are limited or flawed. By doing your review you will avoid duplicating the mistakes of previous researchers.

How do you go about doing library research? Perhaps the best place to begin to locate and study theories is in the textbooks for your other classes. Most textbooks provide condensed, introductory summaries of main theories and identify notable studies and prominent psychologists. However, to find more extensive, up-to-date, and evaluative reviews of theories, you will need to use the psychological research journals. Particularly good places to start are the academic publications *Psychological Review, Psychological Bulletin, Annual Review of Psychology*; the latter two consist primarily of reviews of the literature.

To find original research studies, rather than literature reviews, you will probably need to employ reference indexes such as the *Psychological Abstracts* (summaries of articles published in the psychological literature), the *Social Sciences Citation Index* (organizing journal articles in terms of who has cited or referenced them after their publication), and the *Social Sciences Index* (covering a number of disciplines such as anthropology, psychology, sociology, and social work). The reference librarian at your library can assist you in learning how to use these indexes, as well as accessing computer-based indexes such as *PsycLit.*

Deriving Research Hypotheses

Once the issue or topic is chosen and existing data and theories have been studied, the next step is to state the specific questions or propositions to be investigated. The **research hypothesis** is a succinct statement of the purpose of the study. Examples of research hypotheses are:

- Exposure to aggressive stimuli leads to aggressive behavior.

- The type of material to be learned affects the retention of that material.

- General information leads to the quick identification of an object from a partial glimpse of the object.

- Students who are perceived by their teachers as being similar to them in personality characteristics will receive higher grades than students perceived as being dissimilar.

Research hypotheses are typically stated in *words* rather than in numbers or symbols. This differentiates them from other types of hypotheses you may be used to seeing, such as the null hypothesis or the alternative hypothesis. These types of hypotheses — known as **statistical hypotheses** — are statements of relationships between treatment conditions, expressed in numbers and symbols rather than in words, and are also an important part of the research process. As you will see beginning in Chap. 3 and throughout this book, researchers test statistical hypotheses to make decisions about their research hypotheses.

Independent Variables

The primary purpose of research hypotheses is to state a relationship between variables. Put simply, a **variable** can be defined as a property that can take different values. In talking about experiments, we distinguish between two classes of variables: independent variables and dependent variables. We will discuss independent variables in this section and dependent variables in the next.

As noted earlier, an experiment consists of two or more treatment conditions. The actual treatment conditions in an experiment are usually determined by the manipulations specified in the research hypothesis. A research hypothesis may state, for example, that variations in the amount of a particular drug will have differential effects on behavior, or that different kinds of drugs will have differential effects on behavior. *Variations in amount*, in the first example, and *different kinds of drugs*, in the second example, are descriptive phrases referring to the treatment conditions included in the two experiments designed to test these hypotheses. However, these phrases are not detailed enough to define the treatment conditions sufficiently. The researcher would have to provide more information — specifying the dosage variations in the first example, naming the particular drugs to be administered in the second — to clearly delineate the different treatment conditions in these two experiments.

A number of different terms are used to refer to the treatment conditions included in an experiment. Most commonly, the treatment conditions are called, collectively, the **independent variable**. In the first of our examples, variations in amount constitute the independent variable of the experiment, while in the second, variations in drug type constitute the independent variable. The independent variable comprises the range of treatment conditions under the control of the experimenter. The term *under control* means *manipulated by* or *varied by* the experimenter. For this reason, the independent variable is also known as the *manipulated variable* or the *treatment variable*. Alternative terms are also used to refer to the treatment conditions themselves — that is, the differences in treatment administered to the subjects in the experiment. These terms are **treatments** and **levels** of the independent variable.

A Classification of Independent Variables. We find it useful to classify independent variables on the basis of the *source* of the treatment manipulation. One source of manipulation is the task; variations in some characteristic of the task itself constitute a **task variable**. Mazes differing in complexity and different types of conceptual problems are examples of task variables. A second type of independent variable is an **environmental variable**. In this case, the nature of the task is held constant but some aspect of the experimental environment is manipulated. Obvious examples include the temperature, humidity, illumination, and other conditions prevailing in the testing situation.

A final source of manipulation is the *subject*. We discuss two types of such manipulation. The first consists of some sort of temporary psychological or physiological intervention. Giving differential instructions to human subjects is the typical way of manipulating subjects' set, or view, of the task. A substantial portion of the research in social psychology, for example, relies on the use of instructions to create certain attitudes or expectations in different groups of subjects that in turn are expected to influence the performance of the subjects in these groups. An extreme form of instructional manipulation is the use of hypnotism to induce different states in subjects — for example, different mood states — and observe the effects of these induced moods on some task, such as learning, memory, or perception. Drugs are commonly used to induce differential physiological states in subjects. The internal changes produced in the subjects by these various sorts of manipulations are temporary in the sense that the subjects will quickly return to their "normal" selves after the experiment. Thus, we call such manipulations **temporary subject variables**.

The second type of subject manipulation is different in that it involves more or less permanent characteristics of subjects. The effect of intelligence on problem solving and the effect of gender on speed of learning are examples of this class of manipulation. Variables involving such manipulation are variously referred to as **classification variables**, *subject variables, organismic variables*, and *individual-difference variables*. In the context of an experiment, classification variables are manipulated through the *selection* of subjects on the dimension to be studied. To "manipulate" intelligence, for instance, we would have to obtain intelligence scores for a large number of individuals and then select subjects from this pool on the basis of these scores. The independent variable would then consist of subjects grouped together according to the IQ scores — for example, one group might contain subjects with high IQ scores, another might contain subjects with medium IQ scores, and a third subjects with low IQ scores.

Manipulations of this sort — involving classification variables — do not constitute an experiment as we have defined it, however, since the "administration" of the experimental "treatments" is obviously not under the control of the experimenter. The manipulation consists of *classifying* subjects — in our example, with regard to IQ. In an experiment, the independent variable is the only feature of the situation that is allowed to vary systematically from condition to condition. It is this characteristic of an experiment that permits the researcher to infer that a particular manipulation caused systematic differences in behavior observed among the different groups. But when a classification variable is manipulated, the subjects may also differ systematically from level to level with respect to characteristics other than the classification variable. Since such characteristics are not subject to the researcher's control, making an unambiguous statement about cause and effect is impossible where classification variables are involved, unless steps are taken to remove these other differences from the experiment. Experiments with classification variables are examples of **quasi-experiments**, which we will consider in Chap. 16.

Dependent Variables

One of the great advantages of specifying a research hypothesis is that the researcher is prepared to make exacting and careful measurement of some aspect of the behavior observed in conjunction with the manipulation of the independent variable. This selected behavior is called the *response measure*. Any behavior capable of being measured can be a response measure — for example, the speed of completing a task, the number of errors made, or even ratings on a scale. The response measure is often referred to as the **dependent variable**. We use the terms *dependent variable, response measure,* and *response variable* interchangeably.

A choice of response measures exists for most experiments. The experimenter's choice of which response measure to include depends on a number of factors. A response measure should be *readily observable, easily transformable into numbers,* and *economically feasible.* Also, a response measure must actually *measure the behavior* it is supposed to measure. Finally, the response measure must be *stable,* or *reliable,* known to show the least variation under constant experimental conditions. Mechanized recording procedures, which are usually not available for use in an undergraduate project, help to produce stability in the translation of behavior to some numerical index.

Researchers often "solve" the problem of choosing among response measures simply by including several response measures in an experiment. They follow this procedure to preserve some of the richness and complexity of the behavior being studied and to ascertain whether different aspects of the behavior are affected differently by the administration of the treatment conditions. In this book, we will consider only experiments that have a single dependent variable. For experiments in which two or more dependent variables are to be recorded and analyzed, results can be examined as deriving from *separate experiments,* one for each of the response measures.[3]

Conducting the Study

The most difficult components of any research study occur before the first piece of data is ever collected. But, as we hope is clear by now, this work is critical if the study is to have any meaning or value. Reviewing and evaluating existing

---

[3] In fact, most researchers analyze an experiment with multiple response measures in this way. More appropriate *multivariate procedures* are available for analyzing experiments with more than one response measure, but these are complicated, generally require the use of a computer, and are beyond the scope of this book.

theory and research helps to ensure that the study will answer unaddressed questions. Stating the research hypothesis identifies the independent and dependent variables, which may then be translated into specific treatment conditions and measurable aspects of relevant behavior.

Once this work has been carried out, what's next? The researcher is now ready to conduct the study, which consists primarily of collecting data using a particular experimental design. (We consider this stage of research in Sec. 1.3.) Once collected, the data may then be analyzed using statistical methods. There are two main types of statistics we discuss in this book. The first type are what are called **descriptive statistics**; these are statistics designed to describe or summarize a set of data. The most common descriptive statistics are the *mean* and the *standard deviation*. The other type of statistics are what are known as **inferential statistics**. These are statistics designed to make inferences about larger populations. The concept of populations will be discussed in greater detail in Sec. 1.3.

Once the data are analyzed, decisions can be made regarding whether the research hypothesis has been supported. Did you find the results you anticipated? Do the findings *support* your theory? Note the emphasis on the word *support* in the previous sentence. Unfortunately, in any field where one studies complex phenomena, it is impossible for one individual study to "prove" that a theory is true or false. Theories are always tentative, serving an explanatory function until a better theory or explanation is devised.

Reporting Your Results

No research project is complete until it has been summarized in a formal research report and, if appropriate, submitted to a journal for publication or to a convention for presentation to other researchers who are interested in research conducted in the research field. A research report contains sufficient information that the reader will understand the following critical aspects of the study:

- Why the experiment was conducted.

- What research hypotheses were evaluated.

- How the research hypotheses were translated into the methods and procedures of an actual experiment. The detail should be sufficient that the reader could duplicate the experiment exactly.

- What differences were observed among the different treatment conditions (descriptive statistics).

- Which research hypotheses were supported by the results and which were not (inferential statistics).

- What conclusions will be drawn from the experiment and how they relate to relevant theories.

Science is dependent on a steady flow of new research reports so that it can mature and develop. Preparing research reports forces researchers to examine all aspects of their studies critically and in minute detail before they are made available to the scientific community. Errors of reasoning and flaws in the experimental design are sometimes discovered at this stage; if these are then not adequately resolved, they will usually persuade the researcher to place the report in a filing cabinet and return to the laboratory, where he or she will redesign the experiment to correct the flaws and conduct a new, improved study.

1.3 EXPERIMENTAL RESEARCH DESIGN

The specification of the research hypothesis and the identification of the independent and dependent variables provide only a skeletal outline of an experiment. Many specific details must be worked out before experimentation can actually begin. The decisions an investigator makes at this stage can be creative, challenging, and often frustrating.

Characteristics of Experimental Designs

The actual *design* of an experiment is a topic about which we will have a great deal to say. In a statistics book, **experimental design** usually refers to a general plan for conducting an experiment. Experimental designs can differ in a number of ways — for example, in the *number of independent variables* to be manipulated. The most common design for an experiment in which two or more independent variables are manipulated is called the *factorial design*. Most experiments in the contemporary literature of psychological research employ factorial designs. As a consequence, we will discuss the analysis of such designs fully (in Parts Three and Four) to enable you both to understand such experiments when you encounter them in your studies and to design them when you are ready to conduct independent research of your own. In the earlier chapters, however, we will focus on the *single*-variable experiment, because it is simpler to understand and it serves as an important building block for the more complicated factorial design.

A second major way in which experimental designs can differ is in the *method of assigning subjects* to the different treatment conditions. In the simplest procedure, and the one we consider first, an independent group of subjects is assigned to each of the treatments. At the other extreme is a design in which each subject serves in *all* of the treatment conditions. In between are designs in which these features are combined, with the subjects serving in some but not all of the treatment conditions. All these designs are relatively common in psychology, and consequently we give them considerable attention in this book.

Decisions Regarding the Subjects

Several issues regarding the subjects to be studied in an experiment must be considered during the planning stage of a research project. Generally, three decisions must be made at this point: the nature or type of subjects included in the experiment, the selection of these subjects, and the number of subjects needed in the experiment. We consider each decision in turn.

The Nature of the Subjects.   What sort of subjects do we wish to study in an experiment? Should we test animals or humans? Any particular sort of animal or human? Do we want subjects with a particular past history? Do we want individuals at a particular stage of maturation or development? In many cases, the primary factor is *availability*. Students usually test one another as well as friends and relatives, and researchers frequently select student "volunteers" from introductory psychology classes. In the case of two of the authors of this book, we defend our choice of subjects by noting that we want to study basic learning and memory processes, and that these factors are most easily observable in articulate individuals who have developed efficient skills in learning and in using what they have learned. If the nature of our research questions were to change and college students were no longer appropriate as subjects, we would choose other types of individuals — for example, children (to study the development of learning and memory skills) or individuals with head injuries (to study the loss of learning skills and memory ability). In addition to availability, then, theoretical considerations may also play a role in the choice of subjects.

Selecting the Subjects.   By now in your psychology courses, you have often heard of the term *sample*. Most typically, it has referred to a group of people who were part of a research study. The term **sampling**, logically enough, refers to the process of selecting participants for a research project. For many psychologists, the primary goal of research is to build and test theories regarding different phenomena. To accomplish this goal, research is conducted in order to make inferences regarding the phenomenon (its characteristics, its relationship with other variables, and so on) as it exists in a **population**, which may be defined as the total number of possible units or elements that can be included in a study. Even though we wish to make inferences or **generalizations** about a particular population, it is often difficult if not impossible to collect data from all members of that population. As the next best thing, psychologists make inferences about populations based on information collected from a portion, or **sample**, of that population. The goal of sampling, therefore, is to collect data from a representative sample drawn from a larger population to make inferences about that population. The ability to make generalizations about a population from a sample is what is referred to as **external validity**.

Suppose you were conducting an experiment and you wanted to apply the results to all college students in the United States. How could you draw a sample from this population? There are two main categories of sampling strategies, one of which involves a *random selection process* and the other a *nonrandom process*. For example, as a random selection technique you could employ **random sampling**, whereby every member of the population has an equal probability of being selected. In this example, this would involve finding a list of everyone currently enrolled in a college or university in the United States and randomly selecting a sample from this list.

Although random sampling may be the best way for a study to have a representative sample, and therefore to have the greatest external validity, you can see that these strategies require a great deal of time and money. Because of these pragmatic issues, much research in psychology is based on samples obtained through nonrandom selection processes; one example of this is what is known as **availability sampling**.

If you participated in research studies as part of a course requirement, you were introduced to this type of sampling strategy. The psychologist conducting the study collects data from those who choose to participate in it; since this decision is left up to the participant, it is very difficult for the researcher to know how random or representative the sample is. As a consequence, although availability sampling has the advantages of economy of time and money, studies using this technique have a lessened ability to generalize their findings to larger populations.

Most researchers conducting psychology experiments use availability sampling — that is, they identify a sample or pool of subjects who will participate in an experiment — and are not particularly concerned with the loss of external validity resulting from this decision. What researchers *are* concerned about is whether the results of experiments can be *duplicated* or *replicated* by themselves and others. This is another meaning of the concept of external validity, namely, whether the results of a particular independent variable *generalize* to different samples of subjects who serve in essentially the same experiment. We consider this issue at various points throughout this book.

Choosing the Number of Subjects. "How many subjects do we need to include in an experiment?" is a question our students ask us just before they start testing subjects in their research projects. The answer to this question is so simple it seems trite. An experimenter needs as many subjects as are necessary to provide a relatively sensitive test of the research hypothesis. (By *sensitivity*, we mean the ability to detect differences when they are present.) One way to increase the sensitivity in an experiment is to increase the number of subjects.[4] Given that the availability of subjects is generally limited, the experimenter attempts to test as many subjects as possible, but for students this may consist of a relatively small sample. As a result, students are often forced to conclude that their experiments have produced results that are "promising" — that is, results that lean in the direction predicted, but that do not have strong statistical support, since too few subjects were tested. To aid our own students in increasing the sensitivity of their experiments, we encourage them to work jointly on research projects so that they can both broaden the scope of their studies — by increasing the number of treatment conditions — and combine their friends and relatives to add to the number of subjects included in the experiment.

The relative lack of statistical sensitivity resulting from the use of small numbers of subjects — a problem that is usually beyond the control of student experimenters — takes some of the fun out of conducting a research project. You may have an interesting research idea and a perfectly good experiment and by all rights expect to be able to obtain unambiguous conclusions following the statistical analysis. But an insufficient number of subjects may render such conclusions impossible. We will return to the problem of sensitivity in later chapters.

Confounding Variables

The strength of the experimental method depends on our ability to guarantee that only the manipulated variable is permitted to vary systematically from con-

---

[4] We discuss additional ways of achieving sensitivity in Chap. 8.

dition to condition. In cases where other differences are found to have varied along with the treatment differences, we say that a *confounding* exists between any variation associated with the independent variable and these other differences, which are not part of the basic manipulation defining the independent variable. These unwanted factors are called **confounding variables** and usually pose a serious problem for us if they can be shown to influence the behavior under study. If this does happen, we will not be able to distinguish between the effects of the manipulated variable and the effects of the other differences representing the confounding variables. As a result, the presence of confounding variables usually ruins an experiment.

An Example of a Confounding.   Suppose we want to compare the effectiveness of three different methods of teaching arithmetic to elementary school children. For the experiment, we train a different teacher in each method, making sure that in all three methods exactly the same material is covered. The teachers then instruct their classes for two weeks using the method in which they were trained, and the performance of the subjects is assessed by a test made up by the experimenter. The methods of teaching arithmetic constitute the independent variable, and the scores on the proficiency test constitute the dependent variable.

How would you evaluate this experiment? We hope that you can see the rather serious flaws built into this example. Although the manipulated variable consists of the differences in the teaching methods, several other variables may be at work, thus potentially confounding the independent variable under study. One such variable is the ability of the subjects in the different classes. It is highly likely that the classes differed in average ability and training *before* the start of the two-week training period. Disentangling these differences from any differences produced by the three training methods be impossible; thus, training methods and preexisting differences in ability are confounded. Another confounding variable might consist of differences in the abilities of the three teachers. The teachers probably differ in teaching effectiveness, and discriminating these differences from the effects of the three training methods would be impossible. Thus, teacher ability and training methods are confounded.

Another Example.   Perhaps a nonresearch situation may help explain the concept of confounding variables. Recently one of the authors of this book was having problems with the tape deck in his car. For some reason, the sound coming out of the right speaker was full of static. Not wanting to pay for repairs, he took the deck out of the car and poked around — adjusting a screw here, pushing a wire there, cleaning the tape heads. After about three hours, he put the deck back into the car and was pleasantly surprised to find that it worked perfectly. But what was the cause of the improvement? Was it adjusting the screws? Cleaning the tape heads?

Because many different things had been changed, there were many different "causes" for the "effect" of good sound, making it difficult, if not impossible, to give causal credit to any one of them. How could he have identified the real cause of the tape deck's problems? One way may have been to change only one thing at a time before testing the tape deck's sound. That is, he could have cleaned the tape heads, put the deck back in, and seen if it worked. If it did, then he could have said with confidence that dirty tape heads caused the sound problems. If it did not work, then he could have tried something else. Realistically, of course, most of us in this sort of nonresearch situation would not be particularly interested in the laborious process of isolating the *cause* of the effect, but would be content simply with curing the problem. In this case, we would probably find it more efficient to try to remedy all "causes" at once, rather than assess each potential factor one at a time.

Eliminating Confoundings.   Researchers need to be continually on the alert for factors operating in an experiment that may result in a confounding with the independent variable. The obvious first step toward preventing confoundings in your own research is to be constantly aware of the problem. You should examine critically all phases of your planned research to discover possible flaws. Discussing your experiment with others is also often helpful. Kirk (1982, p. 7) suggests that researchers try to list all factors that might affect the behavior under study and to make sure that these are all controlled in some manner in the design of the experiment.

How do we control these potential sources of confoundings, which we will call **nuisance variables** — factors that may vary from condition to condition and influence the dependent variable? One obvious method is to exercise experimental *control* by holding them *constant*, so that they have the same influence on each of the treatment conditions. Common nuisance variables that may be controlled by holding them physically constant throughout the duration of the experiment are certain background characteristics in the experimental situation — such as the testing environment itself (temperature, level of illumination, humidity, and the like), the location of the experiment, the time of day or day of the week of the experiment, the instruments or measures used, and the instructions given to the research participants.

There is no question that holding potentially variable characteristics of the experiment at constant levels prevents the confounding of variables in an unambiguous and straightforward manner. Unfortunately, however, we are not able to "handle" all potential nuisance variables in this way. This happens because we find it difficult or impossible to control many nuisance variables during the course of an experiment and because we are usually not able even to identify all potential nuisance variables in order to hold them constant. For these remaining nuisance variables, we equalize or neutralize their effects by distributing them equally over all levels of the independent variable through the **random assignment** of subjects to the treatment conditions. We discuss this important procedure in Sec. 3.1.

Loss of Subjects

We have argued that confoundings resulting from the operation of nuisance variables must be eliminated either by exercising experimental control over them or neutralizing their impact by randomly assigning subjects to the treatment conditions. What happens when there is inadvertent loss of subjects during the course of experimentation? How does this affect the process of neutralizing nuisance variables? This loss of subjects, known as **subject mortality**, is particularly a concern when subject loss occurs in different amounts for the different conditions. We will consider the implications of this unfortunate circumstance in some detail.

Subjects are lost (or discarded) from an experiment for various reasons. In animal studies, for example, subjects are frequently lost through sickness and other factors. In human studies in which testing is to continue over several days, subjects are discarded when they fail to complete the entire experimental sequence. In a memory study, for instance, some subjects may fail to return a week after the first phase for their final retention test, perhaps because of illness or an unforeseen appointment. Subjects may also be lost when the experimental procedures require that all subjects meet the same performance criterion, such as a certain level of mastery. In this sort of experiment, subjects who fail to meet the previously determined performance criterion are dropped. Another source of losses is the failure of subjects to produce responses that meet the criteria established for the response measure. Suppose we are interested in the speed with which correct responses are made. A subject who fails to give a correct response cannot contribute to the analysis. Or suppose we want to determine the percentage of times in which the errors produced on a task are of a particular type. A subject who fails to make any errors cannot contribute to the analysis. In such situations, then, subjects are eliminated from the experiment because they fail to give scorable responses.

When subject losses occur, it is of critical importance to the interpretation of the experiment that we determine their implication. After all, we have assigned our subjects to the experimental conditions randomly to neutralize the effects of nuisance variables. We are not concerned with the loss of subjects per se, but with this question: Has the loss of subjects, for whatever reason, resulted in a loss of "randomness"? If randomness has been lost, we no longer have the assurance that all nuisance variables have been balanced over the treatment conditions. We must either find a way to restore this balance or simply junk the experiment. No form of statistical juggling will rectify the situation if randomness cannot be restored. If randomness may still be safely assumed, or if it has been restored, we can proceed with the analysis and interpretation of the data.

In each situation, we must determine whether the reason for the subject loss was in any way associated with particular treatments. In animal research, for instance, certain treatment conditions (such as surgery, drugs, high levels of food or water deprivation, exhausting training procedures) may actually be responsible for the loss of the subjects. In such a case, only the strongest and healthiest animals would complete the experiment, and the result would be an obvious confounding of subject differences and treatment conditions: the difficult conditions would contain a larger proportion of healthy animals than the less trying conditions. Replacing the lost subjects with new animals drawn from the same population would not be an adequate solution, since the replacement subjects would not "match" those lost. But if the researcher can show that the loss of subjects was approximately the same for all the treatment conditions or that the loss was not related to the specific treatments, the analysis can continue.

The second source of subject loss — through the failure of subjects to reach a criterion of mastery — poses similar problems. Clearly, subjects who fail to learn the task in an experiment are by definition poorer learners than those who do learn it. If one group suffers a greater loss through failure of mastery, which may very well happen if the conditions differ in difficulty, the subjects in the difficult condition who meet the predetermined criterion will be better learners than those completing the training in the easier conditions. Replacing subjects lost in the difficult condition would not solve this problem, since the replacement subjects would not match the ability of the lost subjects.

Clearly, then, the loss of subjects is of paramount concern to a researcher. If the loss of subjects is related to the phenomenon under study, it destroys the neutralization of nuisance variables normally achieved by random assignment, thus potentially adding a systematic bias or confounding to the differences among the treatment conditions that cannot be disentangled from the influence of the independent variable. This problem is one of experimental design and must be solved by the researcher if the results of the experiment are to have meaning. It is here that knowledge of the subject matter being studied and the practice of others can be helpful.

The Analytical Nature of Experimentation

Not long ago, the two-condition experiment was the typical experiment in psychology. Today, the multiple-condition experiment is dominant, and the simple two-condition study is rarely reported. One reason for this development is that contemporary researchers choose to study a range of treatment conditions rather than to base their conclusions on an experiment with only two levels of an independent variable.

Quantitative Independent Variables. A **quantitative independent variable** is a variable in which the treatment levels differ in *degree* or in *amount* as measured by either a physical or a psychological scale. The number of hours of food deprivation for rats in a maze-learning experiment, the degree of background noise in a signal-detection task, the amount of money given as incentive in a problem-solving task are all examples of quantitative independent variables. In an experiment that has a quantitative independent variable, the variable is usually represented by several levels, or conditions, covering a relatively large range of variation. In the rat experiment, for example, a researcher might include conditions with 0, 1, 12, and 24 hours of food deprivation — and even longer intervals if there is reason to believe that additional changes will be observed after 24 hours. This strategy ensures that the relationship linking changes in the independent variable with changes in the dependent variable will be adequately determined in the experiment.

The research hypothesis associated with a quantitative manipulation consists of a statement that changing a particular independent variable quantitatively will produce a systematic change in the dependent variable. For example, the experimenter might ask, "Will increasing amounts of light affect the detection of a visual pattern?" or, "Will increasing amounts of a particular drug influence the speed of a motor response?" Entertaining such a speculation is sufficient reason for designing an experiment to provide this sort of information. The investigator making the speculation will then conduct analyses to determine the *properties* of this particular relationship. The analytical nature of such an experiment is reflected in the procedures involved in detailing and assessing the components or processes responsible for the observed relationship.

Qualitative Independent Variables. A **qualitative independent variable** is a variable in which the levels differ in *kind* rather than in amount. Qualitative independent variables are easy to recognize, since the specific conditions chosen to define the independent variable cannot be ordered meaningfully on a quantitative scale. Types of drugs, variations in the instructions given to subjects, and differences in teaching methods are examples of qualitative independent variables.

An experiment containing a qualitative independent variable is generally made up of a number of **analytical comparisons**, or, if you will, a number of miniature experiments. Suppose, for example, that we have been asked to assess the usefulness of two different drugs in relaxing hyperactive children in the classroom. The most obvious approach would be to administer the two drugs to two groups of hyperactive children and to compare their relative effectiveness. The independent variable in this experiment is qualitative (kind of drug, not amount). Any difference observed in the classroom between the two groups after the drug is administered is attributed by the researcher to the differential effectiveness of the two drugs. Most investigators would not be satisfied with this simple experiment, however. They would probably include a third level in the experiment, a control condition in which a third group of subjects is given no drug at all. This **control group** (or **placebo group**, as it is often called) adds valuable information to the experiment. More specifically, the control condition helps to rule out the operation of *psychological* factors associated with the experience of serving in an experiment. Let's consider this point in more detail.

The addition of the control group results in three different treatment conditions and the possibility of obtaining answers to several analytical questions from the results of the experiment. Consider three possibilities:

Comparison 1: Control versus drug A
Comparison 2: Control versus drug B
Comparison 3: Drug A versus drug B

You will note that each comparison is in essence a separate two-group experiment incorporated into the design of the overall experiment. Comparison 3, drug A versus drug B, represents the information available from the original two-group experiment we considered initially. Comparisons 1 and 2 both involve the control condition and provide information that would not have been available from the simpler design. That is, comparison 1 permits us to determine whether drug A has a *positive* effect (produces relaxation in the subjects), a *negative* effect (increases hyperactivity), or *no effect* whatsoever (in which case no difference would be discovered between the drug A group and the control group). Comparison 2 assesses the same three possible outcomes with drug B.

Let us summarize the important advantages of including the control condition in this experiment. First, the control condition will lead us to the appropriate conclusion if the two drugs are *equally effective* in reducing hyperactivity.

The two-group experiment, on the other hand, would lead us to conclude that the two drugs do not differ, but we would be unable to tell whether the drugs are equally effective or equally *in*effective in controlling hyperactivity. The addition of the control condition provides us with a means of distinguishing between these two possibilities.

Second, the control condition will give us information about the nature of the two drug effects if the two drug conditions *do* produce a difference on the dependent variable. Suppose drug A is found to be more effective than drug B. Does this mean that drug A has a positive effect and drug B has no effect? No, all we are able to conclude is that drug A is more effective than drug B. In reality, drug A may have no effect while drug B has a negative effect — that is, while drug B increases hyperactivity. The control condition allows us to determine which of these different possibilities is correct.

This example demonstrates how we can increase the analytical power of an experiment by including more than two conditions in the experiment. As you will see, this form of qualitative manipulation can be applied to most of the experiments we will encounter. In Chap. 6, we will introduce statistical procedures by which these kinds of analytical comparisons can be assessed directly. In this section, we set the stage for this future discussion by illustrating how informationally rich even a relatively simple experiment can be, and by emphasizing that in the design and analysis of experiments a researcher can exercise his or her imagination, individuality, and creative powers to the fullest. No two investigators will design an experiment in exactly the same way. Some researchers design experiments that yield important insights, while others construct studies that are less creatively designed. The challenge is to create meaningful and analytically powerful experiments that excite your imagination. Learning how to use an experiment analytically will permit you to enter this rewarding arena, in which new knowledge about behavior is continually being sought and discovered.

While the execution of a research project allows the full expression of imagination and creativity, the success or failure of the whole operation still depends on the proper exercise of *logic* at all stages of the study. First, the research hypothesis must follow logically from the empirical and theoretical background of the study. Next, the specific treatment conditions must adequately reflect the critical elements of the research hypothesis. Third, the experiment must be defined so that only the different treatments are permitted to vary systematically across the conditions — that is, confoundings must be avoided. Also, the statistical analyses must be conducted so as to provide a comprehensive assessment of the results. And finally, the investigator must draw correct inferences in interpreting the statistical analyses and must integrate these new findings with existing knowledge and theory.

Despite these caveats, it is worth remembering that statistical procedures and analyses are only of secondary importance in the discovery of knowledge and that statistical procedures are neutral with respect to the quality of the experiment under analysis. A poorly designed experiment can be just as impeccably and competently analyzed as one that is well designed. In this regard, researchers often view statistics and statistical analyses as *tools* to assist them in drawing statistically justifiable conclusions from a set of data. Success in using these tools is dependent on the underlying logic and creative construction of the experimental design.

1.4 SUMMARY

The establishment of facts and the testing of theory in psychology are dependent on careful and imaginative experimentation. While other research approaches and techniques occupy an important place in our discipline, the experiment is a tool we can use to establish factors that cause behavior.

An experiment begins with the formulation of a research hypothesis. A research hypothesis often represents a test of an existing theory, but other reasons exist for conducting an experiment. For example, investigators may undertake experiments to add to our factual knowledge, to investigate a new independent variable, or to study a new phenomenon, while showing little or no concern for theory testing or even theoretical development. In any case, the research hypothesis provides the focus for the experiment: it dictates the nature of the independent variable to be manipulated, and it probably suggests the nature of the dependent variable as well. Other decisions influence the design of an experiment — for example, the specific methods and procedures to be employed, the type of experimental design to be used, and the subjects to be tested.

The greatest failing of experiments is the inadvertent confounding of independent variables. Confounding occurs when uncontrolled factors, called nuisance variables, vary in conjunction with the manipulation of the independent variable. If any possibility exists that such factors may have influenced the behavior under study, then the experiment is usually ruined and the findings are uninterpretable.

Almost any feature of the task and of the subject's external and internal environment can be manipulated in an experiment. Also, researchers are able to study the effects of psychological variables by giving different instructions to different subjects designed to induce differential sets and motivations. Even relatively permanent characteristics of subjects can be varied in an experiment — these are subject or classification variables — but since in such cases the "manipulations" are not directly under the control of the experimenter, inferences of cause and effect are difficult, if not impossible, to draw from the results of such studies.

Most experimental manipulations are carefully crafted by a researcher to provide answers to the analytical questions posed by research hypotheses. If the manipulation is quantitative in nature — variation in the *amount* of the independent variable — the research hypothesis often includes some speculation concerning the anticipated shape of the function relating the dependent variable to the quantitative manipulation. On the other hand, if the manipulation is qualitative — variation in *kind* rather than amount — the intent of the experiment is to answer a number of specific research questions that use the data from the different treatment conditions in various combinations. Each of the combinations is designed to shed some light on these specific analytical questions.

1.5 EXERCISES

1. Distinguish between an independent variable and a dependent variable. Illustrate your answer with a real or imaginary experiment.

2. What are confounding variables? Why are they a concern in conducting an experiment?

Chapter · 2

PRELIMINARY DATA ANALYSIS

In the preceding chapter, we described the general nature of psychology experiments. In this chapter, we introduce procedures that transform the results of an experiment (the so-called raw data) into a manageable and useful form. This stage can be thought of as a preliminary analysis of the data, that is, an initial examination of how the experiment "turned out." To accomplish this preliminary analysis, the researcher uses the individual data points — the basic scores or observations — to calculate certain quantities that summarize the fundamental characteristics of the results. This process of "refinement" has been called *data reduction*, since it results in the reduction of a large number of observations to a much smaller number of *statistical indices*. These indices — numbers derived from the raw data — are used as indicators or measures to describe and summarize the different sets of scores produced by the experiment.

We introduce two kinds of statistical indices that are particularly useful in summarizing data and in drawing inferences from the results of experiments. The measure we discuss first is used to specify what we might call the "typical" score — a score that is representative of all the scores in any set under consideration. This kind of index is a measure of the centrality, or **central tendency**, of a set of scores. When obtaining a measure of central tendency, we make a simple assumption, which, given past experience, appears to be a safe one: even though the scores vary, they do spread themselves around a point that best describes the data in question. The second kind of index provides a measure of this variation or irregularity in a set of scores. This type of index is a measure of the **variability** — the differences among scores — in a given set. As you will see in later chapters, we use measures of variability to estimate the degree to which chance factors (as opposed to the independent variable) are responsible for any differences observed among the treatment conditions of an experiment.

2.1 THE MEAN AS A MEASURE OF CENTRAL TENDENCY

Definition of the Mean

The arithmetic mean, or **mean** for short, is the primary index of central tendency used in the analysis of experiments. It is defined thus:

$$\text{mean} = \frac{\text{sum of the scores}}{\text{number of scores}} \tag{2-1}$$

Computationally, the mean is simple, especially if you have a hand-held calculator. The scores do not have to be arranged in any particular order, but can be summed just as they are listed in front of you.

Most people are familiar with the concept of the mean because of the averages reported by the media at every flip of a channel or turn of a page. The average score on a midterm examination, the average income of a college graduate, and the team batting averages of baseball players are all common examples of the mean. Conceptually, the mean represents the score value *per subject* or *per observation*. This property of means makes possible the comparison of individuals or groups of individuals — which may vary with regard to the numbers of available observations — on a *common base* or reference point.

Symbolic Representation of the Mean

While presenting the formulas for various calculations, we will also introduce some notation. The notation is merely a shorthand way of representing the various arithmetic operations we need to perform in carrying out these calculations.

The Formula. We have already defined the mean in words as the sum of the scores divided by the number of scores. The next step is to demonstrate how these arithmetical operations can be represented symbolically. Since you may be unfamiliar with some of the expressions used, we will construct the formula for the mean step by step.

We start with the representation of the set of scores from which the mean will be calculated. We use the capital letter Y to symbolize a score or an observation, and a numerical subscript to designate a *particular* score. Thus, Y_1 refers to the first score in a set, Y_2 to the second score in a set, and so on. To refer to all the Y scores *in general* but to no one score in particular, we use the letter i as a subscript instead of a number: Y_i.

Next, we designate the addition of the Y scores by means of the symbol Σ, which is the capital Greek letter *sigma* and means *sum*. We usually "read" this symbol as "take the sum of...," and follow this expression with whatever quantities we want to add. In the case of the mean, we want to take the sum of all the Y scores. Symbolically, this intention is represented by

$$\Sigma Y_i$$

which states, "take the sum of the Y_i scores." Finally, we will represent the number of scores by a lower-case n. Putting all this together, we can write the formula for the arithmetic mean, $\overline{Y}$. (With this notation, $\overline{Y}$ is the symbol for a mean and is read "Y bar." Usually, any symbol with a bar over it indicates a mean.) Thus, the formula is

$$\overline{Y} = \frac{\Sigma Y_i}{n} \tag{2-2}$$

Again, in words this formula defines the mean as the sum of the scores divided by the number of scores.

In most situations, the use of the subscript i is superfluous and conveys no additional information. When this is the case, we drop the subscript and write the formula of Eq. (2-2) more simply as

$$\overline{Y} = \frac{\Sigma Y}{n} \tag{2-3}$$

TABLE 2-1 *A Numerical Example*	
Symbol (Y_i)	*Score*
Y_1	6
Y_2	3
Y_3	4
Y_4	9
Y_5	3

Numerical Example. A set of five scores (that is, $n = 5$) is presented in Table 2-1. Each score is designated by a number subscript representing the ordinal position of the score in the set. The sum of these scores is represented by

$$\Sigma Y = Y_1 + Y_2 + Y_3 + Y_4 + Y_5$$

When the scores are substituted, the formula becomes

$$\Sigma Y = 6 + 3 + 4 + 9 + 3$$

$$= 25$$

Substituting in Eq. (2-3), we calculate the mean as follows:

$$\overline{Y} = \frac{\Sigma Y}{n}$$

$$= \frac{25}{5}$$

$$= 5.00$$

Rounding. We selected the Y scores for this example to produce a mean that would come out evenly, without decimals. With actual data, however, the mean is rarely a whole number. Now that nearly everyone has access to a hand-held electronic calculator, it is possible with minimal effort to produce answers to a large number of decimal places. On the other hand, such accuracy and precision is usually unnecessary in our work, and we drop, or *round off*, the excess digits. Generally, for purposes of calculating and reporting, the value of the mean (and other statistics) is rounded to two or at most three decimal places. In this book, we round each calculation we report, whether a substep in a longer calculation or a final answer, to two decimal places — that is, to the nearest hundredth.[1] (In some cases, when the example is simple and answers purposely come out evenly, we will report the values without a decimal point.)

Authors (and researchers) differ in the particular method they use in rounding numbers. For the sake of simplicity, we have adopted the method that is programmed into most electronic calculators. The only difference is that we will round answers to the second decimal place whereas most calculators round to the limits of the numerical display regardless of the number of decimal places appearing in the answer. The rounding rules are simple:

1. **If the digit in the third decimal place is less than 5, leave the digit in the second place** *unchanged.*
2. **If the digit in the third decimal place is equal to or greater than 5,** *raise* **the digit in the second place by 1.**

These two rules will become clear as you follow through the calculations appearing in this book. Rounding has the advantage of making the arithmetical operations easier to comprehend, especially when the calculations are complex. In nearly all cases, rounding to the nearest hundredth will have no practical effect on our ultimate statistical decisions.

The Mean as a Balancing Point

As an index of central tendency, the mean possesses an interesting characteristic. Suppose we express each score in a set of data as a discrepancy (or difference) from the mean. Thus, scores smaller than the mean would take on negative values, while scores greater than the mean would take on positive values. The unique property of the mean is that the sum of the negative discrepancies *exactly equals* the sum of the positive discrepancies. As a consequence, the sum of the discrepancies — keeping in mind the positive and negative signs — equals zero. We will illustrate this property with the data in Table 2-1, which have been plotted on a number line in Fig. 2-1. The extent to which each score deviates above or below the mean ($\overline{Y} = 5$) is indicated directly underneath the number line. As you can see, the sum of the three Y

---

[1] Technically, we should carry all substeps to three decimal places and round to two only in the last step. This has proved to be confusing to students in the past, and the precision afforded by such a procedure for our purposes is minimal. If you choose to be more precise and carry your calculations out further, you may find that your final answers differ from ours by 1 to 2 percent at the most.

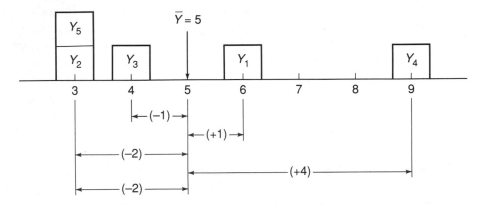

FIGURE 2-1 *Graphic Display of the Deviation of Each Observation (Y) from the Mean of the Observations ($\overline{Y}$). Note that except for sign, the sum of the negative deviations (Y scores falling below the mean) equals the sum of the positive deviations (Y scores falling above the mean).*

scores falling below the mean (sum $= -5$) exactly balances the sum of the two Y scores falling above the mean (sum $= +5$). In symbols,

$$\Sigma(Y - \overline{Y}) = 0 \tag{2-4}$$

As you will see in Sec. 2.2, the mean serves as a reference point against which we can express another important characteristic of a set of scores, the degree to which the numbers vary.

The Median as a Measure of Central Tendency

Occasionally, the median of a set of scores is reported in the research literature as a measure of central tendency. To calculate the median, we begin by arranging the scores in order of magnitude. The **median** is the middlemost score of this ordered set, the score at or above which one-half of the scores lie.

Why would one choose to report the median rather than the mean? For one reason, the median is not influenced by the presence of extreme scores on either side of the dividing point. The only scores critical in the determination of the median are those immediately next to the median; the remaining scores beyond these two transition points have no direct effect on the median value. The mean, on the other hand, *is* influenced by extreme scores, since its value is affected directly by the values of *all* the scores in the set.

Researchers use the median when they feel that extreme scores would tend to obscure the central tendency exhibited by the large majority of the scores if the mean were calculated. For example, when social scientists report the "typical" income of a group of individuals, they usually choose the median as a more representative measure of central tendency than the mean. They make this choice to minimize the influence of a small number of extremely high incomes that would have a distorting effect on the mean.

Experimenters also use the median when some of the scores are unavailable because of time limits set by the researcher. In problem-solving experiments, for example, subjects are frequently given a fixed time to solve a problem, which means that occasionally a few subjects will not solve the problem within the time limit. Under these circumstances, the mean would actually be incalculable, because solution-time scores would not be produced by all subjects. The median usually would be calculated, however, since it does not require the actual values of these extreme and unavailable scores.

If the median is not unduly influenced by extreme scores, why not use it in our analyses instead of the mean? As already noted, the mean plays an essential role in the statistical analysis of experiments, and for this reason we have stressed it most heavily as a measure of central tendency. The median can be used in this role, but its applications are not as extensive as those associated with the mean. However, in purely descriptive research — for example, survey research, demographic research, and the like — the median may actually be more descriptive than the mean because of its relative insensitivity to extreme scores and to missing or incomplete data.

2.2 THE VARIANCE AS A MEASURE OF VARIABILITY

We have seen that one way to characterize a set of scores is to calculate the mean. This index of central tendency can then be used as a basis for comparing different sets of scores. We will be making such comparisons when we begin to analyze the data from experiments. A second way to characterize a set of scores is to determine the extent to which the scores differ from one another. As noted earlier, this characteristic is usually referred to as the variability of a set of scores, but other terms — for example, *deviation, dispersion, spread,* and *scatter* — are often used interchangeably.

Definition of the Variance

Whereas several measures of variability exist, the variance is the most critical for the statistical analysis of experiments. The **variance** is essentially an average of the dispersion, or scatter, of the scores in a set. The dispersion of each score is expressed as a **deviation from the mean**. The more widely scattered the scores in a set are, the larger these deviations will be, and the larger the variance.

Unfortunately, however, a straightforward average of these deviations will be of no use to us. As we illustrated with the data plotted in Fig. 2-1, the sum of the deviations from the mean will be zero for any set of scores, no matter how variable they may be. To solve this problem, we must remove the positive and negative signs associated with this index of dispersion. How can this be accomplished? By *squaring* each of the deviations *before* taking the average.[2] Thus,

> **the variance is defined as an average of the squared deviations from the mean.**

We will now consider the formulas with which we can calculate the variance.

Sum of Squares

The first step in obtaining the variance involves calculating the sum of the squared deviations from the mean, or the **sum of squares** (abbreviated *SS*). Two formulas are commonly given for calculating *SS*. We will first present the **defining formula**, because it perfectly represents in symbols the verbal definition of the sum of squares. We use the other, the **computational formula**, for calculation, since it involves less computational effort and has a wider application in the analysis of experiments.

Defining Formula. We can write the defining formula directly from the verbal definition of a sum of squares. Again, the sum of squares is defined the following way:

   SS = the sum of the squared deviations of all the scores from the mean

Since we already have available symbols for the mean ($\overline{Y}$) and for an individual

---

[2] The squared deviations do not cancel each other when summed, since squaring eliminates the negative deviations. Moreover, the sum will be zero only when there is absolutely no variability, that is, when all the scores have the same value.

TABLE 2-2 *The Steps in Calculating a Sum of Squares*

Basic Observation		Deviation from the Mean ($\overline{Y}$)		Squared Deviation from the Mean	
1. Symbol (Y_i)	2. Score	3. Symbol ($Y_i - \overline{Y}$)	4. Deviation	5. Symbol ($Y_i - \overline{Y}$)²	6. Squared Deviation
Y_1	16	$Y_1 - \overline{Y}$	$16 - 7 = +9$	$(Y_1 - \overline{Y})^2$	$(+9)^2 = 81$
Y_2	2	$Y_2 - \overline{Y}$	$2 - 7 = -5$	$(Y_2 - \overline{Y})^2$	$(-5)^2 = 25$
Y_3	4	$Y_3 - \overline{Y}$	$4 - 7 = -3$	$(Y_3 - \overline{Y})^2$	$(-3)^2 = 9$
Y_4	2	$Y_4 - \overline{Y}$	$2 - 7 = -5$	$(Y_4 - \overline{Y})^2$	$(-5)^2 = 25$
Y_5	11	$Y_5 - \overline{Y}$	$11 - 7 = +4$	$(Y_5 - \overline{Y})^2$	$(+4)^2 = 16$

score (Y_i), we can represent the deviation of any score from the mean as

$$Y_i - \overline{Y}$$

If we introduce the symbol for summation, Σ, we can write the following expression:

$$SS = \Sigma \, (Y_i - \overline{Y})^2$$

Again, we can drop the unnecessary subscript and write the formula more simply as

$$SS = \Sigma \, (Y - \overline{Y})^2 \tag{2-5}$$

Let's make sure that you can "read" this formula. The first symbol to the right of the equals sign, Σ, means "take the sum of," and the expression that follows designates the squared deviation of a Y score from the mean ($\overline{Y}$). Combining these two expressions and reading from left to right, we have, "The sum of squares equals the sum of the squared deviations from the mean."

As a numerical example, consider the set of scores in column 2 of Table 2-2. The calculations specified in Eq. (2-5) are enumerated step by step in the table. First, we need the mean. Substituting in Eq. (2-3), we find

$$\overline{Y} = \frac{\Sigma \, Y}{n}$$

$$= \frac{16 + 2 + 4 + 2 + 11}{5}$$

$$= \frac{35}{5}$$

$$= 7.00$$

Second, we subtract the mean from each score in order to obtain the required deviations. This step is made explicit with symbols in column 3 of Table 2-2 and with numbers in column 4. In passing, you see — as specified in Eq. (2-4) — that the sum of these deviations is zero. That is,

$$\begin{aligned}
\Sigma(Y - \overline{Y}) &= (16 - 7) + (2 - 7) + (4 - 7) + (2 - 7) + (11 - 7) \\
&= 9 + (-5) + (-3) + (-5) + 4 \\
&= 9 - 5 - 3 - 5 + 4 \\
&= 0
\end{aligned}$$

Third, each deviation is squared, as shown with symbols in column 5 and with numbers in column 6. Finally, all the squared deviations are summed. Substituting these squares in Eq. (2-5), we obtain

$$\begin{aligned}
SS &= \Sigma(Y - \overline{Y})^2 \\
&= (9)^2 + (-5)^2 + (-3)^2 + (-5)^2 + (4)^2 \\
&= 81 + 25 + 9 + 25 + 16 \\
&= 156
\end{aligned}$$

Computational Formula. As we stated earlier, the defining formula is usually not used to calculate the sum of squares. Some computational steps in the defining formula can be quite tedious, especially when the mean is not a whole number as it was in our example and when the set of scores is large. The computational formula, which we consider next, requires fewer steps and avoids this problem by dealing directly with the basic raw scores. In this form, the sum of squares is calculated by

$$SS = \Sigma \, Y^2 - \frac{(\Sigma \, Y)^2}{n} \tag{2-6}$$

With this formula, the raw scores are used to obtain two different sums:

1. The sum of the scores themselves, $\Sigma \, Y$
2. The sum of the *squares* of these scores, $\Sigma \, Y^2$

The latter quantity is new, and you should be certain that you understand completely what is involved. To be more explicit,

$$\Sigma \, Y^2 = Y_1^2 + Y_2^2 + Y_3^2 + \cdots$$

Each score is first squared and then the squares are summed. This operation is distinctly different from that specified in the numerator of the second term on the right side of Eq. (2-6), namely, $(\Sigma \, Y)^2$. This latter operation involves a squaring also, not of the individual scores, but of their sum, or total.

Students frequently confuse these two different calculations, and consequently they have difficulty in obtaining correct values for sums of squares. A common problem our students have is that they somehow end up with a *negative* value for the sum of squares. A negative sum of squares is impossible, which becomes obvious when you return to Eq. (2-5), the defining formula for a sum of squares, and note that all deviations — positive and negative — are *squared* before they are sum.

It is important that we not lose you at this point. You must understand sums of squares both conceptually and computationally. We make this emphatic pronouncement because sums of squares are calculated in nearly all the statistical analyses we consider in this book. Thus, sums of squares are vital for your future success, both as a neophyte researcher and as a (sometimes) struggling student.

The calculations themselves, specified in Eq. (2-6), are not complicated. They involve only the simple arithmetical operations of addition, subtraction, multiplication (in the form of squaring), and division. The one step that students identify as the most confusing is the translation of the abstract symbols in the computational formula into the concrete arithmetical manipulations of actual data. In fact, a relatively simple pattern lies behind the computational formulas of *all* sums of squares. However, we will not elucidate this pattern until Chap. 4, when it will be more evident than it would be now. At this point, we will describe — first with symbols and then with numbers — how we calculate the two quantities specified in Eq. (2-6) that are required to obtain the sum of squares.

We will use the data from Table 2-2 as a numerical example so that we can compare the results of applying the defining and computational formulas to the same set of numbers. For convenience, we present the data again on the left side of Table 2-3. On the right side of the table, each score is squared. We are now ready to use the basic scores and the squares of these scores to obtain the sum of squares.

TABLE 2-3 *A Numerical Example of the Computational Formula*

Basic Score		Square of the Basic Score	
Symbol (Y_i)	Score	Symbol (Y_i^2)	(Score)^2
Y_1	16	Y_1^2	256
Y_2	2	Y_2^2	4
Y_3	4	Y_3^2	16
Y_4	2	Y_4^2	4
Y_5	11	Y_5^2	121

With reference to Eq. (2-6), we will calculate the two quantities on the right first. That is,

$$\Sigma Y^2 = Y_1^2 + Y_2^2 + Y_3^2 + Y_4^2 + Y_5^2$$

$$= (16)^2 + (2)^2 + (4)^2 + (2)^2 + (11)^2$$

$$= 256 + 4 + 16 + 4 + 121$$

$$= 401$$

$$\frac{(\Sigma Y)^2}{n} = \frac{(16 + 2 + 4 + 2 + 11)^2}{5}$$

$$= \frac{(35)^2}{5} = \frac{1,225}{5}$$

$$= 245.00$$

We now subtract these numbers as indicated to obtain the sum of squares:

$$SS = \Sigma Y^2 - \frac{(\Sigma Y)^2}{n}$$

$$= 401 - 245.00$$

$$= 156.00$$

Does this number look familiar? Using the computational formula, we have calculated the same value we obtained using the defining formula in the preceding section.

Using a Calculator. The basic operations involved in calculating the sum of squares are at times tedious but are really relatively simple. These operations are repeated over and over in the analysis of data from simple as well as complex experiments. The calculation of $\Sigma\ Y$ and $\Sigma\ Y^2$, called *summing and squaring*, is particularly easy when performed on a calculator designed for statistical use. With this type of calculator, one just enters each score individually and presses the special summation button (sometimes labeled "$\Sigma+$ or "M+"), which "instructs" the calculator to cumulate and store the sum of scores and the sum of the squared scores automatically. Using such a calculator greatly reduces the agony usually associated with statistical calculations. Even a simple (and less expensive) four-function calculator cuts calculation time considerably. Since this type of calculator has no memory, the user has to supply the "memory" and perform the necessary operations in a series of three steps:

1. Sum the scores to obtain $\Sigma\ Y$.

2. Square each score and record each result on a worksheet.

3. Sum the values recorded in step 2 to obtain $\Sigma\ Y^2$.

We have prepared a brief tutorial on using several common electronic calculators to perform the calculations required for this book; it is presented in Appendix C at the end of the book.

Using the Computer. Depending on your resources and those available at your institution, you may have the opportunity to use a computer to conduct some or all of the calculations covered in this text. Whereas there is no question that you should be using the computer when you embark on a major research project — such as an undergraduate honors thesis, a master's thesis, or a doctoral dissertation — you may find your instructor reluctant to encourage using the computer, particularly for an introductory undergraduate course. As you might suspect, instructors differ widely in their sense of the appropriate time to introduce the computer in the classroom. Some believe, for example, that computer use should be integrated with statistical analysis almost at once, and they devote class time or create special sections to ensure that students learn to use the statistical software programs chosen for the class. On the other hand, some feel that they need all the allocated class time simply to cover the substantive statistical material in appropriate detail. They assume that software programs are easily learned once the students know what the programs should be doing for them. We discuss the use of statistical software in Chap. 16.

Variance

The variance is an average, just as the mean is an average. While the mean is calculated by dividing the sum of the scores by the number of scores, n, the variance is calculated by dividing the sum of squares (SS) by a slightly smaller number, the number of scores minus 1, that is, $n - 1$. In symbols,

$$\text{variance} = \frac{SS}{n - 1} \tag{2-7}$$

The divisor is called the **degrees of freedom** (abbreviated **df**). Thus, the variance can be defined as

$$\text{variance} = \frac{SS}{df} \tag{2-8}$$

We will discuss the concept of degrees of freedom more fully in Chap. 4. For the time being, we ask you to accept this definition of variance and not to worry why we divide the sum of squares by $n - 1$ rather than by the more "natural" n.[3]

We can illustrate the calculation of the variance with the data from Table 2-3. From the calculations summarized in the last section, we can substitute directly in Eq. (2-7), that is,

$$\begin{aligned} \text{variance} &= \frac{SS}{n - 1} \\ &= \frac{156.00}{5 - 1} \\ &= \frac{156.00}{4} \\ &= 39.00 \end{aligned}$$

Standard Deviation

The **standard deviation** is often reported instead of the variance. This statistical index is equal to the square root of the variance:

$$\text{standard deviation} = \sqrt{\text{variance}} \tag{2-9}$$

---

[3] Situations exist in which it is appropriate to divide by the number of scores in calculating the variance, but these are rarely found in psychological experimentation. These generally occur when one merely wants to describe the variability of a set of scores and has no interest in extending the findings to any larger group of individuals. In fact, many applied statisticians disregard this distinction and use Eq. (2-8) to define the variance regardless of the ultimate use of the information.

For the current set of data,

$$\text{standard deviation} = \sqrt{39.00} = 6.24$$

The primary advantage of using the standard deviation is that the variability of a set of scores is expressed in terms of the original units of measure. The variance requires that the basic deviation scores be *squared*, changing the unit of measure to a squared quantity. "Unsquaring" the variance by taking the square root restores the measure to a form that is more easily understood and assimilated.

Using a Calculator. Statistical calculators usually provide buttons to calculate the mean and standard deviation directly. After you have become familiar with the basic operations involved in calculating these quantities, you may want to take advantage of these automatic functions. Most calculators provide buttons for *two* standard deviations, one that divides the *SS* by the degrees of freedom ($df = n-1$) and the other by the number of scores (n). You can find out which is which by the simple expedient of calculating *both* and comparing them; the correct button is the one producing the *larger* value. (Remember that we almost always use the standard deviation that uses the degrees of freedom as the denominator.)

You can use the button producing the standard deviation to calculate the variance, simply by squaring the standard deviation; that is,

$$\text{variance} = (\text{standard deviation})^2$$

2.3 ADDITIONAL DESCRIPTIVE TECHNIQUES

The primary role of descriptive statistics, of which the mean and the variance are parts, is to describe "what happened" in an experiment. At this point, we shift from an interest in the mean or the variance of an individual treatment condition to a *comparison* of these descriptive statistics across the different treatment conditions. In addition to examining the means derived from the treatment conditions and testing hypotheses about differences among the means, researchers usually spend considerable time and effort looking at their data from a variety of different angles. They construct tables and graphs, examine distributions of individual scores, and conduct detailed analyses on additional response measures. If you could follow an experienced researcher through the analysis of an entire experiment, you would be amazed at the amount of information that can be extracted by someone who is experienced in working with data. It is difficult to convey the nature and extent of this activity in an abstract discussion. Thus, we can only encourage you to become exposed to concrete examples of experimentation in your studies. If your current course requires you to analyze data collected by you and your classmates, you will soon find that you are inundated with information. If you have the opportunity to conduct your own research, either as a final project in a course or as part of an independent study, your introduction to data analysis and research will be even more thorough.

Tables and graphs are common and efficient ways of displaying summary data from an experiment. Not being statistics, tables and graphs may seem out of place among statistical procedures. In truth, they are such simple and convincing devices for summarizing the results of research that we cannot get along without them. Since they are essential for describing data, we offer some advice on their use and construction.[4]

Tables

Tables are simply organized collections of summary information. Even when the object is to construct a graph, the investigator first makes a table from which to work. Of course, when only a few means are to be reported, including them in the text along with the explanations may make more sense than preparing a formal table. When several pieces of summary data are to be reported, however, listing them in tabular form is a good choice.

Table 2-4 is an example of a table based on a fictitious experiment in which the effects of odors from other animals on the exploratory behavior of kangaroo rats were studied.[5] The general plan of the experiment was to place a rat in an artificial burrow system and to measure the amount of time the rat spent exploring the new surroundings. For the purposes of this study, the different odors were introduced in the burrow by taking sawdust from the cages of other kangaroo rats. The functions of some features of Table 2-4 may seem obvious to you, but many students frequently fail to make use of these basic features when learning to make up tables.

First, the title of the table indicates the table's contents and, in general terms, the source of the data. Even the number of data points for each treatment group is given somewhere in the table, in this case in the title. An informative

---

[4] Most research reports present a given set of data either in a table or a figure, *but not both.* The restriction on duplicating information is made to conserve journal space by eliminating information that would otherwise be redundant.

[5] We wish to thank Dr. Kay Holekamp for suggesting this example.

TABLE 2-4 *Mean Number of Minutes (and Standard Deviations) Spent Exploring by Kangaroo Rats during the 60-Minute Test (n = 7)*

Type of Smell	Mean Minutes	Standard Deviation
Control	37.29	5.68
Unfamiliar smell	24.71	6.21
Familiar smell		
Immediate	5.86	4.63
2-week delay	11.71	5.91
4-week delay	23.14	4.74

title is critical in conveying the contents of the table. However, we often find that students spend the least amount of time on the title.

The group designations are given as brief descriptions of the particular treatment condition. Students are often tempted, in constructing a table, to use group designations from the analysis, such as 1, 2, 3, and so on. These labels are not appropriate for describing the data to others.

The arrangement of the groups in a table conveys information about the design of the experiment. In Table 2-4, for example, the arrangement of the last three conditions emphasizes the fact that three groups were subjected to odors from rats with whom they had previously interacted (the "familiar treatments"), but differed with respect to the period of time following this interaction (immediately following, 2 weeks later, or 4 weeks later). Occasionally, when the experimental design is complex, a table can be useful for outlining the experimental design and showing the sequence of events.

Two advantages of tables are the clarity and succinctness with which critical summary data can be presented — in this case, the means and standard deviations for the five treatment groups. Another advantage is the precision and completeness of the information, which permits readers to conduct statistical analyses not reported in the paper but of interest to them nevertheless.

Graphs

Graphs, which depict relationships between independent and dependent variables by means of lines and points, are also concise summaries of experimental results. Their advantage is that they permit a reader to scan the summary rapidly to identify relationships and trends in the data. Thus, graphs have high impact value — that is, their meaning can be apprehended almost instantly

— which is why they are used so frequently in newspapers, magazines, and television.

Conventions for Graphical Displays.   The primary criterion for assessing a graph is the clarity with which it displays the data. In standard graphs, the independent variable is represented on the horizontal axis (or X axis) and the dependent variable along the vertical axis (or Y axis). The axes must be labeled clearly, and some form of legend or key should be provided to distinguish points that might be confused. (See Fig. 2-3 later in this section for an example of a legend.) As with tables, the title of the figure should tell the reader just what the figure contains. In addition to these conventions, certain others have been more or less adopted in the field of psychology:

1. The length of the vertical axis is approximately three-quarters of the length of the horizontal axis. Severe deviations from this "formula" can result in distortions of meaning — an exaggeration of the treatment differences when the vertical axis is unduly expanded, and a minimization when the vertical axis is unduly compressed.
2. The scale for the dependent variable (and independent variable if the manipulation is quantitative) is assumed to begin with zero, at the left-hand intersection of the horizontal and vertical axes. If the graph includes some "dead space," a break in the scale is often introduced to condense this area. Such breaks must be clearly designated in the figure or the results may be misleading.
3. It is a good idea to enclose the graph on all four sides with the vertical axis on the right marked off in the same units as the vertical axis on the left. This permits a reader to estimate the data points more accurately from the printed version of the figure.
4. A standard deviation can be expressed by a vertical band centered on each condition's mean. The "mark" or "band" above or below the mean for each condition represents the size of one standard deviation for that condition.[6]

Graphing Quantitative Independent Variables.   A quantitative independent variable is an independent variable that consists of a series of points selected from some quantitative dimension. The primary purpose of plotting a quantitative variable is to reveal the *shape* of the function describing the relationship of the independent and dependent variables. Is the relationship approximated

---

[6] Researchers frequently plot the *standard error of the mean* rather than the standard deviation for each group. We will discuss this statistic in Chap. 7.

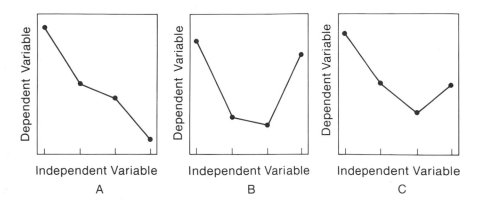

FIGURE 2-2 *Three Examples of the Outcome of a Quantitative Independent Variable.*

by a straight line, or is a curve more appropriate? The example in panel A of Fig. 2-2 is best described as a downward-sloping straight-line, or linear, function while that in panel B of Fig. 2-2 is a so-called U-shaped, or curvilinear, function. Panel C represents a mixture of both linear and curvilinear trends.

Certain conventions govern the graphing of the results of quantitative manipulations. First, intervals depicting treatment conditions are spaced along the baseline in direct proportion to their respective associated scale values. For example, if the values chosen for the independent variable were 2, 4, 6, and 8, the distances between successive points on the horizontal axis — including the origin (0) — would be the same, namely, 2 units each. On the other hand, if the values were 1, 3, 9, and 18, the distances between them on the baseline would be proportional to the differences in the numerical values of the treatment conditions — that is, between 0 (the origin) and 1, 1 unit; between 1 and 3, 2 units; between 3 and 9, 6 units; and between 9 and 18, 9 units. Second, successive data points are connected by straight lines. This type of graph is often called a *line graph*.

Once the independent and dependent variables have been arranged on a piece of graph paper, we are ready to plot the treatment means. To plot the means obtained from any given treatment condition, we start at the location of this condition on the horizontal axis — the point on the horizontal axis representing the numerical value of the independent variable administered to the subjects. Next, we move vertically from this point until the appropriate value of the dependent variable — that is, the treatment mean — is reached on the vertical axis. We place a mark at this location on the graph. After all the means have been plotted, we connect successive points by straight lines. To "read" a graph, we simply note the values on the independent and dependent variables for each point plotted on the graph.

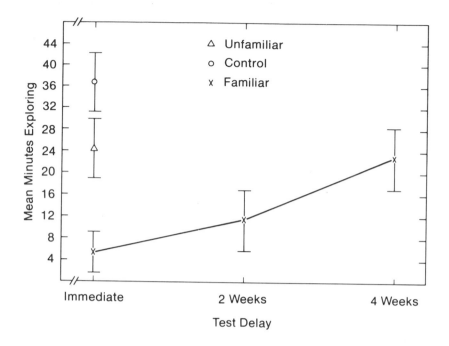

FIGURE 2-3 *Mean Number of Minutes of Exploration Spent by Kangaroo Rats during the 60-Minute Test. Brackets indicate ±1 standard deviation. Based on n = 7 subjects per condition.*

The data from Table 2-4 have been plotted in Fig. 2-3 as an example of a line graph. The first important feature of this graph is that three points are connected with straight lines while two of the groups stand alone. The connected points link the three familiar-smell groups, for which the time of the test (immediate, after 2 weeks, or after 4 weeks) is a quantitative variable (time). The other two groups do not share a common dimension, and are therefore unconnected to the means of the other treatments. Completing the picture are the standard deviations for the treatment conditions; the upper bands represent one standard deviation above and the lower bands one standard deviation below the mean.

Graphing Qualitative Independent Variables. A different sort of graph is used to depict results involving qualitative independent variables — a form of **bar graph**. Consider a hypothetical experiment as an example. Subjects are exposed to a list of common words and instructed to "process" the material in different ways. One group is asked to study the words for a memory test, while the other three groups are not explicitly instructed to memorize the words. One group is asked to report the number of vowels in each word; another

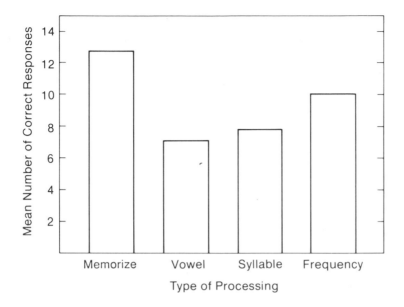

FIGURE 2-4 *Mean Number of Correct Responses (out of 30) for the Four Processing Conditions. Based on n = 26 subjects per condition.*

group, to report the number of syllables in each word; and a third group, to give a "pleasantness" rating for each word. A total of 30 words is presented at a rate of 5 seconds per word. After exposure, subjects are asked to recall the words. The results of the experiment are presented in Fig. 2-4.

The independent variable (type of processing) is a qualitative manipulation — the treatment conditions reflect differences in *kind* rather than in amount. One criterion for determining whether a variable is qualitative or quantitative is that the order in which the treatment conditions are arranged is *not* critical for a qualitative variable, though it is with a quantitative variable. In this example, the four conditions could be arranged in any of the 24 possible orders. In Fig. 2-3, however, which involved a quantitative variable, the conditions are ordered and spaced in the only way possible, namely, that which reflects the underlying ordered dimension of time.

The distinguishing feature of a bar graph is the use of rectangles to depict the value on the dependent variable. The reader obtains the plotted value for each condition by measuring the top of each rectangle against the vertical axis. Despite the fact that bar graphs are appropriate for summarizing data obtained from a qualitative manipulation, most researchers prefer to use line graphs for this purpose. Usually, such data can be presented in a line graph with no problem unless this alternative way of plotting the data could confuse a reader.

Bar graphs and related displays are favored in the pictorial representation of results from opinion surveys and other forms of survey research.

2.4 SUMMARY

An experiment produces a large quantity of "raw" data that, without being "refined" to some degree, will not convey quickly and accurately the findings of the experiment or permit the statistical evaluation of the research hypotheses. In this chapter, we considered at some length two measures that abstract most of the information present in a set of scores, the mean (a measure of central tendency) and the variance (a measure of variability). Not only do these two measures provide a succinct description of a set of scores, but they permit the assessment of hypotheses formed about the possible outcome of an experiment.

The mean is defined as the sum of a set of scores divided by the number of scores in the set. The mean is a point at which the deviations of the scores above are perfectly balanced with the deviations of the scores below. The variance is defined as an average of the squares of these deviations; the standard deviation is the square root of the variance. In the process of calculating the variance, we described the calculation of the sum of squares, a procedure employed often throughout this text.

Tables and graphs are widely used and efficient methods of reporting the outcome of an experiment. The advantages of tables are the precision with which summary statistics can be reported and the ease with which additional measures — especially standard deviations — can be included. The advantages of graphs are their visual impact and the ease with which trends resulting from the manipulation of quantitative independent variables can be displayed.

2.5 EXERCISES [7]

*1. A researcher tested the memory spans of $n = 10$ preschool children and obtained the following data. (Memory span usually refers to the longest

---

[7] Answers to the starred problems are given in Appendix B.

string of random single digits that an individual can reproduce without error.)

8	6
6	7
7	9
7	4
9	7

a. Calculate the mean for this set of scores.

b. Calculate the deviations from the mean $(Y - \overline{Y})$ for each of the scores. Use Eq. (2-4) to verify that the sum of the deviations is zero.

c. Use Eq. (2-5) to calculate the sum of squares for these scores based on the deviations you calculated in part (b).

d. Use the computational formula, Eq. (2-6), to calculate the sum of squares based on the actual Y scores.

e. Calculate the variance and the standard deviation for this set of data.

2. This problem is designed to give you practice with a statistical calculator, which can be used to calculate the mean and standard deviation automatically. Enter the data from exercise 1 into the calculator using the summation button to enter the numbers individually (see your manual for the location of this button) or consult Appendix C.

a. Use the recall function, which is usually invoked with one or two button pushes, to produce ΣY and ΣY^2 (again, see your manual for instructions on how to extract stored information from your calculator). Check your calculator against the values you calculated by hand in exercise 1.

b. Use the appropriate button (or buttons) on your calculator to calculate the mean. Verify your answer against exercise 1(a).

c. Use the appropriate button (or buttons) to calculate the standard deviation. If your calculator is programmed to calculate the two different standard deviations described in Sec. 2.2, calculate both of them and make a note which button (or buttons) produces the standard deviation based on degrees of freedom $(df = n - 1)$ and which produces the standard deviation based on the number of scores (n). The one based on the df, which is the standard deviation we will use throughout this book, will be the *larger* of the two.

d. Obtain the variance of the scores by squaring the standard deviation based on $n - 1$. You should be able to produce this value by instructing the calculator to calculate the correct standard deviation first and then squaring this value. With most calculators, you can calculate the variance without reentering numbers simply by calculating the standard deviation and immediately pressing the "square" button, which on most calculators is labeled "x^2"; the variance should appear in the display.

e. With the variance in the display, you can calculate the sum of squares by multiplying the variance by the degrees of freedom; that is, $SS = (\text{variance})(n - 1)$.

PART • TWO

THE ANALYSIS OF SINGLE-FACTOR EXPERIMENTS

In this part, we present a detailed discussion of the analysis of the most basic experimental design, a design in which a single independent variable (or factor) is manipulated and subjects are randomly assigned to the different treatment conditions. The analysis of this design will serve as a building block for the analysis of more complex — and more typical — experimental designs that we consider later in the book.

Chapter 3 is a general discussion of the logic governing the evaluation of research hypotheses. The principles of hypothesis testing covered in this chapter are applied throughout the book. At first, the logic of this procedure may seem strange, especially if you are unfamiliar with the topic. Thus, we have avoided introducing formulas and numbers, to concentrate, instead, on the overall logic of the operations. We review this logic in later chapters, in the hope that repetition in the context of concrete examples will aid you in integrating the procedure into your general thinking about experimentation.

In Chaps. 4 and 5, we concentrate on the statistical analysis of the basic experimental design just mentioned in which one independent variable is manipulated and subjects are randomly assigned to the different treatment conditions. Chapter 4 covers the formation of an index that reflects the presence of effects of the different treatment manipulations, a process known as the *analysis of variance*. Chapter 5 discusses the methods for determining whether the observed differences among the treatment means can be reasonably attributed to the influence of the independent variable or are most likely due to the operation of chance factors, which can never be completely eliminated from any experiment.

In Chap. 6, we concentrate on the analytical function of hypothesis testing. That is, in Chaps. 4 and 5 we concern ourselves with detecting differences among the treatment conditions, but not with determining which treatments are responsible for the observed effects. The means by which differences among specific treatment conditions can be examined individually are covered in Chap. 6.

Chapter 7 considers two topics that help researchers interpret the results of their experiments. The first consists of making estimates about the treatment population means based on information available from an experiment. The second topic concerns making estimates of the size of the treatment effects observed in an experiment.

Chapter 8 examines in some detail the risks associated with hypothesis testing. As you will see, any decision that results from testing hypotheses — that is, to reject the null hypothesis or to retain it — may be wrong. We discuss these errors and ways of keeping them at a reasonably low level. We also show how to use sample size and the concept of statistical power to achieve control over the sensitivity of an experimental design.

Chapter · 3

THE LOGIC OF HYPOTHESIS TESTING

In Chap. 1, we called your attention to a number of details that you must consider when designing an experiment. Underlying the whole process is the requirement that only the independent variable be permitted to vary systematically from treatment condition to treatment condition. Without elaboration, we simply asserted that this requirement was necessary to prevent a confounding of variables, and we did not discuss how this critical condition is in fact met. The present chapter deals with this problem, as well as with the general logic of hypothesis testing. The ideas, concepts, and arguments developed in this chapter are extremely important for an understanding of the statistical analyses covered in subsequent chapters. You may have to read this chapter several times before you feel comfortable with the topics covered, but this additional study will facilitate your mastery of the later material. The chapters that follow translate this relatively abstract and verbal discussion into the concrete arithmetical operations applied to the data generated by an experiment.

3.1 NEUTRALIZING NUISANCE VARIABLES THROUGH RANDOMIZATION

In any experiment, many variables exert measurable effects on the dependent variable. In the simplest experiment, we single out one of these potential independent variables for manipulation and attempt to neutralize the systematic variation of all the others. Since in the context of the experiment we are not interested in these other variables and must take steps to prevent them from damaging our results through systematic biasing, or confounding, they are often called **nuisance variables**. In Chap. 1 we mentioned two ways of controlling nuisance variables (see pp. 20–21), namely, control through holding a nuisance variable *constant*, and control through spreading the effect of the nuisance variable *randomly* over the treatment conditions. Because of the importance of **randomization** in experimentation, we will consider this concept in more detail at this time.

Neutralizing the Influence of Subject Variables

Suppose we want to study as a research project the effects of different background noises on reading comprehension. We decide to form three treatment conditions: no background noise, and either classical music or popular music playing quietly in the background. Subjects will be given a fixed time to read a particular passage, followed by a test on the material presented in the passage. Suppose we plan to test a total of 15 students living on the same floor of a college dormitory and to place five of them in each of the treatment groups. How can we assign the students to the three groups to prevent confounding the independent variable with other variables — in this case, subject variables?

While many characteristics of the students would probably affect reading comprehension, we will concentrate on an obvious one at first, namely, differences in reading speed. Unless the reading speed of the subjects assigned to the different conditions is controlled in some manner, this factor could potentially confound the effects of the independent variable. That is, without some control, any differences in average comprehension scores observed among the treatment groups are as likely to be due to differences in the reading speeds of the subjects assigned to the groups as to the differences in background noise.

What can be done about this serious problem? An obvious solution would be to employ some form of **matching** of the reading speeds of students assigned to the different conditions, but for the purposes of extending this example to cover unmeasurable nuisance variables, we will assume that we have no adequate way of determining a student's reading speed before the start of the experiment. Thus, matching is out as a solution to this problem.

What if we assigned each student *at random* to the treatment conditions? (By *random* we mean that each subject has an equal chance of being assigned to any one of the treatment conditions.) One thing can be said about this alternative: it is improbable that the groups will be perfectly matched by this method of assignment. The groups will still differ in the average reading speeds of the students assigned to them in a random manner. What sort of solution is this?

The miraculous answer is that random assignment *is* the solution in most experimental designs! Any differences in the average reading speeds of the three conditions introduced by randomly assigning students are typically small. Note carefully that in assigning subjects at random to the treatment conditions, we have used the "roulette wheel" of experimentation to spread the differences in reading speed more or less equally among the treatment conditions. Once we have randomly assigned the subjects, we can introduce statistical procedures to assess the degree to which the average differences resulting from random assignment can reasonably account for the observed differences in behavior.

So far we have considered only a single subject variable, reading speed. But subjects vary in many ways, and at least some of these will affect the dependent variable, reading comprehension. Even if we consider all the subject variables one by one, advancing the argument we offered for the speed variable, we can show that the random assignment of students to the conditions will "guarantee" that any difference among the groups will still reflect only chance factors. That is, since random assignment of subjects to conditions "works" for all subject variables individually, a single random assignment should be sufficient to neutralize *all* effects at the same time.

Neutralizing the Effects of Other Nuisance Variables

How can we neutralize the influence of other types of nuisance variables — for example, time of day, temperature, and the like? Consider time of testing. We could control this factor by running our subjects at only one time or by following a schedule that would balance all times of testing equally across the treatment conditions. As an alternative, we could make up a testing schedule based on the times convenient to us, assigning these times at random to the treatment conditions. (*Random* in this case refers to a method that gives each treatment an equal chance of being assigned to a particular time period.) Time of day would then exert only a random influence on the treatment conditions in our experiment. We could treat other factors in a similar manner in order to transform their influence into random or chance fluctuation as well. Let's see how all of this randomization can be accomplished in practice.

Some Methods of Random Assignment

When the Subjects Are Unknown to the Researcher.   Most research with humans is conducted with students enrolled in introductory psychology classes. An experimenter posts sign-up sheets with possible testing times indicated, and students choose sessions that are convenient to them. Usually an experimenter will know nothing about the subjects until they appear in the laboratory at the appointed time. Under these circumstances, the experimenter decides before starting the study on an assignment procedure that will give all subjects an equal chance of being assigned to any one of the treatment conditions. Suppose the experiment consists of four treatments. The experimenter could let the numbers 1 to 4 stand for the four treatments and simply roll a six-sided die to determine which condition a subject would receive — disregarding all instances in which any irrelevant numbers (in this case, 5 and 6) turned up, of course. Because each of the four relevant numbers (1, 2, 3, and 4) has an equal chance of appearing on a roll of the die, each of the four treatments has an equal chance of being assigned to any given subject. The treatment a subject receives, then, is determined by an independent roll of the die, until near the end of the study, when it is usually necessary to restrict the assignment to ensure that each condition is represented by the same number of subjects.

Table 3-1 shows the results of following this assignment procedure with a total of 20 subjects, who will be divided in equal numbers — that is, five — among four treatment conditions. At the beginning of the process, all four conditions (1, 2, 3, and 4) are equally likely assignments for the first subject (S_1), who happens to be assigned to condition 1. The four conditions

TABLE 3-1 *An Example of Random Assignment of* 20 *Subjects to* 4 *Treatment Conditions*

Subject	Random Assignment	Condition	Code
S_1	1	Treatment 1	1
S_2	2	Treatment 2	2
S_3	1	Treatment 3	3
S_4	4	Treatment 4	4
S_5	1		
S_6	4		
S_7	2		
S_8	3		
S_9	4		
S_{10}	4		
S_{11}	2		
S_{12}	1		
S_{13}	1		
S_{14}	4		
S_{15}	3		
S_{16}	3		
S_{17}	2		
S_{18}	2		
S_{19}	3		
S_{20}	3		

Subject Assignment to Treatments

Treatment			
1	2	3	4
S_1	S_2	S_8	S_4
S_3	S_7	S_{15}	S_6
S_5	S_{11}	S_{16}	S_9
S_{12}	S_{17}	S_{19}	S_{10}
S_{13}	S_{18}	S_{20}	S_{14}

continue to be equal candidates for all subjects through the thirteenth (S_{13}), who becomes the fifth and final subject to be assigned to condition 1. At this point, then, condition 1 is removed from the assignment pool, leaving the other three conditions (2, 3, and 4) as equally likely assignments for the next subject (S_{14}). However, this subject becomes the fifth subject assigned to condition 4, leaving the other two conditions (2 and 3) as equally likely assignments for the next subject (S_{15}). This situation remains in effect until we reach the eighteenth subject (S_{18}) who becomes the fifth subject assigned to condition 2. Because there is only one condition (condition 3) remaining in the assignment pool, this condition is assigned to the last two subjects (S_{19} and S_{20}). The assignment procedure is now complete, with five subjects randomly assigned to each of the four treatment conditions.

Instead of rolling a die or drawing numbers out of a hat, many researchers use a **table of random numbers**, which often consists of a random listing of single-digit numbers (1, 2, ..., 9, and 0) usually produced by a computer programmed to generate strings of random digits. A portion from a much larger random number table can be found in Table A-1 of Appendix A. We enter the random number table "blindly," usually by closing our eyes and placing a finger somewhere on the page, and begin reading a series of single-digit numbers in a left-to-right direction from this starting point. (Actually, the table produces a random string of numbers in any direction.) As the critical digits representing the coded treatments appear in the table — 1 through 4 in our example — we record them on a sheet, which now becomes the assignment sheet for the subjects as they appear in the laboratory. When we come to the end of a row of numbers, we can scan the next row for the code numbers (up or down — either direction is acceptable). We continue this process until we have listed each condition an appropriate number of times.

Block Randomization. Most researchers use a variant of this procedure called **block randomization**. With this method, the treatment schedule is arranged in blocks, with each block containing each treatment once. Suppose we again have four conditions and a total of 20 subjects, which means that we would divide them into five blocks of four subjects each, as we have illustrated on the left side of Table 3-2. Beginning with the first block, we assign a different treatment to each of the four subjects in this block (S_1 through S_4) by some random method — for example, using a table of random numbers, rolling a die, drawing the treatment numbers out of a hat, or the like. From the table, you can see that S_1 will be given condition 3, S_2 will be given condition 2, S_3 will be given condition 1, and S_4 will be given condition 4. This process would be followed again for the second block of subjects (S_5 through S_8) — that is, a different treatment would be randomly assigned to each of the four subjects in this block. We continue this process of randomly assigning the treatments to the subjects within blocks until all five blocks are complete. The right side of Table 3-2 shows the results of these assignments.

You should notice the difference between the two procedures. With the first method, the number of subjects is balanced at the very *end* of the testing schedule, when the number of subjects must be the same in the four conditions. With block randomization, on the other hand, the number of subjects is balanced at the end of *each block*, not just at the end of the schedule of conditions.

There are good reasons for using block randomization. The nuisance variables we are trying to control often follow a cycle or pattern. The variation of temperatures during the day is an obvious example. Less obviously, the flow of subjects volunteering for an experiment may also follow some cycle. Subjects who volunteer early in the school term may be more anxious, more curious, or smarter than those who volunteer later — who knows? Block randomization capitalizes on the cyclic nature of certain nuisance variables and the fact that these variables will tend to have similar effects on subjects appearing within a given block. Because each block contains one instance of each treatment

TABLE 3-2 *An Example of Block Randomization of 4 Treatments for 20 Subjects*

Block	Subject	Random Assignment	Subject Assignment to Treatments			
			Treatment			
			1	2	3	4
Block 1	S_1	3				
	S_2	2				
	S_3	1				
	S_4	4	S_3	S_2	S_1	S_4
Block 2	S_5	4	S_7	S_8	S_6	S_5
	S_6	3	S_{10}	S_{12}	S_9	S_{11}
	S_7	1	S_{14}	S_{15}	S_{13}	S_{16}
	S_8	2	S_{17}	S_{20}	S_{19}	S_{18}
Block 3	S_9	3				
	S_{10}	1				
	S_{11}	4				
	S_{12}	2				
Block 4	S_{13}	3				
	S_{14}	1				
	S_{15}	2				
	S_{16}	4				
Block 5	S_{17}	1				
	S_{18}	4				
	S_{19}	3				
	S_{20}	2				

condition, block randomization will also reduce the variation of nuisance variables from condition to condition and thus increase our chances that the randomization process will be successful.

When the Subjects Are Known to the Researcher. In many studies, researchers know something about the subjects before they are tested in the experiment. In animal research, for example, the subjects have usually been housed in the animal quarters for some time, allowing the researcher to record information about them during this period of confinement. In human research, the researcher may have available information about the subjects' ability from institutional records or a pretest administered on the first day of classes to all students in large introductory classes. Under these circumstances, researchers may use block randomization as a form of *matching* rather than as a way of reducing the influence of cyclic effects in the flow of participants in a study. For example, a researcher might create blocks of similar subjects by matching them on some relevant characteristic, such as IQ or grade point average for humans and age or body weight for animals. Subjects are then assigned to the treatment conditions in the same way we described for the imaginary subjects in Table 3-2. This method of random assignment produces groups of subjects that are closely matched on the subject variable used to create the different blocks.[1]

Whether block randomization has been used to match subjects or not, a researcher still needs to take special steps to determine the *order of testing* the subjects, in addition to deciding which treatment each subject will receive. Suppose we want to assign a pool of 20 animal subjects to four treatment conditions. The only restriction is that an equal number of subjects (five) must be assigned to each treatment. To determine the testing order, we can code the subjects with two-digit numbers — for example, 01, 02, ..., 19, and 20 — and begin reading successive *pairs* of digits from the table of random numbers, searching for the subjects' code numbers. The order of testing the subjects is thus established by the order in which their number codes "turn up" in the sequence of random numbers. That is, the first subject so identified is tested first, the second subject is tested second, and so on. After determining the testing order, we can randomly assign the four treatments to the subjects, in the same manner that we described earlier.

Summary

Researchers create experiments by treating independent groups of subjects differently. A fundamental challenge to an investigator is conducting an experiment in such a way that only the independent variable is permitted to vary systematically from condition to condition. If this challenge is not met, the influence of the independent variable becomes entangled with the systematic variation of the so-called nuisance variables, and discriminating the influence of one from that of the others is generally impossible. In some cases, the researcher controls nuisance variables by holding them constant for all subjects and thus eliminating completely their potential for systematic variation. In most cases, however, experimenters control nuisance variables by assigning the treatment conditions to the subjects randomly, transforming any potential systematic variation of nuisance variables into relatively "harmless" unsystematic, or random, variation. As we will see, this method is not without difficulties,

---

[1] The statistical analysis of experiments employing this form of block randomization is different from the procedures we consider in Chaps. 4 and 5. You can find discussions of the appropriate analysis in most advanced statistics books (see, for example, Keppel, 1991, pp. 298–301).

but these problems can be solved through statistical means. In the next two sections, we consider the logic and rationale that underlie these helpful statistical procedures.

3.2 INDEX OF THE TREATMENT EFFECTS

In principle, you are now ready to design and conduct an experiment. All you would have to do is propose a research hypothesis, translate it into a set of manipulations, select a dependent variable, locate some subjects, minimize the influence of nuisance variables either by holding them constant during the experiment or by spreading their composite effects randomly over the treatment conditions, and, finally, collect the data. After arranging the data in a convenient form for calculations, you would obtain the means of the treatment conditions and ponder their implications. In doing so, you would ask yourself a number of questions: Did the differences among the means turn out as you predicted? How will you integrate these new findings with the findings of others? What experiments are necessary for resolving the new questions raised by the data?

Experimenters are exhilarated rather than disturbed by such questions; it is only natural to be excited and stimulated by the results of a new experiment. So much time elapses between the moment an experiment is conceived and that in which the final piece of data is collected that the question "What now?" is one to be savored.

Once you have calculated the means of the treatment conditions, doubts begin to surface. How will you determine whether the differences you have observed were produced by the differences in the treatment manipulations? Presumably, you will have avoided all serious confounding of relevant variables and neutralized the effects of nuisance variables through appropriate randomization procedures. Wouldn't these precautions guarantee that the differences among the treatment means reflect the effects of your independent variable and that variable alone?

Unfortunately, the answer is no. Chance factors are present in every experiment. It is *always* possible that the differences observed among the treatment means are due entirely to the influence of these chance factors and not to the differential effects of the treatment conditions. Said another way, the outcome of any experiment can always be due to the operation of chance factors alone; differences that seem to be the result of differences in treatments may actually be reflecting the fact that randomization never results in the complete elimination of nuisance variables.

Between-Groups Variability

To ascertain that the results of an experiment are not attributable to chance, we need an index that reflects the effects of the treatments relative to the differences that could reasonably be due to chance. Consider the kinds of information an experiment makes available. First, we have the differences among the treatment means. Using procedures that will be outlined in the next chapter, we can express these differences in terms of a measure of variability. This **between-groups variability** (as it is called[2]) — the differences among the means of the different treatment groups — reflects the potential operation of two factors:

1. The effect of the differential treatments
2. The effect of chance factors

We will refer to the first source of the between-groups variability as the **treatment effects** and the second source as **experimental error**. Thus,

between-groups variability = (treatment effects) + (experimental error)

Students report having difficulty understanding the concept of experimental error. Simply put, experimental error consists of all sources of variability in an experiment that are not taken into account or controlled for. As we have already indicated, individual differences (differences due to subject variables) represent the most important source of experimental error. Variations in the various features of the testing environment (time of day, temperature, noise outside the testing room, and so on) represent a second source. Another source of experimental error is measurement error — the misreading of a dial, a misjudgment that a particular behavior has occurred, an error in recording a response, and so on. A final source of experimental error is the variability with which the experimental treatments are administered. Any given treatment cannot be administered identically to all subjects in that condition. The apparatus might move in and out of adjustment, an experimenter will inevitably

---

[2] Grammatically, we should use *among* rather than *between* when we are referring to differences among three or more groups. To avoid possible confusion, however, we have adopted the more common usage *between* to be consistent with the terminology used by researchers and by authors of other texts on research design and statistical analysis.

read instructions differently each time, experimenter-subject interactions will be different with different subjects, and so on.

Another way to think about experimental error is to consider a situation in which treatment effects are entirely absent. In this situation, would you expect the treatment means to be *identical* (the treatment-group variability equal to zero)? From our discussion in Sec. 3.1, you would expect not — how could the groups be perfectly matched when we use a procedure that assigns the treatment conditions *randomly* to the subjects? Thus, we do expect differences between the group means, even when our independent variable is totally ineffective. This is why we have a problem in making a decision at this point: we cannot tell whether the differences we observe among the treatment means are due to the operation of experimental error alone, or whether the differences reflect the joint operation of experimental error and treatment effects.

Within-Group Variability

Next, consider another source of variability obtainable from an experiment. We have concentrated, for obvious reasons, on the differences among the treatment means. But the scores of the *subjects* who supply the individual data points for each treatment group also differ. Since all subjects within any given treatment group have been given the same treatment condition, theoretically they should all have the same value for the dependent variable. If they vary, this can only be a result of the same chance factors that are at least partially responsible for the between-groups variability. That is, subjects will vary because of the differences — in ability, motivation, time of testing, and temperature — that were partially neutralized by the randomization procedures we used to assign the treatment conditions to the subjects. Thus, a measure of variability that takes into consideration the *variation of subjects treated alike* — the **within-group variability** — will provide an estimate of experimental error. That is,

within-group variability = experimental error

The Treatment Index

To determine whether differences among the treatment means are due to chance, let's use these two measures of variability — differences among the treatment means in one case (between-groups variability) and differences among subjects treated alike in the other case (within-group variability) —

to form a useful index that we call the **treatment index**. We obtain this index by dividing the between-groups variability by the within-group variability:

$$\text{treatment index} = \frac{\text{between-groups variability}}{\text{within-group variability}} \tag{3-1}$$

Some authors define the treatment index as a ratio of *systematic variability* (reflecting in part any systematic effects of the different treatment conditions) to *nonsystematic,* or *error, variability* (reflecting the operation of unaccounted-for or randomly varying nuisance variables). In subsequent chapters, we will refer to the treatment index as the *F* **ratio**.

When Population Treatment Effects Are Absent. Considering the sources that influence the numerator and denominator terms of Eq. (3-1), we can see that the treatment index is responsive to the presence or absence of treatment effects. More specifically, if our independent variable were completely *ineffective*, producing the same effects for all treatment groups, the ratio would consist of one estimate of experimental error (based on the variability among the treatment means) divided by another estimate of experimental error (based on the variability of individual subjects treated alike). Under these circumstances, the ratio would become

$$\frac{\text{experimental error}}{\text{experimental error}}$$

and would be approximately equal to 1.0.

This situation is diagramed in panel A of Fig. 3-1 with a simplified representation of two groups. The vertical boundaries within the body of the figure represent the smallest and largest Y scores for each group, which we can think of as a rough measure of the variability within each group. (If we were dealing with the actual numbers, we could express the variability in terms of the group variances or standard deviations.) As you will see in Chap. 4, we will combine the separate estimates of within-group variability — one from group 1 and the other from group 2 — to provide us with an overall estimate of the experimental error present in the entire experiment. The dot near the center of each pair of vertical limits represents the mean for the corresponding treatment group. Again using procedures covered in Chap. 4, we can use the difference between these two means to estimate the between-groups variability. Because we are

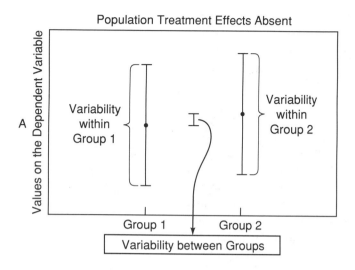

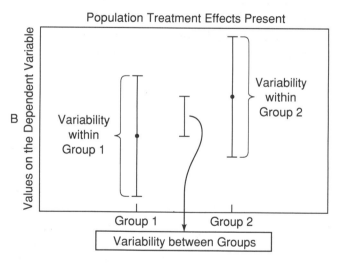

FIGURE 3-1 *A Comparison of Between-Groups Variability and Within-Group Variability when Treatment Effects Are Absent in the Populations (Panel A) and when Treatment Effects Are Present in the Population (Panel B). The between-groups variability is reflected by the differences among the group means, whereas the within-group variability is reflected by the differences among the subjects given the same treatment condition.*

assuming at this point that there are no treatment effects in the population, we have depicted only a small difference between the two group means.[3]

When Population Treatment Effects Are Present.   Consider now what happens to the treatment index when treatment effects are actually present. Under these circumstances, the ratio would consist of

$$\frac{(\text{treatment effects}) + (\text{experimental error})}{\text{experimental error}}$$

and would have a value *greater* than 1.0.

We have represented this particular situation in panel B of Fig. 3-1. We are assuming in this diagram that treatment effects are present in the population; we have depicted them by a larger difference between the two means plotted in the body of the figure. Using procedures we cover in Chap. 4, we would eventually translate this difference into an estimate of between-groups variability, except that in this case, the estimate reflects the population treatment effects in addition to the unavoidable contribution of experimental error. Although we have represented a "real" difference between the two means, there is still variation among the scores of the subjects within each of the groups. This variation, which is reflected by boundaries located above and below the two means, depicts the variability of subjects treated alike and provides an estimate of "pure" experimental error.

Summary.   The treatment index consists of a ratio of between-groups variability to within-group variability. The former is based on the differences among the treatment means, and the latter is based on the variability of subjects treated alike. As we have seen, the treatment index is a numerical index that is sensitive to the existence of treatment effects. More specifically, the index approximates 1.0 when treatment effects are absent and is greater than 1.0 when they are present. This index provides the baseline for chance effects against which observed differences among treatment means can be compared.

---

[3] You may have noticed that the difference between the two means is much smaller than the within-group variation depicted in the figure and wonder why these two estimates of experimental error — between-groups differences and within-group differences — appear to be so different. Without going into the details, we can assure you that the formulas we introduce in Chap. 4 to estimate these two sources of variability will correct for this apparent discrepancy.

3.3 HYPOTHESIS TESTING

Having introduced the treatment index, which reflects the presence or absence of effects of the independent variable, we can turn to the actual testing of hypotheses.

Statistical Hypotheses

The heart of any experiment is the research hypothesis. This construct represents the rationale of an experiment and specifies the kinds of information required to support the hypothesis. To evaluate a research hypothesis *statistically*, however, the researcher forms a set of **statistical hypotheses**. For reasons embedded in statistical theory, the statistical hypotheses are the ones that are assessed and evaluated in the actual statistical analysis. Although the distinction between research and statistical hypotheses may not be clear at this point, be assured that the decision to reject or to retain a statistical hypothesis has direct relevance for the status of the research hypothesis.

Statistical hypotheses, as applied to any given experiment, refer to the hypothetical outcome of the experiment were it administered to an infinitely large number of individuals. (This would never happen, of course, but the situation represents the sort of hypothetical conditions within which statistical theory usually operates.) Let's assume that each of these individuals is randomly assigned to one of the treatment conditions. The set of scores obtained from subjects receiving the same treatment is called a **treatment population**. There is a different treatment population for each condition of the experiment. The mean of a treatment population is called a **population treatment mean** and is designated by the Greek letter μ (pronounced "mu"). A subscript is usually added so that we can designate a particular treatment condition. Thus, μ_1 is the population mean for treatment 1, μ_2 is the population mean for treatment 2, and so on. The symbol μ_i is used to represent any one of the population treatment means.

The differences among the population treatment means — the effects of the independent variable observed in these hypothetical treatment populations — are called the **population treatment effects**. Statistical hypotheses are thus statements concerning the hypothetical state of affairs in the treatment populations. For statistical purposes,

an experiment is assumed to consist of samples drawn *randomly* from the treatment populations

Viewed in this way, the experiment we actually conduct is used to obtain some idea of what the population treatment means are. We must say again that the concept of the treatment populations and the differences among the population treatment means are based on statistical theory, and not a situation we will ever observe or measure. We can still think about the possibility and consider the implications of conceiving of an experiment as consisting of random samples drawn from different treatment populations.

Two statistical hypotheses are involved in the decision-making process called **hypothesis testing**. Taken together, they encompass all possible arrangements of the population treatment means. One of these hypotheses is called the **null hypothesis**, and it specifies only *one* of the possible arrangements, namely, the case when the population means are *equal*. (Obviously, there is only one way this can happen, since the means are identical!) The null hypothesis specifies the *complete absence* of differences among the treatment means, that is, the absence of population treatment effects. The null hypothesis is usually designated H_0, "H" for hypothesis and "0" for null, and is stated in symbols as

$$H_0 : \mu_1 = \mu_2 = \mu_3 = \cdots \qquad (3\text{-}2)$$

or more simply as

$$H_0 : \text{ all } \mu_i\text{'s are equal} \qquad (3\text{-}3)$$

The other statistical hypothesis, referred to as the **alternative hypothesis** and designated H_1, specifies all the remaining ways that the population treatment means might be arranged. In symbols, the alternative hypothesis is represented as

$$H_1 : \text{ not all } \mu_i\text{'s are equal} \qquad (3\text{-}4)$$

Note that the alternative hypothesis is *not* "all μ_i's are different." For example, if you have four treatment conditions, the alternative hypothesis is not that all four conditions differ from each other, but just that some differences exist between conditions. The alternative hypothesis, therefore, encompasses an extremely large number of possibilities, namely, all the possible ways a set of population treatment means can differ. Somewhere, among these various possibilities, we will find our research hypothesis. In Chap. 6, we discuss the ways in which the field of alternative hypotheses can be narrowed drastically so that the investigator can focus more directly on the specific analytical questions originally posed for the study.

Evaluating the Null Hypothesis

Though ultimately our interest lies in the status of the alternative hypothesis, in this section we concentrate on the evaluation of the null hypothesis, since our decision concerning the null hypothesis has direct implication for the alternative hypothesis. The reason for this interconnectedness is that we have placed all possible outcomes into one or the other of two categories, the null category and the alternative category, the latter of which contains our research hypothesis. To gain support for our research hypothesis, therefore, we must *reject the null hypothesis.*

Refer back to Eq. (3-1) and the so-called treatment index. You will recall that this index becomes approximately 1.0 when treatment effects are completely absent in the population. This value is obtained because the measures of between-groups variability and of within-group variability both reflect the operation of experimental error, and

$$\frac{\text{between-groups variability}}{\text{within-group variability}} = \frac{\text{experimental error}}{\text{experimental error}} = 1.0$$

You will also recall that the null hypothesis specifies the *absence* of treatment effects. Thus, if the null hypothesis is true, the treatment index should be approximately 1.0. Consider what happens to the treatment index when the null hypothesis is false and thus treatment differences exist in the population. Under these circumstances, the treatment index will be greater than 1.0, since the numerator term is affected by two factors while the denominator term is affected by only one of these factors; that is,

$$\frac{\text{between-groups variability}}{\text{within-group variability}} = \frac{(\text{treatment effects}) + (\text{experimental error})}{\text{experimental error}}$$

Superficially, our course of action now seems obvious: to reject the null hypothesis whenever the treatment index is greater than 1.0, since the ratio will exceed this value only when treatment effects are present. Unfortunately, however, deciding which hypothesis is supported is not so simple. Evaluating the null hypothesis — that is, deciding whether it should be rejected or retained — is much more complicated than determining whether the value of the treatment index is greater than 1.0.

The complication lies in the nature of the two estimates of experimental error. While both are estimates of the same theoretical quantity, experimental error, they are based on different and independent information derived from the same experiment. More specifically, one estimate is obtained from the variability among the *means* of the treatment groups, whereas the other is obtained from the *scores* of subjects treated alike. Because of the chance factors operating in any experiment — stemming largely from our efforts to neutralize nuisance variables — these two estimates will rarely be identical. Consequently, we cannot expect to be able to reject the null hypothesis whenever the treatment index is greater than 1.0, that is, when the numerator is larger than the denominator.

The solution to this difficulty is to determine the frequencies with which different values of the treatment index are expected to occur by chance and to base our decision to reject or to retain the null hypothesis on this information. Fortunately, a great deal is known about the treatment index and how it varies in size when the null hypothesis is true. In general, as the treatment index increases beyond 1.0, the frequency with which larger values occur by chance decreases rather drastically. That is, *the larger the value of the treatment index, the smaller is the likelihood that the value will in fact have occurred by chance* (and the more it is likely that a treatment effect is actually present).

What sort of evidence would prompt us to reject the null hypothesis? How large and how rare must the treatment index be before we feel confident in concluding that the null hypothesis is probably wrong? In principle, each researcher must make this decision individually. In practice, however, most researchers in psychology agree that a frequency of 5 times out of 100 — that is, a probability of $5/100 = .05$ — is a reasonable cutoff point. Thus, whenever the treatment index exceeds a certain critical value, a value which theory tells us will occur by chance only 5 percent of the time, we will consider such evidence to be *incompatible* with the null hypothesis. By rejecting the null hypothesis, we conclude in effect that the alternative hypothesis represents a more accurate description of the hypothetical treatment populations.

Decision Rules in Hypothesis Testing

The actions to be taken by an experimenter can be summarized as a **decision rule** — an unambiguous statement, prepared before the experiment is begun, that indicates under exactly what circumstances the null hypothesis will be rejected and under what circumstances it will be retained. The general form of the decision rules can be stated as follows:

> **If the treatment index equals or exceeds a value of _____, reject the null hypothesis; otherwise, retain the null hypothesis.**

We explain in Chap. 5 how this critical value of the treatment index is obtained. At this point, however, it is sufficient to say that the value in question is the value of the treatment index that will be exceeded only 5 percent of the time when the null hypothesis is true.

Once the decision rule has been written, the actions we then take are almost mechanical — that is, we calculate the value of the treatment index and follow the procedures outlined by the decision rule. With the latter step accomplished, the statistical operations involved in testing a research hypothesis are concluded, but there remains the important process of assimilating the findings into the body of literature relevant to the topic under investigation. For a researcher, the phase in which the results are interpreted — which occurs after the statistical procedures are completed — is the most critical; all the preceding operations are merely necessary steps in the entire analytical process of experimentation. In this sense, experimental design and statistical analysis are the analytical tools the researcher uses to establish new facts, evaluate (that is, support, reject, or revise) old theories, and create new ones.

A Comment

Table 3-3 summarizes the basic steps involved in the statistical evaluation of the outcome of an experiment that we have presented in this chapter. Purposely, we have not introduced formulas, numbers, and numerical examples — these will come in the chapters that follow. Our point was to describe hypothesis testing in purely verbal terms to explain carefully the logic behind the process. Students tell us that this is not an easy chapter to assimilate, particularly if they have not been exposed to these concepts in other classes. Many find that they do not fully comprehend the process until they are exposed to specific mathematical operations and concrete numerical examples. However, we feel that hypothesis testing should be understood on both the abstract and concrete levels. There is a value to the abstract approach taken in this chapter in that you are forced to concentrate on the logic and are not distracted by the manipulation of numbers. The logic outlined in this chapter is general and applies throughout the book in a variety of experimental contexts and in other statistical procedures. If you are experiencing difficulties with this chapter, we suggest that you move on to Chaps. 4 and 5 and return to this chapter after some practical experience with these concepts.

TABLE 3-3 *The Steps in Hypothesis Testing*

---

1. A research hypothesis is generated as a deduction from theory or from an interesting idea or speculation.

2. Treatment conditions (the independent variable) and a response measure (the dependent variable) are chosen to provide a test of the research hypothesis.

3. An experiment is designed to demonstrate that a relationship exists between the independent variable and the dependent variable.

4. The null and alternative hypotheses are formulated.

5. A decision rule is stated that specifies exactly the circumstances under which the null hypothesis will or will not be rejected.

6. The experiment is conducted, and the treatment index is calculated.

7. If the obtained value of the treatment index equals or exceeds the critical value specified by the decision rule, the null hypothesis is rejected, and the investigator concludes that treatment effects are present.

8. If the obtained value of the treatment index is smaller than the critical value, the null hypothesis is retained.

3.4 SUMMARY

The first step in testing a research hypothesis is to design an experiment in which the influence of known and unknown variables is minimized. If uncontrolled, such "nuisance" variables would result in a systematic bias, that is, a confounding with the independent variable. While it is possible to control nuisance variables by holding them constant, the most common procedure is to spread their effects randomly over all the treatment conditions.

Because of the use of randomization procedures to control the operation of nuisance variables, which is unavoidable in experimentation, any differences observed among the treatment means are influenced to some extent by chance factors. The experimenter must decide whether the differences associated with the treatment conditions are entirely or just partially due to chance.

As a first step in solving this problem, the experimenter determines the value of the treatment index, which will serve as a baseline against which to evaluate the presence or absence of treatment effects. The investigator calculates the treatment index by dividing an estimate of the variability among the treatment means, which is assumed to reflect the operation of potential treatment effects and experimental error, by an estimate of the variability of subjects given the same treatment condition, which is assumed to reflect the operation of experimental error alone. When treatment effects are present, the treatment index should be greater than 1.0; when they are not, the treatment index should be approximately equal to 1.0.

Next we considered in some detail the formulation of two statistical hypotheses: the null hypothesis, which states that the population treatment means are equal; and the alternative hypothesis, which states that not all of the means are equal. The experimenter tests the adequacy of the null hypothesis by applying a decision rule that specifies the circumstances under which the null hypothesis will be rejected — and the alternative hypothesis accepted — and the circumstances under which the null hypothesis will be retained. This rule gives a critical value of the treatment index that divides all possible experimental outcomes into two categories, or regions: one in which they are reasonably likely to have occurred by chance, and one in which they are likely to have been caused by the treatment differences. If the value of the treatment index exceeds the critical value assigned to it in the decision rule, the null hypothesis is rejected and the alternative hypothesis is accepted. Under these circumstances, the experimenter concludes that treatment effects are present. On the other hand, if the index is less than the critical value, the null hypothesis is retained. In the latter case, the experimenter is left with differences that are best interpreted in terms of chance factors.

3.5 EXERCISES

1. The 30 numbers listed in the following table represent the fictitious scores of subjects on a test of quantitative reasoning that was administered on the first day of class; low scores on this imaginary test are assumed to reflect low reasoning ability and high scores to reflect high reasoning ability. Let's assume that the scores are arranged in the order these subjects will eventually report to the laboratory to serve in an experiment you are performing. That

is, the first score represents the test results for the first subject you will test, the second score the test results for the second subject, and so on.

Subject	Test Score	Subject	Test Score	Subject	Test Score
S_1	13	S_7	10	S_{13}	12
S_2	11	S_8	14	S_{14}	11
S_3	16	S_9	15	S_{15}	11
S_4	12	S_{10}	6	S_{16}	4
S_5	11	S_{11}	15	S_{17}	11
S_6	12	S_{12}	10	S_{18}	4

Subject	Test Score	Subject	Test Score
S_{19}	4	S_{25}	11
S_{20}	9	S_{26}	7
S_{21}	3	S_{27}	5
S_{22}	9	S_{28}	2
S_{23}	6	S_{29}	8
S_{24}	7	S_{30}	1

a. Using the random numbers presented in Table A-1 of Appendix A, randomly assign the subjects in equal numbers to three treatment conditions (1, 2, and 3). Calculate the mean for each of the three groups to check how well the random assignment has produced three groups of equal ability on the reasoning test.

b. We noted that block randomization is frequently used when a researcher suspects that there may be cyclic changes in the flow of subjects signing up to participate in an experiment. We actually arranged the 30 scores to reflect a tendency for subjects signing up for the experiment at the start of the academic term — when you will have initiated the study — to have higher reasoning scores than those signing up at or near the end of the term. Use block randomization to assign the 30 subjects to the three treatment conditions. Again, calculate the means. You should find that the differences among the three means obtained with block randomization and the group standard deviations are smaller than those obtained in part (a), illustrating the value of block randomization when cyclic trends are present.

2. What are the reasons for using randomization procedures in an experiment?

3. When you perform an experiment and calculate the group means, why is it possible for the means to differ even though there are absolutely no differences among the corresponding treatment means in the population?

4. What are between-groups variability and within-group variability? What are they made up of? Why is within-group variability an index of experimental error?

Chapter • 4

CALCULATING THE *F* RATIO

We are now ready to consider the statistical analysis of the simplest experimental design, in which a single independent variable is administered to groups of subjects who have been randomly assigned to the treatment conditions. It is common to refer to a single independent variable as **factor *A*** and to call this sort of arrangement a **completely randomized single-factor design**. Our goal is to determine from an experiment a value for the treatment index and to compare the magnitude of this quantity against the results that might reasonably be expected to occur by chance if the null hypothesis were true. The calculation of the treatment index and the process of comparison are referred to together as the **analysis of variance**. The analysis of variance, or **ANOVA**, for short, is an apt name, since the procedure compares measures of variability (variances) that are adapted to our needs in hypothesis testing.

We use two chapters to cover the analysis of variance. In this chapter, we develop the procedures needed to calculate the treatment index, which from this point on we call by its technical name, the **F ratio**.[1] In Chap. 5, we present the statistical evaluation of the null hypothesis.

Taken together, these two chapters cover the basic operations we described more generally in Chap. 3. As we noted, an understanding of these procedures is critical in any discussion of the design and analysis of experiments. Keep in mind that the material we consider in these two chapters will be applied repeatedly in other data analyses.

We suggest that you read Chaps. 4 and 5 quickly first to establish an overall frame of reference. Try not to become too involved with specific points on this first reading; save this kind of attention for your more careful later readings of the material.

4.1 DESIGN AND NOTATION

As a preliminary step, we will examine the nature of the experimental design and consider some of the specialized notation we use to represent the arithmetical steps in ANOVA.

The Basic Design

A representation of the completely randomized single-factor design is presented in Fig. 4-1. Each column represents one treatment condition — the **levels** of factor A — and each cell within each given column represents one of the subjects (designated by the letter s and a numerical subscript) randomly assigned to that treatment condition.

In this example, there are four different subjects randomly assigned to each of the treatment conditions. We use a lowercase a to designate the number of treatment levels in an experiment, and a lowercase n to designate the number of subjects assigned randomly to each treatment level. (We are assuming that an equal number of subjects — also known as the **sample size** — appears in each treatment condition.[2]) In the example in Fig. 4-1, $a = 3$ treatment

---

[1] The F ratio is named after Sir Ronald A. Fisher, who developed the analysis of variance.

[2] Although equal sample size is not a requirement in the single-factor design, experiments are

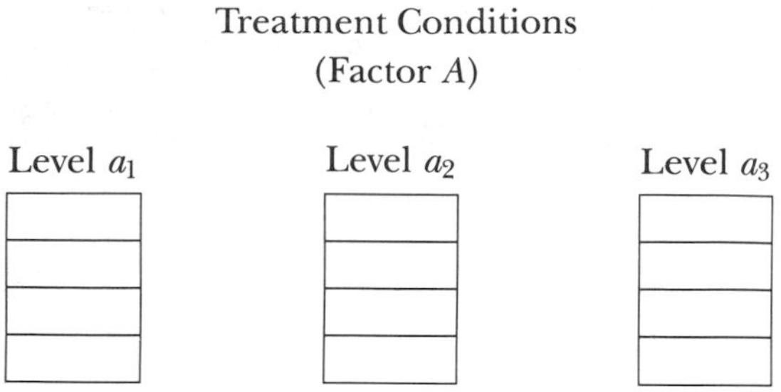

Treatment Conditions
(Factor A)

Level a_1 Level a_2 Level a_3

FIGURE 4-1 *A Representation of the Completely Randomized Single-Factor Design. Each cell represents one subject. In this design, there are 12 subjects; four are assigned randomly to each of the three treatment conditions.*

conditions, and $n = 4$ subjects per condition. We use a subscript with the a to designate a particular treatment level: a_1 refers to the treatment associated with the first-listed condition, a_2 to the second, and so on.

Some Notation to Designate the Means

Consider the nature of the data to be analyzed when an experiment is completed. We would begin by arranging the scores in columns by treatment condition for subsequent calculations. The most obvious information we would want at this stage would be the means for the treatment groups. Let's see how we represent these operations with symbols. The notational system we use for ANOVA is slightly different from the one we introduced in Chap. 2. You need to pay attention to the differences.

The Basic Observations.   The data for a fictitious experiment, with $a = 2$ conditions and $n = 10$ subjects randomly assigned to each condition, are presented in Table 4-1. You will notice that each score is represented by Y and two subscripts separated by a comma. The first subscript designates the treatment condition (1 or 2) and the second the location of each score in the column (1 through 10). Thus, $Y_{1,2}$ refers to the score for the second subject in level a_1,

---

usually designed this way. Using equal sample sizes gives equal weighting or attention to the treatment means in the statistical analysis, a condition that makes the most sense in experimentation. We can compensate for unequal sample sizes in various ways, but it is best to design experiments with equal sample sizes.

TABLE 4-1 *Basic Data from a Fictitious Experiment*

	Level a_1	Level a_2
	$Y_{1,1} = 5$	$Y_{2,1} = 13$
	$Y_{1,2} = 3$	$Y_{2,2} = 9$
	$Y_{1,3} = 4$	$Y_{2,3} = 10$
	$Y_{1,4} = 4$	$Y_{2,4} = 8$
	$Y_{1,5} = 6$	$Y_{2,5} = 9$
	$Y_{1,6} = 1$	$Y_{2,6} = 12$
	$Y_{1,7} = 3$	$Y_{2,7} = 8$
	$Y_{1,8} = 4$	$Y_{2,8} = 12$
	$Y_{1,9} = 6$	$Y_{2,9} = 10$
	$Y_{1,10} = 4$	$Y_{2,10} = 9$
Sums:	$A_1 = 40$	$A_2 = 100$
Number of Subjects:	$n = 10$	$n = 10$
Means:	$\overline{Y}_{A_1} = 4.00$	$\overline{Y}_{A_2} = 10.00$
Grand Sum (T):	$A_1 + A_2 = 140$	
Grand Mean ($\overline{Y}_T$):	7.00	

and $Y_{2,5}$ refers to the score for the fifth subject in level a_2. As you can see, each score is represented by a different pair of subscripts.

The Treatment Sums and Means. A mean is calculated by dividing the sum of a set of scores by the number of scores in the set. To simplify the notation, we will designate the sum of the scores for a treatment condition with a capital A and add a numerical subscript to indicate which condition. Thus,

A_1 = the sum of the Y scores for the subjects assigned to condition a_1

A_2 = the sum of the Y scores for the subjects assigned to condition a_2

Using the data from Table 4-1, we find

$$A_1 = 5 + 3 + \cdots + 6 + 4 = 40$$

$$A_2 = 13 + 9 + \cdots + 10 + 9 = 100$$

The two treatment means are represented as $\overline{Y}_{A_1}$ and $\overline{Y}_{A_2}$, the subscripts clearly distinguishing one treatment mean from the other. Since each treatment condition contains $n = 10$ scores,

$$\overline{Y}_{A_1} = \frac{A_1}{n} = \frac{40}{10} = 4.00$$

$$\overline{Y}_{A_2} = \frac{A_2}{n} = \frac{100}{10} = 10.00$$

The Overall, or Grand, Mean. The final mean we need to designate is the average of all the scores in the experiment. We will use a capital T to represent the grand, or total, sum of the scores. For this example,

$$T = \text{the total sum of the scores}$$

$$= A_1 + A_2 = 40 + 100$$

$$= 140$$

The grand mean, $\overline{Y}_T$, may be calculated simply by dividing the total sum T by the total number of subjects in the experiment, which is $(a)(n) = (2)(10) = 20$.[3] Thus,

$$\overline{Y}_T = \frac{T}{(a)(n)} = \frac{140}{(2)(10)} = \frac{140}{20} = 7.00$$

Comment. The notational system we are beginning to develop in this chapter may be different from the one you might have been exposed to in an earlier book or course. You should make an effort to assimilate the components of the system as we introduce them in this book. Our notational system is designed to simplify the representation of a fairly complex set of arithmetical operations. The advantage of our system will be more evident when we consider the analysis of factorial designs in Part Three.

4.2 PARTITIONING THE TOTAL SUM OF SQUARES

In this section, we examine the very heart of ANOVA, the process by which different sources of variation are identified and isolated for use in hypothesis

---

[3] Some authors use N to designate the total number of observations.

testing. The idea is fundamental to an understanding of the analysis of experimental data. Briefly, we calculate two sums of squares, one that reflects a composite of treatment effects and experimental error and one that reflects the operation of experimental error alone. The isolation of these sources of variability is most easily seen in the single-factor design, although the same basic logic underlies the analysis of the more complicated experimental designs we cover in later chapters.

Basic Deviations

You will recall from Chap. 2 that a sum of squares is based on the deviations of a set of Y scores from their mean. The sums of squares we calculate in ANOVA are also based on analogous deviations. To illustrate, we have plotted the data from Table 4-1 on a number line in Fig. 4-2, using squares with solid lines to represent scores from treatment level a_1 and with dashed lines to represent scores from treatment level a_2. For example, the first score from a_1, $Y_{1,1} = 5$, would appear as a solid square above the number line at 5, while the first score from a_2, $Y_{2,1} = 13$, would appear as a square with dashed lines above the line at 13. All the scores listed in Table 4-1 have been plotted in this fashion in Fig. 4-2. Scores with the same value have been stacked on top of each other. We will now turn our attention to the three means represented immediately below the number line and designated by arrows pointing to their location on the number line. In addition to these we have also designated the location of the sixth score from level a_1 ($Y_{1,6} = 1$).

The purpose of this arrangement of the two sets of scores is to demonstrate graphically an important relationship between an individual score, its relevant treatment mean, and the grand mean. More specifically,

the deviation of any score from the grand mean $(Y - \overline{Y}_T)$ can be partitioned, or divided, into two different deviations: one reflecting the deviation of the score from its treatment mean $(Y - \overline{Y}_A)$ and the other consisting of the deviation of the treatment mean from the grand mean $(\overline{Y}_A - \overline{Y}_T)$.

This relationship for one score $(Y_{1,6})$ is depicted at the bottom of Fig. 4-2. At the very bottom of the figure is a representation of the deviation of this score from the grand mean:

$$Y_{1,6} - \overline{Y}_T$$

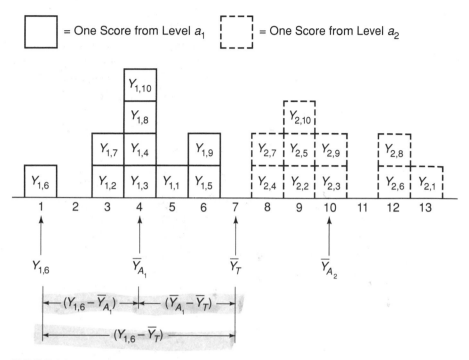

FIGURE 4-2 *A Systematic Arrangement of Scores from Table* 4-1. *The components of deviation for a single score* $(Y_{1,6})$ *from the grand mean* $(\overline{Y}_T)$ *are shown beneath the baseline.*

Just above this deviation we have represented two other deviations, that is, the deviation of this score from its treatment mean,

$$Y_{1,6} - \overline{Y}_{A_1}$$

and the deviation of the treatment mean from the grand mean,

$$\overline{Y}_{A_1} - \overline{Y}_T$$

You can readily see that the first deviation $(Y_{1,6} - \overline{Y}_T)$ is equal to the sum of the other two deviations $(Y_{1,6} - \overline{Y}_{A_1}$ and $\overline{Y}_{A_1} - \overline{Y}_T)$. The "truth" of this relationship can also be demonstrated by means of some simple algebra:

$$
\begin{aligned}
Y_{1,6} - \overline{Y}_T &= (Y_{1,6} - \overline{Y}_{A_1}) + (\overline{Y}_{A_1} - \overline{Y}_T) \\
&= Y_{1,6} - \overline{Y}_{A_1} + \overline{Y}_{A_1} - \overline{Y}_T \\
&= Y_{1,6} - \overline{Y}_T
\end{aligned}
$$

Sums of Squares

The preceding discussion contains hints to how the F ratio (the treatment index) is developed. The two *component deviations* we identified in the last section reflect exactly the sorts of variability we want to capture for the F ratio. That is, the deviation of subjects from their treatment means $(Y - \overline{Y}_A)$ reflects what we called "experimental error" in Chap. 3 — the variation attributable to subjects treated alike, that is, subjects given the same treatment condition. In contrast, the deviation of the treatment means from the grand mean $(\overline{Y}_A - \overline{Y}_T)$ reflects the joint influence of treatments *and* experimental error. You saw in the preceding section that the deviation of a particular score from the grand mean (the **total deviation**) is made up of two component deviations, one based on the deviation of the score from its treatment mean (**within-group deviation**) and the other based on the deviation of the treatment mean from the grand mean (**between-groups deviation**).[4] That is,

$$\begin{array}{ccccc}
\text{total deviation} & = & \text{within-group deviation} & + & \text{between-groups deviation} \\
(Y - \overline{Y}_T) & = & (Y - \overline{Y}_A) & + & (\overline{Y}_A - \overline{Y}_T)
\end{array}$$

We will now apply this relationship to all the scores in the numerical example, as has been accomplished in Table 4-2. To illustrate the calculations for the first subject in level a_1, we have

$$(Y_{1,1} - \overline{Y}_T) = (Y_{1,1} - \overline{Y}_{A_1}) + (\overline{Y}_{A_1} - \overline{Y}_T)$$

$$(5 - 7) = (5 - 4) + (4 - 7)$$

$$(-2) = (+1) + (-3)$$

$$(-2) = (-2)$$

You can clearly see that the total deviation (-2) is equal to the sum of the two component deviations (-2). You should verify this important relationship for a few Y scores until you are convinced of its correctness.

Each column of 20 deviations in Table 4-2 is involved in creating a different sum of squares. You will recall that a sum of squares is based on the sum of the *squared* deviations.[5] If we calculate the sum of squares for the first column

---

[4] Until you become familiar with these terms, you might prefer to refer to the between-groups deviation as the treatment-group deviation to emphasize the logic of the analysis. Both terms refer to the same component deviations, of course — the deviation of the treatment means from the grand mean.

[5] In Chap. 2, we demonstrated that the sum of the *deviations* from the mean is zero, which is why

TABLE 4-2 *Analysis of Component Deviations*

Score	Deviations				
Y	Total $(Y - \overline{Y}_T)$	=	Within-Gp $(Y - \overline{Y}_A)$	+	Between-Gps $(\overline{Y}_A - \overline{Y}_T)$
			Level a_1		
5	(-2)	=	$(+1)$	+	(-3)
3	(-4)	=	(-1)	+	(-3)
4	(-3)	=	(0)	+	(-3)
4	(-3)	=	(0)	+	(-3)
6	(-1)	=	$(+2)$	+	(-3)
1	(-6)	=	(-3)	+	(-3)
3	(-4)	=	(-1)	+	(-3)
4	(-3)	=	(0)	+	(-3)
6	(-1)	=	$(+2)$	+	(-3)
4	(-3)	=	(0)	+	(-3)
			Level a_2		
13	$(+6)$	=	$(+3)$	+	$(+3)$
9	$(+2)$	=	(-1)	+	$(+3)$
10	$(+3)$	=	(0)	+	$(+3)$
8	$(+1)$	=	(-2)	+	$(+3)$
9	$(+2)$	=	(-1)	+	$(+3)$
12	$(+5)$	=	$(+2)$	+	$(+3)$
8	$(+1)$	=	(-2)	+	$(+3)$
12	$(+5)$	=	$(+2)$	+	$(+3)$
10	$(+3)$	=	(0)	+	$(+3)$
9	$(+2)$	=	(-1)	+	$(+3)$

$\overline{Y}_{A_1} = 4$ (Level a_1), $\overline{Y}_{A_2} = 10$ (Level a_2), $\overline{Y}_T = 7$

(total deviation), we find

$$\Sigma(Y - \overline{Y}_T)^2 = (-2)^2 + (-4)^2 + \cdots + (+3)^2 + (+2)^2$$

$$= 4 + 16 + \cdots + 9 + 4$$

$$= 228$$

Applying these operations to the deviations in the second and third columns

we squared these deviations in developing a measure of variability. The same property holds for the three sets of deviations in Table 4-2, as we can demonstrate simply by summing each column of 20 deviations. In each case, the sum is zero.

(within-group deviations and between-groups deviations, respectively), we have

$$\Sigma(Y - \overline{Y}_A)^2 = (+1)^2 + (-1)^2 + \cdots + (0)^2 + (-1)^2$$
$$= 1 + 1 + \cdots + 0 + 1$$
$$= 48$$

$$\Sigma(\overline{Y}_A - \overline{Y}_T)^2 = (-3)^2 + (-3)^2 + \cdots + (+3)^2 + (+3)^2$$
$$= 9 + 9 + \cdots + 9 + 9$$
$$= 180$$

We can now show that the sum of squares based on the total deviations is made up of the other two sums of squares based on the within-group and between-groups component deviations. More specifically,

$$\Sigma(Y - \overline{Y}_T)^2 = \Sigma(Y - \overline{Y}_A)^2 + \Sigma(\overline{Y}_A - \overline{Y}_T)^2 \qquad (4\text{-}1)$$
$$228 = 48 + 180$$
$$= 228$$

In words, it is the case that

the sum of the squared total deviations equals the sum of the squared within-group deviations plus the sum of the squared between-groups deviations.

If we use SS to designate the sum of the squared deviations from a mean, this statement becomes

$$SS_{total} = SS_{within-groups} + SS_{between-groups} \qquad (4\text{-}2)$$

In an even simpler shorthand notation, we have

$$SS_T = SS_{S/A} + SS_A \qquad (4\text{-}3)$$

where the subscript T stands for "total," S/A for "subjects within the A treatment groups," and A for the "variability among the A treatment means." Table 4-3 presents a summary of the different sets of symbols and special terms we have introduced in this section.

TABLE 4-3 *A Summary of Special Symbols and Terms Used to Represent the Basic Deviations and Corresponding Sums of Squares Involved in the Analysis of Variance*

Total Deviation	=	Within-Group Deviation	+	Between-Groups Deviation
$(Y - \overline{Y}_T)$	=	$(Y - \overline{Y}_A)$	+	$(\overline{Y}_A - \overline{Y}_T)$
$\Sigma(Y - \overline{Y}_T)^2$	=	$\Sigma(Y - \overline{Y}_A)^2$	+	$\Sigma(\overline{Y}_A - \overline{Y}_T)^2$
SS_{total}	=	$SS_{within\text{-}groups}$	+	$SS_{between\text{-}groups}$
SS_T	=	$SS_{S/A}$	+	SS_A

Some Comments on the Sums of Squares. Before we turn to a consideration of the computational formulas that permit us to calculate these same three sums of squares with relative ease, we wish to highlight certain features of the component deviations in Table 4-2.

First, you should note that all subjects contribute to the determination of the three sums of squares. That is, each subject contributes a total deviation, a within-group deviation, and a between-groups deviation to the determination of the three corresponding sums of squares.

Second, the contribution of the subjects to the SS_A is the same for all subjects in each of the two treatment groups. That is, every subject in a_1 contributes -3 to the treatment-group component, while every subject in a_2 contributes $+3$ to the treatment-group component.

Third, it is important to point out that the within-groups sum of squares, $SS_{S/A}$, is actually a *composite* created by combining, or pooling, the sums of squares for all the treatment groups. To illustrate, the sum of squares for the subjects in the first group is

$$(+1)^2 + (-1)^2 + \cdots + (+2)^2 + (0)^2 = 20$$

and for the subjects in the second group is

$$(+3)^2 + (-1)^2 + \cdots + (0)^2 + (-1)^2 = 28$$

If we combine these two within-group sums of squares, we find

$$20 + 28 = 48 = SS_{S/A}$$

What this demonstrates, then, is that the separate treatment groups provide separate estimates of experimental error — the variability of subjects treated alike — which, for the analysis of variance, are combined to produce the within-groups sum of squares, $SS_{S/A}$. Thus, the within-groups sum of squares represents the *pooled* variability of subjects treated alike, with each treatment condition contributing to its determination.[6]

4.3　SUMS OF SQUARES: COMPUTATIONAL FORMULAS

The formulas we presented in Sec. 4.2 are frequently called *definitional, defining*, or *conceptual formulas*. Although these formulas preserve the logic by which the component deviations are derived, we usually calculate the sums of squares in ANOVA with formulas that are equivalent algebraically but much simpler computationally.

Basic Ratios

The computational formulas for the required SS's are neither intrinsically difficult nor complex. In this textbook, each of the sums of squares will be calculated by adding and subtracting special quantities that we call **basic ratios**. All basic ratios have the same underlying form in the analysis of variance and are calculated in a series of simple arithmetic steps. For this design — the completely randomized single-factor design — only three basic ratios are needed, each involving a different aspect of the data. One basic ratio involves the *individual observations* or *scores* (Y), another involves the *treatment subtotals* (A), and the other involves the *grand total* (T).

Although the three basic ratios are based on different aspects of the data, each of them is calculated following the same series of steps. All basic ratios require the initial *squaring* of an entire set of quantities — either all the Y's, all the A's, or T. The squaring operation is followed by *summing* the squared quantities if more than one is present. Finally, each of these sums may be *divided* by a special divisor. We will illustrate the calculation of each basic ratio with the data presented in Table 4-1.

---

[6] We demonstrate this point in Chap. 5 (p. 128).

The Basic Ratio Calculated from the Individual Scores (Y). The basic ratio based on the Y scores involves only the first two steps, that is, squaring followed by summing; there is no division required in calculating this basic ratio. Using the data from Table 4-1, we calculate

$$\Sigma\, Y^2 = (5)^2 + (3)^2 + (4)^2 + (4)^2 + (6)^2 + (1)^2 + (3)^2 + (4)^2$$
$$+\, (6)^2 + (4)^2 + (13)^2 + (9)^2 + (10)^2 + (8)^2 + (9)^2$$
$$+\, (12)^2 + (8)^2 + (12)^2 + (10)^2 + (9)^2$$
$$= 25 + 9 + 16 + 16 + 36 + 1 + 9 + 16 + 36 + 16 + 169$$
$$+\, 81 + 100 + 64 + 81 + 144 + 64 + 144 + 100 + 81$$
$$= 1,208$$

These calculations are greatly facilitated by using a statistical calculator that permits you to sum a set of squared numbers, such as these, simply by entering each number separately and then pressing a special key (see Appendix C).

The Basic Ratio Calculated from the Treatment Sums (A). The basic ratio involving the A treatment sums requires all three computational steps of squaring, followed by summing, and then dividing. Expressed in symbols, the basic ratio consists of

$$\frac{\Sigma\, A^2}{n}$$

That is, each of the treatment sums (A) is squared, these squared values are then summed, and the resulting sum is divided by the number of scores in each condition (n). Using the data from Table 4-1, we obtain

$$\frac{\Sigma\, A^2}{n} = \frac{(40)^2 + (100)^2}{10}$$
$$= \frac{1,600 + 10,000}{10} = \frac{11,600}{10}$$
$$= 1,160.00$$

The Basic Ratio Calculated from the Grand Sum (T). The basic ratio based on the grand sum T involves only two of the computational steps, squaring and dividing. More specifically, we first square the grand total and then divide by the total number of observations in the experiment, namely, $(a)(n)$. (No

TABLE 4-4 *Special Code Designating Basic Ratios*	
Special Code	*Basic Ratio*
$[Y]$	$\Sigma\,Y^2$
$[A]$	$\dfrac{\Sigma\,A^2}{n}$
$[T]$	$\dfrac{T^2}{(a)(n)}$

summation is possible in calculating this basic ratio, since there is only one grand total.) Illustrating with the data from Table 4-1, we calculate

$$\frac{T^2}{(a)(n)} = \frac{(140)^2}{(2)(10)}$$

$$= \frac{19,600}{20}$$

$$= 980.00$$

Comments on Basic Ratios. Students occasionally confuse basic ratios with sums of squares. We use the basic ratios as tools in calculating the different sums of squares, a way of simplifying the computational formulas for the sums of squares. To further simplify these computational formulas, we will use a special notation or code to designate each basic ratio, as illustrated in Table 4-4. The notation indicating a basic ratio is a pair of brackets, whereas the letter appearing within the brackets identifies a specific basic ratio. As you can see,

$[Y]$ = the basic ratio involving the individual Y scores

$[A]$ = the basic ratio involving the A treatment sums

$[T]$ = the basic ratio involving the grand sum T

Sums of Squares

You will recall from an earlier discussion that the deviation of each score from the grand mean $(Y - \overline{Y}_T)$ is divided into two deviations, namely, the deviation of each score from the treatment mean $(Y - \overline{Y}_A)$ and the deviation of the treatment mean from the grand mean $(\overline{Y}_A - \overline{Y}_T)$. The analysis of variance consists of transforming these deviations into sums of squares, variances, and then the F ratio. We will now indicate how the three sums of squares, which are based on these three sets of deviations, can be calculated by using the basic ratios. We will begin with the total sum of squares (SS_T).

The Total Sum of Squares (SS_T).   We can derive the computational formula for the SS_T from the basic deviations on which this sum of squares is based. More explicitly, the SS_T is based on the following deviation:

$$Y - \overline{Y}_T$$

which immediately implies that we can calculate this sum of squares simply by combining the two basic ratios suggested by this deviation, $[Y]$ and $[T]$. Thus,

$$SS_T = [Y] - [T] \tag{4-4}$$

or, for the sake of completeness,

$$SS_T = \Sigma\, Y^2 - \frac{T^2}{(a)(n)} \tag{4-5}$$

Substituting the quantities we calculated in the last section, we find

$$
\begin{aligned}
SS_T &= [Y] - [T] \\
&= 1,208 - 980.00 \\
&= 228.00
\end{aligned}
$$

which is identical to the quantity we calculated from the actual deviations presented in Table 4-2.

The Between-Groups Sum of Squares (SS_A).   The between-groups, or treatments, sum of squares, SS_A, is based on the deviation of the treatment means from the grand mean, namely,

$$\overline{Y}_A - \overline{Y}_T$$

From this expression, we can derive the computational formula for SS_A as follows:

$$SS_A = [A] - [T] \tag{4-6}$$

Expressed in terms of the actual basic ratios,

$$SS_A = \frac{\Sigma A^2}{n} - \frac{T^2}{(a)(n)} \tag{4-7}$$

Using the values we calculated previously,

$$SS_A = [A] - [T]$$

$$= 1,160.00 - 980.00$$

$$= 180.00$$

The value, too, is identical to the one we calculated in Sec. 4.2.

The Within-Groups Sum of Squares (SS$_{S/A}$).   The within-groups sum of squares, $SS_{S/A}$, is based on the deviation of individual observations from the relevant treatment means; in symbols,

$$Y - \overline{Y}_A$$

The symbols representing this deviation suggest the following computational formula:

$$SS_{S/A} = [Y] - [A] \tag{4-8}$$

or, more fully,

$$SS_{S/A} = \Sigma Y^2 - \frac{\Sigma A^2}{n} \tag{4-9}$$

Substituting our earlier calculations, we find

$$SS_{S/A} = [Y] - [A]$$

$$= 1,208 - 1,160.00$$

$$= 48.00$$

which, again, is equal to the value we calculated from the deviations in Sec. 4.2.

A Summary of the Calculations

The arithmetical operations required by the computational formulas for the three sums of squares are summarized in Tables 4-5 and 4-6. Table 4-5 specifies

TABLE 4-5 *The Arithmetical Operations Performed on Scores or Sums in Forming Basic Ratios*

	1. Score or Sum		2. Squaring		3. Summing (If Relevant)	4. Dividing (If Required)	5. Coding
1. Scores	a_1	a_2			$\Sigma\, Y^2$	$\Sigma\, Y^2$	$[Y]$
	$Y_{1,1}$	$Y_{2,1}$	$Y_{1,1}^2$	$Y_{2,1}^2$			
	$Y_{1,2}$	$Y_{2,2}$	$Y_{1,2}^2$	$Y_{2,2}^2$			
2. Treatment Sums	A_1	A_2	A_1^2	A_2^2	$\Sigma\, A^2$	$\dfrac{\Sigma\, A^2}{n}$	$[A]$
3. Grand Sum	T		T^2		T^2	$\dfrac{T^2}{(a)(n)}$	$[T]$

TABLE 4-6 *Computational Formulas for SS_A, $SS_{S/A}$, and SS_T*

Source of Variability	Basic Deviation	Computational Formula
Treatment Means (SS_A)	$\overline{Y}_A - \overline{Y}_T$	$[A] - [T]$
Subjects Treated Alike ($SS_{S/A}$)	$Y - \overline{Y}_A$	$[Y] - [A]$
Both Components Combined (SS_T)	$Y - \overline{Y}_T$	$[Y] - [T]$

the way in which we "process" the individual observations in the initial steps of calculating the sums of squares. Each row in Table 4-5 concentrates on a different quantity, or aspect of the data, and the calculations that we perform on those particular quantities. Row 1 focuses on the basic observations, Y. As an example, four scores — two for level a_1 and two for level a_2 — are listed in column 1. Row 2 focuses on the treatment sums, A, which are obtained, of course, from the individual observations listed in the first row. In this example, two treatment sums, A_1 and A_2, are listed in column 1 of the table. Finally, row 3 focuses on the grand sum, T, which is obtained either from the scores in row 1 or from the treatment sums in row 2. This quantity is also listed in column 1 of the table.

We have already indicated that column 1 contains three different kinds of quantities: basic observations (Y), treatment sums (A), and the grand sum (T). The remaining columns designate the actual arithmetical operations we perform on these quantities and the order in which we perform them, that is, *squaring* (column 2), *summing* (column 3), and *dividing* (column 4). The *coding* step (column 5) is used to simplify the expression of the formulas for the sums of squares. Look carefully at this table and at the consistent pattern with which the different numbers are manipulated. If you recognize the consistency with which we process these quantities, you will generate a certain rhythm in your calculations that will help demystify the entire computational process involved in analyzing both simple and complex experimental designs.

The final steps in calculating the three sums of squares are summarized in Table 4-6. Each row in this table specifies one of the three sources of variability, first the two component sources (SS_A and $SS_{S/A}$), and then the combination of the two sources (SS_T). The columns of the table indicate the basic deviations on which these sources of variability are based and the computational formulas for the sums of squares expressed in coded form.

4.4 THE ANALYSIS OF VARIANCE

If you have understood the rationale governing the use of the basic deviations, and have followed the various steps involved in calculating the three sums of squares, you are over the worst! The remaining steps in the analysis of variance are relatively simple arithmetically and follow the logic we discussed in Chap. 3.

Calculating Variances (or Mean Squares)

The sums of squares we discussed in the last two sections are not directly usable in calculating the F ratio, because each of the component sums of squares is affected by a different *number* of deviations. For instance, in our example we have two treatment conditions contributing to the between-groups sum of squares, and 10 subjects within each condition contributing to the within-groups sum of squares. The solution to this problem is to adjust each sum of squares for this difference. This *average* sum of squares defines a *variance* (discussed in Chap. 2), but it is called a **mean square** (abbreviated *MS*) when the sum of squares comes from ANOVA. The general formula for a mean square is

$$MS = \frac{SS}{df} \qquad (4\text{-}10)$$

where df refers to the number of **degrees of freedom** associated with the sum of squares (SS). A mean square is still an average, but one that adjusts for the number of degrees of freedom rather than for the number of squared deviations.

Degrees of Freedom

The concept of degrees of freedom can be understood on a number of levels depending on one's interests, background, and formal training in statistics. Most researchers are unfamiliar with the statistical theory and argument used to justify the division of a sum of squares by its degrees of freedom. As a result, they have learned to be satisfied with an understanding of the concept at a less rigorous and demanding level and to accept Eq. (4-10) for the simple utilitarian reason that it lends them statistical advantages. We are encouraging you to adopt a similar philosophy here and to accept the correctness of this definition of a mean square with a considerable amount of faith. We take this approach because a great deal is known about the theoretical properties of mean squares and ratios of mean squares and because we will use this important information in evaluating the null hypothesis.

In general, degrees of freedom can be defined in terms of the number of different elements in a set that are free to vary, meaning that they are not "fixed" by some restrictions placed on them. Suppose we select a set of scores randomly from some larger population. In a sense, each of these scores is free to vary, to take on any of the values present in the population. We could say that the sample contains n independent pieces of information about the nature of the population. We can call these independent pieces of information "degrees of freedom." But what happens when we use information from this sample to estimate characteristics of the population, such as its mean and variance? As you will discover in Chap. 7, we use the mean of the sample to estimate the mean in the population from which the sample was drawn, but this expends one piece of the information available in the sample to estimate the variance. Thus, the number of independent pieces of information, or degrees of freedom, left to estimate the population variance is reduced by 1 and places a restriction on the number of scores that are free to vary.

One way to think about this loss of one df is to consider a simple example. Suppose we randomly select three numbers from a population, 2, 6, and 7. Since each score is free to vary, there are $n = 3$ degrees of freedom at this point. But what happens to the information available in this set of scores when the population mean is estimated from the mean of the sample? In this example, the mean is

$$\frac{2+6+7}{3} = \frac{15}{3} = 5$$

How many of the scores are now free to vary once the mean has been estimated? Only two, because in order for the mean to equal 5, the sum of these scores must be 15, and once two scores have been obtained, the last is already known by subtraction. That is,

$$\text{last score} = 15 - (\text{sum of the first two scores})$$

In this example,

$$\text{last score} = 15 - (2 + 6) = 15 - 8 = 7$$

Thus, once we estimate the population mean from the sample data, only $n - 1$ degrees of freedom — pieces of independent information — are left for the estimate of the variance.

The general rule for computing the df for any sum of squares is

$$df = \left(\begin{array}{c} \text{number of} \\ \text{independent} \\ \text{observations} \end{array} \right) - \left(\begin{array}{c} \text{number of} \\ \text{population} \\ \text{estimates} \end{array} \right) \qquad (4\text{-}11)$$

If there are n observations in a sample, one df is lost when we estimate the population mean. Application of Eq. (4-11) indicates that

$$df = n - 1$$

In the remainder of this section, we apply this definition to the three sources of variability obtained in the analysis of variance.

Between-Groups Sum of Squares. The between-groups sum of squares, SS_A, is based on the deviation of each treatment mean from the grand mean $(\overline{Y}_A - \overline{Y}_T)$. There are a observations — that is, means — contributing to this source of variance. As a result of our estimating the overall population mean from the means of the a treatment conditions, the value of one of the treatment means is "fixed," and one df is lost. In symbols,

$$df_A = a - 1 \qquad (4\text{-}12)$$

Within-Groups Sum of Squares. The within-groups sum of squares, $SS_{S/A}$, is based on the deviation of each individual score from its respective treatment mean $(Y - \overline{Y}_A)$. For any *one* treatment condition, there are n observations. Since one df is lost as a result of estimating the population treatment mean from the mean of this treatment condition,

$$df = n - 1$$

However, in this sum of squares, the separate sums of squares for each group are pooled across all of the treatment conditions. We find the degrees of freedom, therefore, by adding together the df's associated with the different treatment conditions in the experiment. That is,

$$df_{S/A} = (n - 1) + (n - 1) + (n - 1) + \cdots$$

Since there are a treatment conditions, each with $df = n - 1$, and the same number of subjects in each group (n), we can simplify the formula to read

$$df_{S/A} = (a)(n - 1) \tag{4-13}$$

Total Sum of Squares. The total sum of squares, SS_T, is based on the deviation of each individual score from the grand mean $(Y - \overline{Y}_T)$. There are $(a)(n)$ observations in the total experiment. As a result of our estimating the overall population mean from the grand mean of the experiment, the value of one subject's score is "fixed," and one df is lost. Thus,

$$df_T = (a)(n) - 1 \tag{4-14}$$

An alternative formula for df_T derives from the fact that the sum of the component degrees of freedom (df_A and $df_{S/A}$) must equal the total degrees of freedom, df_T, just as the sum of the component sums of squares must equal the total sum of squares. In symbols,

$$df_T = df_A + df_{S/A} \tag{4-15}$$

Computational Formulas for the Analysis of Variance

Table 4-7 gives the computational formulas for the analysis of variance. Each row of the table provides relevant formulas for one of the three sources of variance. The first column of the table lists these three sources. The second

TABLE 4-7 *A Summary of the Analysis of Variance*

Source of Variance	Sum of Squares $(SS)^a$	Degrees of Freedom (df)	Mean Square (MS)	F Ratio
Treatments (A)	SS_A	$a - 1$	$\dfrac{SS_A}{df_A}$	$\dfrac{MS_A}{MS_{S/A}}$
Subjects Within Groups (S/A)	$SS_{S/A}$	$(a)(n - 1)$	$\dfrac{SS_{S/A}}{df_{S/A}}$	
Total (T)	SS_T	$(a)(n) - 1$		

^{a} See Tables 4-5 and 4-6 for computational formulas.

column lists the sums of squares associated with these sources. (See Tables 4-5 and 4-6 for the computational formulas for these sums of squares.) The third column shows the degrees of freedom associated with the sources of variability. The fourth column gives the formulas for the two component mean squares, MS_A and $MS_{S/A}$. (A mean square based on the total sum of squares is not needed and is normally not calculated.) The fifth column gives the formula for the F ratio. The F ratio is formed by

$$F = \frac{MS_A}{MS_{S/A}} \tag{4-16}$$

which consists of an estimate of treatment variability (MS_A) divided by an estimate of the variability of subjects treated alike $(MS_{S/A})$. This latter term is frequently called the **error term** of the F ratio, the term that provides an estimate of the experimental error influencing the differences among the treatment means. That is,

$$F = \frac{MS_A}{MS_{S/A}}$$

$$= \frac{\text{between-groups variability (effect + error)}}{\text{within-groups variability (error)}}$$

A Numerical Example

We can now complete the analysis of variance for the data in Table 4-1. The sums of squares, which we calculated earlier, are presented again in Table 4-8, a summary table of the ANOVA.

TABLE 4-8 *The Summary Table for the Analysis of Variance*				
Source	*SS*	*df*	*MS*	*F*
A	180.00	1	180.00	67.42
S/A	48.00	18	2.67	
Total	228.00	19		

The next step is to calculate the degrees of freedom for the three sums of squares. For this example, there are $a = 2$ treatment conditions and $n = 10$ subjects in each of the treatment groups. Thus,

$$df_A = a - 1 = 2 - 1 = 1$$

$$df_{S/A} = (a)(n - 1) = (2)(10 - 1) = (2)(9) = 18$$

$$df_T = (a)(n) - 1 = (2)(10) - 1 = 20 - 1 = 19$$

These values are listed in the *df* column of the summary table. You should note that

$$df_T = df_A + df_{S/A}$$

$$= 1 + 18$$

$$= 19$$

which must hold for the calculations to be correct.

To obtain the two mean squares, we divide each sum of squares by the appropriate degrees of freedom. That is,

$$MS_A = \frac{SS_A}{df_A} = \frac{180.00}{1} = 180.00$$

$$MS_{S/A} = \frac{SS_{S/A}}{df_{S/A}} = \frac{48.00}{18} = 2.67$$

These quantities are entered into the summary table.

The final step in the calculations is to form the F ratio. From Eq. (4-16),

$$F = \frac{MS_A}{MS_{S/A}} = \frac{180.00}{2.67} = 67.42$$

Given the logic surrounding the evaluation of the F ratio, which we discussed in Chap. 3, you probably suspect that the null hypothesis will be rejected when the F value is as large as this one. While this suspicion is correct, forming decision rules with which we formally evaluate the null hypothesis is still necessary. We cover this step in the next chapter.

4.5 SUMMARY

The process of analyzing a completely randomized single-factor experiment begins with the isolation of two sources of variation in the data: one source reflecting the effects of the different treatments (if any) and the unavoidable effects of experimental error, and the other source reflecting the effects of experimental error alone. We first illustrated how these sources could be expressed as deviations from means, and we then used this information to calculate corresponding sums of squares, SS_A and $SS_{S/A}$. Next, we developed alternative computational formulas that simplify the calculation of these sums of squares. Finally, we showed how to calculate two variances, known as *mean squares* (MS_A and $MS_{S/A}$) in the analysis of variance, from this information. The ratio of the MS_A to the $MS_{S/A}$ forms the treatment index — the F ratio — which we will use in evaluating the null hypothesis. In the next chapter, we describe how this final, but critical, last step is accomplished.

4.6 EXERCISES [7]

*1. Suppose a researcher is interested in the effects of various chemical additives to foods on activity levels in children determined to be hyperactive.

---

[7] Answers to the starred problems are given in Appendix B.

An experiment is designed in which the two conditions consist of food without the additives and the same food but with the additives. Data for two groups of $n = 9$ children consist of a response measure developed especially for the research. The following data are obtained:

No Additives		Additives	
$Y_{1,1}$	31	$Y_{2,1}$	30
$Y_{1,2}$	33	$Y_{2,2}$	28
$Y_{1,3}$	25	$Y_{2,3}$	36
$Y_{1,4}$	28	$Y_{2,4}$	41
$Y_{1,5}$	24	$Y_{2,5}$	29
$Y_{1,6}$	30	$Y_{2,6}$	32
$Y_{1,7}$	31	$Y_{2,7}$	27
$Y_{1,8}$	26	$Y_{2,8}$	35
$Y_{1,9}$	30	$Y_{2,9}$	36
	258		294

(handwritten notes: $a = 2$, $n = 9$, $a(n) = 18$)

a. Calculate the means for the two treatment conditions.

b. Calculate the basic ratios.

c. Find the sums of squares for A, S/A, and T.

d. Write the df statements and determine the degrees of freedom that correspond to these sources of variability.

e. Calculate the mean squares.

f. Construct a summary table and calculate F.

2. In an experiment, subjects were asked to rate on a 5-point scale each of 24 words on a specified attribute. After the words were rated, each subject wrote down as many of the words as he or she could remember. The data consisted of the number of words recalled by each subject. Block randomization was used in the formation of four groups of $n = 16$ subjects each. The subjects in a_1 rated each word on how pleasant its meaning was; in a_2 each word was rated on frequency of usage in the language; in a_3 each word was rated on how pleasant its sound was; and in a_4 each word was rated on how frequently each subject thought its syllables were used in the language. The investigators were interested in whether the differences in the rating tasks would lead to differences in the numbers of words recalled. The results of the study follow.

Pleasantness of Meaning	Frequency of Word	Pleasantness of Sound	Frequency of Syllables
11	7	8	3
11	3	2	4
12	10	8	3
9	7	8	2
10	7	9	5
13	4	4	2
11	8	6	5
9	7	7	5
10	5	7	2
6	7	1	8
13	8	9	4
7	11	3	8
12	8	6	5
12	10	5	7
9	9	11	7
10	8	8	5

Handwritten annotations left of table:

$a = 4$

$n = 16$

$a(n) = 64$

Handwritten column labels and totals:

	A1	A2	A3	A4
ΣY	165	119	102	75
ΣY^2	1761	953	764	413
$\bar{Y}_A$	10.3125	7.4375	6.375	4.6875

Conduct an analysis of variance and determine whether the different treatments had an effect on word recall. To assist you in your calculations, we have indicated the sorts of summary calculations you will need to make to complete the analysis. Though they are not needed for the F ratio, calculate the means for the different treatment conditions. (Save your calculations for exercise 2 in Chap. 5, p. 132; exercise 5 in Chap. 6, p. 163; and exercise 1 in Chap. 7, p. 186.)

3. Before making a decision about an advertising brochure, a publisher ran an experiment to discover whether the responses by readers to certain ads differed. More specifically, he wanted to test responses to three kinds of ads: ads with a color picture, ads with a black and white picture, and ads with no picture. Each ad was inserted in a magazine with other printed material intended to draw attention away from the material being evaluated. Subjects rated the critical ad on an 11-point scale where the higher the number, the greater the preference for the ad. Results for the

21 subjects ($n = 7$ subjects in each condition) are as follows:

Color	Black and White	No Picture
3	4	10
3	7	7
7	5	8
6	3	5
8	9	9
1	8	7
5	7	6

33   43   52

Complete all the necessary calculations for the construction of an analysis summary table. (Save your calculations for exercise 3 in Chap. 5, p. 132; for exercise 3 in Chap. 6, p. 163; and for exercise 2 in Chap. 7, p. 186.)

Chapter · 5

EVALUATING THE F RATIO

It may be helpful at this point to review the basic logic behind the evaluation of the null hypothesis. We start with an experiment in which subjects are assigned randomly to different treatment conditions. From the scores of the subjects on the dependent variable, we calculate two variance estimates, one reflecting the variation among the treatment means (MS_A) and the other reflecting variation among subjects treated alike ($MS_{S/A}$). The MS_A is affected by the effects of the different treatment conditions — if any — in addition to the presence of experimental error. The $MS_{S/A}$, on the other hand, is affected by the presence of experimental error alone. We form a set of two statistical hypotheses: the null hypothesis, which states that the population treatment means are equal — that is, no treatment effects exist — and the alternative hypothesis, which states that not all the population means are equal, or treatment effects do exist. The F ratio — MS_A divided by $MS_{S/A}$ (the so-called error term) — provides a useful way to test the null hypothesis. If the null hypothesis is true, both mean squares will reflect the operation of experimental error, and the value of F will be approximately equal to 1.0. If the null hypothesis is false, the MS_A will reflect the operation of an additional factor — treatment effects — and the value of F will be greater than 1.0.

5.1 THE SAMPLING DISTRIBUTION OF F

Suppose we were able to conduct the same experiment over and over, each time with a different set of subjects. Suppose further that the null hypothesis was in fact true, meaning that no differences existed among the treatment means in the population. Each experiment would yield a perfectly valid value of F; the values would not all be the same, simply because sampling and random assignment would produce a different pattern of differences among the treatment conditions in each experiment. Suppose we arranged these F's in size from small to large and noted the frequency with which each value occurred over an extremely large number of these experiments. We would be able to plot this information in a graph, measuring off the values of F on the horizontal axis and the frequency of occurrence on the vertical axis. The result would be the **sampling distribution** of the F statistic.

An Empirical Determination of a Sampling Distribution

Consider an example of just such a series of experiments conducted by Lewis F. Petrinovich and Curtis D. Hardyck.[1] These investigators did not actually

---

[1] We wish to thank Drs. Petrinovich and Hardyck for making available the results of these experiments.

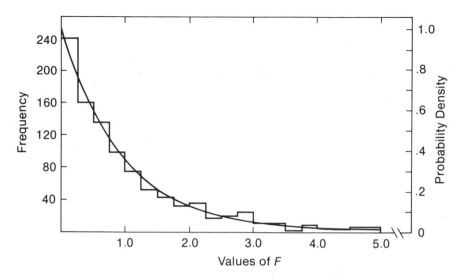

FIGURE 5-1 *A Sampling Distribution of F from Simulated Experiments (Bar Graph) with a = 3 (Treatment Conditions) and n = 15 (Scores Each). The smooth curve is the theoretical sampling distribution of F corresponding to this example.*

perform real experiments, but simulated them with a computer by drawing many random samples, each consisting of 45 scores, from a population of 6,000 scores stored in the memory of the computer. They then divided the 45 scores randomly into $a = 3$ "treatment" groups of $n = 15$ scores each and performed an ANOVA on these data. The 45 scores were then put back into the population, and a new sample of 45 scores was randomly chosen. This second group of scores was also divided randomly into three groups, and an ANOVA was performed. This procedure was repeated until 1,000 such "experiments" had been conducted and analyzed, producing 1,000 F ratios. Experiments using this sort of sampling procedure are referred to as *Monte Carlo studies*.

Since each of the three "treatment" conditions represented a random sample from the *same* underlying population, the null hypothesis is true — that is, the three population "treatment" means are identical. The 1,000 values of F, arranged and grouped according to size, therefore, represent a sampling distribution of the F statistic when the null hypothesis is true. The distribution obtained is plotted in Fig. 5-1. For comparison, the *theoretical* sampling distribution of this F statistic, which is mathematically determined, is superimposed over the results of the sampling study.

The first point to note is the close correspondence between the theoretical sampling distribution (the smooth curve) and that obtained from the Monte

Carlo study. Second, the average value of F is approximately 1.0 ($\overline{F} = 1.09$), which is what should occur if the null hypothesis is true. Finally, as you can see, the frequencies of the F's decline rapidly as the values of F become larger and larger. (We cut the distribution off at $F = 5.0$, because cases of larger values occur so infrequently. The theoretical distribution actually extends to $F =$ infinity.)

Consider the ways in which we can use this information. Although large values of F can and do occur by chance when the null hypothesis is true, they do not happen all that frequently. For example, the largest F observed by Petrinovich and Hardyck in their Monte Carlo study was 8.50. On the basis of their study, we can conclude that an F this size or larger occurred by chance only once in 1,000 sampling studies. What would happen if we obtained an F of 8.50 in an *actual* experiment, where we did not know at the outset whether the null hypothesis was true? Would we conclude that the null hypothesis was true, since an F this large could in fact occur by chance (and did in the illustration) under these circumstances? Or would we note that an F of 8.50 or larger is an *extremely rare event*, and conclude that the null hypothesis is far more likely to be false?

In fact, the latter decision, to reject the null hypothesis, would be justified in such a case. It is simply not reasonable to hold on to the null hypothesis when the probability is so small that a particular F has occurred by chance under the null hypothesis. One time out of a thousand (a probability of $p = .001$) certainly qualifies as an infrequent and rare event. For this reason, we are willing to conclude that an F of 8.50 is evidence — in a word — *incompatible* with the null hypothesis.

In this discussion, we have focused on the largest F obtained from the Petrinovich and Hardyck Monte Carlo study. As noted in Chap. 3, most researchers would find a probability level of $p = .001$, which this example reflects, too stringent a test of the null hypothesis. They would be willing to accept more probable values of F as critical evidence against the null hypothesis.

Given the results of the sampling study, we could start counting the values of F beginning with the largest ($F = 8.50$) and moving toward the smallest until we had tabulated 5 percent of the 1,000 F ratios (5 percent of $1,000 = 50$). You will recall that this particular percentage (5 percent) is the standard against which most researchers assess the null hypothesis. In this example, the critical value of F representing the fiftieth case happens to be 3.23. If we were to conduct our own experiment with the same number of subjects (45) randomly assigned to three different treatment groups, this F value of 3.23 would define the beginning of a region within which the null hypothesis would begin to be questioned. Any value of F above this point, then, would fall into a region within which we would reject the null hypothesis.

A Summary of Terms

Several terms commonly used to refer to different aspects of hypothesis testing are defined graphically in Fig. 5-2. At the top of the figure lies a number line representing all possible values of the F statistic; this scale runs from zero to extremely large numbers. The **critical value** of F is located on this number line and extends down to the bottom of the figure. This critical value is determined by a researcher's personal definition of evidence considered to be incompatible with the null hypothesis; that is, it defines values of F that cannot be reasonably attributed to the operation of chance factors when the null hypothesis is true. This definition of incompatibility is usually stated as a percentage, a proportion, or a probability, and is referred to as the **significance level**. This probability is generally designated by the Greek letter α (**alpha**).

The first row of terms in Fig. 5-2 shows the critical value of F as a point dividing the sampling distribution of F into two parts. If $\alpha = .05$, the critical value of F is such that the proportion of F's occurring *at or above* the critical value is .05. By subtraction, the remaining proportion, the F's falling *below* the critical value, is $1 - .05 = .95$. In symbols, the proportion of cases at or above the critical value is α and that below the critical value is $1 - \alpha$.

The second row of the figure indicates the relationship between the significance level and a researcher's decision concerning the status of the null hypothesis. That is, if the observed F equals or exceeds the critical value of F,

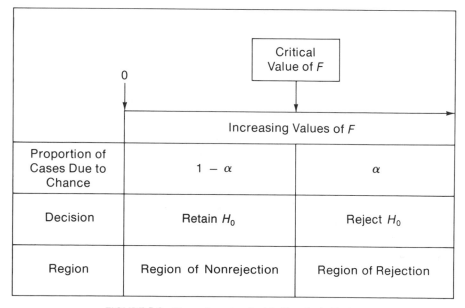

FIGURE 5-2 *Terms Associated with Hypothesis Testing.*

we reject the null hypothesis; if not, we retain it. Finally, the third row gives names to the two categories of *F* defined by the critical value: the **region of rejection** — also known as the *critical region* — for the range of *F* values within which the null hypothesis will be rejected, and the **region of nonrejection** for the range of *F* values within which the null hypothesis will be retained.

5.2 DETERMINING THE CRITICAL VALUE OF *F*

Determining the critical value of *F* is relatively easy when the sampling distribution is available, but what do we do when it is not? The problem is increased immeasurably by the fact that a different sampling distribution of *F* exists for every possible combination of the number of treatment conditions (a) and sample size (n).[2] Although the theoretical sampling distributions for these different situations are known to statisticians and could be made available to researchers in that form, a book containing this information would be enormous. You may have noted that we do not need to plot the entire sampling distribution to determine the beginning of a rejection region — only the critical value. Thus, if some agreement exists among researchers concerning acceptable significance levels (and it does), tables of *critical values* — called an **F table** — can be constructed for all possible combinations of a and n in a relatively small space. Table A-2 in Appendix A is such a table.

Using the *F* Table

To find a critical value in the *F* table, you need three pieces of information:

1. The degrees of freedom for the numerator of the *F* ratio (df_A)
2. The degrees of freedom for the denominator of the *F* ratio ($df_{S/A}$)
3. The significance level (α)

Look at the *F* table in Appendix A (Table A-2). You will find that numerator df's are listed in the columns and denominator df's are listed in the rows. You may notice that not all combinations of df's are available in this table. Most

---

[2] The shapes of these different *F* distributions can be quite different from the one depicted in Fig. 5-1, depending both on the number of treatment conditions and the number of subjects per condition.

F tables are abbreviated in some way or another to conserve space. Little is lost, however, since deletions in either numerator or denominator degrees of freedom occur only where changes in critical values of F are small with increases in df.[3] Within each row of Table A-2, you have a choice between two significance levels, $\alpha = .05$ or $\alpha = .01$. Critical values of F are listed in the body of the F table. (Values for the most commonly chosen significance level, $\alpha = .05$, are printed in boldface type.)

5.3 FORMING THE DECISION RULE

The **decision rule** represents a formal statement of the exact conditions under which the null hypothesis will be rejected. Once stated, a researcher merely needs to apply the rule to the F obtained from an experiment. The decision rule takes the following form:

> **If the obtained value of F equals or exceeds $F_\alpha =$ ____, reject the null hypothesis; otherwise, retain it.**

The critical value of F (F_α) is obtained from the F table. As we saw, this value depends on the degrees of freedom associated with the numerator and denominator terms of the F ratio and the significance level (α).

As an example, consider the analysis of variance we conducted on the data from Table 4-1 (summarized in Table 4-8, p. 101). In this example, $a = 2$ and $n = 10$. The degrees of freedom associated with the numerator term of the F ratio (MS_A) were found to be $df_A = 1$, and the degrees of freedom associated with the denominator term $(MS_{S/A})$ were found to be $df_{S/A} = 18$. If we set the significance level at $\alpha = .05$, we have all the information we need to determine F_α.

Turning now to the F table, the first step is to find the intersection of the column listing $df_{num.} = 1$ and the row listing $df_{denom.} = 18$. You will find two

---

[3] When the critical value of F falls between two rows (or columns) of the table, most researchers follow the practice of choosing the row (or column) with the *smaller* number of degrees of freedom. This choice results in a critical value of F that is slightly larger than it should be. The consequence is a reduced rejection region (and a slightly smaller value for α). Other options are available if this procedure seems unreasonable — for example, linear interpolation (see Lindman, 1974, pp. 18–19) or the use of more extensive tables of F (see, for example, Pearson & Hartley, 1970). This problem is not serious, however, and becomes relevant only when the obtained value of F lies very close to the critical value.

critical values of F at this point of intersection, one for $\alpha = .05$ (in boldface type) and the other for $\alpha = .01$. The value we want is $F_\alpha = 4.41$. This value can now be substituted in the decision rule:

If the obtained value of F equals or exceeds $F_\alpha = 4.41$, reject the null hypothesis; otherwise, retain it.

Consulting Table 4-8, we see that the obtained value of $F = 67.42$ clearly exceeds the critical value of F. Thus, we reject the null hypothesis and conclude that the two population treatment means are different. In a research report, we would omit the lines of reasoning with which investigators are very familiar and simply state, "The F is significant at the 5 percent level of significance." If we wanted to convey more information, we could say, "the means of the conditions were significantly different, $F(1, 18) = 67.42$, at the 5 percent level of significance." This more complete statement gives all the relevant information the *reader* needs to make his or her own decision, and indicates what decision the researcher has made, that is, that the null hypothesis is rejected with $\alpha = .05$.

The decision rule is depicted in Fig. 5-3, which depicts the theoretical sampling distribution underlying this particular experiment.[4] The vertical line drawn at $F_\alpha = 4.41$ locates the critical value of F that ultimately determines our decision concerning the status of the null hypothesis: values falling within the region to the right of the line will result in our rejecting the null hypothesis, whereas values to the left will result in our retaining the null hypothesis.

Some Comments on Format

For a class report, you would probably be expected to include a summary table for an analysis of variance you performed on your data. (Table 4-8 is an example of such a summary.) Such tables are usually omitted from research reports found in the literature, however, unless the analysis is complex. Instead, the outcome of the statistical analysis is generally reported in the text of an article. (An example of how this might be stated was given in the first part of Sec. 5.3.) In addition, researchers are often expected to report the value of the denominator of the F ratio — the error term — to permit readers to perform their own statistical analyses of the data. Using the analysis reported in Table 4-8 as an example, we can report the error term, $MS_{S/A}$, as $MS_e = 2.67$.

---

[4] This is an idealized representation of the theoretical sampling distribution of F for this example.

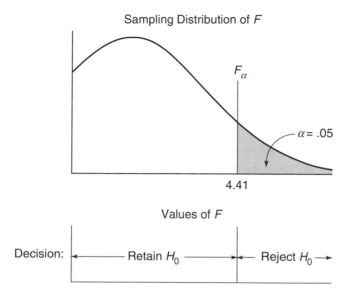

FIGURE 5-3 *The Decision Rule for the Numerical Example Superimposed over the Relevant Sampling Distribution of F.*

A common mistake made by students is to omit the presentation of the treatment means. This is a serious omission, since without the treatment means the results of an experiment are incomplete and relatively uninformative. If the experiment is a simple one, as in the example of Table 4-8, the means can be reported in the body of the text along with the summary of the statistical test. If the experiment is more complex, the means should be reported in a table, properly labeled with regard to the treatments, or, if the treatment conditions consist of a *quantitative manipulation*, in a figure (see pp. 44–50 for examples of tables and figures).

Reporting the Results of Statistical Tests

As you begin to read articles in the research literature, you will find the statistical outcomes of analyses reported in various ways. A recent practice in some journals is to require a researcher to state the particular level of significance adopted — for instance, $\alpha = .05$ — at the beginning of the results section. Once this standard is stated, the outcome of any statistical analysis is then reported as being "significant" or "nonsignificant" — but *not* "*in*significant," which is a value judgment, not a statistical statement. More typically, however, the results of statistical tests are reported in symbols and numbers. Since you will need to understand the meaning of these statements when you come across them in your reading, we pause in our discussion of the analysis of variance to explain some frequently encountered terms. We first consider statements designating significant statistical tests.

Reporting Significant Effects. Significance is often reported by means of $<$, the symbol for *less than*, in conjunction with a probability statement. For example, the statement that a particular analysis is "significant at $p < .05$" (where the letter p stands for the word *probability*) indicates that the obtained value of F falls within the rejection region established for the 5 percent level of significance. We will use this particular format in this book.

Often, significant results are reported with probabilities other than .05. For example, a test might be declared to be "significant at $p < .01$" or even "significant at $p < .001$." Such expressions rarely mean that the researcher originally set his or her personal probability of α at these smaller values. They simply allow the few researchers who *have* adopted these smaller values of α to determine at a glance whether *they* will reject the null hypothesis. It should be noted that if a null hypothesis can be rejected at an α level *smaller* than .05 — for instance, .01 — it would necessarily be rejected at $\alpha = .05$ as well. Thus, the use of this particular format provides information that is useful to the researcher who has adopted the more common 5 percent significance level and to the relatively rare investigator who prefers to use a significance level smaller than 5 percent.

In this regard, you will occasionally see reported what is called the **exact probability** of an F statistic. This probability, obtained from most statistical software programs for the computer, refers to the proportion of the sampling distribution of the F statistic falling at or above the F obtained from an experiment. An $F(2, 45) = 6.39$, for example, has an exact probability of $p = .0036$. Knowing this, one can simply apply one's chosen significance level — for example, $p = .05$ — and reject the null hypothesis if the exact probability is smaller (which it is in this example) or retain the null hypothesis if it is larger. The decision rule in this case becomes

If the exact probability of the observed F is equal to or less than $p = .05$, reject the null hypothesis; otherwise, retain it.

This method of reporting the results of statistical tests has considerable merit, since it results in a clear distinction between an accurate description of the F test provided by the exact probability and a researcher's own decision to reject or retain the null hypothesis.

The habit of some researchers to report different probability levels (.05, .01, .001, and so on) while maintaining a personal probability level of $\alpha = .05$

(which most researchers do) leads to some problems of misinterpretation as to exactly what can be concluded following a test of significance. For example, many researchers have a tendency to assume that a finding which is significant at $p < .01$, say, is actually *more* significant than one that is significant at $p < .05$. Given the logic outlined in Chap. 3, a finding either is significant or is not — one's criterion for these conclusions is specified by the decision rule. The results of two experiments *cannot* be measured against each other in this manner. We discuss an appropriate measure of the size, or magnitude, of the treatment effects in Chap. 7. With this measure, one can compare the size of the treatment effects from one experiment with those from another.

A similar misunderstanding can arise when a researcher reports a finding to be "highly significant," or even "very highly significant," rather than merely "significant." If these adverbs are intended as the verbal equivalents of the probability statements $p < .01$ and $p < .001$, respectively, then there is no problem. But often the researcher is implying with these words that a finding is actually *more significant* than one that is "only" significant at $p < .05$. Again, only *two conclusions* are possible in the reasoning we follow in rejecting null hypotheses, namely, significance and nonsignificance. *Degrees* of significance (for example, significant, highly significant, and very highly significant) are not part of the decision-making process.

In summary, then, the term *significance* has a very precise meaning when applied to statistical tests. A test is statistically significant if the obtained F (or any other test statistic, for that matter) falls within the rejection region determined by a researcher's choice of significance level. *Significance* is not to be interpreted as *importance*, however — a common error among individuals who are unfamiliar with these concepts. The importance of a finding depends on a number of additional factors, including its usefulness in both a practical and a theoretical sense. More information than the outcome of a statistical test is necessary for determining the importance of results from an experiment.

Reporting Nonsignificant Results. Nonsignificance is often denoted by $>$, the symbol for *greater than*, in conjunction with a probability statement. For example, the statement that a particular analysis is "not significant, $p > .05$" indicates that the obtained value of F falls within the region of nonrejection established at the 5 percent level of significance.[5] You may also see the initials "n.s." to designate a nonsignificant result, such as "$F(1, 120) = 1.14$, n.s."

---

[5] Occasionally, you will see a statement that an outcome is not significant at a probability *greater* than .05, that is $p > .10$ or $p > .25$. Such an expression means that the null hypothesis would be retained even if one adopted a relatively lax significance level, for example, $\alpha = .10$ or $.25$, respectively.

5.4 ASSUMPTIONS UNDERLYING THE ANALYSIS

We used the sampling distribution of F — by means of the F table — to find the critical value of F that marks the beginning of the rejection region. In our theoretical justification of this procedure, we assumed that several conditions are met by the data being subjected to statistical analysis. This concept will require a bit of explaining. We start with the notion of treatment populations — extremely large numbers of individuals randomly subjected to the same treatment conditions that constitute our experiment. There is a different treatment population for each of these treatment conditions. A population treatment mean is an average of the scores obtained from the subjects in a given treatment population. As we saw in Chap. 3, the null and alternative hypotheses are statements concerning the relationship among these population treatment means. That is, the null hypothesis states that the population treatment means are equal, and the alternative hypothesis states that not all the population treatment means are the same.

The Three Assumptions

The assumptions underlying the use of the sampling distribution of F consist of statements about additional characteristics of these treatment populations. More specifically, we make three assumptions regarding the individual scores of the subjects present in these hypothetical treatment populations:

1. The scores distribute themselves normally (the **assumption of normality**).
2. The scores show the same degree of variability from treatment population to treatment population (the **assumption of equal variances**).
3. The scores are independent of one another both within each treatment population as well as across the different populations (the **assumption of independence**).

The first assumption is concerned with the particular shape of the frequency distribution of the scores in the treatment populations. This shape, which is defined mathematically and is known as the **normal distribution**, is commonly observed in nature, especially when characteristics being measured are influenced by a large number of independent factors. (The normal distribution is bell-shaped and is familiar to anyone who has read an introductory psychology text or has taken a course that was graded "on the curve.") The second assumption specifies that the different sets of treatment scores are equally variable, that is, have the same variance. This is known as the assumption of **homogeneity of variance**. The final assumption ultimately refers to the absence of systematic bias resulting from nuisance variables operating in the experiment.

Consequences of Violating the Assumptions

How well does a typical experiment meet the requirements of these assumptions, and to what extent do deviations from them jeopardize the procedures we employ in evaluating a null hypothesis? The assumption of independence is generally satisfied through the random assignment of subjects to the treatment conditions, and must be met before others will accept the results of an experiment. However, the other two assumptions — normality and homogeneity of variance — frequently are *not* satisfied in psychological experimentation. For many years, it was believed that even relatively severe deviations from the conditions assumed have little effect on the evaluation process. More recent evidence, however, suggests that violations of the *homogeneity assumption* affect the sampling distribution of F and, consequently, the probability of rejecting the null hypothesis. More specifically, the presence of unequal group variances actually *increases* our chances of rejecting the null hypothesis, which if left uncorrected, increases the significance level from .05, for example, to .10 or greater. (We present an explanation of these effects in Sec. 5.9.)

A Correction for Unequal Variances

Most researchers will want to restore the original significance level when the homogeneity assumption is not met. Whereas several solutions to this problem have been proposed, we will present a relatively simple one based on values listed in the F table. We begin the correction procedure by determining the degree to which the variances for the treatment conditions are different. One such index, $F_{max.}$, consists of a ratio formed by dividing the largest variance in the experiment ($s^2_{largest}$) by the smallest ($s^2_{smallest}$). That is,

$$F_{max.} = \frac{s^2_{largest}}{s^2_{smallest}} \tag{5-1}$$

Research has shown that when $F_{max.}$ *is greater than* 3.0, the sampling distribution of F begins to become sufficiently distorted to seriously affect the decision rule based on the undistorted theoretical sampling distribution of F. We can correct

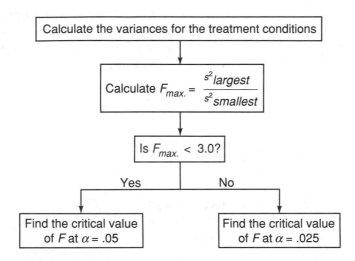

FIGURE 5-4 *Summary of a Procedure for Modifying the Decision Rule When the Homogeneity Assumption is Violated.*

for this distortion by selecting a new critical value of F, which we will call $\boldsymbol{F_{adj.}}$, at a slightly more stringent significance level, namely, $\alpha = .025$.

This correction procedure may be summarized as a series of four steps, which are listed in Fig. 5-4:

1. Calculate the variances for the treatment conditions.
2. Divide the largest variance by the smallest variance to obtain $F_{max.}$.
3. If $F_{max.}$ is less than 3, follow the usual evaluation procedures.
4. If $F_{max.}$ is greater than 3, obtain the new critical F, $F_{adj.}$, by using the values listed in the F table at $\alpha = .025$.

Suppose that $F_{max.}$ is greater than 3 for our numerical example. Applying the steps outlined in Fig. 5-4, we would need to obtain a new critical F, $F_{adj.}$. Because the F table in Appendix A (Table A-2) does not give critical values of F at $\alpha = .025$, we must consult a more extensive F table, such as those presented in advanced statistics books. From such a table, we find that with $df_{num.} = 1$ and $df_{denom.} = 18$, $F = 5.98$ at $\alpha = .025$. The revised decision rule then becomes

If the obtained value of F equals or exceeds $F_{adj.} = 5.98$, reject the null hypothesis; otherwise, retain it.

In comparison, the uncorrected critical value of F is 4.41.

5.5 A COMPLETE NUMERICAL EXAMPLE

In this section, we work through a second numerical example to demonstrate in one place all the calculations required for the analysis of variance.

The Experimental Design

Consider an experiment comparing the effects of three kinds of reinforcement on the performance of children given a series of simple reasoning problems. The independent variable of reinforcement consists of the following three conditions: *praise* for correct responses; *criticism* for mistakes; and *silence* regardless of whether the child answered the problem correctly. A total of 15 third-grade children are assigned randomly in equal numbers ($n = 5$) to the $a = 3$ treatment conditions. The measure of performance (the dependent variable) is the number of correct responses given during the course of testing. The scores from this hypothetical experiment are presented in Table 5-1.

TABLE 5-1 *Preliminary Calculations for ANOVA*

Treatment Conditions	Factor A (Type of Reinforcement)		
	Praise a_1	*Criticism* a_2	*Silence* a_3
Basic Observations	7	9	2
	8	4	7
	6	6	5
	10	9	3
	7	8	5
1. Mean	7.60	7.20	4.40
2. Standard Deviation	1.52	2.17	1.95
3. Sum of Scores	38	36	22
4. Sum of Squared Scores	298	278	112
5. Sum of Squares	9.20	18.80	15.20
6. Variance	2.30	4.70	3.80

Preliminary Calculations

As a first step, we perform certain preliminary calculations in preparation for the analysis of variance. These include the treatment means and standard deviations (both of which we would probably place in a table when we reported our results), as well as the treatment sums and the sum of the squared observations (from which the means and standard deviations are derived). An examination of the means suggests that the children given either praise ($\overline{Y}_{A_1} = 7.60$) or criticism ($\overline{Y}_{A_2} = 7.20$) solved more problems correctly than the children given no reinforcement ($\overline{Y}_{A_3} = 4.40$), but that the nature of the verbal reinforcement (praise versus criticism) does not seem to matter.

As we have already indicated, most researchers would also obtain some measure of variability for each treatment condition as part of their preliminary calculations. The usual measure is the standard deviation, designated s, which can be easily calculated from the information in the table. The first step in calculating the standard deviation is to obtain the sum of squares (SS) for each treatment group. In terms of deviations from the mean ($Y - \overline{Y}_A$), the formula is

$$SS = \Sigma(Y - \overline{Y}_A)^2 \tag{5-2}$$

As an example of the calculations, the sum of squares for the praise condition is equal to

$$
\begin{aligned}
SS &= (7 - 7.6)^2 + (8 - 7.6)^2 + (6 - 7.6)^2 + (10 - 7.6)^2 + (7 - 7.6)^2 \\
&= (-.6)^2 + (.4)^2 + (-1.6)^2 + (2.4)^2 + (-.6)^2 \\
&= .36 + .16 + 2.56 + 5.76 + .36 = 9.20
\end{aligned}
$$

As you saw in Chap. 2, we can use a computationally simpler formula for the sum of squares instead of Eq. (5-2). More explicitly,

$$SS = (\text{sum of the squared scores}) - \frac{(\text{sum of scores})^2}{n} \tag{5-3}$$

Applying Eq. (5-3) to the same set of data, we find

$$SS = 298 - \frac{(38)^2}{5} = 298 - 288.80 = 9.20$$

Once the sum of squares is calculated, finding the variance and the standard deviation is easy. You will recall from Chap. 2 that the

$$\text{variance } (s^2) = \frac{SS}{df} = \frac{SS}{n-1}$$

For the praise condition,

$$s^2 = \frac{9.20}{5-1} = \frac{9.20}{4} = 2.30$$

Finally, the standard deviation of a set of scores is defined as

$$\text{standard deviation } (s) = \sqrt{\text{variance}}$$

For the praise condition,

$$s = \sqrt{2.30} = 1.52$$

The standard deviations for the three conditions are presented in row 2 of the table. For convenience, the sums of squares and variances for the three treatment conditions are given in rows 5 and 6, respectively, if you want to practice the calculations on the data for the other two conditions.

The main reason for calculating measures of variability for each treatment condition is to determine whether the groups show comparable degrees of variability. Whereas an inspection of either the standard deviations (row 2) or the variances (row 6) indicates some variability from group to group, these differences are well within the range of values one would expect if chance factors alone were operating.[6] Nevertheless, we should still check to see if we need to be concerned about any violation of the assumption of equal variances. Following the procedures presented in Sec. 5.4, we can calculate $F_{max.}$ to see if any correction is necessary. We see from Table 5-1 that the criticism condition

---

[6] Most advanced statistics texts present procedures for determining the significance of differences among treatment variances.

has the largest variance ($s_2^2 = 4.70$) and the praise condition the smallest ($s_1^2 = 2.30$). From this information, we can substitute in Eq. (5-1) to calculate $F_{max.}$:

$$F_{max.} = \frac{s_{largest}^2}{s_{smallest}^2}$$

$$= \frac{4.70}{2.30}$$

$$= 2.04$$

Applying the procedures summarized in Fig. 5-4, we find that we do not need to apply a special correction in evaluating the outcome of the F test, because $F_{max.}$ is less than 3.

Calculating Basic Ratios

The second step in the analysis is to calculate the sums of squares, beginning with key quantities, namely, the basic ratios $[Y]$, $[A]$, and $[T]$. The computational formulas for the basic ratios are found in Table 4-5 (p. 95). The formula for $[Y]$ specifies the sum of all the squared observations — $\Sigma\, Y^2$ — which we can obtain either by returning to Table 5-1 and actually summing the 15 squared scores:

$$[Y] = \Sigma\, Y^2$$

$$= (7)^2 + (8)^2 + \cdots + (3)^2 + (5)^2$$

$$= 688$$

or combining the subtotals we calculated in the preliminary calculations reported in row 4:

$$[Y] = 298 + 278 + 112$$

$$= 688$$

Next, in calculating $[A]$, we find

$$[A] = \frac{\Sigma A^2}{n}$$

$$= \frac{(38)^2 + (36)^2 + (22)^2}{5}$$

$$= \frac{1,444 + 1,296 + 484}{5} = \frac{3,224}{5}$$

$$= 644.80$$

Finally, we must obtain $[T]$. For this calculation, we need the grand total, which is most conveniently obtained by adding together the treatment sums appearing in row 3 of the table. That is,

$$T = \Sigma A = 38 + 36 + 22 = 96$$

Now we can calculate

$$[T] = \frac{T^2}{(a)(n)}$$

$$= \frac{(96)^2}{(3)(5)} = \frac{9,216}{15}$$

$$= 614.40$$

Calculating the Sums of Squares

The three quantities we calculated in the preceding section are now used to form the three sums of squares. From the formulas listed in Table 4-6 (p. 95),

$$SS_A = [A] - [T] = 644.80 - 614.40 = 30.40$$

$$SS_{S/A} = [Y] - [A] = 688 - 644.80 = 43.20$$

$$SS_T = [Y] - [T] = 688 - 614.40 = 73.60$$

These values are recorded in the summary table (Table 5-2). As an arithmetical check, we should verify that

$$SS_T = SS_A + SS_{S/A}$$

$$73.60 = 30.40 + 43.20$$

$$= 73.60$$

TABLE 5-2 *Analysis of Variance Summary Table*				
Source	*SS*	*df*	*MS*	*F*
A (Type of Reinforcement	30.40	2	15.20	4.22*
S/A (Error)	43.20	12	3.60	
Total	73.60	14		

* $p < .05$.

The Analysis of Variance

The final steps in the analysis (see Table 4-7, p. 100) are summarized in Table 5-2. First, we calculate the degrees of freedom:

$$df_A = a - 1 = 3 - 1 = 2$$
$$df_{S/A} = (a)(n - 1) = (3)(5 - 1) = (3)(4) = 12$$
$$df_T = (a)(n) - 1 = (3)(5) - 1 = 15 - 1 = 14$$

We then apply the arithmetical check; that is,

$$df_T = df_A + df_{S/A}$$
$$14 = 2 + 12$$
$$= 14$$

Next, we obtain the two mean squares:

$$MS_A = \frac{SS_A}{df_A} = \frac{30.40}{2} = 15.20$$

$$MS_{S/A} = \frac{SS_{S/A}}{df_{S/A}} = \frac{43.20}{12} = 3.60$$

Finally, we are able to find the value of the F ratio:

$$F = \frac{MS_A}{MS_{S/A}} = \frac{15.20}{3.60} = 4.22$$

We start the evaluation process by formulating the null and alternative hypotheses:

$$H_0 : \text{all } \mu_i\text{'s are equal}$$

$$H_1 : \text{not all } \mu_i\text{'s are equal}$$

We test the null hypothesis by determining those values of F that would persuade us to reject H_0 and those to retain it. From the F table (Table A-2), we find the critical value of F, which defines the dividing point between these two decisions, to be $F(2, 12) = 3.89$ at the 5 percent level of significance. We can now formally state the decision rule:

If the obtained value of F equals or exceeds $F_\alpha = 3.89$, reject the null hypothesis; otherwise, retain the null hypothesis.

Applying the decision rule to the data of the experiment, the obtained $F = 4.22$ leads us to reject the null hypothesis and conclude that the independent variable produced significant differences in the number of problems correctly solved by the children. We can indicate this decision by entering a footnote to the summary table stating that $p < .05$, which is a common way of informing others that the F is significant at the 5 percent level of significance.[7]

If you were conducting this study, how would you report the results of this analysis? One way would be to say the following:

An analysis of variance was conducted to test the hypothesis that subjects receiving different types of reinforcement would differ in their performance on a series of reasoning problems. From the results of this analysis, $F(2, 12) = 4.22$, $p < .05$, it was concluded that the reinforcement variable produced a significant effect.

---

[7] If $F_{max.}$ had been greater than 3.0, we would need to use the adjusted critical value, $F_{adj.}$, which is the value of F at $\alpha = .025$, rather than the usual .05. From a more extensive table than is presented in Table A-2 of Appendix A, we find $F(2, 12) = 5.10$. The adjusted decision rule would become

If the obtained value of F equals or exceeds $F_{adj.} = 5.10$, reject the null hypothesis; otherwise, retain the null hypothesis.

As you can see, an application of this adjustment would have *changed* our conclusion from rejecting the null hypothesis to retaining it. Fortunately, the correction was not necessary because $F_{max.}$ was less than 3.

You should note that this example of a summary includes several important pieces of information:

a discussion of *why* the analysis was conducted;
a statement of *what type* of analysis was performed;
a report of the *numerical outcome* of this particular analysis; and
a *conclusion* regarding the null hypothesis.

An Alternative Method for Calculating the Error Term. We can calculate the error term for this analysis, $MS_{S/A}$, in an alternative way by averaging the individual variances obtained for the respective treatment groups. Using the variances appearing in row 6 of Table 5-1, we find

$$MS_{S/A} = \frac{s_1^2 + s_2^2 + s_3^2}{a}$$

$$= \frac{2.30 + 4.70 + 3.80}{3} = \frac{10.80}{3} = 3.60$$

which is identical to the value of $MS_{S/A}$ we obtained in the normal fashion. In addition to providing a useful arithmetical check, this equivalency illustrates the fact that the $MS_{S/A}$ is actually an average of the separate within-group variances, each of which provides an estimate of experimental error for its respective condition.[8]

5.6 SPECIAL ANALYSIS WITH TWO TREATMENT CONDITIONS

Most experiments in psychology consist of more than two treatment conditions, although there was a time when the typical experiment contained only two different treatments. As you now know, the analysis of variance can be used to analyze experiments with any number of conditions, including, of course, the two-group experiment. In those early years, however, researchers used a

---

[8] We offered a related argument in Chap. 4 when we demonstrated that the within-groups sum of squares ($SS_{S/A}$) is a composite of the sums of squares for the individual treatment groups (see pp. 89–90).

statistical test called Student's t, or the **t test**, to analyze the results of two-group studies.[9]

The interesting point is that the t test is a special case of the F test. To be more specific, if you were to conduct a t test and an F test on the data from the same two-group experiment, you would reach *exactly the same conclusions.* The reason the conclusions would be identical is that the two statistical tests are algebraically equivalent, that is,

$$F = (t)^2 \quad \text{and} \quad t = \sqrt{F} \tag{5-4}$$

One could argue that there is no compelling need to study the t test today, since the two tests are equivalent in the two-group situation and the F test can be applied in situations where the t cannot be used. Nevertheless, we feel you should have some familiarity with this procedure, as an aid in understanding references to the t test you will encounter when you examine the research literature and as a touchstone with the past if you were exposed to the t test in previous courses.

The t Test

We will illustrate the t test using the data for the two-group experiment we introduced in Chap. 4. The data are presented again in Table 5-3. The F statistic, as you know, consists of the ratio of two variances (or mean squares), the variance in the numerator based on deviations of the treatment means from the grand mean and the variance in the denominator on deviations of individual Y scores from their treatment mean. The t test also consists of a ratio, but in this case, the numerator is based on the actual *difference between the two means* and the denominator on a standard deviation reflecting experimental error. More specifically,

$$t = \frac{\overline{Y}_{A_1} - \overline{Y}_{A_2}}{\hat{\sigma}_{diff.}} \tag{5-5}$$

where $\overline{Y}_{A_1}$ and $\overline{Y}_{A_2}$ represent the two means being compared and $\hat{\sigma}_{diff.}$ is the estimate of experimental error in the context of the t test. This last quantity, which is called the **standard error of the difference between two means**, is

---

[9] "Student" was the pseudonym for W. S. Gosset, who developed the t test.

TABLE 5-3 *Data from a Two-Group Experiment*

	a_1	a_2
	5	13
	3	9
	4	10
	4	8
	6	9
	1	12
	3	8
	4	12
	6	10
	4	9
Sum (A)	40	100
$\Sigma\, Y^2$	180	1,028
Mean $(\overline{Y}_A)$	4.00	10.00
Variance (s^2)	2.22	3.11

based on the two within-group variances and may be calculated as follows:

$$\hat{\sigma}_{diff.} = \sqrt{\frac{s_1^2}{n_1} + \frac{s_2^2}{n_2}} \qquad (5\text{-}6)$$

where s_1^2 and s_2^2 are the variances for the two groups and n_1 and n_2 are corresponding sample sizes, which, in the examples we consider in this text, are equal.

Let's apply the *t* test to the data in Table 5-3. First, we calculate the difference between the two means:

$$\overline{Y}_{A_1} - \overline{Y}_{A_2} = 4.00 - 10.00 = -6.00$$

Next, we obtain the standard error of the difference between the two means:

$$\hat{\sigma}_{diff.} = \sqrt{\frac{s_1^2}{n_1} + \frac{s_2^2}{n_2}}$$

$$= \sqrt{\frac{2.22}{10} + \frac{3.11}{10}} = \sqrt{.22 + .31} = \sqrt{.53}$$

$$= .73$$

The value for t is

$$t = \frac{\overline{Y}_{A_1} - \overline{Y}_{A_2}}{\hat{\sigma}_{diff.}}$$

$$= \frac{-6.00}{.73}$$

$$= -8.22$$

To determine the significance of a t, we need a special table, which can be found in Table A-3 of Appendix A. This table lists critical values of t for two significance levels, $\alpha = .05$ and $.01$, and for various numbers of degrees of freedom. The df in this numerical example are given by

$$df_{diff.} = (n_1 - 1) + (n_2 - 1)$$

$$= (10 - 1) + (10 - 1)$$

$$= 18$$

This particular table gives only positive values of t, but this presents no problem, because the t distribution is symmetrical, which means that the critical value for a negative t, such as the one we obtained, is identical to the one for a positive t except for the sign. From the t table, then, we find $t(18) = 2.10$ for the 5 percent significance level. The decision rule becomes

If the observed value of t, disregarding sign, equals or exceeds $t(18) = 2.10$, reject the null hypothesis; otherwise, retain the null hypothesis.

In our example, $t = -8.22$. Applying the decision rule, we reject the null hypothesis and conclude that the difference between these two means is significant. Furthermore, by looking at the two means (4.00 and 10.00), we can conclude that the mean at a_2 is significantly greater than the mean at a_1.

We indicated earlier that F and t are algebraically equivalent. Using Eq. (5-4), we find

$$F = (t)^2 = (-8.22)^2 = 67.57$$

The F we calculated with the same set of data was 67.42; the small discrepancy between the F we calculated directly and the one obtained from Eq. (5-4) is the result of rounding.

5.7 SUMMARY

The final steps in the analysis consist of the evaluation of the F ratio. From the tabled values of the F statistic, which are based on theoretical sampling distributions of F, we are able to obtain the critical value of F. This value sets the lower boundary of the range of F's within which we will reject the null hypothesis. If the F we obtain from an analysis falls within this range — if it is equal to or greater than the critical value of F — we reject the null hypothesis and conclude that some treatment effects are present in the population. If the observed F is smaller than the critical value, we retain the null hypothesis.

Certain theoretical assumptions underlie the process of evaluating the F ratio: the scores of individual subjects in the hypothetical treatment populations distribute themselves normally, show the same degree of variability, and are independent. We discussed the consequences of violating the assumption of equal variances (the homogeneity assumption) in some detail and introduced a procedure that provides a new critical value of F ($F_{adj.}$) to replace the usual one when severe differences among the group variances are discovered.

We also considered an equivalent statistical procedure to F, the t test, which may be conducted when one is interested in the difference between two means. We prefer the F to the t test because of its more general application to the analysis of experiments.

5.8 EXERCISES [10]

*1. For exercise 1 in Chap. 4 (p. 102), find the critical value of F from the F table (Table A-2). Is the obtained F statistically significant?

2. a. For exercise 2 in Chap. 4 (p. 103), find the critical value of F from the F table. Is the obtained F significant?
    b. Calculate $F_{max.}$. Is it necessary to make a correction in the decision rules for differences among the treatment variances?

3. For exercise 3 in Chap. 4 (p. 104), find the critical value of F from the F table. Is the obtained F significant?

4. An instructor decides to create an artificial set of data in which no treatment

---

[10] Answers to the starred problems are given in Appendix B.

effects are present. She does this by extracting a string of 30 digits from Table A-1 (the table of random numbers), arbitrarily assigning the first 10 scores to a_1, the next 10 to a_2, and the last 10 to a_3. The data follow.

a_1	a_2	a_3
3	0	3
6	8	5
0	7	4
3	4	2
0	0	3
7	7	0
0	7	1
4	9	0
1	7	5
4	1	9

a. Conduct an analysis of variance with this set of data.
b. Suppose the instructor made up a different set of data for each of the students in her statistics class. Would you expect any of the students to obtain a significant F? Explain.

5. The purpose of this experiment is to study the effects of scents from other animals on the exploratory behavior of kangaroo rats. The experiment, which is described more fully in Sec. 6.2, consists of $a = 4$ treatment conditions, with $n = 7$ animals assigned randomly to each of the conditions. The dependent variable is the amount of time (in minutes) that each animal spent exploring the artificial burrow during a 60-minute period. Some hypothetical data are presented.

Control a_1	Unfamiliar Scent a_2	Familiar-Immediate a_3	Familiar-Delay a_4
33	33	6	22
31	19	0	15
33	34	0	30
38	21	10	24
47	20	8	23
42	22	12	21
37	24	5	27

a. Calculate the means and the standard deviations for the different treat-ment conditions.
b. Conduct an analysis of variance on these data.
c. Do the group variances differ sufficiently to require an adjustment of the rejection region? Explain.

Note: Save your answers for exercise 4 in Chap. 6 and for exercise 2 in Chap. 8.

5.9 APPENDIX: AN EXPLANATION OF THE CORRECTION FOR UNEQUAL VARIANCES

As we stated in Sec. 5.4, recent evidence indicates that violations of the homo-geneity assumption alters the sampling distribution of F and directly affects our decision-making process. In fact, when group variances are not equal, our chances of rejecting the null hypothesis are inflated considerably from our stated level of significance. Let's see how this occurs and how an apparently more stringent significance level restores our original α level.

The curve in panel A of Fig. 5-5 represents the sampling distribution of F when the *variances are homogeneous.* As you have seen, we use this distribution to locate the critical value of F that indicates the beginning of the rejection region. Theoretically, this region contains 5 percent of the F's we would obtain if we repeatedly conducted the same experiment and the null hypothesis was true; in addition, we would expect the average value of the F's in this distribution to equal approximately 1.0. For a point of reference, we have drawn in the critical value of F for the numerical example we considered in Sec. 5.4 ($F_\alpha = 4.41$), for which $df_{num.} = 1$ and $df_{denom.} = 18$, and indicated that 5 percent of the F's from this sampling distribution have values of 4.41 or larger.

The curve in panel B of Fig. 5-5 represents the sampling distribution of F when the homogeneity assumption is *not* met — that is, the *variances are not equal.* The main point to notice is that this sampling distribution is shifted to the right and that considerably more F's now fall within the rejection region we established with the F table based on the theoretical sampling distribution of F presented by panel A. The extent to which F's migrate into the rejection region depends on the degree to which the homogeneity assumption has been

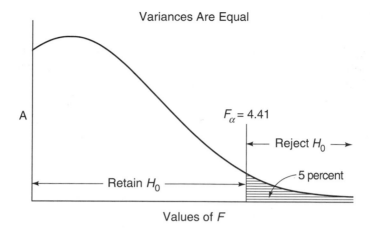

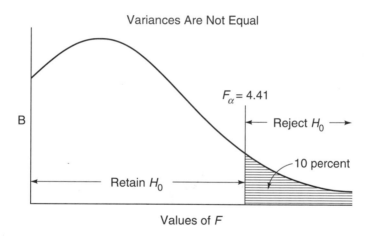

FIGURE 5-5 *The Sampling Distribution of F When the Variances Are Equal (A) and When the Variances Are Not Equal (B). $F_\alpha = 4.41$ is the critical value of $F(1, 18)$ when the homogeneity assumption is met.*

violated. We have indicated in panel B that 10 percent of the F's now fall in the rejection region, the approximate value reported by researchers investigating this problem with Monte Carlo studies (see, for example, Wilcox, 1987). If we have an experiment with unequal variances, then, we should expect to reject the null hypothesis 10 percent of the time, rather than the 5 percent expected when $\alpha = .05$. In other words, in this situation, α is actually equal to .10 rather than .05.

The Effect of $F_{adj.}$

We can correct for the changed rejection region, depicted in panel B, by selecting a new critical value of F, called $F_{adj.}$, at a more stringent significance level, $\alpha = .025$. The effect of this change is shown in Fig. 5-6.

The two sampling distributions from Fig. 5-5 are reproduced in Fig. 5-6. The critical value is now $F_{adj.} = 5.98$, rather than $F_\alpha = 4.41$. We obtained this value from an F table that provides information for the adjusted significance level

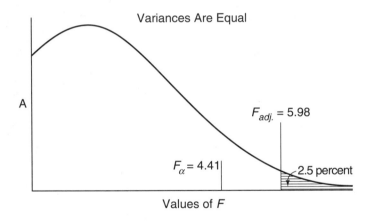

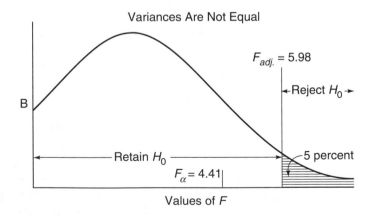

FIGURE 5-6 *An Illustration of How the Correction Procedure Compensates for the Inflationary Effects of Unequal Variances.* $F_{adj.} = 5.98$ *is the critical value of* $F(1, 18)$ *for* $\alpha = .025$.

(α = .025).[11] (For comparison purposes, we have also indicated the critical value of F for the 5 percent level of significance, 4.41, in the two figures.) Consider now what this new critical value accomplishes when the homogeneity assumption is not met. With reference to panel B in Fig. 5-6, which represents the *actual* sampling distribution of F when the variances are not equal, you can see that the start of the new rejection region has shifted to the right when compared to Fig. 5-5 and corrects for the inflationary effects produced by this violation. As a result of this adjustment, then, the new rejection region although appearing to be more stringent, now contains the 5 percent of the F's that we use to reject the null hypothesis and approximately restores our intended significance level.[12]

---

[11] You can find F tables that include α = .025 in most advanced books on research design and statistical analysis.

[12] The correction is not exact in the sense that the resulting significance level will be 5 percent for all possible violations of the homogeneity assumption. The correction is sufficiently accurate to provide a solution that will be acceptable to most researchers.

Chapter • 6

ANALYTICAL COMPARISONS IN THE SINGLE-FACTOR DESIGN

In Chap. 5, you saw how the F ratio and the theoretical sampling distribution of the F statistic are used to evaluate the adequacy of the null hypothesis, which states that the population treatment means are equal. To evaluate this hypothesis, we obtain the MS_A, which reflects the presence of treatment effects in the population in addition to experimental error. The fact that each treatment condition contributes to the calculation of the MS_A suggests that this mean square represents a sort of *average* of the differences among the treatment means. For this reason, the F ratio formed to evaluate this null hypothesis is often called the **overall**, or **omnibus**, **F test**.

We considered these statistical procedures in detail, since they constitute the first in a series of building blocks leading to the analysis of more complicated experimental designs. However, the test of this particular null hypothesis is of limited value to most researchers. A rejection of this hypothesis indicates very little about the adequacy of the research hypotheses that generated the experiment in the first place. For example, suppose we have four treatment means and find a statistically significant F ratio based on the differences among these means. The significant omnibus F test indicates that at least two means are significantly different from one another. We do not know, however, *which* means differ significantly from each other or whether more than one such difference is significant.

In this chapter, we concern ourselves with the evaluation of more specific null hypotheses — hypotheses that correspond directly to the research hypotheses. We refer to these more focused statistical tests as **analytical comparisons** to stress the fact that they *are* analytical. While the procedures described in Chap. 5 can lead to the conclusion that some differences among the treatment means are present in the population, they do not enable us to determine which means are different or which means are the same. As analytical comparisons do permit us to discover such information, they provide the researcher with an extremely valuable tool for pinpointing the source or sources of differences observed in an experiment.

6.1 THE NATURE OF ANALYTICAL COMPARISONS

An analytical comparison can be defined as a statistical test in which the number of means to be compared is smaller than the total number of treatment groups. The most common type of analytical comparison is one in which two of the treatment means in a larger experiment are isolated and compared. By restricting attention to the difference between these two treatments, we focus on an analytical subpart of the overall treatment effects. Analytical comparisons are performed because of this obvious *specificity*. A significant omnibus *F* simply indicates that differences among the means are present; analytical comparisons allow us to determine which differences are responsible.

Planned versus Unplanned Comparisons

Analytical comparisons permit us to assess the specific research hypotheses we form in the planning stages of an experiment. Such comparisons are usually called **planned comparisons**, because they are in fact *planned* before the start of the experiment. We refer to the set of planned comparisons as the *analysis plan* that will govern the critical part of the statistical analysis. The primary requirement is that the analysis plan be formulated *before* the data are collected. Since most researchers form, or at least imply, an analysis plan when they specify their research hypotheses and design their experiments to test them, this approach is really the typical and preferred way of analyzing the results of an experiment.

In contrast, **unplanned comparisons**, also known as **post hoc** or **multiple comparisons**, are comparisons that are suggested *after* the data are examined. Although such comparisons must also reflect meaningful questions, they are for a number of reasons not specifically predicted before the start of an experiment and are, in this sense, unplanned. Unfortunately, there is little agreement among researchers as to the "appropriate" way to evaluate the significance of unplanned comparisons. We will consider this and related problems in Chap. 8.

6.2 AN EXAMPLE OF THE RELATIONSHIP BETWEEN RESEARCH HYPOTHESES AND ANALYTICAL COMPARISONS

An Experiment

As an example, consider a hypothetical experiment based on a study proposed by a student as a possible research project.[1] The purpose of this experiment is to study the effects of scent markings from other animals on the exploratory

---

[1] We wish to thank Dr. Kay Holekamp for suggesting this example.

behavior of kangaroo rats. It is known that many rodents depend on scent markings in the wild to establish territory and to identify friend or foe. Kangaroo rats are ideally suited for study, since they spend a great deal of time depositing smelly secretions on objects in their environment and seem to be greatly influenced by odors and smells in their everyday behavior. The general plan of the experiment is to place a rat in an artificial burrow system made of Plexiglas tubing and to measure the amount of time the rat spends exploring the new surroundings. The treatment conditions are differentiated by the different scents introduced in the artificial burrow from sawdust taken from the cages of other kangaroo rats.

Three Research Hypotheses. Three research hypotheses are to be tested in this experiment:

1. Kangaroo rats will avoid environments in which the scents of unfamiliar kangaroo rats are present.
2. Kangaroo rats will avoid environments in which the scents come from kangaroo rats with whom they have lost a territorial battle.
3. With sufficient time, kangaroo rats no longer associate a particular scent with the winners of the earlier territorial battles.

The Experimental Design. The experiment is designed around these three hypotheses. To test the first hypothesis, two treatments are to be contrasted: a control condition, in which sterile sawdust is placed in the testing apparatus, and a condition in which the sawdust is taken from a cage that housed a kangaroo rat that had never been in contract with the the rat being tested. We will refer to these two treatments as the *control condition* and the *unfamiliar condition*, respectively. Any difference between these two conditions will be attributed to the presence or absence of an unfamiliar scent in the artificial burrow.

To test the second hypothesis, a third condition is introduced in which the sawdust is taken from the cage housing a rat with whom the animal being tested has just fought a territorial battle and lost. We will refer to this treatment as the *familiar-immediate condition*. The comparison most relevant to the second research hypothesis is between the *familiar-immediate* and *unfamiliar* conditions. Because the basic difference between these two conditions is the *source* of the sawdust — from a stranger (unfamiliar) or from a foe (familiar-immediate) — any difference between them in exploratory behavior will be attributed to this difference.

To test the third hypothesis — that a rat will eventually forget the smell identifying a previous winner of a territorial fight — the experiment must include at least two "familiar" conditions, differing only in the time elapsed between the occurrence of the territorial defeat and the testing in the artificial burrow. Any difference in the exploratory behavior of the animals in these two conditions will be attributed to the forgetting of the presumably negative experience. For this example, we have included a familiar condition in which the testing is delayed by four weeks, a delay judged to be sufficient to allow appreciable forgetting to occur. We will refer to this condition as the *familiar-delay condition.*

Students have pointed out a potential confounding in this design. That is, subjects in the two familiar conditions fight a territorial battle, whereas subjects in the control and unfamiliar conditions do not. It is possible, therefore, that this particular difference in experience may contribute in unknown ways to any comparison between either one of the familiar conditions and either of the other two conditions. One way to remove this confounding is to have *all* the kangaroo rats lose a territorial battle so that this particular experience is part of all four treatment conditions and, consequently, cannot contribute to any differences that may be obtained when the groups are compared.

Summary of the Conditions. The experiment consists of $a = 4$ treatment conditions. Each research hypothesis focuses attention on a different portion of the experimental design. The first hypothesis is tested by comparing the control and the unfamiliar conditions, the second by comparing the unfamiliar and the familiar-immediate conditions, and the third by comparing the two familiar conditions (immediate versus delay).

You may have noticed that two of the treatment conditions are involved in evaluating more than one research hypothesis. That is, the unfamiliar condition is used in testing the first two research hypotheses, while the familiar-immediate condition is used in testing the last two research hypotheses. The possibility that specific treatment conditions can be "shared" among two or more research hypotheses means that fewer treatment conditions need to be included in the study. Studying each research hypothesis as an independent two-group experiment would require (3 experiments) $\times$ (2 groups) = 6 treatment conditions; including them in one experiment requires only 4 conditions. This multiple use of treatment conditions saves time, energy, subjects, and other resources.

The complete experimental design is summarized in Table 6-1. We refer to the four treatment conditions either as the levels of the experiment — a_1, a_2, and so on — or by their descriptive titles. In an actual experiment, equal numbers of kangaroo rats would be assigned at random to the different treatment conditions. In response to the confounding we have described, we will assume that immediately before testing, the rats in the control and unfamiliar conditions are subjected to the unsuccessful territorial battle, to

TABLE 6-1 *A Summary of the Experimental Design in the Kangaroo-Rat Study*

Level	Condition	Treatment
a_1	Control	Sterile sawdust in apparatus
a_2	Unfamiliar	Sawdust from a rat "stranger"
	Familiar	Sawdust from a familiar dominant rat
a_3	Familiar-Immediate	Immediately after fight
a_4	Familiar-Delay	Four weeks after fight

remove a potential confounding that could occur if only the rats assigned to the two familiar conditions were given this experience before being observed in the artificial burrow.[2]

Analytical Comparisons

Before we examine more closely the analytical comparisons we outlined in the last section, it is instructive to consider again the nature of the conclusion we can reach when we reject the overall, or omnibus, null hypothesis, which you learned to evaluate in Chap. 5. You will recall that rejection of the overall null hypothesis,

$$H_0 : \mu_1 = \mu_2 = \mu_3 = \mu_4$$

leads to the acceptance of what we can now refer to as a *nonspecific* alternative hypothesis,

$$H_1 : \text{ not all } \mu\text{'s are equal}$$

Thus, rejecting the omnibus null hypothesis merely tells us that some differences exist in the population. We are permitted to conclude that some differences between the treatment means are present, but not specifically which ones.

In contrast, let's consider the nature of the information we obtain from the three analytical comparisons. Corresponding to each research hypothesis is an analytical comparison, which can be represented in terms of a set of statistical hypotheses. This relationship is made explicit in Table 6-2. All four treatment

---

[2] This example appeared originally as exercise 5 in Chap. 5 and is presented again as exercise 4 at the end of this chapter.

TABLE 6-2 *Three Research and Statistical Hypotheses*			

Relevant Experimental Design	**Statistical Hypotheses**

Analysis of the Overall Treatment Effects

Control	Unfam.	Fam.-Imm.	Fam.-Delay	
a_1	a_2	a_3	a_4	
				$H_0 : \mu_1 = \mu_2 = \mu_3 = \mu_4$
				$H_1 :$ not all μ's are equal

Comparison 1: Do Rats Avoid Unfamiliar Scents?

a_1	a_2			
				$H_0 : \mu_1 = \mu_2$
				$H_1 : \mu_1 \neq \mu_2$

Comparison 2: Do Rats Avoid Familiar Scents?

	a_2	a_3		
				$H_0 : \mu_2 = \mu_3$
				$H_1 : \mu_2 \neq \mu_3$

Comparison 3: Do Rats Forget Familiar Scents?

		a_3	a_4	
				$H_0 : \mu_3 = \mu_4$
				$H_1 : \mu_3 \neq \mu_4$

conditions are shown at the top of the table — these are the conditions being compared when we conduct the omnibus test. Consider the first research hypothesis, that kangaroo rats will tend to avoid environments in which the odor of an unfamiliar kangaroo rat is present. As you can see in the table, this analytical comparison literally isolates the two relevant conditions, the control and unfamiliar conditions (level a_1 versus level a_2), from the other two. We evaluate this comparison by forming the following set of statistical hypotheses:

$$H_0 : \mu_1 = \mu_2$$

$$H_1 : \mu_1 \neq \mu_2$$

Using procedures we will discuss later in this chapter, we perform an F test that allows us to directly evaluate the significance of the difference between the two relevant means. If we reject the null hypothesis, we will accept the alternative hypothesis and conclude that the two means are different.

As illustrated in Table 6-2, we assess the other two research hypotheses the same way. Again, you can see the usefulness of these analytical comparisons — they isolate the data relevant to a specific research question and set the stage for the statistical assessment of any differences observed between the two means.

In short, the omnibus F test is an *indirect* way of testing the explicit research hypotheses that occupy a central position in the design of most experiments. In contrast, planned comparisons of the sort we considered in Table 6-2 provide a *direct assessment* of these research hypotheses. We are now ready to consider how analytical comparisons can be evaluated statistically in the analysis of variance. We will restrict our attention to the analysis of the difference between two means, since this is the type of analytical comparison you will most frequently encounter in the psychological literature.[3]

6.3 ANALYZING DIFFERENCES BETWEEN PAIRS OF MEANS

As noted, the statistical analysis of the difference between two means is the most common type of analytical comparison. In this section, we will consider the analysis of **pairwise comparisons**, which are created when we compare one treatment mean with another. Because two means are compared, the variability associated with them is based on two deviations, as would be true in a single-factor experiment with two treatment conditions. Consequently, the mean square based on the difference between two means has associated with it a *single* degree of freedom, that is, $df = (2 - 1) = 1$. Thus, we often refer to such comparisons as **single-df comparisons**.

The statistical analysis of pairwise comparisons is particularly simple: we form an F ratio in which the numerator is based on the actual difference between the two means and the denominator is the error term from the overall analysis, $MS_{S/A}$.

---

[3] See Keppel (1991, pp. 138–139) for a discussion of a less common analysis that focuses on a subset of three or more treatment means drawn from a larger experiment.

The Computational Formulas

We begin the analysis by isolating the two relevant means and subtracting them. We will represent the resulting difference as

$$\hat{\psi} = \overline{Y}_{A_i} - \overline{Y}_{A_{i'}} \qquad (6\text{-}1)$$

where the subscripts i and i' refer to the two treatment conditions being compared.[4] We transform this information into a *comparison sum of squares* with the following formula:

$$SS_{A\,comp.} = \frac{n(\hat{\psi})^2}{2} \qquad (6\text{-}2)$$

The reason for the value 2 in the denominator of Eq. (6-2) will become clearer after you read the section "Computational Formula for Complex Comparisons" and understand the operations specified in Eq. (6-9). As we have noted already, this sum of squares is associated with 1 df; thus,

$$MS_{A\,comp.} = \frac{SS_{A\,comp.}}{1} = SS_{A\,comp.} \qquad (6\text{-}3)$$

We are now ready to calculate the F for this comparison, which is particularly easy because the error term for single-df comparisons in this design comes from the overall analysis. More specifically,

$$F_{A\,comp.} = \frac{MS_{A\,comp.}}{MS_{S/A}} \qquad (6\text{-}4)$$

The degrees of freedom for $F_{A\,comp.}$ are determined as usual by the df's associated with the numerator and denominator mean squares — in this case, $df_{num.} = 1$ and $df_{denom.} = df_{S/A}$. The statistical justification for using the $MS_{S/A}$ as the error term comes from the assumption that the variances of the treatment groups are the same, or homogeneous. If this assumption is not met, separate error terms may be required for each of the comparisons we evaluate (see Keppel, 1991, pp. 123–128).

---

[4] The new symbol in Eq. (6-1), $\hat{\psi}$, is the Greek letter psi ("sigh"), which is commonly used to represent the difference between two means. The "hat" or "caret" above the symbol indicates that the quantity is an estimate of the corresponding difference in the treatment populations.

A Numerical Example

We will illustrate the computational procedures with the experiment we analyzed in Chap. 5 (see Table 5-1, p. 122). In that study, children attempted to solve problems under three different conditions of reinforcement, namely, praise, criticism, or silence; $n = 5$ children were assigned randomly to each of the $a = 3$ treatment groups. The results of the statistical analysis, which are presented again in Table 6-3, revealed a significant omnibus F. An inspection of the treatment means, also presented in the table, suggests that while praise and criticism both produced more correct solutions than did silence, the two groups receiving the two kinds of verbal reinforcement (praise or criticism) do not seem to differ. The significant omnibus F, of course, does not tell us which of these differences is significant — all we know at this point is that the three treatment means are not the same.

Let's consider first the comparison between praise and silence. From Table 6-3, we find the difference between the two means to be

$$\hat{\psi}_1 = \overline{Y}_{A_1} - \overline{Y}_{A_3} = 7.60 - 4.40 = 3.20$$

We calculate the sum of squares for this comparison by substituting in Eq. (6-2), which gives us

$$SS_{A_{comp.1}} = \frac{n(\hat{\psi}_1)^2}{2}$$

$$= \frac{(5)(3.20)^2}{2} = \frac{(5)(10.24)}{2} = \frac{51.20}{2}$$

$$= 25.60$$

Completing the analysis, we find

$$F_{A_{comp.1}} = \frac{MS_{A_{comp.1}}}{MS_{S/A}}$$

$$= \frac{25.60}{3.60} = 7.11$$

The degrees of freedom associated with the numerator ($MS_{A_{comp.1}}$) is 1; the df associated with the denominator ($MS_{S/A}$) is 12 (see Table 6-3). From Table A-2,

TABLE 6-3 *Numerical Example of Pairwise Comparisons*

Source	SS	df	MS	F
A	30.40	2	15.20	4.22*
S/A	43.20	12	3.60	
Total	73.60	14		

* $p < .05$.

$$\overline{Y}_{A_1} \text{ (Praise)} = 7.60 \quad \overline{Y}_{A_2} \text{ (Criticism)} = 7.20 \quad \overline{Y}_{A_3} \text{ (Silence)} = 4.40$$

Comparison 1: Praise versus Silence

$$\hat{\psi}_1 = 7.60 - 4.40 = 3.20$$

$$SS_{A_{comp.1}} = \frac{(5)(3.20)^2}{2} = \frac{51.20}{2} = 25.60$$

$$F_{A_{comp.1}} = \frac{25.60}{3.60} = 7.11$$

Comparison 2: Criticism versus Silence

$$\hat{\psi}_2 = 7.20 - 4.40 = 2.80$$

$$SS_{A_{comp.2}} = \frac{(5)(2.80)^2}{2} = \frac{39.20}{2} = 19.60$$

$$F_{A_{comp.2}} = \frac{19.60}{3.60} = 5.44$$

Comparison 3: Praise versus Criticism

$$\hat{\psi}_3 = 7.60 - 7.20 = .40$$

$$SS_{A_{comp.3}} = \frac{(5)(.40)^2}{2} = \frac{.80}{2} = .40$$

$$F_{A_{comp.3}} = \frac{.40}{3.60} = .11$$

we obtain the critical value of F, $F(1, 12) = 4.75$ for the 5 percent level of significance. Applying the decision rule,

If $F_{A_{comp.1}} \geq 4.75$, reject the null hypothesis; otherwise, retain the null hypothesis.[5]

Since the $F_{A_{comp.1}}$ of 7.11 is greater than 4.75, we reject the null hypothesis. Furthermore, by examining the treatment means, we conclude that the children receiving praise for correct answers solved significantly more problems than children who were told nothing about their performance.

The steps in this analysis are summarized in Table 6-3, together with the results of the other two comparisons. Because each $F_{A_{comp.}}$ is based on the same df's, the critical values for all the $F_{A_{comp.}}$'s are the same (that is, 4.75). From the numbers presented in the table, we see that criticism also significantly facilitates performance ($F_{A_{comp.2}} = 5.44$) and that praise and criticism produce apparently equivalent results ($F_{A_{comp.3}} = .11$).

The Relationship between F and t

Researchers sometimes use the t test rather than the F test to evaluate single-df comparisons. These two tests are equivalent, provided we use the same estimate of error variability in their calculation. The $F_{A_{comp.}}$ specified by Eq. (6-4) uses the error term from the overall analysis ($MS_{S/A}$) as the estimate of error variability (see p. 147 for a justification of this procedure). If the t test is based on the same estimate of error variability, then

$$F_{A_{comp.}} = (t)^2 \qquad (6\text{-}5)$$

and the two procedures will lead to the same conclusions. That is, a difference that is significant at the 5 percent level of significance with the F test will also be significant at the same level of significance with the corresponding t test, and vice versa.[6]

---

[5] The symbol $\geq$ is mathematical shorthand for "greater than or equal to."

[6] Some researchers prefer to use a t test based on a different estimate of error variability — that is, one obtained from the two groups involved in the comparison. Under these circumstances, the equivalence indicated by Eq. (6-5) will *not* hold. We examine the t test more closely in an appendix to this chapter (Sec. 6-7).

6.4 MORE COMPLEX ANALYTICAL COMPARISONS

Most analytical comparisons consist of the analysis between pairs of treatment means, which we have called *pairwise comparisons*. Occasionally, we will find it useful to make more complex comparisons in which an average of two or more groups is compared with either a single group or an average of two or more other groups. We will refer to comparisons of this sort as **complex comparisons**. Although more than two means are involved in a complex comparison, the comparison itself is still between *two* means. Using the kangaroo rat study as an example, suppose we wanted to compare the mean of the control condition $(\overline{Y}_{cont.})$ with the mean produced by averaging all three conditions receiving a scent of some sort $(\overline{Y}_{av.\ scent})$. In this case, the difference in which we are interested is

$$\hat{\psi} = \overline{Y}_{cont.} - \overline{Y}_{av.\ scent}$$

and the comparison focuses on a difference between two means. Because two means are being examined, the comparison is associated with 1 df.

Computational Formula for Complex Comparisons

The computational formula we presented in Sec. 6.3 for pairwise comparisons is a simplified version of a more general formula that will also work for complex comparisons. Central to this formula is the way we express the difference between the two means being compared. Let's examine this new procedure with the numerical example we considered in Sec. 6.3.

From the analysis summarized in Table 6-3, we found a nonsignificant difference between the two groups receiving some form of verbal reinforcement $(F_{A\ comp.3} = .11)$. Given this finding, many researchers would conduct a complex comparison between the *combined verbal conditions* and the *silence condition*, either instead of the two pairwise comparisons between each verbal condition and the silence condition or in addition to them. We are interested, then, in evaluating the significance of the following difference:

$$\hat{\psi} = \frac{\overline{Y}_{A_1} + \overline{Y}_{A_2}}{2} - \overline{Y}_{A_3} \qquad (6\text{-}6)$$

$$= \frac{7.60 + 7.20}{2} - 4.40$$

$$= 7.40 - 4.40$$

$$= 3.00$$

Expressing a Difference as a Sum of the Weighted Means. This straightforward way of expressing the difference between the combined verbal conditions and the silence condition can be transformed into a less intuitive form that will prove useful to us in translating the difference into a sum of squares. Consider the following alternative to Eq. (6-6):

$$\hat{\psi} = \left(+\tfrac{1}{2}\right)\left(\overline{Y}_{A_1}\right) + \left(+\tfrac{1}{2}\right)\left(\overline{Y}_{A_2}\right) + (-1)\left(\overline{Y}_{A_3}\right) \qquad (6\text{-}7)$$

The essence of Eq. (6-7) is that the difference between two means is expressed as the sum of the **weighted treatment means**. That is, each treatment mean is multiplied, or "weighted," by special numbers called **coefficients** (which we will discuss in more detail in the next section). That is,

$$\overline{Y}_{A_1} \text{ is multiplied by the coefficient } +\tfrac{1}{2}$$

$$\overline{Y}_{A_2} \text{ is multiplied by the coefficient } +\tfrac{1}{2}$$

$$\overline{Y}_{A_3} \text{ is multiplied by the coefficient } -1$$

We do obtain the same difference using Eq. (6-7) and the coefficients. More specifically,

$$\hat{\psi} = \left(+\tfrac{1}{2}\right)(7.60) + \left(+\tfrac{1}{2}\right)(7.20) + (-1)(4.40)$$

$$= 3.80 + 3.60 - 4.40 = 7.40 - 4.40$$

$$= 3.00$$

We will use lower-case c with numerical subscripts to refer to the coefficients associated with specific conditions. The general formula for $\hat{\psi}$, then, becomes

$$\hat{\psi} = (c_1)(\overline{Y}_{A_1}) + (c_2)(\overline{Y}_{A_2}) + (c_3)(\overline{Y}_{A_3}) + \cdots \qquad (6\text{-}8)$$

where c_1 is the coefficient for $\overline{Y}_{A_1}$, c_2 is the coefficient for $\overline{Y}_{A_2}$, and so on. We will now use these coefficients, in conjunction with other information, to calculate the sum of squares for this comparison.

The Comparison Sum of Squares. A general computational formula for the sum of squares associated with a single-df comparison is given by the following equation:

$$SS_{A\ comp.} = \frac{n(\hat{\psi})^2}{\Sigma\ c^2} \qquad (6\text{-}9)$$

where the c's refer to the coefficients with which we weight the treatment means; in our present example, the coefficients are

$$c_1 = +\tfrac{1}{2}, \quad c_2 = +\tfrac{1}{2}, \quad \text{and} \quad c_3 = -1$$

Except for the expression in the denominator, however, which specifies the sum of the squared coefficients, Eq. (6-9) is identical to Eq. (6-2), which we used for pairwise comparisons.

We can now complete the calculations specified in Eq. (6-9). More specifically,

$$\begin{aligned}
SS_{A\ comp.} &= \frac{(5)(3.00)^2}{\left(+\tfrac{1}{2}\right)^2 + \left(+\tfrac{1}{2}\right)^2 + (-1)^2} \\
&= \frac{(5)(9.00)}{.25 + .25 + 1} = \frac{45.00}{1.5} \\
&= 30.00
\end{aligned}$$

Remember, even though this comparison involves three treatment conditions, only *two* means are actually being compared — the mean for the combined verbal conditions, on the one hand, and the mean for the silence condition, on the other. Therefore, the df for this sum of squares equals 1, as is the case with the pairwise comparisons we considered in Sec. 6.3. From this point on, we duplicate the steps we followed in evaluating pairwise comparisons. Substituting in Eq. (6-4), we find

$$\begin{aligned}
F_{A\ comp.} &= \frac{MS_{A\ comp.}}{MS_{S/A}} \\
&= \frac{30.00}{3.60} \\
&= 8.33
\end{aligned}$$

The critical value of $F_{A_{comp.}}(1, 12) = 4.75$. The decision rule becomes

If $F_{A_{comp.}} \geq 4.75$, reject the null hypothesis; otherwise, retain the null hypothesis.

Since we reject the null hypothesis, we can conclude that the combined verbal conditions produced significantly *more* correct solutions than the silence condition.

Comments on Constructing Coefficients

Students report some difficulties in constructing coefficients. They also report that with a bit of practice, the procedure becomes almost automatic. We offer some comments to assist you in constructing sets of coefficients.

Coefficients for Pairwise Comparisons. With pairwise comparisons you have the option of using Eq. (6-2), which does not require coefficients, or Eq. (6-9), which does. Both will give the same answer. The coefficients for a pairwise comparison have the form

$$+1, -1, 0, 0, \text{ etc.}$$

where $+1$ is assigned to one of the means entering the comparison and -1 is assigned to the other; zeros are assigned to any remaining means that are not involved in the comparison. The coefficients for the first comparison in Table 6-3 are

$$+1, 0, \text{ and } -1$$

for the praise, criticism, and silence conditions, respectively. We can use these coefficients to produce the difference between the praise and silence conditions; that is,

$$\hat{\psi} = (c_1)(\overline{Y}_{A_1}) + (c_2)(\overline{Y}_{A_2}) + (c_3)(\overline{Y}_{A_3})$$

$$= (+1)(7.60) + (0)(7.20) + (-1)(4.40)$$

$$= 7.60 - 4.40$$

$$= 3.20$$

If we substitute in Eq. (6-9), we find

$$SS_{A\,comp.} = \frac{n(\hat{\psi})^2}{\Sigma\,c^2}$$

$$= \frac{(5)(3.20)^2}{(+1)^2 + (0)^2 + (-1)^2} = \frac{(5)(10.24)}{1 + 0 + 1}$$

$$= \frac{51.20}{2}$$

$$= 25.60$$

which is identical to the sum of squares we obtained with Eq. (6-2) (see p. 148).

Constructing a Set of Coefficients. The procedure we will describe for constructing a set of coefficients for any single-*df* comparison is foolproof. At first you will probably be dependent on it, but as you gain experience you will find that you are able to write the coefficients directly from the research hypothesis.

We will present the construction rules in the context of an example. Suppose an experiment has the following $a = 6$ treatment conditions:

Drug A		Drug B			No Drug
Batch 1	Batch 2	Batch 1	Batch 2	Batch 3	Control
a_1	a_2	a_3	a_4	a_5	a_6

The first two conditions consist of two samples or batches of drug A obtained from a pharmaceutical supplier. The next three conditions consist of three batches of another drug (drug B), and the last condition is a no-drug control condition. Suppose we want to compare drug A with drug B. Thus, we will compare the mean of the two drug A conditions (a_1 and a_2) with the mean of the three drug conditions (a_3, a_4, and a_5); the mean for the control condition (a_6) will not enter this particular comparison. Coefficients for this comparison may be constructed by using the following set of rules:

1. *Verbalize the comparison.* We start with a verbal statement of the research hypothesis. For this example, the statement could be this: "We predict that drug A and drug B will differ in their effects on performance."

2. *Express the comparison in symbols.* In this step, we translate the description of the comparison into a difference between two means, which provides a clear and unambiguous statement of the nature of the comparison under consideration. For this example,

$$\overline{Y}_{Drug\ A} - \overline{Y}_{Drug\ B} = \frac{\overline{Y}_{A_1} + \overline{Y}_{A_2}}{2} - \frac{\overline{Y}_{A_3} + \overline{Y}_{A_4} + \overline{Y}_{A_5}}{3}$$

3. *Isolating the coefficients.* We can use the expression in step 2 to determine a set of coefficients appropriate for this — or any — single-*df* comparison. We will obtain three subsets of coefficients: (*a*) one subset to be used with all the means to the left of the minus sign, (*b*) another subset to be used with all the means to the right of the minus sign, and (*c*) a third subset to be used with means that do not appear in the expression. For either set of means listed in the expression, the coefficient is equal to the fraction

$$\frac{1}{\text{number of means}}$$

In addition, we will arbitrarily give each coefficient to the left of the minus sign a *positive* value and each coefficient to the right a *negative* sign.[7] Thus, the coefficient for each of the *two* means on the left of the minus sign is $+1/2$ and the coefficient for each of the *three* means on the right is $-1/3$. The coefficient for means not entering into a comparison is *zero*. Thus, the entire set of coefficients is

$$c_1 = +\tfrac{1}{2}, c_2 = +\tfrac{1}{2}, c_3 = -\tfrac{1}{3}, c_4 = -\tfrac{1}{3}, c_5 = -\tfrac{1}{3}, \text{ and } c_6 = 0$$

Although these coefficients can be used to calculate the sum of squares for the comparison, transforming the fractional coefficients into whole numbers is generally more convenient. This transformation, which is optional, is accomplished in the final step.

4. *Eliminate fractional coefficients.* We remove the fractional coefficients by multiplying the entire set obtained in step 3 by the *lowest common denominator* (the smallest number divisible by all the denominator terms) of the set of fractions. In this example, the lowest common denominator is 6.

---

[7] The signs can be reversed without affecting the statistical assessment of a comparison. (See exercise 1 for this chapter for a demonstration of this property of coefficients.)

To obtain whole numbers, we simply multiply each of the fractions by 6. The two different fractional coefficients thus become

$$(6)\left(+\tfrac{1}{2}\right) = +3 \quad \text{and} \quad (6)\left(-\tfrac{1}{3}\right) = -2$$

Finally, we can write the complete set of coefficients:

	a_1	a_2	a_3	a_4	a_5	a_6
c_i :	+3	+3	−2	−2	−2	0

5. *Review and check.* This system will permit you to obtain a set of coefficients with which to extract the desired information from your data.[8] One important characteristic of a set of coefficients is that *the individual coefficients must sum to zero.* That is,

$$\Sigma\, c_i = 0 \tag{6-10}$$

Thus, as a check on our calculation, we substitute the coefficients in Eq. (6-10) to verify that they actually do sum to zero:

$$\Sigma\, c_i = (+3) + (+3) + (-2) + (-2) + (-2) + (0) = 0$$

This property of coefficients is expressed graphically as a seesaw in Fig. 6-1. Let's suppose the line in the figure is a wooden plank and that we will locate 2-pound bricks, representing the coefficients as physical objects, on the plank at appropriate distances from the zero or balancing point. Using the coefficients we obtained in step 4 (+3, +3, −2, −2, −2, and 0), we would place two of the bricks 3 feet to one side of zero (representing the two positive coefficients), three of the bricks 2 feet to the other side of zero (representing the three negative coefficients), and one brick directly over zero (representing the single zero coefficient). Arranged this way, the seesaw would be in perfect balance.

---

[8] This is not the only set that will serve this function, however. We could also use, for example, the fractional coefficients we obtained in step 3. On the other hand, we need only one set of coefficients, and this particular set has the computational advantages of avoiding fractions while producing the smallest products possible without fractional coefficients, which in turn give us smaller numbers in our calculations.

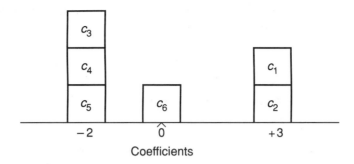

FIGURE 6-1 *Equation (6-9) Represented as a Seesaw in Balance. (See the text for an explanation.)*

You really need to use this construction scheme only for complex comparisons, as in the example cited, because the coefficients for pairwise comparisons are always

$$+1, -1, 0, 0, \text{ etc.}$$

Whatever set you use, however, you must use the *same set* of coefficients to define the two quantities in Eq. (6-9) that involve coefficients — namely, $\hat{\psi}$ in the numerator and $\Sigma\ c^2$ in the denominator. For example, if you use fractional coefficients to define the $\hat{\psi}$ you plan to substitute in Eq. (6-9), you must use the same fractional coefficients for the denominator term; if you prefer to use transformed coefficients to define $\hat{\psi}$, you must use these transformed coefficients for the denominator term. If you fail to use the same set to define $\hat{\psi}$ and the coefficients in the denominator, Eq. (6-9) will give you the wrong answer for $SS_{A_{comp}}$, as exercise 1d at the end of this chapter illustrates.

Trend Analysis

Comparisons that focus on the difference between two means are ideally suited for use with *qualitative* independent variables of the sort we considered in this and earlier chapters. They are less useful or revealing when the independent variable represents a *quantitative* manipulation, where the variation among the treatment conditions represents differences in *amount* rather than in kind. That is, rather than examine separate comparisons between pairs of means, which is the way researchers usually approach the analysis of qualitative independent variables, they prefer instead to plot the means obtained with a quantitative independent variable in a graph and look for overall trends in the data.

As an illustration, let's look at the results of an actual experiment reported by Grant and Schiller (1953). In this experiment, human subjects were trained to respond in a certain way to the presentation of a 12-inch circle.[9] Following training, they were randomly assigned to $a = 7$ different groups, each of which was tested with a different stimulus. One group was tested with the original training circle (12 inches), whereas the others were tested with circles differing in size — three were smaller than the original circle (circles with diameters of 9, 10, and 11 inches) and three were larger (circles with diameters of 13, 14, and 15 inches). The outcome of this experiment is presented in panel A of Fig. 6-2, where we have plotted the individual treatment means and interconnected each two successive data points with a straight line.

Grant and Schiller were not interested in comparing the response to one stimulus size against the response to another, in a series of pairwise comparisons, but in determining whether one or two relatively *simple mathematical trends* could reasonably characterize the overall relationship between the independent and dependent variables. Consider, for example, the same means plotted in panel B of Fig. 6-2. This time we have left the individual data points unconnected and drawn a straight line that seems to achieve a reasonable balance among the means.[10] As you can see, this straight line reveals a general tendency for values on the dependent variable to increase steadily as the size of the test stimulus increases from 9 inches to 15 inches. This is an example of a **linear trend** — a mathematical relationship between two variables that is described by a straight line.

It is obvious that the line we have drawn does not describe or fit the data all that well. On the other hand, one could argue that the scattering of the means above and below the line may only reflect the operation of experimental error, which is the inevitable result of randomly assigning the subjects to the different treatment conditions. A procedure called **trend analysis** is designed to identify general trends that underlie the relationship between a quantitative independent variable and the dependent variable, which are obscured to some degree by the presence of experimental error. We discuss trend analysis in Appendix D.

---

[9] Grant and Schiller used a classical conditioning procedure in which subjects were trained to give a galvanic skin response (GSR) upon the presentation of the stimulus.

[10] This line was produced by a statistical procedure that determines the single straight line that best fits the entire set of data points. One can approximate this *line of best fit*, as it is called, by taking a ruler and moving it around on the graph until the line seems to be in geometric balance, with about half of the means falling above the line and half falling below the line.

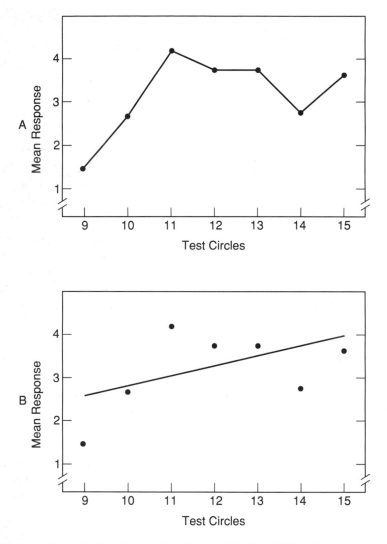

FIGURE 6-2 *A Plot of the Data Reported by Grant and Schiller (1953). (A) Outcome of the experiment as it would be presented in a summary graph or figure. (B) Best-fitting straight line that reflects an overall linear trend in the relationship between the independent and dependent variables.*

6.5 SUMMARY

We pointed out that the overall, or omnibus, analysis of variance can tell us only whether the treatment means are the same or not; the test does not identify the particular means that are responsible for a significant overall *F*. We argued that most researchers are more interested in answering a series of analytical or meaningful questions than in assessing the significance of the overall F. Background considerations — such as a fact, theory, or speculation — lead a researcher to form a number of research hypotheses. An experiment is then designed to provide meaningful and relevant answers to the researcher's questions. In this chapter, we discussed analysis techniques that permit us to evaluate statistically hypotheses that focus directly on these research questions.

We distinguished between comparisons that are planned before the start of an experiment and comparisons that are not. The primary focus of this chapter was on the analysis of planned comparisons. Unplanned comparisons will be discussed in Chap. 8.

The most common type of analytical comparison is one that examines the differences between two different treatment means — so-called pairwise comparisons. Complex comparisons, which are less common than pairwise comparisons, contrast an average of two or more groups with a single group or an average of two or more groups. Both types of comparisons can be conceptualized as a miniature experiment with two conditions, one for each of the means being compared in the analysis. For this reason, pairwise and complex comparisons have $df = 1$ as in an actual two-group experiment; both kinds of comparisons are often called single-df comparisons.

We first introduced some specialized formulas for evaluating pairwise comparisons and then presented more general formulas for evaluating any single-df comparison — pairwise or complex. Both analyses produce a sum of squares that reflects a particular difference between two means. We evaluate the significance of this difference with an F ratio in which we use as an error term the within-groups mean square obtained from the overall analysis of variance, $MS_{S/A}$.

We briefly considered a special analytical technique that researchers often use to analyze the results of a quantitative independent variable. This procedure, called *trend analysis*, consists of identifying relatively simple mathematical trends that seem to underlie the relationship between the independent and dependent variables.

6.6 EXERCISES [11]

*1. In discussing the construction of coefficients for single-df comparisons, we noted that you will obtain the same $SS_{A_{comp}}$ for a complex comparison regard-

---

[11] Answers to the starred problems are given in Appendix B.

less of whether you use fractional coefficients or whole numbers created by multiplying the fractions by their common denominator. This problem will demonstrate that this in fact is the case. Let's continue with the example from Sec. 6.4, which consisted of $a = 6$ treatment conditions: two batches of drug A, three batches of drug B, and a control condition. Suppose we obtained the following means, which are based on $n = 6$ subjects randomly assigned to each condition:

Drug A		Drug B			No Drug
Batch 1	Batch 2	Batch 1	Batch 2	Batch 3	Control
a_1	a_2	a_3	a_4	a_5	a_6
10.00	12.00	6.00	7.00	5.00	8.00

a. Calculate the sum of squares associated with a comparison between the two drugs, using the coefficients we calculated in Sec. 6.4 $(+\frac{1}{2}, +\frac{1}{2}, -\frac{1}{3}, -\frac{1}{3}, -\frac{1}{3},$ and $0)$.

b. Calculate the comparison sum of squares using the set of coefficients from part (a), but with the signs reversed (that is, $-\frac{1}{2}, -\frac{1}{2}, +\frac{1}{3}, +\frac{1}{3}, +\frac{1}{3},$ and 0).

c. Calculate the comparison sum of squares using the set of coefficients from part (a), but with the fractions removed by multiplying by 6 (that is, $+3, +3, -2, -2, -2,$ and 0).

d. As a demonstration that you must use the same set of coefficients to calculate $\hat{\psi}$ and to substitute in Eq. (6-9), use the value for $\hat{\psi}$ from part (a) and the coefficients from part (c) and substitute these quantities in Eq. (6-9). Compare your answer with the value you obtained in parts (a) through (c).

*2. Let's assume that the error term for the data in exercise 1 is $MS_{S/A} = 4.00$.

a. Test the significance of the comparison between the two drugs.

b. Although the difference between the two drugs is significant in part (a), you will need to conduct additional comparisons to determine whether the two drugs considered separately are significantly different from the control condition. Test the significance of the comparison between drug A and the control and of the comparison between drug B and the control.

c. Although of little interest, test the significance of the difference between the combined drug conditions (levels a_1 through a_5) and the control.

d. As an example of a pairwise comparison, test the significance of the difference between the two batches of drug A. Calculate the sum of squares two ways: with the specialized formula for pairwise comparisons, Eq. (6-2); and with the general formula for single-*df* comparisons, Eq. (6-9).

3. Exercise 3 in Chap. 4 consisted of an experiment in which subjects rated three kinds of advertisements: ads with a color picture, ads with a black-and-white picture, and ads with no pictures. Test the significance of the following comparisons:
   a. Color versus black and white
   b. Ads with a picture (color and black and white combined) versus ads with no picture
   c. Color versus no picture
   d. Black and white versus no picture

4. In Sec. 6.2, we considered an experiment investigating the effects of different scents on the exploratory behavior of kangaroo rats. Using the data from exercise 5 in Chap. 5, conduct the three analytical comparisons that follow. In each case, state clearly what conclusions you can draw from the outcome of the analysis.
   a. The control condition versus the unfamiliar condition
   b. The unfamiliar condition versus the familiar-immediate condition
   c. The familiar-immediate condition versus the familiar-delay condition

5. In exercise 2 for Chap. 4, we presented an experiment in which subjects rated words on a specific attribute and then attempted to recall the words after the rating was completed. Different groups of subjects rated the words on the following attributes: how pleasant a word's meaning was, how frequently the word is used in the language, how pleasant its sound was, and how frequently its syllables are used in the language. Test the significance of the following three comparisons:
   a. A comparison of the two "pleasantness" ratings (meaning and sound) with the two "frequency" ratings (word and syllable)
   b. The "meaning" treatment versus the other three
   c. Word frequency versus syllable frequency

6.7 APPENDIX: USING THE *t* TEST TO ANALYZE SINGLE-*df* COMPARISONS[12]

We mentioned in Sec. 6.3 that the *t* test is sometimes used by researchers for evaluating single-*df* comparisons instead of the *F* test we presented in this chapter. In this appendix, we show that both procedures lead to equivalent conclusions when $MS_{S/A}$ is used to estimate experimental error and discuss another procedure — the use of *directional hypotheses* — that you may find mentioned occasionally in research reports appearing in the literature.

The *t* Test

In Sec. 5.6, we demonstrated that $F = (t)^2$ in the context of an actual two-group experiment. We can write the formula for the *t* test for use with single-*df* comparisons extracted from a larger study as follows:

$$t = \frac{\overline{Y}_{A_i} - \overline{Y}_{A_{i'}}}{\hat{\sigma}_{diff.}} \tag{6-11}$$

where the numerator consists of the difference between two treatment means and the denominator represents the standard error of the difference between two means. Within the context of a larger experiment, we are usually permitted to base our estimate of $\hat{\sigma}_{diff.}$ on the error term we calculated in the overall analysis of variance, namely, $MS_{S/A}$, rather than on the variances of the two groups involved in the comparison. (The latter procedure is appropriate when the group variances are not equal or homogeneous.)

Let's look at the formula we presented in Chap. 5 for estimating the standard error in an actual two-group experiment:

$$\hat{\sigma}_{diff.} = \sqrt{\frac{s_1^2}{n_1} + \frac{s_2^2}{n_2}}$$

To adapt this equation to the present multigroup experiment, we simply substitute the error term from the overall analysis of variance, which is an *average* of the group variances, for the individual group variances appearing in this

---

[12] This appendix is intended for students in advanced courses on research design and statistical analysis. Your instructor may wish to omit this material in more introductory courses.

equation. More specifically,

$$\hat{\sigma}_{diff.} = \sqrt{\frac{MS_{S/A}}{n_i} + \frac{MS_{S/A}}{n_{i'}}}$$

With equal sample sizes, and after a little algebraic manipulation, the formula becomes

$$\hat{\sigma}_{diff.} = \sqrt{\frac{MS_{S/A}}{n} + \frac{MS_{S/A}}{n}}$$

$$= \sqrt{\frac{MS_{S/A} + MS_{S/A}}{n}}$$

$$= \sqrt{\frac{(2)(MS_{S/A})}{n}} \qquad (6\text{-}12)$$

As an example, we will calculate the comparison between praise and silence for our experiment in Sec. 6.3. The difference between the two relevant means is given in Table 6-3 (3.20). All we need to calculate the standard error is sample size ($n = 5$) and the value for $MS_{S/A}$ (3.60). From Eq. (6-12), we find

$$\hat{\sigma}_{diff.} = \sqrt{\frac{(2)(MS_{S/A})}{n}}$$

$$= \sqrt{\frac{(2)(3.60)}{5}} = \sqrt{\frac{7.20}{5}} = \sqrt{1.44}$$

$$= 1.20$$

Substituting in Eq. (6-11), we have

$$t = \frac{\overline{Y}_{A_1} - \overline{Y}_{A_3}}{\hat{\sigma}_{diff.}} = \frac{3.20}{1.20} = 2.67$$

The critical value of t is found in Table A-3 of Appendix A under the df associated with the *overall* error term, that is, $df_{S/A} = 12$. From the t table, we find $t(12) = 2.18$. The decision rule becomes

If the observed value of t, disregarding sign, $\geq t(12) = 2.18$, reject the null hypothesis; otherwise, retain the null hypothesis.

Because the observed t of 2.67 is greater than the critical value of 2.18, we conclude that the difference between these two means, praise versus silence, is significant. To show the equivalence of t and F, we simply substitute the two values we have calculated with these data in Eq. (6-5) and show

$$F_{A_{comp.}} = (t)^2$$

$$7.11 = (2.67)^2 = 7.13$$

The slight discrepancy is the result of rounding error.

Directionality of the t Test

You will occasionally come across what are called **directional** and **nondirectional** t **tests**, particularly in conjunction with planned comparisons.[13] These terms refer to two different sets of statistical hypotheses that can be used in the analysis of the difference between two means. Consider the set of statistical hypotheses we established for the comparison between praise and silence:

$$H_0 : \mu_1 = \mu_3$$

$$H_1 : \mu_1 \neq \mu_3$$

The null hypothesis (H_0) states that the two population treatment means are the same. The alternative hypothesis (H_1) on the other hand, states that there is a difference between the two means, but does not specify whether μ_1 is greater than or less than μ_3; it simply states that the two means are not equal ($\neq$). Rejecting the null hypothesis permits us to conclude that the two means are different *regardless* of the actual direction of the difference. This is the way most researchers couch their statistical hypotheses, even though their theory may predict a particular direction of the difference. We call this sort of statistical hypothesis a *nondirectional alternative hypothesis* — the test is sensitive to a difference in either direction.

In contrast, a *directional alternative hypothesis* specifies a particular direction for the difference. In this case, the alternative hypothesis would be

$$H_1 : \mu_1 > \mu_3$$

if the researcher believes that the mean for the praise group will be *larger* than the mean for the silence group, or, the reverse,

$$H_1 : \mu_1 < \mu_3$$

---

[13] They are also called **two-tailed** and **one-tailed** t **tests**, respectively, for reasons that depend on an understanding of the statistical theory behind the t test, which we do not cover in this book.

when hypothesizing that the mean for the praise group will be *smaller* than the mean for the silence group.

The advantage of a directional test over a nondirectional one is an increased sensitivity for detecting a difference occurring in the predicted direction. On the other hand, the issues surrounding the decision to use a directional test are complex and beyond the scope of this book.[14]

---

[14] For further discussion on this issue, see Hays (1988, pp. 270–277) and a collection of relevant articles in a book by Kirk (1972, pp. 276–290).

C h a p t e r · 7

ESTIMATING POPULATION
MEANS AND EFFECT SIZE

This chapter considers two topics that play an important role in the design of experiments and the interpretation of their results. We begin by introducing the statistical process of *estimation,* in which we make educated guesses about characteristics of a population from a sample drawn randomly from that population. The other topic we discuss concerns measures of the *size of the treatment effects* we observe in an experiment, which we will use to supplement the information provided by the *F* test.

7.1 INTERVAL ESTIMATION IN EXPERIMENTS

In discussing the construction of graphs in Chap. 2, we indicated that we can represent the degree of variability in each treatment group by placing a vertical band one standard deviation above and one standard deviation below each treatment mean. (See Fig. 2-3, p. 48, for an example.) Alternatively, researchers often plot another measure of variability, such as the *standard error of the mean* or a *confidence interval*, both of which are based on the group standard deviation. In this section, we will consider these alternative measures that are part of an area of inferential statistics called **estimation**.

True estimation, in which one attempts to estimate the mean of a population on the basis of a sample drawn from that population, assumes that a **random sample** has been drawn from that population. The treatment groups in experiments are *not* random samples, but instead are collections of subjects who are *randomly assigned* to the treatment conditions. The value of random sampling, which is of central importance to survey research, for example, is in our ability to extend, or generalize, the information gleaned from the sample to the population as a whole. Nevertheless, we can operate as if the treatment groups were random samples drawn from corresponding treatment populations and use estimation procedures to provide us with useful information from our experiments.

The estimate of a population treatment mean from a random sample's mean is not expected to hit the population value exactly. As a result of the sampling process, where chance factors determine which members of the population will be selected, a single sample mean will probably underestimate or overestimate the population mean by some finite amount. Since any single estimate is influenced by this chance error, or **sampling error**, a single estimate, or **point estimate**, is of little value by itself. An estimate that specifies the *degree of accuracy* involved in the estimate is preferred. An **interval estimate**, as this sort of estimate is called, takes the form of a range of values within which the population parameter is said to be "contained" (or "covered") with a certain degree of confidence.

Standard Error of the Mean

Suppose we assume that one of our treatment groups is a random sample drawn from a larger treatment population. Statistical theory tells us that the treatment mean is our best estimate of the population treatment mean. However, we also know that this estimate will be in error because of the chance processes operating when we constitute a random sample. We can obtain some estimate of this sampling error by using the standard deviation of the group to estimate the variability of subsequent estimates of the mean obtained by repeated random sampling from the same treatment population. This distribution of sample means is called a **sampling distribution of the mean**. Figure 7-1 depicts this situation and the relative frequency with which different values for the mean will occur through repeated random sampling. The mean of the sam-

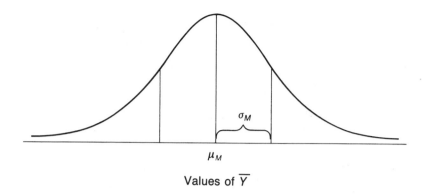

Values of $\overline{Y}$

FIGURE 7-1 *The Sampling Distribution of the Mean*

pling distribution (μ_M) is equal to the mean of the population of the scores (μ); that is,

$$\mu_M = \mu \tag{7-1}$$

The shape of the sampling distribution of means in Fig. 7-1 is described as a **normal distribution**. The distribution of sample means will come closer and closer to the shape of a normal distribution as the number of sample means increases and as the sample size of each mean increases.[1]

The variance of this sampling distribution — a variance based on the sample means — provides a measure of the extent or size of the sampling error. We will designate this quantity by the symbol σ_M^2. The *standard deviation* of this distribution is more useful than the variance in interval estimation and is given a special name, the **standard error of the mean**. That is,

$$\text{standard error of the mean } (\sigma_M) = \sqrt{\sigma_M^2} \tag{7-2}$$

In words, the standard error of the mean is the standard deviation of the sampling distribution of the mean. We have indicated the size of the standard error of the mean in Fig. 7-1 as the distance from the mean (μ_M) to either of the two vertical lines in the figure.

---

[1] This principle of a transition to a normal distribution is known as the **central limit theorem**, a fundamental conception in statistical theory.

Estimating the Standard Error of the Mean.   We can estimate the standard error of the mean from sample data by using the simple formula

$$\hat{\sigma}_M = \frac{s}{\sqrt{n}} \qquad (7\text{-}3)$$

The numerator of this formula is the standard deviation (s) obtained from the sample data, and the denominator is the square root of the sample size, n.

   As an example of the calculations, consider the experiment comparing the effects of different types of reinforcement on problem solving that we originally presented in Chap. 5. From Table 5-1 (p. 122), we obtain the following information for the group of children given praise for correct answers:

$$\text{mean} = 7.60$$

$$\text{sample size} = 5$$

$$\text{standard deviation} = 1.52$$

Using Eq. (7-3), we find that

$$\hat{\sigma}_M = \frac{1.52}{\sqrt{5}} = \frac{1.52}{2.24} = .68$$

We can now construct vertical bands above and below the treatment mean ($\overline{Y}_{A_1} = 7.60$) by simply adding and subtracting the standard error, .68, to and from the treatment mean. The bands are often referred to as **error bars**.

Usefulness of the Standard Error of the Mean.   Either method of constructing the vertical bands — the standard deviation or the standard error — may be used to include a measure of variability in a graphical representation of the results of an experiment. The standard error has the additional advantage of taking into consideration the *precision* with which the means are estimated. That is, the size of the standard error provides an index of how much the means calculated from repeated samples will vary. As you can see from Eq. (7-3), the standard error is influenced by the variability observed in the sample *and* by sample size. A treatment condition with a large sample size will produce a smaller standard error than one with a smaller sample size. In general, we have more confidence in the *stability* of a sample mean when it is calculated from a large sample.

Confidence Intervals

The standard error is also used to construct confidence intervals around treatment means. A **confidence interval** is an interval estimate that is formed in consideration of the degree of risk. It is acknowledged that estimation involves a certain degree of risk. The only way to construct an interval to eliminate the risk entirely would be to make the interval *infinitely wide.* Such an interval would be of no use to a researcher, however; one could specify an infinitely wide interval without ever collecting a random sample! Obviously, this maximum interval must be narrowed to serve as a useful interval estimate. But the narrower the interval, the greater is the possibility that the interval estimate will not include the population mean. In short, we must decide on a compromise in which the size of the interval will be narrowed but the number of erroneous estimates will be kept at a reasonably low level.

The degree of confidence is given by the expression

$$\text{confidence} = (1 - \alpha)(100) \text{ percent}$$

If we let the proportion of erroneous interval estimates we may ever conceivably make be $\alpha = .05$, our interval estimates will be what are referred to as

$$(1 - .05)(100) = (.95)(100) = 95 \text{ percent confidence intervals}$$

Constructing a Confidence Interval. A confidence interval for the mean is based on information estimated from the sample and from certain properties of the sampling distribution of the mean. We need the following pieces of information:

1. The sample mean $(\overline{Y})$
2. The estimated standard error of the mean $(\hat{\sigma}_M)$
3. The value of t obtained from a statistical table

We begin by estimating the population mean $(\hat{\mu})$ from the mean of the sample. This estimate $\hat{\mu}$ will define the center of the confidence interval.[2] The width of the interval above and below $\hat{\mu}$ is found by multiplying $\hat{\sigma}_M$, which we estimate from the sample, by the value of t. Finally, we calculate the lower limit of the

---

[2] As a reminder, the "caret" or "hat" indicates that the mean is an *estimate* of the population mean based on a random sample drawn from the population.

confidence interval by subtracting this product from $\hat{\mu}$, and we calculate the upper limit of the confidence interval by adding this product to $\hat{\mu}$. In symbols,

$$\text{lower limit} = \hat{\mu} - (t)(\hat{\sigma}_M)$$

$$\text{upper limit} = \hat{\mu} + (t)(\hat{\sigma}_M)$$

We can express the formula for the confidence interval more succinctly as follows:

$$\text{confidence interval} = \hat{\mu} \pm (t)(\hat{\sigma}_M) \tag{7-4}$$

where $\pm$ indicates that the product $(t)(\hat{\sigma}_M)$ is both subtracted from and added to $\hat{\mu}$ in determining the lower and upper limits of the confidence interval, respectively.

An Example.   We will illustrate the procedure for constructing a confidence interval with the same example we used to estimate the standard error of the mean previously. We began with the mean (7.60) and standard deviation (1.52) for the group of $n = 5$ children receiving praise for correct answers. We substituted this information into Eq. (7-3) and calculated the standard error of the mean ($\hat{\sigma}_M = .68$). All we need now is the value of t, which we obtain from a table of the t distribution.

The value for t is found in Table A-3 of Appendix A, which we first examined in conjunction with the t test in Chap. 5. As a reminder, the table consists of two columns of numbers, one for $\alpha = .05$ and the other for $\alpha = .01$. The values of t under the heading of $\alpha = .05$ permit the calculation of a 95 percent confidence interval; values of t given under the heading of $\alpha = .01$ permit the calculation of a 99 percent confidence interval.

To find the value of t required for a particular interval estimate, we need to know the degrees of freedom associated with the standard error. This number is given by

$$df_M = n - 1 \tag{7-5}$$

In this example,

$$df_M = 5 - 1 = 4$$

If we decided to construct a 95 percent confidence interval, we would look up the value of t in the table under $df_M = 4$ and $\alpha = .05$; in this case, $t = 2.78$.

We now have the various ingredients required in Eq. (7-4) and can calculate the 95 percent confidence interval. For the lower limit,

$$\hat{\mu} - (t)(\hat{\sigma}_M) = 7.60 - (2.78)(.68)$$

$$= 7.60 - 1.89$$

$$= 5.71$$

For the upper limit,

$$\hat{\mu} + (t)(\hat{\sigma}_M) = 7.60 + (2.78)(.68)$$

$$= 7.60 + 1.89$$

$$= 9.49$$

The 95 percent confidence interval is specified by a set of values ranging between 5.71 and 9.49.

For purposes of illustration, we will calculate the 99 percent confidence interval with the same data. An inspection of the t table indicates that $t = 4.60$ at $\alpha = .01$. For the two limits,

$$\hat{\mu} \pm (t)(\hat{\sigma}_M) = 7.60 \pm (4.60)(.68)$$

$$= 7.60 \pm 3.13$$

The value for the lower limit is

$$7.60 - 3.13 = 4.47$$

and the value for the upper limit is

$$7.60 + 3.13 = 10.73$$

Note that the 99 percent confidence interval is larger than the 95 percent confidence interval (a range of 6.26 versus a range of 3.78). This is just as it should be, of course, since a larger interval is more likely to include the population mean within its limits than a smaller one.

Comments

A Clarification. Interval estimates take the form of confidence intervals. A confidence interval consists of a specification of a range of values within which we say, with a certain degree of confidence, that the population mean occurs. The population mean itself does not shift around, but it is difficult to locate because our *estimates* of it will vary. That is, means from samples randomly chosen from the same population are not expected to be the same, and, consequently, neither will be the confidence intervals that are based on them. In effect, we are saying that out of a large number of intervals determined in the same way, 95 percent (or any other degree of confidence) of them will include the population mean.[3]

Sharpening Interval Estimates. We can reduce the width of any chosen confidence interval — that is, sharpen the interval estimate — simply by increasing the number of scores on which the interval is based. Increasing the sample size (n) has two effects. First, the estimate of the standard error of the mean becomes smaller. An inspection of Eq. (7-3),

$$\hat{\sigma}_M = \frac{s}{\sqrt{n}}$$

indicates that $\hat{\sigma}_M$ decreases as sample size increases. From Eq. (7-4), that is,

$$\text{confidence interval} = \hat{\mu} \pm (t)(\hat{\sigma}_M)$$

we can see that the confidence interval will become smaller as $\hat{\sigma}_M$ becomes smaller. Second, you can see from an inspection of Table A-3 that the value of t becomes smaller as the df_M increases. Since df_M depends on sample size $(df_M = n - 1)$, the t value will decrease as sample size is increased, and, as a consequence, it too contributes to a smaller interval estimate.

An Alternative Estimate of the Standard Error. Some researchers prefer to use the error term from the overall analysis of variance ($MS_{S/A}$) rather than the standard deviation for each group to estimate the standard error of the mean. That is,

$$\hat{\sigma}_M = \sqrt{\frac{MS_{S/A}}{n}} \tag{7-6}$$

The justification for this alternative is that the $MS_{S/A}$ is an *average* of the group variances and as such may offer a better estimate of $\hat{\sigma}_M$, provided that we can

---

[3] Be careful not to confuse *confidence level*, which is associated with interval estimation, with *significance level*, which is associated with hypothesis testing. The two concepts are different. Confidence level refers to the proportion of times confidence intervals constructed in the same way will include a parameter (usually the mean); significance level refers to the probability with which an experimenter is willing to reject the null hypothesis when in fact it is correct.

reasonably assume that the treatment variances are the same. We will illustrate this approach with the same example we have been using in this section. From Table 5-2, we find $MS_{S/A} = 3.60$. We then substitute this value in Eq. (7-6) to estimate the standard error of the mean. To illustrate,

$$\hat{\sigma}_M = \sqrt{\frac{3.60}{5}} = \sqrt{.72} = .85$$

We use the degrees of freedom associated with the overall error term ($df_{S/A} = 12$) to obtain the value for t (2.18 for $\alpha = .05$). Substituting in Eq. (7-4), we find

$$\text{confidence interval} = \hat{\mu} \pm (t)(\hat{\sigma}_M)$$

$$= 7.60 \pm (2.18)(.85)$$

$$= 7.60 \pm 1.85$$

7.2 THE MAGNITUDE OF TREATMENT EFFECTS

To set this topic in a relevant context, imagine the following situation. You are just completing the data analysis for a project that you and a partner have been working on for a course requirement. You have done all the calculations carefully, and have finally obtained the F for the most important part of your study. Turning quickly to the table of F values, you find that the null hypothesis can be rejected at $p < .05$, the level of significance you chose at the outset of the study. Relief sets in and then a bit of self-satisfaction at having produced a significant effect. A classmate walks in and asks how your project turned out, and you report that you found significant results for your major hypothesis at $p < .05$. You ask in turn, "How did you do?" She replies, "We got significance at the .001 level!" — whereupon your smile disappears and the glow of $p < .05$ fades in comparison with $p < .001$.

As we pointed out in Chap. 5, comparing outcomes in terms of probability levels is an inappropriate use of hypothesis testing. Since such comparisons are made frequently in the research literature, however, there is reason to stress the point. For example, a report may contain such phrases as "a highly significant F," used not only to substitute for "$p < .01$," but also as a thinly disguised code for "big" or "highly important." At times, a researcher trying to convince a skeptic of the importance of an effect might even add, "It was significant beyond the .001 level."

Unfortunately, level of significance tells us nothing about the magnitude or the size of the outcome of an experiment. It would be convenient if the F statistic worked in this way, but it does not. As we indicated in Chap. 5, the level of significance is the risk one takes in being wrong when rejecting the null hypothesis.

The Problem with the F Ratio

The F test provides important and necessary information concerning the presence or absence of treatment effects — differences among treatment means — in the population. A significant F ratio permits the inference that treatment effects are present — that the null hypothesis is *false*. The primary problem with the F ratio is that its size is directly related to sample size:

The size of the F ratio increases as sample size increases.

We can demonstrate this relationship with a numerical example. Suppose we took the data from Table 5-1 and simply duplicated each of the Y scores to double the sample size from $n = 5$ to $n = 10$, without changing the means of the $a = 3$ treatment groups. The "new" data set is presented in Table 7-1, together with the details of the ANOVA. The outcome of the analysis conducted on the original set of scores produced an F of 4.22 ($p < .05$). The F based on the scores in Table 7-1 is 9.50 ($p < .01$). This larger F is not due to an increase in the differences among the means — they are the same in the two examples — but primarily to the increase in sample size.

Our point here is not to downplay an interest in comparing magnitudes of treatment effects; comparisons of this sort are certainly legitimate. What we are arguing for is the use of an index of the magnitude of the treatment effects that is not directly affected by the number of subjects in the different treatment groups — an index other than the size of the F.

An Estimate of Treatment Magnitude

The index most commonly used to estimate the **magnitude of treatment effects** in experiments consists of a ratio relating the variability attributed to the

---

TABLE 7-1 *Effect on F of Doubling the Sample Size*

	a_1		a_2		a_3	
	7	7	9	9	2	2
	8	8	4	4	7	7
	6	6	6	6	5	5
	10	10	9	9	3	3
	7	7	8	8	5	5
Mean	7.60		7.20		4.40	
Sum	76		72		44	
ΣY^2	596		556		224	

Basic Ratios

$$[Y] = \Sigma Y^2 = 596 + 556 + 224 = 1,376$$

$$[A] = \frac{\Sigma A^2}{n} = \frac{(76)^2 + (72)^2 + (44)^2}{10} = \frac{12,896}{10} = 1,289.60$$

$$[T] = \frac{T^2}{(a)(n)} = \frac{(76 + 72 + 44)^2}{(3)(10)} = \frac{(192)^2}{30} = \frac{36,864}{30} = 1,228.80$$

Summary of the Analysis

Source	SS		df	MS	F
A	$[A] - [T] =$	60.80	2	30.40	9.50*
S/A	$[Y] - [A] =$	86.40	27	3.20	
Total	$[Y] - [T] =$	147.20	29		

* $p < .01$.

---

treatment manipulations to the total variability in the experiment; that is,

$$\text{treatment magnitude} = \frac{\text{treatment variability}}{\text{total variability}}$$

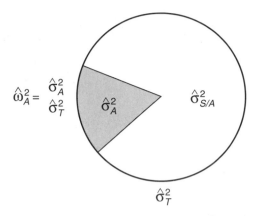

FIGURE 7-2 *A Representation of Estimated Omega Squared $(\hat{\omega}_A^2)$ as a Proportion of the Total Variability in an Experiment.*

To obtain this ratio, we have to estimate *population variances* from the data of an experiment. The ratio itself is simple to express. If we let

$$\hat{\sigma}_A^2 = \text{the estimated population treatment effects}$$

$$\hat{\sigma}_{S/A}^2 = \text{the estimated population error variance}$$

then the estimate of treatment magnitude may be expressed by the following formula:

$$\text{estimated magnitude of treatments } (\hat{\omega}_A^2) = \frac{\hat{\sigma}_A^2}{\hat{\sigma}_A^2 + \hat{\sigma}_{S/A}^2} \qquad (7\text{-}7)$$

The expression $\hat{\omega}_A^2$ is called **estimated omega squared**. As you can see, this index defines size or magnitude as a proportion of the total variability $(\hat{\sigma}_A^2 + \hat{\sigma}_{S/A}^2)$ that is associated with the treatment manipulations $(\hat{\sigma}_A^2)$.

The meaning of this index is diagramed in Fig. 7-2. The entire circle represents the total variability $(\hat{\sigma}_T^2)$, which has been divided into two component parts — the estimated population treatment effects $(\hat{\sigma}_A^2)$ and the estimated population error variance $(\hat{\sigma}_{S/A}^2)$. Clearly, estimated omega squared $(\hat{\omega}_A^2)$ can be interpreted as a *proportion* of the total variability — that is, the proportion of the total variability that is associated with the treatment conditions — and we can say that the larger this proportion the stronger are the treatment effects observed in an experiment.

Let's examine this index a little more closely. A nonexistent effect will produce a value hovering around the minimum theoretical value of .00, while actual treatment effects will produce values between .00 and the maximum theoretical value of 1.00. Estimates of omega squared from actual experiments rarely exceed $\hat{\omega}_A^2 = .25$, however. In fact, a review of the psychological literature reveals that the value of $\hat{\omega}_A^2$ averaged over a large number of studies is about .06 (Sedlmeier & Gigerenzer, 1989). A major reason why estimates of omega squared tend to be about .06 is the substantial contribution of experimental error, which places a damper on the index. Suppose that $\hat{\sigma}_A^2 = 1$ and $\hat{\sigma}_{S/A}^2 = 4$. Such a situation would give us

$$\hat{\omega}_A^2 = \frac{1}{1+4} = \frac{1}{5} = .20$$

Suppose instead that $\hat{\sigma}_{S/A}^2 = 20$ rather than 4 while $\hat{\sigma}_A^2$ remained the same. Under these circumstances,

$$\hat{\omega}_A^2 = \frac{1}{1+20} = \frac{1}{21} = .05$$

which represents a sizable drop from the first value of .20. We can push the estimate even lower by increasing the error component further. Since we must live with the reality of substantial amounts of uncontrolled variability in our experiments, we must be content with the seemingly small values of estimated omega squared our research will reveal.

Estimates of Population Variances. You will recall that the treatment mean square (MS_A) is influenced by two theoretical components, population treatment effects and experimental error, and that the within-treatments mean square ($MS_{S/A}$) is influenced only by experimental error. If we subtract $MS_{S/A}$ from MS_A, we obtain a quantity that reflects the effects of the treatments with the influence of experimental error "removed." That is,

$$MS_A - MS_{S/A} = [(\text{treatment component}) + (\text{experimental error})]$$

$$-(\text{experimental error})$$

$$= \text{treatment component}$$

With this argument as background, we can understand the statistical formula for the actual estimate of the population treatment effects:

$$\hat{\sigma}_A^2 = \frac{(df_A)(MS_A - MS_{S/A})}{(a)(n)} \tag{7-8}$$

In addition to the necessary subtraction of $MS_{S/A}$ from MS_A, Eq. (7-8) specifies some other arithmetical operations that are needed to transform sample data to population estimates — multiplying the difference by df_A and dividing it by $(a)(n)$ — but the underlying logic of the critical operation, the subtraction of $MS_{S/A}$ from MS_A, still remains. The other variance component, the estimated population error variance, comes directly from the analysis without any modification; that is,

$$\hat{\sigma}^2_{S/A} = MS_{S/A} \tag{7-9}$$

A Numerical Example. We will illustrate the calculations with the data from the experiment studying the effects of different types of reinforcement on problem solving. We need the following information from the statistical analysis summarized in Table 5-2 (p. 126): $MS_A = 15.20$, $MS_{S/A} = 3.60$, $a = 3$, and $n = 5$. Substituting these values in Eq. (7-8), we obtain

$$\hat{\sigma}^2_A = \frac{(df_A)(MS_A - MS_{S/A})}{(a)(n)}$$

$$= \frac{(3 - 1)(15.20 - 3.60)}{(3)(5)}$$

$$= \frac{(2)(11.60)}{15} = \frac{23.20}{15}$$

$$= 1.55$$

From Eq. (7-9), we obtain

$$\hat{\sigma}^2_{S/A} = MS_{S/A}$$

$$= 3.60$$

Finally, we can substitute these two variance estimates in Eq. (7-7) to obtain an estimate of the magnitude of the treatment effects ($\hat{\omega}^2_A$):

$$\hat{\omega}^2_A = \frac{\hat{\sigma}^2_A}{\hat{\sigma}^2_A + \hat{\sigma}^2_{S/A}}$$

$$= \frac{1.55}{1.55 + 3.60} = \frac{1.55}{5.15}$$

$$= .30$$

This estimate tells us that 30 percent of the total variance is accounted for by the experimental treatments. Thus, not only is the difference between the three treatment conditions significant statistically, but this difference represents a very sizable effect.[4]

An Alternative Measure of Treatment Magnitude. An alternative to estimated omega squared is often reported in research articles. This index is called R^2 and is based on sums of squares rather than on estimated population variances.[5] More specifically,

$$R^2 = \frac{SS_A}{SS_A + SS_{S/A}} = \frac{SS_A}{SS_T} \qquad (7\text{-}10)$$

Extracting the relevant information from the analysis summary (Table 5-2), we find

$$R^2 = \frac{30.40}{30.40 + 43.20} = \frac{30.40}{73.60}$$
$$= .41$$

This measure indicates that 41 percent of the total variability (as indexed by SS_T) is associated with the variability of the treatment groups (as indexed by SS_A). We have diagramed this relationship in Fig. 7-3, where the circle represents the total sum of squares, which is divided into two components: the sum of squares reflecting the effects of the independent variable and error variance (SS_A) and the sum of squares reflecting effects of error variance alone ($SS_{S/A}$). The index R^2, then, may be viewed as the proportion of the total variability attributed to the differences among the treatment means. As with estimated omega squared, the larger the proportion, the stronger are the treatment effects observed in an experiment.

Because of the way these two measures of effect size are defined, the value of R^2 will always be greater than the value of $\hat{\omega}_A^2$ (.41 versus .30).[6] The main advantage of this alternative measure is its simplicity. Researchers prefer to use estimated omega squared with data from experiments, however, although you will occasionally see R^2 reported instead.

---

[4] You will recall that the average estimated omega squared reported in the psychological literature is .06; a value of .30 is considered quite large. On the other hand, one can always distort reality with fictitious data!

[5] The R^2 statistic is the squared multiple correlation coefficient and is primarily used as a measure of strength in correlational studies.

[6] For an elaboration of the mathematical relationship between $\hat{\omega}_A^2$ and R^2, see Maxwell, Camp, and Arvey (1981).

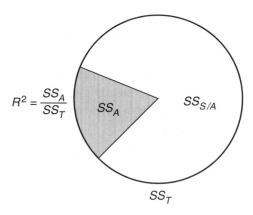

FIGURE 7-3 *A Representation of R^2 as a Proportion of the Total Sum of Squares in an Experiment.*

Using Estimated Omega Squared in Research

Estimated omega squared enables us to estimate the relative strength with which an independent variable produces changes in behavior. Since the value of $\hat{\omega}_A^2$ ranges from .00 to 1.00 and is not affected by sample size, we can make direct comparisons across related research studies conducted with different sample sizes. Together with the F statistic, this index helps to round out the picture of a set of experimental results and should be reported along with the results of the statistical test.

Researchers can use this index in a number of ways — for example, in developing systematic research programs by identifying independent variables that strongly affect behavior. The index can also be useful in the decision-making process that follows the completion of an experiment — for instance, in educational research, medical research, and industrial research, where the primary goal is often to *apply* the results of experimentation to the "real world." In the realm of applied research, the *size* of the effect may actually take on more importance than the results of the statistical test.

Researchers frequently refer to estimates of treatment magnitude as "small," "medium," or "large." This classification, which was proposed by Cohen (for example, 1988, pp. 284–288), defines these terms as follows:

A "small" effect produces an $\hat{\omega}_A^2$ of .01.
A "medium" effect produces an $\hat{\omega}_A^2$ of .06.
A "large" effect produces an $\hat{\omega}_A^2$ of .15 or greater.

While these definitions give us some perspective with which to interpret values of $\hat{\omega}_A^2$ reported in the literature, they should not be used judgmentally to describe experimental findings. *Size* should not be equated with *importance*. A "small" effect, for example, may represent an effect of extreme theoretical importance. For most of us, then, the index is a *supplement* to the statistical test. It contributes to our understanding of a particular manipulation.[7]

7.3 SUMMARY

This chapter presented two topics that assist researchers in interpreting their results, namely, estimating population treatment means and determining the strength or magnitude of the treatment effects observed in an experiment. Both sets of procedures provide information that is not conveyed by the outcome of the F test. Whereas the F test allows us to evaluate the status of the null hypothesis and leads to a yes-or-no decision with regard to the presence of population treatment effects, these other two procedures help us describe the *nature* of the treatment effects.

We first considered methods and procedures we can employ to estimate the population treatment means from the data of an experiment. These estimates usually consist of an interval or a range of values, based either on the standard error of the mean or on the standard error combined with tabled statistical information. The second type of interval estimate is called a *confidence interval* — a range of values within which the population mean is said to be contained with a certain level of confidence. Confidence refers to the probability with which confidence intervals constructed in the same manner would actually contain the population mean.

We discussed next a measure called *omega squared*, which we use to estimate the relative size, or magnitude, of the treatment effects. We argued that the size of the observed F does not provide this useful information directly, while an estimate of omega squared does.

---

[7] We should mention that measures of treatment magnitude have been criticized (see, for example, Keppel, 1991, pp. 66–68; O'Grady, 1982).

7.4 EXERCISES[8]

*1. This problem is based on the data from exercise 2 in Chap. 4 (p. 103).
   a. Calculate the mean and standard deviation for each of the treatment conditions.
   b. Calculate the standard error for each of the treatment conditions.
   c. Use the separate standard errors you calculated in part (b) to construct 95 percent confidence intervals for the respective population treatment means.
   d. Use the standard error based on the $MS_{S/A}$ from the overall analysis of variance to construct the 95 percent confidence interval for each of the population treatment means.

2. This problem is based on the data from exercise 3 in Chap. 4 (p. 104).
   a. Calculate the mean and standard deviation for each of the treatment conditions.
   b. Calculate the standard error for each of the treatment conditions.
   c. Use the separate standard errors you calculated in part (b) to construct the 95 percent confidence interval for each of the population treatment means.
   d. Use the standard error based on the $MS_{S/A}$ from the overall analysis of variance to construct the 95 percent confidence interval for each of the population treatment means.

*3. We have argued that the only function of the F statistic is in evaluating the status of the null hypothesis and stressed that the size of F cannot be used as an index of the *magnitude* of the treatment effects assessed by the F test. We demonstrated this point in this chapter by showing that the size of the F ratio can be increased simply by using larger sample sizes (see p. 178). In Sec. 7.2, we introduced two estimates of treatment magnitude — estimated omega squared $(\hat{\omega}_A^2)$ and R^2 — that *do* reflect the size of the treatment effects without being unduly influenced by differences in sample sizes, as is the F ratio.
   a. Calculate $\hat{\omega}_A^2$ and R^2 from the information appearing in Table 7-1 (p. 179).
   b. Compare the two estimates you obtained in part (a) with those we presented in this chapter, which were based on the information appearing in Table 5-2 (see pp. 182–183). What can you conclude from this comparison?

4. Calculate $\hat{\omega}_A^2$ and R^2 from the information provided in Table 4-8 (p. 101).

---

[8] Answers to the starred problems are found in Appendix B.

Chapter 8

ERRORS OF HYPOTHESIS TESTING AND STATISTICAL POWER

By now you have become quite practiced in hypothesis testing and probably apply the decision rules to the F's you calculate without ever questioning the logic of the procedure that we first discussed in Chap. 5. In this chapter, we return to this topic and examine the risks we take when we decide to reject or to retain the null hypothesis. First, we consider in detail what these risks are — there are two such risks we will discuss — and see how they are related and what can be done to minimize their contribution to the decision process. Next, we discuss the special risk that can occur when we conduct two or more analytical comparisons within the context of a single experiment, and practical ways of dealing with it. Finally, we show how to use sample size and the concept of statistical power to achieve control over the sensitivity of an experimental design.

8.1 STATISTICAL ERRORS IN HYPOTHESIS TESTING

We have hinted in our discussion of hypothesis testing that researchers make wrong decisions from time to time. We can now be even more emphatic:

We can never be certain — one way or another — whether we have made the right decision after applying the decision rules to the results of an experiment.

Students often find this rude fact disillusioning and rather hard to accept; they would much prefer to deal with certainties. Unfortunately, however, complete certainty is unknown in psychological research and, for that matter, in any other field of science that utilizes methods of statistical inference in its day-to-day operations. We tolerate this reality by determining as accurately as possible the *extent* of our uncertainties, that is, the magnitude of our errors of statistical inference. In this section, we are concerned with the nature of the errors surrounding the process of hypothesis testing.

In hypothesis testing, we make dichotomous, yes-no decisions. The decision rule we follow in evaluating the null hypothesis ultimately tells us to do one of two things — either to reject the null hypothesis or to retain it. Also, as we have noted, the statistical basis for these decisions is essentially probabilistic, which means that we take a calculated risk of being wrong with every decision we make. We discuss two risks or errors of hypothesis testing in this section. These are unimaginatively called type I and type II errors, evidently because of the order in which they were discovered and amplified.

Type I Error: The Risk in Rejecting the Null Hypothesis

Type I error is the easiest both to understand and to control, and it occurs whenever we *incorrectly reject* the null hypothesis. In discussing the sampling distribution of the F statistic (see Fig. 5-1, p. 109), we noted the important relationship that exists between the frequency of occurrence by chance and the size of the F ratio: expected frequencies decrease as the size of F increases. In order to reject the null hypothesis, which is the primary way we establish new facts from experiments, we must select a critical region of F, thereby dividing the range of all possible values of F into two regions. One of these, the rejection of nonrejection, extends from the lowest possible value of F (zero) to the critical value and contains the range of values of F that we are willing to attribute to the operation of chance factors. The values in this region represent differences among treatment means that might very well have occurred by chance alone. If the value of F falls within this region, we do *not* reject the null hypothesis; we retain it. The other region, the region of rejection, extends from the critical value to the largest possible value of F (infinity) and contains the range of values of F that we are *not* willing to attribute to the operation of chance factors. When the F falls within this region, we *reject* the null hypothesis.

If we follow this procedure every time we wish to perform an F test, will we ever make a mistake when we reject the null hypothesis? The answer is yes.

> **We will make a mistake whenever the null hypothesis is true and we reject the null hypothesis.**

That is, if the population treatment means are in fact *equal* (that is, if the null hypothesis is true), we will be in error if we reject the null hypothesis and conclude that they are *not all equal* to one another. In such a case, the decision to reject the null hypothesis will be the wrong decision. This error of inference is called *type I error* and has been described as "seeing too much in the data" (Anderson, 1966, p. 72).

Most of the time we will not make this error, however. We will do so only when the null hypothesis is true *and* the F falls within the rejection region. The reason for the comparative rarity of type I error is that the theoretical probability with which F will fall *by chance* in the rejection region is relatively small (usually $\alpha = .05$). Thus, we will make a type I error a small percentage of the time — the exact amount being specified by our choice of significance level. We will make the *correct* inference the rest of the time, that is, 95 percent of the time (assuming we have set $\alpha = .05$).

In summary, type I error is the logical consequence of hypothesis testing. It can occur only when two situations are *both present*, namely, when

1. The null hypothesis is true *and*
2. We reject the null hypothesis.

Type I error is a risk associated with *rejecting* the null hypothesis. We will now consider another kind of error — **type II error** — which is a risk associated with *retaining* the null hypothesis, rather than rejecting it.

Type II Error: The Risk in Retaining the Null Hypothesis

Whereas the focus of type I error is the *null* hypothesis, the focus of type II error is the *alternative* hypothesis. Suppose the alternative hypothesis is *true*, which means that some differences among the treatment means do exist in the population. Given this happy event, can anything go wrong if we follow the procedures for testing the adequacy of the null hypothesis? Again, unfortunately, the answer is yes. Suppose some differences exist among the population treatment means (that is, the alternative hypothesis is *true*). Under these circumstances,

> **we will make a mistake whenever the alternative hypothesis is true but we retain the null hypothesis.**

In this case, we should *reject* the null hypothesis and conclude that some differences exist, but we fail to do so and therefore make the wrong decision. We will make a type II error whenever two situations are *both present*:

1. The alternative hypothesis is true *and*
2. We *retain* the null hypothesis.

Type II error, then, is an error caused by our failure to reject the null hypothesis when the alternative hypothesis is true. This type of error has been described as "not seeing enough in the data" (Anderson, 1966, p. 72). What is the probability of making a type II error? As you will see in the next section, the answer is not as simple as it was for the type I error; the exact probability is affected by a number of factors that we discuss in the section titled "Controlling Type II Error."

	Nature of the Population Treatment Effects	
Experimenter Decision	All μ_i's Are Equal (H_0 Is True)	Not All μ_i's Are Equal (H_0 Is False)
Reject H_0	Type I Error	Correct Decision
Retain H_0	Correct Decision	Type II Error

TABLE 8-1 *Experimenter Decision and the Nature of Treatment Effects in the Population*

Beta and Power.   We use some special terms to describe type II error. The size of the error itself is designated by the Greek letter β (**beta**). We usually express type II error as a probability, based on the frequency with which this error would be made if we repeated the experiment over and over a large number of times. **Power** refers to the converse side of type II error, the probability with which a *correct* decision will be made — that is, rejecting the null hypothesis when the alternative hypothesis is true. Another way of describing power is that it is the probability of detecting differences when they exist. In symbols,

$$\text{power} = 1 - (\text{type II error})$$

$$= 1 - \beta \qquad (8\text{-}1)$$

The relationship between power and β is obvious: any *decrease* in type II error (β) will result in an *increase* in power.

Decision and Type of Error: A Clarification

You should now understand what we meant by stating that a certain degree of uncertainty surrounds hypothesis testing. Researchers make errors of inference, but fortunately they make correct decisions as well. Table 8-1 summarizes the circumstances under which errors and correct decisions occur. Hypothesis testing is concerned with two theoretical possibilities:

1. The treatment means in the population are equal — that is, the null hypothesis (H_0) is true.
2. At least some of the means are different — that is, the alternative hypothesis (H_1) is true.

Taken together, these two hypotheses encompass all the possible ways in which the treatment means may exist in the population. These two hypotheses are represented in the last two columns in Table 8-1.

Hypothesis testing results in one of two possible decisions: either we reject the null hypothesis or we retain the null hypothesis. These two decisions are represented in the last two rows of the table.

Depending on the status of the treatment means in the population — which, of course, we do not know — we will either make an error or make a correct decision.

If the hypothesis we decide on reflects or describes the population, our decision is correct; if it does not, an error is made.

First consider the consequences of rejecting the null hypothesis (see the row labeled "Reject H_0"). With respect to the situation indicated in the first column — that the population treatment means are equal (that is, H_0 is true) — we will make a type I error when our decision is to reject H_0 and conclude that differences are present when, in fact, they are not. On the other hand, regarding the situation indicated in the second column — that the population treatment means are not all the same (that is, H_1 is true) — we would be making a correct decision.

Next, examine the consequences of retaining the null hypothesis (see the row labeled "Retain H_0"). If the situation indicated in the first column is correct — that the population treatment means are equal — we will make the correct decision by retaining the null hypothesis. On the other hand, if the situation indicated in the second column is correct — that the population means are not all the same — we will make a type II error, because we are not rejecting the null hypothesis when it is false.

This table makes clear the fact that it is not logically possible to make *both* types of error in testing a null hypothesis. We are permitted to make only *one* decision in hypothesis testing — either to reject or to retain the null hypothesis. Once we have made that particular decision, we are susceptible to only *one* of the types of errors: a type I error if our decision is to reject the null hypothesis, or a type II error if our decision is to retain the null hypothesis.

Controlling the Two Types of Error

Fortunately, we can take steps in designing and analyzing our experiments to control, or *minimize,* these two potential errors. We consider the control of type I error first.

Controlling Type I Error.   The probability of making a type I error is determined by the significance level we choose for the experiment. In this sense, then, the probability with which a type I error might occur — that is, the "size" of the type I error — is under our *direct* control. If we are greatly concerned about making this particular error, we can simply lower the rejection probability from, for example, $\alpha = .05$ (5 times in 100) to $\alpha = .01$ (1 time in 100). To clarify, consider the theoretical sampling distribution of F we have drawn in panel A of Fig. 8-1. The vertical line labeled F_α defines the start of the rejection region and the values of F that will lead us to reject the null hypothesis. This region also represents the degree of risk we are willing to take when we reject the null hypothesis — that is, the probability of type I error.

Suppose we adopt a more stringent significance level — for example, $\alpha = .01$ instead of the more common $\alpha = .05$. How would we need to change panel A to represent this situation? Assuming that the F_α in the figure depicts the critical value of F for the 5 percent level of significance, we would need to move F_α to the *right* until the tail of the F distribution contains only 1 percent of the F's we expect to occur when the null hypothesis is true. This new significance level is shown in panel B. There is a price we pay for being particularly concerned about type I error, however, and this is an increase in the other kind of error, namely, type II error. We consider the effect on type II error next.

The Consequences of Controlling Type I Error.   Consider next the curve drawn in panel C of Fig. 8-1. This curve represents the theoretical distribution of F when the alternative hypothesis is *true*.[1] You will note that we have extended the vertical line (F_α) from panel A to intersect with the curve in panel C. What happens when we obtain an F to the *left* of F_α? The decision is to *retain* the null hypothesis, but this is clearly an error if the alternative hypothesis is true. The area to the left of F_α in panel C, then, represents β, or type II error. Alternatively, what happens when we obtain an F to the *right* of F_α? In this case, we reject the null hypothesis and *accept* the alternative hypothesis, which is the correct decision, of course. The area to the right of F_α represents *power*. You can see pictorially the meaning of Eq. (8-1), which specifies the relationship between power and beta.

Suppose we decide to use the 1 percent level of significance. Consider now the effect of this decision to reduce type I error on type II error, which is displayed in panel D. You can clearly see that by moving F_α to the right, which is how we reduce type I error, we directly *increase type II error* (and *decrease*

---

[1] The exact shape and location of this distribution depends on a number of factors, including the actual difference between the population treatment means. In general, the distribution is more spread out than the F distribution as we have depicted it in the drawing.

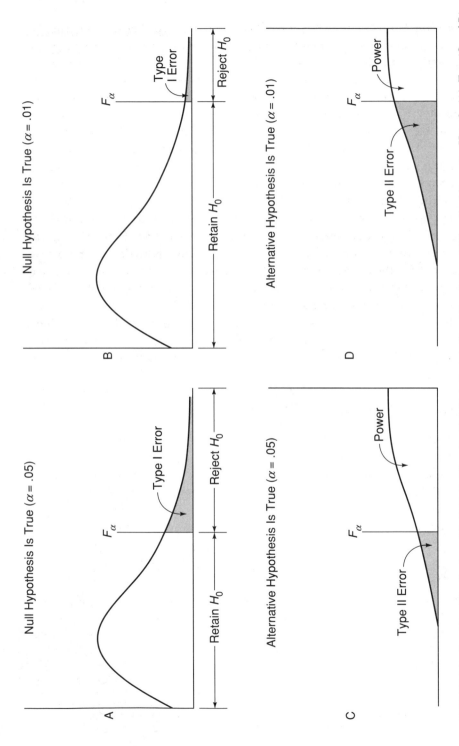

FIGURE 8-1 *Sampling Distribution of the F Ratio When the Null Hypothesis Is True (A and B) and When the Alternative Hypothesis is True (C and D). The critical value of F (F_α) is shown for the 5 percent level of significance (A) and the 1 percent level of significance (B). (The probabilities associated with the three areas of interest are: type I error = α, type II error = β, power = 1 − β.)*

power).In short, any decision we make about controlling type I error will always be at the expense of type II error. Let's now consider ways that we may control type II error.

Controlling Type II Error. Whereas we control the magnitude of type I error directly through our choice of significance level (α), we control type II error *indirectly* through a variety of means. One possibility is to *increase* the rejection region — for example, setting $\alpha = .10$ instead of $.05$. More specifically, if we move F_α to the *left*, which is what we would need to do to enlarge the rejection region, we automatically decrease type II error and increase power. Unfortunately, most psychological researchers have adopted the 5 percent level of significance, which means that this option is not effectively open to us if we want to see our research published in professional journals!

Fortunately, there are other ways we can control type II error which do not have the effect on type I error that adopting a larger value for α has. These procedures increase the size of the F ratio relative to what it would have been otherwise, thereby increasing a researcher's chances of rejecting the null hypothesis and thereby avoiding a type II error. Generally, a researcher achieves this increase in power by taking certain steps in designing the experiment. The following is a list of four such techniques and a description of how they produce an increase in the size of the F ratio:

1. *Increasing sample size.* Increasing the number of subjects assigned to the treatment conditions leads to an increase in the size of the numerator term (MS_A) relative to that of the denominator term ($MS_{S/A}$) of the F ratio and, consequently, to an increase in the size of the obtained F.[2] An increase in sample size also increases the number of degrees of freedom for the denominator term — $df_{S/A} = (a)(n-1)$ — leading to a smaller critical value of F. (You can verify this for yourself by turning to the F table and seeing what happens to the critical value of F as you move *down* any column.) While the benefits of increasing sample size are obvious, this method of decreasing type II error is often difficult to implement because of (*a*) cost, especially when the subjects are animals; (*b*) availability, if the number of subjects with which to conduct the research is limited; or (*c*) time, since testing more subjects takes more time. We will discuss the process of choosing a sample size in Sec. 8.3.

---

[2] You may recall that we illustrated this point in Chap. 7 when we increased the sample size for a numerical example from $n = 5$ to $n = 10$, simply by duplicating each of the scores (see p. 178). Whereas doubling sample size this way had no effect on the treatment means, we demonstrated that F increased from 4.22 to 9.50.

2. *Increasing the size of the treatment effects.* In choosing specific treatment conditions, one can try to select treatments that are most likely to produce big effects. When this technique is used successfully, the numerator term of the F ratio is increased as a result of an increase in the size of the observed differences among the treatment means.

3. *Decreasing the amount of experimental error.* A decrease in the amount of experimental error present in an experiment produces an increase in the size of the F ratio by decreasing the size of the denominator term relative to the numerator term. A researcher generally accomplishes this result by attempting to restrict the variation of nuisance variables controlled through random assignment of subjects to conditions. A common example is the use of homogeneous subjects — subjects who are matched on relevant subject variables. There are statistical procedures, such as the *analysis of covariance*, that reduce the size of the error term on the basis of information that is available about the subjects before the start of the experiment. This approach is complicated and is usually covered only in more advanced books.

4. *Using a more sensitive experimental design.* In this context, *sensitivity* refers to the ability to detect any effects that may exist in the treatment populations. In general, increasing the sensitivity of experiments leads to larger F ratios through a reduction in the size of the denominator term of the F. One way is to turn to designs that use the same subject in some or even all the treatment conditions; we discuss these types of designs in Part Four.

The Meaning of Proof in Hypothesis Testing

We should clarify the statement "to reject the null hypothesis" at this point. Earlier we stated that to reject the null hypothesis is to accept the alternative hypothesis. However, this does not mean we have unequivocally proved that the alternative hypothesis is "true." In the first place, when we reject the null hypothesis, we do so with the full knowledge that such a decision will be in error a small but still finite percentage of the time (type I error). Second, while a particular theory may have predicted the differences observed in an experiment, rejecting the null hypothesis does not necessarily prove that theory. Other theories might make the same prediction. As Underwood and Shaughnessy (1975) put it,

> the results may be said to confirm or support the deduction from the theory, or they may be said to be consonant with theoretical expectations, but a theory is never said to be proved by a result (p. 154).

For these reasons, *proof* is generally considered too strong a word to refer to the rejection of the null hypothesis and acceptance of the alternative hypothesis.

The statement "retain the null hypothesis" is also frequently a source of confusion. You may have noted that we have avoided saying "*accept* the null hypothesis." Why are we inconsistent with our terminology? If the alternative hypothesis can be accepted, why not the null hypothesis? The answer is the practical impossibility of "proving" that no differences in treatments exist in the population. Our experiment may have been insufficiently sensitive to detect the differences in the population. Perhaps if we had used more subjects, employed a more sensitive design, exerted more precise control over the nuisance variables, chosen different levels for our independent variable, and so on, we would have rejected the null hypothesis.

By saying that we "retain the null hypothesis," we are in essence recognizing that a more powerful, or sensitive, experiment might have detected differences in the population treatment means, which consequently resulted in the rejection of the null hypothesis. When we accept the alternative hypothesis, we know how often we will be wrong — that is, we know the probability of the type I error. When we retain the null hypothesis, we cannot accept this with the same degree of confidence. We must wait for additional information from more powerful experiments to provide a more adequate test of the null hypothesis. Until such experiments have been conducted, researchers are often willing to act as if they have in fact accepted the null hypothesis — by revising theory or by turning to a different problem — even though they are still confronted with the problem of demonstrating unequivocally that differences do not exist.[3]

8.2 CUMULATIVE TYPE I ERROR

We have defined type I error as the probability of rejecting the null hypothesis when in fact this hypothesis is true. Although we did not stress the point earlier, this probability applies specifically to the particular statistical test under consideration. The proper term for denoting this probability is **per comparison**

---

[3] Some applied methodologists have suggested procedures that will allow us to "accept" the null hypothesis, but a discussion of them is beyond the scope of this book (see, for example, Keppel, 1991, pp. 89–90).

type I error, which we will designate α_{PC} in this discussion. To be more specific,

> **per comparison type I error (α_{PC}) refers to the probability of committing a type I error for an *individual* statistical test.**

The statistical test referred to can be the omnibus null hypothesis or an analytical hypothesis of the type we discussed in Chap. 6.

Familywise Error

Another kind of type I error becomes relevant when we perform more than one statistical test in the complete analysis of an experiment. We will refer to this kind of error as **familywise (*FW*) type I error**.

> **Familywise type I error refers to the probability of committing type I errors over a set of statistical tests.**

Consider, for example, a situation in which we conduct two statistical tests in the analysis of an experiment. Assuming that we have set $\alpha_{PC} = .05$ in both cases, the probability is .05 that we will commit a type I error on the first test, and the probability is .05 that we will commit a type I error on the second test. This is what is meant by per comparison type I error — each test is considered separately and independently from the others. The point of reference for this error is the *individual statistical test.*

But what if we shift our point of reference to the *set* of two comparisons and to the probability of committing a type I error in this set? Familywise type I error occurs whenever a type I error is made on *any* of the tests in the set. Where two statistical tests are conducted, familywise type I error can occur in three possible ways, namely,

> as a type I error on the first test only
> as a type I error on the second test only
> as a type I error on both tests

With three or more statistical tests in the set, the number of such possibilities increases dramatically.

The Relationship Between Per Comparison and Familywise Errors

Familywise type I error is directly related to the number of statistical tests included in an experiment. With the probability of a per comparison type I error set at α for each of the statistical tests considered separately,

familywise type I error is approximately equal to the *sum* of the separate per comparison probabilities.

In symbols, familywise type I error (α_{FW}) is approximated by

$$\alpha_{FW} = (c)(\alpha_{PC}) \tag{8-2}$$

where c represents the number of comparisons or statistical tests involved and α_{PC} is the probability selected to evaluate each of the comparisons. With two tests, for example, *FW* type I error is approximately equal to $(2)(.05) = .10$; with three tests, *FW* type I error is approximately equal to $(3)(.05) = .15$; and so on. Although the exact relationship between the number of statistical tests and *FW* type I error is relatively complicated (which explains why we use the word *approximately*), the general thrust of the concept is simple:

FW **type I error increases as the number of statistical tests increases.**

The greater the number of tests we conduct, the greater the chances that we will commit at least one type I error somewhere in the set.

The point of Chap. 6 was to provide you with the rationale for using planned analytical comparisons in the analysis of your experiments. We hope you are convinced that to be valuable an experiment should include a number of analytical comparisons. But you should also be aware that when more than one statistical test is included in an experiment, the problem of *FW* type I error becomes relevant and of concern to researchers. We turn now to a consideration of the options available for controlling such error.

Controlling Familywise Type I Error

Most solutions to the problem achieve control of *FW* error by reducing type I error for the *individual tests*. To elaborate, per comparison type I error is the probability of falsely rejecting the null hypothesis in a single statistical test.

Suppose we make it more difficult to reject the null hypothesis for a comparison — for example, simply by lowering the significance level from 5 percent to 1 percent. Two consequences will result: a reduction in the probability of type I error for each comparison, and a resultant decrease in *FW* type I error. This decrease occurs because of the direct relationship between per comparison and *FW* type I errors — a decrease in the first necessarily produces a decrease in the second.

This general solution to the problem of *FW* type I error — that is, a reduction of type I error for the individual tests making up the analytical set of comparisons — is not without cost, however. If we make it more difficult to reject the null hypothesis — which is what happens when we control *FW* type I error — we necessarily decrease our ability to detect actual differences existing in the population. That is, any control of *FW* type I error leads to an increase in type II error.

There is no clear way around this problem, which is one reason why many techniques for controlling *FW* type I error have been developed. A researcher must be concerned with both types of error. Any plan of analysis represents a conscious balancing of each type. At the moment, we cannot offer an easy way to achieve this balance; in fact, this issue is a highly controversial topic for investigators in most fields of research. Given the introductory nature of this book, we will not discuss this complication, but offer instead a simplified — and reasonable — method for selecting statistical procedures based on whether a comparison is *planned* before the start of an experiment or *unplanned*, that is, suggested by the data following experimentation.

Evaluating Planned Comparisons

Fortunately, researchers generally agree on the way to treat *FW* type I error with respect to planned comparisons:

Ignore the theoretical increase in *FW* type I error and reject the null hypothesis at the usual *per comparison* probability level.

This course of action implies a level of tolerance for *FW* type I error generally acceptable to researchers in the field of psychology.[4] It is based on the assumption that the planned comparisons represent the primary purpose of

---

[4] As you might suspect, not all experts agree with this pronouncement and some recommend instead some version of a correction technique called the *Bonferroni test* or the *Dunn test* (see Keppel, 1991, pp. 167–169).

an experiment and were central in its design, and that the number of planned comparisons in any given experiment will be reasonably small. Some experts suggest that the number should not exceed the number of degrees of freedom associated with the MS_A, that is, 1 less than the number of treatment conditions. A "natural" limit to the number of planned comparisons is also imposed by the implied requirements that a comparison be *meaningful* and *central* to the purposes of the experiment. Designs do differ in their analytical power — the number of meaningful comparisons they can answer — but the number is still limited.

In any case, planned comparisons occupy an honored place in the analysis of an experiment. They may be tested regardless of the statistical significance of the omnibus null hypothesis, and they are evaluated on their own merits, independently of other comparisons, at the uncorrected significance level, that is, the per comparison probability, α. The critical value of F for planned comparisons, F_α, is determined by the α chosen, the $df_{num.}$ associated with the comparison, and the $df_{denom.}$ associated with the error term ($MS_{S/A}$).

Evaluating Unplanned Comparisons

Unplanned, or post hoc, comparisons do not usually occupy the same favored position enjoyed by planned comparisons. Unplanned comparisons are considered "opportunistic" in the sense that they can capitalize on chance factors that side with one condition over another. As a consequence, many researchers take precautions against becoming overly "zealous" in declaring that a particularly attractive difference between means is significant. Such precautions reflect the researcher's realization that a larger number of unplanned comparisons could have become "interesting" if chance factors had operated differently.

Thus, it is with respect to unplanned comparisons that adjustment techniques to control familywise type I error are generally applied. As we have indicated, such techniques "work" by making it more difficult for the researcher to assert that the results of unexpected comparisons — unplanned when the experiment was designed — are significant. We will consider three correction techniques designed to exert control over *FW* type I error in three different situations.

The Scheffé Test. The **Scheffé test** (Scheffé, 1953) was developed to allow a researcher to conduct any and all comparisons, whether pairwise or complex, while preventing *FW* error from exceeding some arbitrarily chosen level. That is, if $\alpha_{FW} = .05$ (the level chosen by most researchers), the Scheffé test guarantees that the probability of *FW* type I error will not exceed .05, no matter how many comparisons a researcher chooses to make.

The Scheffé test is quite simple to apply. An *F* for any comparison is evaluated against a special critical value of *F*, which we will refer to as F_S. This critical value is given by the following formula:

$$F_S = (a - 1)F(df_A, df_{S/A}) \qquad (8\text{-}3)$$

where *a* is the number of treatment conditions in the experiment and $F(df_A, df_{S/A})$ is the *critical value* of *F* for the overall, or omnibus, analysis of variance (*not* the *F* that is calculated from the data). The critical value for the *F* in Eq. (8-3) is found in the *F* table for $df_{num.} = df_A$, $df_{denom.} = df_{S/A}$, and $\alpha = .05$ (usually).[5]

As an example, suppose we performed an experiment with $a = 5$ treatment conditions and $n = 9$ subjects assigned randomly to each group. The means for the treatment groups are presented in Table 8-2, together with an abbreviated summary of the overall analysis, which reveals a significant omnibus *F*. As an illustration of the Scheffé test, let's compare the average of two of the groups (a_1 and a_5) with the average of the other three groups (a_2, a_3, a_4). The first average is $(13 + 11)/2 = 12$, and the second average is $(8 + 7 + 9)/3 = 8$. A convenient set of coefficients with which to calculate the comparison sum of squares is $+3, -2, -2, -2, +3$.[6] We use Eq. (6-9) to calculate the sum of squares associated with this comparison; that is,

$$SS_{A\ comp.} = \frac{n(\hat{\psi})^2}{\Sigma\ c^2}$$

where the following conditions hold:

$$n = \text{sample size (9)}$$

$$\hat{\psi} = \text{the sum of the means weighted by the coefficients}$$

$$\text{chosen to reflect the comparison } (+3, -2, -2, -2, +3)$$

$$\Sigma\ c^2 = \text{the sum of the squared coefficients}$$

We will calculate the components of Eq. (6-9) first to simplify the operations.

---

[5] One's choice of α at this point determines the maximum probability of α_{FW}. Most researchers using the Scheffé test choose to set $\alpha_{FW} = .05$.

[6] You may want to review the procedures for constructing coefficients, which we covered in Chap. 6 (pp. 155–158).

TABLE 8-2 *Numerical Example*

Experimental Outcome

	a_1	a_2	a_3	a_4	a_5
Mean	13	8	7	9	11

Summary of the Analysis

Source	df	MS	F
A	4	52.20	4.02*
S/A	40	13.00	

* $p < .05$.

Thus,

$$\hat{\psi} = (+3)(13) + (-2)(8) + (-2)(7) + (-2)(9) + (+3)(11)$$

$$= 39 - 16 - 14 - 18 + 33$$

$$= 24$$

$$\Sigma c^2 = (+3)^2 + (-2)^2 + (-2)^2 + (-2)^2 + (+3)^2$$

$$= 9 + 4 + 4 + 4 + 9$$

$$= 30$$

Substituting these values in Eq. (6-9), we find

$$SS_{A\,comp.} = \frac{(9)(24)^2}{30} = \frac{(9)(576)}{30} = \frac{5,184}{30}$$

$$= 172.80$$

The next step is to form an F ratio. Since we are still contrasting only two means in this comparison, the df for the $SS_{A\,comp.}$ is 1 and the $MS_{A\,comp.} = 172.80/1 = 172.80$. The F ratio, which is specified in Eq. (6-4), becomes

$$F_{A\,comp.} = \frac{MS_{A\,comp.}}{MS_{S/A}} = \frac{172.80}{13.00} = 13.29$$

Normally, this F would be compared with the critical value of $F(1, 40)$, which at $\alpha = .05$ is 4.08. For the Scheffé test, however, we determine the critical value of F_S by substituting in Eq. (8-3), which requires the critical value of F from the overall analysis in its calculation; from Table A-2, we find $F(4, 40) = 2.61$. Substituting in Eq. (8-3), we find

$$F_S = (a - 1)F(4, 40)$$
$$= (5 - 1)(2.61) = (4)(2.61)$$
$$= 10.44$$

We can now write the decision rule for this example of the Scheffé test:

If $F_{A\,comp.} \geq 10.44$, reject the null hypothesis; otherwise, retain the null hypothesis.

Since the F for this comparison, $F_{A\,comp.} = 13.29$, exceeds this critical value specified by the Scheffé test ($F_S = 10.44$), we reject the null hypothesis and conclude that the average of groups a_1 and a_5 is significantly greater than the average of the other three groups.

You can understand how the Scheffé test maintains the FW type I error at $\alpha_{FW} = .05$ for all possible comparisons simply by comparing the critical value for the *uncorrected F*, $F(1, 40) = 4.08$, with the Scheffé correction, $F_S = 10.44$. You can see that it will be considerably more difficult to reject the null hypothesis with unplanned comparisons than it is with planned comparisons. It is this difference in the size of the two critical values of F that is responsible for the control of FW type I error. More specifically, the use of a larger critical value of F ($F_S = 10.44$) means that fewer unplanned comparisons will be declared significant and, consequently, that fewer type I errors will be made. This reduction in the number of type I errors for all possible unplanned comparisons is how the Scheffé test controls FW type I error. The next two procedures we consider exert a smaller correction for unplanned comparisons by restricting the *number* of comparisons that will be considered.

The Tukey Test. The **Tukey test** (Tukey, 1953) was designed to provide a correction for familywise type I error that is tailored to a smaller set of unplanned comparisons, namely, one consisting exclusively of differences between *pairs* of treatment means, which we have called *pairwise comparisons* — not complex comparisons such as the one computed in the previous section.[7] As with the

---

[7] You will often find reference to a related procedure, the *Newman-Kuels test*. The test is generally not recommended, because of its failure to control *FW* type I error under all circumstances (see Eniot & Gabriel, 1975; Ramsey, 1981).

Scheffé test, we calculate $F_{A\,comp.}$ in the usual manner, but evaluate its significance with a corrected value of F that we will call F_T. As an example, let's compare the means for the first two groups ($\overline{Y}_{A_1} - \overline{Y}_{A_2} = 13 - 8 = 5$). Substituting this difference — that is, $\hat{\psi} = 5$ — in the special formula for pairwise comparisons, Eq. (6-2), we find

$$SS_{A\,comp.} = \frac{n(\hat{\psi})^2}{2}$$

$$= \frac{(9)(5)^2}{2} = \frac{(9)(25)}{2} = \frac{225}{2}$$

$$= 112.50$$

Next, we calculate the F for this comparison:

$$F_{A\,comp.} = \frac{112.50}{13.00} = 8.65$$

The formula for calculating the special F for the Tukey test is given by

$$F_T = \frac{(q_T)^2}{2} \tag{8-4}$$

where q_T is an entry in the table of the **Studentized range statistic**, found in Table A-4 of Appendix A. If you look at Table A-4, you will see that three quantities enter into the determination of q_T: df_{error} (the df associated with $MS_{S/A}$), k (the number of treatment means — a in this design), and α_{FW} (the probability of the FW type I error chosen for the experiment — usually .05). For this example,

$$df_{error} = 40$$

$$k = 5$$

$$\alpha_{FW} = .05$$

and the value we find in Table A-4 is 4.04. Substituting in Eq. (8-4), we find

$$F_T = \frac{(4.04)^2}{2} = \frac{16.32}{2} = 8.16$$

The decision rule based on the Tukey test becomes

If $F_{A\,comp.} \geq 8.16$, reject the null hypothesis; otherwise, retain the null hypothesis.

Since $F_{A_{comp.}} = 8.65$, we reject the null hypothesis and conclude that the mean for the first group is significantly greater than the mean for the second. We use the same decision rule to evaluate any of the pairwise comparisons we wish to examine.[8]

The Dunnett Test.   The **Dunnett test** (Dunnett, 1955) is also used with pairwise comparisons, except that the set in this case consists of differences between one mean (usually a control or baseline condition) and each of the others (usually experimental or special treatment conditions). Because the potential size of this set is smaller than the one targeted for by either the Tukey test (all pairwise comparisons) or the Scheffé test (all possible comparisons), the correction for *FW* type I error is less severe with the Dunnett test. Again, we calculate $F_{A_{comp.}}$ in the usual manner, but evaluate the significance of the difference with a special F, F_D, which is easily calculated from the following formula:

$$F_D = (q_D)^2 \tag{8-5}$$

where q_D is an entry in Table A-5, which we will discuss in the context of a numerical example.

As an example, suppose that level a_1 is a control group that receives no special treatment and the other levels are experimental groups that receive different drugs. Although we would usually be interested in comparisons of the control with each of the experimental groups, we will illustrate the process with one of these comparisons, namely, a_1 versus a_4 ($\hat{\psi} = 13 - 9 = 4$). Substituting in Eq. (6-2), we find

$$SS_{A_{comp.}} = \frac{(9)(4)^2}{2} = \frac{(9)(16)}{2} = \frac{144}{2}$$

$$= 72.00$$

The value of F becomes

$$F_{A_{comp.}} = \frac{72.00}{13.00} = 5.54$$

---

[8] If you wish to test all pairwise differences, you may want to use an alternative formula that expresses the Tukey correction in terms of the *minimum difference* between two means that is significant. The formula for this difference, $\bar{d}_T$, is as follows:

$$\bar{d}_T = q_T \sqrt{MS_{S/A}/n}$$

For this example,

$$\bar{d}_T = (4.04)\sqrt{13.00/9} = (4.04)\sqrt{1.44} = (4.04)(1.20) = 4.85$$

Any pairwise difference that equals or exceeds this minimum difference ($\bar{d}_T = 4.85$) is significant.

We calculate the Dunnett correction with Eq. (8-5), which requires a special statistic, q_D, which we obtain from Table A-5 of Appendix A. The tabled statistic is determined by the total number of conditions (k) — which includes the control and all the conditions that will be compared with the control — the degrees of freedom associated with the error term (df_{error}) and the value chosen for FW type I error (α_{FW}). For this example,

$$df_{error} = 40$$

$$k = \text{control} + 4 \text{ experimental conditions} = 5$$

$$\alpha_{FW} = .05$$

and the value we find for q_D in Table A-5 is 2.54. The critical value of F for the Dunnett test becomes

$$F_D = (2.54)^2 = 6.45$$

On the basis of this information, the decision rule becomes

If $F_{A_{comp.}} \geq 6.45$, reject the null hypothesis; otherwise, retain the null hypothesis.

This comparison is not significant.[9]

Recommendations

Table 8-3 provides a summary of the correction procedures we have considered in this section. We start with the evaluation of planned comparisons, where we recommend no special correction for FW type I error — each planned comparison is evaluated as a separate test, with $\alpha = .05$. To test the significance of

---

[9] We can express the Dunnett correction in terms of the minimum difference between two means that is significant. The formula for this difference, $\bar{d}_D$, is as follows:

$$\bar{d}_D = q_D \sqrt{(2)(MS_{S/A})/n}$$

For this example,

$$\bar{d}_D = (2.54)\sqrt{(2)(13.00)/9} = (2.54)\sqrt{2.89} = (2.54)(1.70) = 4.32$$

Any pairwise difference that equals or exceeds this minimum difference ($\bar{d}_D = 4.32$) is significant.

TABLE 8-3 *Comparison of the Familywise Correction Techniques for an Example with $a = 5$ treatments and $n = 9$ subjects per treatment*

Statistical Procedure	Pool of Potential Comparisons	Critical Value of F
Planned Comparisons	A limited number of planned comparisons, central to the main purpose of the experiment	4.08
Scheffé Test	All possible comparisons, including any mixture of pairwise and complex comparisons	10.44
Tukey Test	All possible pairwise comparisons	8.16
Dunnett Test	All possible comparisons between a control, or baseline, condition and the other conditions	6.45

planned comparisons, we need the critical value of F, which for the numerical example is found in Table A-2 under

$$df_{num.} = 1$$

$$df_{denom.} = 40$$

$$\alpha_{PC} = .05$$

This value, 4.08, is entered in the last column of Table 8-3.

Because unplanned comparisons in principle involve a relatively large number of potential comparisons — particularly in comparison with planned comparisons — we recommend that they be evaluated more stringently to keep *FW* type I error within reasonable bounds. The method we recommend, however, depends on the size of the pool of *potential* comparisons from which the unplanned comparisons are presumably drawn. That is,

if the pool includes a mixture of pairwise and complex comparisons, use the Scheffé test;

if the pool includes all pairwise comparisons, use the Tukey test; or

if the pool includes the pairwise comparisons between one group and several other groups, use the Dunnett test.

These recommendations and the corresponding F's from the numerical example are presented in Table 8-3. A comparison of these F's clearly shows how the different correction techniques control *FW* type I error — namely, by narrowing the size of the rejection region. The amount of this adjustment is dictated by the size of the pool of potential comparisons from which the unplanned comparisons are drawn. The disadvantage of these procedures is the substantial loss of power we introduce when we make the rejection region smaller. These F's also show the distinct advantage of *planned comparisons*: an unadjusted significance level and no loss of power.

8.3 USING POWER TO ESTIMATE SAMPLE SIZE

Psychologists have largely ignored power in designing their experiments. We base this conclusion on several studies which estimated the typical power of published research (see, for example, Sedlmeier and Gigerenzer, 1989). We have already considered ways by which we can design experiments with more power (see pp. 195–196), but we have not discussed how we can estimate what our power may be *before* the start of an experiment. We believe that a power estimate is a necessary step in planning an experiment to ensure that type I and type II errors are in reasonable balance. Why design experiments that provide extremely tight control over type I error (usually $\alpha = .05$) but relatively loose control over type II error (for example, $\beta = .50$ or higher)? Once we have decided on the basics of an experiment — the nature of the treatment conditions, the type of experimental design, and the control of nuisance variables — we usually have only one path that we can follow in order to increase power, namely, to increase the sample size.

Power and Sample Size

Suppose you have designed an experiment with $a = 4$ treatment conditions and estimate that the population treatment effects reflect an omega squared of .06. You will recall from Chap. 7 (Sec. 7.2) that an estimated omega squared ($\hat{\omega}_A^2$) of .06 represents a "medium" effect size and that this value is also the average size of the treatment effects generally reported in the psychological research liter- ature (Sedlmeier & Gigerenzer, 1989). Figure 8-2 indicates the relationship between power and sample size for this particular situation, under two levels of significance, $\alpha = .05$ and .01. Consider first the curve for the 5 percent sig- nificance level (the lower curve). You can begin to see why we need substantial sample sizes even to approach what we might think is reasonable power.

What if you wanted your power to be .80 (that is, you wanted an 80 percent chance of detecting differences when they exist)? How many subjects would you need in each of the $a = 4$ treatment conditions? To use Fig. 8-2, move

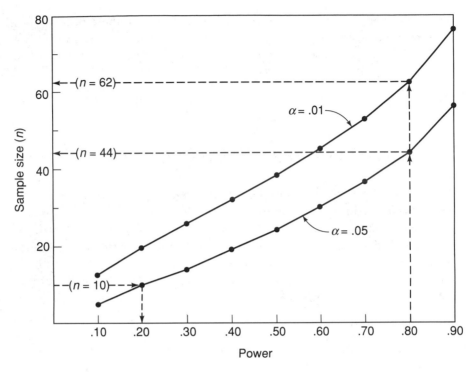

FIGURE 8-2 *The Relationship between Power and Sample Size for an Experiment with a = 4 Treatment Conditions and an Estimated Effect Size of $\hat{\omega}_A^2 = .06$ for Two Levels of Significance ($\alpha = .05$ and .01).*

along the bottom axis until you reach the .80 value for power, and then move up along the dashed line to the point until you intersect the $\alpha = .05$ curve. If you move along the dashed horizontal line extending from the point of intersection to the left until it reaches the vertical axis, you will find that it would take $n = 44$ subjects per condition — or $(a)(n) = (4)(44) = 176$ total — to achieve a power of .80. The upper curve indicates the relationship between power and sample size for the 1 percent significance level. Adopting this more stringent significance level leads to a hefty increase in sample size if we want to maintain power at a particular level. If you continue to move up along the dashed line from power = .80 to the $\alpha = .01$ curve and then along the dashed line from this point to the left, you will find that you would need $n = 62$ subjects per condition (248 total) to achieve the desired power of .80.

Students in our classes conducting experiments for the first time often think a sample size of $n = 10$ would certainly be sufficient to provide a reasonable control of type II error. Let's see how much power is associated with this sample size using our example in which we expect to find a "medium" effect size of $\hat{\omega}_A^2 = .06$. We start by locating $n = 10$ on the vertical axis of Fig. 8-2 and follow the dashed line to the right until it intersects with the curve labeled $\alpha = .05$. The power associated with this situation ($n = 10$ and $\alpha = .05$) is indicated by the value on the baseline immediately below this point — namely, power $= .20$. Consider what this information tells us about our chances of detecting assumed differences among the population treatment conditions with a sample size of $n = 10$: if we were to conduct this same study five times, say, only *one* of the experiments ($1/5 = .20$) will be significant at the the 5 percent level of significance *when an effect is actually present in the treatment populations.*

We hope you agree that the prognosis for an experiment with $n = 10$ is dismal, strongly suggesting that the experiment should not be undertaken unless one substantially increases sample size. This is exactly why we need to conduct a power analysis of any proposed experiment: so that we do not commit ourselves to a design that stands little chance of producing a significant effect. We will now describe how we can go about making an educated guess concerning the sort of sample size we will need to provide us with sufficient power to be able to detect the treatment effects we hope to discover with our proposed experiment.[10]

Estimating Sample Size Needed to Achieve a Selected Power

Before we can determine the desired power of a proposed experiment, we must be able to say something about the nature of the findings we hope to detect. We will consider an approach to this problem that uses estimates of the magnitude of the treatment effects we expect to obtain (omega squared) as the basis for choosing a sample size that will achieve the desired degree of power. Although more precise methods are available, this approach will allow us to illustrate clearly the principles involved.[11] A more accurate approach is illustrated in an appendix at the end of this chapter.

Estimating Omega Squared from Relevant Research.   In many situations, we may be able to make a reasonable estimate of the size of the treatment effects that we would like to detect with an experiment. In some cases, we can base our

---

[10] We will discuss what constitutes a "reasonable" amount of power at a later point in this section.

[11] You can find more detailed discussions of using power to estimate sample sizes in a variety of references, including, for example, Cohen (1988); Keppel (1991, Chap. 4); and Kraemer and Thiemann (1987).

estimate for our proposed study on estimates of omega squared reported for similar experiments in the research literature.[12] We could raise (or lower) this estimate, of course, if we believed that our experiment would produce larger (or smaller) treatment effects than those reported in these studies. If we can find no relevant studies to provide us with an estimate of omega squared, we might consider conducting a "pilot" study — a small preliminary version of the proposed experiment — to help us estimate the magnitude of the treatment effects we can expect to find when we eventually complete the main experiment. We would then use this estimate of omega squared, based on the pilot study, to help us determine the sample size necessary to obtain the power we hope to achieve in the main experiment.

Using Cohen's Size Categories to Estimate Omega Squared. The strategies for estimating omega squared from actual research — that is, from relevant experiments in the literature or from a pilot study — are realistic approaches for substantial research projects, such as honors theses and graduate research leading to master's theses and Ph.D. dissertations, in which there is reasonable time to search the literature or to conduct a pilot study. For undergraduates, however, who must complete their research projects within a single quarter or semester, there is usually insufficient time to pursue either of these strategies. As a practical alternative, we can use the metric proposed by Cohen (for example, 1988) that allows us to categorize treatment effects roughly according to size, which we presented earlier in Sec. 7.2. To repeat, Cohen offers the following terms to characterize the sizes of effects in the behavioral sciences:

A "small" effect produces an $\hat{\omega}_A^2$ of .01.
A "medium" effect produces an $\hat{\omega}_A^2$ of .06.
A "large" effect produces an $\hat{\omega}_A^2$ of .15 or greater.

What you need to do is to choose a value for omega squared that you (and your research colleagues, instructor, or research adviser) feel represents a realistic estimate for the study you propose and the treatment effects you expect to find.

---

[12] A convenient formula for estimating omega squared from published data is one that is based on the reported value of F:

$$\hat{\omega}_A^2 = \frac{(a-1)(F-1)}{(a-1)(F-1) + (a)(n)}$$

The Risk of Overestimating Omega Squared. You should avoid the temptation of assuming that your proposed experiment will produce a "large" effect, unless you have good reasons to do so. Using an unrealistically large estimate of omega squared will work against your attempt to achieve a certain degree of power. Suppose, for example, that you used a value of $\hat{\omega}_A^2$ of .15 (a "large" effect) to estimate the sample size you would need to produce power = .80, when you should have used a value of $\hat{\omega}_A^2 = .06$ instead (a "medium" effect). Without going into the details, we determined for our example that we would need a sample size of $n = 16$ to achieve power = .80 for the unrealistically "large" effect ($\hat{\omega}_A^2 = .15$); if we should have in fact anticipated a "medium" effect ($\hat{\omega}_A^2 = .06$), the power we would achieve with a sample size of $n = 16$ would be approximately .33 — a sharp drop in power and a particularly low value for any scientific investigation.

Using Omega Squared to Estimate Sample Size. Let's assume that we decide to describe the estimated treatment effects in our example as "medium" — that is, we anticipate that our experiment will produce an estimated omega squared of at least $\hat{\omega}_A^2 = .06$. We enter this estimate in the following formula:

$$n' = \phi^2 \left(\frac{1 - \hat{\omega}_A^2}{\hat{\omega}_A^2} \right) \tag{8-6}$$

where n' is the estimated sample size we wish to determine, the quantity ϕ (phi) is a statistic that we will obtain from Table A-6 in Appendix A, and $\hat{\omega}_A^2$ is our estimate of the size of the treatment effects. Table A-6 contains a set of curves, each distinguished by the degrees of freedom associated with the *numerator* of the F ratio; these consist of $df_{num.} = 1$ through 9, 12, and 24. Because our example contains $a = 4$ groups, we would use the curve labeled "3" ($df_{num.} = 4 - 1 = 3$) in Table A-6, which we have duplicated in Fig. 8-3.[13]

For this problem, let's assume that we want to set power = .80. All we need now is to locate .80 on the vertical axis of Fig. 8-3 and to visually extend a horizontal line to the right until it intersects with the power curve. From this point of intersection, we visually extend a vertical line down to the baseline, where we can then read the value for ϕ; in this case, $\phi = 1.7$. We can now easily estimate the sample size by substituting the appropriate values into Eq. (8-6);

---

[13] Table A-6 is a simplified set of power functions constructed from the table reported by Rotton and Schönemann (1978) and the charts published by Pearson and Hartley (1972). We based our adaptation on one of the power functions reported in these sources — that is, $df_{denom.} = 60$ — which provides reasonable information for most applications. You should consult these more comprehensive tables and charts if you require more accurate information.

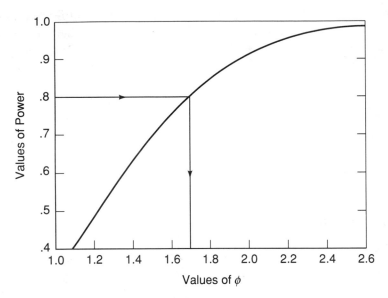

FIGURE 8-3 *An Example of Using Table A-6 to Estimate ϕ for a Particular Degree of Power (.80) for an Experiment with a = 4 Treatment Conditions — i.e., $df_A = 3$.*

that is,

$$n' = \phi^2 \left(\frac{1 - \hat{\omega}_A^2}{\hat{\omega}_A^2} \right)$$

$$= (1.7)^2 \left(\frac{1 - .06}{.06} \right)$$

$$= (2.89) \left(\frac{.94}{.06} \right) = (2.89)(15.67)$$

$$= 45.29$$

It appears that we will need at least 46 subjects per condition to achieve power = .80 when the anticipated results are of "medium" size.

Comments

We have illustrated how to estimate sample size so that an experiment can achieve a reasonable level of statistical power. The procedure required us to come up with some estimate of the nature of the anticipated results in terms of the expected size of the treatment effects. We simply cannot ignore the reality thrust upon us by these estimates of sample size — that is, we usually need considerably more subjects than we ever expect. If we fail to establish a reasonable control of type II error, however, our experiments are often simply a waste of time. If we want to declare certain results significant, we have to design our experiments so that they stand a reasonable chance of "cooperating" with our hopes and expectations. Our "guarantee" for producing results that are significant statistically is the sample size we ultimately decide upon, which we estimate with a consideration of the size of the treatment effects we expect to obtain and the power we want to achieve.

Choosing an Acceptable Level of Power. While there is general agreement among researchers concerning an acceptable level of type I error — namely, $\alpha = .05$ — there is no such consensus concerning an acceptable level of type II error or power. In the absence of such agreement, we offer the recommendation of Jacob Cohen (for example, 1965, pp. 98–99; 1988, pp. 53–56) and others (for example, Hinkle & Oliver, 1983; Keppel, 1991, p. 75; and Kirk, 1982, p. 144) that power be set at .80 for most research in the behavioral sciences. What we are proposing, then, is that we design experiments that are expected to produce significant results 80 percent of the time and nonsignificant results 20 percent of the time.

You might wonder why we have not suggested setting power at a higher level than .80, perhaps .90 or even .95, to reduce even further the probability of a type II error in our research. The reason for proposing .80 is a practical one: using a higher level will usually require more subjects than most researchers can afford to obtain in an experiment. If you return to Fig. 8-2 (p. 210), which depicts the relationship between power and sample size for an experiment producing a "medium" effect ($\hat{\omega}_A^2 = .06$), you will find that increasing power from .80 to .90 requires an increase in sample size from 44 to 57 for $\alpha = .05$ and from 62 to 77 for $\alpha = .01$. These increases in sample size might simply be too great for your research budget to bear.

If you find that the sample size you need to achieve power of .80 is simply too large for your research budget, you might consider lowering the power slightly to .75 or even to .70. We do not recommend reducing sample size to a value that produces a power any lower than .70, however. In our opinion, any power below .70 represents poor science. What is the point of initiating an experiment that has low power? It is unlikely that we will achieve significance with such an experiment and — if we do — that others will be able to duplicate our results. Science must be based on solid research findings, and experiments with low power do not produce dependable, or reliable, findings.

Other Ways of Controlling Power. In this section, we have focused only on sample size as a way to control power. You should remember that you can take other steps to achieve the same goal of reasonable design sensitivity — such as strengthening the manipulations defining the treatment groups, reducing the impact of nuisance variables, and choosing more sensitive designs and statistical procedures. We discussed these different procedures in Sec. 8.1 (see pp. 195–196).

Power and "Trivial" Findings. Achieving statistical significance is not the only factor that we must consider in designing an experiment, however. In addition, we should consider the *importance* of the anticipated treatment effects from both a theoretical and a practical viewpoint as well. Theoretical importance refers to the effect our findings will have on the current explanations of the behavioral phenomena we are studying and not necessarily to the *size* of the treatment effects. A "small" effect, for example, may help decide between two theories that differ in only one critical aspect. Theoretically, it may be important to decide between the two explanations one way or another, regardless of the sample size needed to achieve reasonable power.

Practical importance, on the other hand, refers to the success we will achieve by applying the results of our experiment beyond the laboratory setting to the real world. Perhaps a new drug is significantly better than an older drug in treating some ailment but the *size* of the difference is so small that we question the cost of recommending the new drug over the old. It is here that concerns for effect size or magnitude, as indexed by omega squared or R^2, become directly relevant for the applied researcher. Under these circumstances, a researcher may be interested primarily in "medium" or "large" effects and set sample size for his or her experiments with effects of this size in mind.

Our point is that concerns for effect size (the *strength* of the treatment effects) and for power (the *sensitivity* of an experiment in detecting these effects) should be considered *simultaneously* when an experiment is under development and decisions are being made concerning sample size.

8.4 SUMMARY

This chapter dealt with the sorts of risks that are associated with hypothesis testing and steps that may be taken to minimize those risks. One such risk, type I error, is the error committed when the null hypothesis is falsely rejected. The probability of this error is called the *significance level* and is set by the researcher at a fairly low value (for example, $\alpha = .05$) before the start of the experiment. The other error is type II error, which is committed when the null hypothesis is retained and the alternative hypothesis is true. The researcher controls this error indirectly by designing the experiment to be reasonably sensitive to the existence of treatment effects in the population.

We also considered the fact that type I errors cumulate when two or more statistical tests are conducted within a given experiment. Most researchers agree that if these tests represent meaningful comparisons that are planned in accordance with preexperimental hypotheses, they should be evaluated without concern for the contribution that they make to familywise type I error. On the other hand, many investigators feel that familywise type I error should be controlled when comparisons are unplanned — suggested and conducted only after the data have been examined. We presented three procedures for controlling this error, depending on the size of the underlying pool of comparisons from which those tested by the researcher were presumably drawn.

Finally, we illustrated how a researcher can manipulate sample size to control the probability of type II error. This procedure requires an estimate of the size of the anticipated treatment effects, in the form of either omega squared or R^2. Armed with this estimate, we can choose a sample size that will provide us with reasonable power for detecting these anticipated results.

8.5 EXERCISES [14]

*1. Exercise 1 in Chap. 6 consisted of an experiment in which there were two batches of drug A, three batches of drug B, and a control condition. Exercise 2 in the same chapter asked you to test the significance of several comparisons. Now that you have been exposed to the concept of cumulative type I error — that is, familywise type I error — you will realize that these tests were treated as *planned comparisons* in the sense that you evaluated each F without correcting for the fact that you performed several F tests. There is nothing "wrong" with this procedure, because we recommend using uncorrected F tests for planned comparisons that are meaningful and central to the purposes of the experiment. We will use the same data to give you practice in applying the three techniques we presented in this chapter

---

[14] Answers to the starred problems are given in Appendix B.

for controlling *FW* type I error associated with *unplanned comparisons*. In each case, we will ask you to evaluate the *F* as a *planned comparison* — that is, without correction — and then to evaluate the same *F* with one or more of the correction techniques we covered in this chapter.

    a. Evaluate the complex comparison between the two drugs, first as a planned comparison and then with the Scheffé test.

    b. Let's assume that the researcher would like to compare all five of the drug groups (a_1 through a_5) with the control group (a_6). Evaluate each of these five comparisons first as a planned comparison and then with the Dunnett test.

    c. Suppose the researcher decides to test some pairwise comparisons that were not included as planned comparisons. This often occurs when the primary, or planned, analyses are completed and a researcher begins looking at other comparisons that seem interesting and worthy of testing. Use the Tukey test to evaluate the following pairwise comparisons:

a comparison between a_1 and a_2

a comparison between a_1 and a_3

a comparison between a_1 and a_6

2. Exercise 5 in Chap. 5 was concerned with the analysis of an experiment investigating the effects of different scents on the exploratory behavior of kangaroo rats. Conduct the following analyses on these data:

    a. Evaluate the comparison between the control condition (a_1) and the unfamiliar condition (a_2) without a correction for *FW* type I error — that is, as a planned comparison.

    b. Evaluate the same comparison using the Dunnett test, treating a_1 as a control condition (a group that receives no scent from other kangaroo rats) and the other three conditions (a_2 through a_4) as experimental conditions (groups that receive scents from other kangaroo rats).

*3. Suppose you determined that the power of the results produced by a particular experiment is .60. What does this value tell you about the type II error associated with this study? What can you say about your chances of obtaining a significant *F* under these circumstances?

*4. Let's assume you are planning an experiment with $a = 5$ different treatment conditions and need to make a decision on sample size. After examining the results of related experiments reported in the literature, let's assume you conclude that a realistic effect size that you could expect to produce with your proposed experiment is somewhere between "small" ($\hat{\omega}_A^2 = .01$) and "medium" ($\hat{\omega}_A^2 = .06$).

    a. What sample size will you need to achieve a power of .80 at the 5 percent level of significance for this estimated effect size (use $\hat{\omega}_A^2 = .03$)?

    b. As you have discovered, the sample size required in part (a) is quite large and would probably exceed your resources. One way out of this dilemma is to settle for a lower degree of power. Suppose you decide that the lowest possible power you are willing to accept with this experiment is .70. What sample size do you need now?

    c. You will probably agree that the new sample size you calculated in part (b) is probably still too large to continue with the project as planned — you certainly would not want to reduce power below .70! What options are now open to you? You could reexamine your estimates of effect size. Is it possible that your proposed experiment might produce a larger effect than those found by others? Alternatively, you might be able to modify the specific treatments in such a way as to increase the size of the treatment effects but not change the purpose of your study. In any case, let's assume you now feel that a "medium" ($\hat{\omega}_A^2 = .06$) effect size is a more realistic estimate. What sample size will you need to achieve power $= .80$?

5. Suppose you are planning an experiment for a class project with a group of students and you have reached the point at which you need to decide how many subjects you will assign to each of the treatment conditions. Let's suppose that your group has decided to study the effects of various background noises on reading comprehension — specifically, silence, soft recorded conversation, light classical music, and musical selections recorded from a local "top-40" FM radio station. Your group expects to find a "large" effect ($\hat{\omega}_A^2 = .15$) as a result of these manipulations.

    a. Estimate the sample size you will need to achieve a power of .90, using the 5 percent level of significance.

    b. Suppose you feel that a "large" effect is not a realistic estimate and argue for using a "medium" effect ($\hat{\omega}_A^2 = .06$) to estimate sample size. What sample size will your group need now to achieve the same degree of power?

    c. Let's assume that the sample size you calculate for part (b) is simply not possible to achieve by your group given the time available to complete the study. As you argue back and forth, your group begins to agree that perhaps the original estimate of the size of the anticipated treatment effects was too large, but not as small as you suggested. You decide now that an $\hat{\omega}_A^2 = .10$ is a realistic compromise. What sample size do you now need?

    d. Although your group is delighted by the drop in estimated sample size in part (c), some members of your group still feel that steps could be taken to reduce the estimated sample size some more. They suggest that the group could "live" with a small decrease in power — for example, from .90 to .80. What sample size do you now need?

8.6 APPENDIX: AN ALTERNATIVE METHOD FOR ESTIMATING SAMPLE SIZE [15]

In Sec. 8.3, we considered a method for estimating the sample size of an experiment required to achieve a particular level of power. The basis for this method was an estimate of the size of the treatment effects (omega squared) that we hoped to detect with the experiment. We then demonstrated how we could use this estimate of treatment magnitude in conjunction with a special statistical table (Table A-6) to determine the appropriate sample size. The primary advantage of this method lies in its simplicity — all we need is an estimate of treatment magnitude. On the other hand, its simplicity is also a disadvantage, because it fails to take into consideration the specific pattern of the treatment means that theory or other considerations suggest.[16]

The method we consider in this appendix requires us to make a rough guess at what the population treatment means might be and to estimate error variance in the population. You should use a reasonable estimate of the treatment means. If feasible, you could assign some realistic value to one of the conditions — for example, a baseline or control condition — and then set the other means with reference to it. Alternatively, you might base your estimates on the means found with similar work reported in the literature or on preliminary data collected in preparation for the main experiment.

---

[15] This appendix is intended for students in advanced courses on research design and statistical analysis. Instructors may wish to omit this material in courses where time does not permit discussion.

[16] It is possible to translate certain patterns of anticipated differences among the treatment means into the omega squared estimate, which provides a more accurate estimate of sample size under these circumstances (see Keppel, 1991, pp. 82–85).

Estimating the Population Treatment Means.   We will illustrate the first method by estimating the mean for the control group (a_1) at $\hat{\mu}_1 = 20$ and then selecting values for the three experimental groups (a_2 through a_4) with reference to this mean. From the logic of the study, suppose we predicted the following:

> the first experimental group will score one unit higher on the dependent variable (that is, $\hat{\mu}_2 = 20 + 1 = 21$);

> the second experimental group will score two units lower ($\hat{\mu}_3 = 20 - 2 = 18$); and

> the third experimental group will score three units lower ($\hat{\mu}_4 = 20 - 3 = 17$).

The specific value we choose for the control group mean is not important. What is critical is the number of units the other means would fall above or below this reference condition.

Estimating the Population Treatment Variance ($\hat{\sigma}_A^2$).   Once we have estimated the population treatment means, we then use them to obtain a variance, called $\hat{\sigma}_A^2$, which is calculated as follows:[17]

$$\hat{\sigma}_A^2 = \frac{\Sigma(\hat{\mu}_i - \hat{\mu}_T)^2}{a} \tag{8-7}$$

where

$$\hat{\mu}_i = \text{a population treatment mean}$$

$$\hat{\mu}_T = \text{the mean of the population treatment means}$$

$$a = \text{the number of treatment means.}$$

To illustrate, we begin by calculating $\hat{\mu}_T$; that is,

$$\hat{\mu}_T = \frac{20 + 21 + 18 + 17}{4} = \frac{76}{4} = 19$$

---

[17] Since the following formula uses means, it has a different form than the one we presented in Chap. 7, Eq. (7-8), which used mean squares from the results of an experiment.

Substituting in Eq. (8-7), we find

$$\hat{\sigma}_A^2 = \frac{(20 - 19)^2 + (21 - 19)^2 + (18 - 19)^2 + (17 - 19)^2}{4}$$

$$= \frac{(1)^2 + (2)^2 + (-1)^2 + (-2)^2}{4}$$

$$= \frac{1 + 4 + 1 + 4}{4} = \frac{10}{4}$$

$$= 2.50$$

Estimating the Population Error Variance. The other piece of information we need is an estimate of the variability in the treatment populations — that is, the population error variance. We can usually estimate this quantity from the error term of a related experiment we have performed, an experiment reported in the literature, or even from a pilot study we conduct as a check on the specific conditions of the experiment. Let's assume that we estimate the error variance to be

$$\hat{\sigma}_{S/A}^2 = MS_{S/A} = 16$$

Estimating the Sample Size. To complete the process of estimating the sample size, we need to do the following:

specify the degree of power we wish to achieve with our experiment;

transform this value into a special statistic, ϕ, which we easily accomplish with the help of Table A-6;

enter all three pieces of information — more specifically, $\hat{\sigma}_A^2$, $\hat{\sigma}_{S/A}^2$, and ϕ — into the following equation:

$$n' = \phi^2 \left(\frac{\hat{\sigma}_{S/A}^2}{\hat{\sigma}_A^2} \right); \tag{8-8}$$

and, finally, solve for the estimated sample size (n').

Completing the Example. We already have estimates for $\hat{\sigma}_A^2$ (2.50, based on estimated treatment means of 20, 21, 18, and 17) and $\hat{\sigma}_{S/A}^2$ (16). We obtain ϕ from Table A-6 in Appendix A, which we described in Sec. 8.3 (see pp. 213–214). For this problem, let's assume that we want to set power = .80. All we need now is to locate .80 on the vertical axis and to visually extend a horizontal line to the right until it intersects with the appropriate power curve ($df_{num.} = 3$). From this point of intersection, we visually extend a vertical line down to the baseline, where we can then read the value for ϕ; in this case, $\phi = 1.7$. We can now easily estimate the sample size by substituting the appropriate values into Eq. (8-8); that is,

$$n' = \phi^2 \left(\frac{\hat{\sigma}_{S/A}^2}{\hat{\sigma}_A^2} \right)$$

$$= (1.7)^2 \left(\frac{16}{2.50} \right) = (2.89)(6.40)$$

$$= 18.50$$

We have determined that a sample size of 18 or 19 (or a total of $4 \times 18 = 72$ subjects for the experiment) is associated with power $= .80$ for this particular anticipated outcome of the experiment.

PART · THREE

THE ANALYSIS OF FACTORIAL DESIGNS

In this part, we consider the design and analysis of factorial experiments, studies in which two (or more) independent variables are manipulated simultaneously. Factorial designs are economical in the sense that they provide the same information available from two single-factor experiments. Perhaps more importantly, they also provide information that cannot be derived from single-factor studies, namely, the way in which the independent variables combine to influence behavior. For this reason, factorial experiments are much more common in psychology than are single-factor experiments. They permit researchers to study behavior under conditions in which independent variables are varied simultaneously rather than one at a time, as with single-factor experiments. The research setting in factorial experiments is thus more realistic than that in single-factor studies.

In Chap. 9, we introduce the simplest form of the factorial design, in which subjects serve in only one of the treatment conditions to which they have been randomly assigned. The analysis of this design utilizes the material in Part Two and will serve as a building block for analyzing more complex designs. The main new concept introduced in this chapter — one that is unique to the factorial design — is interaction.

In Chap. 10, we indicate how the analysis of the results of a factorial experiment can be used to identify the conditions or combinations of conditions responsible for significant differences revealed by the methods presented in Chap. 9. These special analyses serve the same function for the factorial design as the analyses we covered in Chap. 6 serve for the single-factor design.

Chapter • 9

INTRODUCTION TO THE ANALYSIS OF FACTORIAL EXPERIMENTS

The experiments we have considered so far share one characteristic: they involve the manipulation of a single independent variable. Also, in each of these examples, more than two treatment conditions were included in the experiment. This feature, as we saw in Chap. 6, permitted us to answer several research questions within the context of a single experiment. Clearly, single-factor experiments can be designed to provide a great deal of useful information in the analysis of a particular problem.

However, a limit does exist on the amount of information single-factor experiments can provide. Through single-factor experiments we study the effects of independent variables *one at a time*. Therefore, by using this design we can determine a great deal about which independent variables influence the behavior, but not about what happens when two or more of these variables are permitted to vary simultaneously in a systematic fashion. Single-factor experiments represent an important first step in the analysis of a research topic, but usually researchers turn to experiments that offer a more faithful and comprehensive picture of the behavior under study. **Factorial experiments**, in which two or more independent variables are manipulated at the same time, provide the means of determining how those independent variables jointly influence the behavior under study.

9.1 THE FACTORIAL EXPERIMENT

Factorial designs are quite common in psychology. We discuss only the simplest form of the factorial design — the two-factor design — in this book, but more complicated designs are reported in the contemporary research literature. A good grounding in the design and analysis of two-factor experiments will help you understand more complex designs. As you will see, the two-variable factorial is built on the single-factor design, and much of the material already covered in this book applies directly to this design. The only new concept is that of interaction, explored in detail in a later section. By the same token, factorial designs with more than two independent variables are built on the two-variable factorial; the only complication is the increase in the number of interactions possible with more independent variables.[1]

The Advantages of Factorial Designs

Factorial designs have several distinct advantages over their single-factor counterparts. In this section, we discuss each of these advantages in turn.

Joint Manipulation of Independent Variables. The essence of the factorial design is the joint manipulation of two or more independent variables. Two advantages result from this feature of factorial designs. The first is a relative richness in the experimental setting compared with the environments in which single-factor studies are normally observed. While we should realize that experimentation cannot duplicate the constantly varying patterns of natural events associated with a particular behavior, factorial designs are a better approximation than single-factor designs. Furthermore, the factorial design permits a researcher to disentangle independent variables that are intertwined in the natural environment, and to establish the causal links between each of the variables and behavior. Thus, factorial experiments have all the virtues of the experiment discussed in Part Two, but are less artificial than single-factor studies.

Interaction. A second consequence of the joint manipulation of two independent variables is the opportunity to determine how the two independent variables *combine* to influence behavior. As you will discover, it is possible for the pattern of results we observe with one of the independent variables to change when another independent variable is included in a factorial design. When such a change occurs, we say that the two independent variables **interact**, or that an **interaction** is present.

The presence of interaction sets *qualifiers* on any description of the effects of a particular independent variable: we are not able to speak about the influence of one independent variable without also specifying how the second independent variable complicates the results. Information about how independent variables combine to influence behavior — in other words, whether they interact — is simply not attainable from single-factor experiments. Thus, the possibility of determining interaction represents a unique advantage of the factorial design. We discuss this important concept more fully in Sec. 9.2.

---

[1] You may find the following references useful for their coverage of more complex designs: Keppel (1991); Kirk (1982); Myers and Well (1991); and Winer, Brown, and Michels (1991).

The Basic Design

In the single-factor design, each treatment condition consists of a different *level* of a single independent variable or factor. In the two-variable factorial design, each treatment condition consists of a different *combination* of the levels of *two* independent variables. Note that we use a new term to refer to the treatment a particular group of subjects receives in the factorial design. Previously, we used the term *treatment conditions* to refer to the distinguishing characteristics of the different levels in a single-factor experiment. In the context of the factorial design, we use the term **treatment combinations** to stress the fact that the distinguishing characteristics of the different treatments result from the combination of two independent variables.

The Factorial Arrangement.   Consider the graphic representation of a factorial design in Fig. 9-1. One of the independent variables, factor A, consists of $a = 3$ levels (designated a_1, a_2, and a_3); the other independent variable, factor B, consists of $b = 2$ levels (designated b_1 and b_2). We usually refer to a factorial design in terms of the numbers of levels associated with the two independent variables. In this particular example, the design is called a 3×2 factorial design (read "three-by-two"). In general, we refer to the factorial design with two independent variables as an $A \times B$ factorial design (read "A-by-B").

We find the total number of treatment combinations by multiplying the number of levels associated with one factor by the number of levels associated with the other. Thus, in the example, $(a)(b) = (3)(2) = 6$ treatment combinations are obtained through the systematic pairing of the levels of the two independent variables. A factorial design, then, contains all possible combinations of the levels of one factor with the levels of the other.

Factorial designs can be distinguished by the way in which subjects are

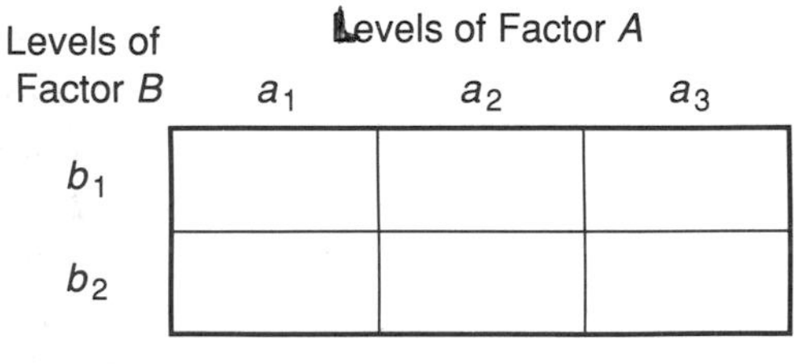

FIGURE 9-1   *An Example of a 3×2 Factorial Design.*

assigned to the various conditions of an experiment. By far the simplest design is one in which equal numbers of subjects (n) are randomly assigned to each of the $(a)(b)$ treatment combinations. This type of design, the subject of this chapter, is called the **completely randomized two-variable factorial design**. We consider other types of factorial designs in Part Four.

Each cell in Fig. 9-1 represents one of the unique treatment combinations a subject might receive. Consider the three treatment cells in the first row. All three cells are associated with the level b_1 treatment, but they differ with regard to the level of factor A with which the b_1 treatment is combined. That is, the first cell represents a treatment resulting from the combination of level a_1 with level b_1, the second cell a combination of level a_2 with level b_1, and the third cell a combination of level a_3 with level b_1. As an illustration, let's return to the example we first presented in Chap. 5 in which third-grade children solved a set of simple reasoning problems. In this experiment, factor A consisted of three conditions of verbal reinforcement, namely, praise, criticism, and silence. As a second independent variable, factor B, suppose we manipulate the *difficulty* of the problems — one level consisting of simple problems and the other level consisting of complex problems. In the first row, then, the three treatment combinations would consist of the following:

a group of subjects receiving praise (level a_1) for solving simple problems (level b_1) — the first cell

a group of subjects receiving criticism (level a_2) for solving simple problems (level b_1) — the second cell

a group of subjects receiving silence (level a_3) for solving simple problems (level b_1) — the third cell

We can enumerate the specific treatment combinations represented by the remainder of Fig. 9-1 in the same way. Briefly, the three cells in the second row are all associated with the complex problems (level b_2). Thus, from left to right, the first group receives praise for solving the complex problems, the second group receives criticism for solving the complex problems, and the third group receives silence for solving the complex problems. In total, six groups represent all possible combinations of the two independent variables. This systematic blending of the two independent variables is the defining characteristic of a factorial design.

Component Single-Factor Experiments. Consider Fig. 9-2, which represents the factorial shown in Fig. 9-1 as two **component single-factor experiments**. Each

Type of Reinforcement (Factor *A*)

a_1 (Praise) a_2 (Criticism) a_3 (Silence)

Component
Experiment b_1
(Simple Problems)

Type of Reinforcement (Factor *A*)

a_1 (Praise) a_2 (Criticism) a_3 (Silence)

Component
Experiment b_2
(Complex Problems)

FIGURE 9-2 *The Factorial Design Expressed as Two Component Single-Factor Experiments.*

experiment consists of the manipulation of the same three levels of factor *A* (reinforcement conditions). The experiments differ systematically, each being conducted in conjunction with a different level of factor *B* (problem difficulty). Thus, component experiment b_1 consists of three treatment conditions differing in the type of verbal reinforcement administered for solving problems, but all the subjects in this experiment receive the simple reasoning problems (level b_1). Component experiment b_2 consists of the same three reinforcement conditions, but in this case all the subjects receive the complex problems (level b_2).

Each of these experiments represents a perfectly acceptable study and could be conducted by itself as a single-factor design — in fact, we used component experiment b_1 as an example of a single-factor experiment in Chap. 5. Whereas such a study provided useful information about the effects of different types of verbal reinforcement on solving simple reasoning problems, it would have nothing to say about the role of problem difficulty in solving reasoning problems. Only when the two component experiments are conducted *simultaneously* in a factorial experiment can we study systematically the joint effects of these two independent variables.[2]

---

[2] We could have made the same argument by "slicing" the factorial along the *columns* rather than the *rows* of Fig. 9-1. In this case, we would obtain three component experiments, each involving a manipulation of problem difficulty (factor *B*), but each differing in the type of verbal reinforcement given to the subjects.

Examples

Factorial experiments can be created from almost any single-factor experiment. Sometimes two particular independent variables are chosen because they have been shown to be important variables in single-factor experiments and studying their combined effects in a factorial experiment seems natural. More specifically, investigators make predictions in the form of research hypotheses about how the treatment effects found with one of the independent variables will be influenced by systematic changes in the other independent variable.

You just saw one example of a reasonable factorial experiment based on an earlier single-factor experiment when we combined a second independent variable — problem difficulty — with the original independent variable (type of reinforcement). This 3 × 2 factorial experiment is presented in panel A of Fig. 9-3. As we have already noted, the children in the original study received relatively simple problems to solve. From the analyses we conducted in Chap. 6 (see Table 6-3, p. 149), we found the following pattern of results with the simple problems:

Praise produced significantly more correct solutions than did silence.

Criticism produced significantly more correct solutions than did silence.

Praise and criticism did not differ significantly.

Do you think that we would find this same pattern of results with *complex* problems if we performed the complete factorial design? Perhaps the children would become frustrated by the complex problems and respond more to praise than to criticism. On the other hand, criticism might sufficiently add to their frustration, thereby producing significantly *fewer* correct solutions than either praise or silence. Alternatively, both types of verbal reinforcement might interfere with the children's performance. If we performed this factorial experiment, we would be able to determine which of these possible outcomes is correct.

As a second example, let's suppose the original experiment was conducted entirely with *girls* as subjects. What would happen if these same conditions were administered to *boys* as well? Would the same general pattern emerge, or would important differences be found? Suppose that third-grade boys are less influenced by adult authority figures than are third-grade girls; then the boys might not be affected to the same degree by these particular manipulations. The design of this experiment is a 3 × 2 factorial and is presented in panel B of Fig. 9-3. Factor *A* consists of the three reinforcement conditions, while factor *B* consists of the gender of the children tested. The design allows us

A. Reinforcement × Problem Difficulty

	a_1 (Praise)	a_2 (Criticism)	a_3 (Silence)
b_1 (Simple)			
b_2 (Complex)			

B. Reinforcement × Gender

	a_1 (Praise)	a_2 (Criticism)	a_3 (Silence)
b_1 (Girls)			
b_2 (Boys)			

C. Reinforcement × Age

	a_1 (Praise)	a_2 (Criticism)	a_3 (Silence)
b_1 (First Grade)			
b_2 (Third Grade)			
b_3 (Fifth Grade)			
b_4 (Seventh Grade)			

FIGURE 9-3 *Three Examples of Factorial Designs.*

to determine whether the three reinforcement conditions have the same or different effects on girls and boys.

As a final example, consider what might happen if the same three reinforcement conditions (factor A) were administered to groups of children differing in age. The children in the original example were selected from the third grade. Would we expect to obtain the same pattern of results using first-grade children? Perhaps the younger children would be more influenced by the reinforcement conditions than the older ones; if so, the results would differ with younger children. Given this possibility, then, we could certainly justify a factorial experiment in which the three reinforcement conditions (factor A) were conducted with subjects of different ages (factor B). Moreover, if we suspected that a trend would show itself as a function of age, we might consider increasing the number of levels of factor B to include fifth-grade and seventh-grade children as well. The resulting 3×4 factorial is presented in panel C of Fig. 9-3.

Factorial experiments often seem to evolve from single-factor experiments, where the influence of a particular independent variable is studied in relative isolation. The results of the simpler experiment are incorporated into a theoretical explanation of some sort, and this explanation may suggest additional single-factor experiments that could yield more information on the phenomenon under study. More often than not, however, the development of a theoretical explanation will also suggest factorial manipulations, whereby a second independent variable is expected to change or to duplicate the pattern of results obtained in the original single-factor experiment. The three examples in Fig. 9-3 evolved in just this way. We expanded some features of the original study — the problem difficulty, gender, and age — to provide a second independent variable. Then, without much elaboration, we indicated how each factorial experiment combining these different independent variables with the three reinforcement conditions might change the pattern of results originally observed in the single-factor experiment. Students generally have little difficulty in proposing factorial experiments, especially once they have analyzed and interpreted the results of a single-factor study.

9.2 MAIN EFFECTS AND INTERACTION

The means of the different treatment combinations reflect the possible presence of three kinds of treatment effects. As we have noted, one possible effect is interaction, which specifically considers the joint influence of the two independent variables. The other two possible treatment effects, which are known as the **main effects** of factor A and factor B, *disregard* this joint influence. Instead, main effects comprise the separate effects of each independent variable — *averaged over the levels of the other*. We consider the nature of each of these potential sources of treatment effects in turn.

Main Effects

We will center this discussion on an example that is based on an actual series of experiments reported by Janak, Keppel, and Martinez (1992). Let's suppose a researcher is interested in the possibility that certain drugs administered some time after training will enhance memory for the training task when subjects are tested 24 hours later. The subjects are laboratory rats trained on a simple avoidance task in which they are first placed in an apparatus and then given 30 seconds to enter a distinctive adjoining chamber and avoid an electric shock. The next day the rats are tested 10 more times in the avoidance apparatus; the dependent variable consists of the number of times each animal avoids the shock over these testing trials.

The experiment is a 3×3 factorial design. One of the independent variables, *time* (factor A), consists of the time after training that different groups of rats are given an injection of some sort. More specifically, rats receive an injection either immediately (0 hours) or after a delay of 2 hours, or after a delay of 4 hours. The other independent variable, *substance* (factor B), consists of the nature of the injected substance — either an inert substance (saline) or one of two drugs (cocaine or lidocaine). The saline condition serves as a control, or baseline, condition against which the effects of the drugs can be assessed. From theory and previous research, it is expected that cocaine will lead to improved performance on day 2 whereas lidocaine (a local anesthetic) will produce little or no improvement.

Consider the results of this hypothetical 3×3 factorial experiment in Table 9-1. The means within the body of the table represent the basic outcome of the experiment — the average score for each of the $(a)(b) = (3)(3) = 9$ treatment combinations. As noted at the beginning of Sec. 9.2, the main effect of an independent variable is based on means obtained when we average the results of the experiment over the different levels of the other independent variable. We obtain the overall mean for each level of factor A (the timing of the injection) by summing the three cell means within that level (the corresponding *column* in Table 9-1) and dividing by the number of means. The

TABLE 9-1   *An Example of No Interaction*

Substance (Factor B)	Time after Training (Factor A)			Mean
	0 h (a_1)	2 h (a_2)	4 h (a_3)	
Saline (b_1)	4.5	2.5	2.0	3.0
Cocaine (b_2)	8.0	6.0	5.5	6.5
Lidocaine (b_3)	5.5	3.5	3.0	4.0
Mean	6.0	4.0	3.5	4.5

overall mean at level a_1 (the immediate condition), for example, is

$$\overline{Y}_{A_1} = \frac{4.5 + 8.0 + 5.5}{3} = \frac{18.0}{3} = 6.0$$

This mean represents the average performance of *all* the subjects in the experiment that received an injection immediately after training on the first day; the specific condition of factor B is unimportant at this point. The overall means for all three levels of factor A are presented in the final row of Table 9-1. These means are called the **column marginal means**.

We obtain the overall means for factor B (the substance in the injection) in a similar manner, namely, by summing the three cell means within each level of factor B (the *rows* in Table 9-1) and dividing by the number of means. The overall mean at level b_3 (lidocaine), for example, is

$$\overline{Y}_{B_3} = \frac{5.5 + 3.5 + 3.0}{3} = \frac{12.0}{3} = 4.0$$

This mean represents the average performance of *all* the subjects who received the lidocaine injection, disregarding the time when the injection was administered. This mean and the other two means of factor B are presented in the final column of Table 9-1. These means are called the **row marginal means**.

Main effects are based on the deviations of the marginal means from the mean of all the subjects in the experiment, that is, the grand mean ($\overline{Y}_T$). The main effects are equivalent to the information we would obtain from single-factor experiments involving the *separate manipulation* of the independent variables. For factor A and the column marginal means, for example,

The mean for all subjects injected immediately after training (level a_1) is $\overline{Y}_{A_1} = 6.0$.

The mean for all subjects injected 2 hours after training (level a_2) is $\overline{Y}_{A_2} = 4.0$.

The mean for all subjects injected 4 hours after training (level a_3) is $\overline{Y}_{A_3} = 3.5$.

In essence, these three means constitute a single-factor experiment for factor A. The only difference is that here we are creating the single-factor experiment from a factorial experiment by disregarding the treatments associated with factor B. The means show that in general the rats receiving an injection immediately after training performed best on the next day in comparison with the rats receiving injections after either 2 or 4 hours, which appeared not to differ. (We would need to conduct several analytical comparisons to substantiate these observations, of course.)

Similarly, the row marginal means (3.0, 6.5, and 4.0) represent a single-factor experiment for factor B. In this case, we create the single-factor experiment by disregarding when the injections were administered (factor A). It appears that both cocaine (6.5) and lidocaine (4.0) enhance performance on the second day, relative to the control (3.0), but that the enhancement is greater for rats injected with cocaine than with lidocaine. (Again, we would need to assess these comparisons statistically before we could make firm conclusions about the outcome of the experiment.)

So far, you have seen that we can determine the separate overall effects of the two independent variables by examining the differences within the two sets of marginal means. In a later section, you will discover that the computational formulas for the sums of squares representing the main effects of factor A and factor B are almost identical to the formulas we encounter in the analysis of an actual single-factor experiment.

Interaction

When we determine any given main effect, which represents the effects of one independent variable averaged over the levels of the other, we are essentially ignoring the effects of the second independent variable. "Main effects" have essentially the same meaning as "treatment effects" in the single-factor analysis of variance, and they are calculated in an analogous manner.

Interaction, on the other hand, is specifically concerned with the *joint effects* of the two independent variables. As we have already indicated, interaction is unique to the factorial design; it cannot be studied in single-factor experiments. Interaction is the one new concept introduced by the factorial experiment. The concept of interaction is important, because it links the two-variable factorial with designs involving three or more independent variables, and it enters into the theoretical thinking on which a great deal of contemporary psychological research is based. In an effort to illustrate this important concept clearly, we consider two sets of data, the first with no interaction and the second with a clear interaction present.

An Example of No Interaction. Besides conducting the actual statistical calculations, it is usually a good idea to plot all the treatment means obtained in a factorial experiment in a figure that permits us to appraise the joint effects of the two independent variables easily. Figure 9-4 is a pictorial representation of the means for the individual treatment combinations listed in Table 9-1. The levels of factor A (the time when the injection occurred) are designated on the horizontal axis of Fig. 9-4, and average values of the dependent variable (mean number of avoidances) are represented on the vertical axis. The means for the individual treatment combinations are plotted separately row by row for each level of the other independent variable, factor B (substance in the injection). Thus, the three levels of factor B are represented by the three solid lines in the figure.

Let us plot this information step by step. The means from the first row of the table are all associated with the saline injection (level b_1). To plot each mean graphically, we coordinate the appropriate level of factor A (represented by the horizontal axis) with the numerical value of the mean (represented by the vertical axis). As an example, the mean for the group receiving the saline injection immediately after training (level a_1) is 4.5 avoidances. We locate the mean on the graph by moving directly up from a_1 on the horizontal axis to the point directly opposite the value 4.5 on the vertical axis. We plot the mean for the group receiving the saline injection 2 hours after training (level a_2), 2.5, in the same way, directly above a_2 on the horizontal axis and directly opposite 2.5 on the vertical axis. We plot the mean for the group receiving the saline injection 4 hours after training (level a_3), 2.0, in a similar fashion, but above a_3 on the horizontal axis. We then connect the three points just plotted by straight lines and label them "saline." Next, we plot, connect, and label as "cocaine" the three means in the second row of the table (the means at level b_2) in the same manner. Finally, we plot, connect, and label as "lidocaine" the three means in the third row of the table (the means at level b_3). (For future comparison purposes, we have also plotted the main effect of factor A, obtained from the column marginal means in Table 9-1, using open circles and dashed lines to connect them.)

Each interconnected set of means depicts the results of one component single-factor experiment involving the manipulation of factor A. Three component experiments make up this factorial study, one for each level of factor B.

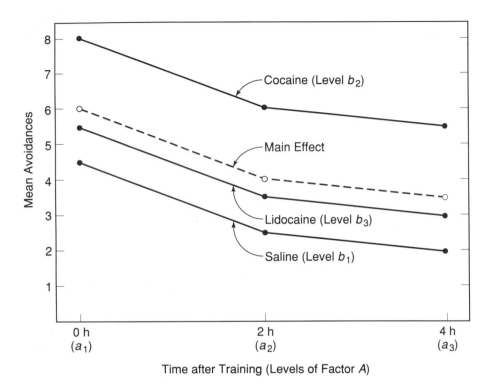

FIGURE 9-4 *An Example of No Interaction (from Table 9-1).*

The results of these component experiments are referred to by the sometimes confusing term **simple effects of factor A**.[3] Thus, the set of points labeled "saline" are called the simple effects of factor A at level b_1. Similarly, the set of points labeled "cocaine" are called the simple effects of factor A at level b_2; and so on.

It is important to distinguish between simple effects and main effects. Both terms refer to the effects of manipulating one independent variable — factor A in this case — with the other independent variable disregarded. The main effect of factor A, for example, disregards the effects of factor B by *averaging* the cell means, a procedure that removes factor B from the picture. The simple effects of factor A also disregard the effects of factor B, not by combining the levels, but by holding them *constant*. For example, the simple effect of factor

---

[3] To add to the confusion, many authors refer to simple effects as *simple main effects.*

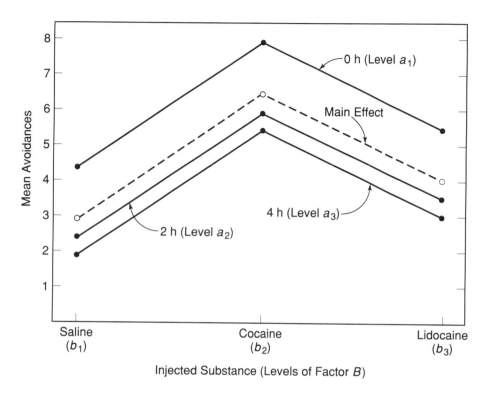

FIGURE 9-5 *An Example of No Interaction (from Table 9-1).*

A at level b_1 restricts our attention to the outcome of the experiment for the three groups of rats receiving the saline injection.

Now that we have plotted the data, we can examine the graph for interaction. The simplest procedure is to compare the three simple effects. If the simple effects show the *same pattern* of differences, no interaction is present. On the other hand, if the simple effects show *different patterns* of differences, an interaction is present. In Fig. 9-4, for example, the three simple effects of factor A have exactly the same shape — that is, they exhibit the same pattern of differences. Said another way, the three lines are *parallel* to each other. Thus, in Fig. 9-4, *no interaction* is present. The simple effects of factor A are the *same* at all levels of factor B.

We would reach exactly the same conclusion if we placed the *other* independent variable on the horizontal axis and plotted the corresponding simple effects within the body of the figure. To illustrate, we have replotted the means from Table 9-1 in Fig. 9-5, with the substance variable (factor B) on the horizontal axis. In this case, we plotted the means for each *column* separately in

TABLE 9-2 *An Example of Interaction*

| Substance (Factor B) | Time after Training (Factor A) | | | Mean |
	0 h (a_1)	2 h (a_2)	4 h (a_3)	
Saline (b_1)	3.0	3.0	3.0	3.0
Cocaine (b_2)	8.5	6.5	4.5	6.5
Lidocaine (b_3)	6.5	2.5	3.0	4.0
Mean	6.0	4.0	3.5	4.5

the graph, one set of means representing the simple effects of factor B for the subjects receiving the injection immediately (level a_1), another representing the simple effects of factor B for the subjects receiving the injection after 2 hours (level a_2), and the third representing the simple effects of factor B for the subjects receiving the injection after 4 hours (level a_3). In this alternative way of viewing the outcome of this experiment, you again can see that interaction is not present: the three curves are *parallel*, which means that the pattern of differences between the different substances injected after training is the same regardless of when the injection was administered.

An Example of Interaction. As a second example, consider a new set of data from the same hypothetical experiment presented in Table 9-2. Note that the marginal means in Table 9-2 are identical to the marginal means in the previous example (Table 9-1). Thus, the main effects for factor A and factor B are the same in the two examples. There is a big difference, however, in the means of the treatment combinations presented in the body of the table. The simple effects of factor A (the time when the injection was administered) for the data in Table 9-2 have been plotted in Fig. 9-6 in exactly the same manner as they were plotted in Fig. 9-4 for the data presented in Table 9-1. That is, the means in the first row of the table have been plotted, connected, and labeled "saline" in the figure, and this set of points represents the simple effects of factor A at b_1. The means in the other two rows have been plotted in a similar fashion; these two sets of points represent the simple effects of factor A at b_2 and at b_3.

Let us examine the differences between Fig. 9-4 and Fig. 9-6. In the first example (Fig. 9-4), all of the simple effects showed the *same* pattern of differences; in the second example (Fig. 9-6), however, the results of each component experiment show a *different* pattern of differences. This observation is clearly reflected by the fact that the three sets of interconnected points are

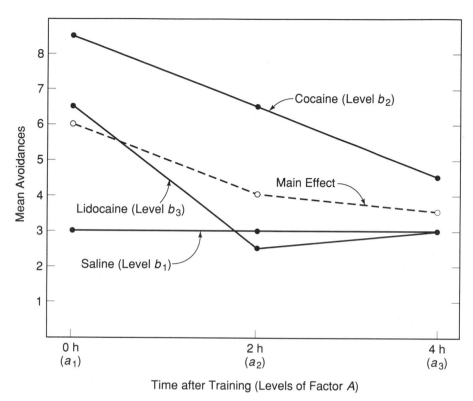

FIGURE 9-6 *An Example of Interaction (from Table 9-2).*

not parallel, as they were in the first example. This is an illustration of *interaction.* The results indicate that the effects of when the injection is administered (factor *A*) certainly depend on the particular substance administered in the injection. For the saline condition (level b_1), for example, the timing of the injection has no effect at all, while for both drug conditions, there is a progressive drop in performance with increasing delays between training and injection. Moreover, this drop in performance is much more dramatic for the animals injected with lidocaine (level b_3) than those injected with cocaine (level b_2).

Clearly, a pictorial representation is extremely useful in inspecting data for the presence of interaction. Interaction is absent when the functions depicting the simple effects are parallel; an interaction is present when the functions are not parallel. Because of the chance factors that operate in every experiment, we cannot make a definitive statement about an interaction until we have conducted the appropriate statistical analysis. Still, the opportunity to spot a potentially significant interaction simply by inspecting a plot of the means is useful.

A Definition of Interaction.   Interaction can be defined in various ways. These definitions are not really different; rather, they emphasize different aspects of the same concept. For example, we can define interaction in terms of the *independent variables*:

> **An interaction is present when the effect of one of the independent variables on the dependent variable is not the same at all levels of the second independent variable.**

Alternatively, we can define interaction a little more formally in terms of the *simple effects*:

> **An interaction is present when the simple effects of one of the independent variables are not the same at all levels of the second independent variable.**

Let's look back at Fig. 9-6 to verify that these two related definitions accurately describe the outcome of the experiment we have been discussing. Examining the simple effects one at a time, we can readily see that the effect of the timing variable (factor *A*) is not the same for the three substances — that is, there is no effect at all for saline, a progressive decline in performance for cocaine, and a sharper decline, followed by little change after 2 hours, for lidocaine.

Another way to define interaction is in terms of the *main effect* of either independent variable:

> **An interaction is present when the main effect of an independent variable is not *representative* of the simple effects of that variable.**

To illustrate this definition, refer back to Fig. 9-6 where we also plotted the main effect of factor *A*, using the column marginal means from Table 9-2. If we compare the main effect against each of the simple effects, we see that the pattern of results reflected by the column marginal means (the main effect) is quite different from the patterns observed with saline and lidocaine and slightly different from the pattern observed with cocaine, each considered separately (the simple effects). In any case, we can clearly state that the main effect is not representative of the corresponding simple effects.[4] Stated another way, any conclusions that are based on the main effects will not fully describe the

---

[4] In contrast, see how the main effect mirrors the simple effects in Fig. 9-4, where there is no interaction. In this case, the main effect *is* representative of the simple effects.

data. The presence of interaction means that the influence of each of the independent variables must be interpreted with the levels of the other one in mind. We consider the interpretation of interaction in Chap. 10.

9.3 IDENTIFYING BASIC DEVIATIONS

Central to an understanding of the analysis of variance is the systematic subdivision of the total sum of squares — based on the deviation of each individual score from the grand mean $(Y - \overline{Y}_T)$ — into a number of component sums of squares. The factorial design is more complicated than the single-factor design, and this complexity is reflected in the fact that the total sum of squares is divided into *four* components, rather than the *two* isolated in the single-factor experiment. We can elucidate the logic of this division more easily if we treat it as a series of steps. We start by calculating the means.

Calculating the Means

The factorial design yields four sets of means, each representing a different aspect of the data: the interaction (the means for the treatment combinations), the two main effects (the two sets of marginal means), and the grand mean. We will illustrate the calculation of these means with a very simple example, namely, a 2×2 design with $n = 2$ subjects randomly assigned to each of the $(a)(b) = (2)(2) = 4$ treatment combinations. The design is depicted in the top part of Table 9-3. A data matrix for this example is given in the next part of the table, where we have identified the two Y scores for each of the four groups. The special notation we have included in the data matrix allows us to identify specific individuals and information about the treatment groups.

Starting with the data matrix, consider the subscripts assigned to each Y score. The first two subscripts identify the relevant levels of factors A and B, whereas the third subscript specifies this score for an individual subject within any given column uniquely. The nature of each treatment combination is specified by a blending of the appropriate levels of the two factors. The first treatment combination, $a_1 b_1$, refers to the group of subjects that receives level a_1 in combination with level b_1; the second, $a_1 b_2$, refers to the group of subjects that receives level a_1 in combination with level b_2; and so on. We need to add up the Y scores in each group to calculate the group means. Each group sum

TABLE 9-3 *Notation for the Two-Factor Design*

Experimental Design

Factor A

Factor B	a_1	a_2
b_1		
b_2		

Data Matrix

	$a_1 b_1$	$a_1 b_2$	$a_2 b_1$	$a_2 b_2$
	$Y_{1,1,1}$	$Y_{1,2,1}$	$Y_{2,1,1}$	$Y_{2,2,1}$
	$Y_{1,1,2}$	$Y_{1,2,2}$	$Y_{2,1,2}$	$Y_{2,2,2}$
Sum:	$AB_{1,1}$	$AB_{1,2}$	$AB_{2,1}$	$AB_{2,2}$

AB Matrix

Levels of Factor B	Levels of Factor A			Marginal Sum
	a_1		a_2	
b_1	$AB_{1,1}$	$+$	$AB_{2,1}$	$\rightarrow$ B_1
	$+$		$+$	$+$
b_2	$AB_{1,2}$	$+$	$AB_{2,2}$	$\rightarrow$ B_2
	$\downarrow$		$\downarrow$	$\downarrow$
Marginal Sum	A_1	$+$	A_2	$\rightarrow$ T

is designated by the capital letters AB and subscripts that identify the treatment combination. For example, $AB_{1,1}$ is the sum for the treatment combination $a_1 b_1$. We calculate the corresponding means by dividing each sum by n, the sample size. The mean for this group is designated as $\overline{Y}_{A_1 B_1}$, with the subscripts again clearly indicating the nature of the treatment combination.

The other sets of means are based on different combinations of groups, as you saw in Sec. 9.2 — means reflecting the A main effect $(\overline{Y}_A)$, the B main effect $(\overline{Y}_B)$, and the grand mean $(\overline{Y}_T)$. An easy way to calculate these means and to set the stage for the analysis of variance is to arrange the AB treatment sums in what we will call an **AB matrix,** which is presented in the bottom part of Table 9-3. The basic entries within the body of this matrix (often called the *cells* of the matrix) are the AB sums we obtained from the data matrix. The plus signs and arrows in the AB matrix indicate the systematic way in which the AB sums are added to produce row and column marginal totals. Three sets of sums are produced by these operations. One set consists of the A sums, which we obtain by summing across the levels of factor B, that is, by adding the AB sums in each *column* of the matrix. The two A sums — A_1 for level a_1 and A_2 for level a_2 — are indicated as column marginal totals in the table. A second set of sums consists of the B sums, which are obtained by summing across the levels of factor A, that is, by adding the AB sums in each *row* of the matrix. The two B sums, B_1 for level b_1 and B_2 for level b_2, are shown as row marginal totals in the table. The final sum is the grand total (T), which we obtain from the AB matrix by adding together either set of marginal totals, as indicated in the table. (It is a good idea to sum both sets of marginal totals for a simple check of your calculations.)

We can now convert the various treatment sums in the AB matrix into corresponding means, simply by dividing each sum by the appropriate number of observations. That is,

$$\overline{Y}_{AB} = \frac{AB}{n}, \quad \overline{Y}_A = \frac{A}{(b)(n)}, \quad \overline{Y}_B = \frac{B}{(a)(n)}, \quad \text{and} \quad \overline{Y}_T = \frac{T}{(a)(b)(n)}$$

A numerical example is presented in Table 9-4 to illustrate the nature of the quantities appearing in the data matrix and the AB matrix. We have kept the calculations simple so that you can determine easily whether you understand the summing operations symbolized by the notational system. You will soon be using these procedures to calculate sums of squares for the analysis of variance.

Initial Division of the Total Deviation ($Y - \overline{Y}_T$)

As explained in Chap. 4 for the single-factor design, the deviation of a Y score from the grand mean (the *total deviation*) can be divided into two components: the deviation of the treatment mean from the grand mean (the *between-groups deviation*) and the deviation of the Y score from its treatment mean (the *within-group deviation*). We can state the relationship generally as follows:

$$\begin{array}{ccccc} \text{total deviation} & = & \text{between-groups deviation} & + & \text{within-group deviation} \\ Y_{ij} - \overline{Y}_T & = & (\overline{Y}_{A_i} - \overline{Y}_T) & + & (Y_{ij} - \overline{Y}_{A_i}) \end{array}$$

TABLE 9-4 *An Example of the Data Matrix and the AB Matrix*

Data Matrix

	Treatment Combinations			
	$a_1 b_1$	$a_1 b_2$	$a_2 b_1$	$a_2 b_2$
	2	8	9	3
	5	6	6	1
Sum:	7	14	15	4

AB Matrix

	Factor A		
Factor B	a_1	a_2	Sum
b_1	7	15	22
b_2	14	4	18
Sum	21	19	40

Let's now turn to the factorial design. To begin extracting deviations for this design, it is convenient to think of the factorial initially as a single-factor experiment, with the "treatments" consisting of the $(a)(b)$ treatment combinations rather than the A treatment conditions in an actual single-factor design. If we do this, we can extend the analysis of deviations summarized in the last paragraph to the factorial. That is, we can divide the deviation of each Y score from the grand mean in the factorial design into a between-groups deviation and a within-group deviation. Specifically,

$$\text{total deviation} = \text{between-groups deviation} + \text{within-group deviation}$$
$$Y_{ijk} - \overline{Y}_T = (\overline{Y}_{AB_{ij}} - \overline{Y}_T) + (Y_{ijk} - \overline{Y}_{AB_{ij}})$$

The only difference between these two subdivisions is the addition of "B," which is needed to reflect the factorial design.

Applying the logic presented in Chap. 4 for the single-factor experiment, we can say that a sum of squares based on the between-groups deviations is influenced by two factors, a "treatment effect" and experimental error; and that a sum of squares based on the within-group deviations is influenced only by experimental error. The sum of squares based on this latter division is designated S/AB to reflect the fact that it represents the variability of subjects within each of the $(a)(b)$ treatment combinations. While the within-groups sum of squares $(SS_{S/AB})$ will prove to be useful in the analysis of variance, the between-groups sum of squares will not. The reason is that this particular "treatment effect" is not an informative quantity, because any differences between the treatment combinations may be the result of three different theoretical quantities, namely,

a main effect of factor A
a main effect of factor B
an interaction of the two factors

To be useful, therefore, the between-groups deviation must be divided further into these more meaningful components.

Further Division of the Between-Groups Deviation ($\overline{Y}_{AB} - \overline{Y}_T$)

To reiterate, the between-groups deviation contains three meaningful components, the main effects of factor A, and factor B, and interaction. The two main effects are easily expressed as deviations from the grand mean:

$$A \text{ main effect} = \overline{Y}_{A_i} - \overline{Y}_T \tag{9-1}$$

$$B \text{ main effect} = \overline{Y}_{B_j} - \overline{Y}_T \tag{9-2}$$

The interaction effect is a bit more complicated, but involves familiar quantities nevertheless:

$$\text{interaction effect} = \overline{Y}_{AB_{ij}} - \overline{Y}_{A_i} - \overline{Y}_{B_j} + \overline{Y}_T \tag{9-3}$$

This somewhat puzzling expression is the result of some simple algebraic manipulation in which we redefine the interaction effect as a *residual* deviation. That is, we start with the following expression:

$$\text{between-groups deviation} = A \text{ main effect} + B \text{ main effect}$$
$$+ \text{ interaction effect}$$

Next, with a little algebraic manipulation, we can express the interaction effect as

$$\text{interaction effect} = \text{between-groups deviation} - A \text{ main effect}$$
$$- B \text{ main effect}$$

which redefines interaction as a residual effect. That is, the interaction effect represents whatever is left of the between-groups deviation once we have subtracted the two main effects. If we now substitute deviations for the three quantities specified on the right side of the equation, we obtain

$$\text{interaction effect} = (\overline{Y}_{AB_{ij}} - \overline{Y}_T) - (\overline{Y}_{A_i} - \overline{Y}_T) - (\overline{Y}_{B_j} - \overline{Y}_T)$$

Removing the parentheses gives us

$$\text{interaction effect} = \overline{Y}_{AB_{ij}} - \overline{Y}_T - \overline{Y}_{A_i} + \overline{Y}_T - \overline{Y}_{B_j} + \overline{Y}_T$$

If we delete the first two grand means $(\overline{Y}_T)$ (since they cancel each other) we find

$$\text{interaction effect} = \overline{Y}_{AB_{ij}} - \overline{Y}_{A_i} - \overline{Y}_{B_j} + \overline{Y}_T$$

which is identical to Eq. (9-3).

Summary. We can now combine the two steps in the subdivision of the total deviation. More specifically,

$$Y_{ijk} - \overline{Y}_T = (\overline{Y}_{A_i} - \overline{Y}_T) + (\overline{Y}_{B_j} - \overline{Y}_T)$$
$$+ (\overline{Y}_{AB_{ij}} - \overline{Y}_{A_i} - \overline{Y}_{B_j} + \overline{Y}_T)$$
$$+ (Y_{ijk} - \overline{Y}_{AB_{ij}}) \tag{9-4}$$

In words, the deviation of a subject from the grand mean can be broken down into four separate components:

1. The main effect at level a_i
2. The main effect at level b_j
3. The interaction effect at the combination of levels a_i and b_j
4. The effect of random error: the deviation of the subject from the appropriate treatment mean

These components and the steps we followed in dividing the total deviation are summarized in Table 9-5. Starting at the top, we first divided the total deviation into two parts, the between-groups deviation and the within-group deviation. We then further divided the between-groups deviation into its component parts: the main effect of factor A, the main effect of factor B, and the interaction effect. Each of these components reflects a different and useful aspect of the results. All that remains is to derive the computational formulas with which these component deviations will be transformed into sums of squares for the analysis of variance.

TABLE 9-5 *Dividing the Total Deviation into Component Deviations*

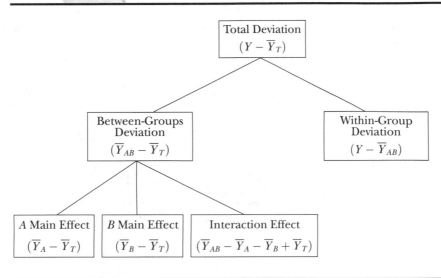

9.4 THE ANALYSIS OF VARIANCE

The next step in the process would be to calculate the various sums of squares, but we will delay this discussion until Sec. 9.5. In this section, we will outline the remaining steps in the analysis so that you can understand the total process in a general sense, before attending to the computational details.

Sums of Squares

The deviations specified in Eq. (9-4) could be applied to each individual subject in the experiment. We could calculate the necessary sums of squares for the analysis simply by squaring these deviations and summing them. Instead, we will calculate the sums of squares with relatively simple computational formulas, which we will present in Sec. 9.5. For the time being, let's assume that we have obtained each of the sums of squares and are ready to complete the analysis.

Degrees of Freedom

The computational formulas specifying the degrees of freedom associated with the different sources of variance obtained in the analysis of the factorial design of variability

TABLE 9-6 *Two-Factor Analysis of Variance*

Source	SS^a	df	MS	F
A	SS_A	$a - 1$	$\dfrac{SS_A}{df_A}$	$\dfrac{MS_A}{MS_{S/AB}}$
B	SS_B	$b - 1$	$\dfrac{SS_B}{df_B}$	$\dfrac{MS_B}{MS_{S/AB}}$
A × B	$SS_{A \times B}$	$(a-1)(b-1)$	$\dfrac{SS_{A \times B}}{df_{A \times B}}$	$\dfrac{MS_{A \times B}}{MS_{S/AB}}$
S/AB (error)	$SS_{S/AB}$	$(a)(b)(n-1)$	$\dfrac{SS_{S/AB}}{df_{S/AB}}$	
Total	SS_T	$(a)(b)(n) - 1$		

interaction (left margin annotation for A × B)

of variance (left margin annotation for Total)

a Computational formulas for the sums of squares are found in Table 9-9.

are placed under *df* in Table 9-6. As we have pointed out before, the number of degrees of freedom associated with any mean square is equal to the number of observations on which the mean square is based minus the number of population estimates required in the process. The degrees of freedom statements for the two main effects (A and B) and for the total source of variability represent straightforward applications of this rule. That is,

$$df_A = a - 1, \quad df_B = b - 1, \quad \text{and} \quad df_T = (a)(b)(n) - 1$$

In addition, the degrees of freedom for the within-groups source (S/AB) conform to this rule in the same way as did the within-groups source in the single-factor experiment (see p. 99). More specifically, we start by specifying the *df* associated with the variability of the *Y* scores within any one of the treatment combinations, namely,

$$df = n - 1$$

The sum of squares for the within-groups source, $SS_{S/AB}$, is actually a composite of the separate sums of squares for the individual treatment groups. As a consequence, the degrees of freedom for the within-groups source, $df_{S/AB}$, is the corresponding composite of the separate degrees of freedom. That is,

$$df_{S/AB} = (n - 1) + (n - 1) + (n - 1) + \cdots$$

Because there are $(a)(b)$ treatment combinations, we can represent this composite more simply as

$$df_{S/AB} = (a)(b)(n - 1) \tag{9-5}$$

The degrees of freedom for the interaction source $(A \times B)$ are the product of the degrees of freedom associated with the two sources represented in this interaction. More specifically,

$$df_{A \times B} = (a - 1)(b - 1) \qquad (9\text{-}6)$$

We will not describe the logic behind the calculation of the degrees of freedom for this particular source, but you can be sure that the general rule for calculating degrees of freedom holds in this case even if its application is not immediately obvious.[5]

Mean Squares and *F* Ratios

The mean squares required for the analysis are designated under *MS* in Table 9-6. All mean squares are calculated by dividing the sum of squares by the appropriate number of degrees of freedom.

Three *F* ratios are obtained from this analysis, one for each of the two main effects and the other for the $A \times B$ interaction. Each ratio is formed by dividing the appropriate mean square by the within-groups mean square, $MS_{S/AB}$.

Hypothesis Testing

Statistical Hypotheses. Our evaluation of the significance of each of the three factorial tests — the two main effects and the interaction — follows the same pattern as that of the treatment effects in the single-factor design. First, we form three sets of statistical hypotheses. Each set follows the same pattern, namely, the null hypothesis (H_0) specifies the absence of any effect, whereas the alternative hypothesis (H_1) specifies that an effect is present. To illustrate, for the main effect of factor *A*,

$$H_0 : \quad \text{all } \mu_i\text{'s are equal}$$

$$H_1 : \quad \text{not all } \mu_i\text{'s are equal}$$

---

[5] See Keppel (1991, pp. 212–213) for an explanation of Eq. (9-6).

The μ_i's refer to the A population treatment means, which are defined by averaging the population means for the treatment combinations over the levels of factor B. We form a similar set of hypotheses for the main effect of factor B:

$$H_0 : \quad \text{all } \mu_j\text{'s are equal}$$

$$H_1 : \quad \text{not all } \mu_j\text{'s are equal}$$

The μ_j's refer to the B population treatment means, which are defined by averaging the population means for the treatment combinations over the levels of factor A. The statistical hypotheses for the $A \times B$ interaction can be expressed as follows:

$$H_0 : \quad \text{interaction effects are completely absent}$$

$$H_1 : \quad \text{some interaction effects are present}$$

Evaluating the Null Hypotheses. Each source of variance in which we are theoretically interested — A, B, and $A \times B$ — is assumed to reflect the possible presence of two components: (1) main effects or interaction effects and (2) experimental error. Each of the null hypotheses specifies the complete absence of main effects or interaction effects in the population. When the null hypothesis is true, the first component will equal zero, leaving only variation due to experimental error. On the other hand, when the null hypothesis is false (and the alternative hypothesis is true), the first component becomes relevant. In this case, the mean square under consideration is now influenced both by systematic effects, in the form of main effects or interaction, and by experimental error, which is present no matter which statistical hypothesis is correct.

The within-groups mean square, $MS_{S/AB}$, is based on the variability of subjects treated alike — in this factorial design, subjects that are given the same treatment combination. Consequently, any variation measured with this mean square represents the degree of experimental error present in the experiment.

The three F ratios specified in Table 9-6 are used to test the three null hypotheses. If the null hypothesis is true in any one of these tests, the numerator mean square reflects experimental error, as does the denominator mean square, and the value of F is expected to be approximately 1.0. If the null hypothesis is false, the numerator mean square will be systematically larger than the error term, and the value of the F ratio is expected to be greater than 1.0. We will now use information derived from the F distribution to form decision rules specifying the circumstances under which we will reject the null hypothesis.

Decision Rules. We need to form different decision rules for each of the null hypotheses under consideration, but we can obtain them all from the following statement:

If the obtained value of $F \geq F(df_{effect}, df_{S/AB})$, reject the null hypothesis; otherwise, retain the null hypothesis.

To find the critical value of F for any one of the factorial effects, we substitute the appropriate degrees of freedom for the numerator term (df_{effect}) and the denominator term ($df_{S/AB}$), enter the F table, and locate the value of F listed at the particular significance level we have chosen for our research. We will illustrate the formulation of the decision rules in the numerical example presented in Sec. 9.6.

9.5 CALCULATING SUMS OF SQUARES

The computational formulas for the necessary sums of squares follow a familiar pattern. We start with *basic ratios* that perform the same set of operations (squaring, summing, and dividing) either on the individual Y scores or on sums obtained from them. We calculate the sums of squares by adding and subtracting these ratios in the patterns indicated by the various sets of deviations specified in Eq. (9-4).

Basic Ratios

The basic ratios formed in the calculation of sums of squares all have the following form:

$$\frac{\Sigma \, (\text{score or sum})^2}{\text{divisor}} \tag{9-7}$$

With reference to Table 9-3 (p. 246), the "scores" specified in Eq. (9-7) are the individual Y observations found in the data matrix, and the "sums" are the different totals and subtotals found in the AB matrix. The application of Eq. (9-7) to each of these quantities is specified systematically in Table 9-7. Since these arithmetical operations should be familiar by now, we comment on them only briefly.

1. Basic Score or Sum (from the Appropriate Matrix)	2. Squaring	3. Summing (if relevant)	4. Dividing (if required)	5. Coding
Y_{ijk}	Y_{ijk}^2	ΣY^2	ΣY^2	$[Y]$
AB_{ij}	$(AB_{ij})^2$	$\Sigma (AB)^2$	$\dfrac{\Sigma (AB)^2}{n}$	$[AB]$
A_i	A_i^2	ΣA^2	$\dfrac{\Sigma A^2}{(b)(n)}$	$[A]$
B_j	B_j^2	ΣB^2	$\dfrac{\Sigma B^2}{(a)(n)}$	$[B]$
T	T^2	T^2	$\dfrac{T^2}{(a)(b)(n)}$	$[T]$

TABLE 9-7 *The Arithmetical Operations Performed on Scores or Sums*

All the calculations begin with the quantities listed in column 1 of Table 9-7, namely, Y_{ijk}, AB_{ij}, A_i, B_j, and T. In the next three columns, the arithmetical operations specified by Eq. (9-7) are performed on each set of scores or sums. As you can see, the same three steps are performed on each of the quantities. That is, each score or sum is first *squared* (column 2), then *summed* if there is more than one squared quantity in the set (column 3), and finally *divided* to form the various basic ratios needed for the calculation of the sums of squares (column 4). The divisor for each basic ratio is specified by the following rule:

Whenever you square a total for the numerator, you will divide by the number of scores that went into the total.

To elaborate, the AB sums are based on n observations, the A sums are based on $(b)(n)$ observations, the B sums are based on $(a)(n)$ observations, and the grand sum (T) is based on $(a)(b)(n)$ observations. The Y scores require no division, of course, because they are each based on one observation. As you can see, then, the calculations are no more complicated than those we performed in the analysis of single-factor experiments. Each ratio is appropriately coded in column 5 to simplify the specification of the computational formulas for the sums of squares.

To illustrate these calculations in as simple a manner as possible, in Table 9-8 we have performed each step in the calculation of the ratios with the data matrix appearing in Table 9-4 (p. 248) — a simple example consisting of a 2×2 factorial with $n = 2$ subjects assigned to each of the four treatment

		TABLE 9-8 *An Example of the Calculation of the Basic Ratios*[a]		
1. Basic Score or Sum	2. Squaring	3. Summing	4. Dividing	5. Coding
$Y_{ijk}:$ 2 8 9 3 5 6 6 1	4 64 81 9 25 36 36 1	256	256	$[Y]$
$AB_{ij}:$ 7 15 14 4	49 225 196 16	486	$\dfrac{486}{2} = 243.00$	$[AB]$
$A_i:$ 21 19	441 361	802	$\dfrac{802}{(2)(2)} = 200.50$	$[A]$
$B_j:$ 22 18	484 324	808	$\dfrac{808}{(2)(2)} = 202.00$	$[B]$
$T:$ 40	1,600	1,600	$\dfrac{1,600}{(2)(2)(2)} = 200.00$	$[T]$

[a] See Table 9-4 (p. 248) for the source of the data.

combinations. Column 1 lists the actual quantities on which each basic ratio is based. More explicitly, the first row gives the individual scores for each of the four treatment combinations. The second row specifies the four AB sums obtained from the data matrix; we have listed the sums in the same arrangement in which they appeared in the body of the AB matrix in Table 9-4. The third row gives the two A sums, while the fourth row gives the two B sums; again they are arranged in the same pattern in which they appeared as marginal totals in Table 9-4. Finally, the last row gives the grand sum of all the scores. The results of each series of calculation steps — squaring, summing, and dividing — are presented in the remaining columns of Table 9-8. Be sure to follow each step in the table until you are certain that you know where the basic scores and sums come from and how they enter into the determination of the basic ratios used in this particular analysis of variance. In Sec. 9.6, we consider a more comprehensive example, but the steps followed there are no more complicated conceptually than those illustrated in Table 9-8.

Sums of Squares

The particular patterns in which the basic ratios are combined to produce the sums of squares are indicated by the deviations specified in Eq. (9-4). For convenience, we have presented each of these deviations again in column 2 of Table 9-9. The computational formulas for the different sums of squares, which are obviously based on the relevant set of deviations, are presented in

TABLE 9-9 *The Computational Formulas for the Sums of Squares*

1. Source	2. Basic Deviation	3. Computational Formula[a]
A	$\overline{Y}_{A_i} - \overline{Y}_T$	$[A] - [T]$
B	$\overline{Y}_{B_j} - \overline{Y}_T$	$[B] - [T]$
$A \times B$	$\overline{Y}_{A_iB_j} - \overline{Y}_{A_i} - \overline{Y}_{B_j} + \overline{Y}_T$	$[AB] - [A] - [B] + [T]$
S/AB	$Y_{ijk} - \overline{Y}_{A_iB_j}$	$[Y] - [AB]$
Total	$Y_{ijk} - \overline{Y}_T$	$[Y] - [T]$

[a] $[A] = \dfrac{\Sigma A^2}{(b)(n)}, [T] = \dfrac{T^2}{(a)(b)(n)}, [B] = \dfrac{\Sigma B^2}{(a)(n)}, [AB] = \dfrac{\Sigma(AB)^2}{n}$, and $[Y] = \Sigma Y^2$.

coded form in column 3 of the table. The first four rows of the table designate the component sources of variability we normally extract from this particular factorial design; the last row designates the total amount of variation reflected in the results of an experiment.

We illustrate the use of these computational formulas with the preliminary calculations presented in column 4 of Table 9-8. Specifically,

$$SS_A = [A] - [T]$$

$$= 200.50 - 200.00$$

$$= .50$$

$$SS_B = [B] - [T]$$

$$= 202.00 - 200.00$$

$$= 2.00$$

$$SS_{A \times B} = [AB] - [A] - [B] + [T]$$

$$= 243.00 - 200.50 - 202.00 + 200.00$$

$$= 40.50$$

$$SS_{S/AB} = [Y] - [AB]$$

$$= 256 - 243.00$$

$$= 13.00$$

$$SS_T = [Y] - [T]$$

$$= 256 - 200.00$$

$$= 56.00$$

As a check on the calculations, we verify that the sum of the component sums of squares equals the total sum of squares. That is,

$$SS_T = SS_A + SS_B + SS_{A \times B} + SS_{S/AB} \tag{9-8}$$

$$56.00 = .50 + 2.00 + 40.50 + 13.00$$

$$= 56.00$$

Rather than complete the analysis of variance with this simplified data set, we will illustrate the entire ANOVA with a more comprehensive example, which follows.

9.6 A NUMERICAL EXAMPLE

The Experiment

We began this chapter by describing a factorial experiment in which factor A consisted of three different types of verbal reinforcement (praise, criticism, and silence) and factor B consisted of two levels of problem difficulty (simple or complex). The subjects were third-grade children. At that time, we considered a number of different ways the experiment might turn out. We know from the original experiment, presented in Chap. 5 as a single-factor experiment involving the three reinforcement conditions and simple problems, that whereas both praise and criticism resulted in more correct solutions than did silence, the two conditions did not differ significantly. The present example allows us to determine if we would find this same pattern of results with *complex* problems.

The design, then, is a 3×2 factorial producing a total of $(a)(b) = (3)(2) = 6$ treatment combinations, which consist of the following:

	Praise (a_1)	Criticism (a_2)	Silence (a_3)
Simple (b_1)	Praise-Simple	Criticism-Simple	Silence-Simple
Complex (b_2)	Praise-Complex	Criticism-Complex	Silence-Complex

Sample size for this example is $n = 5$. Thus, the total number of children tested in the experiment is $(a)(b)(n) = (3)(2)(5) = 30$.

Preliminary Analysis

The numbers of reasoning problems the individual children solved correctly are presented in Table 9-10. The scores for the children receiving simple problems (level b_1) are shown in the first three columns, while the scores for the children receiving the complex problems (level b_2) are in the last three columns. The particular reinforcement conditions are indicated at the top of each column of Y scores. We will first conduct some preliminary analyses of these data to provide us with the totals we will need for calculating the sums of squares and with useful summary statistics, namely, the means and the standard deviations for the different groups.

TABLE 9-10 *Numerical Example: Data Matrix and Preliminary Analyses*

	Praise Simple a_1b_1	Criticism Simple a_2b_1	Silence Simple a_3b_1	Praise Complex a_1b_2	Criticism Complex a_2b_2	Silence Complex a_3b_2
	7	9	2	6	4	1
	8	4	7	5	3	3
	6	6	5	6	0	6
	10	9	3	10	1	2
	7	8	5	8	2	4
1. AB_{ij}:	38	36	22	35	10	16
2. ΣY_{ijk}^2:	298	278	112	261	30	66
3. $\overline{Y}_{A_iB_j}$:	7.60	7.20	4.40	7.00	2.00	3.20
4. s_{ij}:	1.52	2.17	1.95	2.00	1.58	1.92

Calculating the Means and Standard Deviations. The first step in the analysis of any set of data is to calculate the sum of each group of scores (the *AB* sums) and the sum of the squares of these scores $(\Sigma\, Y^2)$. These two sets of sums are given in rows 1 and 2 at the bottom of the data matrix. From this information, we can calculate the means and standard deviations for the six treatment combinations. We will use the data from the group at $a_1 b_2$ (praise-complex) to illustrate the calculation of the mean $(\overline{Y}_{A_1 B_2})$ and the standard deviation $(s_{1,2})$. More specifically,

$$\overline{Y}_{A_1 B_2} = \frac{AB_{1,2}}{n} = \frac{35}{5} = 7.00$$

$$s_{1,2} = \sqrt{\frac{\Sigma(Y_{1,2,k} - \overline{Y}_{A_1 B_2})^2}{n-1}}$$

$$= \sqrt{\frac{(6-7)^2 + (5-7)^2 + (6-7)^2 + (10-7)^2 + (8-7)^2}{5-1}}$$

$$= \sqrt{\frac{(-1)^2 + (-2)^2 + (-1)^2 + (3)^2 + (1)^2}{4}} = \sqrt{\frac{16}{4}} = \sqrt{4}$$

$$= 2.00$$

As we demonstrated in Chap. 5 for the single-factor design, we can calculate the standard deviation with less computational effort by using a formula based on the Y scores and the group sum:

$$s_{1,2} = \sqrt{\frac{\Sigma Y_{1,2,k}^2 - \dfrac{(AB_{1,2})^2}{n}}{n-1}}$$

$$= \sqrt{\frac{261 - \dfrac{(35)^2}{5}}{5-1}}$$

$$= \sqrt{\frac{261 - 245}{4}} = \sqrt{\frac{16}{4}} = \sqrt{4}$$

$$= 2.00$$

The means and standard deviations for all of the treatment groups are presented in the last two rows of Table 9-10.

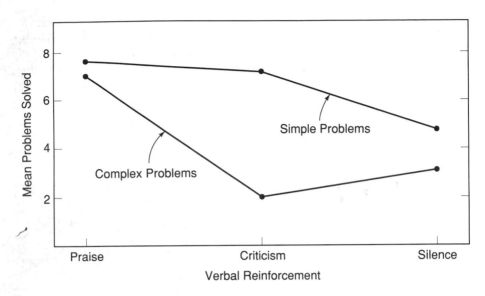

FIGURE 9-7 *Mean Number of Problems Solved as a Function of Verbal Reinforcement and Problem Difficulty (from Table 9-11).*

TABLE 9-11 *Table of Means*				
	Verbal Reinforcement			
Problem Type	Praise (a_1)	Criticism (a_2)	Silence (a_3)	Average
Simple (b_1)	7.60	7.20	4.40	6.40
Complex (b_2)	7.00	2.00	3.20	4.07
Average	7.30	4.60	3.80	—

Tabular and Pictorial Representation.   A convenient way of studying the outcome of a factorial experiment is through a table of means, such as Table 9-11. In this table, we can examine the main effects (the column and row marginal means) and the simple effects (the means in the body of the table) together. It is usually a good idea to plot the means for the treatment combinations for a visual check of the data. To illustrate, we have plotted the means in Fig. 9-7, marking off the reinforcement conditions on the horizontal axis and the response measure on the vertical axis.[6] The potential presence of the interaction is apparent at a glance.

What we see with our eyes, either as a set of treatment means in a table or as a plot of these means in a figure, must be assessed statistically. Main effects and interactions must represent variation that cannot be reasonably accounted for by the operation of experimental error. We now turn to the steps that lead to the analysis of variance.

Sums of Squares

Calculating the Basic Ratios.   The first step in determining the sums of squares is calculating the basic ratios specified in Table 9-7 (p. 256). The first basic ratio listed in Table 9-7 consists of the sum of the squared Y scores, which we can obtain by summing the subtotals in row 2 of Table 9-10. That is,

$$[Y] = \Sigma \, Y^2$$

$$= 298 + 278 + 112 + 261 + 30 + 66$$

$$= 1,045$$

Next, we enter the AB treatment sums from Table 9-10 into the body of an AB matrix, which we have done in Table 9-12. We now can conveniently calculate the remaining basic ratios with the various totals and subtotals in this matrix.

---

[6] We have spaced the three reinforcement conditions equally on the horizontal axis, and connected the three means within the two sets of problems. Technically, this plot of the data is appropriate only for *quantitative* independent variables, where the spacing between successive levels of the variable has a physical or psychological scale of reference. The appropriate way to represent the data is in the form of a *bar graph* (see Chap. 2, pp. 48–50). However, since our intent is to provide a visual check for interaction, and since no one is really confused or misled by the "liberties" taken in this means of plotting the data, we recommend that you use this device in mulling over your data. A bar graph simply does not serve this function well.

TABLE 9-12	*AB Matrix*			
	Praise (a_1)	Criticism (a_2)	Silence (a_3)	Sum
Simple (b_1)	38	36	22	96
Complex (b_2)	35	10	16	61
Sum	73	46	38	157

Substituting in the formulas specified in column 4 of Table 9-7, we find

$$[AB] = \frac{\Sigma(AB)^2}{n}$$

$$= \frac{(38)^2 + (36)^2 + (22)^2 + (35)^2 + (10)^2 + (16)^2}{5}$$

$$= \frac{1{,}444 + 1{,}296 + 484 + 1{,}225 + 100 + 256}{5} = \frac{4{,}805}{5}$$

$$= 961.00$$

$$[A] = \frac{\Sigma A^2}{(b)(n)}$$

$$= \frac{(73)^2 + (46)^2 + (38)^2}{(2)(5)} = \frac{8{,}889}{10}$$

$$= 888.90$$

$$[B] = \frac{\Sigma B^2}{(a)(n)}$$

$$= \frac{(96)^2 + (61)^2}{(3)(5)} = \frac{12{,}937}{15}$$

$$= 862.47$$

$$[T] = \frac{T^2}{(a)(b)(n)}$$

$$= \frac{(157)^2}{(3)(2)(5)} = \frac{24,649}{30}$$

$$= 821.63$$

Calculating the Sums of Squares. Next, we add and subtract the results of these calculations in the patterns specified in Table 9-9 (p. 258) to obtain the required sums of squares. Using the values for the basic ratios we have just calculated, we find the following results:

$$SS_A = [A] - [T]$$

$$= 888.90 - 821.63$$

$$= 67.27$$

$$SS_B = [B] - [T]$$

$$= 862.47 - 821.63$$

$$= 40.84$$

$$SS_{A \times B} = [AB] - [A] - [B] + [T]$$

$$= 961.00 - 888.90 - 862.47 + 821.63$$

$$= 31.26$$

$$SS_{S/AB} = [Y] - [AB]$$

$$= 1,045 - 961.00$$

$$= 84.00$$

$$SS_T = [Y] - [T]$$

$$= 1,045 - 821.63$$

$$= 223.37$$

Source	SS	df	MS	F
TABLE 9-13 *Summary of the Analysis*				
A (Reinforcement)	67.27	2	33.64	9.61*
B (Problem Type)	40.84	1	40.84	11.67*
$A \times B$	31.26	2	15.63	4.47*
S/AB	84.00	24	3.50	
Total	223.37	29		

* $p < .05.$

The values for these sums of squares are entered in a summary table (Table 9-13). As a check on the calculations, we should verify that the component sums of squares add up to the total sum of squares. That is,

$$SS_T = SS_A + SS_B + SS_{A \times B} + SS_{S/AB}$$

$$223.37 = 67.27 + 40.84 + 31.26 + 84.00$$

$$= 223.37$$

Final Calculations

Degrees of Freedom. The formulas for determining the degrees of freedom associated with the different sums of squares are presented in Table 9-6 (p. 252). Running through these calculations briefly, we find

$$df_A = a - 1$$

$$= 3 - 1$$

$$= 2$$

$$df_B = b - 1$$

$$= 2 - 1$$

$$= 1$$

$$df_{A \times B} = (a-1)(b-1)$$
$$= (3-1)(2-1) = (2)(1)$$
$$= 2$$

$$df_{S/AB} = (a)(b)(n-1)$$
$$= (3)(2)(5-1) = (3)(2)(4)$$
$$= 24$$

$$df_T = (a)(b)(n) - 1$$
$$= (3)(2)(5) - 1 = 30 - 1$$
$$= 29$$

We enter these numbers in Table 9-13. As an arithmetical check, we verify that

$$df_T = df_A + df_B + df_{A \times B} + df_{S/AB}$$
$$29 = 2 + 1 + 2 + 24$$
$$= 29$$

Mean Squares and F Ratios. Table 9-6 indicates how we form the mean squares and F ratios. We calculate the mean squares by dividing the sums of squares by their corresponding degrees of freedom. The results of these calculations are presented in Table 9-13.

We obtain the F ratios by dividing the respective mean squares potentially reflecting systematic variance — namely, MS_A (the main effect of factor A), MS_B (the main effect of factor B), and $MS_{A \times B}$ (the interaction of the two factors) — by the within-groups mean square, $MS_{S/AB}$. These results are presented in the final column of the summary table.

Evaluating the Null Hypotheses

We evaluate the null hypothesis for each of the three factorial treatment effects by comparing the corresponding F we just calculated with the critical value of F (F_α) that is specified by the appropriate decision rule. The general form of the decision rules, which we presented in Sec. 9.4, is as follows:

If the obtained value of $F \geq F(df_{effect}, df_{S/AB})$, reject the null hypothesis; otherwise, retain the null hypothesis.

We will now apply this general rule to each of the three factorial treatment effects in the order that the relevant F's are listed in Table 9-13.

To determine the status of the null hypothesis for the A main effect, we need a critical value of F with $df_A = 2$ in the numerator and $df_{S/AB} = 24$ in the denominator. From the Table A-2, we find $F(2, 24) = 3.40$ at the 5 percent level of significance. The decision rule becomes the following:

If the obtained value of $F_A \geq F_\alpha = 3.40$, reject the null hypothesis; otherwise, retain the null hypothesis.

Since the F for the A main effect ($F_A = 9.61$) exceeds the critical value, we reject the null hypothesis and conclude that the main effect of reinforcement is significant.

For the B main effect, the combination of degrees of freedom is $df_B = 1$ and $df_{S/AB} = 24$; the critical value of $F(1, 24) = 4.26$. The decision rule becomes

If the obtained value of $F_B \geq F_\alpha = 4.26$, reject the null hypothesis; otherwise, retain the null hypothesis.

In this case also, the F we obtained ($F_B = 11.67$) exceeds the critical value, and we conclude that the main effect of problem difficulty is significant.

To determine the status of the interaction null hypothesis, we need a critical value of F with $df_{A \times B} = 2$ and $df_{S/AB} = 24$; the critical value of $F(2, 24) = 3.40$. The decision rule becomes

If the obtained value of $F_{A \times B} \geq F_\alpha = 3.40$, reject the null hypothesis; otherwise, retain the null hypothesis.

The obtained value of $F_{A \times B} = 4.47$ exceeds the critical value, and we reject the interaction null hypothesis, concluding that statistically significant interaction effects are present in the data.

Interpreting the Results of the Analysis

We have completed the first stage in the analysis of a factorial experiment, but we are not finished. We need to begin the analytical process of discovering what factors are responsible for the significant F's we discovered in the overall analysis. You will recall that we reached a similar point in the analysis of the single-factor design — a significant omnibus F does not specify which conditions or levels of the independent variable are significantly different from each other. Therefore, in the case of the single-factor design, the analytical process consists of a number of single-df comparisons that examine meaningful differences between means. Because of the nature of the factorial design, the analytical process is more complex. We consider some of the possible approaches to the detailed analysis of a factorial experiment in the next chapter.

Assumptions

The theoretical assumptions underlying the analysis of the single-factor design — concerning the normality of distribution, homogeneity of variance, and independence of the scores in the treatment conditions — apply equally to the analysis of the factorial design (see pp. 118–120 for a discussion of these assumptions). As we noted in Chap. 5, violating the assumption that treatment populations are normally distributed does not appear to have any practical significance for the statistical analysis of an experiment and that the independence assumption is generally met through the random assignment of subjects to conditions. The same conclusion holds true for these two assumptions with the factorial design.

You may recall from Chap. 5 that the remaining assumption, that of equal treatment-group variances, does have an influence on our evaluation of the F ratio when the variances are unequal. The solution we recommended was to calculate $F_{max.}$ (the ratio of the largest variance to the smallest variance) and to use a slightly more stringent significance level (for example, $\alpha = .025$) to determine the critical value of F ($F_{adj.}$) when $F_{max.}$ is greater than 3.0, rather than the usual 5 percent level of significance. This strategy is summarized in Fig. 5-4 (p. 121).

We can use the same strategy for evaluating the three F's we obtain from factorial designs. More specifically, we first obtain the variances for all the treatment groups, select the largest and smallest among them, and then calculate the value for $F_{max.}$. If $F_{max.}$ is less than 3.0, we evaluate all three F ratios in the usual way, that is, at the 5 percent level of significance. On the other hand, if $F_{max.}$ is greater than 3.0, we simply use an adjusted critical value of

F ($F_{adj.}$) for each of the F's. As with the single-factor design, we find $F_{adj.}$ by determining the value of F listed in an F table at $\alpha = .025$.

Magnitude of Factorial Effects

In Chap. 7, we introduced an index that reflects the magnitude or size of the treatment effects in a single-factor experiment. This index, estimated omega squared ($\hat{\omega}_A^2$), is used to provide additional information about the degree to which the total variability among subjects ($\hat{\sigma}_T^2$) can be accounted for by the variability due to the treatment effects ($\hat{\sigma}_A^2$). Estimates of omega squared for factorial effects — for the main effects and interaction — are obtainable from the data of a factorial experiment. Unfortunately, the formulas for obtaining these estimates are complex, and there is disagreement concerning the measures that are most appropriate for factorial experiments.[7]

9.7 SUMMARY

In the factorial experiment, two (or more) independent variables are manipulated simultaneously. Factorial designs are economical in that they provide the information that would be obtained in two single-factor experiments. However, factorial experiments also provide information that cannot be derived from single-factor studies, namely, how the independent variables combine to influence behavior. A concept that specifies the nature of this combination is interaction.

Two new terms are necessary for describing factorial design and interaction: *main effects* and *simple effects*. A main effect consists of the effects of one independent variable *averaged* over the levels of the other independent variable. A simple effect, on the other hand, consists of the effects of one independent variable considered *separately* for each level of the other independent variable. An interaction exists when the simple effects of an independent variable are not the same.

The factorial design is widely used in contemporary psychological research. The design permits investigators to move beyond a single-dimensional view of behavior, the view provided by single-factor experiments, to a richer and more revealing multidimensional view. In this chapter, we have considered only the

---

[7] See Keppel (1991, pp. 221–224) for a presentation of the different formulas and a discussion of the problem.

simplest form of the factorial, two independent variables with independent groups of subjects serving in the different treatment combinations. Designs become more complicated as subjects serve in more than one treatment condition (some form of within-subjects design) and when additional independent variables are combined to form higher-order factorial experiments. The design we considered in this chapter is basic to the analysis of more complex designs. Thus, the two-variable factorial design is an important addition to the research tools a modern-day investigator in psychology must possess to contribute effectively to the developing trends of the science.

9.8 EXERCISES[8]

*1. Complete the analysis of variance for the data appearing in Table 9-4 and partially analyzed in the text.

*2. Imagine an experiment in which two kinds of tasks were used, an easy task and a difficult task. The time subjects took to perform a task was measured (in seconds) under conditions in which the number of distractors was varied at three levels. A 2×3 factorial design resulted in which a_1 was the easy task and a_2 was the difficult task. The three levels of increasing numbers of distractors are represented by b_1, b_2, and b_3, respectively. The data are as follows:

$a_1 b_1$	$a_1 b_2$	$a_1 b_3$	$a_2 b_1$	$a_2 b_2$	$a_2 b_3$
5	5	4	5	9	5
6	4	3	4	5	8
2	3	6	4	3	9
4	4	8	5	7	10
2	5	2	6	3	10
4	5	2	3	8	6
1	6	2	8	5	7
6	7	5	2	8	3
9	5	2	3	6	8
4	7	3	3	8	6
4	4	5	4	9	11
8	3	3	2	6	6
5	4	4	8	6	6

[8] Answers to the starred problems are given in Appendix B.

a. Calculate the mean and standard deviation for each of the treatment combinations.
b. Construct the AB matrix for the analysis.
c. Perform the necessary steps for the analysis, and construct the analysis summary table. Determine whether the obtained F's are greater than the critical values. (Since the degrees of freedom for the denominator are not found in the F table, use the critical values of F listed for the nearest smaller denominator df.)
d. Calculate F_{max}.. Should you change how you evaluate the outcome of your analysis? Explain.

*3. A major research technique in the field of behavioral genetics is to breed animals selectively on the basis of particular characteristics exhibited by the animals and then to observe the relative performance of the offspring. Suppose an experiment is conducted in which three strains of rats are to be compared.[9] One strain was obtained by selectively breeding rats that performed exceptionally well in a maze-learning task (the "bright" rats); a second strain was obtained by selectively breeding rats that performed quite poorly in the same task (the "dull" rats); and a third strain consisted of rats that were bred without regard for their maze-learning performance (the "mixed" rats). One group from each strain was raised under "enriched" conditions, and a second group was raised under "impoverished" conditions. The enriched environment consisted of a large cage containing objects for the animals to play with; the impoverished environment consisted of a similar cage containing nothing except the bare essentials of rat life (food and water dispensers). Following six months of exposure to one of the two environments, all the rats were tested in a standard laboratory maze. There were eight rats randomly assigned to each of the environments from each of the three strains. The learning scores (trials needed to learn the maze) are as follows:

---

[9] This example is based on two independent lines of research conducted by Dr. Mark R. Rosenzweig and Dr. Robert C. Tryon.

Environment	Strain (Factor A)		
(Factor B)	Bright	Mixed	Dull
Enriched	4 2	5 9	5 10
	5 3	4 10	5 11
	4 4	3 5	7 14
	10 4	7 5	4 11
Impoverished	6 5	5 12	5 14
	11 5	11 10	10 13
	11 4	14 10	17 8
	3 9	13 7	15 15

a. Calculate the means and standard deviations for the different treatment combinations.

b. Conduct an analysis of variance on these data, testing for the main effects of strain and environment and their interaction.

c. What conclusions can you draw from this analysis?

4. The first two tables in this chapter presented the means from a fictitious 3×3 factorial in which interaction was either present (Table 9-2) or not present (Table 9-1). For this problem, let's assume that sample size was $n = 10$ for each example. Transform each set of nine cell means into corresponding AB treatment sums and enter each set into an AB matrix. Using the sums in each AB matrix, calculate the sums of squares for the two main effects and the $A \times B$ interaction for each example. What you should discover is that when comparing the two examples the sums of squares for the two A main effects will be identical, as will those for the two B main effects, because the marginal column and row means are identical in the two examples. You should also find that $SS_{A \times B}$ equals zero for the sum of squares based on Table 9-1 and some positive number for the sum of squares based on Table 9-2. (You may wish to save these calculations for exercises 3 and 4 in Chap. 10.)

5. Suppose an experiment was conducted in which children from three different grades in school (first, third, and fifth grades) were given a reading test with instructions designed to produce either low or high motivation in the children. We have created eight possible outcomes for this study. In each case, the cell means are presented on the left, with spaces provided for you to write in the row and column marginal means. You should plot the results of each example in the blank graph presented to the right of the cell means. Finally, on the right, you should indicate which of the factorial effects — that is, main effect of grade, main effect of motivation, and the interaction of grade and motivation — may be present in the results. (Answer either

yes or no.) To get you started, we have provided the answers for part (a).

a.

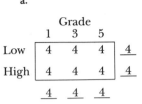

	Grade			
	1	3	5	
Low	4	4	4	4
High	4	4	4	4
	4	4	4	

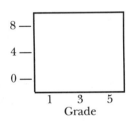

Main Effect of Grade? __No__

Main Effect of Motiv.? __No__

Interaction? __No__

b.

	Grade			
	1	3	5	
Low	2	4	6	__
High	2	4	6	__
	__	__	__	

Main Effect of Grade? ____

Main Effect of Motiv.? ____

Interaction? ____

c.

	Grade			
	1	3	5	
Low	6	6	6	__
High	2	2	2	__
	__	__	__	

Main Effect of Grade? ____

Main Effect of Motiv.? ____

Interaction? ____

d.

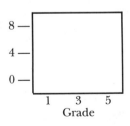

	Grade			
	1	3	5	
Low	4	6	8	__
High	0	2	4	__
	__	__	__	

Main Effect of Grade? ____

Main Effect of Motiv.? ____

Interaction? ____

e.

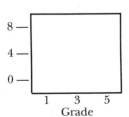

	Grade			
	1	3	5	
Low	2	4	6	__
High	6	4	2	__
	__	__	__	

Main Effect of Grade? ____

Main Effect of Motiv.? ____

Interaction? ____

f.

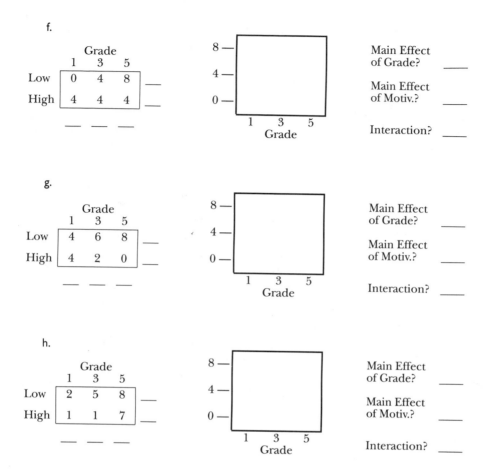

	Grade 1	3	5	
Low	0	4	8	—
High	4	4	4	—
	—	—	—	

Main Effect of Grade? ____

Main Effect of Motiv.? ____

Interaction? ____

g.

	Grade 1	3	5	
Low	4	6	8	—
High	4	2	0	—
	—	—	—	

Main Effect of Grade? ____

Main Effect of Motiv.? ____

Interaction? ____

h.

	Grade 1	3	5	
Low	2	5	8	—
High	1	1	7	—
	—	—	—	

Main Effect of Grade? ____

Main Effect of Motiv.? ____

Interaction? ____

6. This problem is based on an experiment we considered in Chap. 6 as a single-factor study in which kangaroo rats were allowed to explore an artificial burrow in which different scents had been placed. We will include three of the conditions from Chap. 6 as one of the independent variables (factor A) in this problem — namely, a *control* condition (a_1) in which no odor was introduced, an *unfamiliar* condition (a_2) in which the odor from a stranger was introduced, and a *familiar* condition (a_3) in which the odor came from a kangaroo rat that had successfully defeated the subject in a territorial battle.[10] The other independent variable (factor B) consists of two age groups, a group of *young* kangaroo rats (b_1) and a group of *adult* kangaroo rats (b_2). The design is a 3×2 factorial, with each treatment

---

[10] We referred to the last condition as the *familiar-immediate* condition in Chap. 6.

combination containing $n = 7$ subjects. The question of interest is whether the two age groups will show the same or different patterns of behavior in response to the three different scent conditions. The data are as follows:

Young Rats (b_1)			Adult Rats (b_2)		
Control (a_1)	Unfamiliar (a_2)	Familiar (a_3)	Control (a_1)	Unfamiliar (a_2)	Familiar (a_3)
46	41	34	33	32	6
40	44	32	31	19	0
27	31	48	33	36	0
34	29	37	38	20	10
39	47	45	47	20	8
37	28	48	42	22	12
26	43	30	37	24	5

a. Calculate the mean and standard deviation for each of the treatment combinations.

b. Conduct an analysis of variance on these data. (You may wish to save these calculations for exercises 5 through 7 in Chap. 10.)

c. What conclusions can you draw from this analysis?

Chapter · 10

ANALYTICAL COMPARISONS IN THE FACTORIAL DESIGN

The analysis covered in Chap. 9 evaluated the status of three null hypotheses, one for each effect normally extracted from the results of a factorial experiment. Each of these null hypotheses specified the *complete absence* of treatment effects in the population:

1. The null hypothesis for the A main effect stated that all the μ_i's are equal.
2. The null hypothesis for the B main effect stated that all the μ_j's are equal.
3. The null hypothesis for the $A \times B$ interaction stated that no interaction effects are present.

Rejecting any one of these null hypotheses permits us to accept an alternative hypothesis, which states that either *some* population means are different or *some* interaction effects are present. Consequently, a statistically significant F test in a factorial experiment has exactly the same status as a statistically significant overall F test in a single-factor test: knowing that the test is statistically significant is important, but the information is relatively useless by itself. We must turn to other sorts of analyses to obtain more specific information from the data. Chapter 6 was devoted to a discussion of detailed analyses that serve this purpose for the single-factor experiment. This chapter performs a similar function for the factorial experiment.

10.1 INTERPRETING *F* TESTS IN THE FACTORIAL DESIGN

Researchers generally test the three factorial effects — the two main effects and the interaction — and report the outcome of these tests in their writeups of the research. You will undoubtedly do the same. When it comes to *interpreting* the results, however, there is a rational sequence in which we test null hypotheses in the factorial design.

Logical Order of Interpreting the Tests

Logically, the first null hypothesis to be evaluated is the $A \times B$ interaction. This test receives priority because its outcome usually determines the researcher's next step. A significant interaction requires the researcher to analyze and interpret the data with respect to the *combination* of the two independent variables; a nonsignificant interaction indicates that the investigator can treat the factorial experiment as two independent, noninteracting *single*-factor experiments.

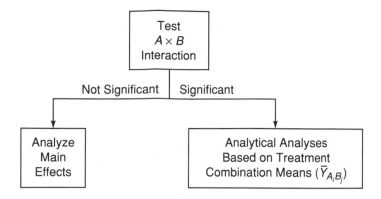

FIGURE 10-1   *The Order of Hypothesis Testing in the Factorial Design.*

These two courses of action, which depend on the significance or nonsignificance of the test for interaction, are summarized in Fig. 10-1.

Starting at the top of the figure, you can see that a significant interaction generally leads a researcher to analyses dealing with the means for the specific treatment combinations (the $\overline{Y}_{AB}$'s), found within the body of the AB matrix of means. These analyses, which we will discuss beginning in Sec. 10.3, help to pinpoint the *locus* of the interaction, that is, to identify the treatments or combinations of treatments responsible for the significant interaction. A nonsignificant interaction, on the other hand, indicates that the results of the experiment can be more appropriately analyzed and interpreted with procedures that disregard the influence of one independent variable on the other — that is, procedures based on the marginal means (the $\overline{Y}_A$'s and $\overline{Y}_B$'s) rather than on the specific treatment means (the $\overline{Y}_{AB}$'s). In other words, where interaction is not significant, we interpret each main effect as if it had come from a single-factor experiment and apply the analytical analyses we discussed in Chap. 6 for that design. We consider the adaptation of these analyses in Sec. 10.2.

Clearly, the test for interaction is most critical. It determines whether the average effects of the separate independent variables — the main effects — are representative or descriptive of the results of the component single-factor experiments that make up the factorial design (that is, the simple effects). If the average effects are *not* representative, we concentrate on the specific treatment means and the interpretation of the significant interaction. If they *are* representative, we focus our attention on the average effects of the two independent variables and interpret the experimental results in terms of the main effects.

Interpreting the Results of the Numerical Example

Let's look again at the results of the numerical example we analyzed in Chap. 9. For convenience, the AB matrix of means and the analysis summary are presented in Tables 10-1 and 10-2, respectively. All three of the F tests are significant. Since the $A \times B$ interaction is significant, following the procedure for interpreting these tests outlined in Fig. 10-1, we turn our attention to the means for the specific treatment combinations.

Simple Effects of Verbal Reinforcement (Factor A). The most common way to proceed at this point is to examine systematically the *simple effects* of one of the independent variables at each level of the other independent variable. In terms of Table 10-1, this might consist of isolating the means in each *row* of the table, for example, and determining the effects of the reinforcement variable (factor A) on the performance of the children when they were attempting to solve either the simple problems (the row labeled b_1) or the complex problems (the row labeled b_2). The value of this analysis is that it focuses on the effects of one of the independent variables (reinforcement, in this case) with the other independent variable (problem type) *held constant.*

As you can see by examining the three means in each of the two rows of Table 10-1, the patterns of results observed with the two types of problems are quite different. That is, while both praise (7.60) and criticism (7.20) facilitate the solving of simple problems in comparison with silence (4.40), only praise (7.00) facilitates the solving of complex problems in comparison with silence (3.20), whereas criticism seems to have inhibited performance (2.00).

Simple Effects of Problem Type (Factor B). We can also look at the other set of simple effects, the effect of problem type separately for each of the three reinforcement conditions (levels of factor A). For the praise condition (a_1), for example, the children perform slightly better with the simple reasoning problems (7.60) than with the complex problems (7.00). This difference is considerably greater for the children in the criticism condition (a_2) — that is,

TABLE 10-1 *Table of Means*

Problem Type	Praise (a_1)	Criticism (a_2)	Silence (a_3)	Average
	Verbal Reinforcement			
Simple (b_1)	7.60	7.20	4.40	6.40
Complex (b_2)	7.00	2.00	3.20	4.07
Average	7.30	4.60	3.80	—

cell means

marginal means

TABLE 10-2 *Summary of the Analysis*

Source	SS	df	MS	F
A (Reinforcement)	67.27	2	33.64	9.61*
B (Problem Type)	40.84	1	40.84	11.67*
A × B	31.26	2	15.63	4.47*
S/AB	84.00	24	3.50	
Total	223.37	29		

* $p < .05$.

7.20 versus 2.00 for the simple and complex problems, respectively. The children in the silence condition (a_3) show a difference somewhere between that of praise and criticism (4.40 versus 3.20 for the simple and complex problems, respectively).

Main Effect of the Reinforcement Variable.   It is instructive to examine the main effect of the reinforcement variable to see why it is of little interest to us in interpreting the outcome of this numerical example, given the significant interaction. More specifically, consider the three column marginal means reflecting the main effect of factor A. We see that when we combine the data for the simple and complex problems, praise is higher than criticism ($7.30 - 4.60 = 2.70$ problems) and criticism is slightly higher than silence ($4.60 - 3.80 = .80$ problems). However, neither of these findings reflects the *actual* outcome of the experiment. That is, the 2.70 overall difference between praise and criticism is *not representative* of the corresponding differences found when we consider the effects of the other independent variable, problem type: for simple problems, the difference between praise and criticism is .40 problems, while for complex problems, the difference is 5.00 problems. In neither case is the difference even close to the 2.70 problems that the column marginal means reveal. Similarly, the .80 overall difference between criticism and silence is not representative of the differences we observed within the body of the table: for the simple problems, this difference is 2.80 problems, while for the complex problems, the difference is actually reversed (-1.20 problems). In short, the main effect of factor A represents a statistical *average* that disregards an important feature of the data — that the effects of verbal reinforcement on problem solving *depends* on problem difficulty.

Main Effect of Problem Type.   A consideration of the main effect of problem type, which is revealed by the row marginal means, indicates that when we combine the data over the three reinforcement conditions, the children performed better with the simple problems (6.40) than with the complex problems (4.07), a difference of 2.33 problems. But this particular finding does not take into consideration that the *magnitude* of the difference between simple and complex problems depends on the nature of the reinforcement the children received, which is what we discovered in the preceding paragraph. That is, what we found was a difference of .60 problems for praise, a difference of 5.20 problems for criticism, and a difference of 1.20 problems for silence. Again, interpretation of the main effect obscures the fact that an interaction is present.

10.2 THE DETAILED ANALYSIS OF MAIN EFFECTS

As mentioned earlier, if the interaction is not significant, we would then turn our attention to the interpretation of the main effects. The detailed analysis of main effects essentially treats the results of the factorial experiment as equivalent to two separate single-factor experiments — the *A* main effect being viewed as a single-factor experiment where factor *A* is manipulated (paying no attention to factor *B*), and the *B* main effect being viewed as a single-factor experiment where factor *B* is manipulated (paying no attention to factor *A*).

In Chap. 6, we stated that most independent variables are manipulated to permit more than one meaningful question to be answered through detailed analyses of the data. We called such analyses *analytical comparisons.* As you have seen, analytical comparisons are possible whenever three or more treatment levels make up the independent variable. For continuity, we will illustrate these analyses in the context of the numerical example from Chap. 9, even though the analyses themselves are not particularly appropriate, because of the significant interaction.

Forming Main Comparisons

A significant main effect allows us to conclude only that the relevant marginal means are not all the same. We need to conduct more analytically focused comparisons to pinpoint the features of the independent variable that are responsible for the significance of the overall main effect. We will use the term **main comparisons** to refer to analyses that examine portions of a main effect.

Our numerical example was a 3×2 design consisting of three types of reinforcement administered to children attempting to solve either simple or complex reasoning problems. Assume that the interaction was not significant in this example (even though it was) and that we wish to conduct analytical comparisons on the marginal means formed by collapsing over the data from the levels of the other independent variable. As we saw in Chap. 6, we can extract several interesting comparisons involving the levels making up the reinforcement variable, namely, praise, criticism, and silence. Exactly the same questions can be translated into main comparisons involving the relevant marginal means (the $\overline{Y}_A$'s). For example, we could use the silence condition (level a_3) as a point of reference against which we could separately assess the effects of praise (level a_1) and of criticism (level a_2). Other meaningful comparisons are possible — for example, a comparison between the two types of verbal reinforcement (praise versus criticism), and a comparison between the silence condition and an average of the two "verbal" conditions. The specific comparisons chosen for analysis depend on one's research hypotheses, of course.

Since the other main effect in this example consists of only two treatment levels (simple and complex), it cannot be divided into any main comparisons. That is, with just two treatment levels, the main effect tells us all we can discover from this independent variable. If additional sets of problems had been included in the factorial experiment — for example, problems of medium difficulty — then analytical comparisons involving factor B would have been possible as well.

Computational Formulas

The computational formulas for main comparisons represent a direct translation of the corresponding formulas we used to conduct single-df comparisons in the single-factor design. We will consider the analysis of two types of main comparisons, one based on differences between two marginal means (*pairwise main comparisons*) and the other on differences produced when one or both of the means are obtained by averaging two or more marginal means (*complex main comparisons*). We will consider pairwise main comparisons first.

Pairwise Main Comparisons. We calculate the comparison itself ($\hat{\psi}_A$) simply by subtracting one of the relevant marginal means from the other and then use this difference to translate this information into a sum of squares. As an illustration, we will calculate the sum of squares associated with the difference between praise and silence. From Table 10-1 (p. 280), we find the difference to be

$$\hat{\psi}_A = \overline{Y}_{A_1} - \overline{Y}_{A_3} = 7.30 - 3.80 = 3.50$$

The formula for the comparison sum of squares is as follows:

$$SS_{A\,comp.} = \frac{(b)(n)(\hat{\psi}_A)^2}{2}$$

(10-1)

This formula is identical to Eq. (6-2) except for the addition of b in the numerator, which is necessary to take into consideration the fact that we collapsed the data over the b levels of factor B in calculating the marginal means. Substituting in Eq. (10-1), we find

$$SS_{A\,comp.} = \frac{(2)(5)(3.50)^2}{2} = \frac{122.50}{2} = 61.25$$

Because $df_{A\,comp.} = 1$, $MS_{A\,comp.} = SS_{A\,comp.} = 61.25$. The error term for main comparisons comes from the overall analysis of the factorial.[1] That is,

$$F_{A\,comp.} = \frac{MS_{A\,comp.}}{MS_{S/AB}}$$

(10-2)

From the summary of this analysis (Table 10-2), we find $MS_{S/AB} = 3.50$. Substituting in Eq. (10-2), we find

$$F_{A\,comp.} = \frac{61.25}{3.50} = 17.50$$

From Table A-2, looking under $df_{num.} = 1$ and $df_{denom.} = df_{S/AB} = 24$, we find the critical value of $F(1, 24) = 4.26$ at the 5 percent level of significance. The decision rule becomes

If $F_{A\,comp.} \geq 4.26$, reject the null hypothesis; otherwise, retain the null hypothesis.

The F for the main comparison (17.50) exceeds this value, and by looking at the marginal means, we conclude that the children receiving praise solved significantly more problems than those receiving no verbal reinforcement (silence).

---

[1] You will recall from Chap. 6 that we also used the error term from the overall analysis to evaluate analytical comparisons in the single-factor design.

Complex Main Comparisons. In Sec. 6.4, we introduced a different formula to calculate complex single-*df* comparisons — one based on special *coefficients* that are designed to reflect the comparison. Suppose we wanted to combine the data for the children receiving some kind of verbal reinforcement (praise or criticism) and compare the average of these two groups with the mean for the children receiving no verbal reinforcement (silence). We can express this complex comparison as a sum of the *weighted means* as follows:

$$\hat{\psi}_A = (c_1)(\overline{Y}_{A_1}) + (c_2)(\overline{Y}_{A_2}) + (c_3)(\overline{Y}_{A_3}) + \cdots \tag{10-3}$$

where the *c*'s are coefficients reflecting the comparison of interest. For this example, the set $(+\frac{1}{2}, +\frac{1}{2}, -1)$ expresses the difference between the combined verbal conditions (praise and criticism) and the nonverbal condition (silence).[2] Applied to our example,

$$\hat{\psi}_A = \left(+\frac{1}{2}\right)(7.30) + \left(+\frac{1}{2}\right)(4.60) + (-1)(3.80)$$

$$= 3.65 + 2.30 - 3.80 = 2.15$$

We then substitute the results of these calculations in the following formula:

$$SS_{A_{comp.}} = \frac{(b)(n)(\hat{\psi}_A)^2}{\Sigma \, c^2} \tag{10-4}$$

For this example,

$$SS_{A_{comp.}} = \frac{(2)(5)(2.15)^2}{\left(+\frac{1}{2}\right)^2 + \left(+\frac{1}{2}\right)^2 + (-1)^2}$$

$$= \frac{(10)(4.62)}{.25 + .25 + 1} = \frac{46.20}{1.50} = 30.80$$

From this point, the procedures for pairwise and complex main comparisons are the same. More specifically, we use Eq. (10-2) to obtain

$$F_{A_{comp.}} = \frac{MS_{A_{comp.}}}{MS_{S/AB}} = \frac{30.80}{3.50} = 8.80$$

The numerator and denominator degrees of freedom are the same as in the pairwise example, which means we use the same decision rule to evaluate the *F*.

---

[2] You may wish to review the relevant material in Sec. 6.4 on how to construct sets of coefficients for single-*df* comparisons.

(Remember, even though this comparison involves three conditions, the comparison itself tests the difference between *two* means.) Since our $F_{A\,comp.}$ of 8.80 is greater than the critical value of 4.26, we can conclude that the difference between the combined verbal conditions and the silence condition is significant; more specifically, children receiving some kind of verbal reinforcement solved more problems (5.95) than children receiving silence (3.80).

Comment

The computational formulas for the main comparisons involving factor B are nearly identical to those we have just covered for factor A. For example, the formula for pairwise main comparisons, Eq. (10-1), becomes

$$SS_{B\,comp.} = \frac{(a)(n)(\hat{\psi}_B)^2}{2} \qquad (10\text{-}5)$$

As you can see, the only changes are in converting the symbols in the equation to reflect the factor B instead of factor A. Similarly, the formula for complex main comparisons, Eq. (10-4), becomes

$$SS_{B\,comp.} = \frac{(a)(n)(\hat{\psi}_B)^2}{\sum c^2} \qquad (10\text{-}6)$$

The F's for these comparisons are formed by dividing the mean square for a main comparison ($MS_{B\,comp.}$) by the error term from the overall analysis ($MS_{S/AB}$). In all other respects, analyses of the main comparisons of the respective independent variables are the same.

10.3 ANALYZING SIMPLE EFFECTS

The unique advantage of the factorial design is that it affords us the opportunity to examine the way in which two independent variables combine to influence the behavior under study. When an interaction is present, it becomes appropriate to conduct analyses that identify the factors that are acting in the interaction, thereby helping to isolate its source.

A common way to accomplish this task is to examine the pattern of results associated with one of the independent variables as the other independent

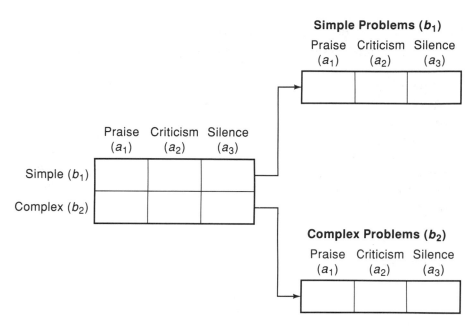

FIGURE 10-2 *A Representation of the Extraction of Simple Effects from the Overall Factorial Design.*

variable is changed systematically. This pattern, of course, represents what we call the *simple effects* of an independent variable. Interaction, you will recall, exists if the simple effects are different, that is, if the pattern of results for one of the independent variables is not the same at all levels of the other independent variable. The analysis of simple effects, then, focuses on the *cell means* in the body of the *AB* matrix, rather than on the marginal means used in the analysis of significant main effects. The goal is to pinpoint the specific combinations of the two independent variables responsible for the significant interaction.

The intent of the analysis is summarized in Fig. 10-2. The factorial design on the left is a representation of our numerical example. The analysis of one set of simple effects — the simple effects of the reinforcement variable — is illustrated on the right as two component experiments in which the reinforcement variable is manipulated under two different conditions. In the upper experiment, the three reinforcement conditions (factor A) are administered in conjunction with a particular level of factor B — that is, the simple reasoning problems (level b_1). In the lower experiment, the same three conditions are administered, but this time in conjunction with the other level of factor B — the complex reasoning problems (level b_2). The analysis of the simple effects would consist in this case of two significance tests: one to test the null hypothesis that the three treatment means at level b_1 are equal, and a second to test the null hypothesis that the corresponding treatment means at level b_2 are equal.

The main characteristic of this analysis is that it simplifies the original factorial manipulation by focusing on the effects of one of the independent variables while the other is held constant. These separate analyses are quite different from the corresponding analysis of the main effects, where the variation of one of the independent variables is analyzed with data that have been combined over the levels of the other independent variable. The analysis of the main effect *obscures* the interaction; the analysis of simple effects *illuminates* the interaction.

Computational Formulas

As you have seen in Fig. 10-2, the analysis of simple effects transforms the factorial design into a set of single-factor experiments. Fortunately, this transformation extends to the computational formulas we use for the actual analysis. That is, with slight modification, the formulas for the analysis of simple effects are identical to the formulas for the analysis of an *actual* single-factor design.

Suppose we wish to test the simple effect of factor A at level b_1. Table 10-3 presents an AB matrix in which we have highlighted the sums involved in calculating this particular simple effect. To emphasize the fact that the computational formula for this analysis is equivalent to the analysis of a single-factor design, we will temporarily change the notational system from one using the factorial symbols to one appropriate for a single-factor experiment. The factorial symbols representing the relevant sums from the AB matrix are presented in the row of Table 10-4 labeled "factorial symbols." Consider the symbols in the row labeled "single-factor symbols." What we have done is to change each AB sum to an A sum, with quotation marks added around the single-factor

---

TABLE 10-3 *Sums Involved in Calculating the Simple Effects of Factor A*

| Factor B | Factor A | | | Sum | Effect |
	a_1	a_2	a_3		
b_1	$AB_{1,1}$	$AB_{2,1}$	$AB_{3,1}$	B_1	$\longmapsto$ A at b_1
b_2	$AB_{1,2}$	$AB_{2,2}$	$AB_{3,2}$	B_2	$\longrightarrow$ A at b_2
Sum	A_1	A_2	A_3	T	$\longrightarrow$ A Main Effect

TABLE 10-4 *Notation to Represent the Sums Involved in the Analysis of the Simple Effects of Factor A at Level b_1*

	a_1	a_2	a_3	Sum
Factorial Symbols	$AB_{1,1}$	$AB_{2,1}$	$AB_{3,1}$	B_1
Single-Factor Symbols	"A_1"	"A_2"	"A_3"	"T"

symbols to remind us that these are special symbols designed for this analysis. The formula for the sum of squares, which we will refer to as "A at b_1," can now be written as follows:

$$SS_{A \text{ at } b_1} = \frac{\Sigma(\text{"}A\text{"})^2}{n} - \frac{(\text{"}T\text{"})^2}{(a)(n)} \tag{10-7}$$

Except for the quotation marks, then, this formula is identical to the one we introduced in Chap. 4 for the overall analysis of the single-factor design:

$$SS_A = \frac{\Sigma A^2}{n} - \frac{T^2}{(a)(n)}$$

Translated back to the factorial notation, Eq. (10-7) becomes

$$SS_{A \text{ at } b_1} = \frac{\Sigma(AB_{i1})^2}{n} - \frac{B_1^2}{(a)(n)} \tag{10-8}$$

As in a single-factor experiment, the degrees of freedom for each simple effect equal 1 less than the number of treatment conditions entering into the analysis:

$$df_{A \text{ at } b_j} = a - 1 \tag{10-9}$$

The mean squares for simple effects are obtained as usual, by dividing each sum of squares by the appropriate df:

$$MS_{A \text{ at } b_j} = \frac{SS_{A \text{ at } b_j}}{df_{A \text{ at } b_j}} \tag{10-10}$$

The error term for each of these mean squares is the error term from the original analysis, $MS_{S/AB}$. That is,

$$F_{A \text{ at } b_j} = \frac{MS_{A \text{ at } b_j}}{MS_{S/AB}} \tag{10-11}$$

The computational formulas for the simple effects involving factor B are formed in an analogous fashion. That is, we dissect the AB matrix into separate columns — each column representing one of the simple effects of factor B. Since each set of data is equivalent to a single-factor experiment involving the manipulation of factor B, we conduct the analysis with that design in mind. We will illustrate this process in the next section.

A Numerical Example

We will use the numerical example to illustrate the calculations for both sets of simple effects. We will calculate first the simple effects of the reinforcement variable (factor A).

Evaluating the Simple Effects of Factor A.   The AB matrix of sums from the analysis we conducted in Chap. 9 is presented again in the upper portion of Table 10-5. We will consider first the simple effect of the different types of verbal reinforcement given to the children attempting to solve simple reasoning problems (level b_1). The steps involved in this analysis are summarized in the lower portion of Table 10-5. We start by isolating the portion of the data that is relevant for this analysis — namely, the sums in the first row of the AB matrix, as illustrated in the table. We then substitute this information in Eq. (10-8) to calculate the sum of squares, as illustrated in the table. The remainder of the analysis, also summarized in the table, consists of a straightforward substitution in the relevant formulas presented in the preceding section. The error term for the simple effect ($MS_{S/AB} = 3.50$) comes from the overall analysis we conducted in Chap. 9. The critical value of $F(2, 24) = 3.40$, and the decision rule becomes

If $F_{A \text{ at } b_1} \geq 3.40$, reject the null hypothesis; otherwise, retain the null hypothesis.

Applying this rule to the analysis summarized in Table 10-5, we conclude that the reinforcement variable has a statistically significant effect with the simple reasoning problems.

The relevant information for calculating the sum of squares for the corresponding simple effect for the children receiving the complex problems

TABLE 10-5 *The Analysis of the Simple Effects of the Reinforcement Variable (Factor A) for the Children Receiving the Simple Reasoning Problems (Level b_1)*

AB Matrix

	Praise	Criticism	Silence	Sum
Simple	38	36	22	96
Complex	35	10	16	61
Sum	73	46	38	157

Steps in the Analysis

1. Calculate $SS_{A\ at\ b_1}$:

$$\frac{\Sigma(AB_{i1})^2}{(n)} - \frac{(B_1)^2}{(a)(n)} = \frac{(38)^2 + (36)^2 + (22)^2}{5} - \frac{(96)^2}{(3)(5)}$$

$$= \frac{3,224}{5} - \frac{9,216}{15}$$

$$= 644.80 - 614.40 = 30.40$$

2. Calculate $df_{A\ at\ b_1}$:

$$a - 1 = 3 - 1 = 2$$

3. Calculate $MS_{A\ at\ b_1}$:

$$\frac{SS_{A\ at\ b_1}}{df_{A\ at\ b_1}} = \frac{30.40}{2} = 15.20$$

4. Calculate $F_{A\ at\ b_1}$:

$$\frac{MS_{A\ at\ b_1}}{MS_{S/AB}} = \frac{15.20}{3.50} = 4.34$$

5. Evaluate $F_{A\ at\ b_1}$ with $F_{crit.}$ ($df_{num.} = df_{A\ at\ b_1}$, $df_{denom.} = df_{S/AB}$):
$F_{crit.}(2, 24) = 3.40$; reject the null hypothesis.

(level b_2) is found in the second row of the AB matrix in the upper portion of Table 10-5. Following the analogous procedures outlined in the table, we find

$$SS_{A\ at\ b_2} = \frac{(35)^2 + (10)^2 + (16)^2}{5} - \frac{(61)^2}{(3)(5)}$$

$$= \frac{1,581}{5} - \frac{3,721}{15} = 316.20 - 248.07$$

$$= 68.13$$

$$df_{A \text{ at } b_2} = 3 - 1 = 2$$

$$MS_{A \text{ at } b_2} = \frac{68.13}{2} = 34.07$$

$$F_{A \text{ at } b_2} = \frac{34.07}{3.50} = 9.73$$

Using the same decision rule, we conclude from this analysis that the reinforcement variable also has a statistically significant effect with the complex reasoning problems. We will come back to these two findings in a moment. For convenience, we have summarized the results of these two analyses in Table 10-6.

Evaluating the Simple Effects of Factor B. We evaluate the simple effects of the problem type (factor B) in the same way. This time, however, our interest is directed to the sums in the individual columns, as we have illustrated in Table 10-7. As you can readily see, each column is equivalent to a single-factor experiment in which problem type is manipulated; the nature of the reinforcement the children receive is held constant in the column. Each column represents a different simple effect; we have highlighted the first column, which reflects the simple effect of problem type for the children receiving praise for correct responses.

We can easily adapt Eq. (10-8) to accommodate the simple effects of factor B rather than of factor A by simply substituting "b's" for "a's" and the reverse. As an illustration, the computational formula for the simple effect of factor B at level a_1 (the highlighted column in Table 10-7) becomes

$$SS_{B \text{ at } a_1} = \frac{\Sigma(AB_{1j})^2}{n} - \frac{A_1^2}{(b)(n)} \qquad (10\text{-}12)$$

Table 10-8 illustrates the calculations for this sum of squares and the remainder of the analysis, which parallels the procedures we followed in the analysis of

TABLE 10-6 *Analysis of the Simple Effects of Factor A*				
Source	SS	df	MS	F
A at b_1	30.40	2	15.20	4.34*
A at b_2	68.13	2	34.07	9.73*
S/AB		24	3.50	

* $p < .05$.

TABLE 10-7	Sums Involved in the Calculation of the Simple Effects of Factor B			

	Factor A			
Factor B	a_1	a_2	a_3	Sum
b_1	$AB_{1,1}$	$AB_{2,1}$	$AB_{3,1}$	B_1
b_2	$AB_{1,2}$	$AB_{2,2}$	$AB_{3,2}$	B_2
Sum	A_1	A_2	A_3	T
	$\downarrow$	$\downarrow$	$\downarrow$	$\downarrow$
Effect	B at a_1	B at a_2	B at a_3	B Main Effect

the simple effects of factor A. The degrees of freedom for this simple effect are

$$df_{B \text{ at } a_1} = b - 1 \tag{10-13}$$

For our example, then, $df_{B \text{ at } a_1} = 1$. The remainder of the analysis is summarized in Table 10-8. The critical value of $F(1, 24) = 4.26$, and the decision rule becomes

If $F_{B \text{ at } a_1} \geq 4.26$, reject the null hypothesis; otherwise, retain the null hypothesis.

Applying this rule to the F we just obtained leads to the conclusion that the nature of the problems (simple versus complex) did not produce a significant effect for the subjects receiving praise.

Adapting Eq. (10-12) to the other two columns of Table 10-8, we find

$$SS_{B \text{ at } a_2} = \frac{(36)^2 + (10)^2}{5} - \frac{(46)^2}{(2)(5)}$$

$$= \frac{1,396}{5} - \frac{2,116}{10} = 279.20 - 211.60$$

$$= 67.60$$

$$SS_{B \text{ at } a_3} = \frac{(22)^2 + (16)^2}{5} - \frac{(38)^2}{(2)(5)}$$

$$= \frac{740}{5} - \frac{1,444}{10} = 148.00 - 144.40$$

$$= 3.60$$

TABLE 10-8   *The Analysis of the Simple Effects of Problem Type (Factor B) for the Children Receiving Praise (Level a_1)*

AB Matrix

	Praise	Criticism	Silence	Sum
Simple	38	36	22	96
Complex	35	10	16	61
Sum	73	46	38	157

Steps in the Analysis

1. Calculate $SS_{B \text{ at } a_1}$:

$$\frac{\Sigma(AB_{1j})^2}{(n)} - \frac{(A_1)^2}{(b)(n)} = \frac{(38)^2 + (35)^2}{5} - \frac{(73)^2}{(2)(5)}$$

$$= \frac{2,669}{5} - \frac{5,329}{10}$$

$$= 533.80 - 532.90 = .90$$

2. Calculate $df_{B \text{ at } a_1}$:

$$b - 1 = 2 - 1 = 1$$

3. Calculate $MS_{B \text{ at } a_1}$:

$$\frac{SS_{B \text{ at } a_1}}{df_{B \text{ at } a_1}} = \frac{.90}{1} = .90$$

4. Calculate $F_{B \text{ at } a_1}$:

$$\frac{MS_{B \text{ at } a_1}}{MS_{S/AB}} = \frac{.90}{3.50} = .26$$

5. Calculate $F_{crit.}$ ($df_{num.} = df_{B \text{ at } a_1}$, $df_{denom.} = df_{S/AB}$):

$F_{crit.}(1, 24) = 4.26$; retain the null hypothesis.

The remaining steps in the analysis are summarized in Table 10-9. The results of these three analyses, then, indicate that the simple reasoning problems are easier to solve than the complex ones only for the children receiving criticism (the simple effect of B at a_2).

Comments on the Analysis

Researchers do not always calculate the simple effects with both independent variables, as we did in the previous section. In many situations, for example, one

TABLE 10-9 *Analysis of the Simple Effects of Factor B*				
Source	SS	df	MS	F
B at a_1	.90	1	.90	.26
B at a_2	67.60	1	67.60	19.31*
B at a_3	3.60	1	3.60	1.03
S/AB		24	3.50	

* $p < .05$.

of the independent variables will be the most "natural," useful, or potentially revealing — the manipulation that will be the easiest to explain. On the other hand, the purpose of these analyses is to understand the nature of the interaction, and frequently we gain insights by evaluating both sets of simple effects.

The analysis of the simple effects of factor A indicated that verbal reinforcement produced significant variation among the treatment conditions for simple as well as complex problems (see Table 10-6). What does this tell us about the nature of the interaction? Because the interaction is significant, we know that the simple effects are *different* from each other. Furthermore, the present analysis tells us that when they are considered individually, *both* simple effects are significant. Although important, however, this information is somewhat lacking. Look again at the cell means presented in Table 10-1 (p. 280) and plotted in Fig. 9-7 (p. 262). The pattern of differences for the simple problems suggests that both praise and criticism result in more correct solutions than silence and that the two forms of verbal reinforcement are about equal. The pattern of differences for the complex problems, on the other hand, is quite different — this time only praise appears to surpass silence, and criticism even falls below this reference group.

The statistical tests we just conducted allow us to conclude that *some* differences among the means are present in each of the two rows, but they do not indicate *which* differences are significant. Each of these tests evaluates the *omnibus* simple effect of factor A, and, as we know from previous discussions, omnibus tests do *not* identify the treatments responsible for the significant F's. *We need to conduct further analyses of the two significant simple effects — analyses that help to identify the treatment conditions responsible for the significant overall effects.* In Sec. 10.4 we will show how to obtain this information, which is vital to the interpretation of the significant interaction.

The analysis of the other set of simple effects does not have this problem, because each simple effect is based on only *two* treatment conditions — namely, simple versus complex problems. The analysis we summarized in Table 10-9 indicates that the complex problems are statistically more difficult than the simple problems, but only for the children receiving verbal *criticism*; the other two forms of reinforcement (praise and silence) do not produce differences that are statistically significant.

10.4 ANALYZING SIMPLE COMPARISONS

We confronted the problem of interpreting a significant omnibus F test in Chap. 6, where we introduced the use of single-*df* comparisons to identify those differences responsible for the significant effect. We will use the same approach for further analyzing significant *simple* effects in a factorial experiment. Again, we will treat this analysis as an actual single-factor experiment, which means that we will conduct a number of meaningful single-*df* comparisons on the data producing significant simple effects. We will call tests of this sort conducted on significant simple effects **simple comparisons** — *comparisons* to be continuous with the single-factor design, and *simple* to indicate that the comparisons represent a detailed analysis of simple effects. We will consider the analysis of simple comparisons within the context of our numerical example.

Analyzing Pairwise Simple Comparisons

Given the analogy between the analysis of simple effects and that of single-factor designs, we can easily evaluate simple comparisons by viewing a set of row or column means as the product of an actual single-factor design and then apply the computational formulas of Chap. 6 to obtain the desired sums of squares.

For example, suppose we wanted to compare the praise and criticism conditions, for the children receiving the complex problems (level b_2). The relevant means for this analysis are highlighted in the upper portion of Table 10-10. The formula for a pairwise comparison conducted with data from an actual single-factor design was given by Eq. (6-2); that is,

$$SS_{A_{comp.}} = \frac{(n)(\hat{\psi}_A)^2}{2}$$

where $\hat{\psi}_A$ is the pairwise difference between two means. As you can probably anticipate, we can easily adapt this formula for the analysis of **pairwise simple**

TABLE 10-10 *The Analysis of a Pairwise Simple Comparison*

AB Matrix of Means

	Praise	Criticism	Silence
Simple	7.60	7.20	4.40
Complex	7.00	2.00	3.20

Steps in the Analysis

1. Calculate $\hat{\psi}_{A \text{ at } b_2}$:

$$7.00 - 2.00 = 5.00$$

2. Calculate $SS_{A\,comp.\text{ at } b_2}$:

$$\frac{(n)(\hat{\psi})^2}{2} = \frac{(5)(5.00)^2}{2} = \frac{125.00}{2} = 62.50$$

3. Calculate $MS_{A\,comp.\text{ at } b_2}$:

$$\frac{SS_{A\,comp.\text{ at } b_2}}{df_{A\,comp.\text{ at } b_2}} = \frac{62.50}{1} = 62.50$$

4. Calculate $F_{A\,comp.\text{ at } b_2}$:

$$\frac{MS_{A\,comp.\text{ at } b_2}}{MS_{S/AB}} = \frac{62.50}{3.50} = 17.86$$

5. Evaluate $F_{A\,comp.\text{ at } b_2}$ with $F_{crit.}(df_{num.} = 1, df_{denom.} = df_{S/AB})$:

$$F_{crit.}(1, 24) = 4.26; \text{ reject the null hypothesis.}$$

---

comparisons. More specifically,

$$SS_{A\,comp.\text{ at } b_j} = \frac{(n)(\hat{\psi}_{A \text{ at } b_j})^2}{2} \tag{10-14}$$

where $\hat{\psi}_{A \text{ at } b_j}$ refers to the pairwise difference between the two means specified by this comparison at a particular level of factor B (level b_j). From Table 10-10, we calculate the difference between praise and criticism for the children receiving the complex problems, $\hat{\psi}_{A \text{ at } b_2} = 7.00 - 2.00 = 5.00$, and substitute this information in Eq. (10-14). This substitution and the remaining steps in the analysis are presented in the bottom portion of Table 10-10. The critical value of $F(df_{num.} = 1, df_{denom.} = 24)$ is 4.26, and the decision rule becomes

If $F_{A_{comp.} \text{ at } b_2} \geq 4.26$, reject the null hypothesis; otherwise, retain the null hypothesis.

The F is significant, and we conclude that the children receiving praise solve significantly more complex problems than do those receiving criticism.

Analyzing More Complex Simple Comparisons

We have called single-df comparisons that are based on averages of two or more groups *complex comparisons.* The reason for the distinction is that the computational formula for complex comparisons is more complicated than the one for pairwise differences, because it is necessary to take the nature of the complex comparison into consideration. This adjustment is taken care of by the coefficients designed to represent any given comparison.

As an example, suppose we wanted to compare the silence condition with an average of praise and criticism for the children receiving simple problems (level b_1). A set of coefficients representing this **complex simple comparison** consists of $+\frac{1}{2}$, $+\frac{1}{2}$, and -1. Using these coefficients to calculate the actual difference, we find

$$\hat{\psi}_{A \text{ at } b_1} = (c_1)(\overline{Y}_{A_1 B_1}) + (c_2)(\overline{Y}_{A_2 B_1}) + (c_3)(\overline{Y}_{A_3 B_1})$$

$$= \left(+\tfrac{1}{2}\right)(7.60) + \left(+\tfrac{1}{2}\right)(7.20) + (-1)(4.40)$$

$$= 3.80 + 3.60 - 4.40 = 3.00$$

We then use this difference and the squared coefficients to calculate the sum of squares by substituting in the following formula:

$$SS_{A_{comp.} \text{ at } b_1} = \frac{(n)(\hat{\psi}_{A \text{ at } b_1})^2}{\sum c^2} \tag{10-15}$$

These calculations are summarized as the first three steps in Table 10-11. After this point, both the pairwise and complex comparisons are treated identically. The remaining steps in the analysis are summarized in Table 10-11. Since the obtained F is greater than the critical value of F (4.26), we can conclude that the superiority of the combined verbal conditions over the silence condition is significant for the children receiving the simple reasoning problems.

TABLE 10-11 *Steps in the Analysis of a Complex Simple Comparison*

1. Calculate $\hat{\psi}_{A\ \text{at}\ b_1}$:

$$(c_1)(\overline{Y}_{A_1 B_1}) + (c_2)(\overline{Y}_{A_2 B_1}) + (c_3)(\overline{Y}_{A_3 B_1}) =$$
$$\left(+\tfrac{1}{2}\right)(7.60) + \left(+\tfrac{1}{2}\right)(7.20) + (-1)(4.40) = 3.00$$

2. Calculate $\Sigma\ c^2$:

$$c_1^2 + c_2^2 + c_3^2 = \left(+\tfrac{1}{2}\right)^2 + \left(+\tfrac{1}{2}\right)^2 + (-1)^2 = 1.50$$

3. Calculate $SS_{A\ comp.\ \text{at}\ b_1}$:

$$\frac{(n)(\hat{\psi}_{A\ \text{at}\ b_1})^2}{\Sigma\ c^2} = \frac{(5)(3.00)^2}{1.50} = \frac{45.00}{1.50} = 30.00$$

4. Calculate $MS_{A\ comp.\ \text{at}\ b_1}$:

$$\frac{SS_{A\ comp.\ \text{at}\ b_1}}{df_{A\ comp.\ \text{at}\ b_1}} = \frac{30.00}{1} = 30.00$$

5. Calculate $F_{A\ comp.\ \text{at}\ b_1}$:

$$\frac{MS_{A\ comp.\ \text{at}\ b_1}}{MS_{S/AB}} = \frac{30.00}{3.50} = 8.57$$

6. Evaluate $F_{A\ comp.\ \text{at}\ b_1}$ with $F_{crit.}$ ($df_{num.} = 1$, $df_{denom.} = df_{S/AB}$):

$$F_{crit.}(1, 24) = 4.26;\ \text{reject the null hypothesis.}$$

10.5 AN OVERALL PLAN OF ANALYSIS

Figure 10-3 presents a plan for the comprehensive analysis of a factorial experiment.[3] As we stated in this chapter, the first step in the analysis of a factorial should be a test of the significance of the overall $A \times B$ interaction. (See pp. 278–279 for an explanation of this point.) Depending on the significance of the interaction effect, two different courses of action are open to us. If the $A \times B$ interaction is significant, we proceed with the analysis of simple

---

[3] We discuss an alternative analysis plan, which is not as common as the one summarized in Fig. 10-3, in an appendix at the end of this chapter.

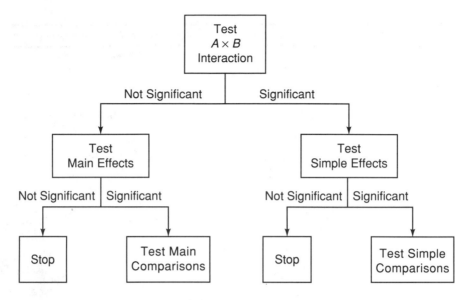

FIGURE 10-3 *A Summary of the Comprehensive Analysis of a Factorial Experiment.*

effects. Depending on the particular analyses that are significant as a result of these examinations, the researcher might undertake simple comparisons to pinpoint even more precisely the source (or sources) of the significant $A \times B$ interaction. These various steps are specified on the right side of Fig. 10-3.

If the $A \times B$ interaction is not significant, a researcher will generally turn to an examination of the two main effects. At this point, the analysis will closely resemble the analysis of a single-factor experiment. If a main effect is significant, analytical comparisons of the sort we originally described in Chap. 6 will be conducted on the marginal treatment means. These steps are specified on the left side of the figure.

No analysis plan is ever as rigid as the one outlined in Fig. 10-3. We offer this particular plan more as a summary than as a mandatory course of action. Specific research hypotheses and questions — that is, planned comparisons — will still be assessed statistically regardless of the status of the overall $A \times B$ interaction or the two overall main effects. You should use this summary to guide your thinking in the planning stages of an experiment to remind you of the possible ways in which a factorial experiment can be analyzed. Above all, the figure illustrates that a researcher involved in such an analysis proceeds logically, exploring each significant effect until it is necessary to stop.

You may have noticed that we have not mentioned the issue of familywise (or cumulative) type I error in this discussion. Whereas correction techniques are available for reducing familywise type I error in the detailed analysis of factorial experiments, most researchers do not use them. Instead, they seem more concerned about isolating and detecting the factors responsible for significant interactions and main effects than about any increase in type I error resulting from this process. Corrections for familywise type I error work against this goal by making it more difficult to identify these critical factors, which is why researchers are reluctant to use them. In essence, then, researchers view the systematic analysis of a factorial experiment, summarized in Fig. 10-3, in the same way they view planned comparisons in the single-factor design — that is, as a comprehensive analysis strategy formed during the planning stage of a study that should not be affected by concerns for cumulative type I error.

10.6 SUMMARY

This chapter considered the questions a researcher might explore after completing the overall analysis of a factorial experiment, which was described in the preceding chapter. These additional analyses are usually required to identify the specific factors contributing to any significant main effect or interaction. We began by emphasizing the critical role that the test for interaction plays in the interpretation of the results of a factorial experiment. That is, a significant interaction directs our attention to the cell means and analyses of the simple effects, whereas a nonsignificant interaction directs our attention to the marginal means and detailed analyses of the main effects.

We first discussed the analysis of main effects, which is usually undertaken when the interaction is not significant. This consisted of single-df comparisons performed on the relevant set of marginal means. The analysis of these main comparisons, as they are called, is equivalent to a corresponding analysis based on an actual single-factor study, except that the data are derived from one independent variable in a factorial design and are combined over the levels of the other independent variable.

The remainder of the chapter covered analyses that are appropriate when we discover in the overall analysis that the $A \times B$ interaction is significant. We argued that whereas a significant interaction allows us to conclude that interaction effects are present, its discovery does not indicate which aspects of the interaction are critical. An analysis of simple effects — a widely used technique — permits the localization of interaction effects. An analysis of simple effects treats the factorial as a set of single-factor experiments. Such an analysis is most useful when theory specifies the presence of a simple effect at one level of the other independent variable and the absence of a simple effect of an independent variable at another level. Such theoretical expectations can be statistically assessed through an analysis of simple effects. Frequently, a significant simple effect is further analyzable through the use of simple comparisons, a technique that is quite similar to those discussed in Chap. 6 for the detailed analysis of single-factor experiments.

We briefly consider in an appendix to this chapter an alternative way of analyzing interaction, the analysis of interaction contrasts. Rather than treat the factorial as a set of single-factor experiments, the investigator conducts an analysis of interaction contrasts within the context of the factorial design. Interactions specified by interaction contrasts are often used in isolating or identifying the sources contributing to a significant overall $A \times B$ interaction.

10.7 EXERCISES [4]

*1. The analysis of variance conducted on the data from the factorial experiment appearing in exercise 3 of Chap. 9 (p. 272) revealed that the two main effects were significant whereas the interaction was not. This means, of course, that we can interpret the outcome of this experiment by considering the main effect of each independent variable individually, without reference to the other. Because factor A consists of three different strains of laboratory rats ("bright," "mixed," and "dull"), we can conduct several main comparisons to help us in interpreting the results of this experiment. (Factor B consists of only two levels — enriched and impoverished environments — and can be analyzed no further.) Conduct the following main comparisons:

    a. "Bright" versus "dull" rats

    b. "Bright" versus "mixed" rats

    c. "Dull" versus "mixed" rats

*2. Exercise 2 in Chap. 9 (p. 271) revealed a significant interaction of task difficulty (factor A) and the number of distractors (factor B).

    a. Conduct an analysis of the simple effects of task difficulty for the three distractor conditions. What have you learned from this analysis?

---

[4] Answers to the starred problems are given in Appendix B.

b. Conduct an analysis of the simple effects of the number of distractors for the two task conditions. What have you learned from this analysis?

c. Given the outcome in part (b), test the following simple comparisons:

(1) A pairwise comparison between levels b_2 and b_3

(2) A complex comparison between level b_1 and the other two levels combined

3. Table 9-1 (p. 237) presents the means from a fictitious 3×3 factorial. For this problem, let's assume that the sample size was $n = 10$. Transform the nine cell means into an AB matrix of treatment sums. (You may have performed this step in answering exercise 4 in Chap. 9.)

a. Conduct an analysis of variance on these data, assuming that $\Sigma\, Y^2 = 2,325$ for the entire data set.

b. Conduct an analysis of the following main comparisons:

(1) A comparison between saline and lidocaine

(2) A comparison between saline and cocaine

(3) A comparison between cocaine and an average of saline and lidocaine

4. Table 9-2 (p. 242) presents the means from the same fictitious 3×3 factorial considered in exercise 3. Again, assume that sample size was $n = 10$ and transform the means into a corresponding AB matrix of treatment sums. (You may have performed this step in answering exercise 4 in Chap. 9.)

a. Conduct an analysis of variance on these data, assuming that $\Sigma\, Y^2 = 2,395$ for the entire data set.

b. Conduct an analysis of the simple effects of the time variable (factor A) for the three substance conditions.

c. Conduct an analysis of the simple effects of the substance variable (factor B) for the three delay conditions.

d. For each significant simple effect in part (c), perform the following simple comparisons:

(1) A comparison between saline and lidocaine

(2) A comparison between saline and cocaine

(3) A comparison between cocaine and an average of saline and lidocaine

5. Exercise 6 in Chap. 9 (p. 275) presented the results of a factorial experiment in which young and adult kangaroo rats were given 60 minutes to explore an artificial burrow in which different scents were introduced.

a. Conduct an analysis of the simple effects of the age variable (factor B) for the three scent conditions.

    b. Conduct an analysis of the simple effects of the scent variable (factor A) for the two age groups.

    c. For the significant simple effect in part (b), perform the following simple comparisons:

        (1) A comparison between the control and unfamiliar conditions

        (2) A comparison between the unfamiliar and familiar conditions

*6. Exercise 5 provided you with practice in conducting the more common way of studying interaction, namely, an analysis of simple effects, which — if they are significant — is usually followed by an additional analysis of simple comparisons. This problem has been included for those readers who have studied the appendix to this chapter on interaction contrasts (Sec. 10.8). Factor A readily lends itself to the examination of two such analyses, one created by focusing on the comparison between the control and unfamiliar conditions and the other on the comparison between the unfamiliar and familiar conditions.

    a. Create a 2×2 AB matrix in which the scent variable is represented by the control and unfamiliar conditions and the age variable by the young and adult animals.

    b. After examining the relevant data in the matrix (or in a plot of the means), describe the nature of this interaction contrast. Describe the interaction two ways, one in terms of the difference between the two scent conditions and the other in terms of the difference between the two age groups.

    c. Test the significance of the interaction contrast.

    d. Given the outcome in part (c), we would probably be interested in testing each of the differences making up the interaction contrast separately. We will concentrate on the effect of the two scent conditions on the young and adult kangaroo rats.

        (1) Is the difference between the control and unfamiliar conditions significant for the young rats?

        (2) Is the difference between the control and unfamiliar conditions significant for the adult rats?

7. This problem deals with the other interaction contrast mentioned in exercise 6, namely, the interaction between the unfamiliar and familiar conditions and the young and adult rats.

    a. Create a 2×2 AB matrix in which the scent variable is represented by the unfamiliar and familiar conditions and the age variable by the young and adult animals.

    b. After examining the relevant data in the matrix (or in a plot of the means), describe the nature of this interaction contrast. Describe the interaction two ways, one in terms of the difference between the two scent conditions and the other in terms of the difference between the two age groups.

c. Test the significance of the interaction contrast.

d. Given the outcome in part (c), we would probably be interested in testing each of the differences making up the interaction contrast separately. We will concentrate on the effect of the two scent conditions on the young and adult kangaroo rats.

(1) Is the difference between the unfamiliar and familiar conditions significant for the young rats?

(2) Is the difference between the unfamiliar and familiar conditions significant for the adult rats?

10.8 APPENDIX: ANALYZING INTERACTION CONTRASTS [5]

Another type of analysis is useful in examining the data from a factorial experiment. In contrast with an analysis of simple effects, where the factorial is analyzed as a set of component single-factor experiments, this alternative procedure preserves the factorial nature of the manipulation and concentrates instead on a number of smaller, component *factorial* designs. We will concentrate on a special type of analysis created when the component factorial forms a 2×2 design. An interaction based on such a component factorial is called an **interaction contrast**.

Creating Interaction Contrasts from the Overall Factorial Design

The top portion of Table 10-12 shows the results of our numerical example. Below this matrix, we have created out of the original 3×2 factorial design a

---

[5] This appendix is intended for students in advanced courses on research design and statistical analysis. Instructors may wish to omit this material in more introductory courses.

TABLE 10-12 *An Example of an Interaction Contrast*

	Praise	Criticism	Silence
Simple	7.60	7.20	4.40
Complex	7.00	2.00	3.20

	Praise	Criticism
Simple	7.60	7.20
Complex	7.00	2.00

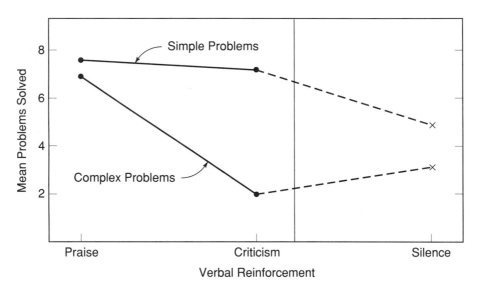

FIGURE 10-4 *An Example of an Interaction Contrast. (The means contributing to the interaction contrast are plotted on the left; the two means not contributing to the interaction contrast are plotted on the right.)*

"miniature" 2×2 factorial experiment by omitting the two silence groups from the analysis. We have highlighted the outcome of this miniature experiment in Fig. 10-4 by emphasizing this portion of the results with solid lines. As you can see, this transformation has produced a smaller experiment consisting of the two levels of factor A we have isolated (praise and criticism) and the two levels of the original factor B (simple and complex). This new factorial, derived from the larger 3×2 factorial design, focuses on one particular aspect of the original manipulation of factor A, namely, the difference between the two kinds of verbal reinforcement.

The interaction of this new design provides more detailed information about the original $A \times B$ interaction, specifically, whether the difference between praise and criticism changes with an increase in the difficulty of the problems. The significant overall $A \times B$ interaction we calculated in Chap. 9 does not give us this particular information directly. All we know from that analysis is that interaction effects are present — but not which ones are present. An examination of the data from the treatment combinations contributing to the interaction contrast, on the other hand, focuses directly on this question and suggests that an interaction is present: there is little difference between praise and criticism with the simple reasoning problems, but the difference increases substantially with the complex problems. If we were to conduct a statistical analysis with the data entering into this interaction contrast, which we will present shortly, we would find that this component interaction is significant.

Most large factorial experiments can be profitably transformed into a number of interaction contrasts, each one focusing on a different aspect of the $A \times B$ interaction.[6] To illustrate with the numerical example, consider the three interaction contrasts presented in Table 10-13. Each one is based on a different pairwise comparison involving the reinforcement variable — namely, praise versus criticism, praise versus silence, and criticism versus silence. As a consequence, each corresponding interaction contrast focuses on a different aspect of the overall $A \times B$ interaction. Let's consider each of the interaction contrasts in turn:

The first interaction contrast involves *praise and criticism* and allows us to determine whether the difference between these two types of verbal reinforcement depends on the type of reasoning problems.

The second interaction contrast involves *praise and silence* and allows us to determine whether the difference between praise and the absence of verbal reinforcement depends on the type of reasoning problems.

The third interaction contrast involves *criticism and silence* and allows us to determine whether the difference between criticism and the absence of verbal reinforcement depends on the type of reasoning problems.

---

[6] In this appendix, we consider *pairwise* interaction contrasts formed by isolating four relevant treatment combinations from the larger design — such as the one diagrammed in Table 10-12. More complex analyses are possible, but these are beyond the scope of this book. You can find useful treatments of interaction contrasts and other procedures in an article by Boik (1979) and in most advanced books on data analysis (see, for example, Keppel, 1991, Chap. 12; Kirk, 1982, pp. 371–379; and Myers & Well, 1991, pp. 188–194).

TABLE 10-13 *Additional Examples of Interaction Contrasts Based on the Numerical Example*

	Interaction Contrasts			Specific Research Questions
	Praise	Criticism	Silence	
Simple				Is the difference between praise and criticism the same for simple and complex problems?
Complex				

	Praise	Criticism	Silence	
Simple				Is the difference between praise and silence the same for simple and complex problems?
Complex				

	Praise	Criticism	Silence	
Simple				Is the difference between criticism and silence the same for simple and complex problems?
Complex				

Computational Procedures

A simple way to conduct the analysis of an interaction contrast is to treat the analysis as an actual 2 × 2 factorial design and then apply to this special arrangement of the data the procedures we would normally follow in the analysis of a factorial design. More specifically, we create a 2 × 2 factorial and use the computational formulas from Chap. 9 to calculate and evaluate the interaction. Let's see how easily this analysis is accomplished.

We will illustrate the analysis with the interaction contrast formed by isolating praise and criticism. We start by creating a special 2 × 2 AB matrix in which both independent variables are represented by two levels — praise and criticism (factor A) and simple and complex (factor B). This matrix is presented in Table 10-14, with notational symbols on the left and the relevant treatment sums on the right. From this point on, we can treat this AB matrix as having been produced by an actual factorial experiment in which both independent variables consisted of two levels.

Table 10-15 summarizes the computational steps involved in evaluating the significance of this interaction contrast. We begin with the basic ratios (step 1), which are calculated in the usual fashion, remembering that $a = 2$ (not 3) for this analysis. In step 2, we calculate the interaction sum of squares. (As you can see, the computational formula for this sum of squares is identical to the

TABLE 10-14 *Forming the AB Matrix for an Interaction Contrast*

Notational Symbols				Numerical Example			
	a_1	a_2	Sum		Praise	Criticism	Sum
b_1	$AB_{1,1}$	$AB_{2,1}$	B_1	Simple	38	36	74
b_2	$AB_{1,2}$	$AB_{2,2}$	B_2	Complex	35	10	45
Sum	A_1	A_2	T	Sum	73	46	119

TABLE 10-15 *Steps in the Analysis of an Interaction Contrast*

1. Calculate the Basic Ratios:

$$[AB] = \frac{\Sigma(AB)^2}{n} = \frac{(38)^2 + (36)^2 + (35)^2 + (10)^2}{5}$$

$$= \frac{4,065}{5} = 813.00$$

$$[A] = \frac{\Sigma A^2}{(b)(n)} = \frac{(73)^2 + (46)^2}{(2)(5)} = \frac{7,445}{10} = 744.50$$

$$[B] = \frac{\Sigma B^2}{(a)(n)} = \frac{(74)^2 + (45)^2}{(2)(5)} = \frac{7,501}{10} = 750.10$$

$$[T] = \frac{T^2}{(a)(b)(n)} = \frac{(119)^2}{(2)(2)(5)} = \frac{14,161}{20} = 708.05$$

2. Calculate $SS_{int.\ cont.}$:

$$[AB] - [A] - [B] + [T] = 813.00 - 744.50 - 750.10 + 708.05 = 26.45$$

3. Calculate $df_{int.\ cont.}$:

$$(a-1)(b-1) = (2-1)(2-1) = (1)(1) = 1$$

4. Calculate $MS_{int.\ cont.}$:

$$\frac{SS_{int.\ cont}}{df_{int.\ cont.}} = \frac{26.45}{1} = 26.45$$

5. Calculate $F_{int.\ cont.}$:

$$\frac{MS_{int.\ cont.}}{MS_{S/AB}} = \frac{26.45}{3.50} = 7.56$$

one we used in Chap. 9.) The remaining steps summarized in Table 10-15 also involve the same computational formulas we followed in Chap. 9. Because the interaction contrast is based on a 2 × 2 factorial, the number of degrees of freedom associated with the interaction is $df_{int.\ cont.} = 1$. The F is formed with $MS_{int.\ cont.}$ in the numerator and the $MS_{S/AB}$ from the original analysis in the denominator. The critical value of this F, which is based on $df_{num.} = 1$ and $df_{denom.} = df_{S/AB} = 24$, is $F(1, 24) = 4.26$. The decision rule becomes

If $F_{int.\ cont.} \geq 4.26$, reject the null hypothesis; otherwise, retain the null hypothesis.

We conclude that the interaction contrast is significant.

Additional Analyses

As we discussed in Sec. 10.3, we usually follow the discovery of a significant interaction with an analysis of the simple effects, in an analytical attempt to identify the factors responsible for the significant interaction. We usually follow this same strategy when we discover a significant interaction contrast.

Let's see how we apply this procedure to the significant interaction we calculated in the previous section. Consider carefully what this significant interaction contrast allows us to conclude up to this point: the difference between the two forms of verbal reinforcement depends on the type of reasoning problems the children receive. The analysis does *not* tell us anything directly about the significance of either of the two differences. Although an inspection of Table 10-14 suggests that the difference will not be significant for the simple problems and probably will be significant for the complex problems, we will still need to evaluate these observations statistically before we can reach any firm conclusion with regard to the status of either of these two differences.

One way to conduct these additional analyses is to isolate each row of the special AB matrix and treat that specific set of data as a separate single-factor design. This approach to uncovering the factors responsible for a significant interaction is called an *analysis of the simple effects*, which we can apply to any factorial design regardless of size. The fact that that this miniature 2×2 design has been extracted from the larger factorial does not change the basic logic underlying this approach to the detailed analysis of a significant interaction.

What we will do next with our significant interaction contrast, then, is to isolate the data appearing in the first row of the AB matrix in Table 10-14, which reflects the difference between praise and criticism for the children receiving the simple problems, and use Eq. (10-8) to calculate the sum of

TABLE 10-16 *Summary of the Analysis of Simple Effects*

Source	SS	df	MS	F
Praise versus Criticism for Simple Problems	.40	1	.40	.11
Praise versus Criticism for Complex Problems	62.50	1	62.50	17.86*
S/AB		24	3.50	

* $p < .05$.

squares; more specifically,

$$SS_{A \text{ at } b_1} = \frac{\Sigma(AB_{i1})^2}{n} - \frac{(B_1)^2}{(a)(n)}$$

$$= \frac{(38)^2 + (36)^2}{5} - \frac{(74)^2}{(2)(5)}$$

$$= \frac{2,740}{5} - \frac{5,476}{10} = 548.00 - 547.60$$

$$= .40$$

The corresponding sum of squares for the second row, which reflects the difference between praise and criticism for the children receiving the complex problems, becomes

$$SS_{A \text{ at } b_2} = \frac{\Sigma(AB_{i2})^2}{n} - \frac{(B_2)^2}{(a)(n)}$$

$$= \frac{(35)^2 + (10)^2}{5} - \frac{(45)^2}{(2)(5)}$$

$$= \frac{1,325}{5} - \frac{2,025}{10} = 265.00 - 202.50$$

$$= 62.50$$

These two sums of squares are entered in Table 10-16 for the final steps in the analysis. The degrees of freedom for each sum of squares is 1. The F's are formed by dividing each mean square by the $MS_{S/AB}$ from the overall analysis. The critical value for these two F's, which is based on $df_{num.} = 1$ and $df_{denom.} = df_{S/AB} = 24$, is $F(1, 24) = 4.26$. The decision rule becomes

If $F \geq 4.26$, reject the null hypothesis; otherwise, retain the null hypothesis.

We conclude that the difference between praise and criticism is significant only with the complex problems.[7]

---

[7] Exercises 6 and 7 provide you with practice in analyzing interaction contrasts.

PART · FOUR

THE ANALYSIS OF WITHIN-SUBJECTS DESIGNS

In this part, we consider designs that are widely utilized in the behavioral and social sciences because of their economical use of subjects and their greater statistical power, particularly when compared with the completely randomized designs we covered in Parts Two and Three. These designs are ones in which subjects serve in more than one or even in all of the treatment conditions. Because the variations of treatments representing an independent variable are administered to the same subjects in these designs, we call them *within-subjects designs* — designs in which the effects of an independent variable are reflected by differences observed *within* subjects. Completely randomized designs, in which subjects receive only one treatment, are called *between-subjects designs* — designs in which the effects of an independent variable are reflected by differences observed *between* subjects.

In Chap. 11, we consider the simplest type of within-subjects design, namely, a design in which subjects receive all levels of a single independent variable. We examine in detail the way in which this important experimental design "works" for two reasons: because undergraduate students frequently choose this sort of design for an undergraduate class project, independent study, or an honors thesis; and because it serves as a building block for the more complex designs that graduate students and professional experimenters choose for their research.

Chapters 12 and 13 show how we can extend the within-subjects design to factorial experiments. Chapter 12 focuses on the *mixed within-subjects factorial design*, which represents a mixture or blending of between-subjects and within-subjects designs. This is accomplished by having subjects receive some but not all of the treatment combinations created by the factorial design. Chapter 13, on the other hand, considers the analysis of a "pure" within-subjects factorial design in which subjects receive *all* of the factorial treatment combinations. You will encounter both types of within-subjects factorial experiments in the contemporary research literature of the behavioral and social sciences.

Chapter · 11

THE SINGLE-FACTOR WITHIN-SUBJECTS DESIGN

The simplest type of experimental design is one in which subjects are assigned randomly to the different conditions in the experiment and are given only one of the treatments. As we noted in Chap. 4, this type of design is called a *completely randomized design*; another term is **between-subjects design**. Both terms emphasize the primary characteristics of this design, namely, that subjects are assigned randomly to the different conditions and that treatment effects are associated with differences between independent groups of subjects. Frequently, however, researchers use a different type of design, whereby the *same* subject serves in *all* the treatment conditions rather than just one. This second type of design is called a **repeated-measures**, or a **within-subjects design**. Again, both terms stress the basic nature of this design — specifically, that repeated measurements are taken on the same subjects and that treatment effects are associated with differences observed within each of the subjects.

The within-subjects design has become the typical design used to study such phenomena as learning, transfer of training, and practice effects of all sorts. In a learning experiment, for example, subjects may receive a series of study-test trials and performance is charted as a function of these trials; trial number becomes the independent variable in this type of experiment. But use of this design is not limited to learning studies. Researchers studying other topics use the within-subjects design because it is characteristically efficient and sensitive, especially in comparison with an equivalent between-subjects design. Students are often forced by circumstances to use the within-subjects design for their research projects because the number of subjects available to serve in their experiments is limited. Because this design is so prevalent, you should understand its advantages and disadvantages and be able to analyze data from experiments of this type. Fortunately, the analysis is not difficult and is based on procedures discussed in earlier chapters.[1]

---

[1] The analysis of within-subjects designs can be complicated, however, especially when the underlying assumptions of the analysis are not met. We will ignore these considerations in this book and provide references to more detailed discussions when appropriate.

11.1 REDUCING ERROR VARIANCE

While one reason for using a within-subjects design is a scarcity of subjects, researchers also use this type of design to minimize the amount of experimental error (error variance) operating in their experiments. As we discussed in Chap. 8, any reduction in error variance will produce an *increase in power*. To highlight this important advantage of the within-subjects design, we discuss in this section various ways in which error variance may be reduced.

Holding Nuisance Variables Constant

In Chap. 3, we discussed the method of reducing error variance by holding nuisance variables constant. Many environmental variables — for example, temperature, humidity, level of illumination, and background noises — can be held constant through the use of regulating devices and the construction of experimental apparatus, and others can be controlled through the careful administration of conditions — for instance, through standardizing the experimental procedures and testing at certain hours.

Using Matched Subjects

Holding nuisance variables constant through experimental control is one means of reducing error variance. In most experiments, however, the primary source of error variability is the subjects. Controlling, or at least reducing, the effects of subject variability in an experiment requires special attention.

Using **matched subjects** — matched on characteristics assumed to be relevant to the behavior under study — is equivalent to using some form of physical control to hold environmental factors constant. Two types of matching exist. The first type consists of forming a group of "homogeneous" subjects, subjects who possess roughly the same talents or abilities or characteristics deemed important for the experiment. These subjects are then assigned randomly to the different treatment conditions. This type of matching is illustrated in Fig. 11-1, in which the group, or "pool," of subjects is formed on the basis of similar college grade-point averages (GPA's). The experimenter then randomly assigns subjects from this homogeneous pool to the $a = 3$ groups that receive the different treatment conditions. This technique can result in a considerable reduction in the size of the error term calculated for a completely randomized design — $MS_{S/A}$ in the single-factor design and $MS_{S/AB}$ in the two-variable factorial design.

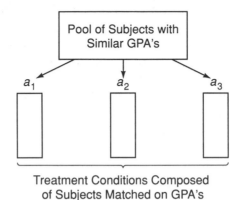

FIGURE 11-1 *Representation of a Design in Which Subjects are Grouped on the Basis of Grade-Point Average (GPA) to Form a Homogenous Pool and Then Randomly Assigned to the Three Levels of Factor A.*

A second type of matching is accomplished in small sets, or *blocks*, as the sets are usually called. A block of subjects consists of a group of subjects matched closely on a relevant characteristic, for example, grade-point average in college. Different values of the matching variable are used to group subjects in different blocks. Once the blocks are formed, subjects within each block are assigned randomly to the different treatment conditions. This type of matching, which is called a **blocking design**, is diagramed in Fig. 11-2. In this case, subjects are first grouped in three blocks according to GPA's and then assigned from each pool to the $a = 3$ treatment conditions. The final design is a *factorial experiment*, in which factor A is the manipulated independent variable and factor B is the blocking variable (in this case, GPA).

The blocking design is generally preferred, since finding small groups of matched subjects (blocks) is easier than finding a large one (a single homogeneous group). Furthermore, the results of an experiment utilizing matched blocks are assumed to have considerable generality, since they are based on the performance of subjects varying widely on the matching characteristic from block to block. In contrast, the results of an experiment using a *single* group of matched subjects may be of limited generality, since the results may be specifically related to the particular type of subject chosen for the study — say, for example, students with high grade-point averages.

Certain problems are associated with the matching procedure. First, as mentioned, finding a sufficiently large number of matched subjects for a single homogeneous group of subjects is often difficult. Second, identifying charac-

Three Pools of Homogeneous Subjects

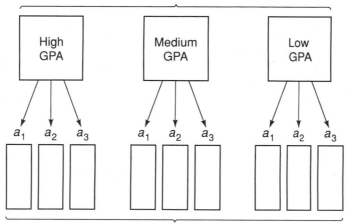

Three Treatment Conditions Each Composed of
Three Matched Groups of Subjects

Factorial Representation of the Blocking

Treatment

	a_1	a_2	a_3
b_1			
b_2			
b_3			

GPA

FIGURE 11-2 *Representation of a Blocking Design with Three Pools of Subjects Grouped According to Grade-Point Average (GPA) from Which Subjects Are Randomly Assigned to the Three Levels of Factor A.*

teristics that are relatively easy to obtain and, more important, strongly related to the dependent variable can also present problems. Unless a close relationship exists between the matching variable and the dependent variable, the reduction in error variance from matching will be slight and the efforts expended to achieve the matching will have been wasted. Unfortunately, a lack of relationship between the matching variable and the dependent variable is all too common in psychological research.

Using the Same Subject

The most typical method for reducing error variance is to use the same subject in all the treatment conditions. This results in a perfect "matching" across conditions, reducing error variance. However, some problems are associated with this type of design as well. The primary problem is the influence of residual or **carryover effects** from previous conditions on the responses of subjects to the currently administered treatments. When the actual purpose of the research is to study the residual effects of a prior treatment, as in transfer-of-training studies, we do not have to be concerned with the presence of carryover effects. But when residual effects are *not* the purpose of the study, they need to be controlled or eliminated so that the influence of the independent variable may be observed without distortion or contamination. Failing to deal with this problem results in a confounding of the independent variable and the carryover effects from previous testing.

To illustrate, suppose we are comparing the effects of two different drugs on a motor-coordination task in a within-subjects design. All subjects perform the task twice, once after receiving drug A and once after receiving drug B. Suppose that half of the subjects receive drug A first, followed by drug B, and that the other half receive drug B first, followed by drug A. Unless the lingering effects of the first drug subjects receive are completely dissipated before the second drug is administered, we will not be able to disentangle the influence of these carryover effects on the motor-coordination task from the effect of the second drug. That is, subjects receiving drug A second will be influenced by both drug A as well as to any lingering effects of drug B; similarly, subjects receiving drug B second will be influenced by drug B in addition to the lingering effects of drug A. Unless steps are taken to eliminate the residual effects of the first drug *before* the second drug is administered, the data obtained in this part of the experiment are probably worthless.

Frequently, researchers are able to convince themselves that carryover effects are not a problem — they either assume that such effects do not exist or that they have been minimized by allowing sufficient time for the effects of earlier treatments to dissipate. In the example of the two drugs, we might schedule the sessions several days apart to allow the substance administered previously to be eliminated from the body. Another procedure, used in operant-conditioning research, is to bring each subject back to some predetermined level before starting the next treatment. We consider some solutions to carryover effects and related problems in Sec. 11.6.

In spite of the need to eliminate or minimize carryover effects, the within-subjects design is still widely used by both professional researchers and students.

In the following section, we consider the logic behind the analysis of data collected in this sort of experiment.

11.2 LOGIC OF THE ANALYSIS OF WITHIN-SUBJECTS DESIGNS

In this section, we will compare the single-factor between-subjects design with the corresponding within-subjects design and show how the latter design reduces error variance.

The Basic Design

Table 11-1 is a comparison between the two types of designs. While both examples contain the same number of observations — three in each treatment condition — they differ in the number of subjects needed to produce them. The between-subjects design on the left has $(a)(n) = (3)(3) = 9$ subjects. As indicated in the table, each subject in this design (S_1 through S_9) receives only one of the treatment conditions. The within-subjects design on the right has $n = 3$ subjects; each subject receives all three treatment conditions, as the table indicates by listing a single subject in all the treatment cells for any given row. As you will see, this change in the nature of the basic experimental design affects the formal statistical analysis.

TABLE 11-1 *A Comparison of Between-Subjects and Within-Subjects Designs*

Between-Subjects Design			Within-Subjects Design		
a_1	a_2	a_3	a_1	a_2	a_3
S_1	S_4	S_7	S_1	S_1	S_1
S_2	S_5	S_8	S_2	S_2	S_2
S_3	S_6	S_9	S_3	S_3	S_3

A Numerical Example of a Within-Subjects Design

We will use a simple numerical example to illustrate how a within-subjects design allows us to reduce error variability. As a point of reference, we will consider first an example of a between-subjects design. Table 11-2 presents the fictitious data matrix for the between-subjects design we depicted on the left side of Table 11-1. As you can see, there are $a = 3$ treatment conditions, each containing $n = 3$ observations; the scores for this example were produced by nine different subjects. The individual Y scores appear in the body of the data matrix, and the column totals are the A treatment sums for the three treatment conditions. The steps in calculating the sums of squares are indicated below the data matrix. Of critical interest to us are the two sums of squares, $SS_A = 6$ and $SS_{S/A} = 52$.

Table 11-3 presents the same set of data, this time cast as a within-subjects design. Look carefully at the differences between this data matrix and the one for the between-subjects design in Table 11-2. More specifically, the first row contains the three Y scores for the first subject, the second row contains

---

TABLE 11-2 *An Example of a Between-Subjects Design*

Data Matrix

	a_1	a_2	a_3
	9	7	5
	3	3	0
	3	2	4
Sum:	15	12	9

Calculating Basic Ratios

$$[T] = \frac{T^2}{(a)(n)} = \frac{(36)^2}{(3)(3)} = \frac{1,296}{9} = 144$$

$$[A] = \frac{\Sigma A^2}{n} = \frac{(15)^2 + (12)^2 + (9)^2}{3} = \frac{450}{3} = 150$$

$$[Y] = \Sigma Y^2 = (9)^2 + (3)^2 + \cdots + (0)^2 + (4)^2 = 202$$

Calculating Sums of Squares

$$SS_A = [A] - [T] = 150 - 144 = 6$$

$$SS_{S/A} = [Y] - [A] = 202 - 150 = 52$$

TABLE 11-3 *The Example from Table* 11-2 *as a Within-Subjects Design*

	a_1	a_2	a_3	Sum	Mean
s_1	9	7	5	21	7
s_2	3	3	0	6	2
s_3	3	2	4	9	3
Sum	15	12	9	36	4

the three Y scores for the second subject, and so on; this is different than the between-subjects design where the 9 Y scores came from 9 different subjects. In addition, we have added a column to the right of the data matrix in which we have entered the sum of the Y scores for each of the three subjects, labeled "sum" in the table. From the information in this column, we can easily calculate the average performance for each subject, which we have entered in the final column of this matrix. We could calculate $SS_{S/A}$ from the data in this matrix, of course, but the variation represented by this sum of squares does not provide an appropriate estimate of error variability for this design. The reasoning behind this statement reflects the distinctive advantage of using the same subjects in all treatment conditions. Let's see why.

In the between-subjects design, since subjects are randomly assigned to the treatment conditions, differences between the treatment means may be entirely due to chance. As a consequence of this assignment process, any differences we may observe among the treatment means must reflect the joint operation of these chance differences and any treatment effects that may be present in the treatment populations. Thus, the MS_A reflects both chance variation (which we variously call *experimental error* or *error variance*) and potential treatment effects. We use the $MS_{S/A}$ to estimate the operation of chance factors alone and form the F ratio, $MS_A \div MS_{S/A}$, to provide us a way of deciding whether treatment effects are present or not. By now, this should be a familiar argument!

Consider next the within-subjects design and the chance factors that may be operating to influence the treatment means. Because the *same subject* serves in each of the treatment conditions, a major source of uncontrolled variability found in the between-subjects design — that due to the random assignment of *different subjects* — is simply not present in the within-subjects design. We can determine the degree to which the $MS_{S/A}$ overestimates chance factors operating in the within-subjects design and then remove this variation from the analysis. One way to do this is to use a subject's average performance ($\overline{Y}_S$) to estimate the degree to which the subject is *consistent* from treatment to treatment and then remove this estimate from the individual Y scores for all subjects. By removing an estimate of a subject's consistency from the Y scores, we leave behind the chance factors that are *not* consistent, variation that *does* contribute to the differences we observe among the treatment means.

We can understand how this works by subtracting each subject's mean from the three relevant Y scores in Table 11-3. For example, the mean for the first subject is $\overline{Y}_{S_1} = 7$. If we subtract 7 from each of this subject's three Y scores, we produce the following "new" Y scores:

$$9 - 7 = 2$$

$$7 - 7 = 0$$

$$5 - 7 = -2$$

These adjusted Y scores are entered in the first row, s_1, of Table 11-4. We obtain corresponding adjusted scores for the other two subjects by subtracting their means, $\overline{Y}_{S_2} = 2$ and $\overline{Y}_{S_3} = 3$, from their respective Y scores. The results of these subtractions are presented in the next two rows of the table.

Let's look at the transformed data matrix more closely. The totals for each subject are now 0, which indicates clearly that consistent individual differences between subjects have been removed from the data set. The treatment totals (3, 0, and −3) may seem strange, but they still reflect the same differences among the treatment conditions as do the sums based on the original Y scores in Table 11-3. We can see this most clearly by comparing the pairwise differences between treatment means. The means for treatment conditions a_1 through a_3, respectively, are 5, 4, and 3 for the original Y scores and 1, 0, and −1 for the transformed Y scores. Each of the three pairwise differences for the two sets of scores are as follows:

	a_1 vs. a_2	a_1 vs. a_3	a_2 vs. a_3
Original Y scores:	$5 - 4 = 1$	$5 - 3 = 2$	$4 - 3 = 1$
Transformed Y scores:	$1 - 0 = 1$	$1 - (-1) = 2$	$0 - (-1) = 1$

As you can readily see, we have not changed the basic outcome of the experiment by subtracting each subject's mean from the three Y scores.

Suppose we now calculate SS_A and $SS_{S/A}$ from this set of transformed data, as summarized in the bottom portions of the table. If you compare these sums of squares with those we calculated in Table 11-2, you will find that the two SS_A's are identical, which is what we would expect from our examination of the pairwise differences in the preceding paragraph. However, the $SS_{S/A}$ from the within-subjects design is dramatically reduced by the removal of consistent subject variability (10 versus 52).

TABLE 11-4   *The Within-Subjects Design with the Average Performance of Subjects Removed from the Individual Y Scores*

Transformed Data Matrix

	a_1	a_2	a_3	Sum
s_1	2	0	−2	0
s_2	1	1	−2	0
s_3	0	−1	1	0
Sum	3	0	−3	0

Calculating Basic Ratios

$$[T] = \frac{T^2}{(a)(n)} = \frac{(0)^2}{(3)(3)} = 0$$

$$[A] = \frac{\Sigma A^2}{n} = \frac{(3)^2 + (0)^2 + (-3)^2}{3} = \frac{18}{3} = 6$$

$$[Y] = \Sigma Y^2 = (2)^2 + (0)^2 + \cdots + (-1)^2 + (1)^2 = 16$$

Calculating Sums of Squares

$$SS_A = [A] - [T] = 6 - 0 = 6$$

$$SS_{S/A} = [Y] - [A] = 16 - 6 = 10$$

Pictorial Representation of the Analysis

We can represent the logic behind the analysis of a within-subjects design pictorially, by means of a pie chart. Consider the chart on the left of Fig. 11-3, which represents the analysis of a single-factor between-subjects design. The total variability in the analysis (SS_T) is encompassed by the entire circle. In the usual analysis, this variability is divided into two parts, that associated with the differences among the treatment means (SS_A) and that associated with the pooled variability of subjects within their own treatment groups ($SS_{S/A}$). We have divided the circle in two parts to represent this basic subdivision, basing the relative sizes on the assumption that the SS_A will account for a substantially smaller proportion of the total variability than the $SS_{S/A}$.

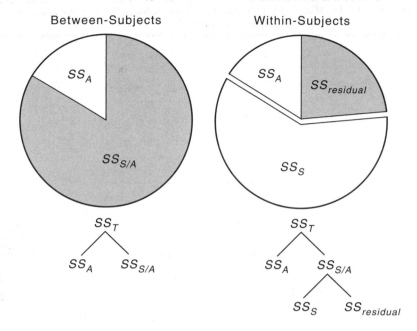

FIGURE 11-3 *Two Representations of the Analysis of Two Single-Factor Designs: A Pictorial Representation (Upper Portion) and a Symbolic Representation (Lower Portion).*

The chart on the right represents the analysis of a single-factor within-subjects design. We begin by identifying the variability associated with the differences among the treatment means (SS_A) as contributing to part of the circle. To reflect the special feature of the within-subjects design, however, we must divide the remaining portion of the circle, which represented $SS_{S/A}$ in the between-subjects design, into *two* parts — one part that represents the variability due to the consistent individual differences among the subjects and another part that represents behavior that is not consistent. We will call the first sum of squares SS_S and the second sum of squares $SS_{residual}$, to emphasize the leftover, or residual, quality of this source of variability. This residual variability, then, is our best estimate of chance variation — error variance — in a within-subjects design and will be used to calculate the denominator for the F ratio in the analysis of variance.

As you can readily see from the diagram, the within-subjects design achieves its smaller error term — that is, its increase in sensitivity — by isolating and removing a source of variability that *cannot* influence the differences among the treatment means. This consistent behavior of subjects (SS_S) is in reality the relative advantage or disadvantage in performance we expect to observe for each subject in *all* the treatment conditions; if this advantage (or disadvantage) affects all treatment conditions equally, it has no influence on the differences among the treatment means. This is why we subtracted SS_S from $SS_{S/A}$: we remove this constant variation, which does not affect the differences among the treatment means, and leave any chance variation that does ($SS_{residual}$). In the next section, we will show in more detail how the analysis proceeds. As you will see, there is a labor-saving computational way of removing consistent performance from the analysis of the data in a within-subjects design.

11.3 COMPUTATIONAL FORMULAS FOR THE ANALYSIS OF VARIANCE

In this section, we present the computational formulas for the analysis of variance; we will illustrate the calculations in Sec. 11.4. We begin with the sums of squares.

Sums of Squares

Notation. Table 11-5 summarizes the notational system we use to represent quantities critical for the statistical analysis of the within-subjects design. Notice that the system corresponds exactly to the one we use for the between-subjects design except for the marginal sums listed for each *row*, namely, S_1, S_2, and S_3. These sums are simply the *totals* for each subject.

Basic Ratios. The key ingredient in the calculation of the sums of squares is the basic ratios, which are distinguished by a series of arithmetical operations — squaring, summing, and dividing — conducted separately on the Y scores and the various sums specified in Table 11-5. We encountered three of these in the analysis of the between-subjects design (pp. 90–92). As a reminder,

$$[Y] = \Sigma\, Y^2, \quad [A] = \frac{\Sigma\, A^2}{n}, \quad \text{and} \quad [T] = \frac{T^2}{(a)(n)}$$

Exactly the same ratios are required for the analysis of the within-subjects design. In addition, one more ratio is needed, which is based on the sum of

TABLE 11-5 *Notational System for the Within-Subjects Design*

| Subjects | Levels of Factor A | | | Sum |
	a_1	a_2	a_3	
s_1	$Y_{1,1}$	$Y_{2,1}$	$Y_{3,1}$	S_1
s_2	$Y_{1,2}$	$Y_{2,2}$	$Y_{3,2}$	S_2
s_3	$Y_{1,3}$	$Y_{2,3}$	$Y_{3,3}$	S_3
Sum	A_1	A_2	A_3	T

the scores for each subject. This ratio is calculated as follows:

$$\text{✳} \quad [S] = \frac{\Sigma \, S^2}{a} \quad \text{✳} \qquad (11\text{-}1)$$

This value is the sum of all the squared subject totals divided by a, the number of treatment conditions.

Combining Basic Ratios. As depicted in Fig. 11-3, we divide the total sum of squares (SS_T) into three parts, namely,

$$SS_T = SS_A + SS_S + SS_{residual} \qquad (11\text{-}2)$$

The first two sums of squares listed in Eq. (11-2), SS_T and SS_A, are calculated just as they were in the between-subjects design; that is,

$$SS_T = [Y] - [T]$$
$$SS_A = [A] - [T]$$

The third sum of squares — the **subject sum of squares** (SS_S) — is based on the deviation of each subject's average score ($\overline{Y}_{S_j}$) from the grand mean ($\overline{Y}_T$). As we saw in Chap. 4, the computational formula for a sum of squares can be derived from the deviations defining that quantity. In the present case, the deviation is $\overline{Y}_{S_j} - \overline{Y}_T$, and the computational formula is

$$SS_S = [S] - [T] \qquad (11\text{-}3)$$

We can obtain the final sum of squares, $SS_{residual}$, by the following subtraction:

$$SS_{residual} = SS_{S/A} - SS_S \qquad (11\text{-}4)$$

Same calculations as Table 4-4

TABLE 11-6 *A Summary of the Analysis of the Within-Subjects Design*

Source	Sums of Squares[a]	df	MS	F
Treatments (A)	$[A] - [T]$	$(a-1)$	$\dfrac{SS_A}{df_A}$	$\dfrac{MS_A}{MS_{A \times S}}$
Subjects (S)	$[S] - [T]$	$(n-1)$	$\dfrac{SS_S}{df_S}$	
Residual (A × S)	$[Y] - [A] - [S] + [T]$	$(a-1)(n-1)$	$\dfrac{SS_{A \times S}}{df_{A \times S}}$	
Total	$[Y] - [T]$	$(a)(n) - 1$		

[a] $[A] = \dfrac{\Sigma A^2}{n}$, $[T] = \dfrac{T^2}{(a)(n)}$, $[S] = \dfrac{\Sigma S^2}{a}$, $[Y] = \Sigma Y^2$.

As a result of this subtraction, $SS_{residual}$ now reflects the chance factors operating in the within-subjects design. To be consistent with the treatment of the within-subjects design in advanced statistics texts, we will also refer to this sum of squares as $SS_{A \times S}$.

While we could obtain the residual sum of squares by subtracting the two sums of squares indicated in Eq. (11-4), we will calculate this quantity "directly" by using basic ratios rather than sums of squares. By applying some simple algebra to the computational formulas for $SS_{S/A}$ and SS_S, we can transform Eq. (11-4) into

$$SS_{residual} = SS_{S/A} - SS_S$$
$$= ([Y] - [A]) - ([S] - [T])$$
$$= [Y] - [A] - [S] + [T] \qquad (11\text{-}5)$$

which represents the computational formula for the residual sum of squares, $SS_{A \times S}$, expressed entirely in terms of basic ratios. The computational formulas for this and the other sums of squares needed for the analysis are presented in Table 11-6. Except for $[S]$, all the basic ratios specified in the table are identical to those required for the between-subjects design.

Expressing the Residual Sum of Squares as an Interaction. A single-factor within-subjects design is actually a type of *factorial* design, in which one of the variables is the independent variable (factor A), of course, and the other is a *subject variable* (factor S). Consider again the within-subjects data matrix in Table 11-5. You can readily see that each level of factor A is paired with all three "levels" (that is, the three subjects) of factor S — the basic requirement of a factorial design. Viewing the within-subjects design as a factorial allows us to refer to the treatment sum of squares as the *main effect of factor A* and to the subject sum of squares as the *main effect of subjects*. In addition, we can view the residual sum of squares as an *interaction* of the two factors — that is, an $A \times S$ interaction.

We can think of this interaction two ways. First, there is the computational formula for $SS_{residual}$, which was expressed in Eq. (11-5) as

$$SS_{residual} = [Y] - [A] - [S] + [T]$$

Note the similarity between this formula and the computational formula for the $A \times B$ interaction:

$$SS_{A \times B} = [AB] - [A] - [B] + [T]$$

Second, we can plot the Y scores in a graph and examine the nature of the $A \times S$ interaction, in the same way we plot the means for the treatment combinations and examine the nature of the $A \times B$ interaction from an actual factorial experiment. To illustrate, we have plotted the Y scores from Table 11-3 (p. 323) in Fig. 11-4. In this graph, we have placed the levels of factor A on the horizontal axis and plotted the three Y scores for each of the three subjects within the body of the figure. Visually, interaction is reflected by curves that are not parallel. As you can see in Fig. 11-4, the three curves — one for each subject in this example — are not parallel, which means that there is an $A \times S$ interaction (that is, an interaction between factor A and factor S).

The Analysis of Variance

Degrees of Freedom. The degrees of freedom associated with each source of variance in the analysis of the within-subjects design are presented in the third column of Table 11-6. We explained in Chap. 4 that the number of degrees of freedom associated with any variance estimate is equal to the number of observations on which the variance is based minus the number of population estimates required in the process. For the treatment source (A), which is based on a treatment means, one df is lost through the estimate of the overall population mean, and $df_A = a - 1$. For the subjects source (S), which is based on n subject means, one df is also lost as a consequence of our estimating the overall population mean, and $df_S = n - 1$ (where n is the number of subjects in the experiment). While the logic is not obvious, we obtain the number of degrees of freedom for the residual source ($A \times S$) by multiplying together the degrees of freedom for treatments and subjects. That is,

$$df_{A \times S} = (df_A)(df_S) = (a - 1)(n - 1) \tag{11-6}$$

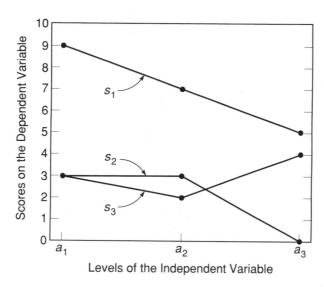

FIGURE 11-4 *Expressing the Residual Sum of Squares in a Within-Subjects Design as an A × S Interaction.*

Mean Squares and F Ratio. The final steps of the analysis, calculating the mean squares and the *F* ratio, are summarized in the last two columns of Table 11-6. We test the omnibus null hypothesis,

$$H_0 : \mu_1 = \mu_2 = \mu_3 = \cdots$$

by calculating

$$F = \frac{MS_A}{MS_{A \times S}} \tag{11-7}$$

and applying the following decision rule:

If the obtained value of $F \geq F(df_A, df_{A \times S})$, reject the null hypothesis; otherwise, retain the null hypothesis.

We usually do not test the significance of the subject source, for two reasons. First, the test itself requires certain assumptions that generally are not tenable in most behavioral research. Second, even if justified, a significant main effect of subjects simply would tell us that the subjects in the experiment did not perform equally — hardly a surprising finding to psychologists, who find that subjects differ on most tasks with which they are confronted.

Assumptions. The assumptions underlying the analysis of the within-subjects design are more complicated than those for the between-subjects design, discussed in Chap. 5. In addition to the assumptions of the between-subjects design (pp. 118–120), we must add the requirement that the subjects show the same degree of consistency for all possible pairs of treatments. A discussion of the consequences of violating these assumptions is beyond the scope of this book, and you may wish to refer to more advanced books that offer a full discussion of this topic (see, for example, Keppel, 1991, pp. 351–353).

11.4 A NUMERICAL EXAMPLE

Consider a fictitious experiment in which an undergraduate decides to investigate factors that might influence performance in a game of Scrabble. In a "normal" game of Scrabble (not the more expensive, deluxe version) players face different sides of a square game board and attempt to construct words on the board with letters they have drawn from a large pool of letters. After doing quite poorly in a game with friends, our student suspects that she was at a disadvantage facing the board from the back and being forced to read the letters and words on the board upside down. She decides to conduct a simple experiment to test her speculation.

Details of the Experimental Design

Let's assume that the student researcher plans to ask some of her friends to help her with this project. She first considers using a between-subjects design in which she would randomly assign friends to one of the four positions around the board — front, back, left, and right. Although this type of design is entirely appropriate, she becomes worried about the large differences in her friends' Scrabble-playing capability and the relatively large number of subjects she would need to create an experiment with reasonable power. She turns instead to a within-subjects design, which is ideally suited to a situation in which there may be large individual differences and a relative scarcity of subjects.

Translating the experiment to a within-subjects design, she decides to have four of her friends play four games of Scrabble, each time from a different orientation with respect to the board. This arrangement solves the problem of large individual differences, because each of her friends will play one game from each of the four orientations — spreading their abilities equally over the four treatment conditions. How should she decide to arrange her friends

TABLE 11-7 *An Example of Counterbalancing*

Subjects	Games			
	1	2	3	4
s_1	a_1	a_2	a_3	a_4
s_2	a_3	a_1	a_4	a_2
s_3	a_2	a_4	a_1	a_3
s_4	a_4	a_3	a_2	a_1

a_1 = front a_2 = back
a_3 = left a_4 = right

each time around the game board? One possibility would be to assign them randomly to the four orientations and then shift them systematically around the table on the next three games. This would mean that the friends would always follow and precede the same persons, however. A better way to control the seating would be to use a procedure that would break up the order of turns and still ensure that each friend played the game from a different orientation each time. Such an arrangement is given in Table 11-7. The order of the games is listed above the columns, and the orientation that each friend is assigned is listed within the body of the table. The second subject, for example, is seated at position a_3 (left) in the first game, at position a_1 (front) in the second game, at position a_4 (right) in the third game, and at position a_2 (back) in the final game. This is an example of **counterbalancing**, a procedure we will discuss more fully in Sec. 11.6. For the time being, you should simply note that the order of turns is completely mixed up — which you can see by looking at the position assignments within each column of the table — while still having each friend sit at a different position each time.

The experimenter finds four friends who are willing to help her with the project and assigns them randomly to the four sequences. The letter pool is scrambled and her friends begin the first game. The game ends when either the letters have all been played or no more moves are possible. The dependent variable consists of the number of points each friend amasses during the course of the game. Because of a concern for the effects of fatigue and boredom, the experimenter decides to conduct the remaining three games on successive days. The results of the experiment are presented in Table 11-8.[2]

---

[2] Readers who are familiar with Scrabble will note that these are relatively low scores. This is not a reflection on the ability of the experimenter's friends, however. We created small scores to reduce the size of the numbers entering into the various calculations.

	Front a_1	Back a_2	Left a_3	Right a_4	Sum
Subjects					
s_1	38	22	30	30	120
s_2	30	21	27	22	100
s_3	17	3	9	11	40
s_4	19	10	18	13	60
Sum	104	56	84	76	320
Mean	26.00	14.00	21.00	19.00	

TABLE 11-8 *Data Matrix for the Numerical Example*

Calculating the Sums of Squares

We calculate the sums of squares in two steps, the basic ratios first and then the sums of squares themselves.

Calculating the Basic Ratios.   There are four basic ratios required for this analysis, one based on the Y scores and three based on the different sums produced when we sum down the columns to produce the treatment sums (A's), across the rows to produce the subject sums (S's), and in both directions to provide the grand sum (T). We now calculate the four basic ratios from the data in Table 11-8:

$$[T] = \frac{T^2}{(a)(n)}$$

$$= \frac{(320)^2}{(4)(4)} = \frac{102,400}{16}$$

$$= 6,400.00$$

$$[A] = \frac{\Sigma A^2}{n}$$

$$= \frac{(104)^2 + (56)^2 + (84)^2 + (76)^2}{4} = \frac{26,784}{4}$$

$$= 6,696.00$$

$$[S] = \frac{\Sigma S^2}{a}$$

$$= \frac{(120)^2 + (100)^2 + (40)^2 + (60)^2}{4} = \frac{29,600}{4}$$

$$= 7,400.00$$

$$[Y] = \Sigma Y^2$$

$$= (38)^2 + (30)^2 + \cdots + (11)^2 + (13)^2$$

$$= 7,736$$

Completing the Calculations.   The patterns in which the basic ratios are combined to produce the required sums of squares are presented in Table 11-6. From the formulas listed in the table,

$$SS_A = [A] - [T] = 6,696.00 - 6,400.00 = 296.00$$

$$SS_S = [S] - [T] = 7,400.00 - 6,400.00 = 1,000.00$$

$$SS_{A \times S} = [Y] - [A] - [S] + [T]$$

$$= 7,736 - 6,696.00 - 7,400.00 + 6,400.00 = 40.00$$

$$SS_T = [Y] - [T] = 7,736 - 6,400.00 = 1,336.00$$

We have entered these values in the summary table of the analysis (Table 11-9). As an arithmetical check, we should verify that

$$SS_T = SS_A + SS_S + SS_{A \times S}$$

$$1,336.00 = 296.00 + 1,000.00 + 40.00$$

$$= 1,336.00$$

TABLE 11-9 *Summary of the Analysis*				
Source	SS	df	MS	F
A (Position)	296.00	3	98.67	22.22*
S (Subject)	1,000.00	3	333.33	
A × S	40.00	9	4.44	
Total	1,336.00	15		

* $p < .05$.

The Analysis of Variance

All that remains is to substitute in the formulas for the degrees of freedom, mean squares, and the F ratio specified in Table 11-6. First, we obtain the degrees of freedom:

$$df_A = a - 1 = 4 - 1 = 3$$

$$df_S = n - 1 = 4 - 1 = 3$$

$$df_{A \times S} = (a - 1)(n - 1) = (4 - 1)(4 - 1) = (3)(3) = 9$$

$$df_T = (a)(n) - 1 = (4)(4) - 1 = 16 - 1 = 15$$

Again, we perform the arithmetical check on these calculations:

$$df_T = df_A + df_S + df_{A \times S}$$

$$15 = 3 + 3 + 9$$

$$= 15$$

The mean squares are calculated by dividing each sum of squares by the appropriate number of degrees of freedom. To illustrate,

$$MS_A = \frac{SS_A}{df_A} = \frac{296.00}{3} = 98.67$$

$$MS_S = \frac{SS_S}{df_S} = \frac{1,000.00}{3} = 333.33$$

$$MS_{A \times S} = \frac{SS_{A \times S}}{df_{A \times S}} = \frac{40.00}{9} = 4.44$$

Finally, we can calculate the omnibus F ratio:

$$F = \frac{MS_A}{MS_{A \times S}} = \frac{98.67}{4.44} = 22.22$$

We look in Table A-2 for the critical value of F at $\alpha = .05$ for $df_A = 3$ and

$df_{A \times S} = 9$ and find $F(3, 9) = 3.86$. We can now form the following decision rule:

If the obtained value of $F \geq 3.86$, reject the null hypothesis; otherwise, retain the null hypothesis.

Since the F we calculated, 22.22, exceeds the critical value specified by the decision rule, we reject the null hypothesis. This analysis reveals that performance in Scrabble depends on where a player sits around the board. Because we tested the omnibus null hypothesis, however, we cannot specify statistically the exact nature of the results. We can make much more specific statements — including the researcher's belief that a person sitting in front of the board has a clear advantage — if the data are subjected to a number of analytical comparisons. We discuss how to conduct these comparisons in the next section.

11.5 ANALYTICAL COMPARISONS

All the analytical techniques discussed in Chap. 6 for asking *meaningful* questions in the analysis of a between-subjects design are applicable in the analysis of a within-subjects design. Conceptually, the formulas for obtaining this information are identical for the two types of designs. The only change is in the nature of the error term used to form the F ratio. We should remind you that it is not necessary to evaluate the omnibus F *before* conducting planned comparisons. If researchers form specific research hypotheses when planning their experiments, they may proceed directly to the evaluation of analytical comparisons. Since the student researcher began with the informal observation that a person sitting in front of the board has an advantage, we present two analyses that focus directly on this expected outcome of the experiment.

Using the Omnibus Error Term

In the between-subjects design, the within-groups mean square ($MS_{S/A}$) was the error term for all comparisons:

$$F_{A_{comp.}} = \frac{MS_{A_{comp.}}}{MS_{S/A}}$$

In the within-subjects design, we will use the error term from the overall analysis ($MS_{A \times S}$) as the error term in evaluating analytical comparisons. That is, we simply calculate

$$F_{A\,comp.} = \frac{MS_{A\,comp.}}{MS_{A \times S}} \tag{11-8}$$

to evaluate the significance of comparisons in the within-subjects design.[3]

Pairwise Comparisons

As an illustration of the procedure, we will analyze two comparisons with the data from the numerical example in Sec. 11.4, which were presented in Table 11-8 (p. 334). The first is a pairwise comparison comparing the performance of subjects playing Scrabble from the front of the board (a_1) and from the back (a_2). The respective means for this comparison are 26.00 and 14.00. We calculate the sum of squares by substituting the relevant information in the following formula, which we originally presented in Chap. 6:

$$SS_{A\,comp.} = \frac{(n)(\hat{\psi}_A)^2}{2} \tag{11-9}$$

where n refers to the sample size ($n = 4$ in this example) and $\hat{\psi}_A$ to the difference between the two means ($\hat{\psi}_A = 26.00 - 14.00 = 12.00$). Substituting these quantities in Eq. (11-9), we find

$$SS_{A\,comp.} = \frac{(4)(12.00)^2}{2} = \frac{576.00}{2} = 288.00$$

Since $df = 1$ for the comparison between two treatment means,

$$MS_{A\,comp.} = SS_{A\,comp.} = 288.00$$

The F ratio, specified by Eq. (11-8), uses the error term from the overall analysis ($MS_{A \times S} = 4.44$) to evaluate the significance of the pairwise difference:

$$F_{A\,comp.} = \frac{MS_{A\,comp.}}{MS_{A \times S}} = \frac{288.00}{4.44} = 64.86$$

---

[3] We suggest using the $MS_{A \times S}$ as the error term for all comparisons, which your instructor may consider appropriate for the goals of the course. For courses in which time permits, we present in an appendix at the end of the chapter an alternative procedure for calculating the error term for an analytical comparison. This procedure, while computationally more complex than the one presented in this section, provides a more accurate error term with which to evaluate the significance of an analytical comparison.

The critical value of F for a single-df comparison is found in the F table under $df_{num.} = 1$ and $df_{denom.} = df_{A \times S}$ (9 in this example) at the appropriate significance level. For this example, then, the critical value of $F(1, 9)$ at $\alpha = .05$ is 5.12. The decision rule becomes

If $F_{A_{comp.}} \geq 5.12$, reject the null hypothesis; otherwise, retain the null hypothesis.

The obtained F falls within the rejection region defined by this critical value of F; we conclude that subjects attained significantly higher scores when sitting in front of the Scrabble board than when sitting to the rear.

Complex Comparisons

Complex comparisons involve differences between two means where one or both of the means are conditions that have been combined for the analysis. An example of such an analysis is a comparison between the front position (a_1) and the combined side positions (a_3 and a_4).[4] For this analysis, we use the general formula for single-df comparisons from Chap. 6, which we present again as Eq. (11-10):

$$SS_{A_{comp.}} = \frac{(n)(\hat{\psi}_A)^2}{\sum c^2} \qquad (11\text{-}10)$$

where n is the sample size, $\hat{\psi}_A$ is the difference between the two means, and c refers to the coefficients with which we compute $\hat{\psi}_A$ (see pp. 151–153). For this example,

$$\hat{\psi}_A = (c_1)(\overline{Y}_{A_1}) + (c_2)(\overline{Y}_{A_2}) + (c_3)(\overline{Y}_{A_3}) + (c_4)(\overline{Y}_{A_4})$$

$$= (+1)(26.00) + (0)(14.00) + \left(-\tfrac{1}{2}\right)(21.00) + \left(-\tfrac{1}{2}\right)(19.00)$$

$$= 26.00 - 10.50 - 9.50 = 26.00 - 20.00$$

$$= 6.00$$

---

[4] It is probably safe to combine the left and right positions, because they both represent positions to the side and they appear not to differ significantly; a pairwise test would bear out this assumption.

$$
\begin{aligned}
\Sigma\, c^2 &= (c_1)^2 + (c_2)^2 + (c_3)^2 + (c_4)^2 \\
&= (+1)^2 + (0)^2 + \left(-\tfrac{1}{2}\right)^2 + \left(-\tfrac{1}{2}\right)^2 \\
&= 1 + 0 + .25 + .25 \\
&= 1.50
\end{aligned}
$$

We now substitute these values in Eq. (11-10) as follows:

$$
SS_{A\,comp.} = \frac{(4)(6.00)^2}{1.50} = \frac{144.00}{1.50} = 96.00
$$

From this point on, we proceed as we did with the pairwise comparison. To illustrate,

$$
F_{A\,comp.} = \frac{MS_{A\,comp.}}{MS_{A \times S}} = \frac{96.00}{4.44} = 21.62
$$

The numerator and denominator degrees of freedom are 1 and 9, respectively, as they were for the pairwise example. Thus, the critical value of F is $F(1, 9) = 5.12$, and we use the same decision rule we established previously. By looking at the relevant treatment means, we can conclude that a person sitting at the front (26.00) has an advantage over persons sitting at the sides of the board (20.00).

11.6 PLANNING WITHIN-SUBJECTS DESIGNS

Now that you have seen how the data from a within-subjects design are analyzed, we can identify the serious difficulties that can arise and must be considered before this design is adopted for an actual experiment. Most of the problems or potential confoundings arise when we do not want carryover or transfer effects to contaminate the various treatment effects being studied.[5] Even when our intention is to use a within-subjects design to study a practice effect such as learning, it is important to consider the possibility of other, unwanted con-

---

[5] We discussed confounding of variables in Chap. 1 (pp. 18–21).

sequences of testing the same subjects repeatedly. Because subjects serve in all the conditions, two problems are possible: (1) that practice will affect the subjects' performance on the task, and (2) that past treatment effects will influence subjects being given a new treatment in the testing series. These two problems, which we will refer to as *general practice effects* and *carryover effects*, are discussed in this section.

Controlling General Practice Effects

The term **general practice effects** refers to changes in performance that occur as subjects progress through the entire experiment. They are called *general* because they do not depend on a particular treatment condition (or conditions), or on a specific sequence of the treatments. We can identify two sorts of practice effects: a general improvement in performance that results as subjects acquire skills associated with the task, and a general decline in performance as subjects become weary, fatigued, or bored. If both types of practice effects are present in an experiment, a combination of the positive and negative factors is at work. It is unlikely that the two will balance each other perfectly, however. In most situations, then, the researcher will be faced with practice effects of some sort. A number of techniques exist for controlling practice effects. We consider the most common methods in this section.

The negative effects of practice can be minimized fairly easily. Experimenters can control fatigue, for example, by allowing subjects to rest sufficiently between successive treatment conditions. Instructions to subjects can minimize boredom by serving to intrigue, motivate, and involve the subjects in the experiment; also, incentives — monetary or otherwise — can be offered to elicit a high level of performance. The positive effects of practice, on the other hand, are not so easily dealt with, since the effects of learning are relatively permanent — thank goodness!

One approach is to use subjects who have had so much practice with the task at hand that they can no longer show improvement. This approach is frequently used in animal research (involving operant conditioning especially), psychophysical research (where subjects are highly trained as reliable and unchanging observers), and information-processing research (where the interest is in the processing of information in what is called a "steady state," a condition reached through considerable practice and training). But where time is insufficient, other methods of controlling practice are necessary.

Controlling Practice Effects by Counterbalancing

Let's suppose that we have designed an experiment in which we expect the subjects to improve as they become more familiar with the task. That is, subjects would do better on the second task than on the first, better on the third task than on the second, and so on. Suppose we presented the treatments in the *same order* for all subjects — for example, a_3, a_2, a_1, and a_4. What could we say about the outcome of the experiment once the data are tabulated and analyzed? The answer is relatively little, because any real effects of the different treatment conditions are influenced, or *confounded*, by the practice effects. You would not be able to know whether any differences you found were due to the treatment conditions themselves or to the *order* in which the conditions were presented.

An Example of Counterbalancing. The solution to this confounding is obvious: vary the sequence for different subjects. The formal technique by which sequence variation is achieved is called **counterbalancing**.[6] To see how this is accomplished, assume that we have three subjects for an experiment and that each receives the three conditions in a different sequence. These three sequences are presented in Table 11-10A. The three columns represent the three testing sessions in which each subject receives the three different conditions (sessions I, II, and III, respectively), and the treatment levels within the body of the table (a_1, a_2, and a_3) represent the particular treatments administered

---

TABLE 11-10 *Two Examples of Counterbalancing*

	A				B		
		Session				Session	
Subject	I	II	III	Subject	I	II	III
1	a_1	a_2	a_3	4	a_1	a_3	a_2
2	a_2	a_3	a_1	5	a_2	a_1	a_3
3	a_3	a_1	a_2	6	a_3	a_2	a_1

---

[6] We considered a form of counterbalancing when we discussed the design of the Scrabble experiment in which we varied the order in which subjects were seated at the four different positions around the board.

to the subjects in these sessions. That is, subject 1 receives the treatments in the order a_1, a_2, a_3; subject 2 receives them in the order a_2, a_3, a_1; and subject 3 receives them in the order a_3, a_1, a_2.

Note the characteristics of this particular arrangement of the conditions. Each subject is given each treatment once *and* each condition appears once in each session. That is, for session I, all three conditions (a_1, a_2, and a_3) are represented. The same is true for session II and for session III. Therefore, the practice effects — whatever they may be — will influence all three conditions equally. To illustrate, suppose we expect all subjects to improve from session I to session II by 10 points. For the first subject, treatment a_2 will gain 10 points from practice; for the second subject, treatment a_3 will gain by the 10 points; and for the third subject, treatment a_1 will gain by 10 points. Each treatment condition benefits equally from the subjects' improvement from session I to session II. A similar argument would be made for any general improvement that may occur from session II to session III. In short, when we combine the data from these three subjects, practice effects will not contribute *differentially* to the treatment averages.

The counterbalancing arrangement in Table 11-10A is one of two that are possible with $a = 3$ treatment conditions. The second is presented in Table 11-10B. Again, in this arrangement each condition is administered once to each subject and is represented once in each of the sessions. By the same rationale that underlies the first arrangement, this counterbalancing scheme neutralizes the practice effects as well.

In an actual experiment, more than three subjects would be tested. In keeping with the logic governing our simplified examples, equal numbers of subjects would be assigned randomly to each of the three sequences of treatments (either arrangement A or arrangement B in Table 11-10). Thus, the total number of subjects would be some multiple of 3, the number of treatment conditions — that is, the sample size could be 3, 6, 9, and so on. It may have occurred to you that we could also use *both* sets of sequences and include all *six* sequences (A and B) in an experiment. Under these circumstances, subjects would then be assigned in multiples of 6 — sample sizes could be 6, 12, 18, and so on.

When all possible sequences are included in an experiment, counterbalancing is said to be *complete*. When only one of the possible arrangements is used, we refer to the counterbalancing as *incomplete*, or, more formally, as a **Latin-square** arrangement. While complete counterbalancing is preferred, since it includes all possible sequences, this technique requires that increasingly large numbers of subjects be tested as the number of treatment conditions increases. For instance, when $a = 3$, six subjects are needed to complete the counter-balancing; when $a = 4$, 24 subjects are needed; and when $a = 5$, 120 subjects are needed! Consequently, most researchers use some form of incomplete counterbalancing to hold the number of subjects at a reasonable figure.

Balancing Pairwise Sequences. You may have noticed with the two counterbalancing arrangements presented in Table 11-10 that certain pairs of conditions were favored over others in the arrangement of the sequences. In the first arrangement, for example, condition a_2 always follows condition a_1. If you examine the other sequences of pairs of conditions in this arrangement you will find that condition a_3 always follows condition a_2, and condition a_1 always follows condition a_3. The same problem exists for the second arrangement, except that different pairs of conditions are favored. More specifically, condition a_3 always follows condition a_1, condition a_1 always follows condition a_2, and condition a_2 always follows condition a_3. Ideally, we would like to have all pairwise sequences equally represented in the counterbalancing arrangement used to control practice effects. An easy way to accomplish this goal in the present case is to use *both* counterbalancing arrangements in determining the sequences in which the conditions are presented. That is, each pairwise sequence is represented *twice* over the total set of six sequences. This is a strong argument for complete counterbalancing.

We can achieve the same pairwise balancing with larger experiments without resorting to complete counterbalancing, which, as we have already noted, can require more subjects than researchers may care to invest in the experiment. The counterbalancing arrangement we presented in Table 11-7 (p. 333) in conjunction with the Scrabble experiment is an example of how this may be accomplished. In this case, there were $a = 4$ conditions, and four sequences were needed to counterbalance the conditions. You will notice that each of the four conditions is followed once by each of the other three conditions, creating a balancing of pairwise sequences.[7]

Carryover Effects

The practice effects we just considered are assumed to be the same for all treatment conditions regardless of the order in which they are presented, which is why we could balance them through some sort of counterbalancing. That is, subjects simply get better at the task — better at playing Scrabble, for

---

[7] Details concerning the construction of counterbalancing arrangements can be found in Keppel (1991, p. 339), Kirk (1982, pp. 309–312), Myers and Well (1991, pp. 344–348), and Winer, Brown, and Michels (1991, pp. 674–679).

example — or decline as they become bored regardless of what tasks they have received previously or are receiving currently. All too frequently, however, this assumption simply does not hold, and we encounter instead influences that are not general, but specific — influences that depend on the *specific* conditions involved. We will call such influences occurring in a sequence of treatments **carryover effects**.[8]

Carryover effects are present when the treatment conditions are affected by the specific conditions appearing before them in the testing sequence. Students frequently confuse carryover effects with practice effects. Practice effects refer to *nonspecific* or *general changes* in performance as the subjects progress through the sequence of treatment conditions they have been assigned; practice effects are assumed to be the same for all the treatment conditions. In contrast, carryover effects refer to *specific* changes that result when earlier treatment conditions continue to influence the performance of subjects when they are given other treatment conditions following the administration of the earlier ones.

Examples of Carryover Effects.   Perhaps the simplest way to emphasize the distinction is to consider an experiment in which the possibility of carryover effects is unambiguous. Earlier in this chapter, we described an experiment in which subjects received two different drugs (drug A and drug B) in a proper counterbalanced order — that is, one half of the subjects received the two drugs in the A-B order and the other half in the B-A order. We noted that if the effects of either drug are not completely dissipated before the other drug is administered, any residual effects from the first drug will continue to influence subjects when they receive the second drug. This is an obvious example of carryover effects that threaten the integrity of the experiment and any conclusions we may wish to draw from the outcome. The only point at which we can assess the unadulterated effects of the two drugs is on the *first* test, of course, where carryover effects are obviously not present; the results of the second test are contaminated by the possibility of carryover effects from the preceding drug condition.

Consider another example in which human subjects either receive criticism for making errors in a learning task or receive no feedback at all during the task. Half the subjects receive the two conditions in the criticism–no feedback order and the other half in the reverse. The subjects receiving the criticism first will probably be extremely apprehensive and suspicious when they are informed that they will no longer be criticized for making errors and will begin the no-feedback treatment with a different attitude and motivation from that of the

---

[8] In the first edition, we referred to carryover effects as *differential carryover effects*.

TABLE 11-11 *Results of a Within-Subjects Design*

Retention Measures	First Test	Second Test
Recall	3.12	4.75
Recognition	7.00	5.00

subjects who receive the no-feedback treatment first. There probably would be no carryover effects for subjects receiving the treatments in the reverse order. In any case, the point we wish to make is that the data from the second half of the experiment again do not provide us with unambiguous information concerning the differential effects of the two treatments.

A third example of carryover effects comes from an actual experiment in which subjects were instructed to study 12 pairs of words for a certain period of time.[9] Two retention measures, designed to show how well subjects had learned the material, were then administered. With both measuring techniques, subjects were shown one member of a pair and required either to *recall* the other member from memory or to *recognize* the other member in a list containing the words used in the experiment. The independent variable was the type of retention measure (recall or recognition), and the dependent variable was the number of words correctly given on the two tests. A within-subjects design was used, with subjects receiving both measures in a counterbalanced order. (Half the subjects received the tests in the recall-recognition order, and the other half received them in the reverse.) Subjects learned a different set of word pairs before each test. The results are given in Table 11-11. Each subject provided two scores, a recall score and a recognition score. The average recall and recognition scores on the tests are shown in the second and third columns of the table.

As you can see by examining the means in each row, both retention measures showed changes from the first to the second test, but these changes were not the same. In fact, the changes were in opposite directions! More specifically, the recall measure showed a gain of 1.63 words (from 3.12 to 4.75 words) while the recognition measure showed a loss of 2.00 words (from 7.00 to 5.00 words). Carryover effects are clearly present. Another way to look at the data is to consider the first and second tests separately. On the first test, when carryover effects are obviously absent, recognition surpassed recall by 3.88 words. In contrast, the difference between recognition and recall was greatly reduced

---

[9] Keppel (1966).

on the second test, the difference now consisting of .25 words. In short, the presence of carryover effects makes questionable any analysis in which the results from the two tests are combined.

Considerations in Planning a Within-Subjects Design.   Researchers must think carefully about the possibility of carryover effects when they contemplate using a within-subjects design. In certain types of research, the within-subjects design is generally rejected as a useful way of increasing power in an experiment. Experiments that are designed to change the way subjects view or solve a task or problem probably are not well suited to within-subjects designs. If you designed an experiment to change a person's attitude toward some belief or conviction, you would not expect to be able to change an attitude one way and then change it another way with a shift in the treatment conditions. If you wanted to compare several kinds of therapy in a clinical setting, it would make little sense having individuals receive one therapy until completion and then shift to another. If you created different treatment conditions in which subjects were misled about the true purposes of the experiment, it is unlikely that they could be deceived again with a different set of instructions.

The major concern in the planning stage of an experiment is whether the results obtained with a within-subjects design will be roughly equivalent to those obtained with an equivalent between-subjects design. If you can expect the results to be basically the same, you would probably choose the within-subjects design because of its sensitivity and convenience. However, if you do not expect the results to be the same, you should choose instead the less efficient, but also less ambiguous, between-subjects design. You can always check the adequacy of a within-subjects design *after* the experiment is completed by examining the differences among the treatment conditions *session by session*. If the results shift or change from one session to another, you would probably have to pay primary attention to the *first* session or test, in which the data obviously are free from carryover effects of any kind.[10]

On a more positive note, carryover effects may themselves lead to some interesting speculations. One might ask why such effects occur and design new

---

[10] You will lose considerable power if you are forced to restrict the analysis to the data from the first session. In the first place, you will lose the advantage of the increased power usually associated with within-subjects designs. More specifically, subjects contribute only *one Y* score at this point in the experiment, creating what amounts to a single-factor *between*-subjects design. Power is also reduced because the treatment effects for this restricted analysis are based on a much smaller number of observations than when they are based on the data from the entire experiment.

experiments to study them specifically. In any case, problems are associated with the within-subjects design in psychology, and these problems must be accounted for in the choice of an experimental design.

11.7 SUMMARY

Minimizing the operation of experimental error is a primary concern in designing any experiment. Between-subjects designs, in which subjects are randomly assigned to a single treatment condition, are particularly vulnerable because of the presence of large differences among subjects who are treated alike. Two types of designs can serve to increase the sensitivity of an experiment by reducing experimental error. One design accomplishes this goal through the use of subjects matched on characteristics assumed to be highly related to scores on the dependent variable. The other, the within-subjects design, achieves this goal by using the same subjects in all the treatment conditions. We have considered the within-subjects design, since it is a superior method of controlling variation due to subjects.

The analysis of data from a within-subjects design is quite similar to that of data from the between-subjects design considered in Part Two. The primary difference lies in the error term, that is, the denominator term of the F ratio. In the between-subjects design, the error term is based entirely on the pooled variability of subjects treated alike. But in using the within-subjects design, the researcher reduces this estimate of experimental error by subtracting a quantity that reflects the consistent performance of each subject over the entire experiment.

While investigators can gain considerable advantages by choosing a within-subjects design over a between-subjects design, some difficulties must be overcome before the former design can be used. First, some research projects are not suited to within-subjects designs. For example, instruction variables (common in social psychology experiments) are not used in within-subjects designs, since subjects are not likely to conveniently disregard the instruction set (or sets) given previously. Second, unless they are the object of study, as in a learning or transfer-of-training experiment, practice effects must be controlled. If left unchecked, these effects result in a confounding with the independent variable. Some method of counterbalancing, in which the use of different sequences ensures that all the treatment conditions will appear equally in all of the testing sessions, is usually used to solve this problem.

Finally, the within-subjects design generally cannot be used where the possibility exists that carryover effects may be operating. The severity of this problem varies from research area to research area, but every within-subjects design should be examined for the presence of carryover effects.

11.8 EXERCISES [11]

1. The within-subjects design requires identification of a new term and calculation of a new sum of squares, which is then removed from the sources of variation to yield the error term.
   a. What is this new term?
   b. Draw a pie chart and identify each source of variation in the within-subjects design. Shade in the segment representing the new source of variation.
   c. Why is the new sum of squares not tested for significance?

2. An important advantage of a within-subjects design is the marked reduction in the size of the error term, produced by isolating and removing consistent individual differences that remain constant from treatment to treatment. Demonstrate the effectiveness of the within-subjects design by analyzing the data from the Scrabble example in Table 11-8 (p. 334) as a *between-subjects* design. That is, assume that each *Y* score is produced by a *different* subject.
   a. Compare the results of the revised analysis with the example in the text.
   b. Which terms in the analysis remain the same? Which is new?
   c. Explain the difference in the outcome produced by the two analyses. That is, which design is more sensitive? Which term or source of variation in the analysis demonstrates the increase in power afforded by the within-subjects design?

*3. In this hypothetical study, the effect of noise on performance in a perceptual task was tested with six subjects. Subjects practiced the task until they reached a level of performance determined by previous research to be ideal. A total of $n = 6$ subjects were tested under $a = 3$ treatment

---

[11] Answers to the starred problems are given in Appendix B.

conditions in a completely counterbalanced order. In condition a_1, subjects performed the task in the absence of noise. Noise was present in the other two conditions, either intermittently, in condition a_2 (the sound of an airplane passing overhead), or constantly, in a_3 (a diesel generator in an adjoining room). The number of errors at the end of each testing session was used as the measure of performance. The following data were obtained:

Subject	No Noise a_1	Intermittent Noise a_2	Constant Noise a_3	
1	17	19	24	60
2	30	26	31	87
3	22	18	27	67
4	23	17	29	69
5	26	20	33	79
6	19	20	25	64
	137	120	169	

a. Conduct an overall analysis of variance on these data.
b. Compare the two noise conditions (a_2 and a_3).
c. Compare the condition without noise (a_1) with the two noise conditions combined.

4. To satisfy a course requirement, an instructor in a computer literacy course wanted to measure progress in learning to use a versatile word-processing program. His intention was to encourage students to use the variety of formatting commands available, particularly by using the macro-writing ability of the program. His plan was to give students five test sessions during which they were to attempt to use the word-processing program to enter a document into the computer. He prepared five different documents, each differing in content but using the same number of formatting instructions. The five documents were arranged in five different orders that were properly counterbalanced. He selected five students who were approximately equally skilled in typing and computer experience; none was familiar with a complex word-processing program. They were given the training manual to study one week before the experiment began, following which time they were given a series of five tests during which they attempted to enter a document into the computer within a one-hour time limit. The dependent variable consisted of the number of different formatting commands the student used in attempting to reproduce

the document with the word-processing program. The scores are as follows:

Students	Test Sessions				
	a_1	a_2	a_3	a_4	a_5
1	5	6	14	19	22
2	2	7	11	18	24
3	1	3	8	25	22
4	6	5	9	18	22
5	6	8	15	22	29

a. Conduct an overall analysis of variance on these data.
b. The analysis in part (a) revealed that the omnibus F is significant, which allows us to conclude that the means are not the same. The instructor is more interested in the nature of the *improvement* and would like to demonstrate that learning has occurred. As a rough demonstration that learning has occurred, test the difference between the first and last tests.
c. As another demonstration that significant improvement has occurred, compare the performance of the subjects on the combined first two with that on the combined last two tests.
d. Many researchers would use a *trend analysis* to examine the nature of the learning exhibited by these students over the five tests.[12] As a first step, plot the means in a graph and connect the points. You will clearly see that the students improve steadily during the course of the experiment. You can capture this improvement by drawing a straight line that seems to best fit the five means in the graph. A trend analysis would focus on the slant or slope of this line and determine whether it is statistically significant. Appendix D shows you how to conduct this analysis and the analysis of more complex trend components. Try to use this procedure to determine whether a significant linear trend component is present.

---

[12] This question is intended for individuals who have studied Appendix D.

11.9 Appendix: Using Separate Error Terms to Evaluate Analytical Comparisons [13]

The analysis of analytical comparisons that we described and illustrated in Sec. 11.5 is based on the assumption that the error term from the overall analysis ($MS_{A \times S}$) provides an appropriate estimate of error variance for any and all single-df comparisons. Occasionally, this assumption does not hold. Let's see why.

Suppose we segregated the data from a within-subjects experiment into a number of smaller experiments, each consisting of two levels. If there were $a = 3$ conditions, for example, we could create three smaller within-subjects experiments, one involving a_1 and a_2, a second involving a_1 and a_3, and a third involving a_2 and a_3. In each case, we could perform a standard analysis of each experiment using only the data relevant to the particular comparison involved. The error term in each case would be *different* because it would be based on a different set of scores. When the assumptions underlying the within-subjects design are met, we can safely assume that any differences among the three error terms — the $MS_{A \times S}$ for the first comparison, the $MS_{A \times S}$ for the second comparison, and the $MS_{A \times S}$ for the third comparison — represent the operation of chance effects. Under these circumstances, we can use the $MS_{A \times S}$ from the *overall* analysis as the error term for all three comparisons, because this mean square is in effect an *average* of the three separate error terms. You may recall that we followed a similar strategy with the between-subjects design (see p. 147).

What happens when these simplifying assumptions do *not* hold for either type of design? For the between-subjects design, we need to construct a separate error term for each comparison based on the variances of the groups entering into the comparison. For the within-subjects design, we will follow the same strategy, using separate error terms calculated from only the data contributing to the comparison involved. Under these circumstances, then, the analysis quite literally consists of a series of "miniature" within-subjects designs, each with $a = 2$ levels (the two conditions entering into the comparison) and each with a different $MS_{A \times S}$ calculated on that particular subset of the data matrix. We will illustrate this procedure with the two comparisons we conducted in Sec. 11.5 — a pairwise comparison and a complex comparison — although the procedure itself is the same regardless of the complexity of the comparison. To anticipate, we first form a special data matrix, called a

---

[13] This appendix is intended for students in advanced courses on research design and statistical analysis. Instructors may wish to omit this material in more introductory courses.

comparison matrix, in which the data relevant for the comparison are isolated. Next, we perform a standard within-subjects analysis with these data, which gives us the correct error term for this particular comparison. We will consider the pairwise example first.

Pairwise Comparisons

The pairwise comparison we examined in Sec. 11.5 consisted of a contrast between the front and back conditions (levels a_1 and a_2). As indicated, we first form a comparison matrix, which in this case involves the scores from the first two levels only. This matrix is presented in Table 11-12. If you refer back to the original data set in Table 11-8 (p. 334), you will see that we have simply extracted the data for the two relevant conditions and placed them in a new matrix. From this point on, we treat the data in this comparison matrix as if we were using a within-subjects design in which factor A is represented by only *two levels.* That is, we have two treatment conditions — front and back — and $n = 4$ subjects, each providing Y scores for both conditions.

The analysis begins by summing in both directions to produce column and row marginal sums. We then calculate the four basic ratios specified in Table 11-6 for the analysis of an ordinary within-subjects design. All we need to remember is that $a = 2$ in this analysis and then apply the standard formulas. More specifically,

$$[T] = \frac{T^2}{(a)(n)} = \frac{(160)^2}{(2)(4)} = \frac{25,600}{8} = 3,200.00$$

$$[A] = \frac{\Sigma A^2}{n} = \frac{(104)^2 + (56)^2}{4} = \frac{13,952}{4} = 3,488.00$$

TABLE 11-12 *A Comparison Matrix for a Pairwise Comparison*

Subjects	Front a_1	Back a_2	Sum
s_1	38	22	60
s_2	30	21	51
s_3	17	3	20
s_4	19	10	29
Sum	104	56	160

TABLE 11-13 *Summary of the Analysis: A Pairwise Comparison with a Separate Error Term*

Source	SS	df	MS	F
$A_{comp.}$	$[A] - [T] = 288.00$	1	288.00	45.50*
S	$[S] - [T] = 521.00$	3	173.67	
$A_{comp.} \times S$	$[Y] - [A] - [S] + [T] = 19.00$	3	6.33	
Total	$[Y] - [T] = 828.00$	7		

* $p < .05$.

$$[S] = \frac{\Sigma S^2}{a} = \frac{(60)^2 + (51)^2 + (20)^2 + (29)^2}{2} = \frac{7,442.00}{2} = 3,721.00$$

$$[Y] = \Sigma Y^2 = (38)^2 + (30)^2 + \cdots + (3)^2 + (10)^2 = 4,028$$

Next we combine these quantities in different patterns to produce the sums of squares for this analysis; this step is summarized in the summary table for the analysis (Table 11-13). The remainder of the analysis should be familiar to you. The critical value of *F*, which is based on this new combination of degrees of freedom, is $F(1,3) = 10.1$. The decision rule is as follows:

If $F_{A_{comp.}} \geq 10.1$, reject the null hypothesis; otherwise, retain the null hypothesis.

Since our obtained *F* of 45.50 is greater than 10.1, we reject the null hypothesis and conclude that the subjects playing Scrabble perform significantly better when they are seated in front of the board than when they are seated to the rear.

Although we arrived at the same conclusion with this analysis as the one based on the simplified procedure, there are some clear differences. First, you should note that the error terms are different (6.33 in this analysis versus 4.44 in the overall analysis). The difference in size of the error terms depends on the nature of a set of data — sometimes the separate error term is larger (as it is in this example) and sometimes it is smaller. This should not come as a surprise, however, since the error term from the overall analysis is an *average* of the error terms from all pairwise comparisons. Second, you should also note that the degrees of freedom for the error term are greatly reduced from 9 in the overall analysis to 3 in the current analysis. This reduction in the degrees of freedom associated with separate error terms decreases power somewhat, which you can appreciate by comparing the critical value for the separate error term (10.1) with the critical value for the error term from the overall analysis

(5.12). This difference in power is usually negligible with the substantially larger sample sizes that are used in actual research. In any case, the issue is not one of power at this point, however, but rather of using the *correct* error term to evaluate the significance of a single-*df* comparison.

Complex Comparisons

We follow the same procedure in evaluating a complex comparison, except that the comparison matrix is not as easy to construct as it is with pairwise comparisons. For pairwise comparisons, we constructed the comparison matrix simply by entering each subject's Y scores for the two relevant treatment conditions in the matrix. For complex comparisons, either one of the means or both of the means involved in the comparison consist of a combination of conditions. In constructing the comparison matrix, we need to apply the comparison at the level of the individual subject and enter the transformed Y scores in the matrix. Let's look at the procedure and work through a numerical example.

As an illustration, we will evaluate the same complex comparison we considered in Sec. 11.5, a comparison of the front condition (a_1) with an average of the two side conditions (a_3 and a_4). We construct the comparison matrix by returning to the original data matrix (Table 11-8) and transforming the Y scores to reflect this comparison for each of the subjects in the experiment. The first subject, for example, produced scores of 38, 22, 30, and 30 for the front, back, left, and right conditions, respectively. We would take the Y score from the front condition (38) and place it in the first column of the comparison matrix (labeled "front" in Table 11-14), and we would average the two Y scores from the left and right conditions — that is, $(30 + 30)/2 = 30.0$ — and place the average in the second column of the comparison matrix (labeled "combined sides"). For the second subject, the score for the "front" condition is 30 and the average for the "combined sides" is $(27 + 22)/2 = 24.5$; these transformed scores are entered in the second row of Table 11-14. The data for the other two subjects are treated similarly.

Look carefully at the completed comparison matrix presented in Table 11-14. Although the scores within the body of the matrix are not exactly Y scores — the scores in the first column are the Y scores from the front condition, of course, whereas the scores in the second column are *average* Y scores calculated from each subject's Y scores for the two side conditions — we can treat them as if they were. Thus, the analysis now follows the procedures we presented for a standard within-subjects design in which $a = 2$ and $n = 4$. We now duplicate the steps we followed for the pairwise comparison. We calculate

TABLE 11-14 *A Comparison Matrix for a Complex Comparison*

Subjects	Front	Combined Sides	Sum
s_1	38	30.0	68.0
s_2	30	24.5	54.5
s_3	17	10.0	27.0
s_4	19	15.5	34.5
Sum	104	80.0	184.0

first the following basic ratios:

$$[T] = \frac{T^2}{(a)(n)} = \frac{(184.0)^2}{(2)(4)} = \frac{33,856.00}{8} = 4,232.00$$

$$[A] = \frac{\Sigma\, A^2}{n} = \frac{(104)^2 + (80.0)^2}{4} = \frac{17,216.00}{4} = 4,304.00$$

$$[S] = \frac{\Sigma\, S^2}{a} = \frac{(68.0)^2 + (54.5)^2 + (27.0)^2 + (34.5)^2}{2} = \frac{9,513.50}{2}$$

$$= 4,756.75$$

$$[Y] = \Sigma\, Y^2 = (38)^2 + (30)^2 + \cdots + (10.0)^2 + (15.5)^2 = 4,834.50$$

The remainder of the analysis is summarized in Table 11-15.[14]

You may have noted that the degrees of freedom for the error term for the complex comparison are the same as those for the pairwise ($df_{A\,comp.\times S} = 3$), which means that we can use the same critical value of $F(10.1)$ and the same decision rule for both analyses. The obtained F is significant, and we conclude that the subjects playing Scrabble perform significantly better when they are seated in front of the board than when they are seated on the sides.

---

[14] You may have noted that the sum of squares for the comparison (72.00) is not equal to the value we obtained for the same comparison in Sec. 11.5 (p. 340) with the simplified procedure (96.00). This apparent discrepancy is a consequence of this special procedure for calculating separate error terms. Keppel (1991, pp. 359–361) presents a correction for removing this discrepancy between the sums of squares calculated by the two procedures. For a more detailed discussion of this method of calculating separate error terms for single-*df* comparisons, see Keppel (1991, pp. 356–361).

TABLE 11-15 *Summary of the Analysis: A Complex Comparison with a Separate Error Term*

Source	SS	df	MS	F
$A_{comp.}$	$[A] - [T] = 72.00$	1	72.00	37.50*
S	$[S] - [T] = 524.75$	3	174.92	
$A_{comp.} \times S$	$[Y] - [A] - [S] + [T] = 5.75$	3	1.92	
Total	$[Y] - [T] = 602.50$	7		

* $p < .05$.

Comment

We have presented two ways to evaluate single-*df* comparisons in the within-subjects design. The simplified method we presented in Sec. 11.5 uses the error term from the overall analysis, $MS_{A \times S}$, for each of the analytical comparisons. Unfortunately, subjects often respond to different treatment conditions in unique ways and cause the average error term to mask the correct estimate of the $MS_{A_{comp.} \times S}$ source of variation. The solution that we presented in this appendix is to compute an error term from the particular data set subject to the comparison, although the calculation labor is increased. Any loss of power due to a decrease in the degrees of freedom associated with the separate error terms must be weighed against the potential increase gained from a more accurate estimate of error variance. In our particular example, both methods — with different error terms and changes in power — led to the same decision to reject the null hypothesis, and so it might seem that all the extra work is not worth the effort. In actual research, in contrast with artificial data created for numerical examples, this convergence of the two procedures does not always occur.[15]

When reading the details of statistical analyses conducted on within-subjects designs reported in the research literature, you should try to determine which approach for the evaluation of analytical comparisons was taken by the authors of the reports. In some cases, the authors will state that separate error terms were used in the analysis. In the other cases, however, you will have to perform some detective work to figure out how the authors formed their F ratios. One

---

[15] Our recommendation to advanced students and professional researchers is to always use separate error terms unless there is strong evidence that the observed differences among them are due entirely to chance factors, in which case the average error term may be used. If you are worried about the loss in power associated with the reduced number of *df* associated with separate error terms, your most responsible course of action is to increase your sample size appropriately to compensate for this loss.

clue is a statement that "separate t tests" were conducted. In most cases, these tests use separate error terms for the analyses and are equivalent to the F tests we presented in this appendix. Another clue is found in the number of degrees of freedom reported for the tests. When separate error terms have been computed, the number of degrees of freedom associated with each of these error terms is $n - 1$. On the other hand, if the average error term from the overall analysis has been used to evaluate the comparisons, the degrees of freedom will equal $df_{A \times S} = (a - 1)(n - 1)$. In our numerical example, where $a = 4$ and $n = 4$, a designation of $F(1, 3)$, $4 - 1$, would indicate that separate error terms were used in the analysis of the single-df comparisons evaluated in an experiment, whereas a designation of $F(1, 9)$, $(4 - 1)(4 - 1)$, would indicate that the average error term was used.

Contemporary experimental research in psychology is characterized by two features. First, the experiments employed are primarily factorial in nature, with two or more independent variables manipulated in the same experiment. As we noted in Chap. 9, factorial designs are attractive because they are economical, extract information on interaction, and provide a more representative view of factors responsible for behavior outside the laboratory than single-factor designs. The second feature of modern experimental research is a growing tendency to introduce repeated measures — that is, to introduce within-subjects designs in which subjects serve in more than one treatment combination. As we mentioned in Chap. 11, the primary advantage of within-subjects designs is their sensitivity. Research can benefit from both of these characteristics when factorial designs include a certain degree of multiple testing — a representation of the same subject in more than one of the treatment conditions. We will consider two types of within-subjects factorial designs in this chapter and the next.

12.1   A COMPARISON OF FACTORIAL DESIGNS

Repeated measures are introduced into factorial designs in two ways, either partially or completely. Both types of designs are depicted in Table 12-1, along with a completely randomized factorial design for purposes of comparison. In each design the same basic 2×3 factorial arrangement is employed, and each design contains the same total number of observations: $(a)(b)(n) = (2)(3)(3) = 18$.

Design A is an example of the *completely randomized factorial design*, in which a different group of $n = 3$ subjects is randomly assigned to each of the treatment combinations. We covered this design in Chap. 9.

Design B is an example of a **"pure," or complete, within-subjects factorial design**. By *complete*, we mean that each of the $n = 3$ subjects receives all the $(a)(b) = (2)(3) = 6$ treatment combinations in some counterbalanced order.[1] We will discuss this type of factorial design in Chap. 13.

The final design in Table 12-1 is an example of a *partial* within-subjects factorial. Here the same six treatment combinations are present, but any given subject serves in only three of them. Moreover, the particular set of three is explicitly specified: one set of subjects (s_1, s_2, and s_3) serves in all three levels of factor B, but only in combination with the a_1 level of factor A, while a different set of subjects (s_4, s_5, and s_6) receives the three levels of factor B in combination with the a_2 level of factor A.

---

[1]   We discussed counterbalancing techniques in Sec. 11.6. Also, an actual experiment would probably contain $n = 6$ subjects (or some multiple of 6) to permit the proper counterbalancing of the treatment combinations. We have used $n = 3$ to simplify the presentation.

TABLE 12-1 *A Comparison of Factorial Designs*

A. *Completely Randomized Between-Subjects Factorial (Chap. 9)*

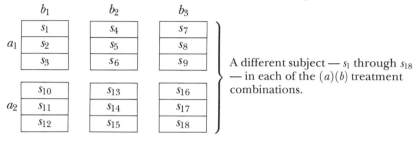

A different subject — s_1 through s_{18} — in each of the $(a)(b)$ treatment combinations.

B. *Pure, or Complete, Within-Subjects Factorial (Chap. 13)*

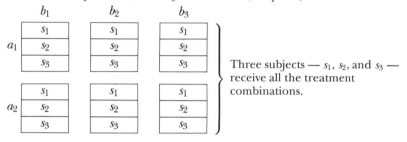

Three subjects — s_1, s_2, and s_3 — receive all the treatment combinations.

C. *Partial, or Mixed, Within-Subjects Factorial (This Chapter)*

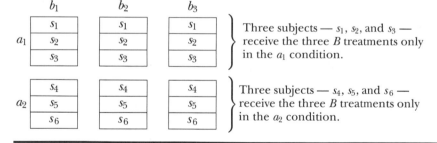

Three subjects — s_1, s_2, and s_3 — receive the three B treatments only in the a_1 condition.

Three subjects — s_4, s_5, and s_6 — receive the three B treatments only in the a_2 condition.

This design combines features of both between-subjects and within-subjects designs. That is, each level of factor *A* contains a different group of randomly assigned subjects. Consequently, this independent variable can be described as being manipulated within the context of a between-subjects design. On the other hand, each level of factor *B* at any given level of factor *A* contains the *same* subjects; this independent variable can therefore be said to be manipulated within the context of a within-subjects design. We refer to this type of within-subjects factorial design as a **mixed within-subjects factorial design,** "mixed" in the sense that it contains elements of both between-subjects and within-subjects designs. Occasionally, you will see this type of design referred to in the literature as a "2 × 3 factorial design with factor A represented as a between-subjects variable and factor B as a within-subjects variable."

Advantages of Within-Subjects Factorials

Although these three designs produce the same kind of information (two main effects and an $A \times B$ interaction) based on the same total number of *observations*, they differ in the numbers of *subjects* required. Table 12-1 shows that the complete within-subjects factorial requires only three subjects, while the mixed factorial consists of six subjects and the complete between-subjects design needs eighteen subjects. In situations where subjects are scarce or expensive, within-subjects designs offer a clear advantage over the between-subjects factorial. They can also save time in studies in which considerable pretraining or complicated instructions are required before any specific treatment is introduced. Such preliminary activities would have to be performed only once for subjects serving in more than one condition, thereby resulting in a significant saving.

The primary advantage of within-subjects designs in general is, of course, their greater *sensitivity* or *statistical power*. That is, within-subjects designs usually require fewer *total observations* than the complete between-subjects factorial to achieve the same degree of sensitivity or statistical power. To create a between-subjects factorial as sensitive as either version of the within-subjects factorial, a researcher would have to make considerably more observations (and thus use many more subjects).

Advantages of the Mixed Factorial Design

Complete within-subjects designs frequently raise difficulties of carryover effects and make large time demands on a single subject. For these reasons, the complete within-subjects factorial is not as common in psychological research as the mixed factorial design, which is frequently and widely represented in the contemporary research literature. Good reasons account for this popularity. We consider three of them.

Minimizing Carryover Effects. First, in contrast with the complete within-subjects factorial, the mixed factorial reduces the number of treatment combinations each subject receives, and this consideration is often important to a researcher. Carryover effects of the sort we discussed in Chap. 11 are usually not as much of a problem in the mixed factorial design as they can be in the complete within-subjects design. In the 2×3 factorial shown in Table 12-1, the mixed factorial requires that subjects serve in three conditions, while the complete within-subjects design requires that subjects serve in six conditions. The more treatment combinations administered to any given subject the greater are the chances that carryover effects will occur.

Studying Learning. Second, the mixed factorial is usually the design of choice when a researcher is studying learning and the processes that influence the speed with which learning takes place. Investigators can often transform a single-factor between-subjects design, where factor A is represented with independent groups of subjects, into a mixed factorial design by testing the subject more than once under the same A treatment condition. For example, factor A might consist of a number of different types of teaching techniques: lecture, video, and discussion. Students are randomly assigned to learn the same material, but using only one of these techniques. The experimenter then systematically tests the subjects during the course of learning to see whether they acquire the task at the same or at different rates. In this example, factor B — a within-subjects factor — consists of *trials*, and the levels are the trial numbers (b_1 is the first trial, b_2 is the second trial, and so on).

An experimenter could choose to avoid a within-subjects design and study the effects of learning with a single-factor experiment. For example, the effects of teaching techniques (factor A) could be measured by combining the measures from all trials into a single score, disregarding the fact that several trials were given. Alternatively, rather than measure performance over several trials, the effects of teaching techniques could be tested on a single trial only. Either approach is a potential waste given the additional information available if the basic experiment is expanded into a mixed factorial in which the individual learning trials become the levels defining factor B. In this case, the groups receiving the different teaching techniques could be compared on the first trial (or on any trial, for that matter) and on rates of acquisition as well as on total learning performance.

For just such reasons, students often turn to mixed factorial experiments for their class projects. A single-factor experiment with independent groups of subjects easily becomes a mixed factorial experiment in which the variable of training trials becomes the second, but within-subjects, factor. The information provided by the mixed factorial is usually worth the time it takes to administer the additional trials. The possibility of discovering an interaction — that the between-subjects independent variable affects the rate at which subjects improve over the training trials — is sufficient justification for using this design in most cases. Discovering the presence of this interaction is simply not possible with the single-factor between-subjects experiment.

Studying Changes over Time.   Finally, another research area that heavily depends on mixed factorial designs is the field of developmental psychology. The developmental process is studied two ways in this field. In one research paradigm, called the **longitudinal study**, a single sample of subjects is studied extensively over a long period of time. The other research paradigm, called the **cross-sectional design**, also studies the developmental changes of the effects of an independent variable (factor *A*), but with *different* samples of subjects drawn from different age groups. This second paradigm, then, represents a mixed within-subjects design.

As an example, consider an experiment conducted by Daniel Slobin (1966) in which subjects were shown pictures depicting some sort of activity together with a sentence describing the objects in the picture. The subjects' task was to indicate whether the sentence accurately described the picture; the dependent variable was the time it took subjects to make a correct decision. Factor *A* consisted of groups of subjects drawn from five different age groups — groups of subjects whose ages were 6, 8, 10, 12, and 20 years. Slobin's other independent variable (factor *B*) consisted of 16 different types of pictures, which all subjects received in different random orders.[2] In short, the experiment was a mixed factorial, with factor *A* (age) the between-subjects variable and factor *B* (picture type) the within-subjects factor. The interest of this research was in the ways the manipulated variable (factor *B*) changed with the developmental variable (factor *A*).

12.2 THE LOGIC OF THE ANALYSIS

You have seen that the mixed factorial design is an ingenious combination of the three designs we have already studied — the between-subjects single-factor design (represented by factor *A* in the mixed design), the within-subjects single-factor design (represented by factor *B* in the mixed design), and the factorial design (represented by the interaction of the two factors). Although we have examined these three aspects of the mixed design separately in preceding chapters, we must now derive all this information from a single design.

---

[2] We have simplified Slobin's study for the purposes of this text.

Two Ways of Dividing the Total Variability

One way to approach the analysis of the mixed factorial design is to remind ourselves of the basic principle we have followed: dividing the total variability (SS_T) into two separable parts, one due to *systematic* treatment effects related to the experimental manipulations and the other due to all *unsystematic* (or uncontrolled) sources of variability that constitute what we have called error variance or experimental error. In addition to this basic breakdown of the total variability, we will also examine another segmentation of the total variability that cuts across the systematic and unsystematic division to isolate *between-subjects variability* and *within-subjects variability*.

It may be useful to anticipate the final outcome of these two sets of subdivisions. We will end up with the three sources of systematic variation, of course, that may be extracted from the results of any two-variable factorial experiment, namely, the main effect of factor A, the main effect of factor B, and the $A \times B$ interaction. Unique to the mixed factorial design, however, is the further subdivision of *unsystematic variability* into two parts, which will be used to evaluate different sources of systematic variability. One of these sources of unsystematic variability — **between-subjects error** — estimates the extent to which chance factors are responsible for any differences observed among the different levels of factor A, the between-subjects factor. The only systematic effect that is based solely on differences between *independent groups* of subjects is the main effect of factor A — that is, differences among the $\overline{Y}_A$ marginal means; consequently, the between-subjects source of error variability will be used as the error term for this systematic effect.

The other source of unsystematic variability — **within-subjects error** — estimates the extent to which chance factors are responsible for any differences observed *within* the same subjects. The only systematic effect that is based solely on within-subjects differences is the main effect of factor B — that is, differences among the $\overline{Y}_B$ marginal means; as a result, the within-subjects source of error variability will be used as the error term for this systematic effect. The remaining systematic effect, the $A \times B$ interaction, is based on *both* sources of systematic variability, which complicates the situation somewhat. For theoretical reasons, however, the within-subjects error is also used as the error term for this systematic effect.

The important and critical point of this additional division of unsystematic variability in the mixed factorial design, then, is that there are two different error terms. From our earlier comparison of single-factor between-subjects design and the corresponding within-subjects design in Chap. 11, we know that the error term for the between-subjects design should be considerably *larger* than the error term for the within-subjects design. As you will soon discover, we find this same difference in the size of the two error terms in the mixed factorial design, which means that factorial effects based entirely on *different groups* of subjects (the main effect of factor *A*) will be evaluated with a larger error term than will factorial effects based at least in part on the *same subjects* (the main effect of factor *B* and the *A* × *B* interaction). Now that you know what to expect, we will discuss in the next section the process of subdividing the total variability.

Systematic and Unsystematic Sources

This first step covers familiar ground. Consider again the analysis of the completely randomized factorial design that we introduced in Chap. 9. The diagram in Fig. 12-1 summarizes the process of subdivision. The entire pie chart represents the total variability in an experiment, which is divided into a number of familiar sources of variability. We see first the division of the total variability into systematic effects, which represent a composite of the usual factorial treatment effects (the two main effects and the interaction), and unsystematic effects, which represent all uncontrolled factors influencing the performance of the subjects in the experiment. This latter source is based on the variability of subjects within each of the factorial treatment groups and is represented by the within-groups sum of squares ($SS_{S/AB}$). For aesthetic reasons, we have allocated half of the pie to the systematic effects and the other half to the unsystematic effects. If we were illustrating the analysis with actual data, the size of the subdivisions would be proportional to the ratio of the effect to the total variability in the experiment.

The diagram also shows that the systematic source of variability is further subdivided into more useful parts — the main effects of the two factors (SS_A and SS_B) and the *A* × *B* interaction ($SS_{A \times B}$). Again, we have arbitrarily assigned equal "slices" to each of the effects; in an actual experiment these slices would vary in size, depending on the proportion of the total variability associated with each of the systematic effects.

Identifying and Dividing Between-Subjects Variation

The analysis of the completely randomized factorial design, which is summarized in Fig. 12-1, represents one of the contributing factors to the analysis of the mixed factorial design — that is, a division of the total variability into systematic variation and unsystematic variation. In this section, we describe the

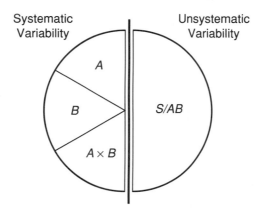

FIGURE 12-1 *Division of the Total Sum of Squares into Systematic and Unsystematic Variability for the Completely Randomized Factorial Design.*

link between the completely randomized *single*-factor design and the mixed factorial and show how we can isolate that portion of the unsystematic variability in Fig. 12-1, which is associated with the between-subjects error term.

We can eliminate the effects of the within-subjects factor (factor *B*) by adding scores across the levels of factor *B* and calculating an average for each subject. When the averages are computed in this manner, we effectively transform the mixed factorial design into an equivalent of a completely randomized single-factor design in which the *between-subjects factor*, factor *A*, is the independent variable.

This arrangement of the data is made explicit in Table 12-2. In part A of the table, we indicate that the three individual *Y* scores for each subject are combined and averaged, to remove any specific information about factor *B* from this aspect of the analysis. We will designate the average scores as $\overline{Y}_{AS}$, with numerical subscripts identifying the specific level of factor *A* and the particular subject. Thus, $\overline{Y}_{A_1 S_1}$ is the average of the individual *Y* scores for the first subject in the group receiving the treatment associated with level a_1.

Consider next the arrangement of the subject means in part B of the table. As you can see, the structural arrangement of the first data matrix is identical to an *actual* single-factor between-subjects design, except that each subject is represented by a *mean* rather than by an individual *Y* score. To emphasize this point, we have substituted *Y* scores for the subject means in the second data matrix, which appears immediately below the first. When transformed this way, the data matrix clearly represents the completely randomized single-factor designs we considered in Part Two. For example, if we calculated the

---

TABLE 12-2 *Transforming the Data Matrix for a Mixed Factorial into a Single-Factor Between-Subjects Design*

A. Calculating the Subject Means:

a_1

	b_1	b_2	b_3		Mean
s_1	Y	Y	Y	$\rightarrow$	$\overline{Y}_{A_1 S_1}$
s_2	Y	Y	Y	$\rightarrow$	$\overline{Y}_{A_1 S_2}$
s_3	Y	Y	Y	$\rightarrow$	$\overline{Y}_{A_1 S_3}$

a_2

	b_1	b_2	b_3		Mean
s_4	Y	Y	Y	$\rightarrow$	$\overline{Y}_{A_2 S_4}$
s_5	Y	Y	Y	$\rightarrow$	$\overline{Y}_{A_2 S_5}$
s_6	Y	Y	Y	$\rightarrow$	$\overline{Y}_{A_2 S_6}$

B. Between-Subjects Variation Represented as a Single-Factor Design:

Using Factorial Symbols:

a_1

s_1	$\overline{Y}_{A_1 S_1}$
s_2	$\overline{Y}_{A_1 S_2}$
s_3	$\overline{Y}_{A_1 S_3}$
Mean	$\overline{Y}_{A_1}$

a_2

s_4	$\overline{Y}_{A_2 S_4}$
s_5	$\overline{Y}_{A_2 S_5}$
s_6	$\overline{Y}_{A_2 S_6}$
Mean	$\overline{Y}_{A_2}$

Using Single-Factor Symbols:

a_1

s_1	$Y_{1,1}$
s_2	$Y_{1,2}$
s_3	$Y_{1,3}$
Mean	$\overline{Y}_{A_1}$

a_2

s_4	$Y_{2,4}$
s_5	$Y_{2,5}$
s_6	$Y_{2,6}$
Mean	$\overline{Y}_{A_2}$

---

deviations of these subject means from the grand mean ($\overline{Y}_{AS} - \overline{Y}_T$), squared the deviations, and summed the squares, we would have a sum of squares that reflects the entire **between-subjects variability** that contributes to the total sum of squares (SS_T) in the mixed factorial design.

Consider an analysis of variance conducted with just this portion of the data, now representing a single-factor between-subjects design. With an actual single-factor design, we would expect to divide the between-subjects variability into two component sources, namely, the effect of factor A and the pooled variability of subjects treated alike, S/A. This is exactly what we obtain when the analysis is conducted within the context of the mixed factorial, except that

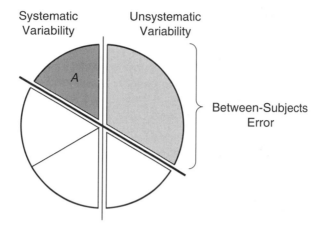

FIGURE 12-2 *Division of the Between-Subjects Variability into Systematic and Unsystematic Parts for the Mixed Factorial Design.*

the terms themselves have names that are more appropriate to this particular design. That is,

between-subjects variability $= A$ main effect $+$ between-subjects error

where the terms to the right of the equals sign, A main effect and between-subjects error, are equivalent to the two component sources we obtain from a single-factor between-subjects design, the effect of factor A and the pooled variability of subjects treated alike (S/A), respectively. We have interpreted this step in Fig. 12-2. As you can see, the part of the circle that appears *above* the slanting line isolates the between-subjects variability. You can see that this upper part of the circle is also divided into systematic and unsystematic parts — that is, the systematic part consists of the A main effect, and the unsystematic part consists of the between-subjects error. Again, the size of these two "slices" is arbitrary for this discussion. We specifically drew the diagonal line to allocate a greater proportion of the unsystematic variability to the between-subjects error (S/A), which represents the outcome observed in the analysis of most mixed factorial designs.

Identifying and Dividing Within-Subjects Variation

We are now able to isolate the **within-subjects variability** that contributes to SS_T in the mixed factorial, which represents the contribution of the single-factor

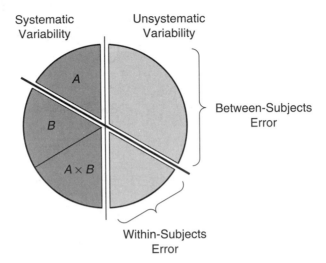

FIGURE 12-3 *Simultaneous Division of the Mixed Factorial into Systematic and Unsystematic Variability and into Between-Subjects and Within-Subjects Variability.*

within-subjects design to the analysis. Each subject in the mixed factorial design produces a total of b Y scores. The within-subjects variability in the mixed factorial is based on the deviation of these scores from the mean for each subject $(Y - \overline{Y}_{AS})$. This variability is depicted in Fig. 12-3 by the part of the circle that appears *below* the slanting line. As you can see, this lower portion of the circle contains the two factorial effects that involve the within-subjects factor — that is, the B main effect and the $A \times B$ interaction — as well as the remaining portion of the unsystematic sources, which we have identified as "within-subjects error."

Summary

Figure 12-3 makes explicit the logic of the analysis of the mixed factorial design.[3] The analysis depends on two major simultaneous subdivisions of the total variability in the experiment — a division into sources of systematic and unsystematic variation and a division into sources of between-subjects variation

---

[3] Exercise 8 provides an example of drawing a pie chart using the data from an experiment.

and within-subjects variation. You can see the principle that is involved: the error term for any given factorial effect depends on whether the effect is based solely on between-subjects variation or at least in part on within-subjects variation. More specifically, the systematic source of between-subjects variation, the A main effect, is tested against the unsystematic source of between-subjects variation, whereas the two systematic sources of within-subjects variation, the B main effect and the $A \times B$ interaction, are tested against the unsystematic source of within-subjects variation.

12.3 ANALYSIS OF VARIANCE

We will now translate the ideas from Sec. 12.2 into the computational formulas with which we will conduct the actual statistical analysis of the mixed factorial design.

Sums of Squares

The computational formulas for the sums of squares are derived from the basic deviations that define the different sources of variability we discussed in Sec. 12.2. We will present these deviations first and then use the symbols defining the respective deviations to indicate the relevant basic ratios to be calculated. The patterns of additions and subtractions tell us how to combine the basic ratios to produce the appropriate sums of squares.

Basic Deviations.   The basic deviations on which the sums of squares for the analysis of the mixed factorial are based are presented in Table 12-3. The deviations for the factorial effects and for the total sum of squares are identical to those we presented in Chap. 9. The only new deviations are those that define the two sources of unsystematic variation, namely, between-subjects error and within-subjects error. We will consider the between-subjects error first.

We use the between-subjects error as the error term to evaluate the main effect of factor A. As discussed in Sec. 12.2 and illustrated in Table 12-2, this source of variability is based on the variability among subjects receiving the same level of factor A, which are then combined over the different groups of subjects receiving different levels of factor A. As we indicated in the earlier discussion, this source of variability is a familiar one — the pooled variability of subjects treated alike, based on the deviation of the average score for each

TABLE 12-3 *Basic Deviations for the Sums of Squares Calculated in the Analysis of the Mixed Factorial Design*

Source	Basic Deviation
A	$\overline{Y}_A - \overline{Y}_T$
B	$\overline{Y}_B - \overline{Y}_T$
$A \times B$	$\overline{Y}_{AB} - \overline{Y}_A - \overline{Y}_B + \overline{Y}_T$
Between-Subjects Error (S/A)	$\overline{Y}_{AS} - \overline{Y}_A$
Within-Subjects Error $(B \times S/A)$	$Y - \overline{Y}_{AB} - \overline{Y}_{AS} + \overline{Y}_A$
Total	$Y - \overline{Y}_T$

subject from his or her group mean; that is,

$$\text{between-subjects error} = \overline{Y}_{AS} - \overline{Y}_A \qquad (12\text{-}1)$$

We designate the between-subjects error S/A to emphasize its connection to an actual single-factor analysis.

We use the within-subjects error, which we designate $B \times S/A$, as the error term to evaluate the two factorial effects based on factor B: the B main effect and the $A \times B$ interaction. We can easily represent the within-subjects error by subtracting the between-subjects error from the total unsystematic variability in the experiment; that is,

$$\text{within-subjects error} = \text{total unsystematic variability}$$
$$- \text{between-subjects error} \qquad (12\text{-}2)$$

The deviation representing the total unsystematic source is $Y - \overline{Y}_{AB}$ — that is, the deviation of each subject from his or her treatment mean.[4] As indicated in Eq. (12-1), the deviation representing the between subjects error is $\overline{Y}_{AS} - \overline{Y}_A$. Substituting these deviations in Eq. (12-2) and then removing the parentheses, we have

$$\text{within-subjects error} = (Y - \overline{Y}_{AB}) - (\overline{Y}_{AS} - \overline{Y}_A)$$
$$= Y - \overline{Y}_{AB} - \overline{Y}_{AS} + \overline{Y}_A \qquad (12\text{-}3)$$

---

[4] You will recall from Chap. 9 that this deviation is the one on which the error term for the completely randomized factorial design (S/AB) was based.

Mixed

TABLE 12-4 *Computational Formulas for the Analysis of Variance in which A Is a Between-Subjects Factor and B Is a Within-Subjects Factor*

Source	Sum of Squares[a]	df	MS	F
A	$[A] - [T]$	$a - 1$	$\dfrac{SS_A}{df_A}$	$\dfrac{MS_A}{MS_{S/A}}$
S/A	$[AS] - [A]$	$(a)(n - 1)$	$\dfrac{SS_{S/A}}{df_{S/A}}$	
B	$[B] - [T]$	$b - 1$	$\dfrac{SS_B}{df_B}$	$\dfrac{MS_B}{MS_{B \times S/A}}$
$A \times B$	$[AB] - [A] - [B] + [T]$	$(a - 1)(b - 1)$	$\dfrac{SS_{A \times B}}{df_{A \times B}}$	$\dfrac{MS_{A \times B}}{MS_{B \times S/A}}$
$B \times S/A$	$[Y] - [AB] - [AS] + [A]$	$(a)(b - 1)(n - 1)$	$\dfrac{SS_{B \times S/A}}{df_{B \times S/A}}$	
Total	$[Y] - [T]$	$(a)(b)(n) - 1$		

[a] $[A] = \dfrac{\Sigma A^2}{(b)(n)}$, $[T] = \dfrac{T^2}{(a)(b)(n)}$, $[AS] = \dfrac{\Sigma(AS)^2}{b}$, $[B] = \dfrac{\Sigma B^2}{(a)(n)}$, $[AB] = \dfrac{\Sigma(AB)^2}{n}$, and $[Y] = \Sigma Y^2$.

Basic Ratios. Except for one new basic ratio, the analysis of the mixed factorial utilizes the same basic ratios as the analysis of the completely randomized factorial design in Chap. 9:

$$[T], [A], [B], [AB], \text{ and } [Y]$$

For convenience, these ratios have been presented again in the footnote to Table 12-4. The new basic ratio involves the one new quantity appearing in this design — the sums for the individual subjects on which the subject means $(\overline{Y}_{AS})$ are based. We will refer to these sums as the *AS* totals. We calculate these totals by summing the *Y* scores obtained from each subject — one for each of the treatment levels of factor *B* a subject receives. Then we simply follow the arithmetical operations specified by the general formula for a basic ratio, namely,

$$\frac{\Sigma(\text{sum})^2}{\text{divisor}}$$

Applied to the combined scores (the *AS* totals), the ratio becomes

$$[AS] = \frac{\Sigma(AS)^2}{b} \tag{12-4}$$

That is, we square the *AS* totals, add up the results, and divide by *b*, the number of observations contributing to each sum.

Sums of Squares. The computational formulas for the sums of squares for the analysis are presented in the second column of Table 12-4. The formulas for the main effects, interaction, and total should be familiar to you from Chap. 9. The formulas for the two error terms are derived from the relevant deviations on which they are based (see Table 12-3). The deviation for the between-subjects error (S/A) was given in Eq. (12-1), namely, $\overline{Y}_{AS} - \overline{Y}_A$; as you can see, the computational formula duplicates this deviation with the basic ratios. The deviation for the within-subjects error $(B \times S/A)$ was given in Eq. (12-3):

$$Y - \overline{Y}_{AB} - \overline{Y}_{AS} + \overline{Y}_A$$

Again, the pattern of combining relevant basic ratios specified in the table for this source is derived from this underlying deviation.

Degrees of Freedom

The degrees of freedom associated with the respective sums of squares are listed in Table 12-4. The degrees of freedom for the factorial effects were also discussed in Chap. 9. To obtain the degrees of freedom for $SS_{S/A}$, the sum of squares for the between-subjects error term, we apply the same logic we used to determine this quantity in the single-factor experiment. That is, the sum of squares is based on the deviation of the mean for each subject from the appropriate treatment mean $(\overline{Y}_{AS} - \overline{Y}_A)$. Because one df is lost as a result of estimating the population treatment mean for any *one* of the treatment groups,

$$df = n - 1$$

Since there are a such groups, however, each with $n - 1$ degrees of freedom,

$$df_{S/A} = (n - 1) + (n - 1) + (n - 1) + \cdots$$
$$= (a)(n - 1) \qquad (12\text{-}5)$$

The formula for the degrees of freedom for $SS_{B \times S/A}$, the sum of squares for the within-subjects error term, may be obtained by subtraction. You will recall from the previous section that we calculated the within-subjects error term by subtracting the between-subjects error term (S/A) from the total unsystematic variability (S/AB), as was expressed in Eq. (12-2). Since any relationship established for $SS_{B \times S/A}$ holds for its corresponding degrees of freedom,

$$df_{B \times S/A} = df_{S/AB} - df_{S/A} \qquad (12\text{-}6)$$

By substituting known quantities for the terms on the right and performing some simple algebra, not outlined here, one can arrive at the compact df statement in Table 12-4, namely,

$$df_{B \times S/A} = (a)(b-1)(n-1) \tag{12-7}$$

Mean Squares and F Ratios

We obtain the mean squares, as usual, by dividing a sum of squares by the appropriate number of degrees of freedom. This step is specified in Table 12-4.

The final stage of the calculations is the formation of the three F ratios. It is here that the two different error terms come into play. In the mixed factorial, the between-subjects error term ($MS_{S/A}$) is used to assess the significance of the A main effect, while the within-subjects error term ($MS_{B \times S/A}$) is used to test the significance of the B main effect and the $A \times B$ interaction. (Figure 12-3, p. 370, illustrates this division into between-subjects and within-subjects components of the analysis.) These F ratios are indicated in the final column of Table 12-4. Note that the arrangement of the sources of variance in Table 12-4 emphasizes the between-subjects and within-subjects portions of the analysis. The A main effect and its error term are listed first and are based on differences between subjects. The remaining factorial effects and their error term are listed next and are based on the repeated measurements taken from the same subjects, that is, differences within subjects.

The statistical hypotheses are the same as those specified in Chap. 9 for the completely randomized factorial experiment (see pp. 253–254). The decision rules follow the same form as those presented in previous chapters. We determine the critical value of F by entering the F table for a specified significance level (α) and combination of numerator and denominator degrees of freedom.

Assumptions underlying the analysis of variance are the same as those for the between-subjects and within-subjects designs (see pp. 118–119 and p. 332, respectively). Researchers tend to be unconcerned with moderate violations of these assumptions, although the consequences of these violations are more serious for the within-subjects portion of the statistical analysis than for the between-subjects portion. For our purposes, however, we will assume that violations have little effect on any conclusions we draw from the statistical evaluation of the data resulting from a mixed factorial experiment.[5]

---

[5] See Keppel (1991, pp. 377–378) for a discussion of the specific assumptions and for procedures to follow in the presence of clear violations.

12.4 A NUMERICAL EXAMPLE

As a numerical example, we will analyze data obtained from a fictitious wine-tasting experiment. The primary question under consideration is whether wines benefit from being opened a half hour or so before being poured and tasted. One of the sacred beliefs of wine buffs is that wines require a "breathing" period to taste their best. A nontechnical justification for this widespread practice is that the early opening allows unpleasant gases and aromas to dissipate and permits a measure of oxidation to occur in the wine. Wine connoisseurs (and most waiters) report that wines definitely improve during the course of a meal or a tasting session. Unfortunately, such evidence is usually contaminated by the fact that changes also take place in the wine taster during the same period as the alcohol takes effect, and therefore any improvement in the taste of the wine might as well be attributed to the changes in the judge as to the effects of a breathing period.

A second independent variable of potential relevance is the type of wine — white or red. Lore has it that red wines benefit more from early opening than white wines. The reasoning is that red wines contain a number of chemical substances that need time to combine with the air to develop fully. Obviously, a well-controlled experiment is required to answer these "important" research questions about the different effects that early opening may have on the two types of wine.

Experimental Design

The design is a 2×3 mixed factorial, with factor A consisting of two types of wine (white and red wine) and factor B consisting of the three breathing conditions (opening periods of 0, 30, or 60 minutes). We will assume that the two types of wines are judged by different groups of subjects. Thus, type of wine represents a between-subjects manipulation and the length of the opening period represents a within-subjects manipulation. There are $n = 5$ subjects randomly assigned to each of the A treatments (types of wine). The response measure consists of a rating on a 10-point scale (1 poor, 10 excellent) of the three wines offered for judgment.

Preliminary Calculations

Summary Matrices. The results of this hypothetical experiment are presented in Table 12-5. The data matrix contains the basic Y scores — the individual

TABLE 12-5 *Matrices Needed for the Analysis*

Data Matrix

	a_1 (White)				a_2 (Red)		
Subjects	(Imm.) b_1	(30 min) b_2	(60 min) b_3	Subjects	(Imm.) b_1	(30 min) b_2	(60 min) b_3
s_1	3	4	2	s_6	10	8	5
s_2	7	5	7	s_7	10	9	7
s_3	4	3	4	s_8	8	6	3
s_4	6	4	4	s_9	7	8	6
s_5	6	6	3	s_{10}	10	7	4
Sum	26	22	20	Sum	45	38	25
Mean	5.20	4.40	4.00	Mean	9.00	7.60	5.00
Variance	2.70	1.30	3.50	Variance	2.00	1.30	2.50
Std. Dev.	1.64	1.14	1.87	Std. Dev.	1.41	1.14	1.58

AB Matrix

	(Imm.) b_1	(30 min) b_2	(60 min) b_3	Sum
a_1 (White)	26	22	20	68
a_2 (Red)	45	38	25	108
Sum	71	60	45	176

AS Matrix

a_1 (White)		a_2 (Red)	
s_1	9	s_6	23
s_2	19	s_7	26
s_3	11	s_8	17
s_4	14	s_9	21
s_5	15	s_{10}	21
Sum	68	Sum	108

ratings for each subject. We have also included for each treatment combination the *AB* sum, mean, variance, and standard deviation. The second matrix is the *AB* matrix, from which we will obtain the basic ratios with which we will compute

TABLE 12-6 *Table of Means*			
Type of Wine (A)	Breathing Period (B)		
	(Imm.) b_1	(30 min) b_2	(60 min) b_3	Average
a_1 (White)	5.20	4.40	4.00	4.53
a_2 (Red)	9.00	7.60	5.00	7.20
Average	7.10	6.00	4.50	

the sums of squares for the factorial treatment effects. The final matrix, the *AS* matrix at the bottom of Table 12-5, isolates the *AS* sums for the respective subjects. To illustrate, the sum of the three *Y* scores for the first subject in level a_1 (s_1) is $AS_{1,1} = 3 + 4 + 2 = 9$, and that for the fourth subject in level a_2 (s_9) is $AS_{2,9} = 7 + 8 + 6 = 21$. We now have all the quantities we need to begin calculating the basic ratios.

Table of Means. Table 12-6 presents the means for the treatment combinations as well as the column and row marginal means on which the two main effects are based. The means within the body of the factorial matrix indicate that, contrary to expectations, neither wine showed an improvement with breathing; in fact, both showed a *deterioration* in judged quality. Moreover, an interaction of the two independent variables appears to be present such that the observed deterioration is much smaller for the white wine than for the red.[6]

Calculating the Sums of Squares

As usual, we obtain the sum of squares by calculating the basic ratios first and then combining them to form the different sums of squares required for the analysis.

Basic Ratios. We will use the entries in the three matrices presented in Table 12-5 to compute the basic ratios we need to obtain the various sums of

---

[6] These findings are fictitious, but they are based on the results of an actual series of experiments reported in *New York Magazine* (1977) by Alexis Bespaloff.

squares. Let's start with the data matrix and calculate the sum of the squared Y scores:

$$[Y] = \Sigma\, Y^2$$

$$= (3)^2 + (7)^2 + \cdots + (6)^2 + (4)^2$$

$$= 1,184$$

We now turn to the AB matrix and calculate the four basic ratios derived from this arrangement of the data. Specifically,

$$[AB] = \frac{\Sigma(AB)^2}{n}$$

$$= \frac{(26)^2 + (22)^2 + \cdots + (38)^2 + (25)^2}{5}$$

$$= \frac{676 + 484 + \cdots + 1,444 + 625}{5} = \frac{5,654}{5}$$

$$= 1,130.80$$

$$[A] = \frac{\Sigma A^2}{(b)(n)}$$

$$= \frac{(68)^2 + (108)^2}{(3)(5)} = \frac{4,624 + 11,664}{15} = \frac{16,288}{15}$$

$$= 1,085.87$$

$$[B] = \frac{\Sigma\, B^2}{(a)(n)}$$

$$= \frac{(71)^2 + (60)^2 + (45)^2}{(2)(5)}$$

$$= \frac{5,041 + 3,600 + 2,025}{10} = \frac{10,666}{10}$$

$$= 1,066.60$$

$$[T] = \frac{T^2}{(a)(b)(n)}$$

$$= \frac{(176)^2}{(2)(3)(5)} = \frac{30,976}{30}$$

$$= 1,032.53$$

Finally, we use the *AS* sums in the *AS* matrix to calculate

$$[AS] = \frac{\Sigma(AS)^2}{b}$$

$$= \frac{(9)^2 + (19)^2 + \cdots + (21)^2 + (21)^2}{3}$$

$$= \frac{81 + 361 + \cdots + 441 + 441}{3} = \frac{3,360}{3}$$

$$= 1,120.00$$

Sums of Squares.   The sums of squares needed for the analysis of variance are specified in Table 12-4. We calculate these values by adding and subtracting the basic ratios in the patterns of combination indicated in the table:

$$SS_A = [A] - [T]$$
$$= 1,085.87 - 1,032.53 = 53.34$$

$$SS_{S/A} = [AS] - [A]$$
$$= 1,120.00 - 1,085.87 = 34.13$$

$$SS_B = [B] - [T]$$
$$= 1,066.60 - 1,032.53 = 34.07$$

$$SS_{A \times B} = [AB] - [A] - [B] + [T]$$
$$= 1,130.80 - 1,085.87 - 1,066.60 + 1,032.53 = 10.86$$

$$SS_{B \times S/A} = [Y] - [AB] - [AS] + [A]$$
$$= 1,184 - 1,130.80 - 1,120.00 + 1,085.87 = 19.07$$

$$SS_T = [Y] - [T]$$
$$= 1,184 - 1,032.53 = 151.47$$

Source	SS	df	MS	F
TABLE 12-7 *Summary of the Analysis*				
A (Type of Wine)	53.34	1	53.34	12.49*
S/A	34.13	8	4.27	
B (Breathing Period)	34.07	2	17.04	14.32*
A × B (Wine × Breathing)	10.86	2	5.43	4.56*
B × S/A	19.07	16	1.19	
Total	151.47	29		

* $p < .05$.

These sums of squares are entered in Table 12-7, the analysis of variance summary table. As an arithmetical check, we should verify that the sum of the component sums of squares equals the total sum of squares. That is,

$$SS_T = SS_A + SS_{S/A} + SS_B + SS_{A \times B} + SS_{B \times S/A}$$

$$151.47 = 53.34 + 34.13 + 34.07 + 10.86 + 19.07$$

$$= 151.47$$

Completing the Analysis of Variance

The degrees of freedom for the different sums of squares are calculated by means of the formulas presented in Table 12-4:

$$df_A = a - 1$$

$$= 2 - 1 = 1$$

$$df_{S/A} = (a)(n - 1)$$

$$= (2)(5 - 1) = (2)(4) = 8$$

$$df_B = b - 1$$

$$= 3 - 1 = 2$$

$$df_{A \times B} = (a - 1)(b - 1)$$
$$= (2 - 1)(3 - 1) = (1)(2) = 2$$

$$df_{B \times S/A} = (a)(b - 1)(n - 1)$$
$$= (2)(3 - 1)(5 - 1) = (2)(2)(4) = 16$$

$$df_T = (a)(b)(n) - 1$$
$$= (2)(3)(5) - 1 = 30 - 1 = 29$$

As an arithmetical check,

$$df_T = df_A + df_{S/A} + df_B + df_{A \times B} + df_{B \times S/A}$$
$$29 = 1 + 8 + 2 + 2 + 16$$
$$= 29$$

We calculate the mean squares for the component sources of variance by dividing each sum of squares by the appropriate number of degrees of freedom. The results of these divisions are presented in Table 12-7. The final step in the calculations is finding the F ratios. For the main effect of factor A, which is based on the between-subjects portion of the statistical analysis,

$$F_A = \frac{MS_A}{MS_{S/A}}$$
$$= \frac{53.34}{4.27} = 12.49$$

The critical value of this F, for which $df_{num.} = 1$ and $df_{denom.} = 8$, is 5.32 at the 5 percent level of significance. Since the obtained F of 12.49 exceeds this critical value, application of the decision rule results in the rejection of the null hypothesis. We conclude that overall, the red wine received significantly higher ratings ($\overline{Y}_{A_2} = 7.20$) than the white wine ($\overline{Y}_{A_1} = 4.53$). As you may have anticipated, however, this conclusion is tempered by the fact that the $A \times B$ interaction is significant.

The other two factorial treatment effects are based on the within-subjects portion of the statistical analysis and thus are assessed by the within-subjects error term, $MS_{B \times S/A}$. Specifically,

$$F_B = \frac{MS_B}{MS_{B \times S/A}}$$

$$= \frac{17.04}{1.19} = 14.32$$

$$F_{A \times B} = \frac{MS_{A \times B}}{MS_{B \times S/A}}$$

$$= \frac{5.43}{1.19} = 4.56$$

Since both F's are associated with the same numbers of degrees of freedom —
$df_{num.} = 2$ and $df_{denom.} = 16$ — both are compared with the same critical value.
At $\alpha = .05$, the critical value of $F(2, 16) = 3.63$. Both F's exceed this value.
Thus, the application of the decision rule results in the rejection of the null
hypothesis in both cases.

Our conclusions at this point are not particularly illuminating, because of
the presence of a significant interaction. We will need to conduct an analysis
of simple effects to establish significantly how the two independent variables
combine to influence the judgments of the wines.

12.5 ANALYTICAL COMPARISONS

As we noted in Chap. 10, an analysis of the main effects and the interaction
usually represents only the first stage in the detailed analysis of a factorial experiment. Different sorts of analytical comparisons are contemplated depending
on the significance or nonsignificance of the $A \times B$ interaction (and the logic
guiding the manipulations that define the levels of the two independent variables). As a general approach to the interpretation of the results of a factorial,
which was summarized in Fig. 10-1 (p. 279), we begin with the $A \times B$ interaction. If the interaction is significant, we then would search for the locus of
the interaction through such statistical techniques as analyses of *simple effects*,
and *simple comparisons*.[7] On the other hand, if the interaction is not significant,

---

[7] We also mentioned another approach to the analysis and interpretation of interaction, the
analysis of *interaction contrasts* (see pp. 305–312), in an appendix at the end of Chap. 10. We

we focus instead on the main effects and their analytical counterparts, *main comparisons*. Examples of these different analyses were presented and discussed in Chap. 10 (see Fig. 10-3, p. 300, for a summary). As you will see, all these analyses are also available for use with the mixed factorial experiment.

We calculate the sums of squares and the mean squares for these analytical comparisons with the same formulas that we described and illustrated in Chap. 10 for the completely randomized factorial design. The only complication occurring in the analysis is the need for different error terms to assess the significance of different analytical comparisons. Given the introductory nature of this book, we will present a simplified procedure for conducting these analyses.[8] We will describe the nature of the error term first and then illustrate their use with the data from the numerical example in the sections that follow.

A Simplified Approach to Error Terms

Table 12-8 indicates which error term we will use to evaluate three different types of analytical comparisons — main comparisons, simple effects, and simple comparisons.

Main Comparisons. As we have already noted, we usually turn our attention to the analysis and interpretation of the *main effects* when the interaction is *not* significant. If a main effect is significant and the factor consists of more than two levels, we would probably examine several meaningful single-df comparisons (*main comparisons*) that reflect differences between relevant marginal row or column means from an AB matrix of means.

As you can see from Table 12-8, the error term we use depends on whether the main comparison involves differences between *different* subjects (factor A) or differences within the *same* subjects (factor B). The appropriate error term for any comparison involving the A marginal means, which we designate $A_{comp.}$, is the between-subjects error term ($MS_{S/A}$), and the error term for any compar-

---

certainly can conduct these often useful analyses with the mixed factorial design, although the selection of an appropriate error term is relatively complex (see Keppel, 1991, pp. 407–415, for a detailed discussion of this analysis).

[8] We feel that the simplified procedure is appropriate for use with class projects, particularly when students are receiving their first exposure to the analysis of relatively complex designs. If your project expands or if you are working on a senior honors thesis or on graduate research, you will need to consult more advanced statistics books for details concerning the error terms for these various analyses. See Keppel (1991, pp. 379–388, 391–415) for a treatment of these issues within a context that is compatible with this book.

TABLE 12-8 *Error Terms for Analytical Comparisons Conducted with the Mixed Factorial Design*

Type of Analysis	Between-Subjects Variability (Analyses Based on Data from Different Groups of Subjects)		Within-Subjects Variability (Analyses Based on Data from the Same Subjects)	
	Source	Error Term	Source	Error Term
Main Comparisons	$A_{comp.}$	$MS_{S/A}{}^a$	$B_{comp.}$	$MS_{B \times S/A}{}^b$
Simple Effects	A at b_j	$MS_{w.cell}{}^c$	B at a_i	$MS_{B \times S/A}$
Simple Comparisons	$A_{comp.}$ at b_j	$MS_{w.cell}$	$B_{comp.}$ at a_i	$MS_{B \times S/A}$

[a] $MS_{S/A}$ is the between-subjects error term from the overall analysis.

[b] $MS_{B \times S/A}$ is the within-subjects error term from the overall analysis.

[c] $MS_{w.cell}$ is the average of the variances (s_{ij}^2) from all the treatment combinations in the design.

ison involving the B marginal means, $B_{comp.}$, is the within-subjects error term ($MS_{B \times S/A}$).

Simple Effects. If the interaction is significant, on the other hand, our attention usually shifts to an evaluation of differences among the means within the body of the AB matrix, rather than main comparisons based on the means in the two margins of the matrix. With a significant interaction, most researchers turn to an examination of the *simple effects* of one or the other of the independent variables, and sometimes of both independent variables. The rationale behind this approach is to pinpoint exactly *where* a given independent variable is having an effect. This goal is facilitated by examining the data for each level of a factor separately, and comparing the results for the different levels.

Researchers usually begin an analysis of simple effects by performing an *omnibus* test in which the overall variation among the treatment means of one factor at a given level of the other factor is evaluated for significance. As indicated in Table 12-8, the error term used in this analysis again depends on whether repeated measures are involved or not. More specifically, if the analysis involves the simple effects of the between-subjects factor (factor A), the error term is a special error term based on the variances for each of the "cells" in the AB matrix ($MS_{w.cell}$), which we will discuss later in this section; whereas if the analysis involves the within-subjects factor (factor B), the error term is the within-subjects factor ($MS_{B \times S/A}$).

Simple Comparisons. Usually when a simple effect is determined to be significant, we follow that finding with one or more meaningful comparisons among the means in the corresponding row or column of the AB matrix of means; we call these *simple comparisons*. If the simple effect is *not* significant, we usually move on to an analysis of another simple effect in the matrix. The selection of error terms again follows a reasonable pattern: if the simple comparison involves the between-subjects factor ($A_{comp.}$ at a particular level of factor B), the error term is the special between-subjects error term ($MS_{w.cell}$); on the other hand, if the simple comparison involves the within-subjects factor ($B_{comp.}$ at a particular level of factor A), the error term is the within-subjects error term from the overall analysis ($MS_{B \times S/A}$). We will now illustrate these analyses briefly with our numerical example. We begin our discussion with the analysis of main comparisons, followed by the analysis of simple effects and simple comparisons.

Analysis of Main Comparisons

As a reminder, we usually turn to a detailed analysis of the main effects when the interaction is not significant. We will disregard this principle with the wine experiment in order to provide an illustration of the procedures involved in conducting main comparisons in the mixed factorial design.

Main comparisons are conducted when the main effect is significant and we want to determine which differences between specific marginal means are significant and which are not. Because factor A in our numerical example consists of only two levels (white and red wine), further analyses are logically not possible. We can still illustrate the procedure that we would follow to analyze main comparisons, however, by treating the two levels of factor A as part of an imaginary larger manipulation even though the result of this analysis will exactly duplicate the main effect of this factor in the overall analysis. Factor B (breathing periods) does not pose this problem, because three periods were included, allowing the possibility of actual main comparisons between the marginal means for this factor.

Between-Subjects Main Comparisons. As we already noted, we will illustrate the analysis of main comparisons involving the between-subjects factor (wine type) by treating the difference between the two marginal means as if this difference represented a single-*df* comparison drawn from a larger set of means. The row marginal means in Table 12-6 give us the following difference between the average ratings given the white and red wines:

$$\hat{\psi}_A = \overline{Y}_{A_1} - \overline{Y}_{A_2} = 4.53 - 7.20 = -2.67$$

Using Eq. (10-1), the formula for a pairwise comparison from Chap. 10, we find[9]

$$SS_{A\,comp.} = \frac{(b)(n)(\hat{\psi}_A)^2}{2}$$

$$= \frac{(3)(5)(-2.67)^2}{2} = \frac{(15)(7.13)}{2} = \frac{106.95}{2}$$

$$= 53.48$$

Because $df_{A\,comp.} = 1$, $MS_{A\,comp.} = 53.48$. According to the entry in Table 12-8, the error term for this main comparison is the between-subjects error term from the overall analysis ($MS_{S/A} = 4.27$). The F becomes

$$F_{A\,comp.} = \frac{MS_{A\,comp.}}{MS_{S/A}} = \frac{53.48}{4.27} = 12.52$$

The critical value of F for $df_{num.} = 1$ and $df_{denom.} = 8$ is 5.32; we conclude that the red wine received significantly higher ratings than did the white.

Complex main comparisons, you will recall, are single-df comparisons in which one or both of the means are averages themselves; they require the use of special coefficients that represent the comparison of interest. We discussed complex main comparisons in Sec. 10.2. We first use the coefficients to express the difference ($\hat{\psi}_A$) as the sum of weighted means; that is,

$$\hat{\psi}_A = (c_1)(\overline{Y}_{A_1}) + (c_2)(\overline{Y}_{A_2}) + (c_3)(\overline{Y}_{A_3}) + \cdots$$

We then enter this difference along with other information in Eq. (10-4),

$$SS_{A\,comp.} = \frac{(b)(n)(\hat{\psi}_A)^2}{\sum c^2}$$

After this point, the procedures for pairwise and complex main comparisons converge and follow the same remaining steps.

Within-Subjects Main Comparisons. The analysis of main comparisons involving the repeated factor (factor B) follows the same steps outlined for the between-subjects factor, except that we use a different error term — $MS_{B \times S/A}$ — to

---

[9] As noted earlier, this main "comparison" is actually the A main effect. The sum of squares for this effect presented in Table 12-7, $SS_A = 53.34$, is identical to the value obtained with Eq. (10-1) except for rounding error introduced during the intermediate steps in the calculations. The two answers will converge if the preliminary calculations are carried to a sufficient number of places.

complete the F test. We will illustrate the procedure with a complex comparison comparing the average ratings of the wines tasted immediately after opening (level b_1) with an average of the wines opened earlier (levels b_2 and b_3 combined). A set of coefficients reflecting this comparison is $1, -\frac{1}{2}, -\frac{1}{2}$. Applying these coefficients to the column marginal means from Table 12-6, we find

$$\hat{\psi}_B = (c_1)(\overline{Y}_{B_1}) + (c_2)(\overline{Y}_{B_2}) + (c_3)(\overline{Y}_{B_3})$$

$$= (1)(7.10) + \left(-\tfrac{1}{2}\right)(6.00) + \left(-\tfrac{1}{2}\right)(4.50)$$

$$= 7.10 - 5.25 = 1.85$$

Substituting in Eq. (10-6) gives us

$$SS_{B\,comp.} = \frac{(a)(n)(\hat{\psi}_B)^2}{\Sigma\,c^2}$$

$$= \frac{(2)(5)(1.85)^2}{(1)^2 + \left(-\tfrac{1}{2}\right)^2 + \left(-\tfrac{1}{2}\right)^2} = \frac{(10)(3.42)}{1 + .25 + .25}$$

$$= \frac{34.20}{1.50} = 22.80$$

The error term for this comparison, which is specified in Table 12-8, is the within-subjects error term from the overall analysis ($MS_{B\times S/A} = 1.19$). The F becomes

$$F_{B\,comp.} = \frac{MS_{B\,comp.}}{MS_{B\times S/A}} = \frac{22.80}{1.19} = 19.16$$

The critical value of F, based on $df_{num.} = 1$ and $df_{denom.} = 16$, is 4.49. We conclude that on the average, wines tasted immediately after opening received significantly higher ratings than wines tasted either 30 or 60 minutes after opening.

Analysis of Simple Effects

We discussed the analysis of simple effects in Sec. 10.3. The analysis of simple effects in the mixed factorial exactly duplicates the steps outlined in Chap. 10, except for the error term, which, as you know, depends on whether the simple effects involve differences between subjects (simple effects of factor A) or

TABLE 12-9 *Sums Used to Calculate the Simple Effects of Type of Wine (Factor A) When Judged Immediately after Opening (Level b_1)*

	(Imm.) b_1	(30 min) b_2	(60 min) b_3
a_1 (White)	26	22	20
a_2 (Red)	45	38	25
Sum	71	60	45

differences within subjects (simple effects of factor B).[10] We will present these analyses quickly; if you need more explanation of some of the details, you may wish to review the relevant discussions in Chap. 10.

Most researchers turn to the analysis of simple effects in an attempt to make sense out of a significant interaction. The fact that the $A \times B$ interaction is significant means that the effect of either one of the independent variables is simply not the same at all levels of the other independent variable. The analysis of simple effects focuses on separate rows or columns in the AB matrix, treating the data as the equivalent of a single-factor experiment involving one factor with the other factor held *constant.*

Between-Subjects Simple Effects. The between-subjects factor in our example is the type of wine — white versus red. An analysis of the simple effects of the type of wine would consist of three analyses, one comparing the two wines immediately after opening (level b_1), one comparing the wines 30 minutes after opening (level b_2), and one comparing the wines 60 minutes after opening (level b_3). We will illustrate the computational procedures with the data from level b_1.

The approach we outlined in Chap. 10 for the analysis of simple effects (pp. 286–290) consisted of isolating the relevant column or row *sums* from the AB matrix and then using formulas that would be appropriate for an *actual* single-factor design, even though this analysis is extracted from a portion of the information produced by the factorial design. We have highlighted the sums from the AB matrix that are relevant for this analysis in Table 12-9.

---

[10] As a reminder, more accurate error terms are available for these analyses, but they are too complex to present in this text. See Keppel (1991, pp. 383–388) for a detailed discussion of error terms used to evaluate simple effects in the mixed factorial.

Substituting in Eq. (10-8), we find

$$SS_{A \text{ at } b_1} = \frac{\Sigma (AB_{i1})^2}{n} - \frac{B_1^2}{(a)(n)}$$

$$= \frac{(26)^2 + (45)^2}{5} - \frac{(71)^2}{(2)(5)}$$

$$= \frac{2,701}{5} - \frac{5,041}{10} = 540.20 - 504.10 = 36.10$$

The degrees of freedom for this analysis are

$$df_{A \text{ at } b_1} = a - 1 = 2 - 1 = 1$$

and so $MS_{A \text{ at } b_1} = 36.10/1 = 36.10$.

As we indicated in Table 12-8, the error term for this simple effect is a special one based on the variances for the individual treatment combinations, which we have termed $MS_{w.cell}$.[11] The variances for each of the "cells" in the AB matrix are found in the original data matrix presented at the top of Table 12-5 (p. 377). We calculate the special error term by taking the average of the variances (s_{ij}^2) from all the treatment combinations in the design:

$$MS_{w.cell} = \frac{\Sigma s_{ij}^2}{(a)(b)} \tag{12-8}$$

Substituting the information from Table 12-5, we find

$$MS_{w.cell} = \frac{2.70 + 1.30 + 3.50 + 2.00 + 1.30 + 2.50}{(2)(3)}$$

$$= \frac{13.30}{6} = 2.22$$

The F then becomes

$$F_{A \text{ at } b_1} = \frac{MS_{A \text{ at } b_1}}{MS_{w.cell}} = \frac{36.10}{2.22} = 16.26$$

The degrees of freedom for the simple effect are

$$df_{A \text{ at } b_1} = a - 1 = 2 - 1 = 1$$

---

[11] One reason the between-subjects error term ($MS_{S/A}$) is *not* appropriate to evaluate this simple effect is that it is based on the average rating for each subject, whereas the analysis of the simple effects is based on the individual Y scores. We correct for this difficulty by working at the level of the individual variances, which are calculated from the Y scores and not the subject means.

TABLE 12-10 *Sums Used to Calculate the Simple Effects of Breathing Periods (Factor B) for Subjects Judging the White Wine (Level a_1)*

	(Imm.) b_1	(30 min) b_2	(60 min) b_3	Sum
a_1 (White)	26	22	20	68
a_2 (Red)	45	38	25	108

whereas the degrees of freedom for the error term are obtained by pooling the *df*'s associated with the individual variances; that is,

$$df_{w.cell} = (n-1) + (n-1) + (n-1) + \cdots$$

$$= (a)(b)(n-1) \tag{12-9}$$

For this example,

$$df_{w.cell} = (2)(3)(5-1) = (6)(4) = 24$$

The critical value of F, for $df_{num.} = 1$ and $df_{denom.} = 24$, is 4.26. We can conclude that when both are tasted immediately after opening, the red wine is rated significantly higher than is the white wine.

Within-Subjects Simple Effects. The formulas for the simple effects of the within-subjects factor (factor B) are essentially the same as those for the between-subjects factor. Suppose we wanted to see whether the different breathing periods had any effect on the white wines (level a_1). As you can see in Table 12-10, this analysis isolates the data in the first row of the AB matrix. Substituting in Eq. (10-12), we find

$$SS_{B \text{ at } a_1} = \frac{\Sigma(AB_{1j})^2}{n} - \frac{A_1^2}{(b)(n)}$$

$$= \frac{(26)^2 + (22)^2 + (20)^2}{5} - \frac{(68)^2}{(3)(5)}$$

$$= \frac{1,560}{5} - \frac{4,624}{15} = 312.00 - 308.27$$

$$= 3.73$$

The degrees of freedom are

$$df_{B \text{ at } a_1} = b - 1 = 3 - 1 = 2$$

and the mean square becomes

$$MS_{B \text{ at } a_1} = \frac{SS_{B \text{ at } a_1}}{df_{B \text{ at } a_1}} = \frac{3.73}{2} = 1.87$$

From Table 12-8, we see that the error term for this simple effect is the within-subjects error term from the overall analysis ($MS_{B \times S/A} = 1.19$). Finally, we calculate the value of F:

$$F_{B \text{ at } a_1} = \frac{MS_{B \text{ at } a_1}}{MS_{B \times S/A}} = \frac{1.87}{1.19} = 1.57$$

The critical value of F, based on $df_{num.} = 2$ and $df_{denom.} = 16$, is 3.63. We would conclude that the three periods of breathing produce differences in the average ratings of the white wines that are not statistically significant.

Analysis of Simple Comparisons

We usually follow the discovery of a significant simple effect with a number of meaningful single-df comparisons, chosen to identify the reasons for the significance of the simple effect. The formulas for the comparison sums of squares are the same for both sets of simple effects, except for obvious changes in notation. The main difference again is in the error terms we use to evaluate the significance of the simple comparisons. We will briefly illustrate both analyses.

Between-Subjects Simple Comparisons. Because the between-subjects factor (type of wine) consisted of only two levels (white and red), the simple effects of this factor can be divided no further. Nevertheless, we will demonstrate the analysis only for purposes of illustrating the techniques for the calculation, even though the F ratio will be identical to that for the corresponding simple effect. If there were more than two levels of the between-subjects factor — white, red, and rosé, for example — then a true simple comparison would be possible.

In the previous section, we examined the simple effect of wine type for wines rated immediately after they were opened. The two means were 5.20 and 9.00, and the difference between them, $\hat{\psi}_{A \text{ at } b_1}$, was $5.20 - 9.00 = -3.80$. Table 12-11 highlights the nature of this analysis. If, for purposes of illustration, we treat these two means as a pairwise simple comparison, we can substitute this

TABLE 12-11 *The Means Contributing to the Analysis of a Simple Comparison Involving the Between-Subjects Factor (Type of Wine)*

	Imm.	30 min	60 min
White	5.20	4.40	4.00
Red	9.00	7.60	5.00

information in Eq. (10-14) to calculate the sum of squares. More specifically,

$$SS_{A \, comp. \; at \; b_1} = \frac{(n)(\hat{\psi}_{A \; at \; b_1})^2}{2}$$

$$= \frac{(5)(-3.80)^2}{2} = \frac{(5)(14.44)}{2} = \frac{72.20}{2} = 36.10$$

Since the number of degrees of freedom for a simple comparison is 1, $MS_{A \, comp. \; at \; b_1} = 36.10/1 = 36.10$. The error term for this analysis is the same error term we calculated for the relevant simple effect ($MS_{w.cell} = 2.22$). The F becomes

$$F_{A \, comp. \; at \; b_1} = \frac{MS_{A \, comp. \; at \; b_1}}{MS_{w.cell}} = \frac{36.10}{2.22} = 16.26$$

The critical value of F, with $df_{num.} = 1$ and $df_{denom.} = 24$, is 4.26. We can conclude that the red wine is preferred to the white wine when it is judged immediately after opening.

Within-Subjects Simple Comparisons.   For the sake of continuity, we will illustrate the analysis of simple comparisons involving the within-subjects factor using the ratings for the white wine, even though the simple effect was not significant and, thus, not justified statistically. Suppose we wanted to compare the average rating obtained immediately after the white wine was opened with the average rating obtained after the 30-minute breathing period. The nature of this analysis is indicated in Table 12-12. This simple comparison is a pairwise comparison, where $\hat{\psi}_{B \; at \; a_1} = 5.20 - 4.40 = .80$. Substituting in the equivalent of Eq. (10-14), we find

$$SS_{B \, comp. \; at \; a_1} = \frac{(n)(\hat{\psi}_{B \; at \; a_1})^2}{2}$$

$$= \frac{(5)(.80)^2}{2} = \frac{(5)(.64)}{2} = \frac{3.20}{2} = 1.60$$

TABLE 12-12 *The Means Contributing to the Analysis of a Simple Comparison Involving the Within-Subjects Factor (Breathing Period)*

	Imm.	30 min	60 min
White	5.20	4.40	4.00
Red	9.00	7.60	5.00

Since $df = 1$, $MS_{B\,comp.}$ at $a_1 = 1.60/1 = 1.60$. According to the simplified procedure for selecting error terms summarized in Table 12-8, the error term is the within-subjects error term from the overall analysis ($MS_{B \times S/A} = 1.19$). The F becomes

$$F_{B\,comp.\ \text{at}\ a_1} = \frac{MS_{B\,comp.\ \text{at}\ a_1}}{MS_{B \times S/A}} = \frac{1.60}{1.19} = 1.34$$

The critical value of F, based on $df_{num.} = 1$ and $df_{denom.} = 16$, is 4.49. The difference between these two breathing periods is not statistically significant.

12.6 SUMMARY

We first discussed three types of factorial designs, which differed in how subjects were represented in the different treatment combinations. In the completely randomized design, which we covered in Chap. 9, subjects are randomly assigned to groups that receive one of the treatment combinations. In the complete, or "pure," within-subjects design, a single group of subjects receives *all* the treatment combinations; we cover the analysis of this design in Chap. 13. In the mixed factorial design, which was the topic of the present chapter, subjects receive all the treatment conditions associated with one of the independent variables (factor *B*) in combination with only one level of the other independent variable (factor *A*).

Mixed factorial designs are extremely common in psychological research. Researchers often choose them to conduct a sensitive or more powerful test when only a small number of subjects are available. In addition, they can easily expand a basic single-factor experiment with independent groups of subjects into a mixed factorial simply by administering a series of learning trials to each of the subjects in the original design. In this case, the variable of trials (a within-subjects factor) becomes a second independent variable in the experiment.

The statistical analysis of the mixed factorial is identical to that required of the completely randomized factorial experiment, except for the error terms. A major part of the chapter was devoted to an explanation of how to identify and construct the error terms.

In brief, a general principle emerged. One error term is used to evaluate the main effect of factor A, which is based on between-subjects differences; this mean square ($MS_{S/A}$) is functionally equivalent to the error term used in the analysis of a completely randomized single-factor experiment, except that it is based on subject means rather than on individual Y scores. A second error term ($MS_{B \times S/A}$) is used to evaluate differences based on the within-subjects factor; this mean square is usually considerably smaller than the between-subjects error term, accounting for the increased sensitivity associated with this type of design.

The final section considered the analytical analyses usually conducted with a factorial experiment. Generally, the nature of these analyses depends on the significance of the $A \times B$ interaction. More specifically, if the interaction is significant, a researcher usually systematically examines a series of simple effects and simple comparisons (when the simple effects are significant); on the other hand, if the interaction is not significant and the main effects are, a researcher examines main comparisons. We showed that the sums of squares for the treatment effects themselves — the main comparisons, simple effects, and simple comparisons — are calculated by means of the formulas presented in Chap. 10, but that the selection of the error term is influenced again by the presence or absence of repeated measures in the data under consideration. We presented a simplified method for selecting error terms that reasonably deals with this complication.

12.7 EXERCISES [12]

*1. An investigator was interested in the effects of the loudness of an auditory message on a person's ability to process messages at different rates of presentation. Previous research indicated that subjects could be tested on messages presented at different rates without any apparent contamination between one rate and another. Thus, the researcher decided to test each subject at each of three rates, slow (b_1), medium (b_2), and fast (b_3). However, individual subjects were tested with only one loudness level, thus, three different

---

[12] Answers to the starred problems are given in Appendix B.

groups of subjects were given respectively either soft (a_1), moderate (a_2), or loud (a_3) auditory messages. The result, of course, was a mixed design with loudness as a between-subjects variable and rate as a within-subjects variable. Rate was completely counterbalanced, requiring six subjects in each loudness condition. The response measure was the number of messages correctly detected. The data for the 18 subjects are as follows:

a_1 (Soft)				a_2 (Moderate)				a_3 (Loud)			
Subject	b_1	b_2	b_3	Subject	b_1	b_2	b_3	Subject	b_1	b_2	b_3
S_1	9	6	5	S_7	15	10	8	S_{13}	12	9	7
S_2	11	9	6	S_8	15	9	7	S_{14}	15	11	7
S_3	11	8	5	S_9	14	6	4	S_{15}	15	12	8
S_4	12	10	10	S_{10}	17	13	11	S_{16}	16	14	12
S_5	12	12	9	S_{11}	11	7	5	S_{17}	17	14	11
S_6	11	11	7	S_{12}	16	10	8	S_{18}	15	13	10

Perform an analysis of variance on these data. To understand the results, construct a graph of the treatment means. How would you summarize the results of the experiment?

*2. Conduct the following analytical comparisons involving the between-subjects factor (loudness of the message) using the data from exercise 1:

    a. An analysis of the simple effects of the loudness factor for the subjects receiving the messages at the slow rate (level b_1)

    b. A simple comparison between moderate and loud messages presented at the slow rate

    c. A simple comparison between soft messages and the combined moderate and loud messages presented at the slow rate

*3. Conduct the following analytical comparisons involving the within-subjects factor (rate of presentation) using the data from exercise 1:

    a. An analysis of the simple effects of the rate factor for the subjects receiving the loud messages (level a_3)

    b. A simple comparison between the slow and medium rates for the subjects receiving the loud messages

    c. A simple comparison between the fast rate and the combined slow and medium rates for the subjects receiving the loud messages

4. Conduct the following analytical comparisons using the data from the numerical example appearing in Table 12-5 (p. 377):

    a. An analysis of the simple effects of wine type when the bottles are opened 60 minutes before the subjects are asked to judge the wines

    b. An analysis of the simple effects of the different breathing periods for the red wines

    c. A simple comparison between the red wines tasted immediately after opening and 60 minutes after opening

5. In exercise 4 of Chap. 11 (pp. 350–351), we presented an experiment conducted by an instructor in a computer literacy course in which he measured the progress students made over five test sessions in learning to use a complex word-processing program. The data presented in Chap. 11 were obtained from subjects who were given a week to study the training manual before they were tested. Suppose the instructor also administered the same experiment to a second group of subjects, who were given the training manual a week before the test but not specifically urged to study the material; essentially, they were left on their own to learn about the program (the method favored by many "experienced" computer users!). The actual design of the experiment, then, is a mixed factorial in which the between-subjects factor (factor A) consists of the different instructions with regard to the training manual — which we will refer to as "manual specified" and "manual unspecified" — and the within-subjects factor (factor B) consists of the five test sessions. Five subjects were randomly assigned to the group receiving the instructions to study the manual and five others were randomly assigned to the group receiving no specific instructions about studying the manual. The data for the two groups are as follows:

Manual Specified (a_1)

Students	b_1	b_2	b_3	b_4	b_5
			Test Sessions		
1	5	6	14	19	22
2	2	7	11	18	24
3	1	3	8	25	22
4	6	5	9	18	22
5	6	8	15	22	29

Manual Unspecified (a_2)

Students	b_1	b_2	b_3	b_4	b_5
			Test Sessions		
6	8	9	9	13	13
7	1	5	15	15	19
8	6	4	6	8	17
9	7	11	15	12	15
10	5	6	9	10	18

Perform an analysis of variance on these data.

6. Analyze the data in exercise 5 to find out whether the group that was urged to study the manual showed significant improvement over the five test sessions.

7. Compare the scores in exercise 5 for the two groups on the first test session to determine if they were comparable at the beginning of the experiment.

8. Using the sums of squares obtained from the overall analysis of the numerical example (Table 12-7, p. 381), draw a pie chart showing the proportion of the total variability (SS_T) that is associated with the various sources of variability normally extracted from the mixed factorial design. Be sure to identify the sources that represent systematic or unsystematic variability, and the sources that represent between-subjects or within-subjects variability.

Chapter · 13

THE TWO-FACTOR
WITHIN-SUBJECTS DESIGN

In Table 12-1, we presented three types of designs in which two independent variables are manipulated factorially. Although these designs provide information about the same factorial treatment effects — the A main effect, the B main effect, and the $A \times B$ interaction — they differ in the extent to which any given subject contributes to this information. At one extreme is the *completely randomized factorial*, in which each subject receives only one treatment combination; and at the other is the *complete*, or *pure, within-subjects factorial*, in which each subject receives *all* the treatment combinations. Between these two extremes lies the *mixed factorial design*, in which subjects receive some, but not all, the treatment combinations. We considered two of these designs in some detail, the completely randomized factorial in Chaps. 9 and 10 and the mixed factorial in Chap. 12. In this chapter, we discuss the complete within-subjects factorial, which we will call the **two-factor within-subjects factorial**.

All the advantages of the single-factor within-subjects design, as well as the disadvantages, extend to the two-factor within-subjects factorial. The primary advantage, of course, is the increase in sensitivity, or power, provided when we examine treatment effects *within the same* subjects rather than *between different* subjects. You will recall that the mixed factorial extended this important benefit to only some of the effects we normally examine in the detailed analysis of a factorial experiment. More specifically, we are able to use the substantially smaller within-subjects error term to evaluate the B main effect and the $A \times B$ interaction in the overall analysis, as well as any main comparisons, simple effects, and simple comparisons involving the within-subjects factor. In contrast, however, we must use a larger, between-subjects error term to evaluate the A main effect in the overall analysis, as well as any main comparisons, simple effects, and simple comparisons that involve the between-subjects factor. The value of the two-factor within-subjects factorial, then, is that it extends increased sensitivity to *all* analyses, not just a subset of these as in the mixed factorial design.

Pure within-subjects factorial designs, in general, are ideal for experiments in which subjects are costly (for example, research with animals), or which involve special human populations (such as clinical or hospital patients), or where long training procedures are needed to prepare subjects before treatments can be applied. Pure within-subjects factorials are also usually the design of choice for experiments dealing with basic skills and sensory capacities, such as reaction time, sensory processes, perception, or a variety of cognitive skills and abilities. Students often find these designs ideal for honors theses and class projects, where the increased sensitivity allows them to reduce the number of subjects they need to create experiments with reasonable power.

The major disadvantage of these designs is the possibility of carryover effects. Although researchers can counterbalance the order of treatment combinations to neutralize any practice effects that may be present, this does not ensure that the effects of earlier treatments are completely dissipated when a new treatment is introduced, a problem we discussed in some detail in Chap. 11.

13.1 THE LOGIC OF THE ANALYSIS

The primary complication in the analysis of the two-factor within-subjects design is that three different error terms are needed to evaluate the two main effects and the $A \times B$ interaction. Whereas the reason for this complication lies deep within statistical theory, it is a direct consequence of the nature of psychological data, which typically exhibit different amounts of unsystematic, or uncontrolled, variability depending on how the data are combined for the different analyses. What this means is that when we combine the Y scores to exhibit the main effect of factor A, for example, these combined scores may reflect a different degree of uncontrolled variability than when we combine the same Y scores to reflect the main effect of factor B or the $A \times B$ interaction. Before you panic at the prospect of three error terms, however, we should hasten to add that the terms for the two main effects are functionally equivalent to the error term we used to analyze the results of a *single*-factor within-subjects design. Thus, the only new procedure introduced with the two-factor within-subjects design is the error term for evaluating the $A \times B$ interaction.

The Basic Design

The basic data matrix representing the data produced by a 2×3 complete within-subjects design is presented in Table 13-1. We have depicted $n = 3$ subjects, and, as you can see, each subject produces a Y score for each of the $(a)(b) = (2)(3) = 6$ treatment combinations.

Constructing Summary Matrices. From this basic matrix, we combine the Y scores in various ways to produce sums that enter into the different analyses. Three additional recombinations of the basic data matrix are necessary. We will illustrate the construction of these matrices using the abstract symbols in Table 13-1. You may want to supplement this discussion by skipping ahead to Table 13-3 (p. 411) and verifying the construction of the matrices with numerical data.

AB Matrix. The column, or AB, sums from the data matrix are entered into the usual AB matrix. For example,

$$AB_{1,1} = Y_{1,1,1} + Y_{1,1,2} + Y_{1,1,3}$$

This matrix will give us the information we need to calculate the sums of squares for the two main effects and the interaction.

TABLE 13-1 *Matrices Needed for the Analysis of the Two-Factor Within-Subjects Design*

Data Matrix

	a_1			a_2		
	b_1	b_2	b_3	b_1	b_2	b_3
s_1	$Y_{1,1,1}$	$Y_{1,2,1}$	$Y_{1,3,1}$	$Y_{2,1,1}$	$Y_{2,2,1}$	$Y_{2,3,1}$
s_2	$Y_{1,1,2}$	$Y_{1,2,2}$	$Y_{1,3,2}$	$Y_{2,1,2}$	$Y_{2,2,2}$	$Y_{2,3,2}$
s_3	$Y_{1,1,3}$	$Y_{1,2,3}$	$Y_{1,3,3}$	$Y_{2,1,3}$	$Y_{2,2,3}$	$Y_{2,3,3}$

AB Matrix

	b_1	b_2	b_3	Sum
a_1	$AB_{1,1}$	$AB_{1,2}$	$AB_{1,3}$	A_1
a_2	$AB_{2,1}$	$AB_{2,2}$	$AB_{2,3}$	A_2
Sum	B_1	B_2	B_3	T

AS Matrix

	a_1	a_2	Sum
s_1	$AS_{1,1}$	$AS_{2,1}$	S_1
s_2	$AS_{1,2}$	$AS_{2,2}$	S_2
s_3	$AS_{1,3}$	$AS_{2,3}$	S_3
Sum	A_1	A_2	T

BS Matrix

	b_1	b_2	b_3	Sum
s_1	$BS_{1,1}$	$BS_{2,1}$	$BS_{3,1}$	S_1
s_2	$BS_{1,2}$	$BS_{2,2}$	$BS_{3,2}$	S_2
s_3	$BS_{1,3}$	$BS_{2,3}$	$BS_{3,3}$	S_3
Sum	B_1	B_2	B_3	T

AS Matrix.   The AS sums are found by summing over the b treatments. For example, $AS_{1,1}$ represents the sum of the three Y scores for s_1 obtained under level a_1, that is, the sum of the first three scores in the first row of the data matrix:

$$AS_{1,1} = Y_{1,1,1} + Y_{1,2,1} + Y_{1,3,1}$$

and $AS_{2,1}$ represents the sum of the three Y scores for the same subject (s_1) under level a_2 — the sum of the last three scores in the first row of the data matrix.

BS Matrix. The BS sums are found by summing over the a treatments. For example, $BS_{1,1}$ is the sum of the two Y scores for the first subject (s_1) obtained under level b_1:

$$BS_{1,1} = Y_{1,1,1} + Y_{2,1,1}$$

and $BS_{2,1}$ represents the sum obtained under level b_2 for the same subject.

Calculation Checks. Each of the three rearrangements of the original data matrix has marginal totals that are duplicated in at least one other matrix. These sums must be identical, and by comparing them we have an initial check on our calculations. For example, the sums for the A treatments, A_1 and A_2, can be found from the AB matrix and the AS matrix. Similarly, the B sums for the levels of factor B and the S sums for the subjects are found in two matrices (AB and BS for the B sums and AS and BS for the S sums). The sum of all the scores, T, appears in each of the three matrices.

Error Term for the A Main Effect

We can transform the two-factor within-subjects design into two single-factor representations, one with factor A as the independent variable and the other with factor B as the independent variable. Consider the AS matrix in Table 13-1, which contains sums obtained by collapsing over the b treatments. Except for the fact that the AS matrix consists of *sums* rather than individual scores, the matrix is identical to that formed with the single-factor within-subjects design (see Table 11-5, p. 328).

Let's consider the information we can obtain from the AS matrix. Because the AS matrix represents a single-factor within-subjects design involving factor A (with factor B disregarded in this matrix), we would expect to obtain the following sums of squares:

- the main effect of factor A, SS_A

- the main effect of subjects, SS_S

- the interaction of factor A and subjects, $SS_{A \times S}$

Continuing with the analogy, we would expect to use the interaction mean square, $MS_{A \times S}$, as the error term to evaluate the main effect of factor A.

Error Term for the B Main Effect

The BS matrix is created by combining the Y scores from the data matrix over the a treatments. As with the AS matrix, the BS matrix resembles the data matrix from a single-factor within-subjects design with factor B as the independent variable. An analysis of this matrix would produce

- the main effect of factor B, SS_B

- the main effect of subjects, SS_S

- the interaction of factor B and subjects, $SS_{B \times S}$

Continuing with the analogy to an actual single-factor within-subjects design, we would expect to use the interaction mean square, $MS_{B \times S}$, as the error term to evaluate the main effect of factor B.

Error Term for the A × B Interaction

You have already seen that the source of the error term for a factorial effect involving one within-subjects factor is the interaction of that factor with subjects — the $A \times S$ interaction for the main effect of factor A and the $B \times S$ interaction for the main effect of factor B. If we simply extend this logic to the $A \times B$ interaction, in which two within-subjects factors are involved, we find that the source of this error term is an interaction between the subjects and the two within-subjects factors — the $A \times B \times S$ interaction. We will calculate the sum of squares for this source, $SS_{A \times B \times S}$, by subtracting all other sources from the total variability in the experiment; the remainder, or *residual*, represents this sum of squares.

The diagram in Fig. 13-1 specifies the sources of variability we will extract from data produced by a two-factor within-subjects factorial. We have arbitrarily divided the circle vertically into two portions, namely, systematic sources of variability and unsystematic sources. The systematic sources consist of the familiar factorial treatment effects: A, B, and $A \times B$. The unsystematic sources consist of all sources of variability that involve the subjects one way or another. As with similar pie charts in Chaps. 11 and 12, the sizes of the "slices" were chosen to clarify the discussion. Based on actual data, the sizes would be proportional to the ratio of the respective sums of squares to the total variability in the experiment (SS_T).

The first source of variability involving subjects, the main effect of subjects (S in Fig. 13-1), is based on an average of *all* the scores produced by each of

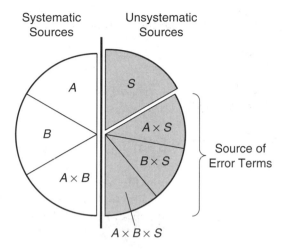

FIGURE 13-1 *Division of the Total Sum of Squares in a Two-Factor Within-Subjects Factorial Design.*

the subjects; this source reflects the average performance of the subjects over all the conditions. Next, we have interactions between the subjects and the two independent variables — that is, $A \times S$ and $B \times S$. As we have already noted, the $A \times S$ interaction is the source of the error term for the main effect of factor A and the $B \times S$ interaction is the source of the error term for the main effect of factor B. The remaining quantity, the $A \times B \times S$ interaction, is the source of the error term for the $A \times B$ interaction. Since the sums of squares for all these sources must add up to equal the total variability in the experiment (SS_T), we can obtain the sum of squares for the $A \times B \times S$ interaction simply by subtracting the sums of squares for all the other sources from SS_T. That is,

$$
\begin{aligned}
SS_{A \times B \times S} = \ &SS_T && \text{(total variability)} \\
&-SS_A && \text{(main effect of factor } A\text{)} \\
&-SS_B && \text{(main effect of factor } B\text{)} \\
&-SS_{A \times B} && \text{(interaction of factors } A \text{ and } B\text{)} \\
&-SS_S && \text{(main effect of subjects)} \\
&-SS_{A \times S} && \text{(interaction of factor } A \text{ and subjects)} \\
&-SS_{B \times S} && \text{(interaction of factor } B \text{ and subjects)} \quad (13\text{-}1)
\end{aligned}
$$

For our purposes, then, the error term for the $A \times B$ interaction is based on the variability left over once we perform the operations specified in Eq. (13-1).

13.2 THE ANALYSIS OF VARIANCE

We discussed the form of the analysis of the two-factor within-subjects factorial in Sec. 13.1. Now, we will fill in the details. We begin with the formulas for the various sums of squares that we must extract from the basic data matrix.

Sums of Squares

As usual, we will present the formulas for the sums of squares in two steps: the formulas for the basic ratios on which the sums of squares are based, followed by the formulas specifying the patterns in which the basic ratios are combined to produce the different sums of squares.

Basic Ratios. Basic ratios, you will recall, are formed by squaring and then summing members of a set of quantities having the same letter designation and dividing by the number of observations contributing to any one of the members in the set. All these sets of quantities are specified in Table 13-1 — namely, Y from the data matrix; AB, A, B, and T from the AB matrix; AS and S from the AS matrix (A and T were already specified in the AB matrix); and BS from the BS matrix (B, S, and T were already specified in other matrices). The formulas for the basic ratios derived from these quantities are presented at the bottom of Table 13-2 for each source of variability we will isolate in the analysis. We will illustrate all these calculations in Sec. 13.3 with a numerical example.

Sums of Squares. The second column specifies the pattern of combination required to calculate each of the sums of squares. The first four sources should be familiar to you from previous chapters — A, B, and $A \times B$ from Chap. 9 and S from Chap. 11. The formula for $SS_{A \times S}$ follows the same pattern as presented

TABLE 13-2 *Computational Formulas for the Analysis of Variance*

Source	Sums of Squares[a]	df	MS	F
A	$[A] - [T]$	$a - 1$	$\dfrac{SS_A}{df_A}$	$\dfrac{MS_A}{MS_{A \times S}}$
B	$[B] - [T]$	$b - 1$	$\dfrac{SS_B}{df_B}$	$\dfrac{MS_B}{MS_{B \times S}}$
$A \times B$	$[AB] - [A] - [B] + [T]$	$(a-1)(b-1)$	$\dfrac{SS_{A \times B}}{df_{A \times B}}$	$\dfrac{MS_{A \times B}}{MS_{A \times B \times S}}$
S	$[S] - [T]$	$n - 1$	$\dfrac{SS_S}{df_S}$	
$A \times S$	$[AS] - [A] - [S] + [T]$	$(a-1)(n-1)$	$\dfrac{SS_{A \times S}}{df_{A \times S}}$	
$B \times S$	$[BS] - [B] - [S] + [T]$	$(b-1)(n-1)$	$\dfrac{SS_{B \times S}}{df_{B \times S}}$	
$A \times B \times S$	$[Y] - [AB] - [AS] - [BS]$ $+[A] + [B] + [S] - [T]$	$(a-1)(b-1)$ $\times(n-1)$	$\dfrac{SS_{A \times B \times S}}{df_{A \times B \times S}}$	
Total	$[Y] - [T]$	$(a)(b)(n) - 1$		

^{a} $[A] = \dfrac{\Sigma A^2}{(b)(n)}, [T] = \dfrac{T^2}{(a)(b)(n)}, [B] = \dfrac{\Sigma B^2}{(a)(n)}, [AB] = \dfrac{\Sigma(AB)^2}{n}, [S] = \dfrac{\Sigma S^2}{(a)(b)},$

$[AS] = \dfrac{\Sigma(AS)^2}{b}, [BS] = \dfrac{\Sigma(BS)^2}{a},$ and $[Y] = \Sigma Y^2.$

in Chap. 11; that is,

$$SS_{A \times S} = [AS] - [A] - [S] + [T]$$

This formula is identical to the one for the single-factor within-subjects design except that $[AS]$, which is based on the AS sums in the two-factor within-subjects design, is substituted for $[Y]$, which is based on the Y scores in the single-factor within-subjects design. The formula for the $SS_{B \times S}$ specifies an analogous pattern of basic ratios, namely,

$$SS_{B \times S} = [BS] - [B] - [S] + [T]$$

You may wish to accept the formula for $SS_{A \times B \times S}$ on faith, of course, simply because it gives the correct answer! On the other hand, if you are courageous and handy with algebraic manipulations, you could verify that the formula for the sum of squares in Table 13-2 is correct by substituting the computational formulas for the relevant sums of squares in Eq. (13-1), which defines this sum of squares as a residual quantity obtained by subtracting all other sources from SS_T, and then simplifying the complex expression that results.

Degrees of Freedom

The degrees of freedom are specified in the third column of the table. Some of these should be familiar. Formulas for main effects (df_A, df_B, and df_S) have the form

$$df_{main\ effect} = \text{number of basic observations} - 1$$

Formulas for interactions consist of products formed by multiplying the degrees of freedom for the factors involved in the interaction. That is,

$$df_{A \times B} = (df_A)(df_B) = (a-1)(b-1)$$
$$df_{A \times S} = (df_A)(df_S) = (a-1)(n-1)$$
$$df_{B \times S} = (df_B)(df_S) = (b-1)(n-1)$$
$$df_{A \times B \times S} = (df_A)(df_B)(df_S) = (a-1)(b-1)(n-1)$$

Mean Squares and *F* Ratios

Mean squares are calculated by dividing each sum of squares by the appropriate number of degrees of freedom, as indicated in the fourth column of Table 13-2. The *F* ratios for the three factorial treatment effects are specified in the last column of the table. As we discussed in Sec. 13.1, there is a different error term for each of the factorial effects. That is,

Source of Factorial Effect	Source of Error Term
A main effect	$A \times S$ interaction
B main effect	$B \times S$ interaction
$A \times B$ interaction	$A \times B \times S$ interaction

13.3 A NUMERICAL EXAMPLE

We are now ready to apply the computational formulas in Table 13-2 to a numerical example.

Experimental Background

We will illustrate the analysis of the two-factor within-subjects design with an example based on an actual experiment conducted by Cynthia Langley and Donald Riley, who were studying the processing of stimuli by pigeons.

Before we present the details of the experiment, we need to describe the nature of the testing situation. On any given trial, a pigeon was presented with the image of a stimulus projected on a central pecking key to which it attended; this stimulus is called the *sample stimulus*. After a fixed amount of time, the sample stimulus disappeared and the pigeon was given a choice between two test stimuli projected on keys placed on either side of the center key, one of which was related to the sample stimulus and one that was different; subjects indicated their choice of stimuli by pecking one of the two side keys. If the pigeon pecked the side key that matched the sample stimulus, it received a small amount of pigeon grain.

One of the independent variables — factor *A*, or *stimulus type* — consisted of two levels: a stimulus containing two elements (for example, a color and a simple shape) or a stimulus containing one element (the color or the shape by itself), which Langley and Riley referred to as *compound* and *element* stimuli, respectively. The other independent variable — factor *B*, or *stimulus duration* — consisted of the length of time the sample stimulus was shown to the pigeon, either 110, 805, or 5,935 milliseconds (1,000 milliseconds = 1 second); we will refer to these durations as *short*, *medium*, and *long*, respectively. A total of $n = 5$ pigeons were tested.

After a lengthy period of pretraining, which was continued until the birds learned to make judgments with a high degree of accuracy, the main experiment began. Each test day started with some warmup trials, followed by a series of test trials. The dependent variable was the number of correct selections made on the test trials. For purposes of our example, we have simplified the original experiment and fabricated some of the data. These changes do not distort the basic findings of their experiment.

Langley and Riley expected the pigeons to perform less well on tests following the presentation of compound stimuli than following element stimuli, because of the increased amount of information the pigeons must process. They also predicted that performance would improve as the length of time for which the sample was shown increased, since the pigeons would have more time to encode information from the sample stimulus and prepare for the test. They offered no specific predictions about the possible interaction of the two variables.

Preliminary Calculations

The design is a 2×3 within-subjects factorial, in which each of $n = 5$ pigeons was tested under each of the $(a)(b) = (2)(3) = 6$ treatment combinations. The data matrix, which contains the basic Y scores, is presented in the upper portion of Table 13-3. Before we embark on the actual analysis, however, we need to conduct a number of preliminary calculations, which include computing the means, variances, and standard deviations. These quantities are presented in the bottom rows of the data matrix.

Summary Matrices. As discussed in Sec. 13.1 and illustrated in Table 13-1 (p. 402), we need to combine the Y scores in the data matrix to form three additional matrices, which contain the sums we will use to calculate the various basic ratios entering into the statistical analysis. These matrices are presented in the bottom portion of Table 13-3. You should make sure that you understand how each summary matrix is constructed by verifying a few of the calculations.

Table of Means. Table 13-4 presents the means for the treatment combinations together with the row and column marginal means on which the main effects are based. An inspection of the marginal means (representing the two main effects) suggests the following general findings: The pigeons performed better with the element stimuli ($\overline{Y}_{A_1} = 33.87$) than with the compound stimuli ($\overline{Y}_{A_2} = 29.93$), and they improved steadily as the interval during which the sample stimulus was displayed was increased from short to long (means of 27.00, 31.30, and 37.40, respectively).

If we examine the means within the body of Table 13-4, we can see that there may be an interaction between stimulus type and stimulus duration. We can comprehend the interaction better by plotting the individual means in a graph, which we have done in Fig. 13-2. We can describe the interaction two ways, depending on which independent variable we favor. In terms of stimulus type (the simple effects of factor A), for example, we could say that the interaction is reflected in the fact that although there is similar performance with the two types of stimuli when they are presented at the short duration (28.00 versus

TABLE 13-3 *Numerical Example*

Data Matrix

Subjects	a_1 (Element) (Short) b_1	(Med.) b_2	(Long) b_3	a_2 (Compound) (Short) b_1	(Med.) b_2	(Long) b_3
s_1	28	31	38	26	28	32
s_2	30	35	40	27	30	34
s_3	26	33	39	24	27	31
s_4	29	35	42	30	35	39
s_5	27	31	44	23	28	35
Sum	140	165	203	130	148	171
Mean	28.00	33.00	40.60	26.00	29.60	34.20
Variance	2.50	4.00	5.80	7.50	10.30	9.70
Std. Dev.	1.58	2.00	2.41	2.74	3.21	3.11

AB Matrix

	(Short) b_1	(Med.) b_2	(Long) b_3	Sum
a_1 (Element)	140	165	203	508
a_2 (Compound)	130	148	171	449
Sum	270	313	374	957

AS Matrix

	a_1	a_2	Sum
s_1	97	86	183
s_2	105	91	196
s_3	98	82	180
s_4	106	104	210
s_5	102	86	188
Sum	508	449	957

BS Matrix

	b_1	b_2	b_3	Sum
s_1	54	59	70	183
s_2	57	65	74	196
s_3	50	60	70	180
s_4	59	70	81	210
s_5	50	59	79	188
Sum	270	313	374	957

26.00), greater performance is shown with the element stimuli as opposed to the compound stimuli at both the medium duration (33.00 versus 29.60) and at the long duration (40.60 versus 34.20).

	Stimulus Duration (Factor B)			
Stimulus Type (Factor A)	(Short) b_1	(Med.) b_2	(Long) b_3	Average
a_1 (Element)	28.00	33.00	40.60	33.87
a_2 (Compound)	26.00	29.60	34.20	29.93
Average	27.00	31.30	37.40	

TABLE 13-4 *Table of Means*

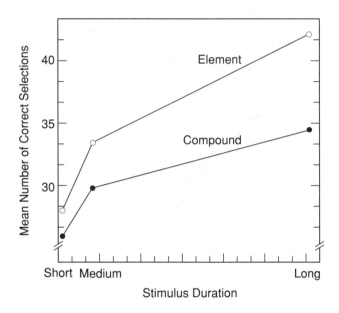

FIGURE 13-2 *Mean Number of Correct Solutions Following Element and Compound Stimuli for Three Stimulus Durations.*

Looking at the possible interaction in terms of stimulus duration (the simple effects of factor B), we could say that the interaction is reflected in a greater increase in performance as stimulus duration lengthens from the short duration to the long duration for the element stimuli than for the compound stimuli. More specifically, performance on the element stimuli increased from 28.00 at the short duration to 40.60 at the long duration (an increase of 12.60 correct responses), whereas performance on the compound stimuli increased from 26.00 to 34.20 (an increase of 8.20 correct responses).

Now that we have some idea of the results of the experiment, we must subject these observations to statistical evaluation.

Calculating the Sums of Squares

Basic Ratios. The basic ratios we will need for the analysis are specified at the bottom of Table 13-2. We will apply these formulas to the values in the different matrices appearing in Table 13-3. Starting with the data matrix, we calculate

$$[Y] = \Sigma Y^2$$
$$= (28)^2 + (30)^2 + \cdots + (39)^2 + (35)^2 = 31,375$$

We will calculate the next set of basic ratios using the sums appearing in the AB matrix. We find

$$[AB] = \frac{\Sigma(AB)^2}{n}$$
$$= \frac{(140)^2 + (130)^2 + \cdots + (203)^2 + (171)^2}{5}$$
$$= \frac{19,600 + 16,900 + \cdots + 41,209 + 29,241}{5} = \frac{156,079}{5}$$
$$= 31,215.80$$

$$[A] = \frac{\Sigma A^2}{(b)(n)}$$
$$= \frac{(508)^2 + (449)^2}{(3)(5)} = \frac{258,064 + 201,601}{15} = \frac{459,665}{15}$$
$$= 30,644.33$$

$$[B] = \frac{\Sigma B^2}{(a)(n)}$$
$$= \frac{(270)^2 + (313)^2 + (374)^2}{(2)(5)}$$
$$= \frac{72,900 + 97,969 + 139,876}{10} = \frac{310,745}{10}$$
$$= 31,074.50$$

$$[T] = \frac{T^2}{(a)(b)(n)}$$

$$= \frac{(957)^2}{(2)(3)(5)} = \frac{915{,}849}{30}$$

$$= 30{,}528.30$$

We now turn to the AS matrix to calculate two more basic ratios:

$$[AS] = \frac{\Sigma(AS)^2}{(b)}$$

$$= \frac{(97)^2 + (105)^2 + \cdots + (104)^2 + (86)^2}{3}$$

$$= \frac{9{,}409 + 11{,}025 + \cdots + 10{,}816 + 7{,}396}{3} = \frac{92{,}291}{3}$$

$$= 30{,}763.67$$

$$[S] = \frac{\Sigma S^2}{(a)(b)}$$

$$= \frac{(183)^2 + (196)^2 + (180)^2 + (210)^2 + (188)^2}{(2)(3)}$$

$$= \frac{33{,}489 + 38{,}416 + 32{,}400 + 44{,}100 + 35{,}344}{6} = \frac{183{,}749}{6}$$

$$= 30{,}624.83$$

Finally, we calculate the one remaining basic ratio from the BS matrix:

$$[BS] = \frac{\Sigma(BS)^2}{(a)}$$

$$= \frac{(54)^2 + (57)^2 + \cdots + (81)^2 + (79)^2}{2}$$

$$= \frac{2{,}916 + 3{,}249 + \cdots + 6{,}561 + 6{,}241}{2} = \frac{62{,}411}{2}$$

$$= 31{,}205.50$$

Sums of Squares. The formulas for the sums of squares we need for the analysis of variance are specified in Table 13-2. As applied to this example, we find

$$SS_A = [A] - [T]$$
$$= 30,644.33 - 30,528.30 = 116.03$$

$$SS_B = [B] - [T]$$
$$= 31,074.50 - 30,528.30 = 546.20$$

$$SS_{A \times B} = [AB] - [A] - [B] + [T]$$
$$= 31,215.80 - 30,644.33 - 31,074.50 + 30,528.30 = 25.27$$

$$SS_S = [S] - [T]$$
$$= 30,624.83 - 30,528.30 = 96.53$$

$$SS_{A \times S} = [AS] - [A] - [S] + [T]$$
$$= 30,763.67 - 30,644.33 - 30,624.83 + 30,528.30 = 22.81$$

$$SS_{B \times S} = [BS] - [B] - [S] + [T]$$
$$= 31,205.50 - 31,074.50 - 30,624.83 + 30,528.30 = 34.47$$

$$SS_{A \times B \times S} = [Y] - [AB] - [AS] - [BS] + [A] + [B] + [S] - [T]$$
$$= 31,375 - 31,215.80 - 30,763.67 - 31,205.50$$
$$+ 30,644.33 + 31,074.50 + 30,624.83 - 30,528.30$$
$$= 5.39$$

$$SS_T = [Y] - [T]$$
$$= 31,375 - 30,528.30 = 846.70$$

These sums of squares are entered in Table 13-5. As an arithmetical check, we should verify that the sum of component sums of squares equals the total sum of squares. That is,

$$SS_T = SS_A + SS_B + SS_{A \times B} + SS_S + SS_{A \times S} + SS_{B \times S} + SS_{A \times B \times S}$$
$$846.70 = 116.03 + 546.20 + 25.27 + 96.53 + 22.81 + 34.47 + 5.39$$
$$= 846.70$$

Source	SS	df	MS	F
A (Stimulus Type)	116.03	1	116.03	20.36*
B (Stimulus Duration)	546.20	2	273.10	63.36*
$A \times B$	25.27	2	12.64	18.87*
S (Subject)	96.53	4	24.13	
$A \times S$	22.81	4	5.70	
$B \times S$	34.47	8	4.31	
$A \times B \times S$	5.39	8	.67	
Total	846.70	29		

TABLE 13-5 *Summary of the Analysis*

* $p < .05$.

Completing the Analysis of Variance

The formulas for the degrees of freedom associated with the different sums of squares are presented in Table 13-2. For this example,

$$df_A = a - 1$$
$$= 2 - 1 = 1$$

$$df_B = b - 1$$
$$= 3 - 1 = 2$$

$$df_{A \times B} = (a - 1)(b - 1)$$
$$= (2 - 1)(3 - 1) = (1)(2) = 2$$

$$df_S = n - 1$$
$$= 5 - 1 = 4$$

$$df_{A \times S} = (a - 1)(n - 1)$$
$$= (2 - 1)(5 - 1) = (1)(4) = 4$$

$$df_{B \times S} = (b - 1)(n - 1)$$
$$= (3 - 1)(5 - 1) = (2)(4) = 8$$

$$df_{A \times B \times S} = (a-1)(b-1)(n-1)$$
$$= (2-1)(3-1)(5-1) = (1)(2)(4) = 8$$
$$df_T = (a)(b)(n) - 1$$
$$= (2)(3)(5) - 1 = 30 - 1 = 29$$

As an arithmetical check,

$$df_T = df_A + df_B + df_{A \times B} + df_S + df_{A \times S} + df_{B \times S} + df_{A \times B \times S}$$
$$29 = 1 + 2 + 2 + 4 + 4 + 8 + 8$$
$$= 29$$

As usual, we calculate the mean square for each of the component sources of variance by dividing each sum of squares by the appropriate number of degrees of freedom. The results of these calculations are presented in Table 13-5. Finally, we are ready to calculate the three F ratios. For the main effect of factor A, we find

$$F_A = \frac{MS_A}{MS_{A \times S}}$$
$$= \frac{116.03}{5.70} = 20.36$$

The critical value of this F, for which $df_{num.} = 1$ and $df_{denom.} = 4$, is 7.71 at the 5 percent level of significance. Since the obtained F of 20.36 exceeds this critical value, we reject the null hypothesis and conclude that overall, the pigeons were more successful with the element stimuli than with the compound stimuli.

Turning next to the main effect of factor B, we calculate

$$F_B = \frac{MS_B}{MS_{B \times S}}$$
$$= \frac{273.10}{4.31} = 63.36$$

The critical value of this F, for which $df_{num.} = 2$ and $df_{denom.} = 8$, is 4.46. Applying the usual decision rule, we conclude that overall, stimulus duration has a statistically significant influence on the performance of the pigeons. Because this is an omnibus test, however, we can say nothing more statistically about the nature of this effect until we conduct more focused main comparisons on the marginal means.

Finally, we have the test of the interaction:

$$F_{A \times B} = \frac{MS_{A \times B}}{MS_{A \times B \times S}}$$

$$= \frac{12.64}{.67} = 18.87$$

The critical value of this F, for which $df_{num.} = 2$ and $df_{denom.} = 8$, is 4.46. Although we can conclude that the interaction is significant, we will need to conduct additional analyses to determine the exact nature of the interaction.

13.4 ANALYTICAL COMPARISONS

As you are by now aware, the completion of the overall analysis of variance of any experiment usually represents only the beginning of the statistical analysis. What follows are the various analyses designed to identify the factors responsible for the significant overall effects. We discussed these analytical comparisons in detail in Chap. 10 for the completely randomized factorial design. We will briefly show how to conduct these same analyses with the two-factor within-subjects design.

A Simplified Approach to Error Terms

A discussion of the selection of appropriate error terms for the detailed analysis of within-subjects designs can be quite complicated and is beyond the scope of this book. We offer instead an approach to these analyses that uses error terms that are simpler conceptually and provide sufficient accuracy for most class projects, independent research projects, and undergraduate honors theses. You should consult more advanced books if your research will become part of the research literature, either as an article in a research journal or deposited in a library as a thesis or a dissertation.[1]

---

[1] See, for example, Keppel (1991, pp. 468–478) for a detailed discussion of these error terms.

TABLE 13-6 *Error Terms for Analytical Comparisons Conducted with the Two-Factor Within-Subjects Design*

Type of Analysis	Source	Error Term
Main Comparisons	$A_{comp.}$	$MS_{A \times S}$
	$B_{comp.}$	$MS_{B \times S}$
Simple Effects	A at b_j	$MS_{A \times B \times S}$
	B at a_i	$MS_{A \times B \times S}$
Simple Comparisons	$A_{comp.}$ at b_j	$MS_{A \times B \times S}$
	$B_{comp.}$ at a_i	$MS_{A \times B \times S}$

The error terms for the different analytical comparisons that we might conduct in a detailed analysis of a two-factor within-subjects design are presented in Table 13-6. The principle behind our approach should be obvious: for main comparisons, we use the error term from the overall analysis that we used to evaluate the relevant main effects (either $MS_{A \times S}$ or $MS_{B \times S}$); and for simple effects and simple comparisons, we use the error term from the overall analysis that we used to evaluate the interaction ($MS_{A \times B \times S}$).

Analysis of Main Comparisons

Main comparisons become relevant when a significant main effect has more than two levels; in this example, only the main effect of stimulus duration (factor B) may serve as a numerical example. Since the analysis is the same for either main effect — except for obvious changes in notation — one example should be sufficient to illustrate the analysis.[2]

Suppose we wanted to compare the short duration with the long duration. Because this is a pairwise comparison, we can simply take the difference between the relevant column marginal means and substitute in Eq. (10-5) to calculate the sum of squares. From Table 13-4, we determine the difference between these two means to be

$$\hat{\psi}_B = 27.00 - 37.40 = -10.40$$

---

[2] We ignore the fact that the $A \times B$ interaction is significant, which usually precludes an analysis of significant main effects, to provide an example of the analysis of main comparisons.

Substituting in Eq. (10-5), we find

$$SS_{B\,comp.} = \frac{(a)(n)(\hat{\psi}_B)^2}{2}$$

$$= \frac{(2)(5)(-10.40)^2}{2} = \frac{(10)(108.16)}{2} = \frac{1,081.60}{2}$$

$$= 540.80$$

Because $df_{B\,comp.} = 1$, $MS_{B\,comp.} = 540.80$. From Table 13-6, we find that the error term is $MS_{B\times S}$ from the overall analysis (4.31). The F becomes

$$F_{B\,comp.} = \frac{MS_{B\,comp.}}{MS_{B\times S}} = \frac{540.80}{4.31} = 125.48$$

The critical value of F, with $df_{num.} = 1$ and $df_{denom.} = 8$, is 5.32. Applying the usual decision rule, we conclude that the overall improvement in performance found between the short and long durations is statistically significant.

Complex single-df comparisons, for which one or both of the means being compared are averages of two or more treatment conditions, require a different formula that defines the difference between two means as a sum of the weighted means, where the weights (c_j) are chosen to reflect the comparison under consideration. As an example, we will compare the performance following the short stimulus duration with an average of the medium and long stimulus durations. If we use the set of coefficients c_j: $+1, -\frac{1}{2}, -\frac{1}{2}$, we find

$$\hat{\psi}_B = (c_1)(\overline{Y}_{B_1}) + (c_2)(\overline{Y}_{B_2}) + (c_3)(\overline{Y}_{B_3})$$

$$= (+1)(27.00) + \left(-\tfrac{1}{2}\right)(31.30) + \left(-\tfrac{1}{2}\right)(37.40)$$

$$= 27.00 - 15.65 - 18.70 = 27.00 - 34.35 = -7.35$$

Substituting in Eq. (10-6), the general formula for single-df comparisons, we obtain

$$SS_{B\,comp.} = \frac{(a)(n)(\hat{\psi}_B)^2}{\Sigma\,c^2}$$

$$= \frac{(2)(5)(-7.35)^2}{(+1)^2 + \left(-\tfrac{1}{2}\right)^2 + \left(-\tfrac{1}{2}\right)^2} = \frac{(10)(54.02)}{1 + .25 + .25}$$

$$= \frac{540.20}{1.50} = 360.13$$

Using the same error term as before,

$$F_{B_{comp.}} = \frac{MS_{B_{comp.}}}{MS_{B \times S}} = \frac{360.13}{4.31} = 83.56$$

Since the critical value of F is the same as in the last example (5.32), this difference is significant, allowing us to conclude that, overall, the pigeons were significantly less successful in selecting the correct stimulus when the duration of the initial stimulus was short than when it was either medium or long.

Analysis of Simple Effects

Most researchers follow the discovery of a significant interaction with analyses of simple effects — analyses involving the effects of one of the independent variables with the levels of the other held constant. While the analyses of the main comparisons were based on the marginal row or column means, the analyses of simple effects focus on the means for the treatment combinations, which are found within the body of the table of means. We will consider two examples of the analysis of simple effects, one for each of the two independent variables.

The simple effects of factor A (type of stimulus) focus on the difference between the element and compound stimuli separately for each of the three duration conditions. We will look at the effect of stimulus type for the medium duration (level b_2). Our approach to this analysis, as we outlined in Chap. 10, consists of isolating the relevant column *sums* in the AB matrix and then using formulas that would be appropriate for a single-factor design. Using the sums in Table 13-3 and substituting in the equivalent of Eq. (10-8), we find

$$
\begin{aligned}
SS_{A \text{ at } b_2} &= \frac{\Sigma(AB_{i2})^2}{n} - \frac{B_2^2}{(a)(n)} \\
&= \frac{(165)^2 + (148)^2}{(5)} - \frac{(313)^2}{(2)(5)} \\
&= \frac{49,129}{5} - \frac{97,969}{10} = 9,825.80 - 9,796.90 = 28.90
\end{aligned}
$$

The degrees of freedom for this analysis are

$$df_{A \text{ at } b_2} = a - 1 = 2 - 1 = 1$$

Thus, $MS_{A \text{ at } b_2} = 28.90$. Using the error term indicated in Table 13-6 ($MS_{A \times B \times S} = .67$), we find

$$F_{A \text{ at } b_2} = \frac{MS_{A \text{ at } b_2}}{MS_{A \times B \times S}} = \frac{28.90}{.67} = 43.13$$

The critical value of F, with $df_{num.} = 1$ and $df_{denom.} = 8$, is 5.32. The simple effect is statistically significant, allowing us to conclude that the performance was significantly better with the element stimulus than with the compound stimulus when the stimuli were presented for the medium duration.

If we were to test the other two simple effects, we would find that the difference for the short duration is not significant while the difference for the long duration is significant. This analysis substantiates our preliminary interpretations of the data in Fig. 13-2, that the interaction is reflected in the fact that the type of stimulus has little or no effect when the stimulus duration is short but that there are relatively large differences in performance in favor of the element stimulus when the duration is medium or long.

The other set of simple effects focuses on the effects of factor B (stimulus duration) separately for the two types of stimuli. We will illustrate the calculations with the simple effects of stimulus duration for the compound stimuli (simple effects of factor B at level a_2). For this analysis, we isolate the data from the second row of the AB matrix of sums and then treat this information as if it had been produced by a single-factor design. Substituting in the equivalent of Eq. (10-12), we find

$$\begin{aligned}
SS_{B \text{ at } a_2} &= \frac{\Sigma(AB_{2j})^2}{n} - \frac{A_2^2}{(b)(n)} \\
&= \frac{(130)^2 + (148)^2 + (171)^2}{5} - \frac{(449)^2}{(3)(5)} \\
&= \frac{68,045}{5} - \frac{201,601}{15} = 13,609.00 - 13,440.07 = 168.93
\end{aligned}$$

The degrees of freedom are

$$df_{B \text{ at } a_2} = b - 1 = 3 - 1 = 2$$

and the mean square becomes

$$MS_{B \text{ at } a_2} = \frac{SS_{B \text{ at } a_2}}{df_{B \text{ at } a_2}} = \frac{168.93}{2} = 84.47$$

According to Table 13-6, the error term for this simple effect is the error term for the $A \times B$ interaction from the overall analysis ($MS_{A \times B \times S} = .67$).

Completing the analysis, we find

$$F_{B \text{ at } a_2} = \frac{MS_{B \text{ at } a_2}}{MS_{A \times B \times S}} = \frac{84.47}{.67} = 126.07$$

The critical value of F, with $df_{num.} = 2$ and $df_{denom.} = 8$, is 4.46. Applying the decision rule, we can conclude that stimulus duration has a significant effect with the compound stimulus. Since this is an omnibus test, we need to conduct additional analyses to document statistically the nature of this significant effect. The other simple effect, the effects of stimulus duration for the element stimulus (B at level a_1), would be calculated the same way.

Analysis of Simple Comparisons

When a significant simple effect is based on more than two treatment conditions, we usually continue the analysis with a few more analytically focused single-df comparisons, called *simple comparisons*. The simple effects of factor A (stimulus type) can be analyzed no further, of course, because this independent variable consists of only two levels, element and compound. The simple effects of factor B (stimulus duration), which consists of three levels (short, medium, and long), can be further analyzed into a number of more focused comparisons. For example, all we know from the analysis we conducted in the previous section is that stimulus duration produces a significant effect with the compound stimulus. Although it is obvious from Fig. 13-2 that there is a progressive increase in performance as stimulus duration is lengthened, we need to confirm this observation statistically.

A simple way to obtain this information would be to conduct two simple comparisons, one comparing the short and medium durations and the other comparing the medium and long durations. We would expect both comparisons to reveal significant differences in favor of the longer duration.[3] We will illustrate the calculations with an analysis of the difference between the medium and long durations. We can find the relevant means in Table 13-4 (29.60 for the medium duration and 34.20 for the long duration); the difference is $\hat{\psi}_{B \text{ at } a_2} = 29.60 - 34.20 = -4.60$. We can now substitute this information in

---

[3] A more satisfying approach to this problem is a specialized procedure designed for the analysis of quantitative independent variables called *analysis of trend*. We discuss this analysis briefly in Appendix D.

Eq. (10-14), the formula for a pairwise simple comparison, as follows:

$$SS_{B \, comp. \, at \, a_2} = \frac{(n)(\hat{\psi}_{B \, at \, a_2})^2}{2}$$

$$= \frac{(5)(-4.60)^2}{2} = \frac{(5)(21.16)}{2} = \frac{105.80}{2} = 52.90$$

Because the number of degrees of freedom for a simple comparison is 1, $MS_{B \, comp. \, at \, a_2} = 52.90$. As indicated in Table 13-6, the error term for this analysis is $MS_{A \times B \times S} = .67$. The F becomes

$$F_{B \, comp. \, at \, a_2} = \frac{MS_{B \, comp. \, at \, a_2}}{MS_{A \times B \times S}} = \frac{52.90}{.67} = 78.96$$

The critical value of F, for $df_{num.} = 1$ and $df_{denom.} = 8$, is 5.32. We can conclude that there is a significant increase in performance when the duration during which the compound stimulus is presented is increased from medium to long. (We would come to the same conclusion if we tested the difference between the short and medium durations.)

13.5 SUMMARY

The two-factor within-subjects design represents a "pure," or "complete," within-subjects design in which subjects receive all the $(a)(b)$ treatment combinations in some counterbalanced or random order of presentation. The advantage of this design over the mixed factorial design is that it extends the increased sensitivity (or power) associated with within-subjects factors to *all* analyses, rather than to a subset. The major disadvantage is the increased possibility that carry-over effects may operate to distort or confound the results of the experiment.

The analysis of the two-factor within-subjects design combines the analyses from earlier designs we considered, namely, the completely randomized factorial design (Chap. 9) and the single-factor within-subjects design (Chap. 11). Each of the factorial treatment effects is evaluated with a different error term. The two main effects, which for statistical purposes are equivalent to two single-factor within-subjects designs, are each tested by an error term based on an interaction of the relevant independent variable and subjects — exactly the same sort of error term we use for analyzing the results of an actual single-factor within-subjects design.

The error term for the $A \times B$ interaction is also an interaction, but a more complicated one based on the interaction of the $A \times B$ interaction itself with subjects — the $A \times B \times S$ interaction. We defined this interaction as a *residual* sum of squares, that is, the variation remaining when we subtract all the other component sums of squares from the total sum of squares.

We concluded the chapter with a discussion of the additional analyses we usually conduct following the completion of the overall analysis. All the analyses available for the completely randomized factorial design may be conducted with the data from a two-factor within-subjects design. The only complication is the need to select the correct error term for any given analysis. We presented a simplified method for selecting error terms in which we use the $MS_{A \times S}$ as the error term for any main comparisons involving factor A, the $MS_{B \times S}$ as the error term for any main comparisons involving factor B, and the $MS_{A \times B \times S}$ as the error term for all simple effects and simple comparisons.

13.6 EXERCISES [4]

*1. The data for a hypothetical experiment are presented in the data matrix that follows. The design is a 2×4 factorial with repeated measures on both factors. Factor A consists of two lists of 30 English words, one containing low-frequency words (level a_1) and the other containing high-frequency words (level a_2). Factor B consists of four learning trials in which subjects first studied the words and then recalled them during a two-minute test period. The words were presented in a different random order on each trial. There are $n = 4$ subjects, of whom half received the list of low-frequency words first, followed by the list of high-frequency words, and the other half received the word lists in the reverse order. The Y scores are the words recalled on each test trial. Conduct an analysis of variance on these data.

	a_1				a_2			
	b_1	b_2	b_3	b_4	b_1	b_2	b_3	b_4
s_1	-8	9	8	12	15	16	17	21
s_2	11	13	14	17	20	22	25	28
s_3	12	18	16	16	20	25	24	25
s_4	5	8	11	11	15	17	19	21

---

[4] Answers to the starred problems are given in Appendix B.

*2. The data in exercise 1 reveal that both main effects are significant, but that the $A \times B$ interaction is not. Consequently, we turn our attention to the analysis of main comparisons. Conduct the following main comparisons involving factor B (learning trials):

    a. A pairwise comparison between trial 1 (b_1) and trial 4 (b_4)

    b. A complex comparison between trial 1 (b_1) and trials 2 through 4 combined (b_2 through b_4)

*3. The numerical example in this chapter produced a significant $A \times B$ interaction, which would usually lead a researcher to an analysis of simple effects.

    a. Test the significance of the simple effect of stimulus duration (factor B) for the element stimuli (level a_1).

    b. Because the simple effect in part (a) is significant, our interest is drawn to additional analyses involving simple comparisons. Test the following:

        (l) A pairwise comparison between short and medium durations

        (2) A complex comparison between the short duration and a combination of the medium and long durations

4. The results of a 3×2 factorial design are presented in the data matrix that follows. A total of $n = 5$ subjects received all of the $(a)(b) = (3)(2) = 6$ treatment combinations. The order of the combinations was randomized for each subject. Analyze the data obtained from this experiment.

	b_1			b_2		
	a_1	a_2	a_3	a_1	a_2	a_3
s_1	17	16	16	17	19	15
s_2	19	6	9	22	28	23
s_3	11	4	9	14	19	16
s_4	10	4	22	10	28	11
s_5	13	10	17	12	21	13

5. The $A \times B$ interaction is significant in exercise 4, which means that we will direct our attention to an analysis of simple effects.

    a. Describe the nature of this interaction in terms of the simple effects of factor A.

    b. Analyze the simple effects of factor A at both levels of the other independent variable.

c. Although not fully justified by the analysis in part (b), test the significance of the comparison between a_2 and the other two levels combined (a_1 and a_3) at both levels of factor B.

d. Describe the nature of the $A \times B$ interaction in terms of the simple effects of the other independent variable, factor B.

e. Analyze the simple effects of factor B at all three levels of the other independent variable.

PART · FIVE

ADDITIONAL STATISTICAL PROCEDURES

In this final part of the book, we consider a number of statistical procedures that fit better here than in earlier sections. In Chap. 14, we present statistical techniques appropriate for use with data that consist of *response categories* rather than scores obtained from continuous measures. An example of a category measure is the division of subjects into two groups: those who learned a given task and those who did not. Each subject in any given treatment condition would then be classified simply as a "learner" or a "nonlearner." The summary data would consist of the frequency or proportion of subjects appearing in the two categories for the different treatment conditions. In all the analyses we discussed in previous chapters, we assumed that a subject's performance was indexed by a number that referred to a location on some continuous scale. Fortunately, we are able to conduct similar sorts of analyses when the dependent variable is in the form of response categories as well.

One important purpose of science is establishing relationships between variables. Throughout this book, we have concerned ourselves with the analysis of *experimental data*, that is, with relationships between independent (or manipulated) variables and behavior. These analyses provide us with evidence we can use in drawing causal inferences about the effect of one variable on another. As mentioned in Chap. 1, another major type of research consists of the discovery of relationships between different aspects of behavior. Using these *correlational methods*, researchers do not vary the antecedent conditions as they do in experimental research; rather, they measure the joint occurrence of different aspects of behavior as revealed in the natural environment or under carefully controlled conditions.

As a consequence of the methodology, the correlational approach usually does not permit investigators to clearly infer causality. On the other hand, correlational relationships serve an important and useful function in the development of psychology and in the real world, where future behavior is predicted on the basis of past performance. In addition, knowing that a relationship between two variables exists is important in itself. Again, as we pointed out Chap. 1, this information can open up new avenues of experimental research designed to determine the causal bases underlying observed relationships. We discuss two basic correlational methods — *correlation* and *regression* — in Chap. 15.

The final chapter (Chap. 16) presents a number of topics that may serve as a supplement to your study of experimentation and research design. One of these topics consists of a description of several types of *nonexperimental research methods* that are widely used in the social and behavioral sciences. Whereas these methods do not permit researchers to infer causation with the certainty that is possible in a properly designed experiment, they do contribute to our understanding of psychology by providing information that usually cannot be obtained by means of an experiment. A second topic we consider concerns the use of the computer in statistical analysis. We present an example of a large and comprehensive statistical software program that is available for use on mainframe computers at most colleges and universities (*SPSS*). This example is not intended to teach you how to use the program, but to show you how the program works and what you have to do to coax it into conducting your analyses. We conclude the chapter with a brief consideration of certain areas of study you might consider exploring to widen your understanding of research and statistical analysis.

Chapter · 14

THE ANALYSIS OF CATEGORICAL DATA

Most experiments in psychology are designed to measure behavior on a more or less continuous scale of measurement. Behavior varies in degree or in amount, and we try to "capture" this variation through the assignment of numbers that reasonably reflect the extent of the behavior observed. At times, however, the behavior under study cannot be measured that precisely. For instance, it may be possible to categorize the behavior in terms of only a small number of categories, each representing either relatively gross performance on the experimental task — for instance, success-failure, completed-incompleted, or type

431

of error — or an attitude toward an issue or a policy, such as agree-disagree, like-dislike, or approve-disapprove. Field research, survey research, and consumer studies often consist of such measurements. Occasionally, however, this sort of response measure is also found in experimental research.

We will consider the analysis of two types of experimental designs in this chapter, the completely randomized single-factor design in Sec. 14.1 and the completely randomized factorial design in an appendix at the end of the chapter (Sec. 14.6). We will introduce the statistical procedures appropriate for the analysis of categorical data within the context of a numerical example.

14.1 ANALYZING COMPLETELY RANDOMIZED SINGLE-FACTOR DESIGNS

In this section, we consider how we can analyze the results of an experiment in which the dependent variable consists of a limited number of categories. The most common examples are **dichotomous classifications** (where there are two categories) — for example, yes–no, pass–fail, solve–not solve — although more than two response categories are certainly possible.

An Experiment

As an example, consider a hypothetical problem-solving experiment in which subjects are required to use a common object (a screwdriver) in an uncommon way (as the weight for a pendulum). Subjects are given a fixed amount of time to solve the problem. Ninety subjects are assigned randomly and in equal numbers to $a = 3$ instructional conditions. One group (a_1) is given no special instructions other than those required to describe the problem; a second group (a_2) is asked to list 10 common uses for a screwdriver; and the third group (a_3) is asked to list 10 uncommon uses for a screwdriver.

It is hypothesized that subjects asked to think of a screwdriver in its usual function will have difficulty using it in an unusual way to solve the problem. On the other hand, subjects asked to think of the screwdriver in an unusual way will be primed for its unusual use in the experimental task. The uninstructed group serves as a baseline or control for performance in the absence of special instructions.

Response Category	No Instruction (a_1)	Common Uses (a_2)	Uncommon Uses (a_3)	Total
TABLE 14-1 *Solvers and Nonsolvers in a Problem-Solving Task*				
Solvers	10	20	24	54
Nonsolvers	20	10	6	36
Total	30	30	30	90

Subjects are given 10 minutes to solve the problem. Since not all the subjects are able to give the correct solution within the 10-minute period, it is possible to divide the subjects in each group into two response categories: those who solve the problem (solvers) and those who do not (nonsolvers).[1] The results of the experiment are presented in Table 14-1, a two-dimensional data matrix called a **contingency table**, with the treatment conditions (factor A) defining one dimension in the table and the response categories (solvers and nonsolvers) defining the other.

The performance of each subject is included within the body of the matrix. All we know is whether a subject solves the problem within the time limit; the number of subjects solving the problem is entered in the first row and the number of subjects not solving the problem is entered in the second row. Column and row totals are also obtained. The column totals provide us with a check to see that we have accounted for all the $n = 30$ subjects in each of the treatment conditions, and the row totals indicate the overall results of the experiment.

Expected Frequencies

The statistical analysis is based on a calculation that compares the **observed frequency** with which a given type of response is given or observed with the **expected frequency** of that response, which is derived from a null hypothesis that asserts that the representation of solvers and nonsolvers will not differ from condition to condition. You should not confuse the expected frequencies entering into the statistical analysis, which are a reflection of the null hypothesis, with your own *expectations* or *research hypotheses* about the outcome of the

---

[1] If all subjects solved the problem, it might be possible to use a time measure (solution time) as the response measure and the analysis of variance to assess the differences observed in the experiment.

experiment, which will form the basis for planned comparisons in the detailed analysis of your study. We will consider planned comparisons in Sec. 14.2.

The first step in the statistical analysis, then, is to estimate the distribution of solvers and nonsolvers if the null hypothesis is in fact true. We can obtain this information by using the row totals to calculate two proportions, one reflecting the proportion of solvers in the *total* sample — disregarding group membership — and the other reflecting the proportion of nonsolvers, also disregarding group membership. With the data in Table 14-1, we find the overall proportion of solvers to be

$$\frac{54}{90} = .60$$

and the overall proportion of nonsolvers to be

$$\frac{36}{90} = .40$$

If the independent variable had no effect on problem-solving performance, we would expect to find approximately 60 percent solvers and 40 percent nonsolvers in *each* of the three treatment conditions. We will now use these two proportions to calculate the necessary expected frequencies (f_E). We obtain these frequencies by multiplying the two overall proportions by the number of subjects in each treatment condition. That is,

$$f_E = (\text{overall proportion}) \times (\text{number of subjects}) \qquad (14\text{-}1)$$

To minimize rounding errors, it is usually better to use the alternative formula,

$$f_E = \frac{(\text{row total})(\text{column total})}{\text{grand total}} \qquad (14\text{-}2)$$

where "row total" refers to the total number of subjects falling into a particular response category (solvers and nonsolvers in our example), "column total" refers to the number of subjects in a given treatment condition ($n = 30$ subjects in each condition), and "grand total" refers to the total number of subjects in the experiment.

To illustrate the calculations, we will compute the expected frequencies for the subjects receiving no special instructions (a_1). From Eq. (14-2), the

TABLE 14-2 *Expected Frequencies Based on the Marginal Totals in Table* 14-1

Response Category	No Instruction (a_1)	Common Uses (a_2)	Uncommon Uses (a_3)	Total
Solvers	18	18	18	54
Nonsolvers	12	12	12	36
Total	30	30	30	90

expected number of solvers is

$$f_{E_{solvers}} = \frac{(54)(30)}{90} = \frac{1,620}{90} = 18$$

and the expected number of nonsolvers is

$$f_{E_{nonsolvers}} = \frac{(36)(30)}{90} = \frac{1,080}{90} = 12$$

The corresponding expected frequencies for the other two treatment conditions are calculated the same way.[2] The expected frequencies for all six cells of the contingency table are presented in Table 14-2. As a useful arithmetical check, we have calculated the totals for the columns and rows; these must equal the corresponding totals obtained with the observed frequencies presented in Table 14-1.

The Chi Square Test Statistic

In comparison with the analysis of variance, the procedures for dealing with categorical data are relatively simple and uncomplicated. We will begin with the computational formula for the general statistic that we will use to compare differences in observed frequencies.

Computational Formula. The null hypothesis is usually evaluated by means of the **chi square test statistic** (*chi* is pronounced "kye," rhyming with "eye."). This statistic, symbolized χ^2, is based on the differences between observed

---

[2] We need perform these calculations only once, because equal numbers of subjects were assigned to each of the treatment conditions ($n = 30$), producing the same pair of expected frequencies for each group. Of course, if the number of subjects were different for each condition, we would have to calculate expected frequencies separately for each condition.

and expected frequencies for each response category.[3] In fact, these two sets of frequencies are the *only* quantities in the computational formula; they are designated f_O (the *observed* frequency for a given response category) and f_E (the *expected* frequency for the same response category). We start by calculating the difference between these two frequencies — that is, $f_O - f_E$ — for each response category. The differences are then squared and the results divided by the appropriate expected frequency (f_E). The chi square statistic simply consists of the sum of these quantities. In symbols,

$$\chi^2 = \sum \frac{(f_O - f_E)^2}{f_E} \tag{14-3}$$

Calculating the Chi Square Statistic.   The next step in the analysis is to calculate the chi square test statistic. Substituting the obtained frequencies (Table 14-1) and the expected frequencies (Table 14-2) in Eq. (14-3), we find

$$
\begin{aligned}
\chi^2 &= \sum \frac{(f_O - f_E)^2}{f_E} \\
&= \frac{(10 - 18)^2}{18} + \frac{(20 - 12)^2}{12} + \frac{(20 - 18)^2}{18} + \frac{(10 - 12)^2}{12} \\
&\quad + \frac{(24 - 18)^2}{18} + \frac{(6 - 12)^2}{12} \\
&= \frac{(-8)^2}{18} + \frac{(8)^2}{12} + \frac{(2)^2}{18} + \frac{(-2)^2}{12} + \frac{(6)^2}{18} + \frac{(-6)^2}{12} \\
&= \frac{64}{18} + \frac{64}{12} + \frac{4}{18} + \frac{4}{12} + \frac{36}{18} + \frac{36}{12} \\
&= 3.56 + 5.33 + .22 + .33 + 2.00 + 3.00 \\
&= 14.44
\end{aligned}
$$

Evaluating the Null Hypothesis

Just as with the analysis of variance, a set of statistical hypotheses is formed in the analysis of categorical data. The null hypothesis (H_0) is evaluated with the

---

[3] Statisticians usually use the Latin letter X to designate the value of the chi square test statistic (X^2), which is calculated from data, and reserve the Greek letter chi to designate the theoretical chi square distribution (χ^2), to which the chi square test statistic refers in hypothesis testing. We have chosen not to follow this convention, to avoid confusion of X with other uses of this letter in this book.

chi square statistic, and the alternative hypothesis (H_1) is accepted if the null hypothesis is rejected. The statistical hypotheses can be stated in terms of the frequencies with which the different classes of responses occur in the different treatment populations. We refer to these sets of frequencies as **response distributions**. The statistical hypotheses can be stated as follows:

H_0: response distributions for all treatment populations are equal
H_1: not all of these response distributions are equal

Where the response distribution consists of only *two* categories, the statistical hypotheses may also be stated in terms of proportions of solvers (or nonsolvers) in the treatment populations. In the present example,

H_0: proportions of solvers in the treatment populations are equal
H_1: not all of these proportions are equal

Under the assumption that the null hypothesis is true, we use the *sampling distribution of chi square* to select a critical value of chi square (χ_α^2) to define the regions of rejection and nonrejection at a selected significance level (α). Like the F statistic, the specific distribution of chi square depends on the degrees of freedom (df). The degrees of freedom for a chi square calculated from a contingency table are given by

$$df = (columns - 1)(rows - 1) \tag{14-4}$$

where "columns" refer to the number of treatment conditions and "rows" to the number of response categories. For this example,

$$df = (3 - 1)(2 - 1) = (2)(1) = 2$$

Critical values of chi square for $\alpha = .05$ and $.01$ are listed in Table A-7 of Appendix A. From this table, we find that the critical value of chi square is 5.99, for $df = 2$, at the 5 percent level of significance. With this information, we form the following decision rule:

If the obtained value of $\chi^2 \geq 5.99$, reject the null hypothesis; otherwise, retain the null hypothesis.

The obtained χ^2 is 14.44. Consequently, we reject the null hypothesis and conclude that the number of subjects solving the problem depends on the instructions they are given at the start of the experiment.

Assumptions Underlying the Chi Square Test

The chi square statistical test is not without its own assumptions and restrictions. We summarize these briefly in the following sections.

Independence. It is assumed that each observation is independent of all other observations in the study. Generally, the researcher meets this assumption by obtaining *one* response from each subject. A common mistake in the use of chi square consists of obtaining two or more responses from subjects and using these frequencies in the analysis. Such a procedure violates the independence assumption. One check on this assumption is to verify that the total number of observations equals the total number of subjects participating in the study. If the observations exceed the subjects, either an arithmetical mistake has been made or the independence assumption has been violated — that is, subjects have been counted more than once.

Expected Frequencies. From a statistical point of view, the information provided in the chi square table (Table A-7) is an approximation for all applications discussed in this chapter. The accuracy is best when the total number of observations is large, for example, more than a 100. The accuracy of the table decreases systematically as the overall sample size decreases in number.

Over the years, a number of so-called rules of thumb have been developed to cope with this problem. They are usually stated in terms of the size of the *expected* frequencies appearing in the data analysis. It appears that the problem is not very serious if 2 or more degrees of freedom are associated with the chi square test statistic. The problem is more serious with 1 degree of freedom, however, and researchers must pay close attention to the size of the expected frequencies and to the "remedial" steps recommended for restoring the accuracy of the statistical test, such as applying *Fisher's exact test* or *Yates' correction for continuity.*[4]

---

[4] Fisher's exact test is generally recommended if one or more of the expected frequencies are smaller than 5 (see Siegel & Castellan, 1988, pp. 103–111 or Hays, 1988, pp. 781–783 for a discussion and illustration of this test). Yates' correction is frequently recommended if any expected frequency falls between 5 and 10, although Wickens (1989, p. 43) points out that the correction may *over* correct and create a loss of power as a consequence.

14.2 CONDUCTING ANALYTICAL COMPARISONS

As was true with the analysis of variance, rejection of the overall null hypothesis does not provide an unambiguous assessment of the results. In the present example, we would like to know a number of things — for example, whether the special instructions had an effect and whether the two types of instructions (common uses versus uncommon uses) produced different results. The first question may be asked several ways, namely, by comparing the control group separately with the two groups receiving special instructions as pairwise comparisons, or by comparing the control with the two instruction conditions combined as a complex comparison. As suggested in Chap. 6, we would hope that such questions would be formed during the planning stage of the experiment and thus qualify as *planned comparisons*. As you will recall, planned comparisons are conducted directly, without reference to the significance or nonsignificance of the overall statistical test.

We evaluate analytical comparisons by taking the data from the original contingency table and entering this information into smaller **comparison contingency tables** that focus on these comparisons directly. We will distinguish between two types of comparisons, one that focuses on the difference between two treatment conditions (a *pairwise comparison*) and another that focuses on the difference between two or more combined conditions and another treatment condition or combination of treatment conditions (a *complex comparison*). We will consider a pairwise comparison first.[5]

Pairwise Comparisons

As an illustration of a pairwise comparison, we will determine whether the proportion of solvers is different for the group asked to give common uses for a screwdriver (a_2) from that for the group asked to give uncommon uses (a_3). We form a special comparison contingency table for this comparison by extracting the relevant information for these two conditions directly from the original data matrix (Table 14-1, p. 433) and treating this new matrix as if it consisted of the results of an experiment consisting of only these two

---

[5] Several ways have been proposed for conducting analytical comparisons extracted from a larger design. The one we present is simpler than the one we discussed in the first edition of this book and is more understandable than the other alternatives. Apparently the different methods produce the same general statistical conclusions when they are applied to the same data set (see Wickens, 1989, p. 272), which is why we have chosen to use the simpler procedure.

TABLE 14-3 *Observed and Expected Frequencies for a Pairwise Comparison of the Two Instruction Conditions*

Observed Frequencies (f_O)

Response Category	Common Uses (a_2)	Uncommon Uses (a_3)	Total
Solvers	20	24	44
Nonsolvers	10	6	16
Total	30	30	60

Expected Frequencies (f_E)

Response Category	Common Uses (a_2)	Uncommon Uses (a_3)	Total
Solvers	22	22	44
Nonsolvers	8	8	16
Total	30	30	60

treatment conditions. The contingency table for this comparison is presented in the upper portion of Table 14-3. As you can see, we have created a 2×2 matrix consisting of the two types of instructions (common and uncommon) and the two categories of responses (solvers and nonsolvers).

The expected frequencies are based on the information appearing in the two margins of the comparison contingency table. We calculate each expected frequency (f_E) by applying Eq. (14-2) to each combination of row and column totals taken from the comparison contingency table. For example, the expected number of solvers for subjects asked to list common uses (a_2) is

$$f_E = \frac{(\text{row total})(\text{column total})}{\text{grand total}}$$

$$= \frac{(44)(30)}{60} = \frac{1,320}{60} = 22$$

and the expected number of nonsolvers in this condition is

$$f_E = \frac{(16)(30)}{60} = \frac{480}{60} = 8$$

The other two expected frequencies, for the subjects asked to list uncommon uses (a_3), are obtained in an identical fashion. All four of the expected frequencies derived from the comparison contingency table are listed in the bottom portion of Table 14-3.

We now use information from both parts of Table 14-3 to calculate the chi square test statistic ($\chi^2_{comp.}$). Substituting in Eq. (14-3), we find

$$\chi^2_{comp.} = \sum \frac{(f_O - f_E)^2}{f_E}$$

$$= \frac{(20 - 22)^2}{22} + \frac{(10 - 8)^2}{8} + \frac{(24 - 22)^2}{22} + \frac{(6 - 8)^2}{8}$$

$$= .18 + .50 + .18 + .50$$

$$= 1.36$$

The degrees of freedom for this comparison are obtained from Eq. (14-4):

$$df_{comp.} = (columns - 1)(rows - 1)$$

$$= (2 - 1)(2 - 1) = 1$$

The table of chi square in the appendix (Table A-7) indicates that a value of 3.84 is required for the 5 percent level of significance. The decision rule becomes

If the obtained value of $\chi^2_{comp.} \geq 3.84$, reject the null hypothesis; otherwise, retain the null hypothesis.

Since the obtained value of 1.36 does not exceed the critical value of chi square (3.84), we retain the null hypothesis and conclude that the evidence is not sufficiently strong to indicate that the different instructions produced differential effects in solving problems.

Given this outcome, our analysis plan would probably call for a complex comparison in which we combine the two instruction conditions — because they appear to have produced equivalent results — and compare the results of this combination with those of the group receiving no specific instructions. On the other hand, if the comparison had been significant, our plan would probably call for separate pairwise comparisons between each instruction group and the group receiving no special instructions.

Complex Comparisons

Complex comparisons are easily extended to the analysis of categorical data. Given the outcome of the comparison between the two special instructions, we are statistically justified in combining these two conditions and comparing the combined results with the control condition. We begin the analysis by constructing a comparison contingency table reflecting this comparison, which is presented in the top part of Table 14-4. If you refer back to the complete experiment (Table 14-1), you can see that we have extracted the data for the control condition (a_1) and placed this information in the first column of the comparison contingency table. You will also see that we have combined the frequencies for the two instruction groups simply by adding the appropriate frequencies for levels a_2 and a_3 and placing the sums in the second column of the comparison contingency table. For the first response category (solvers), for example, we combined the relevant frequencies of 20 and 24 and placed their sum (44) in Table 14-4; for the second response category (nonsolvers), we combined 10 and 6 and placed the sum (16) in the table.

From this point on, we follow the same computational steps we described and illustrated for the pairwise comparison in the preceding section. We start

---

TABLE 14-4 *Observed and Expected Frequencies for a Complex Comparison*

Observed Frequencies (f_O)

Response Category	Control (a_1)	Comb. Instruct.	Total
Solvers	10	44	54
Nonsolvers	20	16	36
Total	30	60	90

Expected Frequencies (f_E)

Response Category	Control (a_1)	Comb. Instruct.	Total
Solvers	18	36	54
Nonsolvers	12	24	36
Total	30	60	90

by calculating the expected frequency for each of the cells in the comparison contingency table by substituting the relevant information in Eq. (14-2). Illustrating the calculations for the solvers in the control condition, we find

$$f_E = \frac{(54)(30)}{90} = \frac{1,620}{90} = 18$$

and for the nonsolvers in the combined instruction condition, we find

$$f_E = \frac{(36)(60)}{90} = \frac{2,160}{90} = 24$$

The other two expected frequencies are obtained in an identical fashion. All of the expected frequencies derived from the comparison contingency table are presented in the bottom part of Table 14-4.

We now use the information in these two tables to calculate the chi square test statistic for this comparison. Substituting in Eq. (14-1), we obtain

$$\chi^2_{comp.} = \sum \frac{(f_O - f_E)^2}{f_E}$$

$$= \frac{(10-18)^2}{18} + \frac{(20-12)^2}{12} + \frac{(44-36)^2}{36} + \frac{(16-24)^2}{24}$$

$$= 3.56 + 5.33 + 1.78 + 2.67$$

$$= 13.34$$

This comparison also has $df_{comp.} = 1$ and, thus, the same critical value of χ^2 as in the last comparison ($\chi^2_\alpha = 3.84$). Applying the same decision rule to this comparison, we reject the null hypothesis and conclude that the instructed subjects in general were more successful with the problem-solving task (the proportion of solvers was $44/60 = .73$) than were the control subjects (the proportion of solvers was $10/30 = .33$).

Some Comments

It is instructive to consider the nature of the conclusions permitted by these comparisons. Taken together, the two comparisons suggest that although the special instructions have a facilitating effect on the solution of this particular problem (the complex comparison), the uniqueness of the uses listed by the subjects given these instructions seems not to be important (the pairwise comparison). Any investigator posing a theory predicting that the different instructions would produce a differential effect would now have to account for this unexpected finding. Perhaps the theory is correct but the manipulation in this experiment was insufficient. The data do contain a nonsignificant "hint" that subjects were more successful in solving the problem after they listed 10 unusual uses ($24/30 = .80$) than after they listed 10 common ones ($20/30 = .67$). Maybe if subjects were asked to list *more* than 10 uses, the difference between the two conditions would widen. On the other hand, perhaps subjects listing common uses of a screwdriver ran out of common ones quickly and shifted to more unusual ones to complete their lists of 10. If this latter possibility were true, then a new experiment requiring only *five* uses might produce results more favorable to the theory.[6]

Whatever the conclusion, it is this sort of speculation that sharpens theory, improves experimental designs, and leads to new and potentially more revealing experiments. But note that these conclusions and speculations do *not* stem from the overall statistical analysis — from which we can conclude only that the three treatment conditions do not all have the same effect — but stem from the *analytical comparisons* that identify specific manipulations responsible for the significant overall chi square. As in Chap. 6, we can see the value of analytical comparisons in both the design and the analysis of experiments. Whether the behavior under study is measured on a continuous scale or in terms of a number of discrete response categories is not critical. All that is required is that an experiment be designed in such a way that these pointed and analytical questions can be examined by the procedures outlined in this section.

14.3 EFFECT SIZE AND POWER

Our discussion of the analysis of experiments with categorical response measures has focused on hypothesis testing — that is, using the chi square statistic to evaluate the significance of the overall differences between treatment conditions and of analytical comparisons that focus on more specific aspects of the experiment. In this section, we will consider additional information that can help us to interpret the results of experiments and to design new experiments based on these findings.

---

[6] One could check on this possibility by examining the last several uses actually produced by the subjects asked to list common uses, to see if their responses became similar to those given by the subjects asked to list uncommon uses.

Measuring Effect Size

We use the chi square test to tell us whether the obtained cell frequencies are statistically different from the expected frequencies. However, the value of the χ^2 we obtain from the calculations does not tell us the size or the strength of the treatment effects detected by the statistical test. You may recall from Chap. 7 that we made this same point with regard to the analysis of variance and the F statistic. The problem is that the value of either test statistic — χ^2 or F — does not unambiguously reflect the size of the treatment effects, for the simple reason that it is also influenced by sample size: the larger the sample size, the larger the value of the test statistic. Thus, a large χ^2 (or F) may represent a truly large effect or it may represent a small effect obtained with a particularly large sample size.

To illustrate the dependence of χ^2 on sample size, suppose we repeated the problem-solving experiment with a much smaller sample size — that is, $n = 15$ subjects — and found exactly the same results we obtained with the original sample size of $n = 30$. The results of this scaled-down experiment, which we have created from the original experiment (see Table 14-1) simply by dividing each cell frequency by 2, are presented in Table 14-5. Without showing the details, we find that the overall χ^2 for the data in Table 14-5 is 7.23, exactly *half* the size (except for rounding) of the χ^2 we calculated for the original experiment (14.44).

What we have demonstrated is that the size of the chi square test statistic is directly proportional to the number of subjects in the experiment, just as the F statistic is affected by sample size in the analysis of variance (see Sec. 7.2, pp. 178–179). As a consequence, a statistically significant χ^2 does not tell us whether the effect is large or small — only that we may reject the null hypothesis. What we need is a measure of treatment magnitude that is *uninfluenced* by sample size so that we can compare the results of experiments with different sample sizes. In addition, we need the measure to help us in making decisions concerning the number of subjects we must test to produce a certain result in a study we are planning (the issue of power) or, as a practical matter in applied

TABLE 14-5 *Observed Frequencies Associated with Reduced Sample Size*

Response Category	No Instruction (a_1)	Common Uses (a_2)	Uncommon Uses (a_3)	Total
Solvers	5	10	12	27
Nonsolvers	10	5	3	18
Total	15	15	15	45

research, in *applying* the results of an experiment to individuals and situations outside of the laboratory.

A Measure of Effect Size.   To simplify our discussion, we will restrict our attention to experimental situations in which the response measure consists of two categories.[7] The index of strength is called the **phi coefficient**, ϕ (phi) and is calculated as follows:

$$\phi = \sqrt{\frac{\chi^2}{N}} \tag{14-5}$$

where χ^2 is the chi square test statistic obtained from the contingency table and N is the *total* number of subjects (not n, the number of subjects in the individual treatment conditions).[8] This measure produces values that range from 0 to 1, indicating the absence of treatment effects to maximum possible effect size, respectively.

As an example, we will use the frequency data from the problem-solving experiment (see Table 14-1, p. 433) in which we obtained a $\chi^2 = 14.44$. The experiment consisted of three treatment conditions, with $n = 30$ subjects assigned to each group. The total number of subjects, then, is $N = (3)(30) = 90$. Substituting in Eq. (14-5), we find

$$\phi = \sqrt{\frac{14.44}{90}} = \sqrt{.1604} = .40$$

We can illustrate that ϕ is not influenced by sample size by estimating the effect size for the data in Table 14-5, which are identical to those in Table 14-1 except that the frequencies are based on a smaller sample size ($n = 15$ rather than $n = 30$). With these data, we found $\chi^2 = 7.23$. Substituting in Eq. (14-5), we obtain

$$\phi = \sqrt{\frac{7.23}{45}} = \sqrt{.1607} = .40$$

which is identical to the value we obtained with the larger sample size.

---

[7] We restrict our consideration of effect size to a case likely to occur in most experimental situations — several treatment conditions and a dichotomous response measure. For cases with more categories or in which both rows and columns of the contingency table both exceed 2, we recommend Cohen (1988, pp. 216–227) or Wickens (1989, Chap. 9).

[8] When the number of treatment conditions is greater than 2, the phi coefficient is technically called *Cramér's ϕ'*. Cramér's ϕ' is used as a measure of effect size with contingency tables containing at least three rows and three columns.

Interpreting Effect Size. To help interpret the meaning of a given value of ϕ, Cohen (1988, pp. 224–226) has assigned the labels "small," "medium," and "large" to specific values of ϕ, in the same manner he assigned these labels to estimated omega squared $(\hat{\omega}_A^2)$ and the analysis of variance (see pp. 184–185).[9] According to Cohen,

> A "small" effect produces a ϕ of .10.
> A "medium" effect produces a ϕ of .30.
> A "large" effect produces a ϕ of .50 or greater.

Accordingly, the outcome of our numerical example, which produced a ϕ of .40, represents an effect size somewhere between "medium" and "large."

Using Power to Estimate Sample Size

Power refers to the probability with which an experiment can detect treatment effects when they are present in the population. We discussed power in detail in Chap. 8 and showed how, in the planning stages, we can select a sample size for an experiment that will ensure a reasonable probability of producing a significant F — that is, will have high power. In this section, we will consider an analogous procedure for experiments with categorical data.[10]

Basing the Calculations on Estimated Outcomes. The key to using considerations of power to choose the sample size of a proposed experiment is in finding a realistic estimate of the minimum effect size we are interested in detecting with the study. Ideally, we could accomplish this task by specifying separately for each treatment condition the proportion of subjects which we expect to fall into each of the two response classifications. We would then use this information — combined with a decision concerning the significance level we would use (usually $\alpha = .05$) and the power we wish to achieve (somewhere between .70 and .80) — to determine the sample size we will need to satisfy these conditions. Alternatively, our guesses of the anticipated outcome might come from similar experiments reported in the research literature or from the data produced by a preliminary, or pilot, experiment we collected before embarking on the primary study.

---

[9] Cohen uses a different symbol, w, to represent the phi coefficient.

[10] Again, we will be assuming that the dependent variable consists of two response categories.

As an example, suppose a researcher is studying the effects of administering a drug on the occurrence of aggression in young hyperactive children. The children will be randomly assigned to receive a pill containing the drug (the drug condition) or a pill containing a neutral substance (the control condition). The children are given the pill in the morning and observed 2 hours later for the occurrence of aggressive behavior during a period of free play in the nursery school where they are enrolled. Trained observers classify the behavior of the children as either aggressive or nonaggressive. On the basis of related research, let's suppose that the researcher expects to find that 70 percent of the children in the control condition and 20 percent in the drug condition will be rated as aggressive. We have entered this estimated outcome in the form of proportions in the upper portion of Table 14-6. To estimate the desired N, we try a few values until we find the one that produces the power we want for our experiment.

Suppose we choose $n = 20$ as our trial sample size per treatment (and $N = 40$). If we multiply this sample size by each of the anticipated proportions in Table 14-6, we create a contingency table that represents the anticipated outcome of the experiment expressed in terms of frequencies. This anticipated contingency table is presented in the middle portion of Table 14-6. The two entries for the control condition, for example, were obtained by multiplying the anticipated proportions for aggressive and nonaggressive behavior by the sample size (20); that is,

$$f_{aggressive} = (.7)(20) = 14 \quad \text{and} \quad f_{nonaggressive} = (.3)(20) = 6$$

Corresponding calculations for the drug condition produce:

$$f_{aggressive} = (.2)(20) = 4 \quad \text{and} \quad f_{nonaggressive} = (.8)(20) = 16$$

Finally, we calculate the expected frequencies for the anticipated outcome of the experiment. The expected frequencies for the four cells are obtained by applying Eq. (14-2) to the column and row totals appearing in the contingency table containing the anticipated results. For the control condition, the expected frequency of aggressive behavior is

$$f_E = \frac{(\text{row total})(\text{column total})}{\text{grand total}} = \frac{(18)(20)}{40} = \frac{360}{40} = 9$$

The expected frequencies for the four cells are presented in the bottom portion of Table 14-6.

TABLE 14-6 *An Example of Using Power to Estimate Sample Size*

Anticipated Outcome Expressed in Proportions

Type of Behavior	Control Condition	Drug Condition
Aggressive	.7	.2
Nonaggressive	.3	.8

Anticipated Outcome Expressed in Frequencies

Type of Behavior	Control Condition	Drug Condition	Total
Aggressive	14	4	18
Nonaggressive	6	16	22
Total	20	20	40

Expected Frequencies

Type of Behavior	Control Condition	Drug Condition	Total
Aggressive	9	9	18
Nonaggressive	11	11	22
Total	20	20	40

The next step in this process is to calculate $\chi^2_{antic.}$ with these anticipated frequencies. Using Eq. (14-3), we find

$$\chi^2_{antic.} = \sum \frac{(f_O - f_E)^2}{f_E}$$

$$= \frac{(14-9)^2}{9} + \frac{(6-11)^2}{11} + \frac{(4-9)^2}{9} + \frac{(16-11)^2}{11}$$

$$= 2.78 + 2.27 + 2.78 + 2.27$$

$$= 10.10$$

Finally, we refer this value of the chi square test statistic to Table A-8 in Appendix A to obtain the power associated with this particular outcome.[11] This table provides curves relating power to anticipated values of the chi square statistic $(\chi^2_{antic.})$ for five different experimental situations distinguished by the df's associated with the chi square test statistic. The top curve (labeled "1") refers to an experiment with $a = 2$ treatment conditions $(df = 1)$, whereas the bottom curve (labeled "5") refers to an experiment with $a = 6$ treatment conditions $(df = 5)$. The middle three curves are appropriate for experiments, from top to bottom, with $a = 3$, 4, and 5 treatment conditions associated with $df = 2$, 3, and 4, respectively. To this table, we locate the value of the anticipated chi square on the baseline $(\chi^2_{antic.})$ and extend a line upward from that point until it intersects the top power function $(df = 1)$; power is read directly off the vertical axis from this point of intersection. Using the value of the χ^2 we obtained from the estimated outcome in Table 14-6 $(\chi^2_{antic.} = 10.10)$, we determine power to be .88.

Presumably we would find this level of power acceptable and plan to use a sample size of $n = 20$ $(N = 40)$ when we conducted the experiment. If we were not satisfied with this estimate of power, however, we would have to try a different sample size, create a new contingency table, calculate $\chi^2_{antic.}$, and use the power chart to determine the power associated with this new trial sample size.

Basing the Calculations on Cohen's Size Categories. If we are unable to make realistic guesses about the specific outcome of a proposed study, we might be able to translate our beliefs about the anticipated outcome in terms of Cohen's size categories of "small," "medium," or "large." You may recall we discussed this same possibility for the analysis of variance in Chap. 8 (see pp. 213–214). All we need to do is to translate the appropriate descriptive adjective that reflects our anticipated results into the phi coefficient (ϕ) and calculate the following:

$$\chi^2_{antic.} = (\phi)^2(N) \tag{14-6}$$

Suppose we expected to find a "medium" effect $(\phi = .30)$ in an experiment with $a = 5$ treatment conditions. We try a trial sample size — for example, $n = 10$ $(N = 50)$ — and substitute these values in Eq. (14-6) to find

$$\chi^2_{antic.} = (.30)^2(50) = (.09)(50) = 4.5$$

Turning to Table A-8 and using the power curve for $df = 4$, we find that power is an unacceptably low value of approximately .37. A doubling of sample size

---

[11] We wish to thank Dr. Thomas D. Wickens for preparing this set of special power charts for us.

($N = 100$) produces a $\chi^2_{antic.}$ of $(.09)(100) = 9.0$ and a power of approximately .67. With a few more trial values, you would find that a sample size of $n = 27$ ($N = 135$) achieves a power of approximately .80.

Comment. Both methods are simple, and both produce estimates of sample size that will be useful in planning an experiment. Whereas most researchers feel uncomfortable about making specific guesses about the anticipated outcome of their experiments, they need to take this step if they want to make intelligent decisions concerning their research. We should point out that the answers we seek concerning sample size do not have to be precise, but simply represent a rough, "ballpark" estimate of the numbers of subjects we may need to produce results that are statistically significant. This information — no matter how approximate or tentative — reduces some of the uncertainty involved in designing an experiment and tells us ahead of time whether the resources we wish to commit to a study are realistic and appropriate, given the nature of the findings we hope to detect.

14.4 SUMMARY

While a great deal of psychological research has been based on behavior that is measured on a continuous scale — a scale that reflects variations in amount — there are many instances reported in the literature in which measurement occurs at a less precise level. In this chapter, we considered statistical procedures appropriate for research in which the dependent variable consists of a number of mutually exclusive classes or categories. Under these circumstances, an observation is placed in one of these classifications with all other observations that satisfy the definition of that response category. The basic data consist of frequency counts, that is, the number of individuals displaying each of the different sorts of behaviors.

The *chi square test statistic* was designed to deal with these sorts of data. We saw how the results of an experiment may be expressed in terms of frequencies — for example, the number of subjects solving or not solving a particular problem — and how this information can be used in evaluating research hypotheses concerning the effects of independent variables on the behavior under investigation. The actual calculations are relatively simple, and the procedures are easily adapted to permit the statistical assessment of analytical comparisons. Procedures are also available to calculate effect size and power with information derived from the chi square test statistic.

14.5 EXERCISES [12]

*1. Suppose an experiment is conducted in a large mental institution comparing the effectiveness of three types of therapy — psychotherapy, chemotherapy, and shock therapy — in treating depressed patients. Eighty patients are randomly assigned in equal numbers to each of four conditions — the three therapy conditions and a control condition of no treatment. After 2 months of treatment (or no treatment), the patients are classified as either "improved" or "not improved." The numbers of patients falling into these two categories for each group are as follows:

Outcome	Psychotherapy	Chemotherapy	Shock Therapy	No Therapy
Improved	14	11	12	5
Not Improved	6	9	8	15

    a. Do the four conditions differ in effectiveness?

    b. What is the effect size associated with these differences?

    c. Are the three therapy conditions differentially effective in treating depressed patients?

    d. If we combine the three therapy conditions, does a significant difference exist between this combined group of subjects and that in the no-therapy control condition?

2. Using the data presented in Table 14-5 (p. 445), verify that the χ^2 we reported in the text is equal to 7.23.

3. In Sec. 14.2, we found that the difference between two instructed groups (a_2 and a_3) was not significant, which led us to an examination of a complex comparison between the control (a_1) and the two instructed groups combined. Let's suppose you were still interested in comparing each of the instructed groups with the control in separate pairwise comparisons.

    a. Compare the results of the control group (a_1) with those of the group instructed to give common uses (a_2).

    b. Compare the results of the control group (a_1) with those of the group instructed to give uncommon uses (a_3).

*4. In the appendix to this chapter (Sec. 14.6), we describe a factorial experiment in which the occurrence of successful births in meadow voles was

---

[12] Answers to the starred problems are given in Appendix B.

studied as a function of two independent variables, the daily administration of saline or a hormone (factor A) and the age of the animals (factor B). The design of the study is diagramed in the upper portion of Table 14-7 (p. 454). Let's assume that each of the four groups of subjects in this 2×2 factorial design contains $n = 20$ subjects and that the following birth data were observed during the course of the experiment:

Response Category	Treatment Conditions			
	saline-young $(a_1 b_1)$	saline-old $(a_1 b_2)$	hormone-young $(a_2 b_1)$	hormone-old $(a_2 b_2)$
Litter	12	8	6	16
No Litter	8	12	14	4

a. As an initial test, determine if the four groups differ in the number of litters they produced.

b. The significant χ^2 in part (a) merely indicates that the four groups do not have the same birth rates. A more appropriate analysis is one that focuses on the treatment effects revealed when we examine the data as a factorial design. Using the arrangements presented in Table 14-7 as a guide, determine which of the following factorial treatment effects is significant:

(1) The overall difference between saline and the hormone (the main effect of factor A)

(2) The overall difference between young and old voles (the main effect of factor B)

(3) The interaction of treatment and age (the $A \times B$ interaction)

14.6 APPENDIX: ANALYZING COMPLETELY RANDOMIZED FACTORIAL DESIGNS

It is not widely known that we can use the chi square test statistic to analyze the results of factorial experiments. As an example, consider a 2×2 factorial experiment on the effects of two independent variables on birth success

TABLE 14-7 *Using the Chi Square Statistic to Analyze the Results of a Factorial Experiment*

Factorial Design

	a_1	a_2
b_1	1	3
b_2	2	4

Contingency Table for the Treatment Conditions

Response Category	Treatment Conditions			
	1 $(a_1 b_1)$	2 $(a_1 b_2)$	3 $(a_2 b_1)$	4 $(a_2 b_2)$
Litter				
No Litter				

Comparison Contingency Tables for the Factorial Treatment Effects

A Main Effect

Response Category	a_1 $(1 + 2)$	a_2 $(3 + 4)$
Litter		
No Litter		

B Main Effect

Response Category	b_1 $(1 + 3)$	b_2 $(2 + 4)$
Litter		
No Litter		

A × B Interaction

Response Category	$(1 + 4)$	$(2 + 3)$
Litter		
No Litter		

in meadow voles.[13] One of the independent variables consisted of the daily administration of saline or a hormone that regulates the reproductive system of these animals; the other was the age of the animals when they were studied ("young" or "old"). For the dependent variable, the animals were classified according to the occurrence of a subsequent birth.

A straightforward way of performing this analysis is to arrange the four cells of the original 2×2 factorial design into a series of comparison contingency tables that represent the three factorial effects we usually extract from this type of design (see pp. 235–245). To illustrate, we will start with the representation of the factorial design presented in the top portion of Table 14-7. For ease of reference, we have assigned the numbers 1 to 4 to identify the four groups making up this factorial design. With a quantitative dependent variable, the four cells of this matrix would contain the means for the different treatment combinations. With a dichotomous dependent variable consisting of two response categories, the cells would contain frequencies or proportions. In order to include the two response categories, we rearrange the 2×2 factorial matrix into the more convenient contingency table in which the columns consist of the four treatment combinations and the rows consist of the two response categories in the factorial experiment ("litter" and "no litter"), which results in the 4×2 contingency table, presented in the middle portion of the table. From this matrix, we would construct three comparison contingency tables, which are created from different combinations of the data produced by the four treatment combinations and represent the three factorial effects.

Consider, for example, the comparison contingency table on the left of the bottom portion of Table 14-7. The first column of this table contains the data from the two treatment groups that received level a_1 (groups 1 and 2), whereas the second column contains the data from the two treatment groups that received level a_2 (groups 3 and 4). Given the way we have combined the treatment groups, a chi square test statistic based on this comparison contingency table provides an assessment of the main effect of factor A. The arrangement of the data on the right provides an assessment of the main effect of factor B. This has been accomplished by entering into the first column of this comparison contingency table the data from the two treatment groups that received level b_1 (groups 1 and 3) and into the second column the data from the two groups that received level b_2 (groups 2 and 4).

The third comparison contingency table focuses on the $A \times B$ interaction. As indicated in the table, we created this arrangement by entering in the first

---

[13] We wish to thank Michael Gorman and Irving Zucker for permitting us to describe this part of a larger study of factors influencing the size of litters in meadow voles.

column the data from groups 1 and 4 and in the second column the data from groups 2 and 3. While not intuitively obvious, this third arrangement does in fact represent the $A \times B$ interaction (see Keppel & Zedeck, 1989, pp. 187–188). To demonstrate, we begin with the definition of interaction in terms of simple effects — that is, interaction is present if the simple effects of one of the independent variables are not the same at all levels of the other independent variable. Translated to our example, we would say that interaction is present if the difference between groups 1 and 3 (the simple effect of factor A at level b_1) is not equal to the difference between groups 2 and 4 (the simple effect of factor A at level b_2). Expressed algebraically,

$$\text{interaction} = (1 - 3) - (2 - 4)$$

If interaction is present, there will be a difference between the two simple effects; if interaction is absent, the difference will be zero. We can express interaction with different combinations of these four groups by first removing the parentheses and then combining the groups differently; that is,

$$\text{interaction} = 1 - 3 - 2 + 4$$
$$= (1 + 4) - (2 + 3)$$

This way of expressing interaction, then — as a difference between groups 1 and 4 combined and groups 2 and 3 combined — corresponds to the way in which we combined groups in Table 14-7.

Once we have have formed the three comparison contingency tables, we can follow the procedures outlined in Sec. 14.2 for evaluating analytical comparisons with the chi square statistic. This consists of calculating three χ^2 test statistics, one based on the data from each of the three comparison contingency tables presented in the bottom portion of Table 14-7.

It is possible to extend this analysis to larger factorial designs, but the procedures are more complex and beyond the scope of this book. The procedure we have illustrated may be applied to the following situations: experiments with dichotomous response measures in which the independent variables consist of two levels only and the sample sizes are equal. Wickens (1989, Chaps. 7 and 11) provides a useful discussion of analyses relevant to factorial experiments.

Chapter · 15

CORRELATION AND REGRESSION

Up to this point, we have focused on the design and analysis of experiments. The unique advantage of such research is our ability to infer *causality* from the results of an experiment. The strength of experimental research is its isolation of the critical factor (or factors) responsible for producing a given set of results through the use of experimental control and random assignment to conditions.

A large portion of psychological research is not experimental, however. Many psychologists are interested in the effects of variables that are not amenable to experimental manipulation. Suppose a researcher hypothesized that there is a relationship between the grades a student receives in college and his or her self-esteem. To investigate this research question using an experiment, we would have to find some reasonable and convincing way of *creating* groups of students with different levels of self-esteem and then observe the effect of these differences on grade-point average (GPA) in college several years later. This would raise two critical questions: (1) can we change a subject's self-esteem by experimental manipulation, and (2) even if we could, is such an intervention morally or professionally ethical?

Since the answer to this latter question is no, to study this issue researchers must locate subjects who *already* differ in self-esteem and then relate these differences to their college GPA's. Let's assume that we find that subjects with low self-esteem obtain lower GPA's than subjects with high self-esteem and that this difference is statistically significant. Would this finding allow us to conclude that high self-esteem "causes" a student to have a higher GPA? Unfortunately, we cannot draw such a conclusion from this finding, because many other differences — in addition to the differences in self-esteem — may have contributed to the differences in college GPA, such as overall intellectual ability, study habits, motivation, and so on.

We refer to studies investigating relationships between sets of measured characteristics of subjects as **correlational research**. In the simplest form of correlational research, which is the focus of this chapter, psychologists study the nature of the relationship between two variables or characteristics of individuals. These characteristics can be *biographical* (for example, age, gender, education, or personal income), *physiological* (height, weight, blood pressure, or other "medical" characteristics), *psychological* (measures of intelligence, personality, or attitudes and opinions), or *behavioral* (any characteristic of behavior that can be observed and measured). We begin by discussing characteristics of correlational research, followed by a consideration of two interrelated statistical measures of the relationship or association between two variables, namely, *correlation* and *regression*.[1]

---

[1] A discussion of more complicated analyses, which involve three or more variables and are

15.1 CHARACTERISTICS OF CORRELATIONAL RESEARCH

Correlational procedures occupy an important place in psychological research, in spite of their limitations in establishing causal relationships unambiguously. The study of *individual differences*, for example, is dependent on correlational information obtained from samples of subjects. Here, the interest is in identifying characteristics on which subjects consistently differ and in establishing relationships among them. Theoretical explanations of differences in personality, for example, are based on information of this sort. Once a relationship has been established, a researcher can also use this information to *predict* one of these characteristics given knowledge of another characteristic or, more typically, a set of characteristics. A common use of prediction using correlational methods, for instance, is the selection of individuals for some future activity — for example, college, skilled jobs, professional schools, and so on — on the basis of information such as school grades and scores on aptitude tests of various sorts.

Distinguishing Features of Correlational Data

The analysis of experiments is directed to the treatment means and not to the individual subject; variability involving subjects is used to calculate the error terms for the statistical analysis. In contrast, correlational research specifically concentrates on the variability of the individual subjects as an object of study and assesses the consistency of subjects on two or more variables.

Absence of Manipulated Variables. The defining characteristic of correlational data is the absence of a true independent variable — that is, differential treatments administered by and under the direct control of the experimenter. The variables included in correlational research are isolated and measured by the investigator, but they are characteristics that occur naturally in the subjects. Students are often initially confused because investigators commonly call one of the variables in correlational research the "independent variable" and the other the "dependent variable." In correlational research, the term *independent variable* refers to the variable or characteristic whose influence on another variable or characteristic is the object of study; and the term *dependent variable*

---

widely reported in the research literature, is beyond the scope of this book. A short book by Edwards (1985) provides a useful introduction to correlational research involving more than two variables.

refers to the variable we are trying to understand or to study. The danger of using these two terms in discussing correlational data is the temptation to infer a causal mechanism or a direction of influence between the two variables — which may in fact underlie the observed relationship but in reality cannot be inferred on the basis of this relationship alone.

To avoid confusion, we will use two neutral terms, **X variable** and **Y variable**, to refer to the "independent" and "dependent" variables, respectively, studied in correlational research.[2] Thus, we can say that a correlational study consists of establishing a relationship between variations in the X variable to variations in the Y variable. In some cases, this designation is purely arbitrary, but in most cases, the X variable will represent the characteristic or attribute whose presumed link to the Y variable is being measured or studied. When viewed this way, researchers often say that they are attempting to *explain* some portion of the variation observed in the Y variable by means of the variation in the X variable. If the goal of the research is selecting individuals for school or for employment, you will often find the X variable referred to as the **predictor variable** and the Y variable as the **criterion variable**. Whatever terms are used, however, we must remember that the presence of a correlation between two naturally occurring variables reflects only an *association* between the two variables and *not necessarily* a causal link.

Plotting the Results of a Correlational Study

The most common way of examining the relationship between two variables in a correlational study is by constructing a **scatterplot** of the data. We will present three scatterplots based on correlational data we have collected in our classes.

Figure 15-1 depicts the relationship between the scores on a test of quantitative skills taken by students on the first day of a statistics course (represented by the X axis) and their combined scores on two midterm examinations (represented by the Y axis). A student is located in the scatterplot on the basis of a *pair* of scores, namely, the student's quantitative score (the X variable) and his or her corresponding midterm score (the Y variable). Be sure you understand how these pairs of scores are located in the scatterplot. One student, for example, obtained a score of 11 on the quantitative test and a combined score of 128 on the two midterms. We charted that person's scores in the scatterplot

---

[2] The X variable corresponds to the variable plotted on the X axis; the Y variable corresponds to the variable plotted on the Y axis (see the section "Plotting the Results of a Correlational Study").

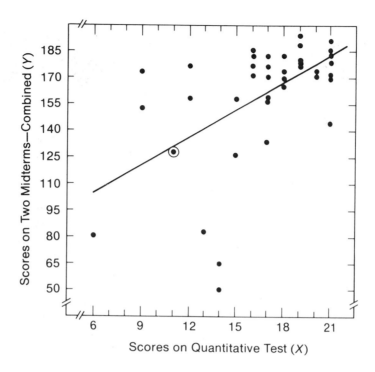

FIGURE 15-1 *An Example of the Relationship Between the Scores on a Quantitative Test (X) and Scores on Two Combined Midterm Examinations (Y).*

by finding 11 on the horizontal axis (scores on the quantitative test) and then moving upward vertically on a line drawn through $X = 11$ until we reached a distance corresponding to 128 on the vertical axis (scores on the combined midterm examinations), where we placed a dot on the graph (we have circled this dot). The scores for the remaining students have been plotted in a similar manner. Note that we shortened both axes to create a square scatterplot just large enough to "capture" all the data points.

The reason for constructing a scatterplot is so that we can tell at a glance the nature of the relationship between the two variables. More specifically, it appears that the two variables are *positively* related: as quantitative skill increases (moving from left to right on the horizontal axis), performance on the two midterms also increases (moving from bottom to top on the vertical axis). The statistical procedures we discuss in this chapter focus on the *linear relationship* between the two variables represented by a special straight line called the **regression line**, which is determined mathematically to best fit the data in the

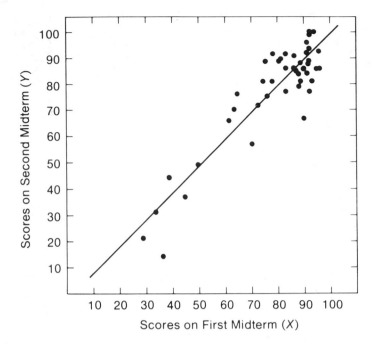

FIGURE 15-2 *An Example of the Relationship Between the Scores on the First Midterm (X) and the Scores on the Second Midterm (Y).*

scatterplot.[3] The line we have drawn in the scatterplot is the regression line for these data. We discuss the regression line in more detail in Sec. 15.3.

The "strength" or "degree" of this linear relationship between the two variables is expressed by a special statistical index that we will consider in Sec. 15.2. Without going into the details at this point, let's just say that the degree of association is reflected by how tightly the data points cluster around the regression line, and that we will use this information to determine whether the linear relationship represents a true relationship in the population or is due entirely to chance factors.

Additional Examples of Scatterplots. Another set of data obtained from this statistics course is plotted in Fig. 15-2. In this case, the two variables consisted of a subject's performance on the two midterm examinations. We designated the scores on the first midterm as the X variable and the scores on the second midterm as the Y variable. In contrast with the previous example relating the

---

[3] The criterion for "best fit" is based on the deviation of the actual data points from the regression line.

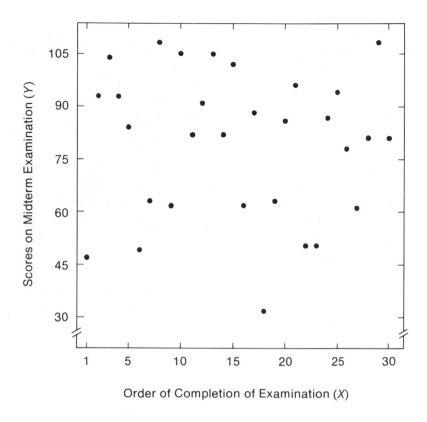

FIGURE 15-3 *An Example of the Relationship Between Order in which a Midterm Is Completed (X) and the Score on the Examination (Y).*

quantitative test and midterm scores (Fig. 15-1), this relationship is more consistent with the data points; the students are more closely clustered around the regression line. This relatively "strong" relationship between the two variables indicates that the students maintain their relative positions on the two tests — students with the highest scores on the first test generally received the highest scores on the second test; conversely, students with the lowest scores on the first test generally received the lowest scores on the second test.

A third set of data examines the relationship between a student's midterm performance and the order in which he or she turned in the test during the examination period. These data are presented in Fig. 15-3. (These data were obtained from a different class from the one producing the other two scatterplots.) What you see is the complete absence of a relationship between the two variables — that is, the data points appear to be scattered about the graph in a haphazard pattern. Students are usually relieved to find out about this lack of relationship, which we have observed in several classes, particularly when they are struggling with a test and observe some of their classmates leaving the room before the end of the examination period.

These three examples illustrate different degrees, or strengths, of linear relationship between two variables. As mentioned earlier, we can see the strength by visualizing the "tightness" of an envelope drawn around the scores. In the absence of any relationship between two variables, the envelope will resemble a circle, which describes the scatterplot in Fig. 15-3. As the linear relationship between the two variables increases, the circle begins to flatten to form an ellipse (a football shape), which is tilted either upward from left to right, when a positive relationship is present, or downward from left to right, when a negative relationship is present. The envelope around the data points continues to flatten as the degree of association increases, until it becomes perfectly flat — that is, a straight line — which happens when the relationship is perfect. Look again at the other two scatterplots. The relationship between the two midterms (Fig. 15-2) represents a considerably stronger association than the one between the quantitative test and the combined midterms (Fig. 15-1). This difference is reflected in the flatter, or "tighter," envelope for the first case than for the second.

Summary

The association or correlation between two variables is an important concept in science. The task of a researcher is to discover relationships between variables and to explain why they are related. When one of the variables is an independent variable manipulated by a researcher, the relationship usually implies that the independent and dependent variables are causally linked. However, when the variables are both observed or measured characteristics of the same group of subjects, the issue of causality is usually uncertain without further study and investigation. Nevertheless, the presence of an association identifies some kind of linkage between the X and Y variables that may be used to help *predict* a subject's score on Y, say, on the basis of his or her score on X.

15.2 LINEAR CORRELATION

We are now ready to consider how we can obtain quantitative measures of the linear association between two variables, X and Y. The index of correlation we consider in this chapter was developed by Karl Pearson — it is variously termed the **Pearson correlation coefficient**, the **product-moment correlation coefficient**, and the **linear correlation coefficient** — and is symbolized by **r**. One way of conceptualizing the correlation coefficient is in terms of *variance*. In relating two variables, we have variance in the X variable and variance in the Y variable. More important, we believe that the two variables have variance in common with each other, that they vary together, or *covary*. The correlation coefficient may therefore be defined as the ratio of the joint variation of X and Y relative to the variation of X and Y considered separately. Since the correlation is in essence a ratio, the product-moment correlation coefficient — or correlation coefficient for short — has two theoretical maximum values for a perfect linear relationship between two variables ($+1.0$ for a perfect positive relationship and -1.0 for a perfect negative relationship) and a theoretical minimum value for the absence of a linear relationship between two variables (0).

In symbols, the product-moment correlation coefficient r is given by the following formula:

$$r = \frac{\text{covariance}(X, Y)}{\sqrt{[\text{variance}(X)][\text{variance}(Y)]}} \qquad (15\text{-}1)$$

Both variance and covariance are based on deviations of individual scores from their respective means. Variance, as you know, is essentially an average of these squared deviations. With correlational data, there are two variances, each reflecting the separate variability of the individual sets of scores — variance (X) and variance (Y). **Covariance**, on the other hand, relates the deviation of each subject's score on the X variable from the mean of the X scores $(X - \overline{X})$ to the corresponding deviation for that subject on the Y variable $(Y - \overline{Y})$. We will consider each of these quantities in detail.

Defining Formulas for Variance and Covariance

Variance (X) and Variance (Y). The variation of the scores on the X variable is based on the deviations of all the X scores from the mean of the X scores. That is,

$$\text{variance}(X) = \frac{\Sigma(X - \overline{X})^2}{df} = \frac{SS_X}{df} \qquad (15\text{-}2)$$

Similarly, the variation of the scores on the Y variable is based on the deviations of all the Y scores from $\overline{Y}$. In symbols,

$$\text{variance}(Y) = \frac{\Sigma(Y - \overline{Y})^2}{df} = \frac{SS_Y}{df} \tag{15-3}$$

By now, both of these formulas should be familiar to you: they present variability as the sum of the squared deviations from the mean divided by the degrees of freedom.

Covariance (X, Y). Although the covariance of the two variables will be a new concept for most readers, it is based on an algebraic blending of what are familiar quantities. More specifically,

$$\text{covariance}(X, Y) = \frac{\Sigma(X - \overline{X})(Y - \overline{Y})}{df}$$

We refer to the numerator term as the sum of the products of corresponding deviations on the X and Y variables, or more simply, as the **sum of products**, abbreviated SP_{XY}. Thus,

$$\text{covariance}(X, Y) = \frac{SP_{XY}}{df} \tag{15-4}$$

Notice the similarity in form between the formulas for variance and for covariance. Variance is a measure that accounts for the deviation of a score (either X or Y) from its mean. Covariance, on the other hand, measures the degree to which these two sets of deviations *vary together*, or *covary*. If the deviations of the X variable tend to be of the same size as the corresponding deviations of the Y variable, the covariance will be large. If the relationship is *inconsistent* — for example, large deviations on X being associated with deviations of *various* magnitudes on Y — then covariance will be small in value. Where a systematic relationship between the two sets of deviations is completely absent, covariance will be zero.

Covariance can be either positive or negative. Covariance is positive when the signs of the paired deviations on X and Y tend to be the *same* (both positive or both negative) and negative when the signs tend to be *different.* The sign of the covariance term determines the sign or the direction of the association between the two variables. That is, if covariance is positive, r will be positive; and if covariance is negative, r will be negative.

Computational Formulas

We will now present the computational formula for calculating the product-moment correlation coefficient. This formula provides the same information as does the defining formula we considered initially as in Eq. (15-1) and has the important advantage of being computationally simpler.

Calculating the Product-Moment Correlation Coefficient. There are several useful computational formulas for r. The one we prefer is based on sums of squares (SS_X and SS_Y) and the sum of products (SP_{XY}). More specifically,

$$r = \frac{SP_{XY}}{\sqrt{(SS_X)(SS_Y)}} \tag{15-5}$$

We will now consider the computational formulas for the three terms required to calculate r with Eq. (15-5).

Calculating the Sums of Squares. Each sum of squares is based on two quantities, the sum of the scores (ΣX and ΣY) and the sum of the squared scores (ΣX^2 and ΣY^2). More specifically,

$$SS_X = \Sigma X^2 - \frac{(\Sigma X)^2}{n} \tag{15-6}$$

$$SS_Y = \Sigma Y^2 - \frac{(\Sigma Y)^2}{n} \tag{15-7}$$

Since these formulas were first presented in Chap. 2, they should be familiar to you by now and require no additional explanation.

Calculating the Sum of Products. The computational formula for SP_{XY} involves the sum of the scores (ΣX and ΣY) and a new quantity, the sum of the *products* of X and Y — that is, $\Sigma(X)(Y)$:

$$SP_{XY} = \Sigma(X)(Y) - \frac{(\Sigma X)(\Sigma Y)}{n} \tag{15-8}$$

Data Layout and Preliminary Calculations. An examination of the computational formulas for the sums of squares and the sum of products will reveal that we need a total of five sums:

two sums involving the X scores: ΣX and ΣX^2
two sums involving the Y scores: ΣY and ΣY^2
one sum involving the products of the pairs of X and Y scores: $\Sigma(X)(Y)$

TABLE 15-1 *Notation for Linear Correlation and Regression*

Subject	(1) Value of X	(2) Value of Y	(3) Product of X and Y
1	X_1	Y_1	$(X_1)(Y_1)$
2	X_2	Y_2	$(X_2)(Y_2)$
3	X_3	Y_3	$(X_3)(Y_3)$
	$\Sigma\,X$	$\Sigma\,Y$	$\Sigma(X)(Y)$
	$\Sigma\,X^2$	$\Sigma\,Y^2$	

$$\Sigma\,X = X_1 + X_2 + X_3 \qquad \Sigma\,Y = Y_1 + Y_2 + Y_3$$

$$\Sigma\,X^2 = X_1^2 + X_2^2 + X_3^2 \qquad \Sigma\,Y^2 = Y_1^2 + Y_2^2 + Y_3^2$$

$$\Sigma(X)(Y) = (X_1)(Y_1) + (X_2)(Y_2) + (X_3)(Y_3)$$

We can facilitate the process of calculating these quantities by arranging the pairs of X and Y scores in two separate columns. These values are symbolized in the columns labeled 1 and 2 in Table 15-1. The subscripts are used to identify members of each pair of values; that is, X_1 and Y_1 constitute the pair of values for the first subject; X_2 and Y_2 constitute the pair of values for the second subject; and so on. From the X values, we obtain their sum, $\Sigma\,X$, and the sum of their squared values, $\Sigma\,X^2$. These two sums are designated at the bottom of column 1. The same set of operations is performed on the Y values, as well, to obtain analogous sums, $\Sigma\,Y$ and $\Sigma\,Y^2$, which are designated at the bottom of column 2. Column 3 consists of the *products* obtained by multiplying each subject's X score by that subject's Y score. The sum of these products is symbolized at the bottom of column 3 as $\Sigma(X)(Y)$. This sum is used in calculating the sum of products, SP_{XY}.

A Numerical Example

Probably all high school students facing the prospect of four (or more) arduous years of additional education wonder how well they will do once they enter college. A reasonable question to ask in this situation is whether there is a significant relationship between one's performance in high school and subsequent performance in college. In setting out to study this question, we might first operationalize "performance" as a student's grade point average (GPA) in high school and college, and then collect some data. Let's assume that we collected this information from a sample of 32 college students after they completed the fourth year of college. This information is provided in Table 15-2.

Preliminary Calculations. We have designated high school GPA as the X variable and college GPA as the Y variable. Table 15-1 makes explicit the nature of the sums we need to extract from the data to calculate the product-moment correlation coefficient. The arithmetical operations performed on the X scores and the Y scores should be familiar to you and we will present them without comment. That is,

$$\Sigma X = 2.5 + 3.9 + \cdots + 3.2 + 3.5 = 106.0$$

$$\Sigma X^2 = (2.5)^2 + (3.9)^2 + \cdots + (3.2)^2 + (3.5)^2 = 354.76$$

$$\Sigma Y = 2.9 + 3.4 + \cdots + 3.2 + 3.4 = 102.0$$

$$\Sigma Y^2 = (2.9)^2 + (3.4)^2 + \cdots + (3.2)^2 + (3.4)^2 = 330.68$$

$$\Sigma(X)(Y) = (2.5)(2.9) + (3.9)(3.4) + \cdots + (3.2)(3.2) + (3.5)(3.4)$$

$$= 7.25 + 13.26 + \cdots + 10.24 + 11.90$$

$$= 340.11$$

Calculating the Sums of Squares. With this information, we can calculate the necessary sums of squares for the correlation. (The means for X and Y have also been calculated and are included in Table 15-2 for descriptive purposes; we will refer to them later in this chapter.) For the X variable,

$$SS_X = \Sigma X^2 - \frac{(\Sigma X)^2}{n}$$

$$= 354.76 - \frac{(106.0)^2}{32} = 354.76 - 351.13$$

$$= 3.63$$

For the Y variable,

$$SS_Y = \Sigma Y^2 - \frac{(\Sigma Y)^2}{n}$$

$$= 330.68 - \frac{(102.2)^2}{32} = 330.68 - 326.40$$

$$= 4.28$$

TABLE 15-2 *Numerical Example: Fictitious High School and College Grade-Point Averages (GPA) from $n = 32$ Students*

Subject	(1) High School GPA (X)	(2) College GPA (Y)	(3) Product (X)(Y)
1	2.5	2.9	7.25
2	3.9	3.4	13.26
3	2.7	2.4	6.48
4	3.8	3.6	13.68
5	3.4	2.8	9.52
6	3.3	3.1	10.23
7	3.6	3.0	10.80
8	3.0	3.7	11.10
9	3.2	3.0	9.60
10	3.7	3.8	14.06
11	3.0	2.5	7.50
12	3.6	3.3	11.88
13	3.4	3.3	11.22
14	2.9	3.4	9.86
15	3.7	3.3	12.21
16	3.5	3.1	10.85
17	3.0	3.3	9.90
18	3.5	2.7	9.45
19	3.1	2.9	8.99
20	3.6	3.2	11.52
21	3.1	3.4	10.54
22	3.3	3.0	9.90
23	3.6	3.7	13.32
24	3.3	2.7	8.91
25	3.4	3.6	12.24
26	3.8	3.1	11.78
27	2.8	3.1	8.68
28	3.3	3.8	12.54
29	3.4	3.7	12.58
30	2.9	2.8	8.12
31	3.2	3.2	10.24
32	3.5	3.4	11.90

$$\Sigma X = 106.0 \qquad \Sigma Y = 102.2 \qquad \Sigma(X)(Y) = 340.11$$
$$\Sigma X^2 = 354.76 \qquad \Sigma Y^2 = 330.68$$
$$\overline{X} = 3.31 \qquad \overline{Y} = 3.19$$

Calculating the Sum of Products (SP_{XY}).   We now begin the ca]
nal quantity we need for Eq. (15-5), namely, SP_{XY}, which was give
as follows:

$$SP_{XY} = \Sigma(X)(Y) - \frac{(\Sigma X)(\Sigma Y)}{n}$$

Substituting the three sums we have calculated in Eq. (15-8), we obtain

$$SP_{XY} = 340.11 - \frac{(106.0)(102.2)}{32}$$

$$= 340.11 - \frac{10,833.20}{32} = 340.11 - 338.54$$

$$= 1.57$$

Calculating the Product-Moment Correlation Coefficient r.   We now have all the
information necessary to use Eq. (15-5) to calculate the product-moment correlation coefficient. To illustrate,

$$r = \frac{SP_{XY}}{\sqrt{(SS_X)(SS_Y)}}$$

$$= \frac{1.57}{\sqrt{(3.63)(4.28)}} = \frac{1.57}{\sqrt{15.54}} = \frac{1.57}{3.94}$$

$$= .40$$

Testing the Significance of a Correlation

Because the correlation coefficient is calculated from data drawn from samples,
we must employ a statistical test in order to make any inference concerning
the presence of a correlation in the population. In this case, the statistical
hypotheses are as follows:

H_0: the population correlation is zero
H_1: the population correlation is not zero

While the null hypothesis can be tested in several ways, including analysis of
variance, we will describe only one, which simply requires the comparison of
r with a critical value listed in a special statistical table. To find the critical
value of r, we choose a value for α (usually $\alpha = .05$) and enter Table A-9 in

Appendix A for the appropriate number of degrees of freedom associated with the correlation coefficient. This number is

$$df_r = n - 2 \qquad\qquad (15\text{-}9)$$

where n equals the number of data pairs in the sample.

In our example, $df_r = 32 - 2 = 30$. For $\alpha = .05$, the critical value of r listed in the table is .35. With this information, the decision rule becomes:

If the obtained value of $r \geq .35$, reject the null hypothesis; otherwise, retain the null hypothesis.

Since our correlation of $r = .40$ exceeds the critical value, we conclude that the positive correlation between grades in high school and in college is statistically significant.

15.3 LINEAR REGRESSION

In the previous section, we established the presence of a significant correlation between high school and college grades. We will have more to say about the interpreting the meaning of this correlation coefficient in Sec. 15.4. We turn next to a consideration of linear regression, which is inextricably entwined with the statistical concepts underlying linear correlation.

Linear correlation refers to the presence of a linear relationship between two variables — that is, a relationship that can be expressed as a straight line. *Linear regression* refers to the set of procedures by which we actually establish that particular straight line, which can then be used to predict a subject's score on one of the variables from a knowledge of that subject's score on the other. Linear correlation helps us understand the nature of the relationship, while linear regression uses this relationship for the purposes of prediction.

The Properties of a Straight Line

We begin by considering two numerical quantities that define, and are used in writing, a formula to describe a straight line: the slope and the intercept.

Slope. **Slope** refers to the angle of a line's tilt relative to one of the axes. Consider the straight line in Fig. 15-4. A straight line can be used to describe changes in the Y variable associated with changes in the X variable. Formally, slope is defined in this way:

$$\text{slope} = \frac{\text{change in } Y}{\text{change in } X}$$

To determine the slope of any line, we must first define *change*. We will concentrate first on the definition of *change in X*. Since the slope is constant for the entire length of the line, we are free to select any two convenient points on the X axis to serve this purpose. We call these two points X_1 and X_2. The numerical difference between these two values of X defines the change in X. That is,

$$\text{change in } X = X_2 - X_1$$

To determine *change in Y*, we extend perpendicular lines from X_1 and X_2 until the two intersect the straight line (the dashed lines from the X axis in Fig. 15-4). We find the values of Y associated with these two points on the line by extending

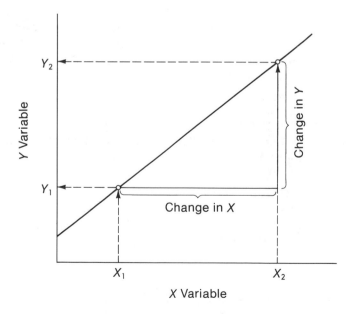

FIGURE 15-4 *An Illustration of the Two Factors Entering into the Determination of the Slope of a Straight Line Specifying the Relationship between Two Variables X and Y.*

lines from these points, parallel to the X axis, until they intersect the Y axis at Y_1 and Y_2. (These two lines are the dashed lines to the Y axis in the figure.) Again, the numerical difference between Y_2 and Y_1 defines the change in Y associated with the corresponding change in X. In symbols,

$$\text{change in } Y = Y_2 - Y_1$$

We calculate the slope by dividing the change in Y by the change in X. That is,

$$\text{slope} = \frac{Y_2 - Y_1}{X_2 - X_1}$$

The numerical value of the slope tells us the rate at which the Y variable changes as the X variable is varied. For example, a slope of 1.0 means that for every change of 1 unit in the X variable, a change of 1 unit also occurs in the Y variable. Values of the slope less than 1 mean that Y changes *more slowly* than X. For example, a slope of .5 indicates that for every unit change in the X variable a half-unit change occurs in Y. On the other hand, slopes greater than 1 indicate that Y changes *faster* than than X. For example, a slope of 2.0 means that for every unit change in the X variable, a 2-unit change occurs in the Y variable.

The *sign* of the slope provides additional information. A **positive slope** indicates that the Y variable changes in the *same* direction as X; in other words, as X increases, Y increases; or as X decreases, Y decreases. A **negative slope** indicates that the Y variable changes in the direction *opposite* to X; that is, as X increases, Y decreases; or as X decreases, Y increases.

Intercept.   The intercept of a straight line refers to the point at which the line crosses the Y axis at $X = 0$. This point is called the **Y intercept**. Suppose a line has a particular slope. A very large number of lines exist with this particular slope; these individual lines differ only in the point at which they intersect the vertical axis at $X = 0$. A few linear functions with the same slope are depicted graphically in Fig. 15-5. The Y intercept can be either positive or negative, depending on whether the line intersects the Y axis above the 0 point (positive) or below it (negative).

The Formula for a Straight Line

It should be clear that once the slope and the intercept of a straight line are specified, the line is completely defined. Only one possible straight line can

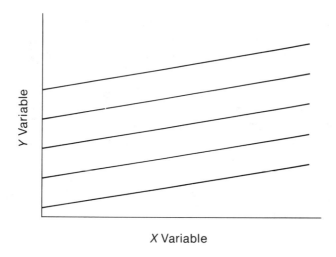

FIGURE 15-5 *Each Line Has the Same Slope but a Different Y Intercept.*

be drawn to those specifications. Stated as a mathematical rule, the formula for a straight line is

$$Y = a + (b)(X) \qquad (15\text{-}10)$$

In this formula,

Y = the calculated value for the variable on the vertical axis

a = the intercept or point at which the line crosses the Y axis at $X = 0$

b = the slope of the line

X = a value for the variable on the horizontal axis

Once this line is specified, we can enter any value of X and calculate the corresponding value of Y specified by the formula.

The Best-Fit Straight Line

We do not expect "real" data to perfectly fit a straight line. Even under the best of circumstances, we would expect some of the data points to fall above the line and some to fall below. The idea behind finding the **best-fit straight line** is to find a line that minimizes as much as possible the amount of variation from the line.[4] Once this regression line is created from a set of data where X and Y are both available, the line — or, more accurately, the equation for the line — can used to *predict* or *estimate* an individual's score on Y solely on the basis of his or her score on X.

We use the regression line to predict Y from a knowledge of X. Without any information about X or the linear relationship between the two variables, our best estimate of an individual's score on the Y variable is the mean of the sample, $\overline{Y}$. A knowledge of an individual's X value and the linear relationship between the X and Y variables permits us to predict with more accuracy. Rather than use the line itself, most researchers use the formula for the regression line — the **regression equation**, as it is called — which has the form

$$Y' = a + (b)(X) \tag{15-11}$$

where Y' is the predicted value of Y, a and b are the characteristics of a line that are estimated from the data, and X is an individual's score on the X variable. The form of Eq. (15-11) is similar to that of Eq. (15-10), but the Y' in Eq. (15-11) indicates that we are dealing with *estimates* of a and b, rather than with the fixed quantities implied in Eq. (15-10). We are ready to describe how we can obtain these various estimates.

Estimating the Slope. Recall that the slope of a straight line is defined in terms of the change in the Y variable associated with a given change in the X variable. When working with data, we use a different definition. We obtain the estimate of the slope, which is often referred to as the **regression coefficient**, from this formula:

$$b = \frac{\text{covariance}(X, Y)}{\text{variance}(X)}$$

which may be rewritten in terms of some of the quantities we introduced in Sec. 15.2. More specifically,

$$b = \frac{SP_{XY}}{SS_X} \tag{15-12}$$

where the formulas for SP_{XY} (the sum of products of X and Y) and SS_X (the sum of squares of the X scores) were given by Eqs. (15-8) and (15-6), respectively.

---

[4] The method of line fitting is called the *method of least squares*, a procedure which reduces the sum of the squared deviations from the line to the smallest amount.

Estimating the Y Intercept. The Y intercept, you will recall, is the point at which the regression line cuts across the Y axis at $X = 0$. The formula for estimating the Y intercept is

$$a = \overline{Y} - (b)(\overline{X}) \qquad (15\text{-}13)$$

where $\overline{Y}$ and $\overline{X}$ are the means based on the sets of Y and X values, respectively, and b is the estimated slope as defined by Eq. (15-12). While not obvious, these calculations ensure that the regression line passes through the point on the scatterplot defined by a pairing of the two means, $\overline{X}$ and $\overline{Y}$.

A Numerical Example

We will illustrate the calculations with the data in Table 15-2. Because we obtained a linear correlation coefficient with these data in Sec. 15.2, all the preliminary calculations we need to determine the linear regression equation have already been computed. We will not repeat these steps here, since you can consult the computational details in that section if you find this necessary.

Calculating the Slope. We calculate the slope of the regression equation (b) by substituting in Eq. (15-12). Using the calculations from Sec. 15.2 (see pp. 469–471), we find

$$b = \frac{SP_{XY}}{SS_X}$$

$$= \frac{1.57}{3.63} = .43$$

This slope means that for every increase of 1 unit in high school GPA (variable X), there is a .43 increase in college GPA (variable Y).

Calculating the Y Intercept. The Y intercept is calculated by substituting in Eq. (15-13), which requires the means for the two sets of scores (presented in Table 15-2) and the slope we have just calculated. Combining this information in the equation, we obtain

$$a = \overline{Y} - (b)(\overline{X})$$

$$= 3.19 - (.43)(3.31) = 3.19 - 1.42$$

$$= 1.77$$

Calculating the Regression Equation. We obtain the regression equation by substituting the estimates of the slope and intercept in Eq. (15-11):

$$Y' = a + (b)(X)$$

$$= 1.77 + (.43)(X)$$

If we want to use this equation to predict a student's college GPA (Y'), we substitute his or her high school GPA (X) and complete the arithmetic. We can also use the regression line itself to estimate college GPA simply by extending a line upward from X until it intersects the regression line and reading the corresponding value of Y' on the Y axis.

In order to draw this regression line, we just choose two convenient values of X and substitute them in the formula for the best-fit straight line. We will choose two points near the extremes of the X variable so that we can draw the regression line with some accuracy. Suppose we use $X_1 = 1$ and $X_2 = 4$ for this purpose. Entering these two values in the regression equation, we find

$$Y_1' = 1.77 + (.43)(1) = 1.77 + .43 = 2.20$$

$$Y_2' = 1.77 + (.43)(4) = 1.77 + 1.72 = 3.49$$

Marking these two points on the scatterplot permits us to draw the regression line and to examine visually how well it describes the relationship between X and Y. The regression line we show in Fig. 15-6 is based on these calculations.

As we mentioned previously, the regression line should pass through the point on the scatterplot lying at the intersection of $X = \overline{X}$ and $Y = \overline{Y}$, within rounding and plotting error. You can confirm this by substituting $\overline{X}$ (3.31) in the regression equation and solving for Y'; the solution must be $\overline{Y}$ (3.19). To illustrate,

$$Y' = 1.77 + (.43)(X)$$

$$= 1.77 + (.43)(3.31) = 1.77 + 1.42$$

$$= 3.19$$

Testing the Significance of the Slope

There is always a possibility that the slope we estimate from the data of a sample may reflect entirely the operation of chance factors. We can assess this

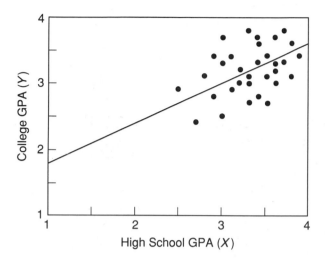

FIGURE 15-6 *A Scatterplot Relating High School Grade-Point Averages (X) and College Grade-Point Averages (Y).*

possibility by evaluating the following set of statistical hypotheses:

H_0: the slope of the population regression line is zero
H_1: the slope of the population regression line is not zero

If we reject the null hypothesis that the slope of the regression line in the population is zero, we conclude that slope is present and that there is a statistical basis for using the linear regression equation to characterize the relationship between the two variables and to predict future performance (Y') from a knowledge of X.

One of the results of the interrelationship between linear correlation and linear regression is that a test of the significance of the product-moment correlation coefficient (r) is equivalent to the test of the significance of the slope of the linear regression line (b). The reason for the equivalency of these two tests is their dependence on the same key quantity, SP_{XY}. Consider the formulas for r and b:

$$r = \frac{SP_{XY}}{\sqrt{(SS_X)(SS_Y)}} \quad \text{and} \quad b = \frac{SP_{XY}}{SS_X}$$

This is why it not necessary to conduct both tests — they test the same underlying null hypothesis. For this reason, then, we will not present a special significance test of the slope; the test of the significance of r presented in Sec. 15.2

is sufficient. We do consider the test of the significance of b in Sec. 15.9, an appendix at the end of this chapter.

15.4 INTERPRETING A CORRELATION COEFFICIENT

By subjecting a correlation coefficient to a test of significance, we determine whether we can conclude that a linear relationship *exists* between two variables. The sign of the correlation coefficient indicates the *direction* of the relationship, and the regression equation provides a formula for *predicting* the Y variable from a knowledge of the X variable. The correlation coefficient also provides us with important additional information that will help us interpret a significant r, namely, the *strength* of the relationship.

Determining the Strength of the Correlation

Researchers often see the presence of a correlation as helping to *explain* some part of the variability of the Y scores. Suppose, for example, that a first-grade teacher observes wide variation in the reading ability of her students and wants to understand why there is such variation. While gazing through her grade book, she notices a relationship between their ages when they entered her class and their reading ability such that the older children seem to be reading better than the younger ones. Discovering this relationship helps to explain why her children are so variable in reading — they differ widely in age. Perhaps there are other factors that might help to further explain these differences, for example, differences in the amount of reading-readiness training the children have received at home and at school, differences in the socioeconomic levels of their families, and so on. Each of these can be correlated with Y (reading ability) and can give her some idea of how strongly any particular X variable is associated with reading ability. Each of these correlations provides the teacher with the potential for understanding why her children differ in reading ability.[5]

---

[5] Researchers pursuing a question such as this would identify a number of X variables and examine their relationship with Y either singly or, more likely, in combination. Correlations between several X variables and a single Y variable are called *multiple correlations*.

We can express the strength of a correlation simply by squari
moment correlation coefficient. The result is the proportior
that is associated with the X variable — that is,

$$\text{strength of the linear association between } X \text{ and } Y = r^2 \qquad (15\text{-}14)$$

Using the correlation we calculated for the relationship between high school
GPA and college GPA, we find

$$r^2 = (.40)^2 = .16$$

What this means is that 16 percent of the variability in students' college grades
is accounted for or explained by the performance of these students in high
school.

This measure of strength is related to measures of *effect size* that we use to
help us interpret the results of an experiment. You will recall that we measured
treatment effect size with a statistic (*estimated omega squared*) that expresses the
variation attributed to the treatment manipulation as a proportion of the total
variation in the experiment (see pp. 178–183). When applied to correlational
research, effect size refers to the covariation of two variables as a proportion
of the variation in either one of them.

We can represent the degree to which one variable explains or predicts the
variability in another variable with two overlapping circles. Each of the circles
in Fig. 15-7 represents the total variability associated with one of the two variables — the circle on the left represents the variability of the X scores, while
the one on the right represents the variability of the Y scores. The *overlapping*,
or shared, area of the two circles represents the strength of the association:
the larger the area of overlap, the greater the strength of the correlation between X and Y. In terms of our example, the two circles in Fig. 15-7 would

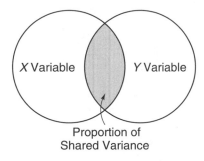

Proportion of
Shared Variance

FIGURE 15-7 *A Venn Diagram Showing r^2 as the Proportion of Variability Shared by Two
Variables (X and Y).*

have an overlap of 16 percent. Two variables that are uncorrelated would be represented by two circles with no area of overlap. This type of representation is called a **Venn diagram** and is a useful way to portray a correlation pictorially.

The three examples of relationships between two variables we considered in Sec. 15.1 represent different degrees of strength. The relationship between scores on a test of quantitative skills and combined midterm scores (see Fig. 15-1, p. 461) produced a correlation of $r = +.52$, which is interpreted to mean that 27 percent — $r^2 = (.52)^2 = .27$ — of the variability of the students on the two midterms is explained by their performance on the quantitative test. The relationship between the two midterm examinations (see Fig. 15-2) produced a correlation of $r = +.91$, which means that 83 percent of the variability observed on the second test is explained or accounted for by the students' performance on the first test. In contrast, the correlation depicted between midterm score and order of completing the examination in Fig. 15-3 is $r = .03$, which implies the absence of a linear relationship between the two variables.

Interpreting Measures of Strength

How should we interpret or characterize this measure of strength? Does the r^2 we observe represent a "weak" relationship in the context of other research or a "strong" one? Jacob Cohen (1988, pp. 79–81) suggests the following classification of this strength measure in correlational research:

A "small" relationship is one in which r^2 is .01 ($r = +.10$ or $-.10$).

A "medium" relationship is one in which r^2 is .09 ($r = +.30$ or $-.30$).

A "large" relationship is one in which r^2 is .25 ($r = +.50$ or $- .50$).[6]

Using Cohen's classification system, we would call the relationship between the quantitative test and the combined midterm scores ($r^2 = .27$) "large" and the relationship between the two midterms ($r^2 = .83$) "extremely large."

---

[6] Given that the maximum value of correlation is $+1.00$ or -1.00, it may surprise you that Cohen defines a "large" relationship as $r = +.50$ or $-.50$. This choice reflects the fact that the relationship between two variables studied in the behavioral sciences is rarely greater than this value.

Residual or Unexplained Variation

We can express the degree to which X and Y are *not* associated by calculating a proportion that we will call **residual variation**.[7] We can obtain this quantity simply by subtracting r^2 from 1:

$$\text{residual variation } = 1 - r^2 \qquad (15\text{-}15)$$

Using our correlation between high school and college GPA's as an example,

$$\text{residual variation } = 1 - (.40)^2 = 1 - .16 = .84$$

What this quantity means is that 84 percent of the variability of the grades of students in college is *unrelated* to their performance in high school. For some, this percentage provides sobering information — there is still a great deal we do not know about why students differ in the grades they receive in college. For others, the same percentage provides a challenge to look for other factors that can improve our understanding of the reasons why some students are successful in college and others are not.

Residual variation is reflected in a scatterplot by the deviation of individual data points from the regression line. This discrepancy between a score (Y) and its vertical distance from the regression line (Y', the estimated score) is referred to as the **error of prediction**. You can see that the errors of prediction are considerably smaller for the relationship plotted in Fig. 15-2 than the ones plotted in Fig. 15-1 or in Fig. 15-6, suggesting a stronger linear relationship in the first example than in the other two.

Factors Influencing the Size of the Correlation Coefficient

A number of factors can influence the size of the correlation coefficient and our inference of the strength of a linear relationship between the two variables. We will consider two of these.

Restriction of the Range of the Variables. You may have noticed that most of the data points from our numerical example are in the upper right corner of the plot (see Fig. 15-6). Why might this occur? One requirement for admittance

---

[7] This proportion is frequently referred to as the *coefficient of nondetermination* or *alienation*.

into college typically is high school GPA; therefore we were not able to include the full range of high school GPA's in our sample, since students with low GPA's have a low likelihood of being admitted into college. Also, you may have noticed that the college GPA data were collected from students after their fourth year in college. Since it is likely that college students with low GPA's may leave school before they reach their fourth year, we also may not have access to the full range of college GPA's.

Not having access to the complete range of possible values in either or both of our variables is what is known as **restriction of range**. What is the implication of restriction of range for correlation? Since restriction of range results in smaller variance in the affected variable, the correlation obtained will generally *underestimate* the actual correlation in the population were there no restriction of range. Ghiselli, Campbell, and Zedeck (1981, pp. 294–306) discuss methods of estimating the unrestricted or population correlation when the researcher believes that restriction of range exists.

Presence of a Curvilinear Relationship. The product-moment correlation coefficient is sensitive to a particular relationship between the two variables — namely, a *linear* one, that is, a relationship that can be expressed by a straight line. Other forms of relationship exist, and a scatterplot can help us to interpret them also. Consider the scatterplot presented in Fig. 15-8. Although the

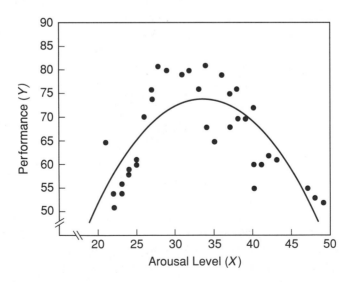

FIGURE 15-8 *An Example of a Curvilinear Relationship without a Significant Linear Correlation. The fictitious data represent an idealized relationship between arousal level (X) and performance on a test (Y).*

correlation between X and Y is near zero ($r = .06$) for these data, we certainly would not want to conclude that a relationship between the two variables does not exist. What we have plotted is an example of a **curvilinear relationship**, in which Y first increases as X increases and then decreases as X increases further. The relationship reflected by the data plotted in Fig. 15-8 is not depicted by a straight line (which is why $r = .06$), but more appropriately by a curve.

Statisticians have developed special indices that are sensitive to the presence of curvilinear relationships between two variables. One such index, the **correlation ratio**, measures the proportion of Y variability that is associated in *any way* with the X variable. This index, also known at **eta squared**, is usually discussed in advanced books on multiple regression and correlation (see, for example, Cohen & Cohen, 1983, Chap. 6; Hays, 1988, pp. 698–701; Keppel & Zedeck, 1989, pp. 50–54; McNemar, 1969, pp. 315–316).

Information Provided by the Means and Standard Deviations

No correlational analysis is complete unless the means and standard deviations of the two variables are examined. The means are particularly useful in the interpretation of the relationship between two response measures obtained at different times. Consider the relationship between the two midterm examinations presented in Sec. 15.1 (see Fig. 15-2, p. 462). The correlation between the two examinations of $r = +.91$ tells us nothing about the average performance of the students on the two tests. That is, students on the average might have scored higher on the second test or lower on the second test — we cannot tell from the correlation coefficient. In actuality, the mean on the first test was slightly higher than the mean on the second (79.20 and 77.32, respectively). Thus, the means provide important information about the relationship between the two variables that is not reflected in the correlation coefficient.

The standard deviations are useful in the interpretation of a nonsignificant, or low, correlation. As noted earlier, the correlation coefficient depends in part on the range or variability of the two variables. An extremely small standard deviation for one of the variables might imply that a restriction of range is having an adverse effect on the size of the correlation coefficient. That is, the obtained correlation will be smaller than the true or population coefficient and, so, will mislead us.

15.5 USING POWER TO ESTIMATE SAMPLE SIZE

You will remember from Chap. 8 that *power* is the probability that a correct decision has been made in rejecting the null hypothesis. When applied to correlation, power is an estimate of the probability we will make a correct decision in rejecting the hypothesis of no linear relationship between two variables. We can use the concept of power to help us estimate the number of subjects we will need to detect a correlation of a particular size.

Estimating a Value of r. The first, and critical, step is to make a reasonable estimate of the value of r we expect to discover in our study. We could determine this value from other research or from theory. If we are unable to be this explicit, we could translate our beliefs about the anticipated r into Cohen's strength categories and give a value of $r^2 = .01$ if we expect to obtain a "small" linear relationship between the two variables, for example, or a value of $r^2 = .09$ or $.25$ if we expect to obtain, respectively, a "medium" or a "large" linear relationship. We will refer to this anticipated value of r as $r_{antic.}$.

Setting a Reasonable Level of Power. After specifying a minimum value of r we expect to detect, we need to establish an acceptable level of power for our proposed correlational study. We suggested in Chap. 8 that power should be set no lower than .70 if we want to stand a reasonable chance of producing a finding that is statistically significant. You will recall that this level of power means that the probability of correctly rejecting the null hypothesis is .70 and of incorrectly retaining the null hypothesis is .30. In our opinion, setting power any lower than .70 is often a waste of resources, because the study is not sufficiently sensitive to detect the findings anticipated by the researcher.

Consulting a Power Chart. Using our acceptable level of power, we consult a power chart or table to obtain a special value, δ (Greek letter *delta*), which we will use in conjunction with our anticipated value of r to estimate the sample size we will need to achieve the level of power we have set. Consider the power chart presented in Table A-10 of Appendix A, which resembles the power charts presented in Tables A-6 and A-8 for use in planning experiments. This chart plots the relationship between δ and power. We begin by locating the power we wish to achieve on the Y axis and moving perpendicularly to the right until we intersect the power function, at which point we read the value of δ found directly underneath on the X axis. This procedure is analogous to the one we followed in using a power chart with experiments (see pp. 213–214). In preparing this chart, we have assumed that researchers will most likely be operating at the 5 percent level of significance. You will need to use other power charts or tables if you plan to set α at some value other than .05.[8]

Solving for Sample Size. As the final step, we solve for sample size simply by entering the information we obtained previously in the following formula:

$$n = \left(\frac{\delta}{r_{antic.}} \right)^2 + 1 \tag{15-16}$$

where $r_{antic.}$ is the estimated value of the correlation coefficient we are proposing to observe with our study and δ is the value we obtain from Table A-10.

An Example. Suppose we expect to find a correlation of $r_{antic.} = +.30$ between the two variables — a "medium" correlation using Cohen's categories; that is, $r_{antic.}^2 = (+.30)^2 = .09$ — and that we want to detect this correlation with a power of .70. From Table A-10, we find $\delta = 2.46$ for this particular power. Substituting this information in Eq. (15-16), we find

$$n = \left(\frac{2.46}{.30} \right)^2 + 1 = (8.20)^2 + 1 = 67.24 + 1 = 68.24$$

What we have discovered is that we will need a sample size of at least $n = 69$ subjects if we want to achieve a 70 percent chance of obtaining a statistically significant correlation of $r = +.30$ at $\alpha = .05$.

15.6 A REPRISE: CAUSATION AND CORRELATION

It seems to be our nature to seek out relationships between variables that permit us to say, "This is the cause of that!" On occasion, the temptation to interpret a significant correlation as somehow imparting causality is almost overwhelming. Two factors seem to lead to this temptation, one having to do with the variables themselves and the other with characteristics of the statistics.

---

[8] You can find power tables relating power and δ for four levels of significance ($\alpha = .10, .05, .02,$ and .01) in a variety of sources (for example, Howell, 1987, p. 582, and Welkowitz, Ewen, & Cohen, 1991, p. 385). Other useful power tables provide estimates of sample size directly (see, for example, Cohen, 1988, pp. 101–102; Friedman, 1982; Kraemer & Thiemann, 1987, pp. 105–112).

Consider the following example. Suppose we were to find that among children a strong negative correlation existed between the number of hours per day spent watching television and reading proficiency. That is, the more time a child spent watching television, the lower was his or her reading proficiency. Most of us would be tempted to impute causation and thus to conclude that watching television *causes* reading ability to be poor.

In this example, one variable, watching television, apparently occurs prior to the development of the other variable, reading proficiency. Learning that the number of hours spent watching television accounted for a substantial proportion of variability in reading proficiency would be of considerable importance. However, neither the strong correlation nor firmly held predispositions justify the inference of causality. Without an experimentally imposed or manipulated variable, we lack control over a potentially large number of other variables also present during the presumed establishment of the relationship between watching television and the development of reading proficiency. In our example, it might be that difficulty in developing the reading skills leads children to compensate by watching television for a large number of hours. In this case, a third variable — difficulty in developing skills — would be responsible for the relationship and not the actual watching of television.

The language used to describe the various statistics associated with correlation also encourages us to make causal inferences from correlational data. When we use r^2, we speak of *variance explained*. It is easy to translate this expression as *producing* or *causing*, even though all that has been established is a statistical *association* between two naturally occurring variables.

However, procedures are available to assist researchers in drawing tentative causal inferences from correlational data. These procedures, which involve the analysis of the patterns taken by a set of correlations, are too complicated to be included in an introductory discussion of correlation.[9] In any case, we must always be skeptical when advertisers, government officials, and even social scientists claim that a certain factor is a *cause* of a particular behavior until we are able to determine the nature of the reported data. If the data come from experiments, causal inference is at least possible. But if the data are correlational, any causal statement is suspect; in such a case, we must look for other sorts of evidence — either more sophisticated correlational procedures or experimental data — with which to substantiate the conclusion.

---

[9]   Three procedures are *cross-lagged panel correlations* (see Neale & Leibert, 1986, pp. 240–245), *path analysis* (for a general presentation, see Kenny, 1979), and *structural modeling* (see Pedhazur, 1982, Chap. 16).

15.7 SUMMARY

This chapter has dealt with the analysis of correlational data, which consist of two (or more) response measures obtained from the same group of individuals; we focused on the correlation of two characteristics, X and Y. The pairs of values for the individual subjects on the X and Y variables are entered into a scatterplot that locates each individual according to his or her values of X and Y. By plotting the data this way, we can easily see the nature of the relationship between the two variables. We concentrated on one type of relationship — the linear one, which expresses the relationship between two variables by means of a straight line. Because correlational research does not involve the active manipulation of independent variables, which is characteristic of experimental research, we are severely limited in our ability to infer a causal link underlying any linear relationship we may establish. Nevertheless, correlational studies provide information about relationships and associations between naturally occurring characteristics of individuals that allow us to study the bases for individual differences, to identify potential causal mechanisms, and to predict success in school or employment on the basis of this information.

Correlation refers to the degree to which two variables *covary*, that is, vary together; linear correlation focuses on a particular form of covariation, one that can be described by a straight line. The statistical index of linear correlation is the product-moment correlation coefficient r, which has a minimum value of 0 in the absence of a linear relationship between X and Y and a maximum value of $+1.0$ or -1.0 when the correlation is perfect. The sign of the correlation coefficient reflects the *direction* of the relationship: a positive sign indicates that as X increases (or decreases), Y changes in the same direction, whereas a negative sign indicates that as X increases (or decreases), Y changes in the opposite direction. The square of the correlation coefficient represents the degree or *strength* of this relationship as a proportion of the total Y variability that is associated with the X variable.

The straight line linking the two variables is the regression line — the line that best fits the data points entered in a scatterplot. The formula for the best-fit straight line, called the *linear regression equation*, is used to predict an individual's score on the Y variable from his or her score on the X variable.

We concluded the chapter with a discussion of the central role of effect size and statistical power in estimating the sample size of any correlational study we may propose. If we fail to include a concern for adequate power during the planning phase of a research project, we may end up with a study in which we will not be able to detect the significance of the sort of correlation we expect to obtain.

15.8 EXERCISES [10]

teacher in high school is interested in the relationship be-
...ght and weight and collects this information from $n = 15$ males in
one of her classes. Arbitrarily, we will designate a student's height (measured
in centimeters) as X and his corresponding weight (measured in kilograms)
as Y. The data are as follows:

Subject	Height (cm) (X)	x^2	Weight (kg) (Y)	y^2	XY
1	150	22500	56	3136	8400
2	154	23716	54	2916	8316
3	168	28224	55	3025	9240
4	162	26244	58	3364	9396
5	152	23104	49	2401	7448
6	155	24025	64	4096	9920
7	178	31684	71	5041	12638
8	163	26569	62	3844	10106
9	173	29929	57	3249	9861
10	179	32041	75	5625	13425
11	174	30276	80	6400	13920
12	165	27225	60	3600	9900
13	182	33124	75	5625	13650
14	183	33489	70	4900	12810
15	160	25600	60	3600	9600
		417741		100888	158630

a. Plot the data in a scatterplot.
b. Calculate the mean and standard deviation for each variable.
c. Calculate SS_X, SS_Y, and SP_{XY}.
d. Calculate the product-moment correlation coefficient, and test its significance.
e. What is the strength of this correlation?
f. Calculate the linear regression equation, and plot the regression line
in the scatterplot.
g. What weight would you predict for a new student in the teacher's class
whose height is 180 cm?

---

[10] Answers to the starred problems are given in Appendix B.

2. An instructor in a statistics course suspected that there would little or no correlation between scores on a take-home test requiring calculating skills and those on an in-class test requiring an understanding of statistical concepts. To test this suspicion, he selected a random sample of his students ($n = 15$) and compared the two sets of test scores using correlational techniques. The data he analyzed were as follows:

Student	Take-Home x	In-Class y	xy
1	73 5329	83 6889	6059
2	68 4624	72 5184	4896
3	66 4356	72 5184	4752
4	56 3136	56 3136	3136
5	66 4356	68 4624	4488
6	78 6084	86 7396	6708
7	57 3249	49 2401	2793
8	56 3136	64 4096	3584
9	64 4096	69 4761	4416
10	56 3136	52 2704	2912
11	61 3721	55 3025	3355
12	51 2601	50 2500	3332
13	68 4624	49 2401	3332
14	79 6241	66 4356	5214
15	59 3481	64 4096	3776
			59421

a. Plot the data in a scatterplot. Do the data support the instructor's contention of little or no relationship between the two types of tests?

b. Calculate the mean and standard deviation for each variable.

c. Calculate the product-moment correlation coefficient, and test its significance.

d. What is the strength of this correlation?

e. Calculate the linear regression equation, and plot the regression line in the scatterplot.

3. As a class assignment, a student determined the number of trials a group of 16 classmates required to learn a list of 11 word pairs. The student noticed that the subjects needed what appeared to be an unusually long time to master the entire list and wondered whether the number correct on the first trial could be used to predict the number of trials necessary to learn the 11 pairs. He obtained the following data:

Subject	Number Correct on Trial 1 (X)	x²	Number of Trials to Learn (Y)	Y²	XY
1	4	16	13	169	52
2	1	1	31	961	31
3	3	9	17	289	51
4	3	9	42	1764	126
5	7	49	18	324	126
6	3	9	12	144	36
7	2	4	17	089	34
8	3	9	33	1089	99
9	7	49	54	2916	378
10	1	1	32	1024	32
11	8	64	5	25	40
12	3	9	33	1089	99
13	8	64	44	1936	352
14	7	49	16	256	112
15	3	9	29	841	87
16	7	49	13	169	91
	70	400	409	13285	1746

a. Plot the data in a scatterplot.

b. Calculate the mean and standard deviation for each variable.

c. Calculate the product-moment correlation coefficient, and test its significance.

d. What is the strength of this correlation?

e. Calculate the linear regression equation, and plot the regression line in the scatterplot.

f. What can the student conclude from this study? Is there any statistical basis for his notion that he could predict how many trials a classmate would need to learn the list from his or her performance on the first trial? Explain.

15.9 APPENDIX: A VARIANCE INTERPRETATION OF LINEAR CORRELATION

This appendix has two purposes. One is to show how the sum of squares of the Y scores can be divided into components in linear regression, as it was in the analysis of variance. The other is to describe a statistical test by which we can determine whether the slope (b) is significantly different from 0. The calculations involved in this test use quantities we have already discussed at some length, namely, SS_X, SS_Y, and SP_{XY}. What is new is the logic of the operations and the ways in which these quantities are combined.

Component Deviations Based on the Y Scores

We use the regression equation to predict Y from a knowledge of X with more accuracy than we can predict it without this knowledge. The question we are trying to answer is "Is this increase in accuracy significant?"

Basic Deviations. The total variation under scrutiny is the variability of the Y scores. We want to determine the portion of this variability that is attributed to linear regression — predictable from a knowledge of a subject's X score — and the portion that is not. Once we make that determination, we can ask whether the portion attributed to linear regression is significantly different from that expected if chance factors alone were operating. As with the analysis of variance, the key factors in this line of reasoning are basic deviations. We are able to express the following important relationship in terms of Y scores:

$$Y_i - \overline{Y} = (Y_i' - \overline{Y}) + (Y_i - Y_i') \qquad (15\text{-}17)$$

In words, the deviation of a Y score from its mean ($Y_i - \overline{Y}$) is made up of two component deviations:

1. The deviation of the predicted Y score from the mean ($Y_i' - \overline{Y}$)
2. The deviation of the actual Y score from the predicted value ($Y - Y_i'$)

The first component represents the degree to which linear regression accounts for variation among the Y scores, while the second component represents the degree to which it does not.

Schematic Representation of the Deviations. The relationship expressed in Eq. (15-17) is represented geometrically in Fig. 15-9. Notice first the location of one of the pairs of scores, X_i, Y_i. This pair is located at the intersection of two lines, one extending from X_i on the X axis (the single vertical line in the figure) and the other extending from Y_i on the Y axis (the uppermost horizontal line in the figure). The point of intersection is labeled (X_i, Y_i) and is indicated by a solid circle. Next, notice the point at which the vertical line drawn from X_i intersects with the regression line. This point is indicated by an unfilled circle.

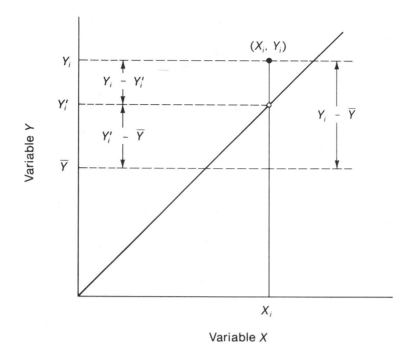

FIGURE 15-9 *A Geometric Representation of Eq. (15-17).*

The dashed line extending from the point of intersection meets the vertical axis at Y_i' — the Y score predicted from X_i and the regression equation. Finally, the bottommost dashed line indicates the position of the mean of the Y scores $(\overline{Y})$ on the vertical axis.

An examination of the vertical distances between the three dashed lines clearly reveals the meaning of Eq. (15-17). Specifically, the distance between the top and bottom dashed lines represents the deviation of Y_i from $\overline{Y}$ and is obviously made up of two components, the distance between the middle and bottom dashed lines $(Y_i' - \overline{Y})$ and the distance between the top and middle dashed lines $(Y_i - Y_i')$.

Computational Formulas for the Component Sums of Squares

The deviations expressed in Eq. (15-17) and depicted schematically in Fig. 15-9 give rise to sums of squares that we can use to evaluate how well a linear function fits the data.

The relationship expressed in Eq. (15-17) for individual Y scores can be extended to sums of squares. That is,

$$SS_Y = SS_{lin.regr.} + SS_{residual} \qquad (15\text{-}18)$$

where SS_Y refers to the sum of the squared deviations of the Y scores from their mean, $SS_{lin.regr.}$ refers to the sum of squares reflecting variability accounted for by linear regression, and $SS_{residual}$ refers to the sum of squares *not* accounted for by linear regression. (This sum of squares reflects the degree of error involved in predicting Y from X on the basis of the regression function.)

The computational formulas for the two component sums of squares are as follows:

$$SS_{lin.regr.} = \frac{(SP_{XY})^2}{SS_X} \qquad (15\text{-}19)$$

$$SS_{residual} = SS_Y - SS_{lin.regr.} \qquad (15\text{-}20)$$

The formulas for the quantities specified in these two equations — namely, SP_{XY}, SS_X, and SS_Y — were presented in Sec. 15.2. We now turn to a numerical example.

A Numerical Example. To illustrate the calculations, we will use the example we presented in Sec. 15.2 in which we correlated high school and college grades. From these earlier calculations (see pp. 469–471), we found

$$SS_X = 3.63, \quad SS_Y = 4.28, \quad \text{and} \quad SP_{XY} = 1.57$$

Substituting first in Eq. (15-19), we determine the sum of squares associated with linear regression:

$$SS_{lin.regr.} = \frac{(1.57)^2}{3.63} = \frac{2.46}{3.63} = .68$$

Finally, we calculate the residual sum of squares by substituting in Eq. (15-20):

$$SS_{residual} = 4.28 - .68 = 3.60$$

These sums of squares are entered in the second column of the analysis of variance summary in Table 15-3.

The Analysis of Variance

We will now use the two component sums of squares to test the hypothesis that the slope of the linear regression line is 0.

TABLE 15-3 *A Summary of the Test for Zero Slope*				
Source	SS	df	MS	F
Linear Regression	.68	1	.68	5.67*
Residual	3.60	30	.12	
Total (Y)	4.28	31		

* $p < .05$.

Degrees of Freedom. The degrees of freedom associated with SS_Y are 1 less than the number of Y scores; that is,

$$df_Y = n - 1 \tag{15-21}$$

Without attempting to explain the reason, we will simply state that 1 degree of freedom is associated with linear regression, or

$$df_{lin.regr.} = 1 \tag{15-22}$$

By subtraction, the degrees of freedom for the residual sum of squares are found to be

$$SS_{residual} = df_Y - df_{lin.regr.}$$
$$= (n - 1) - 1$$
$$= n - 2 \tag{15-23}$$

In the present example,

$$df_Y = 32 - 1 = 31$$
$$df_{lin.regr.} = 1$$
$$df_{residual} = 32 - 2 = 30$$

These numbers are entered in the third column of the summary table (Table 15-3).

Mean Squares. The sums of squares are divided by the appropriate number of degrees of freedom. To illustrate,

$$MS_{lin.regr.} = \frac{SS_{lin.regr.}}{df_{lin.regr.}} \tag{15-24}$$

$$= \frac{.68}{1} = .68$$

$$MS_{residual} = \frac{SS_{residual}}{df_{residual}} \tag{15-25}$$

$$= \frac{3.60}{30} = .12$$

The F Ratio. The statistical hypotheses are as follows:

H_0: the population slope is zero
H_1: the population slope is not zero

The F ratio is

$$F = \frac{MS_{lin.regr.}}{MS_{residual}} \tag{15-26}$$

From the information in Table 15-3, we obtain

$$F = \frac{.68}{.12} = 5.67$$

We evaluate the significance of this F in the usual way. At $\alpha = .05$, and with $df_{num.} = 1$ and $df_{denom.} = 30$, the critical value of F is 4.17. With this information, we can form the decision rule and take the appropriate action. First, we complete the decision rule:

If the obtained value of $F \geq 4.17$, reject the null hypothesis; otherwise retain the null hypothesis.

Since the observed F (5.67) exceeds the critical value, we reject the null hypothesis and conclude that a significant linear relationship is present between high school and college grades.

Standard Error of Estimate. The square root of the residual mean square is called the **standard error of estimate** and is generally included along with the results of a statistical test of slope. Here,

$$\text{standard error of estimate} = \sqrt{MS_{residual}} \tag{15-27}$$

Substituting in Eq. (15-27), we find

$$\text{standard error of estimate} = \sqrt{.12} = .35$$

The standard error of estimate is analogous to the standard deviation of a set of scores. Both statistics are based on the deviation of scores from some reference point, the mean in the case of the standard deviation and the regression line in the case of the standard error of estimate. The standard error of estimate reflects the degree of error involved in predicting a Y score from an X score and a regression equation.

Relating Linear Correlation and Linear Regression

We have pointed out that the product-moment correlation and the slope of the regression line provide interrelated information. Let's examine two of these points of correspondence.

First, we have a correspondence between the two statistical tests. This statistical test is equivalent to the one we described for testing the significance of the correlation coefficient (see pp. 471–472). This is because the slope of the regression line and the correlation coefficient are interrelated mathematically. Thus, either statistical test — evaluation of the significance of r or of b — can be substituted for the other.

Second, we have a correspondence between the two measures of strength of the relationship between the two variables. The measure of strength based on the correlation coefficient is r^2; in Sec. 15.4 we found the strength to be $(.40)^2 = .16$. The measure of strength based on the linear regression line is given by

$$\text{strength of association} = \frac{SS_{lin.regr.}}{SS_Y} \tag{15-28}$$

Theoretically, this index ranges from 0 when no linear relationship exists between X and Y (when $SS_{lin.regr.}$ is equal to 0) to 1.00 when a perfect linear relationship exists (when $SS_{lin.regr.}$ and SS_Y are equal). Using the data from Table 15-3, we find that

$$\text{strength of association} = \frac{.68}{4.28} = .16$$

which is identical to the value we obtained by squaring the correlation coefficient. Expressed in sums of squares, we can understand why researchers often refer to the strength of an association as *explained variability.* The ratio specified by Eq. (15-28) reflects this meaning quite clearly — that is, the proportion of the variability reflected among the 32 college GPA's (the Y scores) that is accounted for by the linear relationship between high school and college grades.

A Second Regression Line

So far we have concerned ourselves with the linear function relating the Y variable to changes in the X variable, and we based our discussion of linear correlation and regression on this particular relationship. For the sake of completeness, we must mention that *two* regression lines are possible with correlational data: a line relating the Y variable to changes in the X variable — which we have emphasized in this chapter — and the reverse, a line relating the X variable to changes in the Y variable. These two regression lines are identical when the correlation between X and Y is perfect and diverge when the correlation is less than perfect.

Some authors introduce the second regression line as an aid to understanding correlation and the relationship between linear regression and correlation.[11] For a variety of reasons, we have chosen not to take this approach. Instead, we simply wish to point out that the two regression lines are possible because relationships based on correlational data are *bidirectional,* which is the primary reason why we find it so difficult to infer from such data a causal linkage between the two variables.

---

[11] One can, for example, calculate r by multiplying the slopes for the two regression lines; that is,

$$r = \sqrt{(b_y)(b_x)}$$

where b_y and b_x are the slopes relating Y to X and X to Y, respectively. We calculate b_x by substituting values we obtained in Sec. 15.2 in an adaptation of Eq. (15-12) as follows: $b_x = SP_{XY}/SS_Y = 1.57/4.28 = .37$. Using the value for b_y we calculated in Sec. 15.3 (.43), we find

$$r = \sqrt{(.43)(.37)} = \sqrt{.16} = .40$$

which is identical to the value we obtained with Eq. (15-5).

Chapter · 16

ADDITIONAL TOPICS

In this last chapter, we consider a number of topics that seem best placed at the end of an introduction to experimental research. We begin with a description of several types of *non*experimental research methods, which contribute substantially to studies in the social and behavioral sciences. We then turn to a brief discussion of the computer and its role in facilitating the analysis of data. Finally, we highlight some areas of study you might consider exploring to widen your understanding of research and statistical analysis.

16.1 NONEXPERIMENTAL RESEARCH

In the experimental approach to research, the administration of the different treatment conditions is under the investigator's direct control; this approach, if implemented properly, permits the investigator to infer causality. A key component of the process of designing experiments is the *random assignment* of subjects to the treatment conditions. We depend on this critical component to neutralize all potential nuisance variables, including individual differences among the subjects, and to justify the use of certain mean squares as error terms in the analysis of variance. The **nonexperimental research** methods we describe in this section, which are in widespread use in the social and behavioral sciences, do not possess this critical feature; as a consequence, they do not permit researchers to infer causation with the certainty that is possible in a properly designed experiment. Nevertheless, along with experimental methods, they contribute to our understanding of psychology. These types of designs are used for exploratory, descriptive, and predictive purposes. We introduce five of the most common types of nonexperimental research designs: correlational designs, quasi-experimental designs, survey research, observational research, and archival research.

Correlational Designs

Correlational research in psychology consists of the search for consistent relationships between two (or more) characteristics of individuals and on occasion to *predict* future behavior on the basis of these relationships. We discussed the simplest form of correlational research — one based on the linear relationship between two variables — in Chap. 15. In this section, we mention some additional correlational procedures to introduce you to the range of uses of correlation.

Special Features of the Data. In all the examples of correlation we have considered in Chap. 15, the X and Y variables have been *continuous* in nature — that is, they could take on any value within a range of values and were measured in what are assumed to be equal units. Occasionally, correlational data do not have this form, but reflect the use of less precise scales. For example, two variables can take the form of *ranks*, each subject in the sample being given a rank indicating his or her relative position on the two variables. This procedure is often employed when the characteristics to be ranked are complex and difficult to measure — for example, leadership skills of executives or the creativity of student art work. Similarly, in the study of social dominance in animals, animals are usually ranked in order of their dominance over those at lower ranks, and researchers frequently assess the dominance rankings under different circumstances, attempting to determine the stability of these rankings in different social situations. Under both of these circumstances, researchers usually compute a **rank-order correlation coefficient**.[1]

In fields of psychological testing or in public-opinion surveys, one of the variables might be *continuous* in nature — say, grade-point average or annual income — while the other is *dichotomous* (having only two values, such as pass or fail, agree or disagree, yes or no). Investigators can analyze data of this sort by calculating a **point-biserial correlation coefficient**, which approximates what *r* would be if *both* distributions were continuous. When both variables are dichotomous in nature, a **phi coefficient** is appropriate.

Edwards (1984, Chap. 7) and Ghiselli, Campbell, and Zedeck (1981, pp. 115–122) offer a useful presentation and discussion of these three alternative measures of correlation. Kirk (1990, p. 190) provides a table in which he summarizes the most common correlation coefficients and gives page references to extended treatments of these indices in other statistics books.

Partial Correlation. In an experiment, we can isolate the effect of a variable of interest to study its effect clearly. We are not able to achieve that same control in correlational designs, but still, we might want to sharpen our understanding of the relationship between two variables. There are instances in which a third variable is known to be associated with the two variables of primary interest and a researcher would like to somehow isolate the effect of the third variable in the analysis. That is, we might be interested in the relationship between two variables after we have *accounted for* or *controlled for* the effect of a third variable by using a procedure called **partial correlation**. Suppose, in our example in Chap. 15 of a correlation between a measure of quantitative skills and the combined scores on two midterms, we became interested in this relationship *independent* of the number of previous courses a student had taken in mathematics. We could collect from each student's record his or her previous formal training in mathematics, and enter that information into an analysis using partial correlation, thereby removing its effect on the resulting correlation between quantitative skills and midterm performance. You will recognize this as a means of gaining some control over variables in a correlational design.

---

[1] The procedure is often referred to as the *Spearman rank-order correlation coefficient*. Data expressed as ranks can also be used in the calculation of the product-moment correlation coefficient, although this approach does involve more computational effort than use of the rank-order correlation.

Multiple Correlation.   The product-moment correlation coefficient and the linear regression equation address the relationship between two variables (X and Y). But what if you wanted to test how well one variable might be predicted from more than one variable? Let's return to our example of high school and college grades. You know from the analysis we conducted in Sec. 15.2 that there is a significant relationship between high school and college grades ($r = .40$). As you also know, the square of this correlation ($r^2 = .16$) means that 16 percent of the variability in college GPA can be accounted for by differences in high school GPA. By necessity this means that 84 percent of the variability in college performance remains unexplained or unpredicted. How could we account for more of the variability in college GPA?

The answer to this question is to use more than one variable to correlate with or to predict college GPA. This is one of the purposes of **multiple correlation and regression**. For example, besides high school GPA, we might want to include a measure of the person's aptitude, such as scores on the Scholastic Aptitude Test (SAT), or perhaps a measure of a person's beliefs about the importance of a college education, or a score measuring the judged quality of the high school education. Multiple regression/correlation (known as *MRC*) looks at the overall relationship between two or more X (or predictor) variables and one Y (or criterion) variable.

The computational effort involved in MRC usually requires computer programs for carrying out the analyses. Several sources can be drawn upon for a discussion and explanation of the procedures, including Edwards (1985), Keppel and Zedeck (1989), Pedhazur (1982), and Stevens (1986).

Factor Analysis.   An extremely useful multiple-correlational technique is **factor analysis**. In this type of correlational research, an investigator starts by examining the performance of a group of subjects on a large number of tests or other observational measures. By means of some fairly complicated procedures, he or she then segregates the sets of scores to form distinctive patterns, or *factors*, of scores. A **factor** in this case consists of a set of scores on two or more tests that are highly correlated among themselves but poorly correlated with other tests or measures. With this procedure, the results of a mammoth testing program — say, a battery of 50 tests given to a large sample of individuals — can be summarized in terms of a smaller, more manageable number of factors.[2] These

---

[2] These techniques are not limited to correlational research. An example of how factor analysis can be used in a topic traditionally thought of as uniquely the domain of *experiments* is found in a paper by Underwood, Boruch, and Malmi (1978).

factors might then be used in a multiple regression equation to predict future behavior or to form hypothetical constructs concerning the nature of the intellect or personality.[3]

Quasi-Experimental Designs

What if you wanted to study the effects of different reading programs on the verbal skills of children? How would you conduct this study? Ideally, you would randomly assign schoolchildren to receive different reading programs and then measure their verbal skills after they had completed their training. However, because children have already been assigned to classrooms, it would probably be unwise to have children in the same class receive different reading programs — a child would see his or her classmates being treated differently, possibly influencing his or her participation. Because of this and other concerns, you might choose a different approach and assign *entire classes* of children to receive different reading programs.

This is an example of **quasi-experimental research** — experimental designs that do not employ random assignment to conditions, but instead use naturally formed or preexisting groups. Quasi-experiments are utilized when an experimenter may not wish or be able (either realistically or ethically) to randomly assign subjects to conditions.

Compared with "true" experiments, quasi-experiments have a number of strengths and weaknesses. One criticism of experiments, resulting from the high degree of control placed upon the experimental setting, is that they do not resemble the real world. Quasi-experiments, conducted outside of the laboratory, often possess a great deal of realism. The findings of quasi-experiments may therefore be directly applicable to solving practical problems.

Unfortunately, the absence of random assignment introduces the possibility that the groups may not be equivalent at the beginning of the study, mitigating our ability to make causal inferences. In the example comparing reading programs, for instance, it is unlikely that the actual classes in the school would have been created by random assignment, but rather by some form of grouping based on characteristics of the children such as reading readiness or academic ability. Consequently, the classes will not be equated on these characteristics

---

[3] Neale and Liebert (1986, pp. 75–78) present a nontechnical discussion of multiple correlation and factor analysis. Kerlinger (1986, Chap. 35) offers a more demanding but still comprehensible discussion of these various procedures.

before the different reading programs are introduced. If these preexisting differences are related to the dependent variable (verbal skills), we may be unable to disentangle these differences from any differential effects related to the different programs.

Another example of quasi-experimentation was conducted by one of the authors of this textbook (Tokunaga, 1985). He was interested in studying the effects of bereavement upon death-related fears and attitudes; more specifically, he wished to test the research hypothesis that as one moves through the stages of bereavement (denial, depression, recovery) after experiencing the death of a close friend, one's own fears of death and dying change. He wished to measure over a 12-month period the "fear of death and dying" of people who had experienced such a loss. However, since it may be possible that other external events might occur during this period that would also affect their scores, he wished to create a control group that would be measured over the same time period and provide information about any changes in the dependent variable that take place during the 12-month period in the absence of the death of a close friend. Understandably, in this situation it was not possible to randomly assign people to the "bereaved" group or the "control" group. Instead, he formed a control group that was matched with the bereaved group on various relevant characteristics such as age, educational level, and number of close friends.

Even when groups are matched on known relevant characteristics, there is always the possibility that differences on other characteristics, which were not matched or controlled, may be present nevertheless. In spite of these and other problems, quasi-experiments still occupy an important place in social science research.[4]

Survey Research

Whether they be "man on the street" interviews, "vote by calling this telephone number," or carefully constructed paper-and-pencil measures, questionnaires and surveys are an integral part of our society. The purpose of **survey research** methods is to obtain information directly from a group of people regarding their thoughts, opinions, beliefs, and attitudes, using this information to represent or estimate the views and beliefs of some larger population.

---

[4] See Campbell and Stanley (1963, 1966) and Cook and Campbell (1979) for a detailed discussion of quasi-experimental designs.

Because the experimenter is not directly manipulating any variables, survey research is not conducted in order to make causal inferences. Rather, the main purpose is to describe a phenomenon, or perhaps to predict future behavior. For example, political pollsters attempt to predict how people will vote in the next election by asking a sample of voters for their preferences.

There are various ways to conduct survey research. For example, surveys may be conducted by the use of interviews, either face to face or by telephone. These interviews, in turn, may also vary in their degree of structure, ranging from closed-ended questions requiring a simple yes or no response to more open-ended questions with no preset "right" or "wrong" answers. Surveys may also be in the form of paper-and-pencil questionnaires, with the data collected either by mail or in person.

Each of these methods — interview versus survey, open-ended versus closed ended — has its strengths and weaknesses. For example, unlike surveys, interviews allow the interviewer to ask follow-up questions and answer any questions the interviewee may have; however, they are also much more time-consuming and expensive to administer. Similarly, open-ended questions provide the respondents the opportunity to elaborate on their feelings and beliefs, yet because of their unstandardized nature they are much more difficult to analyze than closed-ended questions. Judd, Smith, and Kidder (1991) provide a detailed discussion of critical issues in survey research.

Observational Research

We are all constantly observing the world around us. We watch other people, we listen to what they say, and on the basis of these observations we try to infer their feelings, motivations, beliefs, and intentions. Many psychologists engage in **observational research** methods, which differ from everyday observations in that such methods involve the systematic and objective observation of naturally occurring events, with careful record keeping. The purpose of observational research is to study these types of events with little, if any, intervention on the part of the researcher. These methods are thus the opposite of experimental research, which involves experimental control and random assignment to conditions.

Observational research, as you might expect, is conducted not for the purpose of testing causal relationships, but rather to explore or describe a phenomenon. Observational research is often used to study phenomena the researcher either cannot or should not deliberately manipulate. For example, you might be interested in studying aggressive behavior in children; although you cannot ethically force children to hit each other, you may be able to record acts of aggression by observing school playgrounds during recess.

In conducting observational research, researchers must choose whether to directly interact with the subjects being observed; this is the difference between **naturalistic** and **participant observation**. The choice of method is often the pragmatic function of whether one may make the observation without making one's presence known. For example, Rubin (1970) was interested in studying the hypothesis that the more two people are in love with one another, the more openly they communicate. He defined "openness of communication" as the amount of eye contact between couples and measured it in his laboratory by observing couples who reported being in love with each other to varying degrees. By using a one-way mirror, he was able to observe them without their being aware of his presence (his hypothesis was supported, by the way).

There are times when the researcher may not have the luxury of remaining invisible to the person being observed, particularly when the research moves from the laboratory to the outside world. One of the most well-known examples of participant observation in social psychology was provided by Festinger, Riecken, and Schachter (1956). Interested in group dynamics, they wished to study a group that reported receiving a message from aliens in outer space predicting a cataclysmic flood extending from the Arctic Circle to the Gulf of Mexico. Because the group consisted of only 12 members, the researchers could not observe them without first becoming active members in the group. They found that when the predicted flood did not occur, group cohesion surprisingly increased rather than decreased.

Participant observation has both advantages and disadvantages when compared with naturalistic observation. Besides lack of choice, the researcher may prefer to participate in order to actually create the event he or she wishes to study; this is efficient when the event occurs rarely or sporadically. However, one disadvantage of participant observation is that in interacting with the group members, the researcher might change the phenomenon under study. For example, in order for Festinger and his associates to become members of the group, they made up stories of mystical experiences. However, when they did so, members of the group actually thought one of the researchers was an alien!

Archival Research

From the day we are born to the day we die, records of our lives accumulate, seemingly without end. Birth certificates, school records, doctors' records, employment records, marriage licenses, and death certificates — these documents mark important events in one's life. Although psychology may indeed be the science of human behavior, it is not always necessary to directly observe behavior in order to study it. Rather than use explicit behavior, **archival research** methods utilize public records (or archives) as the unit of analysis. Archives are records or documents of the activities of individuals, groups, or organizations. The goal of archival research is to study people by examining recorded information they generate or have generated about them.

In one example of archival research, Phillips (1977) wanted to study the effects of a well-publicized suicide on people's behavior; more specifically, he wished to examine the existence of "copycat" suicides. He hypothesized that a substantial number of deaths due to motor vehicle accidents were actually the result of people's using their cars to commit suicide. In order to study this, he looked at department of motor vehicle records and recorded the number of motor vehicle fatalities occurring over a number of days after a well-publicized suicide. In doing so, he found that the number of fatalities increased significantly, compared with periods without suicides, actually peaking on the third day after the suicide.

Like observational research, archival research is conducted for the purposes of description and exploration, rather than causal relationships. There is no random assignment to conditions or other manipulation — in fact, the experimenter often has absolutely no interaction with the subjects of the study. This is one advantage of archival research — it is *unobtrusive* and *nonreactive* in the sense that the subjects do not come into contact with the researcher. Archival research is also often used to study rare events or phenomena, as well as for studying people whom the experimenter may not have access to. Like observational research, archival research provides the opportunity to study naturally occurring events.

A more pragmatic reason for conducting archival research is the relative ease, efficiency, and economy of collecting data. The researcher does not have to pay or recruit people to participate in the study. Also, information in archives is often based on entire populations over an extended period of time rather than on information obtained from samples at single points in time. Traffic fatality statistics, for example, may be available for entire states or even countries over a 10- or 20-year period.

However, besides the inability to make causal inferences, there are other disadvantages of archival research. The first is what is known as **selective deposit** — biases in the production of the archive. For example, Tetlock (1981) performed a content analysis of the speeches of presidential candidates in terms of what he called "cognitive complexity." One concern in conducting the study was that the speeches were published in newspapers — reporters and editors often do not print speeches verbatim, but choose to print only what they feel is important or noteworthy. A second problem is what is known as **selective**

survival — biases in what archives are available for analysis. Perhaps the most famous example of selective survival was the 18 minutes of tape that somehow disappeared from former President Richard Nixon's recordings of meetings and conversations in the White House. For an excellent discussion of the use of unobtrusive research designs, the student is referred to Webb, Campbell, Schwartz, Sechrest, and Grove (1981).

Summary

The purpose of this section was to provide a brief introduction to different methods of research design. There are several things to note from this discussion. The first is that the particular research design you choose to employ is a function of several factors. Perhaps the most important influence is your research hypothesis, that is, the question you are trying to answer. Whether your goal is to make causal inferences about the relationship between variables or to describe some phenomenon in more depth will play a critical role in determining the most appropriate way of collecting your data. A more pragmatic issue concerns your sample — what is the population about which you hope to make inferences? What degree of access do you have to a representative sample of this population? For example, what if you wished to analyze how people make decisions under pressure? Comparing the decision-making processes of United States senators is much more problematic than studying the processes of college-age males.

The other important thing to notice from reading the previous section is something that wasn't even there. There was no discussion of statistics. Statistics and research design, although obviously related, are in fact separate and independent. Your research hypothesis will influence how you choose to measure or operationalize your variables. How you choose to operationalize your variables, in turn, will influence how you analyze the data.

16.2 USING THE COMPUTER

In this book, we have presented a number of different experimental designs, starting with the single-factor between-subjects design and ending with the within-subjects factorial design. As you have seen, the complexity of the experimental design greatly affects the type and number of questions we can ask from a set of experimental data. But, as you have no doubt observed, increasing the complexity of the research design also leads to more elaborate statistical analyses.

As discussed in Chap. 2, we have chosen to focus on how to analyze experimental designs using hand calculations rather than through the use of computers. The most important reason is that we have tried to emphasize the underlying logic of the basic analyses: what variance is; how variance in a dependent variable may be accounted for by your independent variable (or variables); what the F is, and how it is calculated; and computing planned comparisons based on your research hypotheses and knowledge of theory. Through such an intimate familiarity with the data and procedures, you gain an appreciation of how the components of a statistical analysis are related. We strongly believe that learning how to use the computer to conduct statistical analyses interferes with the development of these critical conceptual abilities, and that students have a very difficult time trying to learn statistics and statistical software simultaneously.

We feel that the real danger of relying on the computer before the meaning and logic of the analyses are fully appreciated and understood by students is a potential loss of creativity in tailoring the statistical procedures to suit their specific research needs and interests. All too often, students consider the results of standard statistical analyses, built into most software programs, as the completion of their data analysis, when in fact, they may represent only the *beginning*, to be followed by the statistical analysis of a number of more focused and analytical questions.

Choosing a Statistical Software Package

Like most computer software, the main function of statistical software packages is to manage, analyze, and display information. There are many different statistical software packages on the market; the comprehensive computer programs leased by most colleges and universities and widely used by students and faculty are SPSS (the Statistical Package for the Social Sciences), BMDP (the Biomedical Data Programs), and SAS (Statistical Analysis System). Generally, you may access these programs from the mainframe computer — by means of either a terminal connected directly to the mainframe computer or a modem intervening between your personal computer and a telephone line connected to the mainframe computer. Because it is the most widely accepted and perhaps easiest to learn, we will focus on SPSS. In learning SPSS, we strongly recommend that you obtain a copy of the SPSS manual; also, *The SPSS Guide to Data Analysis for SPSS* (Norusis, 1990) is an easy-to-read introduction and tutorial that many of our students find useful.

Instructors are frequently asked to recommend statistical software for use by their students and colleagues. The answer to this question depends upon the type of computer (IBM-compatible computer or Apple/Macintosh) owned by the student, his or her computational needs, and the student's budget. Although there are versions of SPSS, BMDP, and SAS available to use with a personal computer, they are extremely expensive. One inexpensive, yet flexible, program we recommend is called MYSTAT.[5] You should certainly consult with your own instructor, who may have definite recommendations (or at least strong personal preferences). You should also seek the advice of classmates who already use the computer for statistical analyses and may be willing to tutor you.

An Overview of the SPSS Statistical Program

The SPSS program is a comprehensive, multipurpose statistical software program that is made up of a large number of separate computational procedures. The user selects from among these procedures by specifying a sequence of explicit *commands* and *subcommands* — each identified by a special word or series of words — that essentially provides the SPSS program with the following information: what procedures to perform, what data to perform them on, when to perform these procedures, and how to report the results of these procedures.

As in many statistical software packages, we will need to create at least one *file* that contains the series of commands we want SPSS to execute, called a *command file*. The data on which these commands will act may be included with the command file — this is our preference — or may be contained in a separate *data file*. We will present an example of a command file in a moment. We can create these files with a word processor and send them to the mainframe computer via a modem, to be stored in some form of "permanent" computer memory that we can summon or access when we enter the mainframe system. Alternatively, we can create these files within the mainframe system itself, using an *editor* devised to facilitate the construction of these files.

Once the files are complete, we then access the SPSS program and ask it to follow the series of instructions specified in our command file. We can

---

[5] The current price of MYSTAT is $5. You can obtain a copy of this program by writing to SYSTAT, Inc., 1800 Sherman Avenue, Evanston, IL 60201, or by contacting the company by telephone at its current number, (312) 864-5670. This program, which is available in IBM-compatible and Macintosh versions, can be used to calculate a variety of statistical procedures, including standard analyses of completely randomized single-factor and two-factor designs (the analyses we cover in Chaps. 4–5 and Chap. 9, respectively).

TABLE 16-1 *Number of Problems Solved (Data from Table 5-1)*		
Factor *A* (Type of Reinforcement)		
Praise a_1	Criticism a_2	Silence a_3
7	9	2
8	4	7
6	6	5
10	9	3
7	8	5

instruct SPSS either to send results (or *output*) of the different commands to the computer screen, or to a printer to produce "hard copy," or a permanent record, of the statistical analysis. This record lists the different commands we included in the command file in the order they were processed by SPSS. Each set of commands is immediately followed by a listing of the outcome of these commands — that is, the results of the different analyses we asked SPSS to perform. We will present examples of output generated by various SPSS commands so that you can see how the results of different statistical analyses are presented. An actual SPSS output contains considerably more information spread over an annoyingly large number of pages. To conserve space, we present an edited version of this output that focuses on those portions of the printout that are of direct concern to us.

Creating a Command File

To provide a brief introduction to SPSS, we will present a command file we created to analyze the data based on the single-factor between-subjects example introduced in Chap. 5. This experiment compared the effects of three different types of reinforcement (praise, criticism, and silence) on children's performance on simple reasoning problems. A total of 15 children ($n = 5$) were randomly assigned to the $a = 3$ treatment conditions. The data, originally presented in Table 5-1 (p. 122), are presented again in Table 16-1.

A copy of an SPSS command file designed to analyze this experiment is shown in Table 16-2. We comment briefly on the function of each command

---

TABLE 16-2 *SPSS Command File for the Overall Analysis of a Completely Randomized Single-Factor Experiment*

TITLE "EFFECTS OF VERBAL REINFORCEMENT: OVERALL ANOVA"

DATA LIST FREE /   ID   COND   PROBS

VARIABLE LABELS   COND   "REINFORCEMENT CONDITIONS"/
                  PROBS   "NO. PROBLEMS SOLVED"

VALUE LABELS   COND 1 "PRAISE" 2 "CRITICISM" 3 "SILENCE"

BEGIN DATA

01	1	7
02	1	8
03	1	6
04	1	10
05	1	7
06	2	9
07	2	4
08	2	6
09	2	9
10	2	8
11	3	2
12	3	7
13	3	5
14	3	3
15	3	5

END DATA

LIST VARIABLES = COND   PROBS

MEANS PROBS BY COND

MANOVA PROBS BY COND (1, 3)/
    DESIGN = COND/

FINISH

---

so you will understand what these somewhat cryptic statements are instructing SPSS to do with the data. We start with the *TITLE* statement, which serves as a reminder of such important details as the type of design, the data set, and the nature of the analysis. The title will be printed on each page of the printout.

Specifying Variables and Descriptive Labels.   The statement *DATA LIST FREE* provides the names of the variables in the data set and indicates how the data set will be organized. If you examine the data set that begins immediately below the statement *BEGIN DATA*, you will see that we have chosen to arrange the data in three columns of numbers:

1. The first column consists of an identification number (1 through 15) assigned to each subject in the data set.
2. The second column identifies the treatment condition each subject received (1 = praise, 2 = criticism, and 3 = silence).
3. The third column contains the actual data (or *Y* scores) — that is, the number of problems solved by each of the children.

There are other ways we can enter a data set. The method we illustrate is called *FREE*.[6] We need to explain this arrangement of the data set to the SPSS program, which we accomplish with the information entered after the "/" that follows *DATA LIST FREE*. Each column of numbers is given a distinctive label — *ID* for identification numbers, *COND* for the treatment conditions, and *PROBS* for the number of problems solved.

The next two statements are optional with SPSS, but we always include them to remind us of what the variables, as well as the values of those variables, represent. So far we have designated the two variables making up our data set *COND* and *PROBS*. The statement *VARIABLE LABELS* gives more meaningful names to these two abbreviations, that is, *reinforcement conditions* for *COND* and *no. problems solved* for *PROBS*. The statement *VALUE LABELS* identifies the specific treatment conditions for the independent variable, that is, 1 = praise, 2 = criticism, and 3 = silence.

The Data Set. The next part of the command file contains the actual data set, arranged as we specified in the statement *DATA LIST FREE*. The data set begins with the statement *BEGIN DATA* and ends with the statement *END DATA*. You would want to proofread this listing very carefully for any errors. A second way of checking for errors is to include the command *LIST VARIABLES* that provides for each subject a list of his or her values on the requested variables.[7]

---

[6] The *FREE* refers to a specific way of organizing the columns: in this case, each line will contain three numbers, the identification number followed by the treatment condition and the *Y* score; the only requirement is that each number must be separated by at least one space — that is, the exact location of the numbers on the line does not matter. Another method, called *FIXED*, specifies exact locations for the different columns of numbers; this method is generally used with large data sets and data sets that contain some missing scores.

TABLE 16-3	Edited Listing of the Data Set Produced with the LIST VARIABLES Command

COND	PROBS
1.00	7.00
1.00	8.00
1.00	6.00
1.00	10.00
1.00	7.00
2.00	9.00
2.00	4.00
2.00	6.00
2.00	9.00
2.00	8.00
3.00	2.00
3.00	7.00
3.00	5.00
3.00	3.00
3.00	5.00

Number of cases read: 15   Number of cases listed: 15

Table 16-3 presents a listing of what SPSS will produce after having processed this command.

Calculating the Means and Standard Deviations. For our first statistical procedure (the *MEANS* command), we have specified the calculation of the means and standard deviations. The word *BY* separates the dependent variable (on its left) from the independent variable (on its right). The means and standard deviations on the dependent variable will be calculated first for the entire set of scores and then separately for each of the three treatment conditions. An edited listing of SPSS output is presented in Table 16-4.

Performing the Omnibus Analysis of Variance. The overall analysis of variance is conducted by issuing the command *MANOVA*, which stands for *multivariate analysis of variance*.[8] This command also uses *BY* to separate the dependent

---

[7] We indicated "= COND PROBS," which requests that only the treatment conditions and the *Y* scores be included in the listing. If we wanted to list all the information in the data set, we would use the command

LIST VARIABLES = ALL

[8] Although the alternative SPSS command *ANOVA* will also perform the analyses we describe in this section, we use the *MANOVA* command because of its ability to analyze complex designs,

---

TABLE 16-4 *Edited Listing of the Means and Standard Deviations Produced with the MEANS Command*

DESCRIPTION OF SUBPOPULATIONS

| | | Criterion Variable | PROBS | NO. PROBLEMS SOLVED | | |
| | | Broken Down by | COND | REINFORCEMENT CONDITIONS | | |

Variable	Value	Label	Mean	Std Dev	Cases
For Entire Population			6.4000	2.2928	15
COND	1.00	PRAISE	7.6000	1.5166	5
COND	2.00	CRITICISM	7.2000	2.1679	5
COND	3.00	SILENCE	4.4000	1.9494	5

Total Cases = 15

---

variable from the independent variable as we saw in the *MEANS* command. In addition, we need to specify the minimum and maximum values of the levels of the independent variable involved in this analysis — in this case, the levels 1 through 3. If there were five levels, the command would be

MANOVA PROBS BY COND $(1, 5)$

The next command, *DESIGN = COND*, is required to initiate the actual statistical analysis. The final command, *FINISH*, terminates the involvement with SPSS. The results of this analysis are presented in Table 16-5.[9] As you can see from the output, the obtained F of 4.22 is identical to that obtained by hand calculations in Chap. 5 (Table 5-2, p. 126). Furthermore, SPSS reports an *exact probability* for this F, or one more extreme, of .041. When reported this way, we do not need to consult an F table, but instead use the following decision rule to evaluate the outcome of the analysis:

If the exact probability of the observed $F \leq .05$, reject the null hypothesis; otherwise, retain it.

---

including factorial experiments and designs that include within-subjects factors (repeated measures).

[9] Please disregard the term *UNIQUE sums of squares*, which is not relevant for the sorts of designs we consider in this book.

TABLE 16-5 *Edited Listing of the Analysis of Variance Produced with the MANOVA Command*

---

* * * * * * A N A L Y S I S O F V A R I A N C E -- DESIGN 1 * * * * * *

Tests of Significance for PROBS using UNIQUE sums of squares

Source of Variation	SS	DF	MS	F	Sig of F
WITHIN CELLS	43.20	12	3.60		
COND	30.40	2	15.20	4.22	.041

Because .041 is less than $\alpha = .05$, we reject the null hypothesis and conclude that the mean numbers of correct solutions are not equal for the three treatment conditions.

Conducting Single-*df* Comparisons

In most cases, we will want to examine a number of comparisons involving specific means. When we considered the detailed analysis of these results in Chap. 6, we considered first the three pairwise comparisons: praise versus silence, criticism versus silence, and praise versus criticism; later, we added a complex comparison between silence and the combined groups receiving some form of verbal reinforcement (praise or criticism). To conduct the same four analyses with SPSS, we simply insert a set of additional commands following the *MANOVA* command included in the original command file presented in Table 16-2. Let's see how we obtain this information from SPSS.

The new command file is presented in Table 16-6. As you can see, this file is an exact duplication of the original command file except for the addition of the new commands, which we have highlighted in the table. The set of commands that produce the analysis of single-*df* comparisons begins with *CONTRAST(COND)*, the *COND* indicating that the contrasts will involve the independent variable. The word *SPECIAL* indicates that we will be defining specific comparisons we want SPSS to make. What follow are three sets of numbers. The first set of numbers consists of three 1's (corresponding to the number of levels of our independent variable) and must be included for the analysis to work properly. The next two rows of numbers consist of sets of coefficients that tell SPSS to make the following comparisons: praise versus silence $(1, 0, -1)$ and criticism versus silence $(0, 1, -1)$. The number of comparisons specified in a *CONTRAST* subcommand must be 1 less than the number of treatment conditions (that is, $df_A = a - 1$), which means that only two of the four comparisons we mentioned earlier may be included in this first set. We

TABLE 16-6 *SPSS Command File for the Single-df Comparisons*

TITLE "EFFECTS OF VERBAL REINFORCEMENT: OVERALL ANOVA"

DATA LIST FREE /   ID   COND   PROBS

VARIABLE LABELS   COND   "REINFORCEMENT CONDITIONS"/
                  PROBS   "NO. PROBLEMS SOLVED"

VALUE LABELS   COND   1 "PRAISE"   2 "CRITICISM"   3 "SILENCE"

BEGIN DATA

01	1	7
02	1	8
03	1	6
04	1	10
05	1	7
06	2	9
07	2	4
08	2	6
09	2	9
10	2	8
11	3	2
12	3	7
13	3	5
14	3	3
15	3	5

END DATA

LIST VARIABLES = COND   PROBS

MEANS PROBS BY COND

MANOVA PROBS BY COND $(1, 3)$/
   DESIGN = COND/

```
CONTRAST(COND) = SPECIAL ( 1      1      1
                           1      0     -1
                           0      1     -1)/
PARTITION(COND) = (1,1)/
DESIGN = COND(1), COND(2)/

CONTRAST(COND) = SPECIAL ( 1      1      1
                           1     -1      0
                           1      1     -2)/
PARTITION(COND) = (1,1)/
DESIGN = COND(1), COND(2)/
```

FINISH

conclude this part of the command file with two additional subcommands, *PARTITION* and *DESIGN*, which are needed to instruct SPSS how to divide the data and to test these subdivisions. We have indicated that there will be two subdivisions:

$$\text{PARTITION(COND)} = (1, 1)$$

and that each one will be tested for significance:

$$\text{DESIGN} = \text{COND}(1), \text{COND}(2)$$

We are interested in two additional comparisons: praise versus criticism (1, −1, 0) and silence versus combined reinforcement (1, 1, −2). We include these in a second CONTRAST subcommand, as indicated in Table 16-6.

The outcome of these analyses is presented in Table 16-7. The results of the two different *CONTRAST* subcommands are reported as *DESIGN 2* and *DE-SIGN 3*, respectively.[10] Comparing the results of the three pairwise comparisons

---

TABLE 16-7 *Edited Listing of the Analysis of Single-df Comparisons*

******A N A L Y S I S   O F   V A R I A N C E -- DESIGN 2 ******

Tests of Significance for PROBS using UNIQUE sums of squares

Source of Variation	SS	DF	MS	F	Sig of F
WITHIN CELLS	43.20	12	3.60		
COND(1)	25.60	1	25.60	7.11	.021
COND(2)	19.60	1	19.60	5.44	.038

******A N A L Y S I S   O F   V A R I A N C E -- DESIGN 3 ******

Tests of Significance for PROBS using UNIQUE sums of squares

Source of Variation	SS	DF	MS	F	Sig of F
WITHIN CELLS	43.20	12	3.60		
COND(1)	.40	1	.40	.11	.745
COND(2)	30.00	1	30.00	8.33	.014

---

[10] SPSS designates each analysis included within the original *MANOVA* command as a separate *DESIGN*, and numbers the analyses consecutively. For this demonstration, we inserted these

with those in Table 6-3, we can see that the three $F_{A\,comp.}$'s (7.11, 5.44, and .11) are the same in both tables. If we compare the results for the complex comparison with the analysis reported in Chap. 6 (see pp. 151–154), we again find the same $F_{A\,comp.}$ of 8.33.

Comment

We do not expect to convince you with this brief illustration that you should immediately replace your humble electronic calculator with a more complicated device that can gain access to a mainframe computer and the SPSS statistical program. SPSS is a complicated program that requires a great deal of effort to reach a point of mastery where you can easily create command files to produce analyses on the first try without error. The advantage of a comprehensive program such as SPSS is the ease with which one can analyze large data sets and data generated from complicated experiments, particularly designs that include within-subjects factors. But you must be willing to spend many hours in learning the meaning and use of the words and phrases that play a key role in extracting specific analyses from the program. You need to decide whether the time required to become competent in using SPSS to analyze a particular data set — your independent study or your honors thesis, for example — is less than the time required to perform the same analyses with a statistical calculator. If you have the luxury of far-distant deadlines, you may find this investment of time worthwhile, especially if you plan to embark upon a research career in which familiarity with SPSS or a similar program is either assumed or highly desirable.[12] One final advantage of an acceptable software program is that once the data are entered accurately, arithmetic and transcription errors are eliminated.

---

two *CONTRAST* subcommands after *DESIGN = COND* in Table 16-6. Consequently, SPSS reports the results of the first set of comparisons as *DESIGN 2* and the second set of comparisons as *DESIGN 3*.

[12] Several books are available that provide useful examples of SPSS command files and computer outputs for a variety of experimental designs (see, for example, Collyer & Enns, 1987; Levine, 1991; Rowland, Arkkelin, & Crisler, 1991; Stevens, 1990; West, 1991).

16.3 AREAS OF FURTHER STUDY

Where do you go from here in your study of research design and statistical analysis? In this section, we consider a number of areas you might investigate as you continue your studies in advanced undergraduate courses or in graduate school.

Continuing Your Study of Experimental Design

We have covered in detail the analysis of the most common experimental designs in psychology, which will serve as building blocks for the analysis of more complicated designs. You have seen how a factorial design with two independent variables grows out of a single-factor design, both in its construction as a set of component single-factor designs, and in its detailed analysis of main comparisons, simple effects, and simple comparisons — analytical procedures designed for the factorial experiment but based on procedures developed for the single-factor design. You have also seen how we can increase the sensitivity of our experiments by using within-subjects designs — designs in which subjects receive all or a portion of the treatment conditions created for the experiment. The designs covered in Parts Three and Four form the building blocks with which more complex experiments are designed and analyzed.[13]

In this book, we have only scratched the surface in the discussion of experimental designs. We will mention briefly some of the more important details we have either omitted or simplified.

More Complex Factorial Designs. We find that once students begin working on a research problem that interests them, they propose experiments that are more complex than the ones we have covered in this book. This complexity is the result of two factors: an increase in the number of independent variables considered relevant by the students, and the use of within-subjects factors as a way of increasing power and reducing the number of subjects needed for their experiments. A factorial experiment with three independent variables (factors A, B, and C) yields a great deal of information, including three main effects (A, B, and C) and a total of *four* interactions — three interactions between the independent variables considered two at a time (known as the *two-way interactions*, $A \times B$, $A \times C$, and $B \times C$), and an interaction of all three independent variables (known as the *three-way interaction*, $A \times B \times C$) — that

---

[13] Keppel (1991, Chap. 22) presents an overall analysis scheme that emphasizes the fact that the analysis of more complex designs may be understood by examining the simpler designs from which they are constructed.

must be analyzed as well. Furthermore, there are additional analyses that are available depending on whether a particular effect is significant.

Because you are familiar with our approach to statistical analysis and our notational system, you may find that the advanced version of this book written by the first author of this text (Keppel, 1991, *Design and Analysis: A Researcher's Handbook*) will help you to analyze higher-order experimental designs such as the one described in the preceding paragraph. *Design and Analysis* is purposefully written to be a direct extension of what you have learned in this text.

Power. All researchers should develop a deep concern for statistical *power*, as has been argued in several sections of this book. The evidence is convincing that most research designs currently used by psychologists are substantially *under* powered, which means that many researchers are failing to find significant *F*'s when treatment effects are in fact present, and that other researchers are failing to replicate significant findings reported in the research literature (see Sedlmeier & Gigerenzer, 1989). You may find the book *Statistical Power Analysis for the Behavioral Sciences* by Cohen (1988) — which considers the issue of power in a wide variety of research contexts — useful when you begin to plan a new study and need to decide how many subjects you should include. A more elementary introduction to this problem is the book *How Many Subjects?* by Kraemer and Thiemann (1987), which many readers may find helpful.

Analysis of Interaction Comparisons. Our coverage of the detailed analysis of interaction focused on a breakdown of the results into simple effects and simple comparisons. We mentioned briefly in Sec. 10.8 a more satisfying way to study interaction: transforming a larger factorial design into a number of smaller factorials to focus on different aspects of the interaction. This type of analysis is given extended treatment in books by Keppel (1991, Chap. 12) and Rosenthal and Rosnow (1985).

More Accurate Error Terms in Within-Subjects Designs. In our discussion of within-subjects designs, we presented a simplified technique for evaluating single-*df* comparisons and simple effects. While we feel this approach is appropriate for an introductory treatment of these analyses, we urge you to consult more advanced treatments of this material if your research blossoms into a potentially publishable paper. The problem is that, in most cases, we need to calculate a *separate* error term for *each* analysis. We broached this topic briefly in Sec. 11.9 within the context of the single-factor within-subjects design, but avoided the problem with the two-factor within-subjects designs because of its complexity. You will find a detailed discussion of this problem and its solution in most advanced statistics books (see, for example, Keppel, 1991; Kirk, 1982; Myers & Well, 1991; Winer, Brown, & Michels, 1991).

Analysis of Covariance.   An additional statistical procedure that provides a way to increase power is the *analysis of covariance.* Briefly, a researcher obtains information about the subjects before they are randomly assigned to the different treatment conditions and then uses this information when analyzing the study to adjust for any chance differences existing prior to the start of the experiment. The benefits from using analysis of covariance include a more precise estimate of the treatment effects and a smaller error term, which of course increases the power of the statistical test. The computational procedures for the analysis of covariance are discussed in most advanced books on statistical analysis.

Learning to Avoid Design Flaws

The conclusions we are able to draw from research depend fundamentally on the care with which we have designed our studies. If a piece of research is poorly designed, our conclusions will be severely limited, regardless of how elegantly we have combined the Y scores in the statistical analysis. Data analysts have a catchy phrase to describe the results from a flawed study: "garbage in, garbage out."

To avoid such problems, we recommend two older, but excellent, books dealing with *experimental design*: a discussion of quasi-experiments by Donald T. Campbell and Julian C. Stanley, which originally appeared as a chapter in a book (1963) but has been reprinted as a separate monograph (1966); and a book by Benton J. Underwood (1957), *Psychological Research*, in which Chaps. 4 and 5 are particularly relevant to the design of experiments. A more recent book by Cook and Campbell (1979) offers advice and guidance in designing field research. Another book that considers issues relevant to the broad research needs of the behavioral scientist is by Neale and Liebert (1986). To obtain experience in analyzing existing studies for possible design flaws, we highly recommend the book by Huck and Sandler (1979). Finally, we should mention a book by Webb, Campbell, Schwartz, and Sechrest (1966), *Unobtrusive Measures*, and its sequel by Webb, Campbell, Schwartz, Sechrest, and Grove (1981), *Non-Reactive Measures in the Social Sciences*, which discuss the role of experimentation in changing the actual behavior under study.

Branching into Other Areas of Research Design

Most graduate students are exposed to a variety of research designs as part of their formal training. Although an investigator's particular area of study may depend almost exclusively on one particular form of research design —

true experiments, quasi-experiments, correlational studies, and so on — he or she should still be aware of the other areas of research. For example, social psychologists might prefer to conduct experiments but still be receptive to a quasi-experiment when random assignment is not feasible, or to a correlational study when direct manipulation is not possible or is unethical. Personality psychologists might prefer to collect and analyze correlational data but be willing to intervene directly by manipulating independent variables when experimental situations are appropriate. In areas such as neuroscience, psychologists study mental and motor disorders produced by accident or disease — conditions that occur in nature rather than through deliberate human intervention, as in experiments. Consequently, they study such classification variables with quasi-experimental designs or correlational designs. Experimental psychologists who deal with experiments almost exclusively might still find that correlational results may add information that supplements and extends the conclusions drawn from experiments.[14]

We urge our students to broaden their training to include at least an informed understanding of the major methodologies of their disciplines. We believe that all graduate students in psychology should possess a working knowledge of both correlational research and experimental design. There are several advanced books that offer an integrated presentation of experimental design and correlational research. Cohen and Cohen (1983) and Pedhazur (1982), for example, achieve the integration by presenting the analysis of variance as a special case derived from the more general correlational approach to data analysis. Keppel and Zedeck (1989), on the other hand, present the two procedures on an equal footing, highlighting their special advantages and disadvantages in specific research situations; they leave the choice of statistical method to the researcher when the two methods are equally appropriate to the analysis of a given set of data.

A Final Thought

Ultimately, we view statistics as consisting of a set of analytical tools created to serve the particular needs of each researcher. It is the responsibility of researchers to understand the nature of these tools and to learn to use them to illuminate their research questions rather than confuse and obscure them. It is to this end that we dedicate this book.

---

[14] Benton J. Underwood (1975), an experimental psychologist and research methodologist, offers a compelling argument for collecting correlational data that provide corroborating evidence for the operation of processes in a natural setting that have been inferred primarily from the results of experiments.

APPENDICES

A p p e n d i x · A

STATISTICAL TABLES

TABLE A-1 *Table of Random Numbers*

Instructions for Use: This table contains 2,500 digits generated by a random process. To obtain a random string of digits, enter the table at a point chosen randomly and record the digits as they are listed in the table. If you need random strings of two-digit numbers, record the numbers two at a time. You may move in any direction in the table as long as your path through the table is determined before you select your starting point.

```
63 73 35 20 05    02 78 59 68 21    39 90 76 98 19    24 61 74 15 34    36 58 68 02 24
66 09 89 21 81    50 03 16 23 18    41 30 54 76 53    89 77 39 66 91    58 57 52 01 19
55 78 43 34 24    78 06 18 87 41    06 85 73 71 64    62 68 43 33 38    23 83 83 38 88
57 55 44 74 82    65 61 17 55 86    12 96 65 07 83    77 97 76 75 71    67 60 86 47 86
41 91 16 20 30    67 34 38 20 14    21 02 57 07 97    20 94 63 58 64    76 11 62 04 62
90 00 04 40 80    22 39 05 26 63    16 44 29 19 62    62 89 68 37 28    45 98 07 34 06
73 14 66 97 68    88 66 44 73 13    15 54 24 48 11    80 79 07 37 71    81 40 94 77 67
28 38 38 62 37    46 07 30 11 56    16 96 51 36 35    84 63 04 81 61    59 32 58 85 74
20 80 06 18 32    13 95 59 62 08    95 01 01 76 88    74 00 36 70 13    10 15 14 46 89
04 85 32 97 44    50 01 32 70 85    39 66 64 10 59    97 39 41 13 46    82 41 43 17 58

28 29 27 01 57    86 38 39 63 24    90 94 51 70 91    08 07 58 60 08    67 44 35 98 47
53 48 24 92 94    03 53 96 15 42    84 31 07 16 79    04 52 70 07 18    08 61 92 80 60
46 74 13 42 72    45 60 54 47 07    21 90 18 87 32    51 35 85 47 53    51 44 15 57 35
37 52 88 74 48    82 74 05 05 44    02 61 38 89 48    17 17 27 36 09    28 89 91 47 96
09 21 40 44 26    72 74 11 36 03    14 56 55 77 99    08 92 37 14 90    40 57 78 32 28
67 27 99 98 71    43 26 00 78 54    90 52 69 02 74    76 00 60 08 95    01 25 80 72 66
42 96 44 70 18    79 50 31 54 30    24 54 11 08 37    27 02 32 43 52    71 33 77 83 28
89 23 14 10 81    61 04 20 46 67    82 82 11 62 83    73 14 90 37 43    46 38 00 29 36
09 92 00 48 30    03 31 43 40 78    20 39 26 11 52    03 38 84 51 49    48 22 16 86 27
06 77 40 12 10    32 79 51 06 80    67 49 41 03 41    56 62 05 70 15    11 95 25 47 48

14 46 74 16 88    24 92 31 78 69    40 38 63 90 22    11 92 17 39 59    23 19 16 86 37
83 04 89 15 47    36 87 12 65 14    84 24 39 69 12    16 17 53 35 18    71 71 30 00 04
81 92 21 06 02    94 80 79 31 77    92 71 95 62 68    23 79 57 66 90    71 10 82 98 90
96 80 87 59 34    72 69 98 19 16    16 73 09 18 96    18 80 37 70 72    78 96 83 48 52
43 36 45 14 47    59 95 71 48 76    73 08 27 30 29    63 27 27 34 67    73 06 91 08 74
19 75 91 02 49    18 39 77 72 60    42 24 74 32 19    27 12 03 69 32    59 80 85 84 83
08 07 97 12 70    57 24 06 76 07    08 49 46 45 20    90 95 16 45 58    99 10 42 65 99
91 77 40 05 08    53 47 42 27 60    43 22 89 44 93    62 00 09 55 40    23 86 21 71 47
37 13 15 48 06    07 29 70 17 41    92 00 24 48 16    19 23 71 40 34    72 84 95 90 29
14 41 39 66 60    77 21 82 55 16    56 85 11 14 16    70 00 58 37 63    59 17 41 11 29
```

TABLE A-1 *Continued*

09 60 07 12 47	99 88 01 56 60	22 95 24 70 12	99 02 39 80 61	82 53 25 07 66
75 83 19 60 55	78 09 47 76 67	25 77 23 98 33	60 56 38 19 62	96 75 34 96 52
09 13 61 69 22	06 40 17 46 74	51 36 78 98 93	95 38 28 41 48	59 70 50 13 69
87 77 74 71 19	01 65 44 76 95	55 59 08 50 54	76 56 64 52 18	25 94 57 85 22
08 39 55 85 17	33 41 06 70 83	52 05 65 17 68	59 39 12 94 95	10 22 32 02 84
64 69 65 77 16	58 20 74 03 86	18 23 26 69 95	04 29 42 94 56	65 63 73 30 02
25 07 40 75 96	84 98 07 87 34	75 38 01 54 63	29 37 43 07 94	61 69 56 38 68
43 33 63 15 85	70 74 32 94 52	91 82 97 52 14	56 73 74 51 99	46 70 45 21 05
35 43 23 49 53	44 67 01 03 68	38 17 19 10 03	37 33 60 39 38	49 69 33 25 80
41 39 12 03 50	69 72 63 38 14	65 79 08 31 65	44 37 85 14 41	85 33 20 24 59
15 84 36 85 93	89 46 33 32 99	13 03 76 79 00	16 64 26 37 81	15 70 33 75 18
53 81 43 10 71	69 81 72 54 08	94 63 68 89 73	09 72 81 59 33	79 61 75 66 86
94 38 20 81 52	45 89 88 71 36	93 93 87 42 44	96 24 52 49 21	27 58 72 54 88
35 88 06 84 31	58 53 91 72 14	49 72 45 10 50	15 52 77 10 87	31 61 84 51 06
93 88 13 29 99	44 22 50 26 27	12 12 22 99 49	14 21 27 93 35	40 69 31 23 40
44 25 22 22 89	08 41 64 73 49	32 77 25 49 39	65 19 29 18 15	03 28 74 47 86
15 62 52 72 07	97 73 04 77 87	43 30 41 70 60	79 61 44 42 58	26 75 99 86 38
61 10 24 35 02	65 91 78 89 77	15 60 32 76 58	40 01 90 97 88	57 97 97 99 97
71 84 84 14 98	79 58 48 21 95	49 75 61 18 47	67 61 56 05 36	59 39 59 41 62
04 10 56 90 17	24 37 09 97 30	59 44 61 94 64	60 88 75 60 01	69 03 73 61 29

TABLE A-2 Critical Values of the F Distribution

Instructions for Use: To find the critical value of F, locate the cell in the table formed by the intersection of the row containing the degrees of freedom associated with the denominator of the F ratio and the column containing the degrees of freedom associated with the numerator of the F ratio. The numbers listed in **boldface type** are the critical values of F at $\alpha = .05$; the numbers listed in lightface roman type are the critical values of F at $\alpha = .01$. As an example, suppose we have adopted the 5 percent level of significance and wish to evaluate the significance of an F with $df_{num.} = 2$ and $df_{denom.} = 12$. From the table we find that the critical value of $F(2, 12) = 3.89$ at $\alpha = .05$. If the obtained value of F equals or exceeds this critical value, we will reject the null hypothesis; if the obtained value of F is smaller than this critical value, we will retain the null hypothesis. See pp. 112–113 for a discussion of the use of the F table in evaluating the null hypothesis.[a]

Degrees of Freedom for Numerator

Den.	1	2	3	4	5	6	7	8	9	10	12	15	20	24	30	40	60	∞
1	**161**	**200**	**216**	**225**	**230**	**234**	**237**	**239**	**241**	**242**	**244**	**246**	**248**	**249**	**250**	**251**	**252**	**254**
	4052	4999	5403	5625	5764	5859	5928	5981	6022	6056	6106	6157	6209	6235	6261	6287	6313	6366
2	**18.5**	**19.0**	**19.2**	**19.2**	**19.3**	**19.3**	**19.4**	**19.4**	**19.4**	**19.4**	**19.4**	**19.4**	**19.4**	**19.4**	**19.5**	**19.5**	**19.5**	**19.5**
	98.5	99.0	99.2	99.2	99.3	99.3	99.4	99.4	99.4	99.4	99.4	99.4	99.4	99.5	99.5	99.5	99.5	99.5
3	**10.1**	**9.55**	**9.28**	**9.12**	**9.01**	**8.94**	**8.89**	**8.85**	**8.81**	**8.79**	**8.74**	**8.70**	**8.66**	**8.64**	**8.62**	**8.59**	**8.57**	**8.53**
	34.1	30.8	29.5	28.7	28.2	27.9	27.7	27.5	27.4	27.2	27.0	26.9	26.7	26.6	26.5	26.4	26.3	26.1
4	**7.71**	**6.94**	**6.59**	**6.39**	**6.26**	**6.16**	**6.09**	**6.04**	**6.00**	**5.96**	**5.91**	**5.86**	**5.80**	**5.77**	**5.75**	**5.72**	**5.69**	**5.63**
	21.2	18.0	16.7	16.0	15.5	15.2	15.0	14.8	14.7	14.6	14.4	14.2	14.0	13.9	13.8	13.8	13.6	13.5
5	**6.61**	**5.79**	**5.41**	**5.19**	**5.05**	**4.95**	**4.88**	**4.82**	**4.77**	**4.74**	**4.68**	**4.62**	**4.56**	**4.53**	**4.50**	**4.46**	**4.43**	**4.36**
	16.3	13.3	12.1	11.4	11.0	10.7	10.5	10.3	10.2	10.0	9.89	9.72	9.55	9.47	9.38	9.29	9.20	9.02
6	**5.99**	**5.14**	**4.76**	**4.53**	**4.39**	**4.28**	**4.21**	**4.15**	**4.10**	**4.06**	**4.00**	**3.94**	**3.87**	**3.84**	**3.81**	**3.77**	**3.74**	**3.67**
	13.8	10.9	9.78	9.15	8.75	8.47	8.26	8.10	7.98	7.87	7.72	7.56	7.40	7.31	7.23	7.14	7.06	6.88
7	**5.59**	**4.74**	**4.35**	**4.12**	**3.97**	**3.87**	**3.79**	**3.73**	**3.68**	**3.64**	**3.57**	**3.51**	**3.44**	**3.41**	**3.38**	**3.34**	**3.30**	**3.23**
	12.2	9.55	8.45	7.85	7.46	7.19	6.99	6.84	6.72	6.62	6.47	6.31	6.16	6.07	5.99	5.91	5.82	5.65

Degrees of Freedom for Denominator

[a] This table is abridged from Table 18 in E. S. Pearson and H. O. Hartley (Eds.), *Biometrika tables for statisticians* (3rd ed., Vol. 1). Cambridge University Press, New York, 1970, by permission of the *Biometrika* Trustees.

Numerator / Denominator

Bold Type is α level of .05

TABLE A-2 Continued

Degrees of Freedom for Denominator	Degrees of Freedom for Numerator																	
	1	2	3	4	5	6	7	8	9	10	12	15	20	24	30	40	60	∞
8	5.32	4.46	4.07	3.84	3.69	3.58	3.50	3.44	3.39	3.35	3.28	3.22	3.15	3.12	3.08	3.04	3.01	2.93
	11.3	8.65	7.59	7.01	6.63	6.37	6.18	6.03	5.91	5.81	5.67	5.52	5.36	5.28	5.20	5.12	5.03	4.86
9	5.12	4.26	3.86	3.63	3.48	3.37	3.29	3.23	3.18	3.14	3.07	3.01	2.94	2.90	2.86	2.83	2.79	2.71
	10.6	8.02	6.99	6.42	6.06	5.80	5.61	5.47	5.35	5.26	5.11	4.96	4.81	4.73	4.65	4.57	4.48	4.31
10	4.96	4.10	3.71	3.48	3.33	3.22	3.14	3.07	3.02	2.98	2.91	2.85	2.77	2.74	2.70	2.66	2.62	2.54
	10.0	7.56	6.55	5.99	5.64	5.39	5.20	5.06	4.94	4.85	4.71	4.56	4.41	4.33	4.25	4.17	4.08	3.91
11	4.84	3.98	3.59	3.36	3.20	3.09	3.01	2.95	2.90	2.85	2.79	2.72	2.65	2.61	2.57	2.53	2.49	2.40
	9.65	7.21	6.22	5.67	5.32	5.07	4.89	4.74	4.63	4.54	4.40	4.25	4.10	4.02	3.94	3.86	3.78	3.60
12	4.75	3.89	3.49	3.26	3.11	3.00	2.91	2.85	2.80	2.75	2.59	2.62	2.54	2.51	2.47	2.43	2.38	2.30
	9.33	6.93	5.95	5.41	5.06	4.82	4.64	4.50	4.39	4.30	4.16	4.01	3.86	3.78	3.70	3.62	3.54	3.36
13	4.67	3.81	3.41	3.18	3.03	2.92	2.83	2.77	2.71	2.67	2.60	2.53	2.46	2.42	2.38	2.34	2.30	2.21
	9.07	6.70	5.74	5.21	4.86	4.62	4.44	4.30	4.19	4.10	3.96	3.82	3.66	3.59	3.51	3.43	3.34	3.17
14	4.60	3.74	3.34	3.11	2.96	2.85	2.76	2.70	2.65	2.60	2.53	2.46	2.39	2.35	2.31	2.27	2.22	2.13
	8.86	6.51	5.56	5.04	4.69	4.46	4.28	4.14	4.03	3.94	3.80	3.66	3.51	3.43	3.35	3.27	3.18	3.00
15	4.54	3.68	3.29	3.06	2.90	2.79	2.71	2.64	2.59	2.54	2.48	2.40	2.33	2.29	2.25	2.20	2.16	2.07
	8.68	6.36	5.42	4.89	4.56	4.32	4.14	4.00	3.89	3.80	3.67	3.52	3.37	3.29	3.21	3.13	3.05	2.87
16	4.49	3.63	3.24	3.01	2.85	2.74	2.66	2.59	2.54	2.49	2.42	2.35	2.28	2.24	2.19	2.15	2.11	2.01
	8.53	6.23	5.29	4.77	4.44	4.20	4.03	3.89	3.78	3.69	3.55	3.41	3.26	3.18	3.10	3.02	2.93	2.75
17	4.45	3.59	3.20	2.96	2.81	2.70	2.61	2.55	2.49	2.45	2.38	2.31	2.23	2.19	2.15	2.10	2.06	1.96
	8.40	6.11	5.18	4.67	4.34	4.10	3.93	3.79	3.68	3.59	3.46	3.31	3.16	3.08	3.00	2.92	2.83	2.65
18	4.41	3.55	3.16	2.93	2.77	2.66	2.58	2.51	2.46	2.41	2.34	2.27	2.19	2.15	2.11	2.06	2.02	1.92
	8.29	6.01	5.09	4.58	4.25	4.01	3.84	3.71	3.60	3.51	3.37	3.23	3.08	3.00	2.92	2.84	2.75	2.57

TABLE A-2 Continued

Degrees of Freedom for Denominator

df																		
19	**4.38**	**3.52**	**3.13**	**2.90**	**2.74**	**2.63**	**2.54**	**2.48**	**2.42**	**2.38**	**2.31**	**2.23**	**2.16**	**2.11**	**2.07**	**2.03**	**1.98**	**1.88**
	8.18	5.93	5.01	4.50	4.17	3.94	3.77	3.63	3.52	3.43	3.30	3.15	3.00	2.92	2.84	2.76	2.67	2.49
20	**4.35**	**3.49**	**3.10**	**2.87**	**2.71**	**2.60**	**2.51**	**2.45**	**2.39**	**2.35**	**2.28**	**2.20**	**2.12**	**2.08**	**2.04**	**1.99**	**1.95**	**1.84**
	8.10	5.85	4.94	4.43	4.10	3.87	3.70	3.56	3.46	3.37	3.23	3.09	2.94	2.86	2.78	2.69	2.61	2.42
22	**4.30**	**3.44**	**3.05**	**2.82**	**2.66**	**2.55**	**2.46**	**2.40**	**2.34**	**2.30**	**2.23**	**2.15**	**2.07**	**2.03**	**1.98**	**1.94**	**1.89**	**1.78**
	7.95	5.72	4.82	4.31	3.99	3.76	3.59	3.45	3.35	3.26	3.12	2.98	2.83	2.75	2.67	2.58	2.50	2.31
24	**4.26**	**3.40**	**3.01**	**2.78**	**2.62**	**2.51**	**2.42**	**2.36**	**2.30**	**2.25**	**2.18**	**2.11**	**2.03**	**1.98**	**1.94**	**1.89**	**1.84**	**1.73**
	7.82	5.61	4.72	4.22	3.90	3.67	3.50	3.36	3.26	3.17	3.03	2.89	2.74	2.66	2.58	2.49	2.40	2.21
26	**4.23**	**3.37**	**2.98**	**2.74**	**2.59**	**2.47**	**2.39**	**2.32**	**2.27**	**2.22**	**2.15**	**2.07**	**1.99**	**1.95**	**1.90**	**1.85**	**1.80**	**1.69**
	7.72	5.53	4.64	4.14	3.82	3.59	3.42	3.29	3.18	3.09	2.96	2.81	2.66	2.58	2.50	2.42	2.33	2.13
28	**4.20**	**3.34**	**2.95**	**2.71**	**2.56**	**2.45**	**2.36**	**2.29**	**2.24**	**2.19**	**2.12**	**2.04**	**1.96**	**1.91**	**1.87**	**1.82**	**1.77**	**1.65**
	7.64	5.45	4.57	4.07	3.75	3.53	3.36	3.23	3.12	3.03	2.90	2.75	2.60	2.52	2.44	2.35	2.26	2.06
30	**4.17**	**3.32**	**2.92**	**2.69**	**2.53**	**2.42**	**2.33**	**2.27**	**2.21**	**2.16**	**2.09**	**2.01**	**1.93**	**1.89**	**1.84**	**1.79**	**1.74**	**1.62**
	7.56	5.39	4.51	4.02	3.70	3.47	3.30	3.17	3.07	2.98	2.84	2.70	2.55	2.47	2.39	2.30	2.21	2.01
40	**4.08**	**3.23**	**2.84**	**2.61**	**2.45**	**2.34**	**2.25**	**2.18**	**2.12**	**2.08**	**2.00**	**1.92**	**1.84**	**1.79**	**1.74**	**1.69**	**1.64**	**1.51**
	7.31	5.18	4.31	3.83	3.51	3.29	3.12	2.99	2.89	2.80	2.66	2.52	2.37	2.29	2.20	2.11	2.02	1.80
60	**4.00**	**3.15**	**2.76**	**2.53**	**2.37**	**2.25**	**2.17**	**2.10**	**2.04**	**1.99**	**1.92**	**1.84**	**1.75**	**1.70**	**1.65**	**1.59**	**1.53**	**1.39**
	7.08	4.98	4.13	3.65	3.34	3.12	2.95	2.82	2.72	2.63	2.50	2.35	2.20	2.12	2.03	1.94	1.84	1.60
120	**3.92**	**3.07**	**2.68**	**2.45**	**2.29**	**2.17**	**2.09**	**2.02**	**1.96**	**1.91**	**1.83**	**1.75**	**1.66**	**1.61**	**1.55**	**1.50**	**1.43**	**1.25**
	6.85	4.79	3.95	3.48	3.17	2.96	2.79	2.66	2.56	2.47	2.34	2.19	2.03	1.95	1.86	1.76	1.66	1.38
∞	**3.84**	**3.00**	**2.60**	**2.37**	**2.21**	**2.10**	**2.01**	**1.94**	**1.88**	**1.83**	**1.75**	**1.67**	**1.57**	**1.52**	**1.46**	**1.39**	**1.32**	**1.00**
	6.63	4.61	3.78	3.32	3.02	2.80	2.64	2.51	2.41	2.32	2.18	2.04	1.88	1.79	1.70	1.59	1.47	1.00

TABLE A-3 *Critical Values of the t Distribution*

Instructions for Use: To find the critical value of t, locate the row in the left-hand column of the table corresponding to the number of degrees of freedom for the statistic you have calculated, and select the value of t listed for your choice of α.[a]

df	$\alpha = .05$	$\alpha = .01$	df	$\alpha = .05$	$\alpha = .01$
1	12.71	63.66	18	2.10	2.88
2	4.30	9.92	19	2.09	2.86
3	3.18	5.84	20	2.09	2.84
4	2.78	4.60	21	2.08	2.83
5	2.57	4.03	22	2.07	2.82
6	2.45	3.71	23	2.07	2.81
7	2.36	3.50	24	2.06	2.80
8	2.31	3.36	25	2.06	2.79
9	2.26	3.25	26	2.06	2.78
10	2.23	3.17	27	2.05	2.77
11	2.20	3.11	28	2.05	2.76
12	2.18	3.06	29	2.04	2.76
13	2.16	3.01	30	2.04	2.75
14	2.14	2.98	40	2.02	2.70
15	2.13	2.95	60	2.00	2.66
16	2.12	2.92	120	1.98	2.62
17	2.11	2.90	∞	1.96	2.58

[a] This table is abridged from Table 12 in E. S. Pearson and H. O. Hartley (Eds.), *Biometrika tables for statisticians* (3rd ed., Vol. 1). Cambridge University Press, New York, 1970, by permission of the *Biometrika* Trustees.

TABLE A-4 Critical Values of the Studentized Range Statistic

Instructions for Use: To find the critical value of q_T, locate the cell in the table formed by the intersection of the row containing the degrees of freedom associated with the error term and the column containing the number of means contributing to the analysis, and select the value of q_T listed for your choice of α_{FW}.[a]

k = Number of Means (Tukey Test)

df_{error}	α_{FW}	2	3	4	5	6	7	8	9	10	11	12	13	14	15	16	17	18	19	20
5	.05	3.64	4.60	5.22	5.67	6.03	6.33	6.58	6.80	6.99	7.17	7.32	7.47	7.60	7.72	7.83	7.93	8.03	8.12	8.21
	.01	5.70	6.98	7.80	8.42	8.91	9.32	9.67	9.97	10.24	10.48	10.70	10.89	11.08	11.24	11.40	11.55	11.68	11.81	11.93
6	.05	3.46	4.34	4.90	5.30	5.63	5.90	6.12	6.32	6.49	6.65	6.79	6.92	7.03	7.14	7.24	7.34	7.43	7.51	7.59
	.01	5.24	6.33	7.03	7.56	7.97	8.32	8.61	8.87	9.10	9.30	9.48	9.65	9.81	9.95	10.08	10.21	10.32	10.43	10.54
7	.05	3.34	4.16	4.68	5.06	5.36	5.61	5.82	6.00	6.16	6.30	6.43	6.55	6.66	6.76	6.85	6.94	7.02	7.10	7.17
	.01	4.95	5.92	6.54	7.01	7.37	7.68	7.94	8.17	8.37	8.55	8.71	8.86	9.00	9.12	9.24	9.35	9.46	9.55	9.65
8	.05	3.26	4.04	4.53	4.89	5.17	5.40	5.60	5.77	5.92	6.05	6.18	6.29	6.39	6.48	6.57	6.65	6.73	6.80	6.87
	.01	4.75	5.64	6.20	6.62	6.96	7.24	7.47	7.68	7.86	8.03	8.18	8.31	8.44	8.55	8.66	8.76	8.85	8.94	9.03
9	.05	3.20	3.95	4.41	4.76	5.02	5.24	5.43	5.59	5.74	5.87	5.98	6.09	6.19	6.28	6.36	6.44	6.51	6.58	6.64
	.01	4.60	5.43	5.96	6.35	6.66	6.91	7.13	7.33	7.49	7.65	7.78	7.91	8.03	8.13	8.23	8.33	8.41	8.49	8.57
10	.05	3.15	3.88	4.33	4.65	4.91	5.12	5.30	5.46	5.60	5.72	5.83	5.93	6.03	6.11	6.19	6.27	6.34	6.40	6.47
	.01	4.48	5.27	5.77	6.14	6.43	6.67	6.87	7.05	7.21	7.36	7.49	7.60	7.71	7.81	7.91	7.99	8.08	8.15	8.23
11	.05	3.11	3.82	4.26	4.57	4.82	5.03	5.20	5.35	5.49	5.61	5.71	5.81	5.90	5.98	6.06	6.13	6.20	6.27	6.33
	.01	4.39	5.15	5.62	5.97	6.25	6.48	6.67	6.84	6.99	7.13	7.25	7.36	7.46	7.56	7.65	7.73	7.81	7.88	7.95
12	.05	3.08	3.77	4.20	4.51	4.75	4.95	5.12	5.27	5.39	5.51	5.61	5.71	5.80	5.88	5.95	6.02	6.09	6.15	6.21
	.01	4.32	5.05	5.50	5.84	6.10	6.32	6.51	6.67	6.81	6.94	7.06	7.17	7.26	7.36	7.44	7.52	7.59	7.66	7.73
13	.05	3.06	3.73	4.15	4.45	4.69	4.88	5.05	5.19	5.32	5.43	5.53	5.63	5.71	5.79	5.86	5.93	5.99	6.05	6.11
	.01	4.26	4.96	5.40	5.73	5.98	6.19	6.37	6.53	6.67	6.79	6.90	7.01	7.10	7.19	7.27	7.35	7.42	7.48	7.55
14	.05	3.03	3.70	4.11	4.41	4.64	4.83	4.99	5.13	5.25	5.36	5.46	5.55	5.64	5.71	5.79	5.85	5.91	5.97	6.03
	.01	4.21	4.89	5.32	5.63	5.88	6.08	6.26	6.41	6.54	6.66	6.77	6.87	6.96	7.05	7.13	7.20	7.27	7.33	7.39
15	.05	3.01	3.67	4.08	4.37	4.59	4.78	4.94	5.08	5.20	5.31	5.40	5.49	5.57	5.65	5.72	5.78	5.85	5.90	5.96
	.01	4.17	4.84	5.25	5.56	5.80	5.99	6.16	6.31	6.44	6.55	6.66	6.76	6.84	6.93	7.00	7.07	7.14	7.20	7.26

[a] This table is abridged from Table 29 in E. S. Pearson and H. O. Hartley (Eds.), *Biometrika tables for statisticians* (3rd ed., Vol. 1). Cambridge University Press, New York, 1970, by permission of the *Biometrika* Trustees.

TABLE A-4 Continued

df_{error}	α_{FW}	2	3	4	5	6	7	8	9	10	11	12	13	14	15	16	17	18	19	20
16	.05	3.00	3.65	4.05	4.33	4.56	4.74	4.90	5.03	5.15	5.26	5.35	5.44	5.52	5.59	5.66	5.73	5.79	5.84	5.90
	.01	4.13	4.79	5.19	5.49	5.72	5.92	6.08	6.22	6.35	6.46	6.56	6.66	6.74	6.82	6.90	6.97	7.03	7.09	7.15
17	.05	2.98	3.63	4.02	4.30	4.52	4.70	4.86	4.99	5.11	5.21	5.31	5.39	5.47	5.54	5.61	5.67	5.73	5.79	5.84
	.01	4.10	4.74	5.14	5.43	5.66	5.85	6.01	6.15	6.27	6.38	6.48	6.57	6.66	6.73	6.81	6.87	6.94	7.00	7.05
18	.05	2.97	3.61	4.00	4.28	4.49	4.67	4.82	4.96	5.07	5.17	5.27	5.35	5.43	5.50	5.57	5.63	5.69	5.74	5.79
	.01	4.07	4.70	5.09	5.38	5.60	5.79	5.94	6.08	6.20	6.31	6.41	6.50	6.58	6.65	6.73	6.79	6.85	6.91	6.97
19	.05	2.96	3.59	3.98	4.25	4.47	4.65	4.79	4.92	5.04	5.14	5.23	5.31	5.39	5.46	5.53	5.59	5.65	5.70	5.75
	.01	4.05	4.67	5.05	5.33	5.55	5.73	5.89	6.02	6.14	6.25	6.34	6.43	6.51	6.58	6.65	6.72	6.78	6.84	6.89
20	.05	2.95	3.58	3.96	4.23	4.45	4.62	4.77	4.90	5.01	5.11	5.20	5.28	5.36	5.43	5.49	5.55	5.61	5.66	5.71
	.01	4.02	4.64	5.02	5.29	5.51	5.69	5.84	5.97	6.09	6.19	6.28	6.37	6.45	6.52	6.59	6.65	6.71	6.77	6.82
24	.05	2.92	3.53	3.90	4.17	4.37	4.54	4.68	4.81	4.92	5.01	5.10	5.18	5.25	5.32	5.38	5.44	5.49	5.55	5.59
	.01	3.96	4.55	4.91	5.17	5.37	5.54	5.69	5.81	5.92	6.02	6.11	6.19	6.26	6.33	6.39	6.45	6.51	6.56	6.61
30	.05	2.89	3.49	3.85	4.10	4.30	4.46	4.60	4.72	4.82	4.92	5.00	5.08	5.15	5.21	5.27	5.33	5.38	5.43	5.47
	.01	3.89	4.45	4.80	5.05	5.24	5.40	5.54	5.65	5.76	5.85	5.93	6.01	6.08	6.14	6.20	6.26	6.31	6.36	6.41
40	.05	2.86	3.44	3.79	4.04	4.23	4.39	4.52	4.63	4.73	4.82	4.90	4.98	5.04	5.11	5.16	5.22	5.27	5.31	5.36
	.01	3.82	4.37	4.70	4.93	5.11	5.26	5.39	5.50	5.60	5.69	5.76	5.83	5.90	5.96	6.02	6.07	6.12	6.16	6.21
60	.05	2.83	3.40	3.74	3.98	4.16	4.31	4.44	4.55	4.65	4.73	4.81	4.88	4.94	5.00	5.06	5.11	5.15	5.20	5.24
	.01	3.76	4.28	4.59	4.82	4.99	5.13	5.25	5.36	5.45	5.53	5.60	5.67	5.73	5.78	5.84	5.89	5.93	5.97	6.01
120	.05	2.80	3.36	3.68	3.92	4.10	4.24	4.36	4.47	4.56	4.64	4.71	4.78	4.84	4.90	4.95	5.00	5.04	5.09	5.13
	.01	3.70	4.20	4.50	4.71	4.87	5.01	5.12	5.21	5.30	5.37	5.44	5.50	5.56	5.61	5.66	5.71	5.75	5.79	5.83
∞	.05	2.77	3.31	3.63	3.86	4.03	4.17	4.29	4.39	4.47	4.55	4.62	4.68	4.74	4.80	4.85	4.89	4.93	4.97	5.01
	.01	3.64	4.12	4.40	4.60	4.76	4.88	4.99	5.08	5.16	5.23	5.29	5.35	5.40	5.45	5.49	5.54	5.57	5.61	5.65

TABLE A-5 *Critical Values of the Dunnett Test*

Instructions for Use: To find the critical value of q_D, locate the cell in the table formed by the intersection of the row containing the degrees of freedom associated with the error term and the column containing the number of means contributing to the analysis, and select the value of q_D listed for your choice of α_{FW}.[a]

		k = Number of Treatment Means, Including Control								
df_{error}	α_{FW}	2	3	4	5	6	7	8	9	10
6	.05	2.45	2.86	3.10	3.26	3.39	3.49	3.57	3.64	3.71
	.01	3.71	4.21	4.51	4.71	4.87	5.00	5.10	5.20	5.28
7	.05	2.36	2.75	2.97	3.12	3.24	3.33	3.41	3.47	3.53
	.01	3.50	3.95	4.21	4.39	4.53	4.64	4.74	4.82	4.89
8	.05	2.31	2.67	2.88	3.02	3.13	3.22	3.29	3.35	3.41
	.01	3.36	3.77	4.00	4.17	4.29	4.40	4.48	4.56	4.62
9	.05	2.26	2.61	2.81	2.95	3.05	3.14	3.20	3.26	3.32
	.01	3.25	3.63	3.85	4.01	4.12	4.22	4.30	4.37	4.43
10	.05	2.23	2.57	2.76	2.89	2.99	3.07	3.14	3.19	3.24
	.01	3.17	3.53	3.74	3.88	3.99	4.08	4.16	4.22	4.28
11	.05	2.20	2.53	2.72	2.84	2.94	3.02	3.08	3.14	3.19
	.01	3.11	3.45	3.65	3.79	3.89	3.98	4.05	4.11	4.16
12	.05	2.18	2.50	2.68	2.81	2.90	2.98	3.04	3.09	3.14
	.01	3.05	3.39	3.58	3.71	3.81	3.89	3.96	4.02	4.07
13	.05	2.16	2.48	2.65	2.78	2.87	2.94	3.00	3.06	3.10
	.01	3.01	3.33	3.52	3.65	3.74	3.82	3.89	3.94	3.99
14	.05	2.14	2.46	2.63	2.75	2.84	2.91	2.97	3.02	3.07
	.01	2.98	3.29	3.47	3.59	3.69	3.76	3.83	3.88	3.93
15	.05	2.13	2.44	2.61	2.73	2.82	2.89	2.95	3.00	3.04
	.01	2.95	3.25	3.43	3.55	3.64	3.71	3.78	3.83	3.88
16	.05	2.12	2.42	2.59	2.71	2.80	2.87	2.92	2.97	3.02
	.01	2.92	3.22	3.39	3.51	3.60	3.67	3.73	3.78	3.83
17	.05	2.11	2.41	2.58	2.69	2.78	2.85	2.90	2.95	3.00
	.01	2.90	3.19	3.36	3.47	3.56	3.63	3.69	3.74	3.79
18	.05	2.10	2.40	2.56	2.68	2.76	2.83	2.89	2.94	2.98
	.01	2.88	3.17	3.33	3.44	3.53	3.60	3.66	3.71	3.75
19	.05	2.09	2.39	2.55	2.66	2.75	2.81	2.87	2.92	2.96
	.01	2.86	3.15	3.31	3.42	3.50	3.57	3.63	3.68	3.72
20	.05	2.09	2.38	2.54	2.65	2.73	2.80	2.86	2.90	2.95
	.01	2.85	3.13	3.29	3.40 '	3.48	3.55	3.60	3.65	3.69
24	.05	2.06	2.35	2.51	2.61	2.70	2.76	2.81	2.86	2.90
	.01	2.80	3.07	3.22	3.32	3.40	3.47	3.52	3.57	3.61
30	.05	2.04	2.32	2.47	2.58	2.66	2.72	2.77	2.82	2.86
	.01	2.75	3.01	3.15	3.25	3.33	3.39	3.44	3.49	3.52
40	.05	2.02	2.29	2.44	2.54	2.62	2.68	2.73	2.77	2.81
	.01	2.70	2.95	3.09	3.19	3.26	3.32	3.37	3.41	3.44
60	.05	2.00	2.27	2.41	2.51	2.58	2.64	2.69	2.73	2.77
	.01	2.66	2.90	3.03	3.12	3.19	3.25	3.29	3.33	3.37
120	.05	1.98	2.24	2.38	2.47	2.55	2.60	2.65	2.69	2.73
	.01	2.62	2.85	2.97	3.06	3.12	3.18	3.22	3.26	3.29
∞	.05	1.96	2.21	2.35	2.44	2.51	2.57	2.61	2.65	2.69
	.01	2.58	2.79	2.92	3.00	3.06	3.11	3.15	3.19	3.22

[a] This table is abridged from C. W. Dunnett, New tables for multiple comparisons with a control, *Biometrics*, 1964, *20*, 482–491, with permission from the Biometric Society.

TABLE A-6 *Power Functions for the Analysis of Variance*

Instructions for Estimating Sample Size: Extend a line from the point on the Y axis that represents the power you wish to achieve until it intersects the appropriate power function for your experiment (df_{effect}) and read the value for ϕ directly underneath this point of intersection. Substitute this value in Eq. (8-6), p. 213, to determine the estimated sample size.[a]

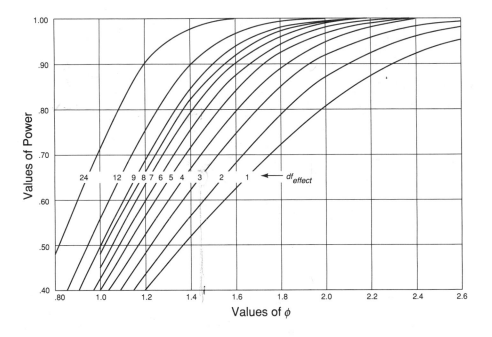

---

[a] The power functions for $df_{effect} = 4, 5, 7, 8,$ and 24 are based on values from Table 30 in E. S. Pearson and H. O. Hartley (Eds.), *Biometrika tables for statisticians* (Vol. II), Cambridge University Press, London, 1972 (by permission of the *Biometrika* Trustees), and those for $df_{effect} = 1, 2, 3, 6, 9,$ and 12 are based on values from Table 1 in J. Rotton and P. S. Schönemann, Power tables for analysis of variance, *Journal of Educational and Psychological Measurement*, 1978, *38*, pp. 213–229 (by permission of the authors and the editor).

TABLE A-7 *Critical Values of the Chi Square (χ^2) Distribution*

Instructions for Use: To find the critical value of χ^2, locate the row in the left-hand column of the table corresponding to the number of degrees of freedom (df) associated with χ^2, and select the value of χ^2 listed for the desired level of significance (α).[a]

df	$\alpha = .05$	$\alpha = .01$	df	$\alpha = .05$	$\alpha = .01$
1	3.84	6.63	16	26.30	32.00
2	5.99	9.21	17	27.59	33.41
3	7.81	11.34	18	28.87	34.81
4	9.49	13.28	19	30.14	36.19
5	11.07	15.09	20	31.41	37.57
6	12.59	16.81	21	32.67	38.93
7	14.07	18.48	22	33.92	40.29
8	15.51	20.09	23	35.17	41.64
9	16.92	21.67	24	36.42	42.98
10	18.31	23.21	25	37.65	44.31
11	19.68	24.72	26	38.89	45.64
12	21.03	26.22	27	40.11	46.96
13	22.36	27.69	28	41.34	48.28
14	23.68	29.14	29	42.56	49.59
15	25.00	30.58	30	43.77	50.89

[a] This table is abridged from Table 8 in E. S. Pearson and H. O. Hartley (Eds.), *Biometrika tables for statisticians* (3rd ed., Vol. 1). Cambridge University Press, New York, 1970, by permission of the *Biometrika* Trustees.

TABLE A-8 *Power Functions for the Chi Square Statistic*

Instructions for Estimating Power for an Anticipated Set of Results: Extend a line from the point on the X axis that represents the value of chi square you expect to obtain with a particular sample size ($\chi^2_{antic.}$) until it intersects with the appropriate power function (df_{effect}) and read the value for power directly opposite this point of intersection.

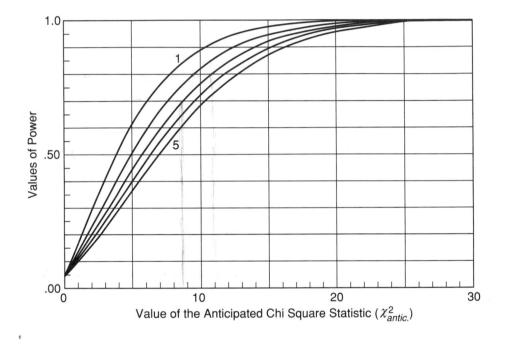

TABLE A-9 *Critical Values of the Product-Moment Correlation Coeffic.*

Instructions for Use: To find the critical value of r, locate the row in the left-ha
column of the table corresponding to the number of degrees of freedom $(df_r,$
associated with r, and select the value of r listed for the desired level of
significance (α).[a]

df_r	$\alpha = .05$	$\alpha = .01$	df_r	$\alpha = .05$	$\alpha = .01$
1	.997	.9999	16	.47	.59
2	.95	.99	17	.46	.58
3	.88	.96	18	.44	.56
4	.81	.92	19	.43	.55
5	.75	.88	20	.42	.54
6	.71	.83	25	.38	.49
7	.67	.80	30	.35	.45
8	.63	.76	35	.32	.42
9	.60	.74	40	.30	.39
10	.58	.71	45	.29	.37
11	.55	.68	50	.27	.35
12	.53	.66	60	.25	.32
13	.51	.64	70	.23	.30
14	.50	.62	80	.22	.28
15	.48	.61	90	.20	.27
			100	.20	.25

[a] $df_r = n - 2$ (where $n =$ the number of pairs of scores).

This table is abridged from Table 13 in E. S. Pearson and H. O. Hartley (Eds.), *Biometrika tables for statisticians* (3rd ed., Vol. 1). Cambridge University Press, New York, 1970, by permission of the *Biometrika* Trustees.

TABLE A-10 *Power Function for the Product-Moment Correlation Coefficient (r)*

Instructions for Estimating Sample Size: Extend a line from the point on the *Y* axis that represents the power you wish to achieve until it intersects the power function and read the value for δ directly underneath this point of intersection. Substitute this value in Eq. (15-16), p. 487, to determine the estimated sample size.

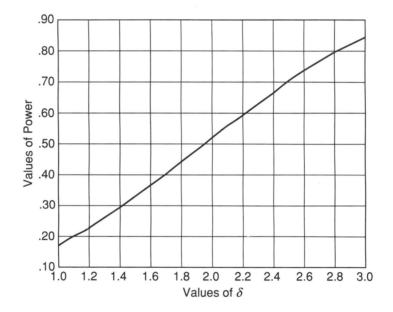

TABLE A-11 *Linear and Quadratic Coefficients for Trend Analysis*

Instructions for Use: The coefficients needed for an analysis of linear and quadratic trend are listed according to the number of treatment levels entering into the analysis. Different numbers of treatment levels are identified in the left-hand column of the table. Coefficients for assessing the degree of linear and quadratic trends are listed in the rows designated in the second column of the table. The underlying assumption in this table is that the levels of the independent variable represent equally spaced points on a quantitative dimension.[a]

Number of Treatment Levels	Nature of Trend	Values of Coefficients									
3	Linear	-1	0	$+1$							
	Quadratic	$+1$	-2	$+1$							
4	Linear	-3	-1	$+1$	$+3$						
	Quadratic	$+1$	-1	-1	$+1$						
5	Linear	-2	-1	0	$+1$	$+2$					
	Quadratic	$+2$	-1	-2	-1	$+2$					
6	Linear	-5	-3	-1	$+1$	$+3$	$+5$				
	Quadratic	$+5$	-1	-4	-4	-1	$+5$				
7	Linear	-3	-2	-1	0	$+1$	$+2$	$+3$			
	Quadratic	$+5$	0	-3	-4	-3	0	$+5$			
8	Linear	-7	-5	-3	-1	$+1$	$+3$	$+5$	$+7$		
	Quadratic	$+7$	$+1$	-3	-5	-5	-3	$+1$	$+7$		
9	Linear	-4	-3	-2	-1	0	$+1$	$+2$	$+3$	$+4$	
	Quadratic	$+28$	$+7$	-8	-17	-20	-17	-8	$+7$	$+28$	
10	Linear	-9	-7	-5	-3	-1	$+1$	$+3$	$+5$	$+7$	$+9$
	Quadratic	$+6$	$+2$	-1	-3	-4	-4	-3	-1	$+2$	$+6$

[a] This table is abridged from Table 47 in E. S. Pearson and H. O. Hartley (Eds.), *Biometrika tables for statisticians* (3rd ed., Vol. 1). Cambridge University Press, New York, 1970, by permission of the *Biometrika* Trustees.

Appendix · B

ANSWERS TO SELECTED CHAPTER EXERCISES

We have attempted to make the answers to the exercises in the first chapters more complete than those in later chapters. When procedures are introduced for the first time, we have made an effort to provide enough information to enable you to check your work for sources of error. In preparing the answers, we followed the rounding rules adopted for this book, which you may want to review if your calculations do not agree with ours (see pp. 32–33). In any case, discrepancies due to differences in rounding will be small and will not affect the outcome of the analysis.

We encourage you to become familiar with your calculator as you begin the first problems so that when more computational effort is required in later problems you will be prepared (see Appendix C on using a statistical calculator). In spite of the seductive ease afforded by hand calculators or computer programs, we cannot overemphasize the usefulness of examining the results of an analysis and comparing different sets of scores. As you gain practice, you will become sensitive to patterns in results and possible errors in computations.

We encourage you to save the work you do for the exercises both for review and because certain problems appear again in subsequent chapters. As you learn new procedures, you will be able to make additional calculations using the same data and thus be able to analyze the data in the exercises more thoroughly.

CHAPTER 2

1. a. *Mean*:

$$\overline{Y} = \frac{\Sigma Y}{n} = \frac{70}{10} = 7.00$$

545

b. *Deviations:*   C. *Sum of squared deviations:*

$8 - 7 = 1$ $(1)^2 = 1$

$6 - 7 = -1$ $(-1)^2 = 1$

$7 - 7 = 0$ $(0)^2 = 0$

$7 - 7 = 0$ $(0)^2 = 0$

$9 - 7 = 2$ $(2)^2 = 4$

$6 - 7 = -1$ $(-1)^2 = 1$

$7 - 7 = 0$ $(0)^2 = 0$

$9 - 7 = 2$ $(2)^2 = 4$

$4 - 7 = -3$ $(-3)^2 = 9$

$7 - 7 = 0$ $(0)^2 = 0$

Note: $\Sigma(Y - \overline{Y}) = 0$ and $\Sigma(Y - \overline{Y})^2 = 20 = SS$.

d. *Sum of squares:*

$$SS = \Sigma\, Y^2 - \frac{(\Sigma\, Y)^2}{n}$$

$$= 510 = \frac{(70)^2}{10} = 510 - \frac{4,900}{10} = 510 - 490.00 = 20.00$$

e. *Variance and standard deviation:*

$$\text{variance} = \frac{SS}{df} = \frac{20.00}{9} = 2.22$$

$$\text{standard deviation} = \sqrt{\text{variance}} = \sqrt{2.22} = 1.49$$

CHAPTER 4

I.   a. *Means:*

$$\overline{Y}_{A_1} = 28.67 \qquad \overline{Y}_{A_2} = 32.67$$

b. *Basic ratios*:

$$[A] = \frac{\Sigma A^2}{n} = \frac{153{,}000}{9} = 17{,}000.00$$

$$[Y] = \Sigma Y^2 = 17{,}248$$

$$[T] = \frac{T^2}{(a)(n)} = \frac{(552)^2}{(2)(9)} = \frac{304{,}704}{18} = 16{,}928.00$$

c. *Sums of squares*:

$$SS_A = [A] - [T] = 17{,}000.00 - 16{,}928.00 = 72.00$$

$$SS_{S/A} = [Y] - [A] = 17{,}248 - 17{,}000.00 = 248.00$$

$$SS_T = [Y] - [T] = 17{,}248 - 16{,}928.00 = 320.00$$

d. *Degrees of freedom*:

$$df_A = a - 1 = 2 - 1 = 1$$

$$df_{S/A} = (a)(n - 1) = (2)(9 - 1) = (2)(8) = 16$$

$$df_T = (a)(n) - 1 = (2)(9) - 1 = 18 - 1 = 17$$

e. *Mean squares*:

$$MS_A = \frac{SS_A}{df_A} = \frac{72.00}{1} = 72.00$$

$$MS_{S/A} = \frac{SS_{S/A}}{df_{S/A}} = \frac{248.00}{16} = 15.50$$

f. *Summary of the analysis*:

Source	SS	df	MS	F
A (Additives)	72.00	1	72.00	4.65
S/A	248.00	16	15.50	
Total	320.00	17		

CHAPTER 5

1. For $\alpha = .05$, $df_A = 1$ and $df_{S/A} = 16$; $F_\alpha = 4.49$. Yes.

CHAPTER 6

1.   a.

$$\hat{\psi} = \left(+\tfrac{1}{2}\right)(10.00) + \left(+\tfrac{1}{2}\right)(12.00) + \left(-\tfrac{1}{3}\right)(6.00) + \left(-\tfrac{1}{3}\right)(7.00)$$
$$+ \left(-\tfrac{1}{3}\right)(5.00) + (0)(8.00)$$
$$= (+5.00) + (+6.00) + (-2.00) + (-2.33) + (-1.67) + 0.00$$
$$= 5.00$$

$$\Sigma\, c^2 = \left(+\tfrac{1}{2}\right)^2 + \left(+\tfrac{1}{2}\right)^2 + \left(-\tfrac{1}{3}\right)^2 + \left(-\tfrac{1}{3}\right)^2 + \left(-\tfrac{1}{3}\right)^2 + (0)^2$$
$$= (+.50)^2 + (+.50)^2 + (-.33)^2 + (-.33)^2 + (-.33)^2 + (0)^2$$
$$= .25 + .25 + .11 + .11 + .11 + .00 = .83$$

$$SS_{A\,comp.} = \frac{n(\hat{\psi})^2}{\Sigma\, c^2} = \frac{(6)(5.00)^2}{.83} = \frac{150.00}{.83} = 180.72$$

b.

$$\hat{\psi} = \left(-\tfrac{1}{2}\right)(10.00) + \left(-\tfrac{1}{2}\right)(12.00) + \left(+\tfrac{1}{3}\right)(6.00) + \left(+\tfrac{1}{3}\right)(7.00)$$
$$+ \left(+\tfrac{1}{3}\right)(5.00) + (0)(8.00)$$
$$= (-5.00) + (-6.00) + (+2.00) + (+2.33) + (+1.67) + 0$$
$$= -5.00$$

$$\Sigma\, c^2 = \left(-\tfrac{1}{2}\right)^2 + \left(-\tfrac{1}{2}\right)^2 + \left(+\tfrac{1}{3}\right)^2 + \left(+\tfrac{1}{3}\right)^2 + \left(+\tfrac{1}{3}\right)^2 + (0)^2$$
$$= (-.50)^2 + (-.50)^2 + (+.33)^2 + (+.33)^2 + (+.33)^2 + (0)^2$$
$$= .25 + .25 + .11 + .11 + .11 + .00 = .83$$

$$SS_{A\,comp.} = \frac{(6)(-5.00)^2}{.83} = \frac{150.00}{.83} = 180.72$$

c.

$$\hat{\psi} = (+3)(10.00) + (+3)(12.00) + (-2)(6.00) + (-2)(7.00)$$
$$+ (-2)(5.00) + (0)(8.00)$$
$$= 30.00 + 36.00 - 12.00 - 14.00 - 10.00 + 0.00 = 30.00$$

$$\Sigma c^2 = (+3)^2 + (+3)^2 + (-2)^2 + (-2)^2 + (-2)^2 + (0)^2$$
$$= 9 + 9 + 4 + 4 + 4 + 0 = 30$$

$$SS_{A\ comp.} = \frac{(6)(30.00)^2}{30} = \frac{5,400.00}{30} = 180.00$$

Note: Parts (a) and (b) differ from part (c) because of rounding error.

d. $\hat{\psi}$ from part (a) = 5.00; Σc^2 from part (c) = 30

$$SS_{A\ comp.} = \frac{(6)(5.00)^2}{30} = \frac{150.00}{30} = 5.00$$

Except for rounding error, exercises 1(a) through 1(c) produced $SS_{A\ comp.} = 180.00$, whereas part (d) gave an incorrect value of 5.00.

2. a. *Drug A versus drug B*:

$$MS_{A\ comp.} = \frac{SS_{A\ comp.}}{df_{A\ comp.}} = \frac{180.00}{1} = 180.00$$

$$F_{A\ comp.} = \frac{MS_{A\ comp.}}{MS_{S/A}} = \frac{180.00}{4.00} = 45.00$$

The critical value of $F_{A\ comp.}(1, 30) = 4.17$; therefore, reject H_0 and, after an inspection of the means, conclude that drug A produced significantly higher scores on the dependent variable than drug B.

b. *Drug A versus control*:

$$\text{coefficients} : +1, +1, 0, 0, 0, -2$$

$$\hat{\psi} = (+1)(10.00) + (+1)(12.00) + (0)(6.00) + (0)(7.00)$$
$$+ (0)(5.00) + (-2)(8.00)$$
$$= 10.00 + 12.00 + 0.00 + 0.00 + 0.00 - 16.00 = 6.00$$

$$\Sigma \; c^2 = (+1)^2 + (+1)^2 + (0)^2 + (0)^2 + (0)^2 + (-2)^2 = 6$$

$$SS_{A\,comp.} = \frac{(6)(6.00)^2}{6} = \frac{216.00}{6} = 36.00; \quad MS_{A\,comp.} = \frac{36.00}{1} = 36.00$$

$$F_{A\,comp.} = \frac{36.00}{4.00} = 9.00; \quad p < .05$$

Drug B versus control:

$$\text{coefficients} : 0, 0, +1, +1, +1, -3$$

$$\hat{\psi} = (0)(10.00) + (0)(12.00) + (+1)(6.00) + (+1)(7.00)$$

$$+ (+1)(5.00) + (-3)(8.00)$$

$$= 0.00 + 0.00 + 6.00 + 7.00 + 5.00 - 24.00 = -6.00$$

$$\Sigma \; c^2 = (0)^2 + (0)^2 + (+1)^2 + (+1)^2 + (+1)^2 + (-3)^2 = 12$$

$$SS_{A\,comp.} = \frac{(6)(-6.00)^2}{12} = \frac{216.00}{12} = 18.00; \quad MS_{A\,comp.} = \frac{18.00}{1} = 18.00$$

$$F_{A\,comp.} = \frac{18.00}{4.00} = 4.50; \quad p < .05$$

c. *Combined drugs versus control*:

$$\text{coefficients} : +1, +1, +1, +1, +1, -5$$

$$\hat{\psi} = (+1)(10.00) + (+1)(12.00) + (+1)(6.00) + (+1)(7.00)$$

$$+ (+1)(5.00) + (-5)(8.00)$$

$$= 10.00 + 12.00 + 6.00 + 7.00 + 5.00 - 40.00 = 0.00$$

Since $\hat{\psi}$ represents the difference between the two means — the combined drug versus the control — and is equal to 0.00, we proceed no further. There is no difference between the two means.

d. *Drug A: batch 1 versus batch 2:*

Eq. (6-2): $SS_{A\,comp.} = \dfrac{n(\hat{\psi})^2}{2}$	Eq. (6-9): $SS_{A\,comp.} = \dfrac{n(\hat{\psi})^2}{\Sigma\,c^2}$
$$\begin{aligned} \hat{\psi} &= \overline{Y}_{A_1} - \overline{Y}_{A_2} \\ &= 10.00 - 12.00 \\ &= -2.00 \end{aligned}$$	$$\begin{aligned} \hat{\psi} &= (+1)(10.00) + (-1)(12.00) \\ &\quad + \cdots + (0)(5.00) + (0)(8.00) \\ &= -2.00 \end{aligned}$$
	$$\begin{aligned} \Sigma\,c^2 &= (+1)^2 + (-1)^2 + \cdots \\ &\quad + (0)^2 + (0)^2 = 2 \end{aligned}$$
$$\begin{aligned} SS_{A\,comp.} &= \frac{(6)(-2.00)^2}{2} \\ &= \frac{24.00}{2} = 12.00 \end{aligned}$$	$$\begin{aligned} SS_{A\,comp.} &= \frac{(6)(-2.00)^2}{2} \\ &= \frac{24.00}{2} = 12.00 \end{aligned}$$
$$MS_{A\,comp.} = \frac{12.00}{1} = 12.00$$	$$MS_{A\,comp.} = \frac{12.00}{1} = 12.00$$

Because the $MS_{A\,comp.}$ is the same (identical) value when calculated from either of the two equations, the corresponding $F_{A\,comp.}$'s will be identical also:

$$F_{A\,comp.} = \frac{12.00}{4.00} = 3.00$$

Since the critical value of $F_{A\,comp.}\,(1, 30) = 4.17$, we retain H_0.

CHAPTER 7

1. *Means, standard deviations, and standard errors:*

	a. Mean	Std. Dev.	b. $\hat{\sigma}_M$	d. $\hat{\sigma}_M$[†]
Pleasantness of Meaning	10.31	1.99	.50	.56
Frequency of Word	7.44	2.13	.53	.56
Pleasantness of Sound	6.38	2.75	.69	.56
Frequency of Syllables	4.69	2.02	.51	.56

[†] *Note:* $\hat{\sigma}_M = \sqrt{\dfrac{MS_{S/A}}{n}} = \sqrt{\dfrac{5.04}{16}} = \sqrt{.3150} = .56.$

Confidence intervals:[†]

	c.	d.
Pleasantness of Meaning	$10.31 \pm (2.13)(.50)$ $= 10.31 \pm 1.07$	$10.31 \pm (2.00)(.56)$ $= 10.31 \pm 1.12$
Frequency of Word	$7.44 \pm (2.13)(.53)$ $= 7.44 \pm 1.13$	$7.44 \pm (2.00)(.56)$ $= 7.44 \pm 1.12$
Pleasantness of Sound	$6.38 \pm (2.13)(.69)$ $= 6.38 \pm 1.47$	$6.38 \pm (2.00)(.56)$ $= 6.38 \pm 1.12$
Frequency of Syllables	$4.69 \pm (2.13)(.51)$ $= 4.69 \pm 1.09$	$4.69 \pm (2.00)(.56)$ $= 4.69 \pm 1.12$

[†] *Note:* for part (c), value for $t(15) = 2.13$; and for part (d), $t(60) = 2.00$.

3. a. *Measures of treatment magnitude:*

$$\hat{\sigma}_A^2 = \frac{(df_A)(MS_A - MS_{S/A})}{(a)(n)} = \frac{(2)(30.40 - 3.20)}{(3)(10)} = 1.81$$

$$\hat{\sigma}_{S/A}^2 = MS_{S/A} = 3.20$$

$$\hat{\omega}_A^2 = \frac{\hat{\sigma}_A^2}{\hat{\sigma}_A^2 + \hat{\sigma}_{S/A}^2} = \frac{1.81}{1.81 + 3.20} = \frac{1.81}{5.01} = .36$$

$$R^2 = \frac{SS_A}{SS_A + SS_{S/A}} = \frac{60.80}{60.80 + 86.40} = \frac{60.80}{147.20} = .41$$

b. You have observed that when the difference between the means remained identical but sample size doubled from $n = 5$ to $n = 10$, the estimated omega squared increased slightly, whereas R^2 remained the same. The small increase in estimated omega squared (.30 for $n = 5$ to .36 for $n = 10$) resulted from the way we "increased" sample size — that is, by doubling the original set of scores.

CHAPTER 8

1. a. *A complex comparison and the Scheffé test*:

From exercise 2 of Chap. 6, the comparison between drug A ($a_1 + a_2$) and drug B ($a_3 + a_4 + a_5$) produced an $F_{A\ comp.} = 45.00$. As a planned comparison, the critical value of $F(1, 30) = 4.17$, and we would reject H_0. Treated as a Scheffé test, we evaluate the observed F against a different critical value, F_S. In this exercise, $F_S = (a - 1)F(df_A, df_{S/A}) = (6 - 1)(2.53) = 12.65$, which means we would also reject H_0 under this more stringent test.

b. *Comparing all drug conditions against the control condition*:

Comparison	$F_{A\ comp.}$	Planned Comparison	Dunnett Test
a_1 vs. a_6	3.00	retain H_0	retain H_0
a_2 vs. a_6	12.00	reject H_0	reject H_0
a_3 vs. a_6	3.00	retain H_0	retain H_0
a_4 vs. a_6	.75	retain H_0	retain H_0
a_5 vs. a_6	6.75	reject H_0	retain H_0

Critical value of $F_{A\ comp.}(1, 30) = 4.17$.
Critical value of $F_D = (2.66)^2 = 7.08$.

The decision for the comparison a_5 versus a_6 changes from "reject H_0" as a planned comparison to "retain H_0" as a comparison subjected to the Dunnett test.

c. *Comparisons involving the Tukey test*:

For these comparisons, $F_T = \dfrac{(q_T)^2}{2} = \dfrac{(4.30)^2}{2} = 9.25.$

Comparison	$F_{A_{comp.}}$	Decision
a_1 vs. a_2	3.00	retain H_0
a_1 vs. a_3	12.00	reject H_0
a_1 vs. a_6	3.00	retain H_0

3. The probability of a type II error is β. Power $= 1 - \beta$, and since power $= .60$, $\beta = 1 - .60 = .40$. The chance of obtaining a significant F is .60; that is, we will obtain a significant F sixty percent of the time.

4. a. $n' = \phi^2 \left(\dfrac{1 - \hat{\omega}_A^2}{\hat{\omega}_A^2} \right) = (1.62)^2 \left(\dfrac{1 - .03}{.03} \right) = (2.62)(32.33) = 84.70$

That is, you will need approximately 85 subjects per treatment condition, for a total of $(5)(85) = 425$ subjects.

b. $n' = (1.45)^2(32.33) = (2.10)(32.33) = 67.89$ or approximately 68 subjects per treatment condition for a total of $(5)(68) = 340$ subjects.

c. $n' = (1.62)^2 \left(\dfrac{1 - .06}{.06} \right) = (2.62)(15.67) = 41.06$ or approximately 41 subjects per treatment condition for a total of $(5)(41) = 205$ subjects.

CHAPTER 9

1. *Summary of the analysis*:

Source	SS	df	MS	F
A	.50	1	.50	.15
B	2.00	1	2.00	.62
$A \times B$	40.50	1	40.50	12.46*
S/AB	13.00	4	3.25	
Total	56.00	7		

* $p < .05.$

2. a. *Means and standard deviations*:

	$a_1 b_1$	$a_1 b_2$	$a_1 b_3$	$a_2 b_1$	$a_2 b_2$	$a_2 b_3$
Mean	4.62	4.77	3.77	4.38	6.38	7.31
Std. Dev.	2.29	1.30	1.83	1.98	2.02	2.29

b. *AB matrix*:

	Factor A		
Factor B	a_1	a_2	Sum
b_1	60	57	117
b_2	62	83	145
b_3	49	95	144
Sum	171	235	406

c. *Summary of the analysis*:

$$[Y] = 2,514; \quad [A] = 2,165.79; \quad [B] = 2,132.69; \quad [AB] = 2,231.38;$$
$$[T] = 2,113.28$$

Source	SS	df	MS	F
A	52.51	1	52.51	13.36*
B	19.41	2	9.71	2.47
$A \times B$	46.18	2	23.09	5.88*
S/AB	282.62	72	3.93	
Total	400.72	77		

* $p < .05$.

Note: $F(1, 72) \cong 4.00$ and $F(2, 72) \cong 3.15$, both read from Table A-2 using $df_{denom.} = 60$, the next smaller entry.

d. *Conducting the $F_{max.}$ test*:

$$F_{max.} = \frac{s^2_{largest}}{s^2_{smallest}} = \frac{(2.29)^2}{(1.30)^2} = \frac{5.24}{1.69} = 3.10$$

Yes, because $F_{max.} > 3.00$. We should adjust the critical value of F by using $\alpha = .025$ instead of $\alpha = .05$.

3. a. *Means and standard deviations*:

	Bright (a_1)	Mixed (a_2)	Dull (a_3)
Enriched (b_1)			
Mean	4.50	6.00	8.38
Std. Dev.	2.39	2.45	3.62
Impoverished (b_2)			
Mean	6.75	10.25	12.13
Std. Dev.	3.15	3.01	4.09

b. *Summary of the Analysis*:

$[Y] = 3,816;$ $[A] = 3,243.50;$ $[B] = 3,212.08;$ $[AB] = 3,392.25;$

$[T] = 3,072.00$

Source	SS	df	MS	F
A (Strain)	171.50	2	85.75	8.50*
B (Environment)	140.08	1	140.08	13.88*
A × B	8.67	2	1.34	.43
S/AB	423.75	42	10.09	
Total	744.00	47		

* $p < .05$.

c. There was no interaction between the two variables. The enriched environment leads to significantly fewer trials to learn the maze. Strain also produced a significant effect, but additional tests are necessary to determine which differences between the three conditions are responsible for the significant omnibus main effect.

CHAPTER 10

1. *Note*: For all comparisons, $MS_{S/AB} = 10.09$ (see exercise 3, Chap. 9).

   a. *"Bright" versus "dull" (levels a_1 and a_3, respectively)*:

   $$\hat{\psi}_A = 5.63 - 10.25 = -4.62$$

$$SS_{A\,comp.} = \frac{(b)(n)(\hat{\psi}_A)^2}{2} = \frac{(2)(8)(-4.62)^2}{2} = \frac{(16)(21.34)}{2} = 170.72$$

Since $df_{A\,comp.} = 1$, $SS_{A\,comp.} = MS_{A\,comp.} = 170.72$.

$$F_{A\,comp.} = \frac{MS_{A\,comp.}}{MS_{S/AB}} = \frac{170.72}{10.09} = 16.92, \quad p < .05$$

b. *"Bright" versus "mixed" (levels a_1 and a_2, respectively)*:

$$\hat{\psi}_A = 5.63 - 8.13 = -2.50$$

$$SS_{A\,comp.} = \frac{(2)(8)(-2.50)^2}{2} = \frac{(16)(6.25)}{2} = 50.00$$

$$F_{A\,comp.} = 4.96, \quad p < .05$$

c. *"Dull" versus "mixed" (levels a_3 and a_2, respectively)*:

$$\hat{\psi}_A = 10.25 - 8.13 = 2.12$$

$$SS_{A\,comp.} = \frac{(2)(8)(2.12)^2}{2} = \frac{(16)(4.49)}{2} = 35.92$$

$$F_{A\,comp.} = 3.56, \quad p > .05$$

2. a. *Analysis of the simple effects of task difficulty (factor A)*:

Note: For SS's use Eq. (10-8); for MS's use Eq. (10-10); for F's use Eq. (10-11). For each simple effect, $MS_{S/AB} = 3.93$ and the critical value of $F(1, 72) \cong 4.00$.

Simple effects of task difficulty at level b_1:

$$SS_{A\,at\,b_1} = \frac{(60)^2 + (57)^2}{13} - \frac{(117)^2}{(2)(13)} = 526.85 - 526.50 = .35$$

$$MS_{A\,at\,b_1} = \frac{.35}{1} = .35 \quad (df_{A\,at\,b_1} = 2 - 1 = 1)$$

$$F_{A\,at\,b_1} = \frac{.35}{3.93} = .09, \quad p > .05$$

Simple effects of task difficulty at levels b_2 and b_3:

$$SS_{A\,at\,b_2} = 16.97; \quad F_{A\,at\,b_2} = 4.32, \quad p < .05$$

$$SS_{A\,at\,b_3} = 81.38; \quad F_{A\,at\,b_3} = 20.71, \quad p < .05$$

A significant interaction does not mean that each of the simple effects represents a significant effect. In this example, task difficulty is significant only with the larger number of distractors (levels b_2 and b_3).

b. *Analysis of the simple effects of the number of distractors (factor B):*

Note: For SS's use Eq. (10-12); for each simple effect, $MS_{S/AB} = 3.93$ and the critical value of $F(2, 72) \cong 3.15$.

Simple effects of the number of distractors for the easy task (level a_1):

$$SS_{B \text{ at } a_1} = \frac{(60)^2 + (62)^2 + (49)^2}{13} - \frac{(171)^2}{(3)(13)} = 757.31 - 749.77$$

$$= 7.54$$

$$MS_{B \text{ at } a_1} = \frac{7.54}{2} = 3.77; \quad F_{B \text{ at } a_1} = \frac{3.77}{3.93} = .96, \quad p > .05$$

Simple effects of the number of distractors for the difficult task (level a_2):

$$SS_{B \text{ at } a_2} = 58.05; \quad MS_{B \text{ at } a_2} = 29.03; \quad F_{B \text{ at } a_2} - 7.39, \quad p < .05$$

Distractors are more effective with the difficult task, but not effective with the easy task.

c. *Analysis of simple comparisons involving the number of distractors for the difficult task (level a_2):*

Note: For each simple comparison, $MS_{S/AB} = 3.93$ and the critical value of $F(1, 72) \cong 4.00$.

(1) *A comparison between levels b_2 and b_3 for the difficult task (level a_2):*

Note: Use the steps outlined in Table 10-10.

$$\hat{\psi}_{B \text{ at } a_2} = 6.38 - 7.31 = -.93$$

$$SS_{B \text{ comp. at } a_2} = \frac{(13)(-.93)^2}{2} = \frac{(13)(.86)}{2} = 5.59$$

$$MS_{B \text{ comp. at } a_2} = \frac{5.59}{1} = 5.59$$

$$F_{B \text{ comp. at } a_2} = \frac{5.59}{3.93} = 1.42, \quad p > .05$$

(2) *A comparison between level b_1 and the other two levels combined for the difficult task (level a_2):*

Note: Use the steps outlined in Table 10-11.

$$\hat{\psi}_{B \text{ at } a_2} = (+1)(4.38) + \left(-\tfrac{1}{2}\right)(6.38) + \left(-\tfrac{1}{2}\right)(7.31) = -2.47$$

$$\Sigma c^2 = (+1)^2 + \left(-\tfrac{1}{2}\right)^2 + \left(-\tfrac{1}{2}\right)^2 = 1.5$$

$$SS_{B \text{ comp. at } a_2} = \frac{(13)(-2.47)^2}{1.5} = \frac{(13)(6.10)}{1.5} = 52.87$$

$$MS_{B \text{ comp. at } a_2} = \frac{52.87}{1} = 52.87$$

$$F_{B \text{ comp. at } a_2} = \frac{52.87}{3.93} = 13.45, \quad p < .05$$

6. a. *The AB matrix:*

	Control (a_1)	Unfamiliar (a_2)	Sum
Young (b_1)	249	263	512
Adult (b_2)	261	173	434
Sum	510	436	946

b. Differences between the control and unfamiliar conditions depend on the age of the rats so that the unfamiliar scent appears more effective with the adult rats than with the young rats.

   Differences between young and adult rats vary depending on the scent conditions. The two age groups appear to differ only when the unfamiliar scent is present.

c. *Summary of the analysis of the interaction contrast:*

$$[AB] = 32,745.71; \quad [A] = 32,156.86; \quad [B] = 32,178.57;$$

$$[T] = 31,961.29$$

$$SS_{int.cont} = [AB] - [A] - [B] + [T] = 371.57$$

Since $df_{int.cont} = 1$, $MS_{int.cont} = SS_{int.cont} = 371.57$

$$MS_{S/AB} = 45.39 \text{ (from exercise 6, Chap. 9)}$$

$$F_{int.cont.} = \frac{371.57}{45.39} = 8.19, \quad p < .05$$

d. *Analysis of the simple effects involving the comparison between the control and unfamiliar conditions:*

(1) *Control versus unfamiliar conditions for the young rats (level b_1):*

$$SS_{A \text{ at } b_1} = \frac{(249)^2 + (263)^2}{7} - \frac{(512)^2}{(2)(7)} = 18,738.57 - 18,724.57 = 14.00$$

$$MS_{A \text{ at } b_1} = \frac{14.00}{1} = 14.00$$

$$F_{A \text{ at } b_1} = \frac{14.00}{45.39} = .31, \quad p > .05$$

(2) *Control versus unfamiliar conditions for the adult rats (level b_2):*

$$SS_{A \text{ at } b_2} = \frac{(261)^2 + (173)^2}{7} - \frac{(434)^2}{(2)(7)} = 14,007.14 - 13,454.00 = 553.14$$

$$F_{A \text{ at } b_1} = \frac{553.14}{45.39} = 12.19, \quad p < .05$$

CHAPTER 11

3. a. *Summary of the analyses:*

$$[T] = 10,082.00; \quad [A] = 10,288.33; \quad [S] = 10,252.00; \quad [Y] = 10,510$$

$$SS_A = [A] - [T] = 206.33; \quad SS_S = [S] - [T] = 170.00;$$

$$SS_{A \times S} = [Y] - [A] - [S] + [T] = 51.67; \quad SS_T = [Y] - [T] = 428.00$$

Source	SS	df	MS	F
A (Noise)	206.33	2	103.17	19.96*
S (Subjects)	170.00	5	34.00	
A × S (Residual)	51.67	10	5.17	
Total	428.00	17		

* $p < .05$.

b. *Comparison of the two noise conditions (levels a_2 and a_3):*

$$\hat{\psi}_A = 20.00 - 28.17 = -8.17$$

$$SS_{A\,comp.} = \frac{(6)(-8.17)^2}{2} = \frac{(6)(66.75)}{2} = 200.25$$

$$F_{A\,comp.} = \frac{200.25}{5.17} = 38.73, \quad p < .05$$

c. *Comparison of "no noise" (level a_1) with the combined noise conditions (levels a_2 and a_3):*

$$\hat{\psi}_A = (+1)(22.83) + \left(-\tfrac{1}{2}\right)(20.00) + \left(-\tfrac{1}{2}\right)(28.17) = -1.26$$

$$SS_{A\,comp.} = \frac{(6)(-1.26)^2}{1.5} = \frac{(6)(1.59)}{1.5} = 6.36$$

$$F_{A\,comp.} = \frac{6.36}{5.17} = 1.23, \quad p > .05$$

CHAPTER 12

1. *Matrices needed for the analysis:*

AB Matrix

	Soft (a_1)	Moderate (a_2)	Loud (a_3)	Sum
Slow (b_1)	66	88	90	244
Medium (b_2)	56	55	73	184
Fast (b_3)	42	43	55	140
Sum	164	186	218	568

AS Matrix

Soft (a_1)		Moderate (a_2)		Loud (a_3)	
s_1	20	s_7	33	s_{13}	28
s_2	26	s_8	31	s_{14}	33
s_3	24	s_9	24	s_{15}	35
s_4	32	s_{10}	41	s_{16}	42
s_5	33	s_{11}	23	s_{17}	42
s_6	29	s_{12}	34	s_{18}	38
Sum	164	Sum	186	Sum	218

Basic ratios:

$$[Y] = 6,578; \quad [A] = 6,056.44; \quad [B] = 6,277.33;$$

$$[AB] = 6,388.00; \quad [AS] = 6,222.67; \quad [T] = 5,974.52$$

Sums of squares:

$$SS_A = [A] - [T] = 81.92$$

$$SS_{S/A} = [AS] - [A] = 166.23$$

$$SS_B = [B] - [T] = 302.81$$

$$SS_{A \times B} = [AB] - [A] - [B] + [T] = 28.75$$

$$SS_{B \times S/A} = [Y] - [AB] - [AS] + [A] = 23.77$$

$$SS_T = [Y] - [T] = 603.48$$

Summary of the analysis:

Source	SS	df	MS	F
A (Loudness)	81.92	2	40.96	3.70*
S/A	166.23	15	11.08	
B (Rate)	302.81	2	151.41	191.66*
A × B	28.75	4	7.19	9.10*
B × S/A	23.77	30	.79	
Total	603.48	53		

* $p < .05$.

2. a. *Analysis of the simple effect of loudness for the messages presented at the slow rate (level b_1):*

$$SS_{A \text{ at } b_1} = \frac{(66)^2 + (88)^2 + (90)^2}{6} - \frac{(244)^2}{(3)(6)} = 3,366.67 - 3.307.56$$

$$= 59.11$$

$$MS_{A \text{ at } b_1} = \frac{59.11}{2} = 29.56$$

$$MS_{w.cell} = \frac{\Sigma s_{ij}^2}{(a)(b)} = \frac{1.20 + 4.67 + \cdots + 3.77 + 4.57}{(3)(3)} = \frac{38.02}{9} = 4.22$$

$$F_{A \text{ at } b_1} = \frac{MS_{A \text{ at } b_1}}{MS_{w.cell}} = \frac{29.56}{4.22} = 7.00, \quad p < .05$$

Note: The critical value of this F, which is found in Table A-2 with $df_{num.} = 2$ and $df_{denom.} = (a)(b)(n - 1) = (3)(3)(6 - 1) = 45$, is approximately 3.23 (using $df_{denom.} = 40$ in the table).

b. *Analysis of the simple comparison between moderate and loud messages (levels a_2 and a_3, respectively) presented at the slow rate (level b_1):*

$$\hat{\psi}_{A \text{ at } b_1} = 14.67 - 15.00 = -.33$$

$$SS_{A \text{ comp. at } b_1} = \frac{(6)(-.33)^2}{2} = .33$$

$$F_{A \text{ comp. at } b_1} = \frac{MS_{A \text{ comp. at } b_1}}{MS_{w.cell}} = \frac{.33}{4.22} = .08, \quad p > .05$$

c. *Analysis of the simple comparison between the soft message (level a_1) and a combination of the moderate and loud messages (levels a_2 and a_3, respectively) presented at the slow rate (level b_1):*

$$\hat{\psi}_{A \text{ at } b_1} = (+1)(11.00) + \left(-\tfrac{1}{2}\right)(14.67) + \left(-\tfrac{1}{2}\right)(15.00) = -3.84$$

$$SS_{A \text{ comp. at } b_1} = \frac{(6)(-3.84)^2}{1.5} = \frac{(6)(14.75)}{1.5} = 59.00$$

$$F_{A \text{ comp. at } b_1} = \frac{59.00}{4.22} = 13.98, \quad p < .05$$

3.   a. *Analysis of the simple effect of presentation rate for the loud messages (level a_3):*

$$SS_{B \text{ at } a_3} = \frac{(90)^2 + (73)^2 + (55)^2}{6} - \frac{(218)^2}{(3)(6)} = 2{,}742.33 - 2{,}640.22$$

$$= 102.11$$

$$MS_{B \text{ at } a_3} = \frac{102.11}{2} = 51.06$$

$$F_{B \text{ at } a_3} = \frac{MS_{B \text{ at } a_3}}{MS_{B \times S/A}} = \frac{51.06}{.79} = 64.63, \quad p < .05$$

b. *Analysis of the simple comparison between slow and medium rates (levels b_1 and b_2, respectively) for the loud messages (level a_3):*

$$\hat{\psi}_{B \text{ at } a_3} = 15.00 - 12.17 = 2.83$$

$$SS_{B \, comp. \text{ at } a_3} = \frac{(6)(2.83)^2}{2} = \frac{(6)(8.01)}{2} = 24.03$$

$$F_{B \, comp. \text{ at } a_3} = \frac{MS_{B \, comp. \text{ at } a_3}}{MS_{B \times S/A}} = \frac{24.03}{.79} = 30.42, \quad p < .05$$

c. *Analysis of the simple comparison between the fast rate (level b_3) and the combination of the slow and medium rates (levels b_1 and b_2, respectively) for the loud messages (level a_3):*

$$\hat{\psi}_{B \text{ at } a_3} = \left(-\tfrac{1}{2}\right)(15.00) + \left(-\tfrac{1}{2}\right)(12.17) + (+1)(9.17) = -4.42$$

$$SS_{B \, comp. \text{ at } a_3} = \frac{(6)(-4.42)^2}{1.5} = \frac{(6)(19.54)}{1.5} = 78.16$$

$$F_{B \, comp. \text{ at } a_3} = \frac{78.16}{.79} = 98.94, \quad p < .05$$

CHAPTER 13

1. *Matrices needed for the analysis*:

AB Matrix

	b_1	b_2	b_3	b_4	Sum
a_1	36	48	49	56	189
a_2	70	80	85	95	330
Sum	106	128	134	151	519

AS Matrix

	a_1	a_2	Sum
s_1	37	69	106
s_2	55	95	150
s_3	62	94	156
s_4	35	72	107
Sum	189	330	519

BS Matrix

	b_1	b_2	b_3	b_4	Sum
s_1	23	25	25	33	106
s_2	31	35	39	45	150
s_3	32	43	40	41	156
s_4	20	25	30	32	107
Sum	106	128	134	151	519

Basic ratios:

$$[Y] = 9,485; \quad [A] = 9,038.81; \quad [B] = 8,547.13;$$

$$[AB] = 9,171.75; \quad [S] = 8,690.13; \quad [AS] = 9,317.25;$$

$$[BS] = 8,851.50; \quad [T] = 8,417.53$$

Sums of squares:

$$SS_A = [A] - [T] = 621.28$$

$$SS_B = [B] - [T] = 129.60$$

$$SS_{A \times B} = [AB] - [A] - [B] + [T] = 3.34$$

$$SS_S = [S] - [T] = 272.60$$

$$SS_{A \times S} = [AS] - [A] - [S] + [T] = 5.84$$

$$SS_{B \times S} = [BS] - [B] - [S] + [T] = 31.77$$

$$SS_{A \times B \times S} = [Y] - [AB] - [AS] - [BS] + [A] + [B] + [S] - [T] = 3.04$$

$$SS_T = [Y] - [T] = 1,067.47$$

Summary of the analysis:

Source	SS	df	MS	F
A (Frequency)	621.28	1	621.28	318.61*
B (Trials)	129.60	3	43.20	12.24*
A × B	3.34	3	1.11	3.26
S (Subjects)	272.60	3	90.87	
A × S	5.84	3	1.95	
B × S	31.77	9	3.53	
A × B × S	3.04	9	.34	
Total	1,067.47	31		

* $p < .05$.

2. *Analysis of main comparisons involving trials (factor B)*

   a. *A comparison between trial 1 and trial 4 (levels b_1 and b_4, respectively):*

   $$\hat{\psi}_B = 13.25 - 18.88 = -5.63$$

   $$SS_{B\,comp.} = \frac{(2)(4)(-5.63)^2}{2} = \frac{(8)(31.70)}{2} = 126.80$$

   $$F_{B\,comp.} = \frac{MS_{B\,comp.}}{MS_{B\times S}} = \frac{126.80}{3.53} = 35.92, \quad p < .05$$

   b. *A comparison between trial 1 and the other trials combined (levels b_2 through b_4):*

   $$\hat{\psi}_B = (+3)(13.25) + (-1)(16.00) + (-1)(16.75) + (-1)(18.88)$$

   $$= -11.88$$

   $$\Sigma\, c^2 = (+3)^2 + (-1)^2 + (-1)^2 + (-1)^2 = 12$$

   $$SS_{B\,comp.} = \frac{(2)(4)(-11.88)^2}{12} = \frac{(8)(141.13)}{12} = 94.09$$

   $$F_{B\,comp.} = \frac{94.09}{3.53} = 26.65, \quad p < .05$$

3. a. *Analysis of the simple effect of stimulus duration (factor B) for element stimuli (level a_1):*

$$SS_{B \text{ at } a_1} = \frac{(140)^2 + (165)^2 + (203)^2}{5} - \frac{(508)^2}{(3)(5)}$$

$$= 17,606.80 - 17,204.27$$

$$= 402.53$$

$$MS_{B \text{ at } a_1} = \frac{402.53}{2} = 201.27$$

$$F_{B \text{ at } a_1} = \frac{MS_{B \text{ at } a_1}}{MS_{A \times B \times S}} = \frac{201.27}{.67} = 300.40, \quad p < .05$$

b. *Analysis of two simple comparisons*

(1) *A simple comparison between short and medium durations (levels b_1 and b_2) for the element stimuli (level a_1):*

$$\hat{\psi}_{B \text{ at } a_1} = 28.00 - 33.00 = -5.00$$

$$SS_{B \text{ comp. at } a_1} = \frac{(5)(-5.00)^2}{2} = \frac{(5)(25.00)}{2} = 62.50$$

$$F_{B \text{ comp. at } a_1} = \frac{MS_{B \text{ comp. at } a_1}}{MS_{A \times B \times S}} = \frac{62.50}{.67} = 93.28, \quad p < .05$$

(2) *A simple comparison between the short duration (level b_1) and a combination of the medium and long durations (levels b_2 and b_3) for the element stimuli (level a_1):*

$$\hat{\psi}_{B \text{ at } a_1} = (+1)(28.00) + \left(-\tfrac{1}{2}\right)(33.00) + \left(-\tfrac{1}{2}\right)(40.60) = -8.80$$

$$SS_{B \text{ comp. at } a_1} = \frac{(5)(-8.80)^2}{1.5} = \frac{(5)(77.44)}{1.5} = 258.13$$

$$F_{B \text{ comp. at } a_1} = \frac{258.13}{.67} = 385.27, \quad p < .05$$

CHAPTER 14

I. a. *Summary of the overall analysis:*

$$\chi^2 = \sum \frac{(f_O - f_E)^2}{f_E}$$

$$= \frac{(14 - 10.5)^2}{10.5} + \frac{(6 - 9.5)^2}{9.5} + \frac{(11 - 10.5)^2}{10.5} + \frac{(9 - 9.5)^2}{9.5}$$

$$+ \frac{(12 - 10.5)^2}{10.5} + \frac{(8 - 9.5)^2}{9.5} + \frac{(5 - 10.5)^2}{10.5} + \frac{(15 - 9.5)^2}{9.5}$$

$$= 1.17 + 1.29 + .02 + .03 + .21 + .24 + 2.88 + 3.18 = 9.02$$

For $df = 3$, the critical value of $\chi^2 = 7.81$ at the 5 percent level of significance; the overall differences among the treatment conditions are statistically significant.

b. *Estimating effect size:*

$$\phi = \sqrt{\frac{\chi^2}{N}} = \sqrt{\frac{9.02}{80}} = \sqrt{.11} = .33$$

c. *A comparison among the three therapy conditions:*

$$\chi^2 = \frac{(14 - 12.33)^2}{12.33} + \frac{(6 - 7.67)^2}{7.67} + \frac{(11 - 12.33)^2}{12.33} + \frac{(9 - 7.67)^2}{7.67}$$

$$+ \frac{(12 - 12.33)^2}{12.33} + \frac{(8 - 7.67)^2}{7.67}$$

$$= .23 + .36 + .14 + .23 + .01 + .01 = .98$$

For $df = 2$, the critical value of $\chi^2 = 5.99$ at the 5 percent level of significance; the overall differences among the three therapy conditions are not statistically significant.

d. *A comparison between the control condition and the combined therapy conditions:*

$$\chi^2 = \frac{(37 - 31.5)^2}{31.5} + \frac{(23 - 28.5)^2}{28.5} + \frac{(5 - 10.5)^2}{10.5} + \frac{(15 - 9.5)^2}{9.5}$$

$$= .96 + 1.06 + 2.88 + 3.18 = 8.08$$

For $df = 1$, the critical value of $\chi^2 = 3.84$ at the 5 percent level of significance; the improvement of patients receiving any therapy is statistically better than the improvement of patients receiving no therapy.

4. a. *Summary of the overall analysis:*

$$\chi^2 = \frac{(12-10.5)^2}{10.5} + \frac{(8-9.5)^2}{9.5} + \frac{(8-10.5)^2}{10.5} + \frac{(12-9.5)^2}{9.5}$$

$$+ \frac{(6-10.5)^2}{10.5} + \frac{(14-9.5)^2}{9.5} + \frac{(16-10.5)^2}{10.5} + \frac{(4-9.5)^2}{9.5}$$

$$= .21 + .24 + .60 + .66 + 1.93 + 2.13 + 2.88 + 3.18 = 11.83$$

For $df = 3$, the critical value of $\chi^2 = 7.81$ at the 5 percent level of significance; the overall differences among the treatment conditions are statistically significant.

b. *Analysis of the factorial design:*

(1) *Main effect of treatment (factor A):*

$$\chi^2 = \frac{(20-21)^2}{21} + \frac{(20-19)^2}{19} + \frac{(22-21)^2}{21} + \frac{(18-19)^2}{19}$$

$$= .05 + .05 + .05 + .05 = .20, \quad p > .05$$

(2) *Main effect of age (factor B):*

$$\chi^2 = \frac{(18-21)^2}{21} + \frac{(22-19)^2}{19} + \frac{(24-21)^2}{21} + \frac{(16-19)^2}{19}$$

$$= .43 + .47 + .43 + .47 = 1.80, \quad p > .05$$

(3) *Interaction of treatment and age:*

$$\chi^2 = \frac{(28-21)^2}{21} + \frac{(12-19)^2}{19} + \frac{(14-21)^2}{21} + \frac{(26-19)^2}{19}$$

$$= 2.33 + 2.58 + 2.33 + 2.58 = 9.82, \quad p < .05$$

CHAPTER 15

Means and standard deviations:

	Height (cm) (X)	Weight (kg) (Y)
Mean	166.53	63.07
Std. Dev.	11.18	9.11

c. *Sums of squares and sum of products:*

$$SS_X = 417,750 - \frac{(2,498)^2}{15} = 417,750 - 416,000.27 = 1,749.73$$

$$SS_Y = 60,822 - \frac{(946)^2}{15} = 60,822 - 59,661.07 = 1,160.93$$

$$SP_{XY} = 158,630 - \frac{(2,498)(946)}{15} = 158,630 - 157,540.53 = 1,089.47$$

d. *Product-moment correlation:*

$$r = \frac{1,089.47}{\sqrt{(1,749.73)(1,160.93)}} = \frac{1,089.47}{\sqrt{2,031,314.05}} = \frac{1,089.47}{1,425.24} = .76$$

For $df_r = 15 - 2 = 13$, critical value of $r = .51$; the correlation is statistically significant, $p < .05$.

e. *Strength of the correlation:*

$$r^2 = (.76)^2 = .58$$

f. *The regression equation:*

$$b = \frac{1,089.47}{1,749.73} = .62$$

$$a = 63.07 - (.62)(166.53) = 63.07 - 103.25 = -40.18$$

$$Y' = -40.18 + (.62)(X)$$

g. $Y' = -40.18 + (.62)(180) = -40.18 + 111.60 = 71.42$ kg

Appendix · C

USING STATISTICAL CALCULATORS

Relatively inexpensive, hand-held electronic calculators are readily available that greatly facilitate the repetitive operations required for calculating sums of squares and provide built-in programs that calculate common statistics such as the mean and the standard deviation. The purpose of this appendix is to show you how to perform certain basic statistical operations with a number of the more popular models available in most student bookstores for prices beginning at less than $15 — at least at the time of this writing. We have also included a more expensive statistical calculator from Hewlett-Packard, because students frequently come to our classes equipped with one of these models, which they have "inherited" from a friend or relative in the physical sciences, engineering, or business, and need some help in using the calculator for statistical applications.

SELECTING A STATISTICAL CALCULATOR

Perhaps the best source for statistical calculators is the student bookstore at your institution. These stores often have a wide selection of brands and models and a knowledgeable staff to help you select a calculator that will perform the calculations you require.

Calculators Designed for the Analysis of Data from Experiments

Calculators with statistical capabilities are usually identified as *statistical* or *scientific* calculators. You should examine the keyboard of the calculator carefully, looking for the following labels printed on, above, or below the keys:

$$\text{mean (or } \overline{X})$$

$$\text{standard deviation } (SD \text{ or } \sigma)$$

$$\Sigma\, X$$

$$\Sigma\, X^2$$

$$n$$

The presence of the first two labels indicates that the calculator will automatically calculate the mean and the standard deviation for a set of numbers after you have entered each one in and pressed a special entry key. The presence of the last three labels is important because it indicates that you will be able to extract from the internal memory of the calculator such vital information as the sum of the scores ($\Sigma\, X$), the sum of the squared scores ($\Sigma\, X^2$), and the sample size (n).[1] You should not consider purchasing a calculator that does not allow direct recovery of these last three quantities, which we use repeatedly in the calculations presented in this book.

Calculators Designed for the Analysis of Correlational Data

The calculators we discuss are designed to facilitate statistical calculations conducted on single sets of numbers, such as those required in this book in the analysis of data from experiments (Chaps. 2 through 14). Slightly more sophisticated calculators are available for use with correlational data in which the calculations are conducted on two sets of numbers (X and Y) arranged as *X-Y pairs*. (We discussed the analysis of correlational data in Chap. 15.) These calculators are distinguished by the inclusion of two sets of letters, X and Y, and labels representing the following operations:

$$\Sigma\, X, \quad \Sigma\, X^2, \quad \Sigma\, Y, \quad \Sigma\, Y^2, \quad \text{and} \quad \Sigma(X)(Y)$$

With these calculators, we enter the numbers by pairs (for example, X followed by Y). When this task is completed, we can obtain any of these five operations

---

[1] You should not be confused by the use of "X" to refer to individual scores. The symbol is arbitrary, of course — we would have used "Y" to correspond to the symbol we use to designate scores on the response measure or the dependent variable.

simply by pressing the appropriate key. That is, pressing

$\Sigma\ X$ and $\Sigma\ Y$ will produce the sums of the X and Y scores, respectively.

$\Sigma\ X^2$ and $\Sigma\ Y^2$ will produce the sums of the squared X and Y scores, respectively.

$\Sigma(X)(Y)$ will produce the sum of products of the pairs of X and Y scores.

These calculators will calculate the mean and standard deviation for both sets of numbers and a variety of statistics required for the analysis of correlational data.[2] Although calculators with these additional functions currently cost approximately $25, they will prove a worthwhile investment if you find yourself working with correlational data; they can, of course, be used with experimental data as well. For an additional $10, then, you will be able to facilitate the calculation of data from experiments as well as from correlational studies.

USING STATISTICAL CALCULATORS TO COMPUTE THE MEAN AND STANDARD DEVIATION

We will illustrate how to use four of the more popular statistical calculators to perform two basic statistical analyses (the mean and standard deviation) and how to obtain two sums ($\Sigma\ Y$ and $\Sigma\ Y^2$) that are needed for the computational formulas for sums of squares entering into the analysis of experiments. Because most calculators use X rather than Y to designate the dependent variable, we will follow this convention in referring to the different operations. We have based this discussion on the least expensive version of each model type currently available in campus bookstores — a reasonable choice given a student's limited budget! Although more expensive versions of the same model type will probably operate similarly, you should check the keyboard for the presence of the symbols representing the critical operations you will want the calculator to perform. Your best source of information is the manual

---

[2] Depending on the calculator, these may include the product-moment correlation coefficient r, the slope of the regression line, the Y intercept, and the capacity to use the regression equation to predict a value for Y (Y') on the basis of a value for X.

that comes with the calculator and the section on calculating the mean and standard deviation. This section will show you how to clear the calculator, enter the numbers, correct errors, calculate the mean and standard deviation, and how to obtain $\Sigma\, X$ and $\Sigma\, X^2$. We suggest that you find a numerical example in the manual and work through it until you can duplicate the answers in the manual. Then try the numerical example in Chap. 2 (see Table 2-2, p. 37).

Some statistical calculators require you to enter the *statistical mode*, which changes the way certain keys work. Most calculators require that you press a *function key*, followed by a second key, to execute an operation or to obtain information stored in the calculator. Some calculators have several function keys. We will use the same numerical example to illustrate how to use the different calculators in the statistical mode. The different sequences of operations for the four calculators are summarized in Table C-1. Each rectangle represents a button press; a series of rectangles represents a sequence of button presses. We have designated function keys with dark shading. The labels we have used for the keys in the table will be found on, above, or below the actual keys on the calculator.

Sharp EL-509D

Entering the Statistical Mode. The first step after turning the calculator on is to enter the statistical mode. This is accomplished by pressing the function key [2nd F], followed by the key labeled [ON/C]; the word *STAT* should be highlighted in the display.

Clearing the Statistical Registers. It is good practice to clear the memory (or *statistical*) registers before you begin to enter a new set of data into your calculator. You may need to read your manual to find out how this is accomplished with your particular model, if our instructions do not seem to work. With the Sharp EL-509D you press the function key [2nd F] first, followed by the key labeled [ON/C] to clear the statistical registers. Because this operation also returns the calculator to the normal operating mode, you will have to reenter the statistical mode by pressing [2nd F], followed by [ON/C].

Entering a Series of Numbers. We are now ready to enter the following series of numbers: 16, 10, 13, and 8. Each number is first entered by using the appropriate number keys followed by pressing the key labeled [M+] on the model we use — check your manual for details. This key instructs the calculator to do two things: (1) to store the cumulative sum of the scores in one statistical register and (2) to store the cumulative sum of the squared scores in another. Each number that you enter will appear in the display; you should take this

TABLE C-1 *Steps in Calculating the Mean and Standard Deviation with Four Statistical Calculators*

Step	Sharp EL-509D	Casio FX-82D	Texas Inst. TI-30 SLR+	Hewlett-Packard 15C
1. Put calculator in statistical mode.	2nd F ON/C (STAT in display)	MODE · (SD in display)	Occurs when you first press Σ+ (STAT in display)	Occurs when you press ON (No special symbol)
2. Make sure the statistical registers are clear.	(See text)	INV AC	INV CSR	f Σ
3. Enter data.	16 M+ 10 M+ 13 M+ 8 M+	16 M+ 10 M+ 13 M+ 8 M+	16 Σ+ 10 Σ+ 13 Σ+ 8 Σ+	16 Σ+ 10 Σ+ 13 Σ+ 8 Σ+
4. Obtain statistics:				
Mean ($\overline{Y}$)	$\overline{X}$	INV $\overline{X}$	INV $\overline{X}$	g $\overline{X}$
Std. dev. (s)	s	INV σ_{n-1}	INV σ_{n-1}	g s
Variance (s^2)	s X^2	INV σ_{n-1} INV X^2	INV σ_{n-1} X^2	g s g X^2
Sum of the scores ($\Sigma\ Y$)	2nd F $\Sigma\ X$	INV $\Sigma\ X$	INV $\Sigma\ X$	RCL 3
Sum of the squared scores ($\Sigma\ Y^2$)	2nd F $\Sigma\ X^2$	INV $\Sigma\ X^2$	INV $\Sigma\ X^2$	RCL 4

opportunity to check for accuracy and to make any necessary correction before you press M+ . After pressing M+ , you will see a new number in the display, which tells you how many numbers you have entered into the calculator up to this point. After entering the four numbers, the number 4 should show in the display.

Calculating the Mean and Standard Deviation. You obtain the mean by pressing the key labeled $\overline{X}$; the mean (11.75) will appear in the display. If the mean does not come out evenly, the answer will be displayed with as many decimal places as can fit in the display. You simply round the answer to the number of decimal places you wish to keep in your calculations. (We round all calculations to two places in this book — see pp. 32–33.) If you need to verify the sample size, press the key labeled n; sample size (4) will appear in the display.

This calculator gives you the option of calculating two different standard deviations, depending on whether the sum of squares is divided by the sample size (n) or by the degrees of freedom ($df = n - 1$). The one appropriate for purposes of statistical inference and for all the calculations in this book uses the df in its calculation. You obtain this standard deviation by pressing the key labeled s; the answer (3.5) will appear in the display. If you want the variance, simply press the "square key," labeled X^2 — *not* the key labeled ΣX^2 — and the variance ($3.5^2 = 12.25$) will appear in the display. If you want the other standard deviation, press the function key $\boxed{\text{2nd F}}$, followed by the key labeled σ; the answer (3.031088..., or 3.03, rounded to two decimal places) will appear in the display. If you are unclear on which standard deviation to use in your statistical calculations, you should use the *larger* of the two.

Obtaining ΣX ***and*** ΣX^2. If you want to use computational formulas to calculate the mean and standard deviation, you will need to obtain the sum of the scores and the sum of the squared scores from the calculator. To retrieve the first sum, press the function key $\boxed{\text{2nd F}}$, followed by the key labeled ΣX; the answer (47) will appear in the display. To retrieve the second sum, press the function key $\boxed{\text{2nd F}}$, followed by the key labeled ΣX^2; the answer (589) will appear in the display.

Casio FX-82D

Entering the Statistical Mode. The first step after turning the calculator on is to enter the statistical mode. This is accomplished by pressing the function key $\boxed{\text{MODE}}$, followed by the key for the decimal point $\boxed{.}$; the letters *SD* (for *standard deviation mode*) should be highlighted in the display.

Clearing the Statistical Registers. It is good practice to clear the memory (or *statistical*) registers before you begin to enter a new set of data into your calculator. You may need to read your manual to find out how this is accomplished with your particular model, if our instructions do not seem to work. With the Casio FX-82D you simply press another function key, $\boxed{\text{INV}}$, followed by the key labeled $\boxed{\text{AC}}$; you will remain in the statistical mode until you formally cancel this mode of operation.

Entering a Series of Numbers. We are now ready to enter the following series of numbers: 16, 10, 13, and 8. Each number is first entered by using the appropriate number keys followed by pressing the key labeled $\boxed{\text{M+}}$ on the model we use, but it may be labeled $\boxed{\text{X}}$ or $\boxed{\text{DATA}}$ — check your manual for details. This key instructs the calculator to do two things: (1) to store the cumulative sum of the scores in one statistical register and (2) to store the cumulative sum of the squared scores in another. Each number that you enter will appear in the display; you should take this opportunity to check for accuracy and to make any necessary correction before you press $\boxed{\text{M+}}$. After pressing $\boxed{\text{M+}}$, you will continue to see the last number until you begin to enter the next number, which will now be shown in the display as you enter it. After entering the four numbers, the last number you entered (8) should show in the display.

Calculating the Mean and Standard Deviation. You obtain the mean by pressing the function key labeled $\boxed{\text{INV}}$, followed by the key labeled $\boxed{\overline{X}}$; the mean (11.75) will appear in the display. If the mean does not come out evenly, the answer will be displayed with as many decimal places as can fit in the display. You simply round the answer to the number of decimal places you wish to keep in your calculations. (We round all calculation to two places in this book — see pp. 32–33.) If you need to verify the sample size, press the function key $\boxed{\text{INV}}$, followed by the key labeled $\boxed{n}$; sample size (4) will appear in the display.

This calculator gives you the option of calculating two different standard deviations, depending on whether the sum of squares is divided by the sample size (n) or by the degrees of freedom ($df = n - 1$). The one appropriate for purposes of statistical inference and for all the calculations in this book uses the df in its calculation. You obtain this standard deviation by pressing the function key $\boxed{\text{INV}}$, followed by the key labeled $\boxed{\sigma_{n-1}}$; the answer (3.5) will appear in the display. If you want the variance, simply press $\boxed{\text{INV}}$ again, followed by "square key," labeled $\boxed{X^2}$ — *not* the key labeled $\boxed{\Sigma\, X^2}$ — and the variance ($3.5^2 = 12.25$) will appear in the display. If you want the other standard deviation, press the function key $\boxed{\text{INV}}$, followed by the key labeled $\boxed{\sigma_n}$; the answer (3.031088..., or 3.03, rounded to two decimal places) will appear in the display. If you are unclear on which standard deviation to use in your statistical calculations, you should use the *larger* of the two.

Obtaining $\Sigma\, X$ and $\Sigma\, X^2$. If you want to use computational formulas to calculate the mean and standard deviation, you will need to obtain the sum of the scores and the sum of the squared scores from the calculator. To retrieve the first sum, press the function key $\boxed{\text{INV}}$, followed by the key labeled $\boxed{\Sigma\, X}$; the answer (47) will appear in the display. To retrieve the second sum, press the function key $\boxed{\text{INV}}$, followed by the key labeled $\boxed{\Sigma\ X^2}$; the answer (589) will appear in the display.

Texas Instruments TI-30 SLR+

Entering the Statistical Mode. No special step is necessary to enter the statistical mode with this calculator. This will happen when you begin to enter a data set to calculate the mean and standard deviation.

Clearing the Statistical Registers. It is good practice to clear the memory (or *statistical*) registers before you begin to enter a new set of data into your calculator. You may need to read your manual to find out how this is accomplished with your particular model, if our instructions do not seem to work. With the TI-30 SLR+ you simply press the function key $\boxed{\text{INV}}$, followed by the key labeled $\boxed{\text{CSR}}$ ("clear statistical register").

Entering a Series of Numbers. We are now ready to enter the following series of numbers: 16, 10, 13, and 8. Each number is first entered by using the appropriate number keys followed by pressing the key labeled $\boxed{\Sigma+}$ on the model we use — check your manual for details. As soon as you press this key, you will automatically enter the statistical mode, which is indicated by the word *STAT* appearing in your display. The $\boxed{\Sigma+}$ key instructs the calculator to do two things: (1) to store the cumulative sum of the scores in one statistical register and (2) to store the cumulative sum of the squared scores in another. Each number that you enter will appear in the display; you should take this opportunity to check for accuracy and to make any necessary correction before you press $\boxed{\Sigma+}$. After pressing $\boxed{\Sigma+}$, you will see a new number in the display, which tells you how many numbers you have entered into the calculator up to this point. After entering the four numbers, the number 4 should show in the display.

Calculating the Mean and Standard Deviation. You obtain the mean by pressing the function key labeled $\boxed{\text{INV}}$, followed by the key labeled $\boxed{\overline{X}}$; the mean (11.75) will appear in the display. If the mean does not come out evenly, the answer will be displayed with as many decimal places as can fit in the display. You simply round the answer to the number of decimal places you wish to keep in your calculations. (We round all calculations to two places in this book — see pp. 32–33.) If you need to verify the sample size, you will need to count the numbers or divide the sum of the scores (read on) by the mean; there is no special key that will produce the sample size directly.

This calculator gives you the option of calculating two different standard deviations, depending on whether the sum of squares is divided by the sample size (n) or by the degrees of freedom ($df = n - 1$). The one appropriate for purposes of statistical inference and for all the calculations in this book uses the *df* in its calculation. You obtain this standard deviation by pressing the function key $\boxed{\text{INV}}$, followed by the key labeled $\boxed{\sigma_{n-1}}$; the answer (3.5) will appear in the display. If you want the variance, next simply press the "square key," labeled $\boxed{X^2}$ — *not* the key labeled $\boxed{\Sigma\, X^2}$ — and the variance ($3.5^2 = 12.25$) will appear in the display. If you want the other standard deviation, press the function key $\boxed{\text{INV}}$, followed by the key labeled $\boxed{\sigma_n}$; the answer (3.031088..., or 3.03, rounded to two decimal places) will appear in the display. If you are unclear on which standard deviation to use in your statistical calculations, you should use the *larger* of the two.

Obtaining $\Sigma\, X$ ***and*** $\Sigma\, X^2$. If you want to use computational formulas to calculate the mean and standard deviation, you will need to obtain the sum of the scores and the sum of the squared scores from the calculator. To retrieve the first sum, press the function key $\boxed{\text{INV}}$, followed by the key labeled $\boxed{\Sigma\, X}$; the answer (47) will appear in the display. To retrieve the second sum, press the function key $\boxed{\text{INV}}$, followed by the key labeled $\boxed{\Sigma\, X^2}$; the answer (589) will appear in the display.

Hewlett-Packard 15C

Entering the Statistical Mode. No special step is necessary to enter the statistical mode with this calculator, because it is continually ready to perform statistical calculations.

Clearing the Statistical Registers. It is good practice to clear the memory (or *statistical*) registers before you begin to enter a new set of data into your calculator. You may need to read your manual to find out how this is accomplished with your particular model, if our instructions do not seem to work. With the HP-15C you simply press the function key labeled $\boxed{f}$ (one of several function keys), followed by the key labeled $\boxed{\Sigma}$.

Entering a Series of Numbers

We are now ready to enter the following series of numbers: 16, 10, 13, and 8. Each number is first entered by using the appropriate number keys followed by pressing the key labeled $\boxed{\Sigma+}$ on the model we use — check your manual for details. The $\boxed{\Sigma+}$ key instructs the calculator to do two things: (1) to store the cumulative sum of the scores in one statistical register and (2) to store the cumulative sum of the squared scores in another. Each number that you enter will appear in the display; you should take this opportunity to check for accuracy and to make any necessary correction before you press $\boxed{\Sigma+}$. After pressing $\boxed{\Sigma+}$, you see a new number in the display, which tells you how many numbers have been entered up to this point. Additional 0's will also appear to the right of the decimal point, depending on the number of decimal places you have programmed into the calculator (see the next paragraph for setting this number).

Calculating the Mean and Standard Deviation. You obtain the mean by pressing another function key, $\boxed{g}$, followed by the key labeled $\boxed{\overline{X}}$; the mean (11.75) will appear in the display. If the mean does not come out evenly, the answer will be rounded automatically to the number of decimal places you wish to show in the display. You set the number of places by pressing the function key $\boxed{f}$, followed by the key labeled $\boxed{\text{FIX}}$ and a number key indicating the number of places you want the calculator to report. For example, the sequence

will give you answers rounded to two places; the sequence

will give you answers rounded to four places. (We round all calculations to two places in this book — see pp. 32–33.) If you need to verify the sample size, press another function key, $\boxed{\text{RCL}}$, followed by the number key $\boxed{2}$; sample size (4) will appear in the display.

This calculator will calculate only one standard deviation directly — namely, the one that uses the *df* in its calculation and is appropriate for purposes of statistical inference and for all the calculations in this book. You obtain this standard deviation by pressing the function key labeled $\boxed{g}$, followed by the key labeled $\boxed{s}$; the answer (3.50) will appear in the display. If you want the variance, you continue by pressing the function key $\boxed{g}$ again, followed by "square key," labeled $\boxed{X^2}$, and the variance ($3.5^2 = 12.25$) will appear in the display.

Obtaining $\Sigma\ X$ and $\Sigma\ X^2$. If you want to use computational formulas to calculate the mean and standard deviation, you will need to obtain the sum of the scores and the sum of the squared scores from the calculator. To retrieve the first sum, press the function key $\boxed{\text{RCL}}$, followed by the number key $\boxed{3}$;

the answer (47) will appear in the display. To retrieve the second sum, press the function key $\boxed{\text{RCL}}$, followed by the number key $\boxed{4}$; the answer (589) will appear in the display.

CALCULATING BASIC RATIOS [3]

Beginning in Chap. 4, you are introduced to a set of repetitive arithmetical operations that we use to calculate the different sums of squares required for the analysis of variance. These operations produce a quantity we call a *basic ratio*. Central to each basic ratio is a squaring-and-summing operation that we can conveniently carry out with a statistical calculator.

Preliminary Calculations

We would begin by arranging the data according to the different treatment conditions, as we have done in Table C-2. We would place our calculator in the statistical mode and then perform the series of preliminary calculations summarized in part 2 of Table C-2. That is, we would first clear the statistical registers and then enter the data into the calculator separately for each group, using the special summation key we described in the preceding section. After entering the Y scores for each group, we would then extract the following information from the calculator:

Calculate the mean $(\overline{Y}_A)$

Calculate the standard deviation (s)

Recall the sum of the scores (A)

Recall the sum of the squared scores $(\Sigma\ Y^2)$

The means and standard deviations provide the descriptive statistics we need to summarize the results for the different treatment conditions. They are calculated in the manner we outlined in the previous section. The sums obtained

---

[3] In preparing this section, we assumed that readers will have read Chap. 4 and Sec. 4.3 in particular.

TABLE C-2 *Calculating the Basic Ratios for the Analysis of a Completely Randomized Single-Factor Experiment*

I. Arrange Data According to Treatment Conditions

a_1	a_2
2	6
3	5
1	4

2. Perform Preliminary Calculations

a. Enter the data for each group, using the summation key.

b. Calculate the mean: $\overline{Y}_{A_1} = 2.00 \qquad \overline{Y}_{A_2} = 5.00$

c. Calculate the standard deviation: $s_1 = 1.00 \qquad s_2 = 1.00$

d. Recall the sum of the scores $\boxed{\Sigma X}$: $A_1 = 6 \qquad A_2 = 15$

e. Recall the sum of the squared scores $\boxed{\Sigma X^2}$: $\Sigma Y^2 = 14 \qquad \Sigma Y^2 = 77$

3. Calculate [A]

a. Enter the treatment sums (A_i) using the summation key.

b. Recall $\boxed{\Sigma X^2}$: $\Sigma A^2 = 261$. [Note: $261 = (6)^2 + (15)^2$.]

c. Calculate [A]: $[A] = \Sigma A^2/n = 261/3 = 87.00$.

4. Calculate [T]

a. Recall $\boxed{\Sigma X}$ from step 3: $T = 21$. [Note: $21 = 6 + 15$.]

b. Calculate [T]: $[T] = T^2/(a)(n) = (21)^2/(2)(3) = 441/6 = 73.50$.

5. Calculate [Y]

a. Locate the subtotals from step 2e.

b. Calculate [Y]: $[Y] = \Sigma Y^2 = 14 + 77 = 91$.

---

from the data entries provide us with the ingredients for two of the basic ratios we need for the analysis of variance: the treatment sums (A), which we obtain by pressing the appropriate keys to recall $\boxed{\Sigma X}$, are used to calculate the basic ratio $[A]$; and the sums of the squared Y scores, which we obtain by pressing the appropriate keys to recall $\boxed{\Sigma\ X^2}$, are used to calculate the basic ratio $[Y]$. The results of these operations are given in parts 2d and 2e of Table C-2, respectively.

Calculating the Basic Ratio [A]

The formula for the basic ratio based on the treatment sums is as follows:

$$[A] = \frac{\Sigma\ A^2}{n}$$

The quantity we need to calculate consists of the sum of the squared treatment sums ($\Sigma\ A^2$). We can obtain this value with the statistical calculator by following the steps summarized in part 3 of Table C-2. We start by clearing the statistical registers and then entering the treatment sums (A_1 and A_2 in this example) as if they were *individual scores* rather than *sums* of scores. After they have been entered, we simply recall the sum of the squared sums — by pressing the keys to produce $\boxed{\Sigma\ X^2}$ — and complete the required calculations.

Calculating the Basic Ratio [T]

The formula for the basic ratio based on the grand total is as follows:

$$[T] = \frac{T^2}{(a)(n)}$$

The key quantity we need, T, is available from the operations we performed in step 3. That is, in the process of summing the squared treatment totals, we also calculated the *sum* of these totals, namely, T. We obtain this quantity by recalling the sum of treatment sums — by pressing the keys to produce $\boxed{\Sigma\ X}$ — and completing the required calculations. These steps are summarized in part 4 of the table.

Calculating the Basic Ratio [Y]

The final basic ratio is based on the individual Y scores; that is,

$$[Y] = \Sigma\ Y^2$$

We can obtain this quantity by locating the sums of the squared Y scores we obtained for the two treatments in step 2e and then combining them. This final calculation is summarized in part 5 of the table.

A p p e n d i x · D

TREND ANALYSIS

Throughout this book we have focused on one type of independent variable, one in which the treatment conditions reflect differences in *kind* or *type* — namely, *qualitative independent variables.* Analytical comparisons appropriate for qualitative manipulations, which assess more focused questions than does the omnibus *F*, tend to consist of contrasting one treatment condition against another. A control condition versus a drug condition, praise versus criticism, and sterile sawdust versus unfamiliar smells are examples of comparisons of this sort we have examined in various chapters in Part Two.

Another type of manipulation involves a *quantitative* manipulation, in which the treatment conditions reflect differences in *degree* or *amount.* For example, a researcher might study the effects of different intensities of background noise on a subject's ability to follow targets projected on a screen, or the effects of different dosages of a drug on the performance of rats in a complex maze. Analytical comparisons appropriate for quantitative manipulations are different from those appropriate for qualitative manipulations. Instead of examining differences between two conditions, which characterizes the way we commonly analyze qualitative independent variables, researchers usually plot the treatment means in a graph and examine the data for relatively simple ways of describing the outcome mathematically. For example, most investigators will want to know whether the data may be described by a *straight line.* Stated another way, they are interested in determining whether a significant **linear trend** is reflected in the data. This general approach to the analysis of quantitative independent variables is called **trend analysis**. We briefly discussed this type of analysis in Chap. 6 (pp. 158–160).

ANALYSIS OF LINEAR TREND

Trend analysis involves a special type of single-*df* comparison, which means that we follow exactly the same steps we outlined in Sec. 6.4 for the analysis of differences between means. The formulas are identical; the only complication is in selecting the appropriate set of coefficients, which may be found in a special table in the Appendix (Table A-11). We will discuss the analysis of linear trend by working through a numerical example.

A Numerical Example

Consider a hypothetical experiment investigating the relationship between the length of a task and the time needed to complete it. Although we would expect to find that longer tasks require more time to learn than shorter ones, we are unable to predict the nature of the relationship. Will the time needed to learn a task increase steadily as the task is lengthened, or will the task become increasingly more difficult? A steady increase in difficulty would imply a linear relationship between length and time to learn, whereas a progressive increase would imply a more complex one.

The task consists of a list of word pairs that subjects must learn completely. There are $a = 6$ different lists consisting of 4, 8, 12, 16, 20, and 24 pairs, each represented by a different group of subjects ($n = 8$) who were assigned randomly to the groups. Length of list, then, is the independent variable, and the average number of trials needed to master the list is the dependent variable. The data are presented in the upper portion of Table D-1. The means, which are presented in the table, have been plotted in Fig. D-1. As you can readily see, there is a strong tendency for the mean number of trials required to learn a list to increase steadily as the length of the list increases.

Our first step is to conduct an overall analysis of variance to determine whether the differences among the treatment means are significant. The analysis, a single-factor between-subjects design (see Chap. 5), is summarized in the remainder of Table D-1. The overall F is significant, and we can conclude that list length affects trials to learn. We can say nothing definitive about the *nature* of this result, because this analysis allows us to conclude only that the means are not the same. We need to conduct additional analyses to reveal the reasons for the significant omnibus F. With a qualitative independent variable, these analyses would consist of a number of meaningful comparisons between selected treatment conditions. With a quantitative independent variable, on the other hand, we can make more precise descriptions with analyses consisting of an overall assessment of linear and perhaps other, more complicated trends.

The Statistical Hypotheses

You may have noticed that we have also drawn a straight line through the means in Fig. D-1 to illustrate how well the data reflect a linear trend — that is, a trend that may be described by a straight line. This line is called the line of "best fit,"

TABLE D-I *Numerical Example: Trials to Learn Lists Consisting of Varying Numbers of Pairs*

Data Matrix

	a_1	a_2	a_3	a_4	a_5	a_6
	2	8	12	23	12	33
	4	10	11	19	25	36
	10	8	7	17	13	26
	3	5	4	14	27	27
	8	3	14	21	17	29
	2	4	10	15	24	31
	6	3	6	13	24	22
	4	4	5	11	19	23
$\overline{Y}_A$:	4.88	5.63	8.63	16.63	20.13	28.38
A:	39	45	69	133	161	227
$\Sigma\, Y^2$:	249	303	687	2,331	3,469	6,605

Basic Ratios

$$[Y] = \Sigma\, Y^2 = 249 + 303 + \cdots + 3,469 + 6,605 = 13,644$$

$$[A] = \frac{\Sigma\, A^2}{n} = \frac{(39)^2 + (45)^2 + \cdots + (161)^2 + (227)^2}{8} = 12,930.75$$

$$[T] = \frac{T^2}{(a)(n)} = \frac{(39 + 45 + \cdots + 161 + 227)^2}{(6)(8)} = 9,464.08$$

Summary of the Analysis

Source	SS	df	MS	F
A (No. of Pairs)	$[A] - [T] = 3,466.67$	5	693.33	40.83*
S/A	$[Y] - [A] = \;\;\;713.25$	42	16.98	
Total	$[Y] - [T] = 4,179.92$	47		

* $p < .05$.

---

because it minimizes the discrepancies between the line and the actual data points plotted in the figure. As you can see, the straight line fits the data point quite well.

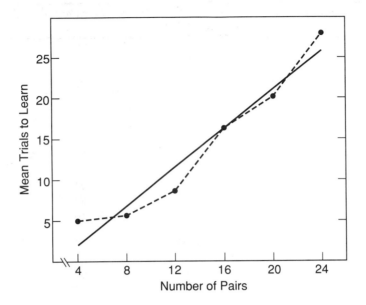

FIGURE D-1 *Mean Trials to Learn Lists Consisting of Varying Numbers of Pairs. The straight line represents the estimated linear relationship between the independent and dependent variables.*

If there is absolutely no linear trend relating the independent and dependent variables, the line of best fit will have no "tilt," or *slope,* and will be parallel to the baseline or *X* axis; under these circumstances, the slope will be *zero.* If there is a positive linear trend, as the means plotted in Fig. D-1 suggest, the line will tilt upward from left to right and the slope will have a positive value. If there is a negative linear trend, the line will tilt downward and the slope will have a negative value. Because of experimental error, however, it is entirely possible that the value of the observed slope of the line plotted in the figure is not statistically different from zero. The analysis of linear trend assesses the following set of statistical hypotheses:

H_0: linear trend is absent (or slope = zero)

H_1: linear trend is present (or slope $\neq$ zero)

Calculating the Linear Sum of Squares

We assess the null hypothesis by calculating an *F* ratio that is sensitive to the presence of linear trend. The key to the analysis is the linear sum of squares ($SS_{A\,linear}$), which we obtain with Eq. (6-9), the general formula for single-*df* comparisons that we introduced in Chap. 6 (see pp. 151–154). That is,

$$SS_{A_{linear}} = \frac{n(\hat{\psi}_{linear})^2}{\Sigma\, c^2} \tag{D-1}$$

where n is the sample size, $\hat{\psi}_{linear}$ is the sum of the treatment means weighted (or multiplied) by a special set of linear coefficients, and c refers to the linear coefficients.

The linear coefficients for this analysis may be found in Table A-11 in Appendix A, which lists coefficients for two different types of trend — linear and quadratic — for experiments with varying numbers of treatment conditions. The set we need for this analysis is found under $a = 6$ treatment levels, in the row labeled "linear," and consists of

$$-5, -3, -1, +1, +3, +5$$

Using the general formula for $\hat{\psi}$, as presented in Eq. (6-8), we now calculate $\hat{\psi}_{linear}$:

$$
\begin{aligned}
\hat{\psi}_{linear} &= (c_1)(\overline{Y}_{A_1}) + (c_2)(\overline{Y}_{A_2}) + (c_3)(\overline{Y}_{A_3}) + \cdots \\
&= (-5)(4.88) + (-3)(5.63) + \cdots + (3)(20.13) + (5)(28.38) \\
&= -24.40 - 16.89 - 8.63 + 16.63 + 60.39 + 141.90 \\
&= 169.00
\end{aligned}
$$

We also need the sum of the squared coefficients for Eq. (D-1):

$$\Sigma\, c^2 = (-5)^2 + (-3)^2 + \cdots + (3)^2 + (5)^2 = 70$$

Substituting in Eq. (D-1), we find

$$SS_{A_{linear}} = \frac{(8)(169.00)^2}{70} = \frac{(8)(28,561.00)}{70} = \frac{228,488.00}{70} = 3,264.11$$

Completing the Analysis

The final steps in the analysis duplicate the procedures we outlined in Chap. 6. Linear trend is associated with one degree of freedom; that is,

$$df_{A_{linear}} = 1 \tag{D-2}$$

Thus, $MS_{A_{linear}} = 3,264.11/1 = 3,264.11$. The F ratio is formed by dividing the linear mean square by the error term from the overall analysis ($MS_{S/A} = 16.98$). The F becomes

$$F_{A_{linear}} = \frac{MS_{A_{linear}}}{MS_{S/A}} \qquad (D\text{-}3)$$

Substituting in Eq. (D-3), we find

$$F_{A_{linear}} = \frac{3,264.11}{16.98} = 192.23$$

The critical value of F (F_α) is found in Table A-2 under $df_{num.} = 1$ and $df_{denom.} = df_{S/A} = 42$. With $\alpha = .05$, we find $F_\alpha = 4.08$ (at $df_{denom.} = 40$). The decision rule is formed in the usual way. More specifically,

If $F_{A_{linear}} \geq 4.08$, reject the null hypothesis; otherwise, retain the null hypothesis.

We reject the null hypothesis and conclude that there is a significant linear relationship between list length and trials to learn — that is, as list length increases, trials to learn increases in a linear fashion.

ANALYZING HIGHER-ORDER TRENDS

Sometimes the relationship between a quantitative independent variable and a dependent variable reflects the presence of more complex, or **nonlinear, trends**. The figure we first presented as Fig. 6-2 (and present again in Fig. D-2), based on an experiment by Grant and Schiller (1953), is just such an example. In that study, subjects were trained to respond to a particular stimulus (a 12-inch circle) and then were tested with circles varying in diameter from 9 inches to 15 inches. Although there is a tendency for the means to increase as the independent variable increases, suggesting the presence of a linear trend, there is a distinct tendency for the means to *decrease* beginning with the 12-inch circle and continuing for the larger test stimuli. This is an example of a form of nonlinear trend called a **quadratic trend** — a trend in this case that appears to look like an inverted U, in which the means first increase as the independent variable increases and later decrease.

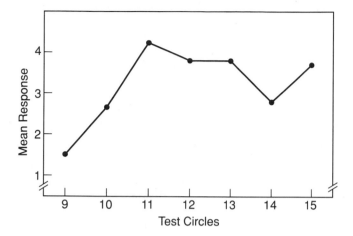

FIGURE D-2 *A Plot of the Data Reported by Grant and Schiller (1953). (See Fig. 6-2, p. 160.)*

Testing for the Presence of Nonlinear Trends

Usually, we need to conduct a preliminary test before determining whether nonlinear trends are present in the data. This preliminary test consists of removing the linear sum of squares from the between-groups sum of squares and testing whether nonlinear trends account for a significant portion of the remaining, or *residual*, sum of squares.

The formula for this residual sum of squares is simply the following:

$$SS_{A_{residual}} = SS_A - SS_{A_{linear}} \qquad (D\text{-}4)$$

Illustrating with our numerical example of the previous section relating learning time to the length of the list, we find

$$SS_{A_{residual}} = 3,466.67 - 3,264.11 = 202.56$$

The degrees of freedom for the residual sum of squares are calculated analogously; that is,

$$df_{A_{residual}} = df_A - df_{A_{linear}} \qquad (D\text{-}5)$$

For this example,

$$df_{A_{residual}} = 5 - 1 = 4$$

The mean square is calculated by dividing the residual sum of squares by the residual degrees of freedom:

$$MS_{A\,residual} = \frac{SS_{A\,residual}}{df_{A\,residual}} \tag{D-6}$$

Since $df_{A\,residual} = 4$, $MS_{A\,residual} = 202.56/4 = 50.64$.

The F ratio is formed by dividing the residual mean square by the error term from the overall analysis ($MS_{S/A}$). In symbols,

$$F_{A\,residual} = \frac{MS_{A\,residual}}{MS_{S/A}} \tag{D-7}$$

The F ratio for our numerical example becomes

$$F_{A\,residual} = \frac{50.64}{16.98} = 2.98$$

The critical value of F is found in Table A-2 under $df_{num.} = 4$ and $df_{denom.} = 42$; using $df_{denom.} = 40$, we find $F_\alpha = 2.61$. The decision rule becomes

If $F_{A\,residual} \geq 2.61$, reject the null hypothesis; otherwise, retain the null hypothesis.

We conclude that the variation remaining among the treatment means after we have removed the linear trend is significant — that is, significant nonlinear trends may be present.

Searching for Significant Nonlinear Trends

The common strategy at this point is to test for the presence of the least complex trend — in this case, a nonlinear trend that contains one "bend," or reversal of direction, such as the inverted U-shaped trend we identified in Fig. D-2. With regard to our numerical example, the bend is reflected by a slight tendency for the means to curve around the straight line (see Fig. D-1), which you can see more easily by tilting the figure until the straight line is horizontal and then examine the pattern of the data points.

The procedure for assessing this type of trend is no more complex than the one we detailed for linear trend. More specifically, we adapt the formulas we presented for the linear analysis simply by substituting a different set of coefficients constructed to detect the presence of this type of nonlinear trend.

These coefficients are also found in Table A-11 under the more technical term of *quadratic trend*. The set for the present example, where $a = 6$, is

$$+5, -1, -4, -4, -1, +5$$

Conducting the Analysis. From this point on, the analysis of the quadratic trend parallels the analysis of the linear trend we conducted in the preceding section. That is, we calculate $\hat{\psi}_{quadratic}$ as follows:

$$\hat{\psi}_{quadratic} = (5)(4.88) + (-1)(5.63) + \cdots + (-1)(20.13) + (5)(28.38)$$

$$= 24.40 - 5.63 + \cdots - 20.13 + 141.90$$

$$= 39.50$$

Substituting in an adaptation of Eq. (D-1), we find

$$= \frac{n(\hat{\psi}_{quadratic})^2}{\Sigma c^2}$$

$$= \frac{(8)(39.50)^2}{84} = \frac{(8)(1,560.25)}{84} = \frac{12,482.00}{84}$$

$$= 148.60$$

As with the linear sum of squares, $SS_{A\,quadratic}$ has 1 df; thus, $MS_{A\,quadratic} = 148.60$. The F becomes

$$F_{A\,quadratic} = \frac{MS_{A\,quadratic}}{MS_{S/A}}$$

$$= \frac{148.60}{16.98}$$

$$= 8.75$$

The critical value of F for quadratic trend is the same as the one we determined for linear trend ($F_\alpha = 4.08$) and the decision rule becomes

If $F_{A\,quadratic} \geq 4.08$, reject the null hypothesis; otherwise, retain the null hypothesis.

We conclude that a significant quadratic trend is present. You would describe this trend as a tendency for learning time to become increasingly longer with the longer lists.

Testing for Additional Trends.   Most researchers would stop after completing this analysis. They could test the sum of squares that remains after subtracting $SS_{A\,linear}$ and $SS_{A\,quadratic}$ from SS_A and continue searching for more complex trends if this new residual variation is significant and stop the search if it is not. The search is often pointless, however, because complex trends are usually too difficult to explain. In practice, then, unless you have theoretical reasons for expecting a particular higher-order trend, we recommend that you restrict your analysis to the linear trend, or, perhaps, the linear and quadratic trends. Trends of greater complexity are rare in psychology and, if discovered, may confuse more than illuminate the interpretation of an experiment.

ADDITIONAL CONSIDERATIONS

We conclude this appendix by mentioning several additional points you should consider if you contemplate conducting a trend analysis of your data.

Planned Comparisons

The procedure we described for conducting a trend analysis in our example assumed that the researcher did not anticipate obtaining a particular trend component, but simply wanted to see whether a relatively simple trend — such as a linear relationship — might be able to describe the outcome of an experiment. Under these circumstances, it makes sense to first test the significance of the omnibus F test; if this test is significant, then more focused, analytical tests would be conducted to reveal the underlying processes responsible for the significant overall effect. On the other hand, if our theory *predicted* the presence of a particular type of trend, we could quite properly treat the assessment of this trend as a *planned* comparison and test its significance without reference to the outcome of the omnibus test.

The Grant-Schiller experiment we discussed in Chap. 6, the results of which are presented in Fig. D-2, is an excellent example of just such a process. Briefly, these researchers expected to find a general *linear* trend reflecting a tendency of subjects to respond more vigorously to more intense stimuli — that is, they expected to find an increase in responding as the size of the circles increased from 9 inches to 15 inches. In addition, they expected a *quadratic* trend, with subjects responding maximally to the stimulus used in training (12 inches) and progressively less strongly to stimuli further removed from this particular stimulus. An inspection of Fig. D-2 suggests that both expectations are corroborated in the data.

Planned trend components can be tested directly, without conducting either the omnibus test or the subsequent tests of residual variation that we described earlier in this appendix. In this regard, then, we treat planned comparisons the same way, regardless of whether they are based on qualitative or quantitative manipulations.

Equal Intervals

While we did not mention it at the time, the trend analysis we described in our main example in this appendix assumed that the intervals represented by successive levels of the independent variable are equal. In the numerical example, the levels increase in equal steps of four pairs — that is, 4, 8, 12, 16, 20, and 24. In the Grant-Schiller experiment, the levels increase in equal steps of 1 inch — that is, 9, 10, 11, 12, 13, 14, and 15. Under these circumstances, we simply use the coefficients presented in Table A-11 to perform linear and quadratic trend analyses. (Coefficients presented in more extensive tables available in most advanced statistics texts to perform more complex trend analyses.)

We can conduct trend analyses with *unequal* intervals, but they are more complicated. Either we go through an involved algebraic procedure of constructing trend coefficients that are appropriate for the spacings present in our experiment, or we turn to an entirely different type of procedure that usually requires the computer. Both of these procedures are described in more advanced books.[1]

Limits to the Conclusions

It is important to realize that a trend analysis is based only on those points on the manipulated continuum that were actually included in the study. We need to be cautious in making any inferences about the shape of the function *beyond* or outside those points. In our example, what would the underlying

---

[1] For a detailed explanation of constructing sets of trend coefficients, see Keppel (1982, pp. 629–633). For the alternative approach, which is conducted within the context of a procedure called *multiple regression and correlation*, see Cohen (1980), Cohen and Cohen (1983), and Keppel and Zedeck (1989, pp. 500–505).

function look like if we had included lists containing 30 or 40 pairs? Would the trend we observed with the data in Table D-1 continue to be largely linear, or would the difficulty of the task become progressively harder, thereby reflecting the presence of a nonlinear trend and accentuate the "bend" in the curve? We cannot distinguish between these two possibilities without having included these more extreme values in the study.

What about making inferences about trend that are based on the values we *have* included in the experiment — are there any limitations there? Let's consider some possibilities. If we include *two* levels, we can detect only a linear trend — any higher-order trends that may be present between these two points will be *invisible* in the sense that they cannot be detected. If we include *three* levels, on the other hand, we can detect both linear and quadratic trends, although not trends of any greater complexity. In summary, then, if we wish to detect the two trends of most interest to researchers in the behavioral and social sciences — linear and quadratic trends — we must include a sufficiently large number of levels (five to seven) of a quantitative independent variable to convince ourselves that these *are* the primary, or prevalent, trends that describe the relationship between the independent and dependent variables.

Glossary

SIGNIFICANT TERMS AND CONCEPTS

AB matrix. A systematic arrangement of the treatment sums in a two-factor design.

Alpha (α). The probability of committing a type I error. See **significance level**; **type I error**.

Alternative hypothesis. The hypothesis that is accepted when the null hypothesis is rejected; represented by the symbol H_1.

Analysis of variance. A statistical analysis involving the comparison of variances that reflect different sources of variability; abbreviated ANOVA.

Analytical comparisons. Meaningful comparisons between two or more treatment conditions that are components of a larger experimental design. These comparisons are direct expressions of specific research hypotheses.

ANOVA. Acronym for *analysis of variance*.

Archival research. A form of research which uses public records as the source of data; a form of unobtrusive research.

Assumption of equal variances. The assumption that the scores show the same degree of variability from treatment population to treatment population; required for proper use of the F tables.

Assumption of independence. The assumption that scores are independent from one another both within each treatment population and across populations.

Assumption of normality. The assumption that the scores making up a treatment condition are distributed normally. See **normal distribution**.

Availability sampling. A sample of convenience, based on subjects available to the researcher; often the population source is not completely defined. This is a common procedure in psychology experiments. See **random sampling**.

Bar graph. A pictorial representation of data in which bars are used to represent data from an experiment involving a qualitative manipulation.

Basic ratios. Quantities entered into the computational formulas for the sums of squares in the analysis of variance.

Best-fit straight line. A line representing the linear relationship between two variables from which the deviations of the actual data are minimized. It is used to make predictions about one variable from another, correlated variable. See **regression equation**.

Beta (β).   The probability of committing a type II error. See **type II error.**

Between-groups deviation.   The deviation of a treatment mean from the overall mean in an experiment ($\overline{Y}_T$). Used in the calculation of the between-groups sum of squares in the analysis of variance.

Between-groups variability.   Differences among the treatment means; reflects the effects of the treatments plus chance factors (experimental error).

Between-subjects design.   An experimental design in which subjects are each randomly assigned to only one of the treatment conditions. It can also be a part of a mixed design.

Between-subjects error.   The estimate of random error used to test the statistical significance of between-subjects sources of treatment variance in the mixed within-subjects factorial design.

Between-subjects variability.   Consists of all systematic and unsystematic sources of variability in a completely randomized design. In a mixed within-subjects factorial design, it consists of the systematic and unsystematic sources associated with the between-subjects portion of the analysis.

Block randomization.   A method of random assignment in which numbers of subjects are balanced over all the conditions at the end of each subject assignment block rather than at the end of the testing schedule; each block contains each treatment once.

Blocking design.   A way of matching subjects in which the subjects are segmented into small groups defined by specified ranges of the characteristic used for matching; used as a means of reducing error variance.

Carryover effects.   The effects of a previously administered condition on a subject's performance on a subsequent condition in a within-subjects design; they are generally not eliminated by counterbalancing.

Categorical data.   Data consisting of a classification of the behavior of subjects into a number of mutually exclusive response categories. See **dichotomous classification**.

Central limit theorem.   A theorem stating that the sampling distribution of the mean approaches the normal distribution in shape as the size of the sample on which the means are based is increased.

Central tendency, measure of.   A statistic that describes the typical score in a distribution of scores. See **mean; median.**

Chi square (χ^2) test statistic.   A statistic based on categorical data in which the observed frequencies with which different classes of responses occur are compared with expected frequencies derived from theoretical or empirical considerations. Sometimes referred to as the *Pearson chi square statistic.*

Classification variable.   An independent variable created by the systematic selection of subjects on the dimension to be studied — for example, intelligence, age, or gender. It is a characteristic which is observed and classified rather than arbitrarily imposed.

Coefficient. A number assigned to a treatment condition that specifies a particular arrangement of treatment means in a single-*df* comparison. Used in the calculation of the sum of squares for the comparison.

Column marginal means. See **marginal means**.

Comparison contingency table. A specialized contingency table used in analytical comparisons conducted in the analysis of frequency data. Used in calculation of a special chi square statistic, χ^2_{comp}.

Complete within-subjects factorial design. A factorial design in which each subject receives all of the treatment combinations. The design results in a need for fewer subjects than a comparable completely randomized factorial and is often used to reduce error variance.

Completely randomized single-factor design. A single-factor experiment in which subjects are each randomly assigned to one of the treatment conditions.

Completely randomized two-variable factorial design. An experiment in which subjects are each randomly assigned to one of the treatment conditions formed from the factorial combination of two independent variables.

Complex comparison. A single-*df* comparison in which at least one of the two means in the comparison is an average of two or more conditions.

Complex simple comparisons. A complex single-*df* comparison used to analyze a significant simple effect. See **complex comparison; simple effect**.

Component single-factor experiments. Single-factor experiments combined to form a factorial design; the basis for the analysis of simple effects.

Computational formula. A formula with which one usually calculates a statistic. Involves less computational effort than the corresponding defining formula.

Confidence interval. A range of values assumed, with a specified degree of confidence, to include a population parameter.

Confounding variables. One or more independent variables that vary systematically with the variable of interest, decreasing the ability to make causal inferences. See **nuisance variable**.

Contingency table. A two-dimensional matrix used with categorical data to classify subjects jointly on the basis of two variables.

Control group. Group assigned to a reference, or baseline, condition consisting of the absence of a specific experimental treatment. Sometimes referred to as a *placebo group* when included in an experiment involving the administration of drugs.

Correlation coefficient (*r*). See **product-moment correlation coefficient**.

Correlation ratio.   A statistical index that detects the presence of any relationship — linear, curvilinear, or more complex — between two variables. Also known as *eta squared*.

Correlational research.   Nonexperimental research consisting of the establishment of relationships between two or more naturally occurring characteristics.

Counterbalancing.   A systematic arrangement of treatment conditions designed to neutralize practice effects. Complete counterbalancing is an arrangement in which all possible combinations of the treatment conditions are included. See **Latin square**.

Covariance.   A measure of the joint variability of two variables.

Criterion variable.   The variable predicted or estimated from another, correlated variable; also called the *Y variable*.

Critical value.   A value obtained from a sampling distribution that specifies the beginning of the region of rejection.

Cross-sectional design.   A technique for studying developmental variables in which subjects differing on a developmental variable such as age are studied at a single point in time.

Curvilinear relationship.   A relationship characterized by a curved line. The presence of a curvilinear correlation can be detected by special indices such as the correlation ratio or eta squared.

Decision rule.   A rule specifying the conditions under which the null hypothesis will be rejected or retained.

Defining formula.   A formula expressing a statistical operation in a form that directly mirrors the meaning of the concept. Actual calculations are usually performed with an equivalent but computationally simpler computational formula.

Degrees of freedom.   The number of independent pieces of information available in the estimation of population parameters; abbreviated *df*.

Dependent variable.   The response measure of an experiment. It is the selected behavior which is measured to gauge the effect of the independent variable. The term also refers to the criterion variable, or *Y* variable, in a correlational study.

Descriptive research.   Research designed to describe with increasing amounts of thoroughness a relation between two or more variables. Descriptive research is closely allied with and sometimes leads to explanatory research.

Descriptive statistics.   Numerical summaries of scores. Descriptive statistics are often used in inferential statistical procedures. These are not to be confused with descriptive research.

Deviation from the mean.   The difference between a number and the mean of the set of numbers to which it belongs.

Dichotomous classification. A response variable consisting of only two values.

Dunnett test. A correction technique designed to hold familywise type I error at some arbitrarily determined level when the comparisons include the difference between one mean and each of the others. See **Tukey test**; **Scheffé test**.

Environmental variable. An independent variable in which some aspect of the physical environment is manipulated

Error bars. Graphical depiction of a measure of variability using bands above and below the mean. Usually the standard error of the mean is the value charted; sometimes the standard deviation is used.

Error of prediction. The discrepancy between an observed score and the score predicted by the linear regression line. It forms the basis for the standard error of estimate. The larger the correlation coefficient, the smaller the error of prediction. See **residual variation**; **standard error of estimate**.

Error term. The denominator of a ratio, such as the F ratio, used to determine the presence of a treatment effect.

Estimated omega squared ($\hat{\omega}_A^2$). A measure of the strength, or the magnitude, of the treatment effects in an experiment. See R^2.

Estimation. Procedures permitting numerical characteristics of a given population to be inferred from information provided by a sample drawn randomly from that population.

Eta squared. The correlation ratio; used to detect the presence of any relationship between two variables.

Exact probability. With respect to the outcome of a statistical test, such as F, t, χ^2, or r, the probability that an obtained value would occur under the null hypothesis; it is the proportion of the sampling distribution falling at or above the obtained value of the statistic. Exact probabilities are typically obtained with computer programs.

Expected frequency. The frequency with which a particular type of response is expected to occur on the basis of theoretical or empirical considerations; used in the chi square test. See **chi square test statistic**.

Experiment. A research methodology designed to permit the inference of cause and effect. Differential treatments are administered to different groups of subjects; performance on a selected response measure is then observed and recorded. Differences observed in the response measure among the treatments that are not reasonably accounted for by experimental error are attributed to the critical differences in the relevant treatments. Also known as *explanatory research*.

Experimental design. The plan of an experiment, including specification of the nature of treatment conditions and methods of assigning subjects to conditions.

Experimental error.   Uncontrolled sources of variability (primarily individual differences) assumed to occur randomly during the course of an experiment.

Explanatory research.   See **experiment**.

Exploratory research.   Research designed to investigate a topic on which little systematic information exists. Its purpose is to give initial information to provide ideas for further, systematic research.

External validity.   Generalization of the results of a research study to a variety or range of conditions over which the particular result might apply.

F_{adj}.   A modified critical value of F used to adjust for the effect of violation of the assumption of homogeneity of variance.

F_{α}.   The critical value of F that marks the regions of rejecting and retaining the null hypothesis for the obtained F statistic.

F_{max}.   A ratio used to determine the degree to which the variances of the treatment conditions are different; consists of a ratio formed by dividing the largest variance in the experiment by the smallest.

F ratio.   A statistical index relating systematic variance to nonsystematic variance. The statistical procedure permitting an assessment of the statistical significance of this ratio is called the *F test*.

F table.   A table listing the critical values of F for different combinations of numerator and denominator degrees of freedom for different levels of significance.

Factor.   A term usually referring to an independent variable. The first or an only variable is designated factor A; the second variable is designated factor B, and so on. The levels of a factor are the specific treatment conditions associated with the factor. When used in the correlational procedure known as *factor analysis*, the term refers to the collection of variables which are correlated more highly with each other than with other variables in a set.

Factor analysis.   A statistical procedure using multiple correlation techniques for analyzing correlational relationships among three or more response measures.

Factorial experiments.   Experimental designs in which two or more independent variables are manipulated at the same time; these permit the examination of interactions.

Familywise type I error.   The probability of committing a type I error over a *set* of statistical tests; approximately equal to the sum of the separate per comparison probabilities. Represented by the symbol *FW*. See **per comparison type I error**.

General practice effects.   See **practice effects**.

Generalization.   In statistics, an inference made from a sample to a population. More generally in research, attempts to extend the findings of a study to other situations and variables. Also known as *external validity*.

Grand mean ($\overline{Y}_T$). The mean calculated from all the observations in a study.

H_0. See **null hypothesis**.

H_1. See **alternative hypothesis**.

Homogeneity of variance. See **assumption of equal variances**.

Hypothesis testing. The formal process by which a decision is made concerning the rejection or retention of the null hypothesis.

Independent variable. The variable manipulated by the experimenter. It is a feature of a task given to subjects or of the external or internal environment.

Inferential statistics. Measures and procedures used to make inferences about population characteristics from samples drawn from those populations; consists of hypothesis testing and estimation of population parameters.

Interaction. The outcome of a factorial experiment in which the effects on behavior of one independent variable change at the different levels of the second independent variable.

Intercept. See *Y* **intercept**.

Interval estimate. See **confidence interval**.

Latin square. A form of counterbalancing frequently used in arranging the orders of presentation of treatment conditions in a within-subjects design; a form of incomplete counterbalancing.

Levels. The different treatment conditions of the independent variable under study in an experiment. In a single-factor design the treatments are described as the levels of factor *A*.

Linear correlation coefficient. See **product-moment correlation coefficient**.

Linear regression line. A best-fit straight line depicting the linear relationship between two variables. It is characterized by two features: slope and intercept. The formula for the best-fit straight line is used to predict one variable from another. See **best-fit straight line**; **regression equation**.

Linear trend. A linear relationship between an independent variable and a dependent variable; a relationship represented by a straight line.

Longitudinal study. A form of research in which a designated group of subjects is studied repeatedly over an extended period of time.

Magnitude of treatment effects. The "strength" of a manipulated variable. The proportion of the total variance due to the independent variable. See **estimated omega squared ($\hat{\omega}_A^2$); R^2; phi coefficient (ϕ); r^2**.

Main comparisons. Focused comparisons of a main effect usually made up of pairwise and complex single-*df* comparisons on appropriate marginal column or row means.

Main effects. The overall effects of one independent variable in a factorial design averaged over the levels of the other independent variable(s).

Marginal means. The means entering into the analysis of main effects in the two-factor design; derived from the *AB* matrix. Also known as the *row* or *column marginal means.*

Matched-subjects designs.   Class of between-subjects designs in which subjects are matched on one or more relevant characteristics; used as a means of reducing error variability.

Matching.   Selecting subjects with similar characteristics to serve in the different conditions of an experiment; a method for reducing error variability.

Mean.   Measure of central tendency; the arithmetic average. The sum of a set of scores divided by the number of scores in the set.

Mean square.   A term for the variances calculated in the analysis of variance. A sum of squares divided by the appropriate number of degrees of freedom.

Median.   A measure of central tendency; the score above or below which half of the scores lie.

Mixed within-subjects factorial design.   A factorial design which is a combination of within-subjects and the between-subjects designs.

Multiple comparisons.   See **planned comparisons**; **unplanned comparisons**.

Multiple correlation and regression.   Correlational procedures involving intercorrelation among three or more variables; abbreviated as MRC.

Naturalistic observation.   A form of observational research in which the observer records information about naturally occurring behavior while attempting not to intervene or affect the behavior in any way; the research is also described as *unobtrusive.*

Negative slope.   With respect to a linear regression line, a relationship reflecting a decrease in the *Y* variable as the *X* variable increases and an increase in the *Y* variable as the *X* variable decreases. A negative slope is associated with a negative correlation coefficient.

Nonexperimental research.   Research which lacks a true independent or manipulated variable. Useful in situations in which it is either not possible or not proper to manipulate the variable of interest.

Nonlinear trend.   Higher-order relationship between two variables. See **curvilinear relationship; quadratic trend**.

Normal distribution.   A theoretical distribution that appears bell-shaped. See **assumption of normality**.

Nuisance variable.   A potential independent variable that is not to be manipulated in an experiment that must be neutralized to prevent confounding with the treatment variable(s). See **confounding variables**.

Null hypothesis.   The statistical hypothesis evaluated by hypothesis testing. Usually expressed as the absence of a relationship in the population and represented by the symbol H_0.

Observational research.   The systematic study of behavior as it occurs naturally in the environment.

Observed frequency. The number of observations falling within a particular response category; used in the chi square test. See **chi square test statistic**.

Omega squared. See **estimated omega squared**.

Omnibus (overall) *F* test. An *F* test evaluating the null hypothesis stating that all the population treatment means in an experiment are equal.

Pairwise comparison. A single-*df* comparison between two means. See **single-*df* comparisons**.

Pairwise simple comparisons. A pairwise comparison involving the treatment means in a single row or column of the *AB* matrix. Used to analyze significant simple effects. See **pairwise comparison; simple effects**.

Paradigms. Logical systems made up of theoretical concepts and research techniques reflecting a predominant way of thinking about a given topic.

Partial correlation. A statistical procedure which removes or controls for the effect of a third variable before testing the relationship between the other variables.

Participant observation. A form of observational research in which the observer's presence is known to the subjects being observed.

Pearson correlation coefficient (*r*). An index of linear correlation devised by Karl Pearson. See **product-moment correlation coefficient**.

Per comparison type I error. The probability of committing a type I error for an individual statistical test. See **alpha (α)**.

Phi coefficient (φ). An index of correlation used in cases where both variables are dichotomous (consisting of two values only); a measure of treatment effect size used in conjunction with dichotomous dependent variables.

Placebo group. See **control group**.

Planned comparisons. Analytical comparisons specified before the start of an experiment.

Point-biserial correlation coefficient. A statistical index of the relationship between one continuous variable and one dichotomous variable (composed of two values only).

Point estimate. A population estimate based on a random sample.

Population. The total number of possible units or elements that can be included in a study.

Population treatment effects. See **treatment effects**.

Population treatment mean. The mean of scores in a treatment population, designated by μ. Statistical hypotheses are statements about the relationship among the population treatment means.

Positive slope. With respect to a linear regression line, a relationship reflecting an increase in the Y variable as the X variable increases and a decrease in the Y variable as the X variable decreases. A positive slope is associated with a positive correlation coefficient.

Post hoc. See **unplanned comparisons**.

Power. The probability of correctly rejecting the null hypothesis, that is, rejecting the null hypothesis when it is false; defined as 1 minus the probability of a type II error.

Practice effects. The systematic change — increase or decrease — in performance over a series of treatment conditions in a within-subjects (repeated-measures) design. A potential bias, usually neutralized through counterbalancing.

Predictive research. Research designed to find out whether the score on a selected measure or a test result corresponds with an external standard of interest. A familiar use is the study of relatively brief tests as an indicator of probable performance in college.

Predictor variable. The variable used to predict or estimate another, correlated variable; also called the *X variable*. It is usually a variable that occurs prior in time to the predicted or criterion variable.

Product-moment correlation coefficient (r). The most common index of the linear relationship between two variables. It ranges from -1.0 to $+1.0$ (perfect negative and perfect positive correlations, respectively); a value of 0 represents the complete absence of correlation. Also referred to as the *Pearson correlation coefficient* and the *linear correlation coefficient*.

Quadratic trend. A higher-order or curvilinear relationship between an independent and a dependent variable.

Qualitative independent variable. Variable whose treatment levels differ in kind rather than in amount.

Quantitative independent variable. Variable whose treatment levels differ in degree or amount as measured on either a physical or a psychological scale.

Quasi-experimental research. Research designs using a naturally formed or preexisting set of conditions. A type of nonexperimental design used when manipulation is either not possible or ethically improper.

r. See **product-moment correlation coefficient**.

r^2. An estimate of the strength of the linear relationship between two variables in a correlational study. It is the squared product-moment correlation coefficient.

R^2. An estimate of the magnitude of treatment effect in an experiment based on the sums of squares rather than estimated population variances. See **estimated omega squared**.

Random assignment of subjects. A procedure by which each subject has equal probability of being assigned to each different treatment condition in an experiment. Also known as *randomization*.

Random sample. A sample randomly drawn from a defined population.

Random sampling. A procedure in which each member of the population has an equally likely chance of being included in the sample.

Randomization. See **random assignment of subjects**.

Rank-order correlation coefficient. An index of linear correlation used with data where both variables take the form of ranks. Also referred to as the *Spearman rank-order correlation coefficient.*

Region of nonrejection. The range of values of a statistic within which the null hypothesis will be retained.

Region of rejection. The range of values of a statistic within which the null hypothesis will be rejected; also known as the *critical region.* The critical region is set by the chosen significance level.

Regression coefficient. A numerical value of the slope of the best-fit straight line describing the relationship between variables. Represented by the symbol *b* in this text.

Regression equation. A mathematical expression describing the relationship between correlated variables; used to predict one variable from another. For linear regression it is the formula for the best-fit straight line which contains two constants — the intercept (*a*) and the slope (*b*) — and two variables, *X* and *Y*.

Regression line. See **linear regression line; regression equation**.

Repeated-measures design. See **within-subjects design**.

Research hypothesis. A hypothesis based on empirical and theoretical considerations that leads to the design of a study. The adequacy of the research hypothesis is evaluated during the course of hypothesis testing.

Residual variation. Deviation of the observed data points from the linear regression line describing the relation between two variables. It is the variation not accounted for by linear regression.

Response categories. A classification of responses used to differentiate subjects in a chi square analysis. See **categorical data.**

Response distribution. A listing of the frequencies with which particular scores or classes of responses occur in a set of observations.

Restriction of range. A condition in which one (or both) of the variables in a correlation problem is restricted with respect to its possible variation. The result is a correlation coefficient which is smaller than it would be without restriction of range; it leads to an underestimation of the population correlation.

Row marginal means. See **marginal means**.

Sample. A subgroup drawn from a larger group of subjects or from a population.

Sample size. The number of subjects assigned to a particular treatment condition or observed in a study.

Sampling. The process of selecting participants for research study. See **random sampling**; **availability sampling**.

Sampling distribution. A frequency distribution of a statistic obtained from an extremely large number of random samples drawn from a specified population.

Sampling distribution of *F*. A frequency distribution of the *F* statistic obtained from an extremely large number of experiments, each consisting of data drawn randomly from treatment populations with identical means and variances.

Sampling distribution of the mean. The frequency distribution of all possible sample means that might be obtained from samples randomly drawn from a particular population of subjects.

Sampling error. The variability of a point estimate of a sample drawn from a population.

Scatterplot. A graphical display consisting of the plotting of subjects' scores obtained from two response measures, designated *X* and *Y*. A useful visual aid in the analysis of correlational data.

Scheffé test. A correction technique designed to keep familywise type I error from exceeding some arbitrarily chosen level regardless of the number of comparisons conducted. It can be used with a mixture of pairwise and complex comparisons. See **Tukey test**; **Dunnett test**.

Selective deposit. A potentially biasing feature of archival information; only selected information is placed in archives, rather than a random sample of the information in question.

Selective survival. A potential bias in archival data; some information is lost from the archives for a variety of reasons.

σ_{diff} . See **standard error of the difference between two means**.

Significance level. The probability (α) with which an experimenter is willing to reject the null hypothesis when in fact it is correct. Also known as the *probability of a type I error*.

Simple comparisons. Single-*df* comparisons designed to analyze statistically significant simple effects; simple comparisons can be either pairwise or complex. See **pairwise comparison**; **complex comparison**.

Simple effects. The variability among the treatment means associated with one independent variable at a particular level of the other independent variable. Useful for determining the basis of a significant interaction. Also known as *simple main effects*.

Simple main effects. See **simple effects**.

Single-*df* comparisons. Analyses of differences between two means, either of which consists of the mean of a single treatment condition or an average of two or more treatment conditions. See **pairwise comparison; complex comparison**.

Slope. With reference to a regression line, the numerical constant representing the change in the value of the predicted variable associated with a unit change in the predictor variable. When a correlation is present the slope is either positive or negative. In this text the slope is represented by the symbol *b*. See **negative slope; positive slope**.

Standard deviation. A measure of variability; the square root of the variance. Expresses variability in terms of the original units of measure.

Standard error of estimate. The square root of the variance of deviations of observed scores on a predicted variable from those predicted by a linear regression equation.

Standard error of the difference between two means. A special combination of the variances of two groups of scores used as a measure of random error in the *t* test. Represented by the symbol $\sigma_{diff.}$.

Standard error of the mean. The standard deviation of the sampling distribution of the mean.

Statistical hypotheses. Hypotheses specifying relationships between population parameters. Usually consist of the null and alternative hypotheses.

Studentized range statistic. A value obtained from a table to calculate the special F_T required for the Tukey test.

Subject mortality. The loss of subjects in a research study. It is of particular concern when it occurs unequally in different treatment conditions.

Subject sum of squares. Used in the within-subjects design to reflect the consistent variability of subjects who serve in all the treatment conditions.

Sum of products. Term referring to the sum of products of paired or corresponding deviations of the X and Y variables. When divided by its associated *df*, it produces the covariance term.

Sum of squares. The sum of squared deviations of scores from their mean. Used in the calculation of the variance.

Survey research. Research methods using questionnaires or interviews to poll or obtain information.

***t* distribution.** A theoretical distribution used in conjunction with the *t* test and in the establishment of a confidence interval for the mean. It varies in shape with the *df* associated with the denominator of the *t* ratio.

t **test.** A statistical test of the difference between two means. Algebraically equivalent to the *F* test.

Table of random numbers. A table of numbers generated by an acceptable random process.

Task variable. An independent variable in which some aspect of a task is manipulated.

Temporary subject variable. A class of independent variables that change a subject's behavior for a short time before the behavior returns to a normal level.

Theory. A set of propositions which summarize, organize, and explain a variety of known facts. Theories are intended to produce a logically consistent summarization as well as to generate new tests and ideas on a given topic.

Total deviation. The deviation of an individual score from the grand mean of an experiment; used to calculate the total sum of squares.

Treatment combinations. The different treatment conditions administered to subjects in the factorial design; all possible combinations of the levels of the two independent variables.

Treatment effects. The differences among the treatment means in the population. A theoretical quantity that cannot be observed directly in an experiment.

Treatment index. A ratio consisting of between-groups variability divided by within-group variability. Examples in this text are the *F* ratio, *t*, and χ^2.

Treatment mean. The mean of the scores of subjects receiving a particular treatment condition in an experiment.

Treatment population. The hypothetical scores of an extremely large number of individuals given a particular treatment condition.

Trend analysis. Analytical comparisons for the detailed analysis of the results of an experiment in which a quantitative independent variable is manipulated. Makes a statistical assessment of linear and higher-order trends by means of special coefficients and the general formula for single-*df* comparisons.

Tukey test. A correction technique designed to hold familywise type I error at some arbitrarily determined level when the set of comparisons consists of pairs of treatment means or pairwise comparisons. See **Dunnett test**; **Scheffé test**.

Two-factor within-subjects factorial design. A within-subjects design in which two factors are studied; there is one group of subjects, receiving all of the treatment conditions.

Type I error. An error of statistical inference that occurs when the null hypothesis is true but is rejected. An error of "seeing too much in the data." See **alpha (α)**; **significance level**.

Type II error. An error of statistical inference that occurs when the null hypothesis is false, but is retained. An error of "not seeing enough in the data." See **beta (β)**.

Unplanned comparisons. Comparisons not specified at the start of an experiment and conducted after the data have been examined. Also known as *post hoc* or *multiple comparisons*. See **planned comparisons**.

Variability. Degree to which differences exist among scores in a distribution. Usually the variance or the standard deviation is used to describe the variability of scores.

Variable. A property that can take different values. In research, variables are classified as independent and dependent.

Variance. A measure of variability; the average of the sum of the squared deviations from the mean (sum of squares divided by *df*).

Venn diagram. A diagram using circles to represent the relationship between sets of scores; used to depict the proportion of variance shared by two variables.

Weighted treatment means. Treatment means multiplied by coefficients specified by single-*df* comparisons.

Within-group deviation. The deviation of the score for an individual subject from the relevant treatment-group mean. Used in the calculation of the within-groups sum of squares in the analysis of variance.

Within-groups variability. A measure of variability based on the variation of subjects treated alike; provides an estimate of experimental error.

Within-subjects design. An experimental design in which subjects receive all the treatment conditions in an experiment; a means of reducing error variance. It can be a single design or part of a mixed design. Also known as a *repeated-measures design*.

Within-subjects error. The estimate of random error used to form the error term for *F* ratios to test the statistical significance of within-subjects sources of variance.

Within-subjects variability. All systematic and unsystematic sources of variability in a within-subjects design or a mixed within-subjects factorial design, based on differences within the same subjects.

X variable. The variable plotted on the *X* axis. In an experiment it is the independent variable. When used in correlational research it is one of the variables correlated with another, often the predictor variable and frequently referred to as the "independent" variable.

$\overline{Y}_T$. See **grand mean**.

Y intercept. The value of the linear regression equation predicting variable Y from variable X when $X = 0$. The point at which the regression line intersects the vertical axis (Y axis). In this text the Y intercept is represented by the symbol a.

Y score. The designation of the basic score or response measure; Y scores make up the data from which summary statistics are extracted and tested.

Y variable. The variable plotted on the Y axis. It is the dependent variable in an experiment. When used in correlational research it is the variable correlated with the X variable(s); it is often the variable predicted, the criterion variable.

REFERENCES

Anderson, B. F. (1966). *The psychology experiment.* Belmont, CA: Wadsworth.

Bespaloff, A. (1977). A corking new wine theory. *New York Magazine,* May 23, 1977, 43–45.

Boik, R. J. (1979). Interactions, partial interactions, and interaction contrasts in the analysis of variance. *Psychological Bulletin, 86,* 1084–1089.

Campbell, D. T., & Stanley, J. C. (1963). Experimental and quasi-experimental designs for research on teaching. In N. L. Gage (Ed.), *Handbook of research on teaching* (pp. 171–246). Chicago: Rand McNally.

Campbell, D. T., & Stanley, J. C. (1966). *Experimental and quasi-experimental designs for research.* Chicago: Rand McNally.

Cohen, J. (1965). Some statistical issues in psychological research. In B. B. Wolman (Ed.), *Handbook of clinical psychology* (pp. 95–121). New York: McGraw-Hill.

Cohen, J. (1980). Trend analysis the easy way. *Educational and Psychological Measurement, 40,* 565–568.

Cohen, J. (1988). *Statistical power analysis* (2nd ed.). Hillsdale, NJ: Erlbaum.

Cohen, J., & Cohen, P. (1983). *Applied multiple regression/correlation analysis for the behavioral sciences* (2nd ed.). Hillsdale, NJ: Erlbaum.

Collyer, C. E., & Enns, J. T. (1987). *Analysis of variance: The basic designs.* Chicago: Nelson-Hall.

Cook, T. D., & Campbell, D. T. (1979). *Quasi-experimentation: Design and analysis issues for field settings.* Chicago: Rand McNally.

Dunnett, C. W. (1955). A multiple comparison procedure for comparing several treatments with a control. *Journal of the American Statistical Association, 50,* 1096–1121.

Dunnett, C. W. (1964). New tables for multiple comparisons with a control. *Biometrics, 20,* 482–491.

Edwards, A. L. (1984). *An introduction to linear regression and correlation* (2nd ed.). New York: Freeman.

Edwards, A. L. (1985). *Multiple regression and the analysis of variance and covariance* (2nd ed.). New York: Freeman.

Einot, I., & Gabriel, K. R. (1975). A study of the powers of several methods of multiple comparisons. *Journal of the American Statistical Association, 70,* 574–583.

Festinger, L., Riecken, H. W., & Schachter, S. (1956). *When prophecy fails.*

Minneapolis: University of Minnesota Press.

Friedman, H. (1982). Simplified determinations of statistical power, magnitude of effect and research samples. *Educational and Psychological Measurement, 42,* 521–526.

Ghiselli, E. E., Campbell, J. P., & Zedeck, S. (1981). *Measurement theory for the behavioral sciences.* New York: Freeman.

Grant, D. A., & Schiller, J. J. (1953). Generalization of the conditioned galvanic skin response to visual stimuli. *Journal of Experimental Psychology, 46,* 309–313.

Hays, W. L. (1988). *Statistics* (4th ed.). New York: Holt, Rinehart & Winston.

Hinkle, D. E., & Oliver, J. D. (1983). How large should the sample be? A question with no simple answer? Or . . . . *Educational and Psychological Measurement, 43,* 1051–1060.

Howell, D. C. (1987). *Statistical methods for psychology.* Boston: PWS-Kent.

Huck, S. W., & Sandler, H. M. (1979). *Rival hypotheses.* New York: Harper & Row.

Janak, P. H., Keppel, G., & Martinez, J. L., Jr. (1992). Cocaine enhances retention of avoidance conditioning in rats. *Psychopharmacology, 106,* 383–387.

Judd, C. M., Smith, E. R., & Kidder, L. H. (1991). *Research methods in social relations* (6th ed.). Fort Worth, TX: Holt, Rinehart & Winston.

Kenny, D. A. (1979). *Correlation and causality.* New York: Wiley.

Keppel, G. (1966). Association by contiguity: Role of response availability. *Journal of Experimental Psychology, 71,* 624–628.

Keppel, G. (1982). *Design and analysis: A researcher's handbook* (2nd ed.). Englewood Cliffs, NJ: Prentice-Hall.

Keppel, G. (1991). *Design and analysis: A researcher's handbook* (3rd ed.). Englewood Cliffs, NJ: Prentice-Hall.

Keppel, G., & Zedeck, S. (1989). *Data analysis for research designs: Analysis of variance and multiple regression/correlation approaches.* New York: Freeman.

Kerlinger, F. N. (1986). *Foundations of behavioral research* (3rd ed.). New York: Holt, Rinehart & Winston.

Kirk, R. E. (1972). Classification of ANOVA designs. In R. E. Kirk (Ed.), *Statistical issues.* Monterey, CA: Brooks/Cole.

Kirk, R. E. (1982). *Experimental design: Procedures for the behavioral sciences* (2nd ed.). Monterey, CA: Brooks/Cole.

Kirk, R. E. (1990). *Statistics: An introduction.* Fort Worth, TX: Holt, Rinehart & Winston.

Kraemer, H. C., & Thiemann, S. (1987). *How many subjects?: Statistical power analysis in research.* Newbury Park, CA: Sage.

Levine, G. (1991). *A guide to SPSS for analysis of variance.* Hillsdale, NJ: Erlbaum.

Lindman, H. R. (1974). *Analysis of variance in complex experimental designs.* New York: Freeman.

Maxwell, S. E., Camp, C. J., & Arvey, R. D. (1981). Measures of strength of association: A comparative examination. *Journal of Applied Psychology, 66,* 525–534.

McNemar, Q. (1969). *Psychological statistics* (4th ed.). New York: Wiley.

Myers, J. L., & Well, A. D. (1991). *Research design and statistical analysis.* New York: Harper/Collins.

Neale, J. M., & Liebert, R. M. (1986). *Science and behavior: An introduction to methods of research* (3rd ed.). Englewood Cliffs, NJ: Prentice Hall.

Norusis, M. J. (1990). *The SPSS guide to data analysis for release 4.* Chicago: SPSS Inc.

O'Grady, K. E. (1982). Measures of explained variance: Cautions and limitations. *Psychological Bulletin, 92,* 766–777.

Pearson, E. S., & Hartley, H. O. (Eds.). (1970). *Biometrika tables for statisticians* (3rd ed., Vol. 1). New York: Cambridge University Press.

Pearson, E. S., & Hartley, H. O. (Eds.). (1972). *Biometrika tables for statisticians* (Vol. II). London: Cambridge University Press.

Pedhazur, E. J. (1982). *Multiple regression in behavioral research: Explanation and prediction* (2nd ed.). New York: Holt, Rinehart & Winston.

Phillips, D. P. (1977). Motor vehicle fatalities increase just after publicized suicide stories. *Science, 196,* 1464–1465.

Ramsey, P. H. (1981). Power of univariate pairwise multiple comparison procedures. *Psychological Bulletin, 90,* 352–366.

Rosenthal, R., & Rosnow, R. L. (1985). *Contrast analysis: Focused comparisons in the analysis of variance.* New York: Cambridge University Press.

Rotton, J., & Schönemann, P. H. (1978). Power tables for analysis of variance. *Educational and Psychological Measurement, 38,* 213–229.

Rowland, D., Arkkelin, D., & Crisler, L. (1991). *Computer-based data analysis: Using SPSS^x in the social and behavioral sciences.* Chicago: Nelson-Hall.

Rubin, Z. (1970). Measurement of romantic love. *Journal of Personality and Social Psychology, 16,* 265–273.

Scheffé, H. (1953). A method for judging all contrasts in the analysis of variance. *Biometrika, 40,* 87–104.

Sedlmeier, P., & Gigerenzer, G. (1989). Do studies of statistical power have an effect on the power of studies? *Psychological Bulletin, 105,* 309–316.

Siegel, S., & Castellan, N. J., Jr. (1988). *Nonparametric statistics for the behavioral sciences* (2nd ed.). New York: McGraw-Hill.

Slobin, D. I. (1966). Grammatical transformations and sentence comprehension in childhood and adulthood. *Journal of Verbal Learning and Verbal Behavior, 5,* 219–227.

Stevens, J. (1986). *Applied multivariate statistics for the social sciences.* Hillsdale, NJ: Erlbaum.

Stevens, J. (1990). *Intermediate statistics: A modern approach.* Hillsdale, NJ: Erlbaum.

Tetlock, P. E. (1981). Pre- to postelection shifts in presidential rhetoric: Impression management or cognitive adjustment? *Journal of Personality and Social Psychology, 41,* 207–212.

Tokunaga, H. T. (1985). The effect of bereavement upon death-related attitudes and fears. *Omega, 16,* 267–280.

Tukey, J. W. (1953). *The problem of multiple comparisons.* Unpublished paper, Princeton University, Princeton, NJ.

Tukey, J. W. (1977). *Exploratory data analysis.* Reading, MA: Addison-Wesley.

Underwood, B. J. (1957). *Psychological research.* Englewood Cliffs, NJ: Prentice-Hall.

Underwood, B. J. (1975). Individual differences as a crucible in theory construction. *American Psychologist, 30,* 128–143.

Underwood, B. J., Boruch, R. F., & Malmi, R. A. (1978). Composition of episodic memory. *Journal of Experimental Psychology: General, 107,* 393–419.

Underwood, B. J., & Shaughnessy, J. J. (1975). *Experimentation in psychology.* New York: Wiley.

Webb, E. J., Campbell, D. T., Schwartz, R. D., & Sechrest, L. (1966). *Unobtrusive measures: Nonreactive research in the social sciences.* Chicago: Rand McNally.

Webb, E. J., Campbell, D. T., Schwartz, R. D., Sechrest, L., & Grove, J. B. (1981). *Nonreactive measures in the social sciences* (2nd ed.). Boston: Houghton Mifflin.

Welkowitz, J., Ewen, R. B., & Cohen, J. (1991). *Introductory statistics for the behavioral sciences* (4th ed.). New York: Harcourt Brace Jovanovich.

West, R. (1991). *Computing for psychologists: Statistical analysis using SPSS and MINITAB.* Chur, Switzerland: Harwood.

Wickens, T. D. (1989). *Multiway contingency tables analysis for the social sciences.* Hillsdale, NJ: Erlbaum.

Wilcox, R. R. (1987). New designs in analysis of variance. *Annual Review of Psychology, 38,* 29–60.

Winer, B. J., Brown, D. R., & Michels, K. M. (1991). *Statistical principles in experimental design* (3rd ed.). New York: McGraw-Hill.

Woodworth, R. S. (1938). *Experimental psychology.* New York: Holt.

Author Index

Subject Index